Across Fortune's Tracks

*The research and writing
of this volume were made possible
by a generous grant from the
William R. Kenan, Jr. Charitable Trust*

ACROSS FORTUNE'S TRACKS

A BIOGRAPHY OF

William Rand Kenan Jr.

WALTER E. CAMPBELL

THE UNIVERSITY OF NORTH CAROLINA PRESS

Chapel Hill & London

The paper in this book meets the guidelines for permanence
and durability of the Committee on Production Guidelines for Book Longevity
of the Council on Library Resources.

Library of Congress Cataloging-in-Publication Data
Campbell, Walter E.
Across fortune's tracks : a biography of William Rand Kenan Jr. /
by Walter E. Campbell.
p. cm.
Includes bibliographical references (p.   ) and index.
ISBN 0-8078-2268-x (cloth : alk. paper)
1. Kenan, William Rand, 1872–1965. 2. Businessmen—United States—Biography.
3. Dairy farmers—United States—Biography. 4. Philanthropists—United States—
Biography. I. Title.
HC102.5.K457C35   1996
338.092—dc20
[B]   95-34702
CIP

This book is one in a series of works commissioned by the
Bicentennial Observance Policy Committee of the University of North Carolina
at Chapel Hill. The University of North Carolina Press gratefully acknowledges
the assistance of the committee in publishing these volumes.

Frontispiece: William Rand Kenan Jr. at the Breakers in Palm Beach, Florida, 1939.
(Henry M. Flagler Museum)

00   99   98   97   96   5   4   3   2   1

For Mary Lee and Elijah

CONTENTS

Acknowledgments, xiii

Chapter 1. The Kenans of North Carolina, 3

Chapter 2. The Crucible of Fortune, 34

Chapter 3. The Ins and Outs of UNC, 49

Chapter 4. Calcium Carbide and Acetylene, 75

Chapter 5. The Columbus of Carbide, 103

Chapter 6. For Better or Worse, 138

Chapter 7. Mary Lily and Her Families, 161

Chapter 8. Between the Tracks, 191

Chapter 9. Up and Down the Line, 209

Chapter 10. War on the Empire, 237

Chapter 11. Shared Knowledge and Self-Esteem, 259

Chapter 12. *Incidents* and the War, 285

Chapter 13. A Place to Come To, 303

Chapter 14. Disembarking, 320

Notes, 333

Bibliography, 387

Index, 403

FIGURES, MAP, & ILLUSTRATIONS

FIGURES

Kenan Family, *4*

Barbee and Hargrave Families, *28*

MAP

The Florida East Coast Railway, 1946, *292*

ILLUSTRATIONS

Liberty Hall, *7*

Kenan home in Wilmington, *10*

Will Kenan, age eight, *11*

Mary Hargrave "Mollie" Kenan, *14*

William Rand "Buck" Kenan Sr., *15*

Will Kenan at Horner's Military Academy, *37*

"Sadie" Green, Mrs. Pembroke Jones, *40*

Mary Lily Kenan, *42*

UNC baseball team, 1894, *58*

Members of the Order of Gim Ghouls, 1892, *61*

Francis Preston Venable, *68*

Will Kenan at graduation from UNC, *73*

Major James Turner Morehead, *76*

Thomas "Carbide" Willson, *78*

Willson electric arc furnaces, *81*

Chemistry laboratory at UNC, 1890s, *84*

The "North Carolina Carbide Boys," *105*

Acetylene Light, Heat and Power Company, *106*

The first Horry electric rotary furnace, *115*

Union Carbide Company, *121*
At Jackson's Sanatarium, *126*
Locks of the Erie Canal at Lockport, *131*
The Flaglers and their wedding guests at Liberty Hall, *136*
Whitehall, *139*
The Kenans at Whitehall, *140*
William and Alice Kenan, *146*
Henry Flagler and Alice Pomroy Kenan, *156*
William and Alice's home in Uppertown, *167*
Dr. Owen Hill Kenan, *170*
Graham Kenan with friends, *195*
Lawrence, Louise, and Lawrence Lewis Jr., *200*
Jessie Kenan Wise and Louise Wise Lewis, *216*
The Breakers Hotel, 1927, *226*
Kenan Memorial Stadium, ca. 1927, *228*
After Louise's second divorce, *232*
Sarah Graham Kenan, *247*
Randleigh Farm on the eve of World War II, *266*
The dairy inn at Randleigh Farm, *267*
Picnic of Western Block "office fellows," Camp Kenan, *286*
Carolina Apartment building and Kenan Memorial Fountain, *311*
W. R. Kenan Jr. in the late 1950s, *321*
Schuyler Beattie and his cat, Chan, *325*

ACKNOWLEDGMENTS

In the spring of 1987 I accepted a one-year appointment as acting director of the Southern Oral History Program at the University of North Carolina at Chapel Hill. One of my first assignments was to draft a funding proposal requested by the William Rand Kenan, Jr. Charitable Trust for a series of interviews with people who had known William Rand Kenan Jr.

The trust agreed to fund the interviews, and though I knew the Kenan name only from the football stadium at Chapel Hill, I agreed to conduct the interviews. Newspaper clippings filled in the most prominent features of the Kenan landscape: Henry Flagler, UNC, and calcium carbide. But I learned a lot more that fall about Kenan, his family, and the reason for the interviews after interviewing his cousin's son, Frank Kenan, and Frank's son, Thomas S. Kenan III, both of whom were trustees of what they called the "WRK Jr. Trust."

The Kenans, I discovered, anticipated the publication of David and Mary Chandler's *The Binghams of Louisville*, a juicy exposé of the alleged circumstances surrounding the death of WRK's sister, Mary Lily Kenan Flagler Bingham. Chandler's book had been printed in the spring, but its publication had been canceled by the Macmillan Publishing Company, the original contractor, after receiving challenges to what the company called the "factual premises" of the book. The book was finally published by Crown Publishers in December 1987, three months after my interviews with Frank and Tom Kenan. I bought the book and was naturally intrigued by its thesis that Mary Lily had been mistreated and possibly murdered by her second husband, Judge Robert Worth Bingham of Louisville, Kentucky.

Two months later, UNC history professor George Brown Tindall asked me at a meeting of the Association of Afro-American Life and History in Durham, North Carolina, if I would be interested in writing a book about Kenan or the Florida East Coast Railway. I immediately sent the trust a proposal for a scholarly biography of William Rand Kenan Jr. Another year passed, however, before I signed a contract.

In the meantime I interviewed a number of Kenan's friends and neighbors in Lockport, New York, and his great-nephew, the late Lawrence Lewis Jr., in Richmond, Virginia. Mr. Lewis's interview was one of the most uncomfortable and rewarding I have ever done. He did not like W. R. Kenan Jr., he was not particularly fond of his Kenan kinfolk, and he fought me at every turn. He also helped me to begin to understand the history of W. R. Kenan Jr., the Kenan family, and the WRK Jr. Trust. More important, he confronted me with an issue I later discussed with my mentors in the history department at Chapel Hill: scholarly freedom. It would be impossible, Lewis said, for me to do an objective biography of WRK Jr.; if the trust funded a book, the trustees would get the story they wanted.

The trust did indeed fund this book, with a grant to the University of North Carolina at Chapel Hill Foundation, Inc., but the trustees must judge for themselves if they got what they wanted. At no time and in no way during this long and complicated project did they or anyone connected with them or the trust make any suggestions about the nature and content of this book. I was given complete freedom to do and write what I pleased—with only two exceptions. First, I had to cut the length of the manuscript in half, which improved the work considerably. Second, I requested but was denied access to two documents: the 1917 autopsy and detective's reports connected with Mary Lily's death. I was allowed to read a recent summary of the detective's report prepared by two friends of the Kenan family, but only after promising not to quote it or contact them. The reader will see in the endnotes my appraisal of the significance of the original documents.

Once I began my deep research on Kenan, it quickly became clear that almost everything that was known about him and his family was based upon hearsay and unwarranted speculation. That is certainly the case with Chandler's two books, *The Binghams of Louisville* and its predecessor, *Henry Flagler*, both of which treat the Kenans as crucial but one-dimensional characters in dramas performed by more powerful figures and families. The same can also be said of the way the Kenans are treated by Chandler's fellow journalist-authors in three subsequent books on the Bingham family: Marie Brenner in *House of Dreams*, Sallie Bingham in *Passion and Prejudice*, and Susan Tifft and Alex Jones in *The Patriarch*.

In bringing Kenan and his family to center stage, I have relied on the holdings of many archives, libraries, museums, and courthouses. I am grateful for the help of the staffs and clerks of Alderman Library at the University of Virginia, Antioch College Library, Atlanta Historical Society, Baker Library at Harvard University, University of California at Berkeley, Chesney Medical Archives at Johns Hopkins University, Chicago Historical Society, Dorothy Whitener Library, Duke University Libraries, Duplin County Courthouse, Duplin County Historical Society, East Carolina University, Filson Club, Florida Power & Light Company, Georgia Historical Society, Hagley Museum and Library, Henry Morrison Flagler Museum, Hoover Institution, Kenan Center, Liberty Hall, Lockport Public Library, Lower Cape Fear Historical Society, University of Maryland at Baltimore, Mercer University, National Archives of Canada, New Hanover County Public Library, North Carolina Collection, North Carolina Division of Archives and History, Niagara County Courthouse, Niagara County Historian's Office, Niagara County Historical Society, Ohio State University, Olive Kettering Library, Orange County Courthouse, Pack Memorial Public Library, Peace College, Pepper Library, Rockefeller Archive Center, St. Augustine Historical Society, Southern Historical Collection at the University of North Carolina at Chapel Hill, Stuart Hall, Washington and Lee University, Washington Memorial Library, and Western Reserve Historical Society.

I am especially grateful for the help I received from Bill Johnston at the Walters Art Gallery; Sam Thomas at the Mary & Barry Bingham Fund; Charles Simmons and Joan Runkel at the Henry Morrison Flagler Museum; Robert S. Conte at the Greenbrier Hotel; David Moltke-Hansen at the Southern Historical Collection; Edward Charron and Jerry Hairel of the CSX Corporation; Jacquelyn Hall at UNC; Jovita Flynn, who transcribed many of the interviews for this project; Kate Torrey and Ron Maner at UNC Press; and Stephanie Wenzel, my copyeditor.

I also want to express my appreciation to all who provided me with written and oral recollections of William Rand Kenan Jr., especially Francis B. Grow, S. Walter Martin, Audrey Raff, Dr. Guila B. Janssen, Lawrence Lewis Jr., and Mary Lily Flagler Lewis. Among the many others to whom I am also indebted for insight, information, and guidance I want to thank Mitchell Blakeley, Rich Boyd, Peter Coogan, Alice Cotten, Jerry Cotten, Amanda Cox, Virginia Pou Doughton, Jane Fagg, William C. Friday, Lorena Garmezy, Tom Graham, Lori Hefner, Charlotte Hoffman, Bertha Ihnat, James Shields Kenan, Thomas S. Kenan III, Nancy Post Lange, Roger Lotchin, Richard Lucas, Megan Mazzocchi, Bill Powell, Bill Reaves, Victor and Nancy Story, Beverly Tetterton, George Tindall, Margaret Truax, Susan Wendler, and Joel Williamson.

Many friends, colleagues, and family members read portions of the manuscript, and for their generosity, criticism, and valuable help I want to thank Susan Block, Maurice Bursey, Audrey Campbell, Mary Lee Campbell, Diane Cobb Cashman, and Jim Leloudis. The readers upon whom I inflicted the heaviest burden, and to whom I owe one of my greatest debts of gratitude, are Matt Hodgson and my friend Steven Channing, both of whom helped make the book shorter and better than I could have on my own.

My father and mother continued throughout this project to show me the love and encouragement they have given me throughout my life. Encouragement, though, is not the word to describe what my son, Elijah, gave me during this project; born while the ink was still wet on the contract, he now wants computer time of his own. But if anyone has the right later to claim repressed memories of the pain and pleasure experienced during the years of this project, it is my wife, Mary Lee, who has invested more in it and me than anyone will ever know. Thank you, Melton, for all you have done.

Across Fortune's Tracks

In the United States fortunes have their own histories.
It is the money, not the achievement, that echoes down the
halls of generations.

LEWIS LAPHAM

Money and Class in America

Life's like that[,] this train. If the station it gets to is [the resort]
Beidaihe you can have a great time. But if the station is just a halt in
the desert with nothing to eat, nothing to drink and nobody around
it's still your station. We didn't lay the track and we can't choose
where to stop.

CHINESE PEASANT

in Zhang Xinxin and Sang Ye,
Chinese Lives: An Oral History of
Contemporary China

The Kenans of North Carolina

William Rand Kenan Jr. was born on April 30, 1872, at his parents' home in Wilmington, North Carolina. He was raised in a family of conservative political activists and swaddled in Old South stories of ardent Lost Cause believers—of men and women whose minds and characters had been shaped by a distinct regional culture. But while he nursed at the nipple of Nicey, his black nanny, and loved to visit Liberty Hall, the old family homeplace in rural Duplin County, he grew to manhood in a different world. He matured in the New South, in a world of national integration, multinational corporations, industrialization, and urbanization.

SUSPENDED BETWEEN TWO WORLDS

Liberty Hall was as close as Kenan came to the Old South, and he remembered it fondly as a place of freedom and frolicking. To him it meant Christmastime, special occasions, and summer vacations. It meant cousins, hog killings, barbecues, and an interesting trip into the countryside: an hour-long train ride—exactly "forty-eight" miles on the Wilmington and Weldon Railroad—was coupled with a wagon ride between Magnolia station and Kenansville, a horse-drawn journey that covered "eight miles via a sandy road and usually took one hour."[1]

The wagon ride eased Will and his family into the slower, more self-sufficient environment that their forebears had been shaping and responding to for almost a century and a half. The first North Carolina Kenans arrived in Wilmington from Ireland (to which they had earlier migrated from Scotland) in the 1730s and migrated up the northeast branch of the Cape Fear River to the area that later became Duplin and Sampson counties. Quickly acquiring huge tracts of land and slaves, they became leaders of a small group of local gentry who dominated the political and economic life of their region both before and after the American Revolution.

Thomas Kenan – m – Elizabeth (Johnson or Johnston)
(ca. 1700–1766)   (d. 1789)

(Gen.) James Kenan – m – Sarah (Love)   7 other
(1740–1810)   (1747–1819)   children

Thomas Kenan – m – Mary (Rand)   Daniel   6 other
(1771–1843)   (1781–1856)   (1780–1840)   children

Owen Rand Kenan – m – Sarah Rebecca (Graham)
(1804–1887)   (1817–1871)

William – m – Mary
Rand   Hargrave
Kenan Sr.   (1842–1916)
(1845–1903)

Annie
Dickson
Kenan
(1843–1906)

James – m – Annie
Graham   Howard
Kenan   Hill
(1839–1912) (1852–1948)

Thomas – m – Sallie
Stephen Kenan   (Dortch)
(1838–1911)   (d. 1916)

Owen
(1872–
1963)

Emily
(1873–
1963)

Thomas
(1878–
1962)
m
Annice
(Hawkins)

Graham – m – Sarah
(1883–   (1876–
1920)   1968)

William
(1872–
1965)
m
Alice
(Pomroy)
(1865–1947)

Jessie
(1870–
1968)
m
Joseph Clisby
Wise

Mary Lily
(1867–
1917)

m–1) Henry M. Flagler
└ 2) Robert W. Bingham

1) Lawrence Lewis

Hugh Lewis 2) – m – Louise – m
Frederick Francis 3)   (1895–1937)

Anne
Hill
(1921–)

Sarah

Frank
Hawkins
(1912–)

Harriet 1) – m – 2)
(Dubose)

Elizabeth
(Price)

James
Graham
(1910–)
m
Anne (Clay)

Agnes
Anne
James
Brutus
Sarah

Thomas   Owen
Stephen Graham

Elizabeth   Annice

Lawrence Jr.
(1917–1995)
m

Janet Patton

Louise Janet Kenan

Mary Lily Flagler
(1920–)
m

1) Fred Pollard
2) James Wiley

Kenan Family

The family's most prestigious and powerful forebear was Will's great-great-grandfather, James Kenan, a hero of the Revolution. James began his political career as sheriff of Duplin County, and in 1765, at age twenty-five, he led a group of angry residents to Wilmington to oppose enforcement of the Stamp Act. He also served in North Carolina's colonial assembly and provincial congresses, led troops against the British throughout eastern North Carolina, chaired the Duplin and Wilmington safety committees, and was eventually appointed brigadier general of the Wilmington militia district. A member of the state constitutional convention in 1788 and 1789, James also served as chairman of North Carolina's Committee of the Whole on Ratification of the United States Constitution and as one of the first trustees of the University of North Carolina. By the time he died in 1810, he had served nine consecutive terms in the North Carolina Senate and was Duplin County's second largest slaveholder with thirty-seven slaves. In 1818 the new county seat was named "Kenansville" in his honor.[2]

Politics also played an important role in the lives of James's two surviving sons. Daniel, the youngest, represented Duplin County in both houses of the state legislature before moving to Quincy, Florida, where he became a large slaveholder and a three-term representative in the territorial legislature. Thomas, James's oldest son, also represented Duplin in both houses of the North Carolina legislature and went on to serve three consecutive terms in the United States Congress as well. Prior to moving to Selma, Alabama, in 1833, moreover, where he served several terms in the Alabama House of Representatives, Thomas Kenan operated Lockland plantation, in southern Duplin County, with fifty slaves.[3]

The only member of Thomas's family to remain in Duplin County was his son Owen Kenan, Will's grandfather, who was supposed to join the family in Alabama after selling Lockland and some slaves. But Owen never moved to Alabama. Elected to the North Carolina legislature in 1834, he served in the general assembly until 1836, when he married Sarah Rebecca Graham, the daughter of Duplin's most prominent planter-physician, Dr. Stephen Graham. Having inherited lots of money, land, and slaves from her wealthy father, Sarah made it possible for her husband, who was also her legal guardian, to maintain and expand the power he inherited in Duplin County. Owen not only profited from the use of her slaves on Lockland and the Graham plantations, but he also leased them to and supervised their work on the Wilmington and Weldon Railroad.[4]

Sarah's wealth also made it possible for Owen to buy or build a large house just outside Kenansville. There, it seems, at Liberty Hall, all four of their children were born: Thomas in 1838, James in 1839, Annie in 1843, and William Rand "Buck" Kenan in 1845. All of the children attended private academies in Duplin County, and all eventually received additional schooling away from home. Thomas spent a year at the Central Military Academy in Selma, Alabama, a year at Wake Forest College, and three years at the University of North Carolina, where he graduated in the spring of 1857. He then studied law at Richmond Hill, North Carolina, before returning to Kenansville and opening his law practice in 1860.

James returned to Chapel Hill that fall for his senior year at UNC, and Buck entered the university as a fifteen-year-old freshman. By the time they returned to Liberty Hall the following spring, North Carolina had seceded from the Union; Thomas was commanding the county's first military company, the "Duplin Rifles"; and their father had more than 100 slaves at work on Lockland plantation alone. James immediately joined his brother Thomas in the Duplin Rifles, but Buck was too young to volunteer. He returned to UNC in the fall of 1861, shortly before his father was elected to the Confederate Congress at Richmond, Virginia.[5]

Buck never graduated from UNC. But he did fall in love with Chapel Hill's wealthiest and prettiest woman. He and Mollie Hargrave became engaged in the spring of 1863, and later that summer, after his brothers were wounded and captured at Gettysburg and after Union troops invaded Duplin County and burned a Confederate sword factory near Liberty Hall, eighteen-year-old Buck Kenan joined the Duplin Rifles. He spent several months in action in eastern North Carolina before returning to Chapel Hill, where on March 28, 1864, he and Mollie were married. The altar was still warm, however, when he returned to the war, and on August 21, while commanding a corps of sharpshooters at Charleston, Virginia, Buck, then a second lieutenant, was wounded. Back in action by November, he was elected adjutant of his regiment and was among its few lucky survivors at Appomattox at the end of the war.[6]

Buck returned to Chapel Hill to live with Mollie and her two brothers, but he did not stay long. Shortly after entering the university in the fall of 1865, he took a bookkeeping job with Willard Brothers, a wholesale grocery firm in Wilmington, where he boarded with Mollie's wealthy kinsman, William H. McRary.[7] How long he worked for the Willards is not clear; according to the local R. G. Dun correspondent, the Wilmington firm was "doing a good Bus" in September 1867 and was "considered punctual and reliable." But by then, it seems, Buck had returned to Duplin County, where in June of that year his and Mollie's first child, Mary Lily, was born.[8]

Buck worked at a variety of jobs in Kenansville, none of which proved prosperous. In October 1868 the local Dun reporter described him as "A yng man just commencing no ppy [property] in his own right that I know of but his father is wealthy & I cons'd 'W.R.K.' perf'y safe"; two months later Buck appeared "pruden[t] cautious and attentive to bus, worth in his own right 25 c/$ [$250]." But by the end of 1869 he was reportedly "out of bus," and in the 1870 census he gave his occupation as life insurance agent.[9]

Liberty Hall, Kenansville, North Carolina, late nineteenth century. (*Incidents* 1)

It was during this period of uncertainty and violence that Buck took up the political activism of his male Kenan forebears—something that Will, his son, never did. He supported the political ambitions of his older brother Colonel Thomas Kenan, who was doing rather well since his return to Liberty Hall from the Union prison at Johnson's Island, Ohio. Thanks to the relatively lenient provisions of presidential Reconstruction, Duplin's voters elected Thomas to the state legislatures of 1865–66 and 1866–67. The wounded Confederate veteran was no hero to the county's black population, however, and in 1868, as a result of Radical Reconstruction and black voting, Thomas, despite the efforts of Buck and the other Kenan menfolk, lost his bid for a seat in the United States Congress. Indeed, according to one newspaper, Thomas "accepted the candidacy, in the face of an overwhelming Republican majority, without any expectation of securing an election, but that he might seize that opportunity to stir up the people of the District and publicly to denounce the mischievous and corrupt policy of the party in power."[10]

Reconstruction witnessed a number of other changes among the Kenans of Liberty Hall. Thomas married Sallie Dortch of Edgecombe County and moved with her to Wilson, North Carolina, where he continued to pursue his political career and to work as an attorney for the Wilmington and Weldon Railroad. Sarah, Buck's mother, died at Liberty Hall shortly thereafter, at about the time that his other brother, James, married Annie Hill of Duplin County. Buck and Mollie had their second child, Jessie, late in 1870 and then decided to build a house in Wilmington. Though it is not clear what prompted their move or what work, if any, Buck initially pursued in the bustling seaport city, he probably sold some insurance and kept the books at Willard Brothers.[11]

Buck and Mollie frequently returned with their children to Kenansville, however, where, unlike the busy streets of urban Wilmington, one was "immediately struck with the quiet and antiquated appearance of things in general." The village was no longer "one of the most flourishing and dashing little towns in North Carolina." The war and Reconstruction had seen to that.[12]

Liberty Hall still looked impressive, however, and its rhythms and rituals remained quite unlike those that shaped the life of Will and his sisters in Wilmington. The house had "large" bedrooms, Kenan later recalled, "many having four-posters and deep feather mattresses. The heating was done by means of wood in fire places, one in each room of the house. There was no refrigeration of any kind. If a chicken was required for dinner, it was killed and cooked immediately. If we had beef or lamb, it was planned ahead when to kill it and the excess over our consumption was sold to the neighbors."[13]

Owen, the former Confederate congressman, still reigned at Liberty Hall, but increasingly his maiden daughter, Annie, her cousin Annie Kinnear, and Martha Cooper, their black cook, ruled there. Though Will had little to say about the two Annies, who later tried to turn Liberty Hall into a retirement home for women, he remembered his grandfather as a generous teacher and a strict Presbyterian Sabbatarian. "My Paternal Grandfather looked upon Sunday as a day of rest, so the noon-day dinner was all prepared on Saturday and, of course, a cold spread was eaten."

Owen tried on other days to teach his grandson about farm ways, profits, and patience. A lifelong leader of the Cape Fear Agricultural Association, he occasionally provided Will with a plot of land at Liberty Hall. "Sometimes when we came up to spend the summer I would plant a garden and work it but as I had to return home in time for school some of the vegetables were not matured; however, I was sure to harvest them and take them home." Owen also paid his grandson to cut and haul wood from the forest and stimulated young Will's interest in the care and feeding of cattle—a pursuit better suited to teaching the lessons of patience and profit. The old patriarch often gave Kenan "a calf which I would raise on his feed and, when grown, I would sell it, keeping the proceeds."

What Will enjoyed most about Liberty Hall was the joyous intensity of playing there with his sisters, cousins, and the servants' children. "Usually all the grandchildren would be there and did we have fun. Negro servants, many of all ages—Martha, the cook, had a large family, all of them living on the place, and, in addition there were several other families living there." The Kenan grandchildren eventually numbered eight: Will and his three sisters, Mary Lily, Jessie, and Sarah (who was born in 1876), and the four children of James and Annie Hill Kenan, Owen, Emily, Thomas, and Graham. While only Mary Lily, the oldest of the eight, could remember their grandmother Sarah, even Graham, the youngest Kenan cousin, who was born in 1883, got to know their grandfather Owen.

Liberty Hall made a marvelous playground for the Kenan cousins and their black playmates. They fed the chickens, gathered eggs, rode horses, and watched the fights of the family's prize gamecocks. They played in and around the big house, the smokehouse, and the shacks of the servants who lived "in the yard." They ran through the fields, walked in the woods, and climbed the trees that surrounded the huge garden. "Each tree belonged to one of the children and they took particular pride in their tree. They could do what they wanted to in their respective trees."[14] Will and his sisters also carved their initials on the kitchen wall and lapped up the desserts prepared by Martha. Her apple pie was his favorite: "The bottom or crust was made and apple sauce put in just before being served, this was covered with a deep layer of whipped cream and it was good."[15]

Visits to Liberty Hall also contrasted with the stricter and more closely supervised routine imposed on Will and his sisters in Wilmington. "At Liberty Hall every one was welcome and we children could do anything." They could even sample the casks in the wine cellar, "a large high ceiling cellar under part of the house. Most unusual for the south in those days." The old cellar had "many large wooden casks containing both hard liquor and many kinds of wine, all made on the place." Its huge key "hung on the wall of the Butler's Pantry. It was about eight inches long and weighed approximately one pound. We children would take it any time and sample every cask in the cellar. There was no way to get the contents out, except through the bung hole in the top side so it was necessary to take a rubber tube and siphon it out, which we did."

Christmas always brought the Kenan clan to Liberty Hall for "a barbecue of both pig and lamb." Will remembered the cooking as a very precise operation: "This was done out of doors by digging a trench 2' wide and 15" deep and 6' long, the fire in the bottom and hickory limbs were laid across the pit above the fire to carry the carcass. . . . The cooking is done rapidly at first in order to brown the meat and hold the juices inside; after that the heat is reduced and the roasting is done slowly. The carcass is turned frequently and basted all the time with a sauce very highly seasoned."

Will also became intrigued with the meat grinder at Liberty Hall while "they were killing the hogs for the winter supply." Not understanding how the grinder worked, he put his "finger into the same and the end of one finger on my right hand came off. I had it sewed on again and it did not give me any trouble thereafter except when playing base-ball on two occasions I got it partly split off."

Kenan's meat grinder story reflects his lifelong assumption that some benign force, be it Providence, Nature, or Fate, he never says, blessed him with the soul of a scientist and engineer. This was evident, he believed, in his aggressive curiosity about how things worked. He may have been born and raised in the South, in a region more noted for hog killings than scientific

110 Nun Street, the Kenan home in Wilmington, North Carolina. (*Incidents* 1)

achievement, but it was not the region that ruled him; it was his predisposition to build and understand things. Indeed, Kenan apparently regarded his childhood injury as an act of both self-realization and self-immolation. It taught him the pain and excitement of being a scientist.

This same general assumption informs Kenan's memories of the house in which he grew up. Yet his description of his "father's house" in Wilmington reflects the cold eye of an engineer and not, as with Liberty Hall, the happy, frolicking child who played all day and slept peacefully in feather beds. He describes the house as if he were reading from its blueprints and places paramount importance on its role as his laboratory, as a place where he discovered and nurtured his natural scientific inclinations. "When I reached about eight years old my job was to keep the wood boxes on the rear verandas (both first and second floors) filled. After a few years of carrying wood upstairs, I rigged up a hoist and purchased a goat and had him haul up all the wood, which was great fun."

Others nourished this predisposition, of course. The man Kenan admired most in life, Harvard-trained engineer Henry Walters, gave him science books, while his own family gave him tools as presents. Yet the actions of others merely buttressed what Kenan considered his innate cathedral of character. "I was always interested in construction and from time to time received many carpenter tools. I built several shacks in the yard, improving and enlarging them from time to time." What was more, Kenan shared this inner light with his boyhood friend Theodore Empie. "Empie and I constructed and installed a telephone circuit between our homes, the first in North Carolina."

If both Liberty Hall and the Nun Street house confirmed for Kenan the

Will Kenan, age eight. (*Incidents* 1)

temperament that fortune apparently granted him, so too, it seems, did the environment of Wilmington itself. He discovered his boatbuilding skills, for example, at the Cape Fear River, just a block or so from his house. He not only "built a model of a boat and fully rigged it," but he also constructed "a canoe and used to carry it back and forth to the river, where we got much pleasure in going all about." At the same time, the port city elicited his natural passion for collecting stamps. "I was interested in a foreign stamp collection and it was our custom to board foreign ships both at the docks and out in the stream to obtain stamps from the members of the crew. I had a very fine collection of about 1,000 varieties and, when I came north to live, left them at home and they simply disappeared."

Kenan may have been a born collector, but he failed to inherit the one attribute shared by most of his family—the ability to make music. Unfortunately this made it impossible for him to participate fully in what became one of the most important aspects of family life at 110 Nun Street. All the white women of the house received some kind of professional instruction in voice, piano, or both, and their singing and piano playing dominate Kenan's recollections of family life in Wilmington. His warmest memory is of his mother, Mollie, at the piano. "She was fond of music and any night a crowd of young people would call and she would play the piano all the evening for us to dance." The family was filled, in fact, with musicmakers, both men and women alike. Mollie's uncle taught violin in Chapel Hill; the Colonel played the guitar; Aunt Annie, the organ; cousin Tom, the cornet and the guitar; and so on, with the exception, of course, of young Will, who admitted he "could not sing nor play any instrument."

This natural deficiency worried Kenan, for it became obvious early that it might do more than render him mute during family musicmaking. It might also ruin his chances to meet and attract women. Kenan first made this connection in a series of incidents that combined his own pubescent stirrings with the debutante parties of his oldest sister. Mary Lily was almost five years older than Will, and "when she came out, or made her debut, it was the usual custom for the young men to serenade the young ladies at night with vocal and instrumental music, especially if some other out of town young ladies were visiting at our house." Kenan could not ignore the ritual's impact on the serenaded debs. "My room was at the end of the hall, second floor, directly over the entrance, had two large windows and was a corner room. It was very favorable to see and hear the serenade, so the girls would all pile into my room, and, of course, wake me up, much to my disgust."

A few years later, Kenan's musical deficiencies threatened to keep him out of the Glee Club at the University of North Carolina, the only college club that guaranteed its members field trips and female audiences throughout the state. Kenan became so intent on making the club, however, that he conceived the idea of performing a tumbling act with several other club members during concert intermissions. The club's director naturally considered such antics "foolish," but Kenan continued to work on him and "eventually persuaded him . . . to come over to the gymnasium and view the performance. We put it on for him and, after that, I became a member of the Glee Club."

The University of North Carolina, Liberty Hall, and the house at 110 Nun Street—Kenan says more about them in the five different editions of his autobiography, *Incidents by the Way*, than he does about his family. He acknowledges his parents as a source of food, clothing, shelter, and presents, and they appear warm and friendly to almost everyone, including their only son. Yet, as presented by Will, they remain rather vague figures, nourishing but neither significant nor instrumental in shaping his life. Kenan remembered his mother as "small of stature but the most energetic person I ever knew. She was always occupied." She "was born and raised at Chapel Hill, N.C., attended the public schools and finished at the Oxford Female Seminary at Oxford, N.C." She played the piano, was "a good housekeeper and a fine seamstress," and "would get in a colored seamstress and, together, they would make most of our clothes, including my clothes, until I was about eight years old." Thrifty, energetic, and skilled in the womanly arts, Mollie would "make friends of anybody."

So, too, would Buck. He "liked people and we had some one to meals almost every day," William recalled. "My father loved good food and always had plenty of the best in the market. He always did the marketing each morning when he went to his office." He also gave his son some spectacular (if potentially dangerous) gifts. "When I was about twelve years old my father purchased a pony for me, a real wild Mustang, never had a bridle nor a saddle on him. They were driven from the range, loaded in cattle cars and brought to Wilmington to be sold. The cowboys would lasso the horse, one around the neck and then the other around the hind leg and throw the horse to the ground, when saddle and bridle was attached and we boys learned to ride by mounting the horse on the ground."

Yet Kenan clearly considered his father a better protector than provider. He says only one thing about Buck's business career: "He was a wholesale merchant of Wilmington, North Carolina." For someone like Kenan, who considered business success a critical measure of one's success in life, this was tantamount to admitting that his father failed as a businessman. Indeed, Buck was obviously more at home in the fighting South, in the homosocial male solace of hunting, drinking, and politics, than he was in church, the business world, or the female-dominated house at 110 Nun Street. "In the summer, when the family was away, he would have several young men to dinner etc. very often," William explained. "He was very fond of young men and a great many used to hang out at our house. There was always wine and hard liquors on the sideboard. . . . He liked a long toddy and frequently had one to which I was always invited. He smoked nearly all the time, cigars and sometimes a pipe."

William particularly remembered his father's reputation as "a great hunter of all kinds of game and with any kind of gun. It seemed to be natural with him. He was the best shot I ever saw." So good, in fact, it was intimidating. "When I was eight years old he gave me a gun (a 16 gauge double-barrelled shot

Mary Hargrave "Mollie" Kenan, Will Kenan's mother, ca. 1885. (NgCHS)

gun) and afterwards I always accompanied him when hunting. He would take a 22 rifle and kill more squirrels than I could with a shot gun. We would hunt ducks in a canoe with a colored boy to paddle us. I sat in the bow and he amidship and I always shot first and if I missed he always knocked them down."

William Rand "Buck" Kenan Sr., Will Kenan's father, ca. 1885. (NgCHS)

Buck was an unusually aggressive protector, in fact, especially in political and military matters. Yet there is little about this history in his son's autobiographies. Kenan wrote nothing about Buck's Confederate sharpshooter days or the most important aspect of his father's life, politics, for he always avoided the topics of politics, the Civil War, and the Kenan family's role in both. Instead he mentions his father's postwar saber-rattling. Buck "was much interested in the National Guard. Organized a company in Wilmington; was its Captain for many years, and then Adjutant of the State Guards. He always went into camp with them each summer and on the rifle range he would take any one's gun and outshoot the whole Regiment."

William also mentioned being "impressed" with Buck's most celebrated example of sharpshooting. "There was a riot of colored men in Wilmington [in 1898] and my father organized a volunteer company of men with all kinds of rifles together with a riot gun on a wagon and they cleaned up the riot very quickly, although they were compelled to kill several persons. He rode the wagon and directed the operation." Although Kenan described himself as a "small boy" at the time of the Wilmington race riot, he was actually twenty-six years old and working for the Union Carbide Company in Sault St. Marie, Michigan.

Kenan's chronological confusion involved more than the misremembering of a seventy-year-old man encumbered with creeping senility at the time he wrote his autobiography. It reflected his basic uneasiness with his southern heritage. Nowhere in surviving documents does this son of former slaveholders mention slavery, the Civil War, race, or Reconstruction—the tumultuous period into which he was born. Even his autobiographies reveal little about the people and places, including the South, that profoundly affected his life. Indeed, *Incidents* is only one side of his story: that of a man more actor and shaper than a person shaped and acted upon. One must therefore turn to other sources to understand Kenan's fuller human side.

BIRTH AND REDEMPTION

Buck Kenan began the last day of April 1872 as he did each day, with Indian clubs and sit-up exercises. Like many urban middle-class Americans of the period, the twenty-six-year-old Wilmington resident had joined the ranks of the postwar physical fitness crusade. He was a devoted practitioner of "muscular Christianity," the belief that "morality was a function of muscularity as well as of piety, and that the best sort of Christians were physically fit."[16]

The ex-Confederate sharpshooter touched his toes with more than morality and piety in mind, though. In addition to anticipating the arrival of another child, Buck contemplated Wilmington's normal election-season nastiness. Night writers had chalked the windows and doors of waterfront stores with the huge initials "K.K.K." A new black militia company, the Wilmington Rifle Guards, had ordered a hundred Springfield rifles and uniforms, and the elite white women of the Ladies Memorial Association had announced plans to unveil their Confederate monument at Oakdale cemetery on Confederate Memorial Day—only days after the city elections.[17]

Buck loved politics almost as much as he admired his oldest brother, Thomas Kenan, and like Thomas, who was running for mayor of Wilson, North Carolina, Buck had recently transferred his political activism from the Duplin County countryside to the city. He had charged headlong into the political world of the state's largest city, where for the past year or so he, Mollie, and their two young daughters, Mary Lily and Jessie, had been living in their new house on Nun Street. Buck was acting as a fourth-ward canvasser for the Conservative (or Democratic) party, and the May 6 elections marked his debut in the political life of Wilmington.[18]

Buck and his friends hoped to win for Wilmington the social and political "redemption" achieved by Conservatives elsewhere in the state. The Republican party was on the run in North Carolina's Piedmont region; Conservatives controlled a majority in both houses of the state legislature; and in March 1871 they impeached and convicted Republican governor William Woods Holden, the first state governor to suffer such a fate. Wilmington's Conservatives wanted to move their city in the same direction: to redeem it from Radical Republican rule. Not only was Wilmington critical to "Conservatives as the home of some of their more important leaders and newspapers. But it was even more important to the Republicans: Despite the fact that their strength lay in the more remote rural areas, the Conservatives controlling almost all towns, at least Wilmington was a Republican stronghold."[19] Thus Buck and his Conservative cohorts faced a difficult task. They wanted to lead Wilmington into the future by appealing to the past—a romanticized history that Buck's son never found interesting.

By the time William Rand Kenan Jr. was born, Wilmington's Conservative and Republican leaders had fixed the municipal elections. That was the opinion, at least, of Conservative leader John Lyon Holmes, Buck's cousin. According to Holmes, a member of the state's Secession Convention, the city races appeared "settled." Six Republican and four Conservative candidates would run for the city's ten-member aldermanic board—an agreement, Holmes noted, that would finally give Conservatives "a representation at the Board, a most important & valuable necessity for the tax payers of the city." As for completely redeeming Wilmington from Republican rule, Holmes appealed to more powerful forces: "I hope & pray that God will send us soon a safe deliverance from this terribly oppressive & unscrupulous party."[20]

The Conservatives also hoped that a deal in Wilmington might strengthen their party's position in North Carolina and the South. The city elections would be followed by the state elections in August and by congressional and presidential contests as well as elections in other states in November. "North Carolina having the first election this summer must be carried, if possible," wrote Conservative North Carolina congressman Alfred Moore Waddell, "but the Radicals will use all the money and every means including, if necessary, some force to carry it. We ought to go into the fight with coats off & sleeves rolled up, determined to win."[21] Buck's cousin agreed: "In the state, District & county Elections," Holmes wrote, "we will work like beavers in this coming elections [*sic*]."[22]

At the time of Will Kenan's birth, Wilmington's economic life was also at a turning point, one that presaged immediate and long-term consequences for both the Kenans and the city. By 1872 the production of rice, the once-abundant staple of the city's riverine and littoral hinterland, was at an all-time low. Where in 1857 Wilmington's mills and merchants cleaned and exported half a million bushels of locally grown rice to Baltimore, New York, and foreign ports, in 1871 only a handful of planters produced a total crop of 10,000 bushels—less than the amount used in North Carolina alone. Nowhere in the state could one northern reporter see "so many evidences of the poverty and ruin brought upon the southern people by the war as along the banks of the Cape Fear River from [Wilmington] to and including Fayetteville. Capital and labor are the great desideratums needed to retrieve these lands from the ruin which the war brought them to."[23]

By 1872 Wilmington was also losing its position as a leading lumber center and the foremost naval stores market in the world. The production and trans-portation centers of both industries were shifting farther to the South, to the ports and pine barrens of Georgia and Florida. Though a few local lumber mills still turned a profit, northern capitalists now found "it much cheaper and easier to purchase lumber farther south."[24] At the same time, the "speculative mania" driving the naval stores industry was collapsing, "leaving the industry awash in low prices. The naval stores market never quite recovered from that debacle; neither for that matter did Wilmington's trade."[25]

Simultaneously, moreover, the city was also feeling the impact of its strate-gic position within the Southern Railway Project. The purpose of the project, which was backed by a syndicate of northern investors, was to create a system of interconnected railroads along the Atlantic Coast, and two of Wilmington's three railroad companies—the Wilmington and Weldon and the Wilmington, Columbia & Augusta (WC&A)—lay at the heart of the syndicate's plans.[26] The Wilmington and Weldon provided connections to the Pennsylvania Railroad and the cities of the Northeast. Its standard-gauge tracks ran between Wil-mington and the Virginia border and connected there with the standard-gauge Virginia lines also being targeted by the project. On the other hand, the WC&A ran on broader, "southern" gauge track and tapped the territory south of Wilmington, giving the syndicate connections to the ports at Charleston and Savannah and to the important inland trade centers of Columbia, Augusta, and Atlanta.

By the spring of 1872, financial control of both roads had passed from the hands of local investors to the syndicate. The officers of the WC&A had been moved into the Wilmington and Weldon's office building in downtown Wilmington, and the syndicate had decided to lease the Wilmington and Weldon to the WC&A. The only North Carolinian with a noticeable managerial and financial position in both roads was their president, Robert Bridgers, who originally sought financial support from syndicate leader William T. Walters of Baltimore. In addition to Walters, a wealthy merchant who was "keenly interested in the raising and transportation of fresh vegetables for eastern markets," the syndicate included other prominent Baltimoreans, a group of New York City capitalists, and the president and vice-president of the Pennsylvania Railroad Company.[27]

Walters was the Wilmington and Weldon's largest stockholder and one of its most important postwar leaders. A strong states' rights man who had also invested heavily in the South's transportation and financial networks before 1860, Walters spent most of the war in Paris with his son, Henry, and his daughter, Jennie—all in exile, it seems, for his pro-Confederate activities in Baltimore. With the sad exception of his wife's death from pneumonia, however, Walters's European sojourn was an exciting one. Before returning to Baltimore with Henry and Jennie in 1865, he became intimately acquainted with many French and English painters and embarked on a second career as a serious collector of European art, especially contemporary French paintings.

Few people shaped the Kenan family's fortunes as much as Walters and his son, Henry. By the spring of 1872 Will's uncle James was acting on the syndicate's suggestion to try some fruit and vegetable crops at Lockland, the old family plantation in Duplin County. Though James and his tenants still concentrated on cotton, corn, tobacco, and naval stores, the majority of which they continued to transport south to Wilmington by water, they also began testing Lockland's suitability for truck farming crops: that is, for produce the syndicate could move by rail to urban centers in the Northeast.[28]

The syndicate's activities were even more important to Owen Kenan, Will's grandfather. The former Confederate congressman had recently opened a sawmill at Cerro Gordo, a stop on the WC&A line in Columbus County, that depended directly on the syndicate to move its lumber and to provide it with business. Its largest client was the Harrisburg Car Factory, which made wooden rolling stock for the Pennsylvania Railroad Company in Harrisburg, Pennsylvania, the home of syndicate member and future senator J. Donald Cameron.[29]

It was Henry Walters, however, the syndicate leader's son, who had the greatest impact on the Kenans of 110 Nun Street. Henry was three years younger than Buck and a very different kind of man. He spent most of the war in Europe, visiting galleries and museums with his father, and in the spring of 1872 he completed his first year of studies in the Lawrence Scientific School at Harvard University.[30]

Walters was "the very first individual" Will could remember outside his own immediate family, and Walters became a "second Father" to him, "the best counselor and friend" Kenan ever had. Indeed, Walters had many of the things Kenan wanted for himself—scientific training, business acumen, and financial success—and provided a role model quite different from Buck. Whereas Buck taught his son to shoot a gun, Walters nourished young Will's interest in science, giving him "many Technical books (from time to time) most of them having been purchased in France." And where Buck suffered repeated business failures, Walters symbolized for Kenan the epitome of business success. He became president of the Wilmington and Weldon's successor, the Atlantic Coast Line Railroad Company (ACL), and one of the wealthiest men in the South. "He was a wonderful executive with natural business ability," Kenan believed, "the most outstanding, all around executive it has been my good fortune to know."[31]

Through railroads and Henry Walters, moreover, Will's oldest sister, Mary Lily, met her future husband, Henry Morrison Flagler. By the spring of 1872 Flagler was well on his way to accumulating the fortune that Will and his sisters later inherited. Flagler had been John D. Rockefeller's business partner since 1867. He had suggested the incorporation of Standard Oil of Ohio in 1870, he had served as its secretary and treasurer since that time, and he was critical to its expansion as "transportation negotiator, legal expert and communicator with Rockefeller on new ideas." When Standard increased its capitalization from 10,000 to 25,000 shares on January 1, 1872, one day before Flagler's forty-second birthday, he held close to 14 percent of the company's stock—second only to Rockefeller.[32]

MYTH AND MEMORY

Will Kenan was only ten days old when the Ladies Memorial Association unveiled its Confederate Memorial at Wilmington's Oakdale cemetery. Speeches and poetry readings commemorated the event, cadets from the Cape Fear Academy drilled and saluted, and the Coronet Concert Band, attired in its new gray and gold-braid uniforms, provided music. It was one of the state's largest and most exciting Lost Cause ceremonies.[33]

Though meant for mourning and mythology, the unveiling also marked a victory of sorts for Buck and his fellow Conservatives. The city elections had gone exactly as planned. Conservative (or Democratic) candidates won four aldermanic seats (their first since 1868), and the Republicans retained the mayor's seat and elected six of their candidates (three black and three white) to the ten-member board of aldermen. While Conservatives had a lot more to do to "redeem" their city completely from biracial Republican rule, the aldermanic victories were an encouraging start; they were cause for celebration.[34]

Buck witnessed the unveiling with other memorialists but did not share the grief and bereavement that many displayed. For him, and for many others like him, the new monument was as much a testament to their own honorable triumph over adversity as it was a memorial to the South's fallen heroes. He also had had a very good week. In addition to helping the Conservatives return to power, he was elected treasurer of the Wilmington YMCA. Even more important, Mollie made it safely through the delivery with a healthy son—the first Kenan grandson.[35]

Will's arrival also coincided with the election of his uncle Colonel Thomas Kenan as mayor of Wilson, North Carolina. A handsome, vigorous man with a fashionable Van Dyke beard, the thirty-four-year-old Colonel had all the right stuff to appeal to the thousand or so residents of this lily-white village. He was a railroad attorney in a railroad town, a Democrat, a former Confederate officer, and a North Carolinian of noble pedigree. He was "a product of the old South," one friend recalled, "when honor, chivalry, courtesy, culture and hospitality were the leading characteristics of her people."[36]

Thomas had arrived in Wilson hoping to make yet another run for Congress, but, ironically, in the months preceding his mayoral nomination the Conservative-controlled legislature altered the racial balance of the state's Second District. In an act of partisan apportionment it removed three counties with white majorities (including Duplin) and added three—Northampton, Halifax, and Warren—that were heavily black and Republican.[37] Yet the creation of the new "Black Second" also strengthened the Colonel's already close ties with Wharton Jackson Green, one of the wealthiest and most powerful Democrats in the new gerrymandered district.

Like Thomas Kenan, Green was a lawyer and a former Confederate officer. Both he and Kenan were also wounded and captured at Gettysburg and spent the rest of the war imprisoned together on Johnson's Island, where they drafted and signed a secret letter to North Carolina governor Zebulon Baird Vance. Full of praise for the governor's stand against the peace movement in their state, the 1864 letter had been signed by other imprisoned North Carolina officers and smuggled out to Vance in the garments of an exchanged prisoner.[38] Following the war, moreover, both Green and the Colonel resumed their legal careers and aligned themselves with the Democratic party and the region's railroad interests. They supported Vance's long and distinguished political career and became lifelong promoters of Confederate history and veterans' organizations. More important, perhaps, at least for the Kenans of Wilmington, Green's oldest daughter played a crucial role in fostering the relationship between Will Kenan's sister Mary Lily and Standard Oil magnate Henry M. Flagler.[39]

Green and the Colonel got their first taste of the political realities of their new province when the Republican district convention met in Wilson in the days that followed Will Kenan's birth. Josephus Daniels later recalled the scene in a style characteristic of the era. "The majority of the delegates were Negroes, with a mere handful of white delegates. As soon as the door of the courthouse was opened, the Negroes crowded in so that there was no room for white participants. . . . Think of five hundred perspiring Negroes packed into a courthouse, wrangling and near-fighting, on a red-hot day!"[40]

Shortly thereafter these eager black voters received a visit from Henry Lane Wilson, the Massachusetts radical running with Ulysses S. Grant. Hoping to prevent the black vote from going to Grant's opponent, Horace Greeley, Lane made his only speech in the state at Wilson, the geographical center of the state's Black Second. But he did not share the platform with the city's new Democratic mayor, Thomas Kenan, who had recently returned with Green from the Baltimore convention endorsing Greeley's candidacy. Like other local Democrats, the mayor watched the future vice-president from "the courthouse and heard from the open windows."[41]

One of the Republican party's most impressive speakers, Frederick Douglass, also visited North Carolina at the time of Will Kenan's birth. The fiery black orator spoke in Wilmington in May 1872, only days before the state elections, and mesmerized the thousands of blacks and whites who heard him speak. So compelling was his message, in fact, that local Conservatives moved quickly to try to counter his appeal to white voters. The *Wilmington Star*, which was owned and edited by the chairman of the Conservative Executive Committee of New Hanover County, alerted its readers to some "Startling Information": Federal marshals planned to vote black men early and then seize the ballot boxes under the pretense of protecting them from a riot. But Conservatives were prepared for such shenanigans, the *Star* promised. The party planned to station two "challengers" in each ward "to check all attempts at illegal voting" and "to take charge of the vehicle provided for bringing Conservative voters to the polls, and to perform other duties as may be necessary to the success of our cause."[42]

Buck acted as a Conservative "challenger" in the city's fourth ward, and between his political duties and whatever he was doing for a job, he spent little time at home. He also failed to reap the political payoff he had hoped for: a state job. Although Conservatives retained their majority in the general assembly, Republican candidates won the governor's office, the lieutenant governor's office, and sixteen additional seats in the state legislature.[43] The only evidence of Buck's livelihood at this time appeared in the *Wilmington Star* in the aftermath of the elections: "FOR RENT: That desirable tenement House (French's Brick Building) on Dock, between Fourth & Fifth Sts., with all the modern improvements—waterworks, etc.—. . . Apply to W. R. Kenan." Revealingly, the building belonged to a leading member of Wilmington's Republican ring, George Zadoc French, a Yankee carpetbagger who arrived in the city with the Union army.[44]

As helpful as they were throughout Buck's business career, the most lasting contribution made by local Republicans to him and his family (as well as to many poor whites in the city) was in the field of education. Republican support for a first-class normal school in Wilmington, the Tileston School, and for the unstinting labors of the school's Yankee leader, Amy Morris Bradley, gave Will and his sisters access to what was arguably the best public education then available in North Carolina and the South.[45]

Many Wilmingtonians initially mistrusted Amy Bradley and her intentions. In addition to being a talented, well-educated woman she was an unmarried, forty-two-year-old, northern-born schoolteacher who actively supported the Union cause. She had nursed the northern injured on boats and battlefields, and she had served as a special agent for the United States Sanitary Commission. She had the power, it was said, to raise "one white finger of her little hand" and thereby command the same attention and allegiance as "the drawn sword of General Grant." Put simply, she appeared to be everything Wilmington's old-line southern aristocrats hated.

All the Kenan children attended Bradley's Tileston School, however, and all of them benefited from it. To the three Kenan sisters the school offered more than instruction in the womanly arts of sewing, singing, and piano and more than the best 3R training then available in North Carolina and the South. It gave them an alternative role model, a woman quite unlike their mother and the vast majority of women in Wilmington society. While Mollie Kenan rarely ventured beyond the spheres of family, home, and church, Amy Bradley made her life in the public arena; and whereas Mollie always deferred to Buck, Bradley challenged men like him and the assumptions he held.

Bradley and her school also shaped the course of Will Kenan's career. In addition to providing him with the rudiments of a classical education, they stimulated his lifelong interest in science and engineering. Bradley firmly believed in industrial education, and she often quoted its proponents in the school newspaper: "It is not the faculties of the mind alone, that should be cultivated," one editorialist wrote. "Skill of hand, a power over things, is very essential to success."[46] And Bradley practiced what she preached. Kenan had access to laboratory equipment at Tileston and to some of the finest, most up-to-date textbooks in mineralogy, botany, geology, physics, zoology, and chemistry.

Will also benefited from Bradley's enthusiasm for higher education and the Tileston students who went North to study science and engineering in college. "Some of the Tileston students having finished a course of study here," she wrote in the school newspaper, "have passed into the Institute of Technology in Boston, Massachusetts, to fit themselves for some special profession." As a spur to those who wished to work with such "a definite object in view," she included a sketch of the MIT curriculum and a report from her former student W. H.

Chadbourn Jr., who scored well on his entrance exams at MIT. "I am in section one—" Chadbourn wrote, "a proof that the training given by Tileston will compare favorably with Chauncey Hall and any of that class of schools."[47]

Bradley opened the doors of the new Tileston School in October 1872, only weeks before the congressional and presidential elections. Located just a block and a half from the Kenan home, the new school drew some 160 students, all white. Most were classified as "poor" and thus were permitted to attend the school free of charge, but others, like Will and his sisters, came from families who "paid" something for their schooling.[48] The facility awed them all. Thanks to the generosity of Mary Tileston Hemenway, Boston's wealthiest female philanthropist, Bradley educated her students in a new two-story brick Italianate structure that "featured individual desks—the first to be seen locally, fancy science equipment, pull down maps, globes, and a huge assortment of fresh new textbooks. Amy hired a one handed black man named Archie Hawes as the building and grounds superintendent. She directed: he perfected, until the campus had neat flower beds and a manicured lawn. Since Amy felt Tileston should be used to its fullest potential, she inaugurated a night industrial school and convinced the City of Wilmington to install free gas lamps to light the entryway."[49]

Many whites made it clear that November that they welcomed the policies of the Republican party, including the educational opportunities offered by people like Bradley and her Republican supporters. Grant and Wilson carried the state for president and vice-president by nearly 25,000 votes (and by 18 votes in Buck's fourth ward), and in the state's congressional races, where Republican candidates tallied more total votes than their Democratic challengers, Republicans won three of North Carolina's eight seats in the U.S. House of Representatives. Clearly the "most serious problem remaining for Democrats was that poorer voters of both races were still uniting to support Republicans. . . . To overthrow Reconstruction thoroughly, Democrats had to break the alliance between poorer whites who wanted more democracy and opportunity and Negroes who were reliable Republican voters."[50]

BUCK IN BUSINESS

Within days of the elections, J. A. Byrne announced in the *Wilmington Star*, "I have this day associated with me in the FIRE INSURANCE BUSINESS, Capt. W. R. Kenan. Capt. Kenan is too well and favorably known to the citizens of Wilmington, and the surrounding country, to require any endorsement or introduction."[51]

Two months later Buck also became part of the "& Company" of Wooten Richardson & Company, a recently organized firm of commission merchants. Whatever clerical skills he brought to the firm were his own, but the capital he invested in it, if any, came from Mollie's portion of the Chapel Hill property sold by her brothers, William and Robert Hargrave. Between December 1872 and May 1873, as plans to reopen the University of North Carolina unfolded, her brothers sold more than $10,000 worth of land and buildings in and around the university village. Indeed, their transactions marked the beginning of a long and fruitful association between the Kenan family's financial fortunes and those of Chapel Hill and the university.[52]

Wooten Richardson's success depended almost entirely on its contacts and contracts with farmers in the countryside and the ability of the city's railroads to facilitate and expand the same. The firm had good rural contacts throughout eastern and Piedmont North Carolina, and in the spring of 1873 the city's railroads provided plenty of reasons for optimism. The Carolina Central Railway Company purchased Wilmington's third railroad company, the Wilmington, Charlotte and Rutherford Railroad Company, and initiated a vigorous construction program designed to reach Asheville, where the road could then join the Tennessee lines that tapped the rich lands of the Ohio River Valley.[53]

Raising hopes even higher still were the activities of the Walters syndicate. Not only had it boosted the business of the WC&A by extending the road into the South Carolina upcountry, but it was also generating great expectations with its larger plans to create a unified rail system along the Atlantic Coast. Indeed, by the time of Will Kenan's first birthday, the syndicate and its investors controlled "thirteen southern railroads, with a combined mileage of 2,131 miles. . . . One main line paralleled the Atlantic Coast; another route followed along the fall line to Atlanta, giving access to the cotton kingdom and port cities of the Gulf of Mexico; another line reached toward the Southwest and transcontinental connections."[54]

VISIONS OF A NEW SOUTH

This period of promise in Buck's business career coincided with the emergence of the philosophical fillips that eventually coalesced into the creed of the New South movement, the only creed of the region his son William ever accepted. Education, sectional reconciliation, industrialization, scientific agriculture, and the influx of labor and capital into the region were measures southern leaders advocated as a way for the South to rebuild its war-ravaged economy and retain what was perceived to be the best of the region's values.[55]

Although no records survive of Buck's direct association with the movement, it is clear that his father and brothers preached and practiced many New South doctrines. One particularly revealing example is Mayor Thomas Kenan's speech at the Wilson Collegiate Institute in June 1873. The Colonel's topic for the occasion was a favorite with North Carolina's earliest New South advocates: the need for industrial, or practical, education. It was also a favorite of those who, like the Colonel and his Kenan kinfolk, wanted to see the University of North Carolina reopened under the control of the Conservative-dominated legislature.

The mayor began his speech with an apology. He had been asked to speak to the young gentlemen of the institute and not, he said, "to the young ladies" who were students. But since he could not pass the latter "unnoticed," the Colonel, a trustee of the institute, complimented "woman" and spoke "of her refining influence and gentle virtues." The handsome speaker then returned to his prepared remarks, which stressed that the South was "compelled" for too many years "to send from home for educated labor, for Engineers, Machinists and Architects." The "times now demanded that this should cease to be so, that our southland was to be built up and developed, rail roads and factories were to be built and they must be built by Southern men, and that, in order to do it, the mechanics of the South must be educated men. . . . That the social heresy which had pervaded Southern Society that manual labor was dishonorable, was exploded, and that the sons of some of North Carolina's most distinguished men were now learning trades in Northern cities."[56] Will Kenan heard this message thousands of times and in many different forms before migrating north with the practical skills he learned at Tileston and the University of North Carolina.

The university was very much on the Colonel's mind, in fact, when he spoke to the boys and girls at the Wilson Collegiate Institute. His speech was part of a widespread effort to mobilize support for a convention called by the North Carolina Department of Education. The purpose of the convention, ostensibly at least, was to consider the general condition of publicly supported education throughout the state, and most of the state's leading educators attended. Among them was the Colonel's friend and former classmate at the university Major Robert Bingham, who had just assumed the headmaster's position at the Bingham School in Mebane, North Carolina, northwest of Chapel Hill.[57]

The convention's underlying purpose, however, was to drum up public support for a ordinance critical to UNC's future. The university had closed its doors in early 1871, some three years after the Reconstruction constitution transferred control of the school from the legislature to the state board of education—a board controlled, in turn, by the governor, a Republican, who also served as the ex officio chairman of the university's board of trustees. The ordinance was designed to eliminate Republican control of the school. If approved by a popular vote in August 1873 and then ratified by the Conservative-controlled general assembly (the body that had proposed it two years earlier), the ordinance would return to the legislature the power to appoint the university's trustees. It was the keystone to reopening the university and thus to reinvigorating the economic interests of those who, like Buck and Mollie Kenan, owned property in the "one-industry" village of Chapel Hill.

The convention was not of one mind about the ordinance, however. Some of the delegates despised UNC's elitist tradition and preferred to see the university replaced by an agricultural and mechanical (A&M) college. Others wanted the school to remain closed so it could not compete with the state's denominational colleges, and others, like Major Robert Bingham, wanted the university reopened but only if it did not draw students from preparatory schools like his own. To the extent that the convention met to facilitate the university's reopening, however, it succeeded, for the voters approved the ordinance in August, and the legislature then made it a constitutional amendment—one that "proved to be the decisive event in the university's 'redemption.' "[58]

THE CHAPEL HILL CONNECTION

Approval of the ordinance was a godsend for the Kenans of Wilmington. Business was dull at Wooten Richardson & Company, and Buck badly needed a bullish market in Chapel Hill real estate. Two years earlier, in the days that followed the legislature's decision to put the university ordinance to a public vote, Buck had used money from Mollie's estate to purchase a one-third interest in Guthrie's Hotel, the only hotel-boardinghouse in the one-industry village.

Few things better symbolize the long and intimate connection of Will and his family with the university and Chapel Hill than the boardinghouse. His great-great-grandfather was one of the university's first trustees, his father and uncles attended school there, and his parents met, married, and lived there too. Through his mother, moreover, he was also a descendant of the Barbee family, the First Family of Chapel Hill. As one local author has written, "Of the families who donated land to the university or who were living in the area when the university was founded, the Barbees were to have the most significant and the most lasting influence."[59]

Mollie's great-grandfather Christopher "Old Kit" Barbee was the largest single contributor of land to the new university, and her grandfather William Barbee was "one of Chapel Hill's leading merchants and probably the richest man in the village as the owner of several plots of land and 69 slaves by 1830."[60] Mollie was born twelve years later, in 1842, the out-of-wedlock daughter of Margaret (one of William Barbee's four daughters) and Jesse Hargrave, who arrived in Chapel Hill bankrupt in 1835. Through hard work and prudent investments, however, including his marriage to Margaret Barbee in February 1843, Mollie's father had become Chapel Hill's leading storekeeper and one of its largest landholders. At his death in 1854 he left his family a thriving mercantile business, a prosperous boardinghouse, a huge suburban plantation, and plenty of money, land, stocks, and slaves.[61]

Mollie was the most sought-after maiden in Chapel Hill by the time Buck entered UNC. Three years older than Buck, her physical appearance was as

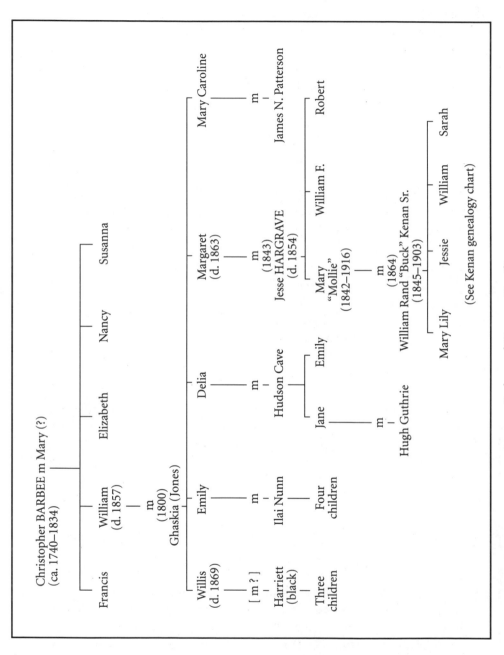

Christopher BARBEE m Mary (?)
(ca. 1740–1834)

Francis

William
(d. 1857)
m
(1800)
Ghaskia (Jones)

Elizabeth

Nancy

Susanna

Willis
(d. 1869)

[m ?]

Harriett
(black)

Three
children

Emily
m
Ilai Nunn
Four
children

Delia
m
Hudson Cave

Jane
m
Hugh Guthrie

Emily

Margaret
(d. 1863)
m
(1843)
Jesse HARGRAVE
(d. 1854)

Mary
"Mollie"
(1842–1916)
m
(1864)
William Rand "Buck" Kenan Sr.
(1845–1903)

Mary Lily

Jessie

William

Sarah

William F.

Robert

Mary Caroline
m
James N. Patterson

(See Kenan genealogy chart)

Barbee and Hargrave Families

appealing as her inheritance. She was "the prettiest and most popular girl" in Chapel Hill, Robert Bingham later wrote. In fact, Bingham claimed, he knew Mollie "very well" and frequently visited her during his student days at the university in the late 1850s, when "half of the college boys thought that they were in love with her and they could not help it."[62]

Mollie's popularity also stemmed from her family's ownership of a boardinghouse in Chapel Hill, one of only three in the village prior to the war. Although the store was sold after her father's death, Mollie's mother kept the popular boardinghouse—a wise move in the flush times of the late 1850s.[63] "With a peak enrollment of 456 students in 1858–1859, the university approached the end of the antebellum period with a student body second in size to Yale among American colleges," and most of the students were forced to seek room and board in the village.[64]

With the onset of the war, however, and the death of Mollie's mother in 1863, the Hargrave boardinghouse entered a decline from which it never recovered. It was probably still standing when Buck returned from Appomattox in the spring of 1865, and it may well have been standing that fall when he and twenty-one other students enrolled in the university; but at some point during this period it burned to the ground. Shortly thereafter he and Mollie left Chapel Hill and ceased to call it home.[65]

They started calling on it for cash instead, selling off lots, plots, and pieces of the vast acreage Mollie and her brothers inherited in and around Chapel Hill. While Buck arranged a few of these transactions, most were handled by Mollie's attorneys, friends, and relatives, including the village's wealthiest merchant, David McCauley. Mollie and McCauley had known each other almost all their lives. McCauley had started work as a clerk in her father's store, he had purchased half of the business after her father's death, and he had married one of Mollie's distant Barbee cousins. More to the point, he had sold Buck the one-third interest in Guthrie's Hotel (whose namesake owner was married to Mollie's cousin), and he would sell Buck and Mollie yet another third of the large hostelry by the time the university reopened in 1875.[66]

THE DEPRESSION OF 1873

Business went from dull to disconcerting at Wooten Richardson in the fall of 1873, and for Buck at least, the excitement engendered by voter approval of the university ordinance quickly faded. The stock market collapsed on September 19, "black Friday," and the following day, "for the first time since its organization in March 1817, the New York Stock Exchange was forced to close. It stayed shut for ten days, and when it reopened, the country quickly drifted into a five-and-a-half-year depression."[67]

The depression ended the first phase of railroad consolidation in the South and devastated the sawmill owned by Will Kenan's grandfather. Although the Walters syndicate managed to hold on to the Wilmington and Weldon Railroad, it did not fare as well with the WC&A. Burdened with a heavy debt structure, declining revenues, and cutthroat competition, the WC&A eventually failed to make its bond payments, forfeited its lease on the Wilmington and Weldon, and went into receivership. At the same time the collapse of the stock market led one of the syndicate's largest investors, the Pennsylvania Railroad, to write off its investments in the holding company and withdraw from the Southern Project. Shortly thereafter the railroad's chief car manufacturer, the Harrisburg Car Factory, stopped ordering lumber from Owen Kenan's sawmill, and by the following spring the former Confederate congressman and his partner were fighting over the assets of the bankrupt firm.[68]

Buck's business survived longer than his father's, but the young bookkeeper stayed busier with social and political activities than he did with the company's ledgers. He took on additional duties at the YMCA and became an active member of the local Freemason's lodge and the St. George and St. Andrew's Athletic Club. He also helped organize two local rifle clubs, and on most Thursday and Friday afternoons he could be found across the Cape Fear River at the rifle ranges on Eagles' Island. In April 1875, moreover, shortly after the arrival of the Reverend Joseph R. Wilson (the father of future president Woodrow Wilson), Buck joined Wilmington's First Presbyterian Church. As William later recalled, "Our family was Scotch Presbyterian so we all went to church and Sunday School every time the bell rang. My father was a Deacon, then an Elder and Treasurer up to the time of his death."[69]

Between work, play, and other public activities, however, Buck spent little time at home. It was a woman's world at 110 Nun Street, and women, both black and white, dominated the early life and memories of William Rand Kenan Jr. Mollie, Mary Lily, Jessie, and Sarah were there, as was Nicey, who according to Kenan "really raised all four children." Nicey even went with Will and the womenfolk on summer vacations—something that his father rarely did. Buck stayed home, William recalled, and entertained "several young men" while Nicey vacationed, as it were, with the rest of the family.[70]

That Kenan wrote little else about black people in his autobiographies suggests the extent to which he ignored two closely intertwined and lifelong obsessions of his father and other Kenan males: politics and race relations. Will Kenan displayed none of the political activism that since colonial times had made the Kenan men arbiters of race and class on the local, state, and regional level. Where his father and uncles lived and breathed politics, where they spent most of their lives creating and reacting to "the Negro Problem," and where they often used racial animosity to redirect and substitute for class divisions, Will Kenan became an engineer who hated politics and thought little about race relations either before or after he left the South and moved to western

New York. To be sure, as one of Union Carbide's first manager-scientists at Niagara Falls and later as a businessman in Lockport, New York, the realities of class, not those of race, confronted Will Kenan.

But if Kenan managed to distance himself from some of the worst aspects of his family and region, he also shared the racist views and assumptions accepted by most Americans for most of our history: that blood carries culture and that black blood carries a culture inferior to that in white society. Kenan encountered these ideas everywhere: at home, in college, in boardrooms, and in New York City, Australia, and Berlin. These assumptions seemed to be confirmed for him in the black people he encountered. The only blacks he ever knew, and with whom he had any contact whatsoever, were "faithful servants": nurses, cooks, maids, and porters—people in socially inferior positions. When one of them, in this case Nicey, showed something more than the patient obsequiousness expected of them, it made an impression on Kenan: "I remember one night at Columbia I was carrying a tin foot tub packed with many hats when I stumped my toe and fell. Everything in the tub flew out and scattered. My nurse was disgusted beyond words."[71]

OPENINGS AND CLOSINGS

Though he was too young during the depression to understand the source of his father's disgust, Will must have sensed that Buck was not happy. In September 1875, as Wooten Richardson continued its downward slide, the University of North Carolina reopened its doors. Rather than bolster Buck's spirits, however, the reopening caused him additional problems.

In December his hotel partner, David McCauley, conveyed to him a two-thirds interest in the Guthrie properties, and Buck, apparently surprised by the indenture, immediately took steps to have it changed. In an affidavit signed by his gun club partner, Buck declared McCauley's conveyance "null and void." It was Mollie, he swore, who owned the hotel properties; he had merely handled her investment in Guthrie's "land and premises, . . . the same having been purchased out of her estate." Buck felt compelled, in fact, "to solemnly dissent from the said deed and publicly declare that I have never accepted the same, and I do hereby disclaim any right title or interest in or to the land and premises therein and thereby attempted to be conveyed."[72]

While the deed controversy added to Buck's embarrassments at Wooten Richardson & Company, the Chapel Hill real estate market, spurred by the university's reopening, helped ease his discomfiture some. One transaction illustrates well the extent to which Mollie not only supported the family financially but how she and Buck also bet on the success of the one-industry village to provide that support. Two weeks after Buck signed his affidavit, Mollie purchased five lots in Chapel Hill from her brother Robert W. Hargrave for $1,500.[73]

Wooten Richardson closed its doors shortly thereafter, however, and Buck was sued by the Bank of Wilmington for writing a bad check. Worse still, his brothers' stars were rising. In Duplin County James was nominated for a seat in the state legislature, and on August 11, 1876, the *Wilmington Star* published a "biographical sketch" of Colonel Thomas Kenan, "the worthy nominee for Attorney General on the Democratic Conservative ticket." Written by a native of Duplin County and originally published in the *Raleigh News*, this "Sketch of Col. Thomas Kenan" emphasized the fortunate, prospective fit of man, family, and character with the needs of the attorney general's office: "There is an elevation of character about him and his family seldom to be found anywhere, and only to be known to be admired. I would to God that *all men*, everywhere, who in this Centennial year aspire to honored position, *were such as he*, for peculation and thievery would know no place in their hearts, and the people of this distracted country would once more rejoice in honest constitutional government."[74]

THE RETURN OF THE DEMOCRACY

Thomas Kenan smiled and stroked his beard as he added up the votes once again. If the rest of the counties voted like Wilson, he would soon be North Carolina's new attorney general, and his good friend Zebulon Baird Vance would be its new governor. It had been a long, hard campaign—one of the most remarkable in memory—and Thomas had just completed "an extended canvass" for the Democratic party. He had made "unremitting exertions" on the party's behalf, and he wanted Vance to hear the good news from Wilson— from the heart of the state's Black Second.[75] "You can rely on 600 Dem. maj. in this Co.," Thomas assured Vance, "(I think it will reach 649). Colored people voted with us in considerable numbers. Whenever a man had an individual preference, he was prevailed on to go the whole ticket so that the result is that Tilden, Vance [the constitutional] amendments & all, run along together."[76]

Buck's brothers did well in the elections of 1876. Thomas won the attorney general's race, and James won a seat in the general assembly. The Democratic presidential ticket also won in North Carolina, Vance recaptured the governorship for the Democrats, and the state's voters approved some thirty amendments that "clearly increased the power of the legislative branch of government, giving it considerable authority over local affairs and enabling the Democratic party to regain virtual control of the state."[77] North Carolina was "redeemed" in the fall of 1876, and in 1877, when the new Republican president, Rutherford B. Hayes, removed the last federal troops in the South, Reconstruction came to an end.

Thomas Kenan served as North Carolina's attorney general for the next eight years, and as such he acted on the New South principles he stressed in his

Wilson Institute speech: education, industrialization, scientific farming, and railroad construction. He conducted numerous inquiries for the governor and the legislature and wrote hundreds of opinions, reports, and memorandums on the constitutionality of laws and taxes involving railroads, the university, the Department of Agriculture, and fertilizer companies. As one of the state's leading post-Reconstruction arbiters, Thomas Kenan helped create North Carolina's modern power triangle of businessmen, universities, and politicians. Beneficial alike to his own, his family's, and the university's financial fortunes, Thomas's contributions to this New South nexus would be supplemented and greatly expanded in the twentieth century by his nieces and nephews and their descendants.

The Crucible of Fortune

Will Kenan heard more than Old South stories and New South promises while growing up. He also received a steady diet of predestination. Preached to him from the Presbyterian pulpit, it was assumed by the people he loved, and evident, he was told, in all that unfolded around him. Yet heaven did not determine his journey, and he knew it. Kenan learned early in life that people both shaped and responded to their environment, that they formed part of a constantly changing nexus of chance, choice, ideas, and action.

Nowhere was this more apparent than in the life of his father. Only the true believer could see the hand of God in Buck Kenan's career. To the extent that Buck succeeded in life, to the extent that he appeared as one of the elected few, it was not in fulfillment of some divine plan. It was through the power and influence of his family and friends. Buck spent most of his business career in the dying profession of commission merchant. He sold supplies and manufactured goods to farmers in eastern North Carolina, sometimes for cash but usually in exchange for the farmers' crops and products, which he then sold anywhere he could. It was one of the oldest and most lucrative professions in the urban seaboard South, but it was fast becoming obsolete there. With the growth of railroads, towns, and stores in the countryside, farmers no longer needed the services of coastal merchants like Buck. They could turn to local, rural merchants instead.

Will must have noticed at an early age that his mother made it possible for his father to fulfill the Victorian male role of provider. Mollie continually sold or mortgaged her Chapel Hill property to back Buck's commission business and to keep their household out of the red. Within a year of losing her investment in Wooten Richardson & Company, she made it possible for Buck to join her brother William "Freddie" Hargrave as a junior partner in the mercantile firm of J. M. Forshee & Company. According to the local Dun reporter this firm was "Comp[osed] of J. M. Forshee who resides in Philad, Pa. W. R. Kenan & W. F. Hargrave of this city neither of them are wor[th] anything but they are active & steady & will no doubt make prompt returns of any consignment made to them."[1]

Uncle Freddie was anything but steady, however, and he soon sold out to Buck and Mollie and headed for St. Louis. Buck immediately changed the company's name to Kenan & Forshee to reflect his majority ownership, but he could do little over the next several years to alter the Dun reporter's description of him and Forshee as "young," "active," "experienced," and "reliable" businessmen of "excellent character" who just happened to have "no cash," "no capital," and "no means."

About 1880, however, Kenan & Forshee entered a period of remarkable growth, which produced several changes for the Kenans of Nun Street. The most immediate adjustment was also the most obvious, at least to Will and his family. They began buying most of their clothes. The change made such an impression on Will that he later mentioned it in his autobiography. Mollie must have felt the same way too, for never again, he recalled, did she have to make the children's clothes.[2]

Buck's business grew because the depression ended and economic conditions improved throughout the country. But he also got a big economic boost from the political power he wielded because of his brother, the Colonel. In 1881, shortly after being reelected as the state's attorney general, Thomas Kenan secured Buck's appointment to one of Wilmington's two most powerful governing bodies: the Board of Audit and Finance. Created by the Colonel and other Democratic Redeemers, this board gave final approval to almost every fiscal decision made by Wilmington's Republican-dominated board of aldermen. It audited the city's accounts and controlled its sinking fund. It fixed the salaries and compensation of municipal employees and officials, endorsed the city's bonds and other obligations, and gave final approval to all municipal contracts.[3] Its members were five of the most powerful men in Wilmington, and Buck became one of the most powerful among them. He was reappointed to the board in 1883, during the Colonel's final years as attorney general, and again in 1889, 1891, and 1893.

Buck's business likewise benefited from a loan Mollie secured for him with a mortgage on one of her largest assets, the 1,300-acre "Barbee plantation" just outside Chapel Hill.[4] Buck used the loan to buy out his partner and go into business alone, and quite a promising business it was. By the time of the 1884 buyout Kenan & Forshee employed four assistants and did between $2 million and $3 million a year in sales.[5]

But Buck could not overcome the economic realities that undermined the function of commission merchants like himself. Although he paid off the mortgage within two years, his business steadily declined in the late 1880s, and he was forced, once again, to turn to Mollie for support, both to back his firm and to help him maintain the comfortable lifestyle to which his family was accustomed. Mollie mortgaged four of her town lots in Chapel Hill, and in September 1892, at the beginning of Will's junior year at UNC, she apparently sold her two-thirds interest in the Chapel Hill hotel.[6]

She could do no more for Buck, however, and during the depression years that followed, he derived his income from the United States government. He served as the highest-paid federal appointee in North Carolina: collector of customs for the port of Wilmington, an appointment that he owed, in part, to the political influence of the Colonel. This lucrative position enabled him and his family to live comfortably during the worst years of the depression, but it lasted only four years (1894–98) and gave him little, if any, time to attend to his failing business. By the time of the Wilmington race riot of 1898 his business prospects appeared bleak indeed, and they improved thereafter only with the aid of Henry Flagler.

If Will learned little from his father about business success, he heard a lot from Buck about working hard and never giving up. Buck repeatedly stressed these themes to the young men who hung out at 110 Nun Street, and in 1884 Will made them the centerpiece of his presentation at Tileston School. He spoke to his schoolmates in the Upper Room, a large "exhibition hall" with a stage, a huge bay window, and room enough for most of Tileston's 240 students. Amy Bradley was impressed. " 'Buckle down Boys' was an admirable lesson given by Willie Kenan," she wrote in the school's newspaper, "I wonder how many of our boys, after such a sermon, have really buckled down and begun work in earnest."[7]

Will adopted Buck's work ethic, but he never followed the seemingly preordained social and political tracks of his father. Buck further grooved the pattern of public pursuits established by his male Kenan forebears in Duplin County.[8] He led Wilmington's oldest and most prominent military company, the Wilmington Light Infantry, and became one of the city's most powerful Democratic officials. He also served the First Presbyterian Church as a deacon and ruling elder; joined the state's oldest and most venerated Masonic lodge, the St. John's Lodge No. 1 of Wilmington; and then left it to form a new lodge, whose members subsequently elected him as their first Master.[9] But Will grew up hating politics and learned to despise the Masons. Though he attended church while living at home, he only occasionally occupied a pew between 1896, when he moved to Niagara Falls, and 1947, when he returned to the Presbyterian church as a tribute to his deceased wife.[10] Nor did he ever, during his five-war lifetime, volunteer for military service or exhibit any interest in military matters.

Buck tried to instill him with the martial spirit, of course, but his most sustained effort to do so, sending Will to Horner's Military Academy in Oxford, North Carolina, apparently backfired. Kenan entered the academy in 1887, when "I was just fifteen years old," and left three years later to begin his

Will Kenan wearing his uniform at Horner's Military Academy. (*Incidents* 1)

freshman year at the University of North Carolina. His recollections of the academy are anything but warm. He describes its setting and architecture but says almost nothing about the people he met there. He also clearly disliked the school's classical and military curriculum. "A retired Army Officer was Drillmaster (Colonel T. J. Drewey) and he also taught Military Tactics. The elder Horner was of the old school and required all kinds of Greek and Latin. I took both for three years and never knew anything about either."[11] As for the school's military regimen, Kenan could muster only slight enthusiasm. "The school was run strictly on a Military basis and was very beneficial from a physical point of view. We had to drill every day but Sunday one and a half hours, do guard duty twice each week for two hours."

That Will was sent to a military academy is not surprising, but the fact that it was Horner's is. Indeed, his presence there raises an interesting and important question: Why did he not go to the Bingham School at Mebane? It also operated on a military basis, and unlike Horner's it had a national reputation. It was, in fact, the most prestigious and popular male preparatory school in North Carolina and the South. Even more compelling, it was run by the family's good friend Major Robert Bingham. The Major knew Mollie well from Chapel Hill. He graduated with Buck's oldest brother from UNC, and he was imprisoned with both of Buck's brothers during the war. His daughters had become good friends with Mary Lily at Peace College in Raleigh, and as head of the Masonic order in North Carolina, Bingham approved Buck's new Masonic lodge in Wilmington and installed him as its first Master.

William offered an answer to this question in his autobiography, which he wrote sixty years after his schooling at Horner's and some thirty years after his widowed sister, Mary Lily Flagler, married the Major's son, Robert Worth Bingham. Although Kenan avoided mentioning the Binghams and their school in his memoirs, he clearly anticipated the question arising in the minds of readers familiar with the long relationship between the two families. Horner's, he explained, "had been suggested to my parents by the Williams family (good friends of theirs) one of the Williams girls having married [one of the school's owner-teachers] Jerome Horner several years before."[12]

Though this personal connection was important to Buck and Mollie, it was Bingham's close connection with two highly publicized events that prompted them not to send their son to the Bingham School. One incident involved Lizzie Turlington, a deaf-mute from Wilmington, who was murdered by Bingham's deaf-mute nephew, Walter Bingham, in December 1886. The other involved Bingham's strong public support for an A&M college in Raleigh.[13]

While the Kenans shared the horror and dismay expressed by many of their fellow citizens toward the highly publicized murder, it was Bingham's promotion of the A&M college that bothered the family the most. The school was chartered in the spring of 1887—in the months that preceded Will's departure for Horner's Military Academy—and its creation threatened the future of UNC and thus the interests of the Kenans themselves. The university lost its major source of state funding, the Land Grant Fund, to the new college, and on several occasions over the next decade or so the university's religious and political opponents did everything possible to cripple it financially and legislate it out of existence. More important, the chartering of the new college marked the beginning of a grassroots farmers' movement that threatened to destroy the power and privilege that both UNC and the Kenan family had long enjoyed.[14]

ALCOHOL, RAILROADS, AND THE ROAD AHEAD

The 1880s proved to be a portentous time for Will and his family, for the decade marked the emergence of some of the most important and lasting forces in their lives. Alcohol was one such force. For much of the decade the Prohibition movement threatened to split and defeat the Democratic party in North Carolina. It "cut across race and party lines and almost undid the political order so carefully constructed by Democratic 'Redeemers.'"[15] Yet alcohol was more than a political issue to the Kenan Redeemers; it was part of their economic and social life. There was always plenty of "wine and hard liquors on the sideboard" at 110 Nun Street, and the family had long been making, drinking, and selling their own wine and liquor at Liberty Hall, where Will and his sisters siphoned off samples from casks in the cellar.[16]

The Kenans found themselves torn, however, between the wet South and the temperance South, between the making and enjoyment of alcohol and the suffering that attended its abuse. Though neither the family nor the region was unique in this ambivalence, alcohol played a crucial role in several of the most important developments in the family's history. It destroyed Jessie's marriage and contributed to both the unhappy life of her only child and the death of Mary Lily in 1917.

On two occasions, moreover, the family suffered public embarrassment from an incident involving Colonel Thomas Kenan's consumption of alcohol. The first grew out of the incident itself, which occurred in Wilson, North Carolina, while Mary Lily was living there with the Colonel and his wife and attending the Wilson Collegiate Institute. The second occurred decades later, when her former schoolmate, newspaper editor Josephus Daniels, recalled it in his autobiography. According to Daniels, a "total abstainer" whose mother led the dry forces in Wilson, the Colonel became the focus of a public debate generated by the antidrink Good Knights of Wilson. The debate erupted in the Daniels home at an "adjourned" meeting of the group when a particularly "zealous" Good Knight asked for an investigation of their fellow member the Colonel, who allegedly "served wine at his table and not only had looked upon

"Sadie" Green, Mrs. Pembroke Jones, at Newport, Rhode Island.
(From Lehr, *"King Lehr"*)

it when it gave color of the cup, but had actually drunk a glass, thereby breaking his pledge 'to touch not, taste not.' "[17]

Daniels, a lifelong antagonist of the Kenan family, could not recall what the investigation showed but believed that the Colonel "withdrew from the organization, saying that he preferred not to belong to the Good Templars if any member of it was poking his nose into other people's affairs." The incident, Daniels claimed, disturbed the Colonel. "The soul of honor, and temperate in his long life, but not a total abstainer when later I knew him well in Raleigh, Colonel Kenan felt keenly the imputation upon him involved in the report and the gossip that ensued."[18]

Alcohol was also closely intertwined with the pleasures and pursuits of the people who helped propel Will and his family across fortune's tracks: Sadie Green and her "two husbands," Pembroke Jones and Henry Walters. Green was the oldest daughter of the Colonel's close friend and political ally Wharton Jackson Green, who abandoned the Black Second in the late 1870s to pursue his political and economic goals at "Tokay," one of the South's largest winegrowing estates, near Fayetteville, North Carolina. In 1882 and again in 1884, in campaigns marked by the Prohibition issue, Green was elected as a Democrat to the United States Congress.[19]

Sadie Green was twenty-four years old, a practicing Roman Catholic, and "beyond question one of the most popular belles in the South" when she arrived in Washington with her father. From Fortress Monroe and Martha's Vineyard to Saratoga and White Sulphur Springs she was a familiar figure at the nation's elite resorts and the focus of many of America's most eligible bachelors. A wealthy North Carolinian, however, brought her belledom to an end. On Thanksgiving Day 1884, in one of the largest and most expensive wedding celebrations in the state's history, she married Pembroke Jones, a handsome Wilmington rice miller who was distantly related to the Kenans and a wealthy heir of the Wilmington and Weldon's founder.[20] Their Fayetteville wedding presaged the ostentatious lifestyle that later made them the subject of the saying "keeping up with the Joneses." More than a thousand dinner guests feasted at Tokay, "whereat the rarest delicacies from many lands and the costliest wines were served in an abandon of profusion."[21]

This lavish merger marked a turning point in the history of the Kenan family, for not long thereafter Pem and Sadie's friend and future lifemate, Henry Walters, moved in with the newlyweds in Wilmington and established a "very intimate" friendship with them and the Kenans of 110 Nun Street. Indeed, Walters eventually bought and shared a mansion with the Joneses just up the street from the Kenans. He acted as a "second Father" to Will Kenan, and he and the Joneses took Will's oldest sister, Mary Lily, on their journeys with her future husband, Henry Flagler, and his second wife, Alice.[22]

Walters had known and probably dated Sadie Green since her schooldays in Baltimore. He had owned stock in the syndicate's two Wilmington railroads since the early 1870s, and he had been a director of the Wilmington and Weldon Railroad since 1882. He was also quite unlike the loud-laughing, joke-telling Jones, a bisexual dandy, it seems, who always sought the spotlight. Walters was a quiet, reserved man who craved privacy and anonymity throughout his life. After graduating from the Lawrence Scientific School at Harvard University, he quickly earned the respect of his father's fellow investors as an efficient, hardworking executive who knew the railroad business from roadbed to boardroom. Indeed, this combination of personal and professional attributes prompted the Wilmington and Weldon's board of directors to make him the first general manager of the ACL in June 1884.[23]

Henry Walters was well acquainted with alcohol and Henry Flagler by the time he moved into the ACL's Wilmington offices. His father had first attained wealth by wholesaling whiskey in Baltimore; his uncle owned one of Baltimore's largest distilleries; and Henry himself pushed for construction of the Wilmington and Weldon's "Fayetteville Cut-off"—a million-dollar extension that proved vital to the success of the Green family's Tokay vineyards. In the case of Henry Flagler, moreover, Walters's father had dealt with the Standard Oil executive since the late 1860s and invested with him and other capitalists in a railroad system between Charleston, Savannah, and Florida—a system, that

Will Kenan's oldest sister, Mary Lily Kenan, ca. 1890. (Thomas S. Kenan III)

is, that would link up with the nine Atlantic Coast Line railroad companies Henry Walters was now managing between Richmond and Charleston.[24]

The two Henrys shared strong interests in the South and worked closely throughout the 1880s to protect and expand them. In addition to investing in marine and rail transportation, they put their money into banks, mining companies, newspapers, petroleum companies, cottonseed mills, and Pem Jones's rice-milling operations.[25] They also worked both sides of the political aisle, uniting Democrats and Republicans in joint economic ventures. In 1886, for example, they backed the formation of the Carolina Oil and Creosote Company in Wilmington, a company that specialized in producing preservatives for railroad ties and dock pilings. The company's officials included several local Democrats with ACL connections, a former Republican mayor of Wilmington, the leader of the Republican machine in Virginia, the secretary of the Treasury under Republican presidents Garfield and Arthur, and the inventors of the creosoting process, Andrew Smith and Ludwig Hansen, the latter the Kenan's next-door neighbor and Buck's future business partner.[26]

Walters also worked closely with Flagler to bring passenger-filled railroad cars down the Atlantic Coast to Florida—something that Walters and Will Kenan later did. Flagler made his first trip to the sunshine state in the 1870s in the company of his ailing wife, Mary Harkness, but not until 1883, two years after her death, did the fifty-three-year-old oil baron visit what soon became the headquarters of his Florida empire: St. Augustine.[27] He was then one of the richest men in America and at a turning point in his life. He had recently remarried, he had already designed and created the Standard Oil Trust, and he was looking for a way to escape the exigencies of New York business and to try his hand at something he could call his own. Although he continued to serve as Standard's secretary and transportation adviser, he started devoting most of his time, energy, and money to Florida, where in December 1885, after almost two years of planning and acquiring land in St. Augustine, construction began on the first of his many hotels, the Ponce de Leon.[28]

It was also about this time that Henry Walters, recuperating from typhoid fever in Pem and Sadie's home, first introduced the Joneses to Henry Flagler. And not long thereafter, it seems, Flagler first saw Will's older sisters entertaining visiting railroad officials at the Jones's home. Jessie played the piano and Mary Lily sang, while other young women smiled and assisted Sadie in serving food, punch, and wine from Tokay's vineyards. They were the best local society had to offer, and if they caught the eye of the wealthy men who watched and listened, and made them think of a potential mate for themselves or their sons, well, so much the better.[29]

Indeed, the frequent visits of wealthy railroad officials help explain why Buck Kenan and Pem Jones took the lead in forming the Cotillion Club in Wilmington in 1887. Though similar in membership and purpose to the city's older L'Arioso German Club—an elite male organization—the Cotillion Club looked beyond the local focus of the older club and beyond the former's occasional dances and suppers. It staged a debutante ball, a ritual imported from the Northeast, which in this case served to mix and match old and new monied families from the North Carolina coast to the Piedmont and beyond.[30]

It was apparently that December, while Will was home from Horner's for Christmas, that the serenaded debs piled into his bedroom and Henry and Alice Flagler witnessed Mary Lily's stage debut before a "fashionable," full-house audience at Thalian Hall, Wilmington's most beautiful building.[31] The dimpled southern diva performed the title role of Violet Knickerbocker, the daughter of an old-line New York aristocrat, in the American-Japanese comic opera *The Little Tycoon*. Her performance drew warm reviews from the *Wilmington Star*:

> The titular part, "The Little Tycoon," first thrusts itself upon us for attention as the central figure of the opera, and Miss Kenan's impersonation of the character was in every way excellent and delighting.
>
> Her splendid voice was never heard to greater advantage, and then she acted in so admirable a manner as to call forth praise and applause upon her every appearance. Every point in the composition that fell to her character was brought out, and she was encored heartily again and again and always most deservedly.[32]

Mary Lily's stage debut coincided with the opening of the Ponce de Leon Hotel in St. Augustine and the first run of the ACL's "Florida Special" from New York. In early January the beautiful new built-to-order train arrived in Wilmington carrying Henry Walters's passengers and Henry Flagler's first hotel guests. As the *Wilmington Star* noted on January 10, "The first of the famed vestibule trains on the Atlantic Coast Line left New York at 9:30 yesterday morning for Jacksonville, Fla., and arrived here at 2 o'clock this morning. After a stop of five minutes at the depot here, the brilliantly illuminated and elegantly appointed train speeded on its way to Jacksonville, where it is expected to arrive this afternoon."[33] Although the St. John's River prevented the "Florida Special" from depositing Flagler's guests directly at the doorstep of his hotel, he quickly overcame this inconvenience by having a bridge built across the river. Significantly, the bridge was constructed with timber treated at the Carolina Oil and Creosote Company's new plant in Fernandina, Florida, where one of Wilmington's wealthiest families, the MacRaes, owned large tracts of land, and the plant's managers included a former Republican politician from Wilmington.[34]

Will Kenan did not meet Henry Flagler during the latter's stops in Wilmington, but he did experience the social and political upheaval that attended the activities of men like Flagler, Henry Walters, and the Kenan Redeemers. Throughout the late 1880s and the 1890s, North Carolina was rocked by an agrarian movement that began in the West and exploded in the South amid a deepening agricultural depression. This movement affected almost every aspect of Will Kenan's life; it defined both the North Carolina and the New South in which he grew up. It took root in local, regional, and national farmers' alliances; blossomed into the Populist party; and resulted, in North Carolina, in an alliance of Republicans and disgruntled Democratic farmers who created a political revolution known as "Fusion."

One of the principal leaders of the agrarian movement was Leonidas Lafayette Polk, a prominent Baptist farmer who was also a bitter enemy of Colonel Thomas Kenan. Polk had led North Carolina's denominational colleges in opposing both the reopening of UNC and the use of the state's Land Grant Fund to do so. He had advocated using the fund instead to create a "farmers' college." More portentous still, Polk resigned as North Carolina's first commissioner of agriculture after feuding with the Colonel and then-governor Vance in the 1870s over the Colonel's advice, as attorney general, for collecting the fertilizer taxes that supported the North Carolina Department of Agriculture and its original Experimental Station at Chapel Hill.[35]

Polk never forgave the Colonel and Vance for their actions, and in January 1887, at a public meeting preceding the realization of his dream for an A&M college, he used the college issue to mobilize the state's farmers into the North Carolina Farmers' Association. The new organization immediately petitioned the legislature for an A&M college and also had a bill introduced to create a railroad commission to provide relief, it was hoped, from the exorbitant rates allegedly charged by railroads on farm goods. The farmers got their college, but the railroads and their lobbyists succeeded in defeating the commission bill.[36]

Polk was not to be trifled with, however, and he quickly expanded his mobilization efforts by merging his organization with a North Carolina chapter of a growing interregional organization, the Farmers' Alliance and Industrial Union. The alliance took up Polk's demand for a railroad commission and grew so rapidly that its leaders decided to back state alliance president Sydenham B. Alexander for the Democratic nomination for governor. Although old-line Democrats succeeded in defeating this hastily organized political move, the party officially endorsed the alliance demand for a railroad commission. And with the election of a farmer-dominated legislature at the end of 1888, the prospects for establishing a commission appeared bright.[37]

Needless to say, these developments alarmed the Kenans and their allies among the state's railroads and moneyed interests, especially the ACL's Henry Walters. A similar commission was already diminishing ACL revenues in South Carolina, and the company expected the same to happen in North Carolina if a commission were created there. Worse still, a railroad commission might disrupt the ACL's ongoing efforts to use its largest and most profitable road, the Wilmington and Weldon, to consolidate the management, operations, and stockholdings of the company's affiliated railroads in Virginia, North Carolina, and South Carolina.[38]

The railroads worked their magic again, however, and with the support of old-line Democrats who abandoned their pledge to support the railroad commission bill, the measure was defeated. Yet the legislature also approved, perhaps as a sop to disgruntled alliancemen, a general tax on all railroad property in North Carolina. While state authorities continued to honor the tax-exempt status conferred on the main line of the Wilmington and Weldon by the company's antebellum charter, they immediately assessed the road for taxes on its branch lines—something former North Carolina attorney general Thomas Kenan had ruled they could not do. Though the money involved was relatively insignificant, ACL officials viewed the move as an opening wedge for further taxation and refused to pay. Thus began a long and heated legal battle between the ACL and the state of North Carolina that eventually wound its way to the United States Supreme Court.[39]

In the meantime, the defeat of the railroad commission bill ignited a storm of agrarian protest. By 1890 some 90,000 farmers belonged to more than 2,000 local alliances in ninety-five North Carolina counties. They also had regional and national allies and a leader of national prominence they could call their own. At a meeting in St. Louis in December 1889—just two months after North Carolina's new A&M college opened for classes—the National Farmers' Alliance elected Polk as its president and published a statement of the organization's goals. The alliance demanded railroad regulation and a variety of fundamental changes in landownership and national fiscal policies, including banking reform, the coinage of silver to inflate the currency, and most far-reaching of all, the establishment of subtreasuries (government warehouses) from which farmers would receive advance payment (in government-backed, legal tender certificates) for crops (mainly cotton) they stored therein. These proposals marked a radical departure from prevailing capitalist practices and gave southern farmers hope of breaking their annual cycle of indebtedness to furnishing merchants like Buck Kenan.[40]

Polk returned from St. Louis agreeing to cooperate with North Carolina's Democratic party but demanding its support for the alliance program, especially the planks on railroad regulation and the subtreasury plan. Some Democrats, including the new editor of the *State Chronicle*, Josephus Daniels, advocated cooperation with the alliance in the 1890 state elections, while others, such as Thomas Kenan, counseled against cooperation. The latter considered the alliance program unconstitutional "class legislation" that would split the Democratic party and lead to the "Negro Domination" that allegedly crippled North Carolina during Reconstruction.[41] Up in Washington, moreover, Polk urged his old enemy Zeb Vance to introduce a subtreasury bill into the senate. Although the North Carolina senator was a leader of the state's old-line Democratic machine, he was also up for reelection in 1891 and thus dependent on the votes of the men elected to the North Carolina legislature in 1890—men, that is, who would almost certainly be alliance supporters.

Vance introduced the subtreasury bill, but in June 1890, as the election season began to heat up, he notified the North Carolina Farmers' Alliance that he could not support the bill. It was unconstitutional, he claimed, and he warned the alliance that continued agitation on the issue would split the Democratic party and return North Carolina to the "African rule" of Reconstruction. Polk responded with a sizzling attack on the Senator in the pages of *The Progressive Farmer*, berating Vance for his opposition to the subtreasury bill and warning him that his days in Washington were numbered if he continued to cross the alliance. As the alliance's secretary wrote to Vance, "The people are restless. We are on the verge of a revolution. God grant it be bloodless. . . . You cannot stand before the tide if it turns in your direction. No living power can withstand it."[42]

The attacks on Vance outraged his old friend and political ally Colonel Thomas Kenan, who wrote the senator pledging his continued support for the embattled lawmaker. The attacks in the " 'Aggressive' Farmer," Kenan wrote, "furnish evidence of the fact that its author is a consummate scoundrel and frightfully inclined towards meanness and malice." Yet Kenan hoped for more of the "same sort" of evidence from *The Progressive Farmer*, believing this would "make the farmers disown the paper as its organ, and solidify them in [Vance's] support." As for the political future of Vance and the Democratic party, Kenan saw them as closely intertwined. "If the question arises, whether you shall be returned to the Senate or the 'Alliance' fail, the latter would have to go; in other words, I think the farmers, notwithstanding the 'Alliance' organization, will not suffer your defeat. You can beat them all. And I don't know but that the best thing we can do for the party is: to make the fight on sending you back to the Senate. Then, we would be sure to win."[43]

The Colonel badly needed and wanted to win. He had recently been appointed clerk of the North Carolina Supreme Court, a position he almost certainly would lose if the alliance won. Indeed, the Colonel needed no such uncertainties at this point, for the job had prompted him to build a beautiful new home in downtown Raleigh less than a block from the magnificent edifice he had helped plan and perfect: the governor's mansion.[44] At the same time the Colonel was worried about the potential impact of an alliance victory on UNC, where he had been serving as a trustee since 1883.[45] Funding, faculty appointments, the new A&M college, and the loss of the Land Grant Funds—all of these controversies had taken their toll on the university and had occurred prior to the political revolution that now seemed certain of placing the school's strongest opponents in control of state government.[46]

Buck Kenan shared many of his older brother's concerns with the alliance threat. The subtreasury plan would further undermine, if not completely destroy, his slumping commission business, while an alliance victory might also mean a slump in Chapel Hill's hotel and real estate business. By coupling funding increases for the A&M college with cuts for the university, the legislature could enhance the competitiveness of both the A&M college and the state's private church schools and thereby reduce the number of students not only entering UNC but also seeking room and board in the university's one-industry village.

By 1890, moreover, Buck had worked his way up from ward "challenger" to the Executive Committee of the Democratic party of New Hanover County, at a time when the alliance was threatening to split the party. He was also presented, in turn, with a particularly disturbing scenario in Wilmington, where a black majority made the city one of the traditional centers of Republican strength in North Carolina. This was clearly on Buck's mind, in fact, when he wrote to Vance to "please send me your speech on the negro question & oblige."[47]

While the Kenans were concerned with defending the regime they helped create in North Carolina, Henry Walters and Henry Flagler worried about the alliance's threat to their railroad interests in the seaboard South. By 1890 the ACL faced considerable opposition up and down the Atlantic Coast. From the seething rhetoric of racist demagogues in South Carolina to North Carolina's tax demands and the anticorporate screeds of farmers and alliancemen, the ACL was under attack. And it looked like things were about to get worse, for the National Farmers' Alliance announced that public ownership of the nation's railroads would be discussed at its convention in Florida at the end of the year. After reading about this "New Kind of Agitation" in the *Richmond Times*, Henry Walters clipped the story and sent it to Henry Flagler, who had recently created a system of Florida railroads known as the East Coast Lines. Flagler acknowledged the clipping in his reply: "I shall watch with interest the action of the Farmers' Alliance, which meets this week at Ocala."[48]

Concern with the alliance was not the only thing that Walters and Flagler now shared with the Kenans, however. By the summer of 1890 Walters was showing a "considerable interest" in eighteen-year-old Will Kenan, and he and the Joneses were also taking Mary Lily along on their railroad and sailing excursions with Henry and Alice Flagler. Indeed, the Flaglers had become so attached to Mary Lily that she was now traveling with them alone. In July, for example, Flagler asked Walters and the Wilmington "Crackers" (Mary Lily and the Joneses) to join him and Alice on the maiden voyage of his new yacht, the *Alicia*. "I have written Pem to try and send us Mary Lily in advance of the rest of the party," Flagler wrote to Walters, "as we are to be alone next week."[49]

It was in this context, then, of social, political, and economic change; of a new state college; and new family relationships that William Rand Kenan Jr. entered the University of North Carolina in the fall of 1890. By the time he received his chemistry degree four years later, the country was in a major economic depression and North Carolina was on the verge of a successful political revolution, one that was not overturned until the end of the century and only then with the violence and racial strife created by men like his father.

The Ins and Outs of UNC

Much of Will Kenan's sense of self-identity emerged from his experiences at the University of North Carolina. He played for the school's athletic teams, managed its baseball team, and held numerous student offices, and he worked with one of the South's leading scientists, Francis Preston Venable, on a series of seminal experiments involving calcium carbide and acetylene. These experiments not only paved the way for a revolutionary new industry; they also enabled Kenan to travel around the world and to become one of Union Carbide's first manager-scientists. They gave him the right, in short, to call himself a scientist, the one thing he desired most in his life. And if they catapulted him far beyond most of the people and concerns of his native North Carolina, they also forged his lifelong commitment to a university with which so much of his self-esteem became inseparable.

THE INS AND THE OUTS

Will Kenan's attendance at college set him apart from the vast majority of Americans in the late nineteenth century. Only 3 percent of Americans between the ages of eighteen and twenty-one attended college in 1890, and the percentage of North Carolinians who did so was even smaller. Fewer than 200 students enrolled at UNC when Kenan began classes in the fall of 1890, and though enrollment grew to 389 by the time he graduated in 1894, the total number of bachelor's degrees awarded in all fields increased by only two: from twenty-seven in 1891 to twenty-nine in 1894. Kenan's bachelor of science degree was one of only seven conferred by the university in the latter year.[1]

Kenan was not a "typical" UNC freshman. He seemed to many people to be mature beyond his years. "Will Kenan was 21 years old when he was born," Henry Flagler later said.[2] He was also assured a prominent place among the "ins" on campus even before he arrived there. His parents owned most of Chapel Hill's largest hotel, and his Uncle Thomas was one of the school's most powerful officials. A trustee of the university since 1883, the Colonel was also president of its Alumni Association and one of only five men on the Executive Committee of university trustees. Will Kenan also arrived in Chapel Hill better prepared for the college classroom than most of his fellow freshmen. He received a solid educational grounding at Wilmington's Tileston School, and if, as he later contended, he gained little intellectual ground at Horner's Military Academy, the academy at least exposed him to Greek and Latin and instilled him with a sense of discipline that helped him meet the challenges of his college coursework.[3]

The observations of one student "out," William Frederick Harding, who both entered and graduated from UNC with Kenan, provide some idea of the extent to which Kenan's connections, temperament, and experience set him apart from the majority of his college classmates. Unlike Kenan, who was born and raised in the city and frequently traveled beyond the confines of his urban birthplace, Harding's arrival at the university coincided with his initial exposure to the changing world beyond the rural countryside. Harding, a resident of Pitt County, took his first train ride "in May of 1890 when I went with the Greenville Guards to Richmond, Va. to attend the unveiling of the Lee Monument. That was the first time I had ever been to a city. Up to that time Goldsboro was the largest town I'd ever seen." Harding's only other exposure to city life occurred during his train trip to the university four months later, in September 1890, when he stopped for "two nights and a day" in Raleigh.[4]

Once in Chapel Hill, moreover, Kenan and Harding occupied dormitory rooms that reflected their respective positions among the ins and outs on campus. Harding moved into the New East Building with his older brother, a sophomore, who arrived on campus shortly after the semester began. Their room cost only $10 per session and was located on the "second floor, East entrance, northeast corner."[5] Kenan also enjoyed the security of rooming with a relative, Owen Kenan, his cousin from Kenansville, but they lived in South Building, the most prestigious campus dormitory since James K. Polk had roomed there during part of his student days. Other South Building ins included the Kenan's next-door neighbors Alexander and William Andrews, whose father was vice-president of the Richmond and Danville Railroad. While neither they nor the Kenans occupied Polk's old room (which was located on the southwest corner of the third floor), they all lived across the hall from it, the Kenans in a room costing $16 per session (on "the third floor north side next to the west corner room") and the Andrews boys in the "corner room" at $20 per session.[6]

Harding also felt less confident than Kenan in the classroom. He considered himself "poorly prepared for college and consequently I had to study very hard to keep up with my classes." He particularly dreaded the written examinations, noting, "I had never had a written examination and I was apprehensive of the result."[7] Kenan strikes a very different tone when recalling his initial approach to the college classroom. "I studied fairly well during my Freshman year. . . . I did not go out for athletics . . . although I did constantly work in the gymnasium and played considerable tennis until I was a fair player." While differences in personality and educational background help explain this contrast in attitudes, so too do economic factors. Unlike Kenan, whose parents had the wherewithal to pay for his college education, Harding had to borrow money and work part-time to attend UNC. He had no time for tennis and no room for failure.[8]

Both young men felt pleased, however, with their performance as freshmen. Harding, a philosophy major, passed all his exams, "making very satisfactory marks. I was then confident that I could keep up with the class and the fear of failure on that score was gone."[9] Kenan, a science major, had "some trouble with French" his first two semesters but scored well in math (99.5 and 99.6) and qualitative chemistry (90 and 85) and average in general chemistry (82 and 75) and English (81 and 70). Although both boys had little trouble keeping up with their classmates, Kenan's roommate and cousin from Kenansville was not so lucky. Owen Kenan flunked out, quit, or failed to show up for his classes in the spring semester and did not return for classes the following fall.[10]

Performing well in the classroom had little or no impact, though, on a student's status as one of the ins on campus. That distinction, initially determined by the student's family background, was confirmed and reinforced by the way he was perceived and treated by his fellow students. It was obvious, for example, in something as simple as the watermelon fight that occurred during Kenan's first month on campus. "The Sophomores have been cutting up in general down here this year," one student reported. "One of the first things they did was to have a watermelon fight, in which they made the freshmen buy the watermelons, and give them to them, but the fresh never even got a taste of them, only the *ins*."[11]

The freshman ins were also first in their class to savor "blacking," the most feared and hoped-for ritual at UNC, and they often emerged from the experience lighter than the rest of their classmates, all of whom eventually had their faces and hands smeared with shoe blacking. As one freshman in, John Lash Gilmer, noted in September 1890, "Last Wednesday night they started out on a blacking tour, and blackened fifteen, of which me and Bowman were of the number, but we got [off] very easy as they did not black us much." Others were not so lucky. "Then last friday night they blacked 23 more and rubbed oil on them, then last night about the lone hour of 2 o'clock they blacked two boys, and tore down their bed and carried it out into the hall."[12]

Harding had to wait "nearly six weeks" for the midnight visit and "was beginning to think that [he] would not receive the accustomed coat of blacking." But late one night six masked and sheeted figures entered his room and confronted him with shoe brush and blacking. Harding "stood mute" as their leader gave commands: " 'Freshman, arise.' I arose. 2nd command, 'Spit in blacking box.' The boy spits in blacking box. 3rd command, 'Rub brush in blacking box.' The boy rubs his brush in the blacking in the box into which his companion had just spat. 4th command, 'Rub brush in freshman face.' Thereupon the boy blacked my face and hands thoroughly, poured out all the water in my room, blew out the lamp and left me smeared hands and face with shoe blacking in the dark with no water—all alone."[13] Harding then ran out into the hall and "found all the other freshmen on my floor had been served the same way and the sting was gone." For him, as for most freshmen, blacking had little symbolic meaning beyond the significance of being accepted at UNC. "We enjoyed it and then felt that we were full fledged freshmen of the University of North Carolina and our right to such a position was permanently fixed on '*The Hill.*' "[14]

Yet blacking did more than give the students a general sense of belonging. It demonstrated the realities of power in their state and region—realities that could transform them, as it were, from masters into servants. While blacking had originated during the antebellum period as a way to humiliate freshman by casting them in the role of black slaves, it had taken on additional meaning by the time Will Kenan entered UNC. The masks, the sheets, and the midnight visits were the unmistakable symbols of the most effective and intimidating instrument of informal, extralegal justice in the postwar South: the Ku Klux Klan. Though the Klan had virtually disappeared by 1890, the growth of the Farmers' Alliance and the introduction by Republicans in Congress of the Lodge Bill (which was designed to restore federal supervision of southern elections) were threatening to disrupt the one-party South that the Klan had helped the Democratic Redeemers establish. Blacking thus served as both a warning and a reminder to this small but potentially powerful group of the state's educated white males: force could and would be used to intimidate anyone—black or white, rich or poor—who stepped beyond the bounds of race and prevailing political orthodoxy.

That this was the larger, intended message of blacking became clear in the weeks that preceded the 1890 state elections. The freshman who bore the brunt of the ritual that September was Will Kenan's distant cousin, a boy named Guthrie, whose prominent Republican family included a member of the Farmers' Alliance who soon become a leader of the Populist party in North Carolina. Poor Guthrie got blacked at least sixteen times during Kenan's first month on campus.[15] Also indicative of blacking's relationship to the wider social and political forces shaping campus activities is its apparent demise during Kenan's final semester as a freshman. In the spring of 1891 in the aftermath of the death of William L. Saunders, the leader of the Ku Klux Klan in North Carolina, Kenan and his classmates approved a resolution that abolished hazing and presumably the attendant ritual of blacking at UNC. Their action coincided with an ominous message to the university from the "farmers' legislature" of 1891, which in addition to creating a railroad commission and increasing taxes for schools, established an A&M college for blacks and a teachers' college for women. In other words, the university now found itself competing for state funds with three other colleges.[16]

Indeed, the antihazing measure represented an attempt by the university's trustees and administrators to offset anticipated funding cuts by increasing the school's enrollment. As Harding suggested, the resolution did not reflect the wishes of the students, most of whom would have relished the chance to blacken incoming freshmen the following fall. "We were to be sophomores for the next year. Dr. Geo. T. Winston had just been elected President of the University, Dr. K. P. Battle having resigned. Dr. Winston was anxious to make an appeal to the people of the state for a large attendance of students and if he could advertise that the sophomore class had abolished hazing, it would be a fine stroke. So the class passed the resolution and it was so advertised."[17]

The struggle between the university and its opponents over money and students became particularly intense during Kenan's college years, as did the social and political unrest out of which it grew. Both help explain his lifelong hatred of politics. The upheaval challenged his family's social position. It ruled his father's life. It angered his uncles. It mortified Henry Walters. It split the state. It divided the students, and it depressed their professors. Indeed, in 1893 the state's denominational colleges came close, with the aid of their Farmers' Alliance allies, to legislating the university out of existence. Politics failed to obey, in short, the general scientific principles Kenan learned at UNC. The irony was, of course, that he owed much of his in-group status to the power and influence of his very political family and campus friends.

Politics pervaded almost every aspect of campus life in the 1890s and tended to separate students from the moment they set foot on campus—not, however, into Republicans and Democrats, for students from Republican backgrounds were rare indeed. Rather, the campus factions resembled the warring wings of the Democratic party. Freshmen immediately got recruited into one of "two political parties—the Conservatives and Tam[m]any." The "conservatives had the majority of the boys," Harding recalled, including members of "D.K.E., S.A.E., Sigma Nu and Kappa Alpha Fraternities and a majority of the non fraternity men," while the Tammany faction "was made up of the other fraternities and other non fraternity men."[18]

Although the campus conservatives tried to confine their membership to the sons of wealthy, prominent families, they needed the support of as many students as possible, for their struggle with Tammany was to some extent the campus equivalent of the contest over issues confronting North Carolina's Conservative Democrats: votes and power. "The issue was college offices,"

Harding explained, "such as Chief Marshal and his assistants, Chief Ball Manager and his assistants, Society officers—that is, officers of the Philanthropic and Dielectic [*sic*] Societies."[19]

Harding never held a student office and remained a nonfraternity man until his senior year, whereas Kenan pledged Sigma Alpha Epsilon his first semester on campus and eventually won election to several student offices, including assistant ball manager, chief ball manager, and secretary and treasurer of his senior class. Kenan's status as a campus conservative was confirmed early in his sophomore year when the brothers of SAE voted him into the fraternity, and the expected spoils followed close behind. He "was elected Sub-Ball Manager for all the Commencement Dances. Was also on the Board of Editors of the Year Book (Known as the Hellenian [in] those days)."[20]

Kenan's confidence and in-group status got another boost early in his sophomore year. In October 1891 in "the absence of Governor Holt, detained on official business, Colonel Thomas S. Kenan, President of the Alumni Association, presided" at the inauguration of the university's new president, George Tayloe Winston.[21] Football returned to UNC that fall, another development aided by Kenan's uncle. The university had competed in organized intercollegiate football since 1888 but had banned further competition in February 1890, primarily as a result of pressure from the school's president, Kemp Battle.[22] Later that year, however, after it became known that Battle would retire from the presidency, a group of students petitioned the faculty for a removal of the prohibition, and in January 1891 the Colonel and UNC's other executive trustees approved a recommendation from professors Francis Preston Venable, Joshua Gore, and Horace Williams "that the students of the university be permitted to take part in inter collegiate athletic contests under the supervision of an advisory committee."[23]

Kenan felt so confident that fall that he tried to leap even further ahead of his classmates. Encouraged by his classroom performance the previous year; by the continued support of his role model, Henry Walters; and by the feeling of being "allowed to get away with most anything," he tried to take two years of courses in one. And he tried to do so while expanding his social activities. He not only made, played on, and managed the baseball team, but he became obsessed with dancing, serving as a leader of the German Club, a campus dance club. "I was extremely fond of dancing and always welcomed a chance to attend at any place far or near. This desire frequently got me into trouble, having cut too many classes, [and] when I was called up before the faculty, I simply acknowledged the coin and left it to my good friends Dr. Venable and Professor Gore, of the faculty, to straighten the matter, which they always did."[24]

Kenan's preoccupation with dancing is not surprising. It was through dances and dancing, after all, that most young people of his class met and mingled with members of the opposite sex, and he had learned from Mary Lily's debutante parties that dancing was the courtship ritual that he performed best. Unable to woo young women with singing or musicmaking, he tried to impress them with his dancing instead.

Dancing, moreover, particularly the various forms of parlor dancing known collectively as the German, played a significant and unifying role in the social life of elite North Carolinians, and few families were more important than the Kenans both in purveying the latest dancing "figures" and in setting the tone, as it were, of high society.[25] Crowds of young people frequently danced in the Kenan home in Wilmington, tripping the light fantastic to Mollie's piano playing, while the Colonel and Aunt Sallie displayed the same openness and gaiety at their home in Raleigh, a beautiful residence that served as "the center of an elegant social circle."[26] Kenan often visited his aunt and uncle during his college days, and he always brought several friends. "If we arrived late at night, the servants would let us in, as they resided in a small house on the lot. We would fill the beds and probably as many cots and next morning by counting the hats in the front hall it was learned how many were in the house."[27]

William owed much of his popularity as a dance leader to his sister Mary Lily, who occupied the highest pedestal in society. Mary Lily was twenty-three years old and at the peak of her reputation as the state's reigning belle when her brother entered college. A short, buxom, and attractive woman, she possessed the ideals of feminine beauty during the Gilded Age. She also sang, acted, and played the piano well and enjoyed one important attribute that none of her potential rivals shared: she was an intimate friend and traveling companion of North Carolina's reigning society leaders, the Pembroke Joneses, and of their fabulously wealthy companions, Henry Walters and the Henry Flaglers. From White Sulphur Springs, West Virginia, to St. Augustine, Florida; Saratoga, New York; and Newport, Rhode Island, Mary Lily socialized at America's most exclusive resorts.

Her experience helped ensure her brother's success as a college dance manager and made Mary Lily a popular guest in cities throughout North Carolina. Exposed to the latest manners and customs of America's socialites, she helped teach the niceties of high society to the folks back home. She was especially familiar with the way the German was performed at White Sulphur Springs, the oldest and most prestigious resort in the South. According to the resort's historian, the German "was an elite dance—that is, since it required formal training in the various 'figures,' it was known in those social classes with the leisure to perfect such maneuvers—and it was a so-called parlor dance, which is to say that it was done best in small groups."[28] And Mary Lily knew every bow and curtsy of the "strictly ordered" German. "White gloves were obligatory, for no gentleman would have dreamed of taking a lady's hand or enclosing her 18-inch waist with bare hands. At least a foot of daylight must come between the partners as they whirled, swooped, reversed and stepped to a polka, a schottishe, or a Strauss waltz."[29]

If Mary Lily helped her brother become a dance leader at UNC, she also boosted the prestige of the society matrons who lured her into their parlors. Quite a few, it seems, succeeded in doing so. She was a "frequent guest" at Blandwood, the famous Morehead mansion in Greensboro, and according to Sam Patterson, whose brother became one of Kenan's closest friends at UNC, she was no stranger to the homes of banking, tobacco, and textile magnates in the central Piedmont.[30] "I had intended going to Charlotte to day," Patterson wrote in February 1890, "but Miss Bessie wrote me several days ago, that Miss Kennan [sic], who has been visiting Mrs. Wm Reynolds in Winston, was then visiting them, & that several gentlemen from Winston were coming down to see Miss Kennan to-day & of course I didn't care to go over there, & sit in the parlor all the time with that great crowd of folks."[31]

William enjoyed the popularity his sister gave him, but neither it nor his faculty and family connections proved strong enough to get him through two years of classes in one. He devoted too much time to dancing and baseball, it seems, to realize his plans of skipping a year of college. Yet he blamed the setback on another source, one that he could not control. "I developed muscular trouble with my eyes," he later wrote, "so gave up the effort and dropped back to '94, the class I entered with."

Kenan's class-skipping plans probably also suffered because of a major family crisis. According to family tradition, the trouble began at a party given by the Hinton family at Midway plantation, eight miles east of Raleigh. Near the end of the party Will's twenty-one-year-old sister, Jessie, accepted the offer of Joseph Clisby Wise, an eighteen-year-old haberdasher from Macon, Georgia, to drive her back to the Colonel's house in Raleigh. But as wagons were wont to do in those days, theirs allegedly broke down, and the star-crossed travelers were forced to spend the night together on the side of the road. Unfortunately, so the story goes, they also were forced to get married.[32]

The wedding took place in Wilmington's First Presbyterian Church on June 15, 1892, two weeks after Will completed his duties as sub-ball manager for the commencement dances at UNC. The ceremony, "solemnized at 9:20 p.m. in the presence of an immense throng of people filling the spacious auditorium and galleries of the large edifice," was performed by the Reverend Peyton H. Hoge, an ambitious young minister who later united Mary Lily and Henry Flagler at Liberty Hall. Although Sarah, Will's youngest sister, played no official role in the ceremonies, Mary Lily acted as Jessie's maid of honor, and Will served as one of Clisby's groomsmen. All of the Kenan aunts and uncles also attended the ceremony, as did all of the Kenan cousins: Emily, Thomas, Graham, and their oldest brother, Owen, Will's freshman roommate, who returned from the College of Physicians and Surgeons in Baltimore to serve as a groomsman.[33]

ATHLETE, GENTLEMAN, AND SCIENTIST

Will Kenan remained an in at UNC until he graduated, and he later described his college years as "the most enjoyable of any. I did not have a care. Was allowed to get away with most anything. . . . If I had my college career to go over again I would not wish to change it one bit."

Many of the most important bits fell into place during the last two years of his college career. Athletics became central to his sense of self-identity, as did his "hard as nails" body and the things it could do: "As a matter of fact," he later wrote, "I do not believe I could have withstood the physical grief of my career, were it not for the resistance built up by my years of athletics." Ultimately, though, it was his work and training as a scientist at UNC that dominated his mature, less physical, and most lasting version of himself.

Kenan made the baseball team his sophomore year but did not play regularly until his junior year, when he started in right field and compiled a 4-0 record as "change pitcher"—that is, as the pitcher who started against the teams UNC expected to beat. He won the opening game of his senior season (the only one he pitched), started twelve of fourteen games in the outfield, and batted .300—his personal best and the third highest average on the team. He was never better than erratic with his glove, however, and ended up tenth on his twelve-member team in fielding percentage his senior year.[34]

Kenan gave his most dazzling display of inconsistency in the two games he played his senior year in front of his "many friends" in Charlotte. His most embarrassing moment as an athlete occurred in the bottom of the ninth inning in the first game against the University of Vermont. Down 6 to 5 to the Tar Heels, Vermont had one man out and one man on when its pitcher, a player named Pond who later became famous as a Baltimore Oriole, came to bat. "We lost the game because of my error," Kenan recalled. "Pond knocked a high fly toward me. The sun was directly in my eyes, and I did not even touch the ball."[35] The play sounded different in the student newspaper. According to the *Tar Heel*, "Pond knocks a beautiful high fly to Kenan, who is wrapped in the arms of Morpheus; the ball strikes the earth with a dull thud, is thrown wild, and all is over for University [of] North Carolina."[36]

But in the second game, the *Tar Heel* continued, "Kenan fully atoned for his errors of the preceding day by gathering in everything that came near him, and making two beautiful running catches"—one of which was the "star play of the evening." Kenan also got three hits in four at-bats and scored one run in UNC's 10 to 3 victory over the University of Vermont.[37]

Kenan made his greatest contribution to Tar Heel baseball off the field, in

Baseball team, UNC, 1894. Kenan is on the front row at extreme left. (NCC)

his role as the team's manager. Elected to the position three years in a row, he pursued it with his typical energy, enthusiasm, and efficiency. In addition to handling the team's equipment and uniforms, he scheduled its games, made its travel arrangements, and secured its members a "training table" at a local restaurant. Yet the job he enjoyed most, the responsibility at which he excelled, was getting the most out of every dollar.

Kenan's most profitable and controversial action involved enclosing the athletic field with a fence. While many believed that the fence would "mar the beauty of the Campus," others agreed with Kenan that the barrier was necessary. The open field made it "utterly impossible to prevent a large part of the crowd from seeing without paying," the *Tar Heel* explained, whereas a fence would make spectators "pay at the gates." A fence would also make it "easier to get other teams to meet us on our own grounds, thereby affording the students and villagers much pleasure and enjoyment," and eliminate the need for fifteen or twenty seating marshals "who, of course, were admitted free of charge, and in this way quite a little sum will be taken in that would be otherwise lost." Also, a fence meant the football team could have "secret practice[s], which were heretofore impossible, but which are of great value for several reasons—affording the team an opportunity to practise [*sic*] its signals and certain plays without the possibility of our opponents learning the same."[38]

After raising money to build the fence, Kenan scheduled several games inside it. Near the end of March 1893, while the fence was being "pushed rapidly to completion," the junior manager "officially announced" the baseball schedule. The *Tar Heel* applauded his work: "From this it can be seen that through the energy of our manager we are to have several games on our home grounds, for which we thank him."[39] Kenan displayed even more aggressiveness his senior year when the effects of a national economic depression threatened the baseball team's finances. He solicited alumni donations and scheduled fourteen games for the team—five more than the previous season.[40]

He also tried to generate as much revenue as he could from these games. Rather than play as many as possible within the fenced field at Chapel Hill, he scheduled at least half of the games in cities throughout North Carolina and Virginia. This not only stimulated widespread interest in university athletics; it also made it possible for the team to make money, to return to Chapel Hill with a share of the gate receipts from large urban crowds. On the other side of the ledger, however, Kenan's ambitious schedule irritated some of the students and forced the university to administer midterm exams a week earlier than the date announced in the school's catalog. The *Tar Heel*, responding to a student who questioned the change, tried to put the best spin on Kenan's actions, claiming that the exams were moved up in order both "to divide the term exactly" and to take "account of some of our baseball games coming so early. It was desired, since athletics are encouraged here, to have such contests when they would interfere less with the student's work."[41]

Many students also disliked Kenan's relentless pursuit of the bottom line. Although he scheduled half of the games in Chapel Hill, he met with "so little success and appreciation" there, the *Tar Heel* explained, that he lost money, "and the result has compelled him to place the games with A. & M. College and Lafayette elsewhere." Kenan thanked the "men who cooperated with him by coming out and upholding college spirit, instead of whining about its decline and sitting in trees, on roofs and all other available places outside the park," but their spirit was not enough. He had to move the remaining "games from University grounds" for financial reasons.

Kenan's decision created such an uproar that he changed his mind and asked the *Tar Heel* to print a retraction shortly before the paper went to press. A column headlined "THE LAFAYETTE GAME TO BE PLAYED HERE" appeared in the same issue that announced just the opposite. "We are glad to announce that Manager Kenan has finally decided not to change the second game with Lafayette, and to have it played here. This was done merely with the desire to give the students an opportunity of seeing one more good game. Now let us all show our appreciation by turning out—not on the roofs of the Physical Laboratory, and the New East Building, or on the South Building steps, and in the Library windows; but let's all fill the grand-stand and the gate-keeper's cashbox. If we do not back our own team, who will?"[42] But the purse-conscious manager was not through yet. He decided at the last minute to play both of the Lafayette games in Greensboro, "because of financial reasons, as too many boys prefer to dead-beat, instead of acting like gentlemen, and pay to see the games."[43]

Kenan's use of the word *gentlemen* speaks volumes about his conception of himself and his experience at UNC. He and his closest friends frequently used the term to distinguish themselves from the rest of the students, and it often escaped their lips in conjunction with the words *athlete, athletics, science,* and *scientific.* Yet in acting on their assumptions of exclusivity, Kenan and his friends provoked a great deal of anger and hostility on campus—feelings that led to a "decline" in college spirit his senior year and to the charge, made in an anonymous editorial in the *Tar Heel,* that the chief source of this decline was "too much *aristocracy* of Athletics here. Like a government of the like nature, it is strong in pride, but mediocre in strength. The common student is not allowed, or sufficiently encouraged, to participate in the working of things, and loses interest, and begins to distrust."[44]

There was an aristocracy of athletics at UNC, and its members promoted and sustained their position through the Order of the Gim Ghouls, a secret society that Kenan joined in October 1892. The Gim Ghouls were leading fraternity boys who practiced elaborate rituals promoting the romantic ideals of chivalry and knighthood while they simultaneously engaged in a somewhat less than noble effort to control the election of fraternity members like themselves to campus offices. The club was one of Kenan's most important college affiliations.

Controlling campus elections was almost certainly the chief motive that prompted Robert Worth Bingham and others to form the exclusive junior-senior club in 1889. Although fraternities dominated both "party" factions on campus, it had become increasingly difficult to have only fraternity men elected to the most prestigious college offices: chief marshall, chief ball manager, and the presidencies of the philanthropic and dialectical societies. Yet by bringing together leading fraternity members from both campus factions, the Gim Ghouls succeeded in forming a voting block that virtually ensured the election of fraternity men to all offices.[45]

By the time Kenan joined the Gim Ghouls, their electoral successes had combined with the political upheaval engulfing North Carolina to raise the tensions between "Frats" and "non-Frats" on campus to the breaking point. As one non-Frat student later noted, the college elections of 1892 marked the demise of the traditional Conservative and Tammany factions on campus: "The two old parties died and two new forces showed themselves—the fraternity men on one side and the non-fraternity men on the other. . . . During the remainder of my career in college the fight was bitter."[46]

To make matters worse, the bad feelings became linked to questions of class

Members of the Order of Gim Ghouls, 1892. Kenan is reclining at front left. His close friend and senior roommate, Charles Baskerville, is on the second row, second from right. (NCC)

and courtship—a linkage that helps explain, perhaps, why the Gim Ghouls emphasized ideals of chivalry and knighthood. As former UNC president Kemp Battle later explained, the situation became "acute when it was alleged that a Frat counseled young ladies to refuse to receive the attention of a non-Frat, because they would thus drive off those of the other party. . . . The non-Frats also charged that their adversaries in all college elections voted together without regard to the merits of the candidates and in general kept themselves aloof from the others, although in birth, breeding, and scholarship they were not a whit superior."[47]

Superior though they may not have been, the members of the Gim Ghoul club assumed they were. As one loose-lipped member confided to his mother shortly after the order was organized, the club "is a select club of boys from all Fraternities, the members of which are all boys of good family & high social position, and so it is an honor to belong to it." The writer said nothing about the club's purpose or its original thirteen members, but he did note that the matter was strictly hush-hush. "We intend to have a Banquet Thursday night of commencement not to cost over $2.00 each. Of course each man will take a girl. This is all a secret, as none of the boys know even of the existence of the 'Ghimghoul Club,' so please don't say anything about it."[48]

The club and its members had a profound impact on Kenan's life both during and after college. Five fellow Gim Ghouls—Robert Bingham, William W. Davies Jr., Shepard Bryan, Hugh Miller, and Charles Baskerville—proved particularly influential. Baskerville, a native of Columbus, Mississippi, became Kenan's closest friend and senior roommate at UNC. He played on and managed the football team, took his Ph.D. under Francis Preston Venable, and served as an instructor in the chemistry department. He also founded and became the first editor of the student newspaper, the *Tar Heel*, and later served as a groomsman, as did Bingham, Davies, and Bryan, at the wedding of fellow Gim Ghoul Hugh Miller. As for Miller, another Venable graduate, he gave Will Kenan a summer job doing fertilizer analyses for Wilmington's Navassa Guano Company in the summer of 1894.[49]

The Gim Ghoul who had the greatest impact on Kenan's life was Robert Worth Bingham, whose father had strongly supported the establishment of the A&M college in Raleigh. Bob or "Rob," as he was known, attended UNC between 1888 and 1890 before transferring to the University of Virginia. Though he and Kenan never attended the university together, their paths crossed many times before and during Kenan's years there. They saw a lot of each other at the 1891 commencement, for example, when Bingham, who always referred to himself as a member of the UNC class of '91, returned to Chapel Hill to celebrate the graduation of his two closest friends and fellow Gim Ghouls, Shepard Bryan and Will Davies.

Then, too, tradition has it that Bingham first courted Kenan's sister Mary Lily at the commencement of 1891. If so, it was a portentous occasion for all concerned. In the spring of 1917, several months after Bingham and Mary Lily's marriage (the second for both), Will Davies would help her draft a secret codicil to her will (leaving Bingham $5 million), and in the months that followed her death in July of that year Shepard Bryan would act as Bingham's go-between in discussions with the Kenan family regarding the codicil and Bingham's alleged complicity in Mary Lily's death. As for Kenan, he may well have been acting as a friend and fellow Gim Ghoul when he decided in the fall of 1917 to have his family drop its investigation of Bingham's alleged connection to the codicil and Mary Lily's death.

In addition to establishing these important relationships, the Gim Ghouls provided Kenan with a sense of what it meant to be a gentleman. From the ideals of chivalry and honor to the rituals of medieval knighthood, these New South city boys attempted to emulate the courtly, noble, and generous behavior attributed by many postbellum novelists and journalists to the so-called aristocrats who had allegedly ruled the Old South's feudal society—a society where, in striking contrast to the urban and industrial realities of late nineteenth-century America, there supposedly had existed a rural, stratified, patriarchal regime that "provided precisely the right niche for each member: each fulfilled his true nature; none was dissatisfied."[50]

Just how much of this popular folderol William swallowed is not clear, but he did drink deeply from the club's cup of knightly conduct. He always displayed impeccable manners and chivalrous behavior; indeed, together with his southern accent, Kenan's politeness would set him apart from the vast majority of men with whom he associated outside the South. While many of these men probably believed, as did one of Kenan's New York secretaries, that the North Carolinian "had exaggerated manners," the women Kenan met and mingled with saw things differently. They "appreciated" his politeness and believed "it came naturally to him." In the opinion of one female observer in Lockport, New York, there was a "romantic chivalry" about Kenan's manners, a "nonverbal communication" that says "to a lady or a little girl, you are a lady, you are special. And it says it better than it can be said verbally. That's the sort of difference between Mr. Kenan's manners, what they said. They were natural and he was trying to say something."[51]

The Gim Ghouls also had much to say about the importance of gentlemanly behavior in athletics—that is, in yet another area of student life they tried to confine to fraternity men. While the origin of the order's name remains unclear (it is currently rendered *Gimghoul*, for instance, rather than *Gim Ghoul*, the spelling most frequently used at the time of its formation), it appears to have been a play on the words *gymnasium* and *ghoul*, the latter derived from an Arabic word meaning demon or spirit of the mountain. All of the Gim Ghouls displayed an intense interest in athletics and could frequently be found in the university's gymnasium, which was then located on the very hill from which Chapel Hill took its name (on a parcel of land that had recently been owned, in part, by Kenan's parents). Put simply, the Gim Ghouls inhabited the gym on the hill of The Hill.[52]

UNC's leading propounders of the athlete-as-gentleman concept were also the two men who had the greatest impact on Kenan's intellectual life at the university: his friend Charles Baskerville and their chemistry professor Francis Preston Venable, both of whom also promoted the application of "scientific" principles to athletic games. Venable was the faculty adviser for sports at UNC and "very fond of athletics," Kenan recalled. He "accompanied the teams on many trips. I always roomed with him when he was along."[53] Venable always stressed, moreover, "The Educational Value of College Athletics"—a lesson that became central to Kenan's own philosophy of education: "I honestly believe one gets a great deal out of college besides book knowledge and I am sure that it is most beneficial to try athletics."[54]

Kenan's beliefs mirrored Venable's contention that sports taught students something they could not get from a "dry and lifeless printed document." The athletic field was like a laboratory, Venable argued, where "some of the most forceful teaching is done . . . by object lessons" and where "certain essential qualities" were cultivated better than they could be from books: "quickness of decision, control of temper, concentration of effort toward a definite end, control and direction of the efforts of others, moderation and abstinence, high ideals of honor, honesty and courtesy."[55]

Similar arguments appeared regularly in the columns of the *Tar Heel*, whose founding editor was Venable's most accomplished student and Kenan's closest friend. In February 1893 in the first issue of the paper, Baskerville announced that the *Tar Heel* would be "published under the auspices of the University Athletic Association" and would be "devoted to the interest of the University at large . . . with especial attention to our own athletic interests, and progress in Football, Baseball, Tennis, etc."[56] Baskerville used the *Tar Heel*, in fact, to champion many of the goals promoted by both his fellow Gim Ghouls and UNC: "The University takes her stand for the best in scholarship and the best in moral and physical man. She will foster all truly, manly sport. She seeks to teach her sons to be wise, skillful and enduring, to be chivalrous in victory and unconquered by defeat, in all things true gentlemen."[57]

Baskerville also wielded the *Tar Heel* as a weapon in the fight against groups, institutions, and individuals who wanted to abolish intercollegiate athletic competition. Indeed, throughout Kenan's college career the Gim Ghouls joined Venable in opposing these forces. George Graham, for example, one of the thirteen original Gim Ghouls, was a star football player and one of the three students who in December 1890 initiated the successful move to overturn the ban on intercollegiate football at UNC.[58] The *Tar Heel* first appeared, moreover, in February 1893 in the aftermath of a spectacular football season at UNC, when the groups most opposed to the university and to intercollegiate athletic contests—the state's denominational colleges and religious bodies—tried to have the state legislature turn UNC into a school for graduate students only, a move that would have doomed the university financially.

It is safe to assume, in fact, that Baskerville started the *Tar Heel* to promote the university's success in athletics and thus to protect the economic benefits it derived from that success. Although the church schools and their supporters were genuinely concerned, as were many of UNC's supporters, with the very real "brutality" of the newest college sport of football, the question of intercollegiate athletic competition also involved the intertwined issues of prestige and money. Young men liked athletic competition, and they liked attending schools that excelled in sports—something that UNC did better than the state's denominational colleges. As the *Tar Heel* noted in the spring of 1893, "It is a safe conjecture to say that the phenomenal record our [football] team made last fall, will attract at least fifty students to the University."[59]

Just how many students were actually attracted, though, and how many of those so attracted would have otherwise chosen, in the absence of such a record, to attend one of the state's denominational colleges is not clear. It is clear, however, that the depression of the 1890s made competition for students more intense than usual, and any factor influencing college choice became extremely important. Indeed, the *Tar Heel*'s prediction appears to have come true: UNC's enrollment increased by more than 50 percent between 1892 and 1893. "We hear that Trinity college opened with 130 students," the newspaper reported in September 1893. "Wake Forest 150, and Davidson 110. The University has 376 students at the present time. We are sorry that the bad times have had such an effect on our sister institutions, but we rejoice that the attendance at the University is larger this year than for 32 years."[60]

The future also appeared bright that fall for Kenan and Baskerville. In September 1893 the Gim Ghoul brothers moved into "quite a pretty suite of rooms" in Chapel Hill "on the Main Street at the east edge of the town."[61] Baskerville, then beginning his final year of Ph.D. studies under Venable, had just capped several months of graduate work at the University of Berlin with a visit to London, while Kenan, a senior chemistry major under Venable, had been promised a carbide job and had just returned from a trip to Niagara Falls and the World's Columbian Exposition at Chicago.

Kenan's trip was a twenty-first birthday present from his father, who had recently been confirmed as the next collector of customs for the port of Wilmington. William had a "grand time" at the fair, especially in the Electricity Building. Even with two semesters of electrical engineering under his belt, he was still astounded by the exhibit's glimpse of the future: Westinghouse's huge new generators and revolutionary electric supply system, "electric stoves, hot plates, washing machines, and carpet sweepers plus electric doorbells, fire alarms and innumerable lighting fixtures."[62]

On his way home from Chicago, moreover, Kenan had stopped at Niagara Falls, where he had gotten a glimpse of both his own future and that of the electric power industry. There, with the backing of J. P. Morgan and other financiers, the Cataract Construction Company was erecting a huge hydroelectric power station to harness the mighty power of the Falls. Still two years from providing electricity, the station eventually housed some of the Westinghouse equipment Kenan saw in Chicago and would generate electrical power both for industries at the Falls and for transmission to Buffalo.[63] More to the point, Kenan would begin working at the Falls in January 1896 as chief chemist and electrical engineer for one of the Niagara power station's principal consumers, the Carbide Manufacturing Company. But on this trip he thought less like an engineer than an accountant. "It certainly is beautiful and well worth seeing," he wrote to his cousin Owen, "but you never saw a place where they try to stick the visitors so. They charge you two prices and nothing is free."[64]

The future of Tar Heel football also appeared bright when Kenan and Baskerville returned to Chapel that fall. Everyone fully expected the team to do as well as the 1892 squad, which had defeated all of its opponents during the regular season except archrival Virginia, a team it had subsequently defeated in Atlanta in a postseason exhibition game witnessed by thousands of people and covered by newspapers throughout the South. Indeed, the Atlanta "punch bowl" victory had produced one of the most uproarious celebrations in the university's history.[65] And Baskerville, who had played on and managed that team, now expected the 1893 squad to "eclipse all former teams."[66]

It may well have been this enticing prospect of honor and glory that prompted Kenan to "make a try" at football in the fall of 1893. He had not done so previously, he later explained, "since I was considered too light, weighing only 142 pounds." He also had arrived at Chapel Hill, as had most of his fellow students, with little or no knowledge of the new sport of football, which, more than any other major American spectator sport, had its origins in colleges and universities. The game had become increasingly popular on many campuses in the late 1880s, and by the early 1890s it was eclipsing baseball as the sport most popular with students. This was certainly the case at UNC, where Kenan remembered having "won a place on the team after two days of practice, playing Right Halfback. . . . I was fast and quick, which helped greatly. In those days The 'Flying Wedge' was the play,—and it was rough! There were no forward or lateral passes, one had to carry the ball."[67]

Kenan actually "won" his position during the middle of the season, and only then because most of the starting players, including Baskerville, were sidelined with injuries. It was a dismal season, in fact, for the overconfident Tar Heels, whose poor performance contributed much to the "decline" in "college spirit" Kenan soon confronted in baseball. Portents of the decline appeared early in the semester in the form of charges that a small group of athlete-aristocrats, specifically fraternity men such as Kenan and Baskerville, controlled sports at UNC. Baskerville tried to disabuse the students of this "mistaken idea" that football was "intended to be confined to the few." He wanted all those "so inclined" to have "the benefit of this most healthful and manly form of exercise." He even promised to provide footballs for daily games between freshmen and sophomores who did not try out for the varsity; also, "Regular inspection of those playing in these games will be made and any man giving promise will be at once transferred to the regular field and a uniform given him."[68]

The football season started well enough, with a 44-0 victory over a hapless Washington and Lee team in Lexington, Virginia. But on the following day five of UNC's "eleven wild-looking, wooley-headed gentlemen caparisoned in blue stockings and dirty-looking foot ball suits" were injured in a 10-4 loss to the Virginia Military Institute. Five of the six remaining starters sustained injuries the following week in Durham, where the Tar Heels lost to the Methodists of Trinity College by a score of 6-4 in the "hardest fought and perhaps most scientific foot ball game ever witnessed in the state." The UNC students did not respond like gentlemen. They mocked the players and floated rumors that the team planned to forfeit the rest of its games. The injured Baskerville was furious. "We are still here and intend to remain until the end of the season," he wrote in the *Tar Heel*. "It is true we are badly broken up, but we no doubt will mend. . . . We have not disbanded; we are not that kind."[69]

At this point, it seems, in the days before UNC's game with the University of Tennessee, Kenan "won" his position on the football team. And he got properly initiated in the Tar Heels' 69-0 victory: "One of the Tennessee men tried to put his knee in my mouth; result, the loss of a front tooth."[70] The next game proved equally lopsided, with the Tar Heels defeating the Baptists of Wake Forest by a score of 44-0. This was also the best game of Kenan's short football career. He recovered a fumble, made at least one unassisted tackle, and gained over 100 yards in eleven carries. "Too much praise cannot be given Rankin, Kenan, Whedbee and 'Kirk' for the way they played," the *Tar Heel* cheered.[71]

The Tar Heels did not fare as well in their last two games, however, the two most important of the year. Lehigh University used "highly developed scientific tactics" to defeat UNC in "the first game a southern team ever played in the great metropolis" of New York City. Kenan did not start against Lehigh; he entered the game only after the recently recovered starting right halfback was reinjured. But he did start the last and most crucial game of the season, against Virginia: the "final championship game in the South." Four thousand people packed Richmond's Island Park to see the Thanksgiving Day game. "The crush became so great that despite the efforts of policemen and marshalls the impatient crowd burst down the gate and some five or six hundred people swept into the park without paying admission." Kenan played well on defense, but did little on offense, carrying the ball ten times for less than thirty yards. His teammates played no better; Virginia won the game 16-0.[72]

Football remained Kenan's favorite sport for the rest of his life, and he showed it by funding the construction of a stadium in Chapel Hill and by establishing a scholarship fund for student athletes at the university. Yet it was his physical and mental investment in science at UNC that came to dominate his memory bank and his sense of who he was. While he quickly learned he would never be more than a mediocre athlete, his experience in the laboratory suggested that he might become a first-rate scientist. Here again, though, there was nothing predestined, as Kenan later intimated, about the intertwining of these forces and their impact on his life. He was simply in the right place at the right time with the right skills and family connections.

Kenan became Frank Venable's constant companion during his junior and senior years at UNC. They shared a room on football and baseball trips, spent hours working on their carbide and acetylene experiments, and often adjourned to the Venable home nearby, where Kenan shared meals and conversation with his hosts and played with their four young children. Part of this

Francis Preston Venable, friend, teacher, and carbide companion to Will Kenan at UNC. (NCC)

camaraderie stemmed from the secrecy imposed on the two men by the Willson Aluminum Company of Spray, North Carolina, which provided them with the material they had identified in the summer of 1892 as calcium carbide. Yet the student and the professor also shared similar backgrounds. Both men came from prominent Old South families; their fathers fought in the Civil War; and despite these connections (or perhaps because of them), they focused on the future rather than the past.[73]

Kenan and Venable also saw in each other the potential to further their own personal goals. Venable was both symbol and substance of that rare southerner Kenan wanted to be, a scientist, and he was one of the best scientists then teaching in the South. After graduating from the University of Virginia, where he helped the South's most prominent chemist, John Mallet, discover aluminum's place in the periodic table, Venable traveled to Germany to start his doctoral studies under some of the world's leading organic chemists. He returned to the United States in 1881, however, to accept the position of professor of chemistry at UNC, only to go back to Germany the following summer to complete his doctorate—an achievement that had made him the first Ph.D. on UNC's teaching faculty.[74]

By the time Kenan entered the university, Venable was widely recognized as an excellent teacher, researcher, and North Carolina booster. He had organized one of the first scientific societies in the South, the Elisha Mitchell Scientific Society, and had founded its journal, both of which he used to stimulate general interest in scientific subjects, to promote the resources of the state, to encourage and publish research, and to present "treatises on scientific subjects" with "the hope of interesting and training up a number of young scientific workers."[75] What was more, the society's journal "set a model for the whole region, indeed the whole country. Through it," Venable's biographer has written, "the University made one of the earliest contributions to higher education in the South, by raising emphasis on the sciences to a level comparable to that accorded the classics."[76] By 1888 the journal was being delivered throughout the United States and the world as part of the university's journal exchange program with 129 other scientific and learned societies.[77]

Kenan also appreciated Venable's success "training up young scientific workers" for employment in both the public and the private sectors. Venable had directed the doctoral work of UNC's first Ph.D., William B. Phillips, who used fertilizer samples from Wilmington's Navassa Guano Company to write his dissertation on the production of superphosphate fertilizers—a dissertation subsequently published in the Mitchell Society's journal. Phillips had then worked as the fertilizer company's chief chemist for two years before returning to the university, where he taught agricultural chemistry and mining until his job was eliminated by the establishment of the A&M college in Raleigh. Another Venable Ph.D., Herbert Bemerton Battle, had been serving since 1887 as professor of chemistry at the Leonard Medical School in Raleigh, as chemist for both the state board of health and the North Carolina Geological Survey, and as state chemist and director of the North Carolina Agricultural and Experimental Station in Raleigh. Hugh Miller, yet another a Venable graduate student who worked with Kenan in the laboratory at UNC, taught chemistry and physics at the A&M college in Raleigh before accepting the position of chief chemist at the Navassa Guano Company in Wilmington.[78]

If Kenan recognized Venable as the perfect mentor, the professor likewise recognized Kenan as someone who might help him promote his own personal, professional, and institutional interests. Venable wanted to move the university beyond its traditional emphasis on the liberal arts. He wanted it to give equal weight to the teaching of science and technology and to advance a curriculum that would serve the interests of both the New South and the industrial nation with which it was inextricably linked. Indeed, Venable wanted to end the South's reputation as a scientific backwater incapable of producing men of science and research—a reputation he had encountered at the 1890 meeting of the American Association for the Advancement of Science. "I have met many men of prominence & they have been nice to me. I felt tickled all over yesterday when the Professor of Chemistry at Cornell incidentally spoke of having mentioned my published work & name in his lectures to his class. I suppose it is an indirect compliment from them also that they have taken me for a northern man who has gone South, . . . & not for a southerner born. They seem to think our native born men very lazy & little likely to excell [sic] in original work."[79]

Kenan seemed to possess the temperament, ability, and connections that could help Venable further many of these goals. He was bright, energetic, mature, and disciplined; he wanted to be a scientist; and he was the nephew of Colonel Thomas Kenan, one of the university's most powerful officials. When one adds the fact that the Kenans were close friends with Major James Turner Morehead, the president of the Willson Aluminum Company, it is easy to understand why Venable chose Will Kenan to work with him on the company's carbide experiments.

These experiments began in the late spring of 1892, after Venable returned to Chapel Hill with several lumps of an unidentified substance produced in the Willson Aluminum Company's electric furnace. The material was handed to him as a "curiosity" during his two-week stay at Spray, where he had been trying to help the company determine the source of its repeated failures to find a cheap process for making pure aluminum in its furnace. Venable brought the material back to Chapel Hill and gave it to Kenan, his lab assistant for the summer, and Kenan, fresh from his duties at his sister Jessie's wedding, began the journey of a lifetime. "This dark colored, spongy mass containing a large amount of graphite had been wheeled out on the dump [at Spray], and when rained on, gave off a small amount of gas with a considerable noxious odor.

This is what Dr. Venable had instructed me to investigate and find out of what it was composed."[80]

While their initial experiments made it "easy to recognize we were dealing with a carbide of calcium," it took them a little longer to answer "the more important question . . . [of] the nature of the gas evolved." According to Kenan he identified the gas as acetylene after "I passed some of this gas through an ammoniacal copper solution and immediately a copious precipitate was produced which was recognized without difficulty as copper acetylide." It was not difficult for the excited researchers to recognize the implications of their findings and what to do next. Venable later wrote, "Here, then was a comparatively cheap and easy method of producing acetylene in any desired quantities and immediately the thought of its illuminating qualities in coal gas and the possibility of using it as an illuminant occurred to me."[81]

The two men continued their research throughout the summer and fall. "On trying a mixture of one part of acetylene with four or five parts of air," Venable explained, "using an ordinary bat-wing burner, the wonderful brilliancy and beauty of the [acetylene] light were revealed. I was, therefore, the first in this country to see this really remarkable light."[82] He let no one else but Kenan see it until March 1893, when at a meeting in Chapel Hill, they revealed it to officials of the Willson Aluminum Company. Also at that meeting, Kenan recalled, he gave the officials "my note book covering the work done," and following "a full discussion of the matter they were to apply for a patent, Dr. Venable was to receive a royalty and I was to have a job."[83]

Things did not go as promised, however. By January 1894, as Kenan began his final semester at UNC, it was obvious he would not have a carbide job waiting for him after graduation, and no royalties would soon be forthcoming for Venable. Their disappointment was not eased by the events of that spring. Indeed, Venable came close to leaving Chapel Hill to accept a teaching position at the University of Texas. The popular professor was tired of the constant attacks on UNC's funding and athletic activities, and it looked like the battle was about to get worse. The economic depression was deepening, so was North Carolina's political crisis, and the state's denominational colleges had stepped up their efforts to ban intercollegiate athletic competition and to cut the university's state funding. Venable pondered long and hard before rejecting the advice of his father, a mathematics professor at the University of Virginia, who urged him to accept the position in Texas. "The denominational colleges in Texas are of very little influence," the elder Venable wrote in February 1894, "therefore can do very little in the way of marring the influence or preventing the growth & expansion of the University [there]."[84]

Also that spring, in the aftermath of Carolina's disappointing football season, relations between Frat and non-Frat students became especially "bitter," and "college spirit" plunged to an all-time low. A group of disgruntled non-

Frat men formed a new student newspaper, the *White and Blue*, and began attacking the *Tar Heel*, accusing it of excessive sports coverage and of helping fraternity "favorites" dominate the most visible student positions on campus, from places on the football and baseball teams to the staff of the *Tar Heel* and campus offices. Indeed, the new paper charged the *Tar Heel* with ignoring the news, pursuits, and aspirations of the majority of the students.[85]

Although the *Tar Heel* continued to dismiss such charges as more apparent than real, and to defend itself as the nonpartisan voice of "the Athletic Association of the University of North Carolina," others saw its competition with the *White and Blue* for what it was, a struggle between Frats and non-Frats. As the *Tar Heel* noted in one of its few references to the new paper, "A recent issue of the *Sewanee Times* has an editorial regarding the present unpleasant condition of affairs here, and states that the *Tar Heel* and the *White and Blue* are two antagonistic weeklies 'each endeavoring to overturn the envied power of the other,' and furthermore that the Tar Heel is the 'avowed organ of the fraternity element at UNC.' Where the *Times* got its information, we are unable to say. It is, however, radically incorrect."[86]

All of these developments increased the already intense pressure Kenan confronted during his final semester as an undergraduate. When he was not practicing baseball, playing it, or managing the team's affairs, he was working on his senior thesis, struggling with German, buying his commencement wardrobe, reading articles for Venable's "Journal Club," preparing a paper to present to the Mitchell Scientific Society, and trying to arrange a summer job.

Kenan's thesis, "The Artificial Production of Petroleum," contains nothing original or revealing, except, perhaps, that it deals with oil, the source of the Flagler fortune he later inherited. It is a ten-page summary of the theories that then prevailed regarding the formation of petroleum, and it ends with a brief, cryptic statement of his argument: "We are able to transform every animal fat into petroleum. No doubt in a few years the artificial production [of petroleum] will be carried on, as the natural wells, especially those of Ohio, seem to be gradually giving out."[87]

The busy senior showed more originality in his presentation before the Mitchell Society, where he, his roommate, and their professor all read papers: Kenan on "his attempt to form double chlorides of the alkalis," Baskerville on "the methods of separating Zirconium and comparing it to that of Titanium," and Venable on "the atomic weight of Zirconium." "The meeting was very interesting and lively," the *Tar Heel* reported, but "there were far less of the students present than there should have been."[88]

By commencement Kenan had secured a one-month summer job in the university laboratory, but he was not sure what he would do after that. "I shall go to work next year if it is possible for me to get a place," he wrote to his cousin Owen. But he did not want to teach, something that his father and

Will Kenan at the time of his graduation from UNC, 1894. (HMFM Archives)

faculty friends were urging him to do. He had neither the desire nor, he believed, the qualifications to do so: "Just imagine me teaching—may be able to instruct the youths in athletics, Foot ball, Base Ball & Tennis but I have some doubts in regard to Latin, Greek, Math &c." And whatever he did would only be temporary. "I shall work one year then continue my study in Chemistry for two and I hope to be able to accomplish something by that time." Yet the voyage ahead was still uncharted. "I have only two exams in June and then I will be a 'Columbus'—just think of it."[89]

Kenan did teach for a year, and he also returned to Chapel Hill for graduate work in chemistry. But unlike Venable and Baskerville, who spent most of their careers as scientists on campus, Kenan spent most of his in the laboratories and offices of the business world. His path to this world was being laid, in fact, even as he and fellow seniors sang their class song and smoked the traditional pipe of peace at commencement. Thomas "Carbide" Willson, the Canadian inventor for whom the Willson Aluminum Company was named, was organizing "a syndicate composed of the biggest gas men and bankers in the United States to carry the [acetylene] gas matter," while out on Long Island Sound, Henry Flagler's second wife was suffering a mental breakdown that would lead him to divorce her and marry Mary Lily Kenan.[90]

CHAPTER 4

Calcium Carbide and Acetylene

There are many different accounts of the discovery and identification of calcium carbide and acetylene in the United States. Kenan always emphasized the
importance of his own and Venable's role in the process, while their good
friend John Motley Morehead advanced his own claims to the discovery by
promoting his father, Major James Turner Morehead, as the man "primarily
responsible for it." In yet another version of the story, one preferred by Cana-
dians, the spotlight falls on Princeton, Ontario, native Thomas Leopold Willson, the winner of Canada's first McCharles Prize—for his calcium carbide and
acetylene discoveries.[1]

Most of the stories of the birth of carbide begin in May 1892 with an accident
at Spray, North Carolina: a dark, crystalline material emerged from the Willson
Aluminum Company's electric arc furnace. What happened next remains a
matter of contention, but the evidence suggests that yet another accident occurred that was followed in turn by the purposive, professional research of Venable and Kenan and a series of developments with far-reaching consequences.

After removing the crystalline material from the furnace, Willson and the
Moreheads ordered the aluminum company's black workers to throw the
apparently worthless product on a nearby garbage pile, where it became covered with peanut hulls and other debris. Sometime later, while relieving himself on the dump, Major Morehead or one of his associates threw a smoldering
cigar butt onto the bubbling, pungent mixture, and the smoke began to rise.
The surprised micturaters rescued the unignited lumps from the dump, and
these blobs and the gas they produced were subsequently identified by Venable
and Kenan at UNC as calcium carbide and acetylene. As apocryphal as parts of
this story may be, it is nevertheless based on traditional accounts of the event
and contains much that is true. The Willson Aluminum Company did produce
the first calcium carbide in the United States, it did so by accident, and the
process involved the contributions of all of the individuals mentioned.[2]

No one made a greater contribution than Major James Turner Morehead.

Major James Turner Morehead, a "great friend" of the Kenan family and one of the organizers of the Willson Aluminum Company at Spray, North Carolina. (NCC)

The second son of North Carolina's wealthiest and most prominent ante-bellum governor, the Major had returned from the Civil War without part of his jawbone but with brighter prospects than most southerners. He had inherited valuable property from his father on the Virginia border near the confluence of the Smith and Dan Rivers, and with the aid of John, his wealthy banker-brother in Charlotte, the Major had done rather well. A cotton gin was followed by cotton and wool carding mills as well as by a spoke and handle factory and other properties at Spray (now part of Eden, North Carolina). In the mid-1880s the Major invested in the uncompleted Cape Fear and Yadkin Valley Railroad, a line projected to run diagonally across the state from Wilmington in the southeast to the mountains in the northwest.[3]

In 1888, however, the failure of London's Baring Brothers forced the Major and his railroad partners to look elsewhere for credit, and finding none, they eventually mortgaged their individual assets to support the railroad. Unfortunately the road fell into receivership and "cleaned out and broke the entire lot of them." By 1890 Morehead's principal creditor, his brother John, had seized the mills and other properties at Spray in lieu of the Major's mounting debts, and with little left but some land and surplus water power at Spray, the busted Confederate veteran went to New York to look for investors to locate an industry on his North Carolina property.

He turned first to Albert R. Ledoux, a former superintendent of the North Carolina Agricultural Station at UNC. Although Ledoux, a prosperous metallurgist, had no interest in returning to or investing in North Carolina, he did refer the Major to August Eimer and a man named Lippert. These two chemists claimed they could make aluminum through a new process involving the electric furnace and electrochemical smelting technique invented by their Canadian friend Thomas Leopold Willson. Morehead then went to Willson, who introduced him in turn to George Frederick Seward, vice-president of the Fidelity and Casualty Company of New York.[4]

Seward was just the kind of contact the Major needed—a wealthy man with powerful connections. His uncle, William H. Seward, had been secretary of state under President Abraham Lincoln, and Seward himself had been one of the nation's leading diplomats to the Far East. During his stay in China, moreover, Seward had met a bright young naval officer, Royal Rodney Ingersoll, who, by the time of Morehead's visit to New York, was head of the ordnance department at the United States Naval Academy and interested with Seward in the overlapping and potentially lucrative projects of Willson, the Canadian inventor. Not only had Willson invented a smelting technique that might be used for making aluminum, but he was also testing aluminum alloys for making guns, big guns, that he hoped to manufacture for the United States government.[5]

The thirty-year-old Willson also had a lot to offer the Major as both an electrical engineer and an inventor. After studying chemistry and physics at the Hamilton Collegiate Institute in Hamilton, Ontario, Willson built one of Canada's first steam-driven dynamos. By 1890 he held numerous patents for improvements to his dynamo, for smelting techniques in electric furnaces, and for various types of electric lights. On the other side of the ledger, however, Willson knew very little chemistry, and he was broke—his creditors constantly "pressing" him "very closely." Having been swindled, moreover, by several prominent patent lawyers, he vowed never to let that happen again, especially since he was attempting to win the hand of Mary Parks, the California cousin of Seward's wife. If anyone made money from one of his inventions, it was going to be Willson himself.[6]

In the spring of 1890, as negotiations continued in New York, the Major

Thomas "Carbide" Willson, the Canadian inventor who investigated and promoted the uses of calcium carbide and acetylene. (Charles Sifton/National Archives of Canada/C-053498)

returned to North Carolina for the graduation of his son, John Motley Morehead, from the University of North Carolina at Chapel Hill. Called "Mot" or "Sober Mot" by his friends, the younger Morehead had previously shown little interest in chemistry, engineering, or science. He wrote his senior thesis on the corn industry in the South and earned special certificates in natural philosophy and natural history in completing his B.A. degree at Chapel Hill. Yet Mot was also a bright young man with no real prospects for immediate employment, and he probably welcomed his father's request to return to Chapel Hill for a year of study under the university's popular chemistry professor, Francis Preston Venable. If everything went well in New York, the Major promised,

Mot could help with the chemical work at the new aluminum company in Spray.[7]

The Moreheads went their separate ways in the fall of 1890, the Major to New York to complete his negotiations with Willson and Seward, and Mot to Chapel Hill to study chemistry under Venable. At this point Mot and Will Kenan first became friends. Their fathers had attended UNC together, the Kenans considered the Major a "great friend" of the family, and Mary Lily frequently visited Blandwood, the Greensboro mansion where the Major was born and where several of his family members still lived.[8] Both young men also belonged to the in group on campus and spent hours in the laboratory. They were probably there together, in fact, in October 1890 when a fire broke out— an incident that their professor described with some amusement. "You can fancy the scene that met me when I came to the room where the fire was. Mott perched up on the hood, coat off and hair redder than ever. Hugh Miller standing below with an iron pipe ready for any emergency & several lesser laboratory lights standing about with water. The fire had already gone out but they were trying to make sure of it & so standing guard."[9]

In the meantime the Major reached an agreement with his northern associates, and on December 2, 1890, he, Seward, and Willson signed the necessary documents for incorporating the Willson Aluminum Company under the laws of the state of New York.[10] Morehead was made president of the firm; Seward, vice-president; and Willson, secretary. The North Carolinian provided land and water power for the new company, the New York insurance executive put up most of the capital, and the Canadian contributed his new smelting process. Willson described their agreement in his response to an interested American investor just a few days later: "The preliminary capital $20,000 cash is subscribed. This simply erects one dynamo of 100–150 horse power with water wheel etc. After this is running and the demonstration of business successful, then from $150,000 to $500,000 will be called in. The small stock subscription at the present (without water [inflating the stock?]) and the 100 shares sold for 125.00 on a premium $8.25 shows how the solid men regard the matter.... Mr. Seward is managing the matter for me and Mr. Seward's standing is sufficient guarantee as to the [?] of my company."[11] If things worked out, Willson continued, he would be glad to welcome other investors.

The Willson Aluminum Company was still trying to work things out by the spring of 1891. It had received its dynamo, but there was no canal trace or waterwheel to power it. The New York chemists, Eimer and Lippert, abandoned the company and returned North, leaving the firm's new head chemist, Mot Morehead, with little to do. "We have a lot of attractions to offer about now with which to kill time," he wrote to a former classmate in June 1891, "they are digging a new canal and putting in a new 200 h.p. water wheel, the Aluminum men have jumped and left a great big dynamo with us.... Besides that we have almost daily games of base-ball."[12]

Just when the Willson Aluminum Company began operations is not clear, but at some point prior to the spring of 1892 the Major hired two black men and several local white boys to work for the company, including two future Union Carbide executives, Jesse King and Edgar F. Price. Willson was certainly not making pure aluminum by then; indeed, "with the exception of a few small globules," Mot Morehead later wrote, "no metallic aluminum was ever produced." The best Willson could do was make alloys of aluminum and copper containing only "10 to 20 per cent of aluminum, and the company was not able to operate at a profit in making this mixture."[13]

Willson appeared much less concerned than the Moreheads with this failure. He hoped to profit from his new smelting technique, to be sure, either by using it or selling it or both, but he was also getting exactly what he wanted: aluminum alloys for his cannon experiments. These experiments apparently contributed, in fact, to the information in Royal Rodney Ingersoll's 1891 publication, *The Elasticity of Guns.* In May 1892, just two weeks after the Willson Aluminum Company accidentally produced calcium carbide, Willson received a patent for a "cannon cylinder" constructed of copper, bronze, and aluminum alloys—what Ingersoll described as "the strongest plan of construction yet invented."[14]

Although the Moreheads later reaped substantial profits from Willson's experiments and contacts, they did not appreciate his performance at the Willson Aluminum Company. He displayed little knowledge of chemistry, he failed to make aluminum, and he constantly shifted his attention from one project to another. According to one Canadian version of the carbide story, however, lazy southerners bore part of the blame. "The Willson Aluminum Company was going broke and the morale of Morehead, Willson and his three assistants was caving in; Willson would lay out work for the day, but, because of growing lethargy, it wasn't always carried out."[15]

The company made its first calcium carbide by accident, after deciding that "it might be possible to produce metallic calcium from a mixture of lime and carbon, and having in hand metallic calcium it might be possible to produce aluminum as a second step by using metallic calcium as a reducing agent." Mot Morehead later offered this version of what happened next:

> There was in the storeroom of the plant at the time a quantity of lime used for whitewashing. This lime was slaked with coal tar which was kept on hand, along with ground carbon, for patching the furnace. No calculations were made as to the proportions of the lime and tar. The slaked lime was merely worked up with all the tar that it would absorb, and it was the merest of luck that the proportions of contained calcium and contained carbon fell within the rather narrow limits which will produce calcium carbide. This mixture was placed in the electric furnace, and subjected to the heat of the arc.[16]

Willson electric arc furnaces at the Willson Aluminum Company in Spray, North Carolina. The company was operating only one furnace—probably the older one on the right—at the time it made the first calcium carbide in the United States. (KC)

The accounts of the birth of carbide trail off in different directions at this point, each emphasizing the crucial role of a different personality. In the most recent Canadian version, it is Willson who nurtured the lime and coal tar mixture and Willson who delivered the black lumps from the furnace, finding, to his astonishment, that "when a chunk fell off the brittle crystalline mass into a bucket of water . . . a gas was released and began to burn with a sooty flame when it ignited on a glowing portion of the sample." Yet this account says nothing about how Willson knew he was witnessing calcium carbide and acetylene, only that he had "discovered the ideal proportions for producing both in bulk using inexpensive materials" and knew "he had the key to industrial success."[17]

Mot Morehead remembered the arrival of carbide somewhat differently. It was standard practice, he wrote, to shut the furnace down before the end of a run in order to withdraw a small quantity of material for analysis. The sample was immediately cooled in water and analyzed, and before completing the run, the material remaining in the furnace was adjusted to achieve the desired proportions of the alloy being produced. This procedure was naturally repeated, Morehead claimed, with the lime and coal tar sample, which "was quenched in a pail of water. It at once gave off large volumes of gas. Judging from the fact that this substance had a crystalline structure and metallic lustre, and when brought in contact with water gave off gas, it was at once concluded that we had produced metallic calcium, which with water, was producing hydrogen, and that at least one step of the process of producing aluminum was accomplished."[18]

But they were wrong. Once the furnace cooled, they placed the remaining product in a bucket of water and ignited the gas released with "a burning piece of oily waste fastened to the end of a fishing pole." The smoke and flame signaled that the gas "could not be hydrogen," Morehead explained, "which burns with a colorless flame, and that the substance was not metallic calcium, but some compound of carbon, as neither water nor metallic calcium contains carbon, and therefore could not produce soot." Thus, the company's "new-born hope of making aluminum, which we had built up on the metallic calcium theory, was dashed to pieces. This all happened on May 2, 1892."[19]

Morehead mentions nothing in this 1922 account, however, about discarding the crystalline lumps or about the peanut hulls, his father urinating on them, and the smoldering cigar butt. He gives no hint, that is, of the story that members of the family still tell today and that was long retold by members of the chemistry department at UNC. Rather, he makes his own claim to fame. He says he identified the lumps as calcium carbide. "I was a graduate of the previous year from the North Carolina State University [UNC], and held the position of chemist with the company. I proceeded at once upon an investigation of the new substance, and determined that it was calcium carbide, but having no apparatus for gas analysis I did not know just what the gas was." So a "sample of this first carbide was sent to Dr. F. P. Venable, Professor of Chemistry at the State University, who analyzed the gas and pronounced it acetylene."[20]

There are a number of peculiar features about Morehead's version of events. Unlike other accounts, which stress the accidental nature of the discovery, his emphasizes the controlled and purposive behavior of the participants. Only the correct combinations of lime and coal tar appear serendipitous. Peculiar too is Morehead's claim that he recognized the material as calcium carbide. Although calcium carbide and acetylene had been discovered and identified decades earlier, and carbide had been produced with lime and coke, it seems very unlikely, given Morehead's superficial knowledge of chemistry and physics in 1892, that he was able to recognize the black lumps as calcium carbide. This leads to two other odd aspects of his account. Morehead not only says that a sample of the carbide "was sent" to Venable, but he also fails to mention Will Kenan's name in connection with the identification of either calcium carbide or acetylene—an omission he continued to make the rest of his life.

Needless to say, Venable and Kenan remembered things differently. The material produced after "Mr. Willson added lime to his mixture . . . was of no value," Kenan recalled, "so it was wheeled out on the dump and it was noticed that when it rained a small amount of gas was evolved and considerable smell was produced." Indeed, according to Kenan, it was this, Willson's failure to make metallic calcium, that prompted the Major to look elsewhere for advice. "Due to the unsatisfactory results Major Morehead obtained the services of Dr. F. P. Venable, the head of the Chemical Department of the University of North Carolina, to see if he could not suggest some means of getting them out of their difficulty."[21] Kenan's story is corroborated by Venable's correspondence from Spray in June 1892.

Venable arrived in the mill village excited but weary from the burdens of final exams and commencement at UNC. He was intrigued with the company's aluminum experiments, and he also needed the money. It was the end of the fiscal year and more than a month before his state salary would be paid; the company was paying him almost twice as much as his salary as a professor; and the Moreheads were feeding and lodging him in their home. Although Venable hated being separated from his wife and four children, he could not ignore this financial and professional opportunity. "I earn my ten dollars a day & think of you and the boys & my two little maidens," he wrote to his wife, "the clothes, the shoes, the food and all the rest of it until our July ship comes home."[22]

The professor was just as perplexed as his employers, however, by their failure to make pure aluminum. "I think perhaps I am helping Mr. Morehead," he wrote to his wife. "I have cleared up two or three things and am directing experiments as if I knew all about it." He hoped to discover something of importance but saw little chance of accomplishing "any very successful work." Still, though, his time was not wasted. "It is all very interesting and I am learning more than I could from six months of book work. . . . When I get a little more time I shall attempt a description of the furnaces & the work we are doing." No matter what happened, he ventured, the Moreheads would not be harmed. "It has cost a large amount of money to get things in their present trim but even if it falls through Maj. Morehead is safe. If it turns out a success somebody is going to be a millionaire."[23]

Venable was referring to the production of aluminum, of course, and not to the discarded crystalline lumps. "I have not been able to accomplish much as yet nor have I hopes of doing much more than proving to the owners of these works that they had better stop experimenting & go to manufacturing the alloys they started out to make. This knowledge will be money in their pockets."[24]

The professor returned to Chapel Hill with some money in his pockets and a few pails of the still-unidentified lumps. "Willson . . . had blundered upon this substance while trying to make Aluminum," the professor later recalled, "and did not know what he had in hand. He gave it to me as a curiosity and I

Chemistry laboratory at UNC, 1890s. (NCC)

set to work upon it and report to him the nature of the body and its probable industrial use. So that really, any mention of the discovery of the substance need not contain my name."[25]

Venable was essentially correct. He and Kenan simply did what chemists were expected to do: they assayed the material to determine what it was. Yet Venable did not feel the same about the acetylene flame, and Kenan, who could only claim a role in the experiments through his professor, always claimed that they deserved credit for both the identification and discovery of calcium carbide and acetylene in the United States.

Kenan later recalled that Venable returned from the Willson Aluminum Company after "making certain suggestions as to the changes in operation and brought back with him to the University at Chapel Hill quite a number of pieces of this waste product and gave them to me with instructions to investigate it and find out what it was composed of. I actually did the work under his instructions, together we discovered that it was Calcium Carbide, determined it's formulae, and made known the fact that acetylene gas could be evolved from it. This work was carried on during the summer and fall of 1892."[26]

Venable immediately notified Willson that the "curiosity" was calcium carbide, but it took him and Kenan longer to identify the gas as acetylene. In the meantime Willson used their information to apply for two patents on the production of calcium carbide, and in September 1892 he sent a case of the material to the famous British scientist Lord Kelvin. Willson told Kelvin that the substance had been identified as calcium carbide, and Kelvin called it that in his reply to Willson in early October, but without mentioning acetylene. "I have seen and tried the calcium carbide, only however so far as throwing it into water and setting fire to the gas which comes off. It seems to me a most interesting substance and I thank you very much for sending it to me."[27]

Willson said nothing to Venable and Kenan about his patent applications and Kelvin correspondence, and they, in turn, said nothing to him about their acetylene discovery. They searched instead for a mixture of air and acetylene that burned brightly but did not explode, for Venable quickly grasped that acetylene might enhance the illuminating qualities of coal gas.[28] By the end of 1892 Venable and Kenan had developed a "brilliant flame" that could be adequately controlled, and in early February 1893, after their "figures were checked and facts recorded," Venable notified Major Morehead that valuable properties had been discovered in the carbide and that all necessary patents should be secured immediately. The professor also asked for permission to publish the discoveries and suggested that Morehead and Willson come to Chapel Hill to observe what had been discovered.[29]

Morehead's response set off a series of events that shaped the legal history of carbide for years to come. After telling Venable he was "pleased to hear of your discoveries, of valuable properties, in the calcium carbide," the Major revealed something the professor was unaware of. "We hold now two patents, covering the mode of production, and whilst, calcium carbide, is specifically mentioned, still it is incidental production, and we wish to have explicit direct protection." Venable, his suspicions aroused by the patent revelations, became even more concerned when the Major asked him to "give us a full statement, of the properties, uses, and advantages of this substance, & also the formula for the carbide—and we will submit it to our patent attorney, and see if any addition or amendments, to our present Patents, can be made & then you can make the publication you speak of."[30] Venable sent the description the Major requested, but without mentioning acetylene, and Willson incorporated the description into his patent application of March 16, 1893—a patent subsequently granted and used on many occasions to establish Willson's claim of priority to the production of calcium carbide.[31]

Only on March 27, 1893, at a meeting in Chapel Hill, did Venable reveal his and Kenan's acetylene discovery. The historic meeting got off to a bad start. The Major was not on the train when it arrived; only his brother-in-law, William R. Walker, and Thomas Willson disembarked. Venable was probably more disappointed than Kenan by the Major's absence. Although he knew Willson and Walker, the Moreheads had been his principal contacts with the Willson Aluminum Company. He had taught Mot at the university, he had worked and lived with him and the Major at Spray, and all of his correspondence had been with the Major. The professor made the best of the situation, however, and invited Willson and Walker to join him and Kenan at the Venable's Chapel Hill home for lunch.[32]

Venable then took the group to his private laboratory on campus, where he and Kenan struck a deal with their visitors before the latter "witnessed the light and were informed of our discovery that acetylene was the gas evolved from the waste product of their furnace."[33] Venable and Kenan were promised jobs with any company Walker and Willson might form to exploit the discoveries, and Venable was guaranteed a percentage of the stock of such a company. While the agreement with Kenan was verbal, arrangements with Venable took the form of a legal contract:

> Memorandum of Agreement entered into this 27th day of March 1893, by and between Dr. F. P. Venable, Thos. L. Wil[l]son, and W. R. Walker, in relation to the organization of a company for the manufacture, application and introduction of calcium and similar carbides,

> Whereas; The Willson Aluminum Co. has been engaged upon the production of calcium carbides and has succeeded in producing it upon a commercial scale, and whereas the said F. P. Venable has been employed by the said Willson Aluminum Co., in chemical research upon said substances, and has among other things discovered a new and valuable commercial use for calcium carbides, and will be engaged upon investigations pertaining to the further commercial development and introduction of said products; Now, therefore, it has been agreed by and between the said F. P. Venable Thos. L. Willson and W. R. Walker, as follows;

> That the said parties will endeavor to organize a corporation to be called a carbide company, of a capitalization of $100,000, more or less, as may be decided to be necessary, and said stock to be proportioned as follows: 51% to go to the Willson Aluminum Co., for its rights to manufacture said carbides, 17% to go to the said F. P. Venable, for and in consideration of his services and all rights and titles to any discoveries he has made or may make in reference to the subject of said carbides, or like material while interested in said company, as owner of said stock, or while in the employment of said company.

> It is further agreed that the said F. P. Venable shall enter the employ of the said company to be formed, at an annual salary of $1,500, beginning with the date of the organization of said company, for such a period of time as may be mutually agreed upon by the said company and said F. P. Venable,

> Further, if during the time and before said organization of said company, said F. P. Venable shall devote time or services in the chemical work and research, upon said subjects beforementioned, then he shall be paid for this

time at the same rate, out of the money which shall be paid into the treasury from the sale of stock of said company.

F. P. Venable
Thomas L. Willson
W. R. Walker[34]

Major Morehead was in New York at the time of the Chapel Hill meeting, trying to find a way to survive in the deepening economic depression. The Willson Aluminum Company still had not made any pure aluminum, and while the carbide appeared to be a potential moneymaker, the company had yet to find a way to exploit its promise and to do anything more than spend money—something that was increasingly hard to find. "Things finally got so desperate that my father got the three of us boys together," Mot Morehead later recalled, "gave us his blessing, paid the other two [Edgar Price and Jesse King] what he could, gave me a little stock in the company for what he owed me, because he had been boarding me all that time, laid off one of the Negroes, helped Price to get a job on a railroad in West Virginia, and me one in a bank in New York, while he continued to operate the plant with Jesse King, and one Negro."[35]

The Major returned to North Carolina shortly after the agreement with Venable was signed, but Mot stayed up North, where he soon lost his position as a banker and started selling electrical goods in New Jersey.[36] In April 1893 Willson and the Major decided that the latter should return to New York to consult with Albert R. Ledoux regarding the results of Venable and Kenan's research. Unfortunately they also hoped to use Ledoux, it seems, to undermine the agreement with Venable.

By the time the Major returned to New York, neither Venable nor the officials of the Willson Aluminum Company felt comfortable with the March 27 "Memorandum of Agreement." Venable believed, and rightfully so, that Willson and Walker might ignore his personal interests when it came time to draw up the necessary patents, charters, and agreements to exploit his and Kenan's discoveries. The agreement said nothing, after all, about acetylene; it mentioned only "carbides." On the other hand, Willson and Morehead needed more than the bright light Venable and Kenan had shown them. They needed a commercial use for the carbide, and they had to have somebody they knew and trusted to help them find one—immediately. Venable had too much to do with the end of the school year approaching, and most important of all, if he did discover a commercial use for the acetylene, Willson and Morehead would be compelled, under the terms of the agreement, to share the profits with him. With Ledoux, of course, there was no such obligation.

Willson's letter to the Major on April 15, 1893, reveals the extent to which deception, tension, and mistrust pervaded these developments. Willson believed that alcohol could be made cheaply from acetylene, and he instructed Morehead, "First have Prof. Ledoux determine the composition of it—gas given off from the Calcium Carbide, whether it is C_2H_2 [acetylene] or not, if not what is it? 2nd To make alcohol from it."[37] The Canadian already knew that the gas was acetylene; Venable and Kenan had told him that. So what, exactly, did he have in mind? Did he doubt their findings and want a second opinion, or was he trying to get around the agreement with Venable by having someone else identify the gas as acetylene? The last paragraph of his letter suggests an answer: "Received letter from Dr Venable in which he says 'I regard my interest as restricted to the burning of this gas' This settles all controversy with alcohol on ?"[38]

But it did not settle Willson's disagreements with the Major. Although both men hoped to profit from the carbide discovery, they differed on the questions of how and when to try to do so. The Major, hounded by his creditors, took the short-term perspective. When approached by an investor who wanted to form a carbide and acetylene company in either England or Scotland, Morehead suggested cutting a deal. But Willson, equally as destitute, urged the Major to be patient: "I believe this is one of the most important of discoveries in organic chemistry and that there is an immense use for this material."[39]

Rather than cut a deal before a commercial use for the carbide had been found, Willson urged the Major to discuss the financial situation with the company's vice-president, George Seward, and "devise some plan whereby this company can be put on a satisfactory financial basis. If there is anything in the carbide, use it for The Willson Aluminum Co's benefit and push it for all it is worth." Using it "to raise 15000 or 20000 dollars" would be a mistake, Willson argued. "More money than that will be needed, it is either a large matter or it is nothing at all. The Willson Aluminum Co's interest lies in a license to manufacture in the United States and until this company does put itself in a commercial position it will be impossible to float any English or European company and any effort in that direction would be futile."[40]

Willson really wanted to devote all of the aluminum company's resources to perfecting the manufacture of his patented cannon cylinder for the United States government. He had been experimenting with the cannon for over two years, and the Willson Aluminum Company, in addition to putting up money for his research, had been making and testing bronze and aluminum alloys for him. By June 1893 the project appeared ready to go. The Carpenter Steel Company had cast the cylinder in New York; Willson had managed "to overcome the prejudice of Navy and Army officers and get their approval" for the new aluminum-bronze gun; and he now possessed all the necessary gun and aluminum patents to protect the project. As usual, though, he lacked the capital to follow through. "As soon as these stringent financial times are over," he wrote to his patent attorney, "I shall organize a company or companies with sufficient capital to carry both the Gun and the aluminum. One company could manufacture the gun and aluminum wanted for the gun. This would necessarily require a large and rich organization, say a company of from five to ten million dollars or separate companies for each."[41]

While the carbide research continued in New York, Willson pushed his business associates to concentrate on the cannon project. In addition to having the Major negotiate a contract to manufacture a prototype of the weapon, he urged Morehead "to get ex secretary of Navy Whitney to take the [cannon] matter in hand."[42] He and his business manager also solicited capital in New York and San Francisco and succeeded in eliciting the support of Lieutenant Commander Royal Rodney Ingersoll, the Naval Academy's ordnance instructor. On June 4, 1893, Ingersoll, who soon became one of Willson's silent partners, wrote the Canadian inventor praising the cannon cylinder: "The value of the invention in my opinion is unquestionable; there is no doubt in my mind that it is the strongest plan of construction yet invented." Indeed, Ingersoll soon repeated this evaluation in the *Proceedings of the Naval Institute* and offered Willson "hope for all the success possible with the [Army and Navy] Departments, and if they will not adopt [the cannon], if at least they can be made to say that the plan has merit, it will help materially in pushing the work along."[43]

Willson did not forget about the carbide, however. He continued baking it in the oven at Spray, keeping some for his own experiments and sending the rest to the Major in New York, where Ledoux's research produced some confusing but potentially useful results. "Mr. Morehead says Dr. Ledoux calls the calcium carbide, calcium acetylide, and that it contains hydrogen," Willson wrote his business manager. That was not what Venable and Kenan had called it, and the term made no sense to Willson either, who was busy preparing yet another patent application for carbide, one that would be more specific with regard to the gas produced by the crystalline material. "While I am not a chemist and so cannot contest [Ledoux's] opinion," Willson continued, "I still hold the composition to be one of Calcium and Carbon principally and would desire to have a claim incorporated in the new application, as the old one to express substantially as follows, 'a compound consisting of carbon and a metal which when thrown into water or other fluid decomposes. The water the oxygen of which unites with the metal and the carbon set fire unites with the Hydrogen and escapes as a gas.' "[44] This was exactly what the UNC chemists had told him, of course, and in June 1893 Willson used their information to apply for a patent on acetylene.[45]

One week later Willson contacted Venable, who had been asking for almost two months for a meeting to discuss the carbide matter. Venable knew nothing, it seems, about Ledoux's research or Willson's new patent application, and there is nothing about these topics in the two surviving letters Willson wrote the professor in the spring of 1893. "When you wrote Mr. Morehead was leaving for New York," Willson explained on June 20. "The Major expects to be in Raleigh on the 28th and then home. I will be very glad to have you come and talk over the carbide matter with Mr. Morehead and hope you have found a commercial side to it."[46]

Venable had not found one, however, and neither had Willson, Ledoux, or the Major. There were no commercial prospects for Willson's cannon project, either, which suffered a devastating blow when Ingersoll was transferred from the Naval Academy to the flagship *Philadelphia* of the Asiatic Squadron. Indeed, Willson appears to have abandoned his hopes for the gun-cylinder project following the departure of Ingersoll, who remained at sea for most of his last fifteen years of service with the navy.[47]

At the same time, the financial fortunes of Major J. T. Morehead sank to an all-time low. He was unable to meet the demands of his creditors, and "they sold him out; cotton mill, real estate, water power and everything else." He did not even "claim the homestead exemption," his son recalled, "and they sold his house, furniture, and everything he had." The Confederate veteran then "packed up a number of glass jars with samples of carbide and left home to sell the product, the patents, or the process. He was 56 years old, broke and discredited; his fortune and property swept away; and he owed some $200,000. His entire capital consisted of $11 in cash, and a faith which surpassed all understanding in the future of carbide."[48]

Willson soon tested the Major's faith. Having stumbled deeper into debt himself, the Canadian left North Carolina and returned to New York, where he presented his old friend August Eimer with some bottles of carbide. The Major would not have approved; Eimer had abandoned his commitments to help with the first aluminum experiments at Spray. Yet the New York chemist now had just what Willson and the Willson Aluminum Company needed. He and his brother-in-law, Otto Paul Amend, were trained chemists and the owners of a successful and well-equipped laboratory that manufactured chemicals, drugs, and scientific equipment, including small gas burners. What was more, Amend, a graduate of Columbia University's school of mining, was working for the Standard Oil Company in the field of oil cracking.[49]

In early January 1894 Willson signed a preliminary agreement with Eimer and Amend. In return for their research and the use of their laboratory facilities he guaranteed them a share of any profits that arose in connection with the commercial use of the carbide. Willson assured the Major the agreement would be profitable for all concerned. "I have found a direct and present use for calcium carbide which will permit of development to an unlimited extent. I have signed a preliminary contract looking to its extensive use in the immediate future." Willson refused, however, to say to what use he planned to put the carbide, and he did not provide any details about the agreement. "The terms of my contract require that the whole matter be kept secret," he wrote. "I can only give you the names of the parties with whom I have signed a contract. They are Eimer & Amend."[50]

The Major read Willson's letter with mixed emotions. The wily Canadian had cut a deal behind his back, but at least it sounded more promising than the Major's own recent efforts to hawk the carbide discovery. The North Carolinian had offered "a half, then two-thirds, then three-quarters, then 80 per cent of the whole thing to the Pintsch Company for $5,000" and had then offered "the whole business to the Springfield Gas Machine people for $5,000 and neither would buy it."[51] Although the Major had no idea what Willson would be using the carbide for, and there was no contract as yet between Willson's new firm and the Willson Aluminum Company to make the carbide, the Canadian not only ordered the Major to make a ton of it, but he also promised Morehead that the "new firm of Eimer Amend and Willson will take the entire product of the Aluminum Co as far as the carbide is concerned. . . . I expect this will now make a commercial business for the Aluminum Co," Willson stroked Morehead, "and I shall be very glad if it shall become a very profitable one for you."[52]

It took most of February 1894 for Willson to complete his negotiations with all of the principals involved, and by the middle of the month he had worked out a contract with Willson Aluminum in which the company was "not required to furnish me or my nominees with the carbide exclusively. The Co can sell to anyone," he promised the Major, "and if you can develop a business personally for the use of the carbide, why it will be a matter of congratulation and furnish another outlet for the sale of carbide by the Aluminum Co."[53]

Willson signed a contract with the company at the end of the month, shortly after signing his agreement with Eimer and Amend. If the Willson Aluminum Company now failed to prosper, it was not his fault. "Look at the facts," he wrote to the Major. "The Willson Aluminum Company has employed Dr. Venable, Dr. Ledoux, Prof. Pitkin and I have personally put the matter before Sir William Thomson [Lord Kelvin] and the results have been a complete failure to find a commercial use for the carbide. . . . So it seems to me the Aluminum Co is indebted to me for giving them a business it could not otherwise get. It is also in my power to give the Aluminum Co a product to manufacture for which there is unlimited sale or market and which does not offer the small difficulties the manufacture of carbide does."[54] It was now up to the Major to carry things through. "If the Willson Aluminum Co will now go at this business I put in its way and turns out the stuff, there is an immense fortune for each of us in it."[55]

Willson did not return to North Carolina. He moved into a Brooklyn boardinghouse to be nearer to Eimer and Amend's laboratory, where the pace of research now became frenzied. "The old saying that 'It never rains good or bad but without it pours' is exemplified in our case," Willson wrote to the Major. "I can sell more of the carbide than we can see our way to make just now." While Eimer and Amend had constructed an apparatus "to make gallons of [the] 'Product'" Willson never identified, the latter experimented with acetylene under pressure and even "succeeded in liquefying the gas . . . and froze the liquid acetylene so we could handle it quite conveniently. The frozen acetylene looks like snow and is so cold that it will blister your hands."[56]

By the spring of 1894 Eimer and Amend had as many as six people at work in their laboratory on carbide experiments with cyanide, chlorine, nitrogen, silicon nitride, and the carbonates of magnesium, barium, and strontium. While all of these experiments eventually provided profitable uses for the carbide, the acetylene research showed the most immediate promise of profit. Not only could the gas be used, as Venable envisioned, as a substitute for oil in the enrichment of city coal gas, but also, as Venable and Kenan had discovered almost a year earlier, acetylene could be made to burn with a flame more brilliant than that produced by coal gas, the major source of illumination in the homes, businesses, and streets of America.[57]

By March, moreover, the laboratory had developed an acetylene lighting system for railroad cars that was the "simplest, lightest, cheapest and altogether the best for car lighting yet devised," Willson bragged to Morehead. "The system is perfect, practical and is a beautiful one in comparison with the present manner of doing the lighting. I shall develope it." And so he did. Before long he was discussing the question of rights and prices with "the lawyers for the man who wants the calcium carbide for car lighting. . . . There is no telling how large a matter this will become," he wrote excitedly to the Major. "I shall be very careful in the papers . . . and I will make it our business that they are right. I believe I am dealing with the Standard Oil Co."[58]

THE GAS MEN

Will Kenan was one month out of college and vacationing with his mother and sisters at Morehead City, North Carolina, when the grandson of the man for whom the ocean resort was named, Major James T. Morehead, received some exciting news from Thomas "Carbide" Willson. Rather than continue to wait for Standard Oil to make him a proposition, the Canadian was busy "organizing a syndicate composed of the biggest gas men and bankers in the United States to carry the gas matter." This syndicate, he assured the Major in July, would "give the Willson Aluminum Co. orders for making the carbide in quantity so great that will give you and all your friends all you can do. . . . I tell you now to throw aside everything else, do not let one hour go to waste. . . . When the names of this syndicate are known it will cause a sensation in gas circles throughout the whole country."[59]

The gas matter that Willson found so exciting was essentially the same one Venable and Kenan had demonstrated to him two years earlier: acetylene's potential as an illuminant. As Willson bragged to his patent attorney in June, "I have made a most wonderful invention of gas for illumination—superior to any other gas or even electric light." Willson's use of the word *invention* reveals the distinction he apparently made between his own research and that done by Venable and Kenan. Whereas the Chapel Hill researchers had generated a bright acetylene flame by mixing acetylene and air in a 1:4 ratio, and whereas they had pumped the mixture to a Bunsen burner through an old, foot-operated bellows pump at UNC, Willson had generated a flame of equal brilliance by using a modified gas-burning apparatus to suck in pure acetylene and air at a 4:1 ratio.[60]

The Canadian installed and experimented with the apparatus in his New York City boardinghouse and found it "simpler than that of all other systems of gas apparatus for private installation and for the private consumer." He even used the apparatus to exhibit the acetylene "light in the parlor of this house which my landlady very kindly permitted me to use for the purpose of seeing if I can raise money to enable me to sell my English patents."[61]

Willson's boardinghouse experiments made it possible to calculate and compare for the first time the relative costs and benefits of acetylene and city water gas. Using a gasometer "to hold 1 cubic foot of gas and ¼ cubic foot air," Willson found this 4:1 mixture "burns with a 1ft burner for 1 hr and gives a magnificent light in quality and in quantity more than you get from 10 cubic feet of city gas per hr. Thus 1 lb carbide = 4 cub ft [acetylene] gas, or 8000 cubic ft per ton and this more than equals 80,000 cubic ft of city gas, therefore if we sell at $80.00 per ton [of carbide] to consumer our gas will be equivalent to city gas at $1.00 per thousand to consumer."[62] In communicating these findings to Morehead, Willson tried to dispel the notion that Venable and Kenan might have a claim on the syndicate. "None of us have ever realized these facts before. Now let us make the most of it."

The prospect of making the most of the carbide matter and making it quickly prompted Willson to turn to the gas men rather than deal with Standard Oil. The Canadian desperately needed money. He had several outstanding claims against him in North Carolina, where the sheriff was threatening to "advertise and sell out my household goods." At the same time Standard Oil demanded an "exclusive right" to use the carbide for illuminating purposes, including the acetylene car lighting, and refused to negotiate further without such a right. "Their persistence in this matter is annoying to me," Willson complained to Morehead, "and I hereby notify you as president of the Willson Aluminum Co not to commit the Willson Aluminum Co to sell the carbide to them exclusively. Because this is a most valuable right more so than either you or I knew before."[63]

Willson found his negotiations with the gas men the "quickest . . . I have ever had and the most practical," and at the end of July he and the Major arranged for the men to travel from New York to Danville, Virginia, where a "special train" would meet and carry them to the Willson Aluminum Company's plant in nearby Spray, North Carolina. "This will be the most important and influential body of men you have ever had [in] your section of country," the Canadian wrote the Major from New York. "After the men arrive at Spray, they will want to see you mix the lime and carbon matter together and make a run. Have the furnace so you can pull it down to take out the carbide after the run is over so that they can see the whole process. You will want to show them as good stuff as you can make economically. We have to show an actual cost of production about $30.00 per ton and a five or ten ton daily output."[64]

The gas men put their money down, and Willson and Morehead divvied up the rights to carbide and acetylene throughout the world. The Major received "all rights within the United States and its dependencies," while the Canadian received "all rights in other countries of the world." Morehead "immediately interested a group of business men, some in New York and some in Chicago, in the formation of a company [the Electro Gas Company of New York] to acquire under the U.S. Patents the right to make, use and sell calcium carbide, and to license others so to do, limited to the use of carbide and acetylene for the generation of light, heat and power."[65]

Willson, who had recently filed patent applications for carbide and acetylene in Canada, immediately sold the patent rights for the British empire (excluding Canada), and the man who bought them hired the Major's son, John Motley Morehead, to travel to Leeds, England, to erect a carbide plant there. By September 1894 Willson was negotiating for "property in Canada in view of the Gas business and . . . preparing to expend some fifteen to twenty thousand dollars upon it."[66]

BETWEEN STUDENT AND TEACHER

That same September, Will Kenan took up residence in Radford, Virginia, as a "Master" at the all-male St. Albans School. He was there only because "my father and my friends of the University of North Carolina faculty both considered it a very good experience," but he pursued his duties with characteristic energy and enthusiasm. He taught math and science, "was captain and coach of the football team, played Left Halfback, ran the gymnasium two hours each day except Sunday, played Left Field and Change Pitcher on the baseball team; was also leader of the German Club. I never worked so hard in my life! . . . I also took a correspondence course in Electrical Engineering, for future use."[67]

Several of Kenan's students were older and bigger than he was, and they quickly put him to the test. They talked and laughed during his lectures, and he "protested vigorously but without results." Then one day, while explaining a geometry problem at the blackboard, he decided to teach the troublemakers a lesson. "There were several of the older boys in the front seats not paying any attention to what I was saying and were disturbing the class. I concluded it was time to put an end to such doings, so I kept on talking and, at the same time, I walked over behind one of the larger boys at the end of the front seat, took him up bodily and really threw him out of the door. This had a grand effect."

The pugnacious pedagogue also asserted his control on the football field. Early in preseason training, the short, hard-bodied Kenan, always ready to prove himself bigger than his size, "purposely let the smaller boys tackle me when carrying the ball and dodge[d] the larger ones so they would sprawl on the ground and every one would laugh and when they would carry the ball I would tackle them by their show [sic] strings and throw them as if I was attempting to make a hole in the ground. From that time on I never had any more trouble."

Kenan never felt particularly comfortable, however, in his role as a teacher. As his maiden aunt, Annie, wrote to another family member, "Wm Kenan seems delighted with his new abode [but] says he can't become accustomed to being addressed as Proff." He did not relish all of his teaching duties, either. "Am in the midst of examinations here," he wrote to his cousin Owen in mid-December. "Never imagined how much trouble it was to correct a pile of poorly written papers."[68]

If Kenan heard any news at all about corporate developments of carbide, he got it from Venable, who with his new laboratory assistant Thomas Clarke, "refined and extended the experiments on calcium carbide and acetylene" during the fall of 1894. In early January 1895, moreover, Venable wrote the Major demanding that the Willson Aluminum Company now honor its 1893 agreement with him. Morehead acted shocked. "I shall regret it if we do not see things alike," he answered Venable, "but I do not see where you have a claim upon the Willson Aluminum Company. We are manufacturers of the carbide, and our position is that of looking for consumers of the article. We have engaged to sell the Electro Gas Company of New York a few hundred tons, but we have no stock in this Company and are not interested beyond their being a possible purchaser of the carbide from us."[69]

The Major then went on to assert, in either a poorly or strategically worded explanation, "My recollection of the paper of March 27th 1893, signed by you, Mr. Thomas L. Willson and W. R. Walker, was formulated before these gentlemen knew what it was you had to disclose and was predicated that this discovery should be a new one and of sufficient value to have an immediate commercial use, and that upon this a company should be organized with sufficient funds to manufacture that for which a use and market had been found." But, Morehead continued, "When it was found that an error had been made in estimating the product of the gas at ten points too much, I understood that the matter was abandoned at that stage. The developments did not reach the commercial status, and we sought a customer in another direction."[70] Just what this "error" was, however, and who made it, the Major did not say; but one has to assume that he was referring to the difference between Willson's mixture of acetylene and oxygen and the combination used by Venable and Kenan.

In any event, Willson had already filed one of the two major acetylene patents under which both the Electro Gas Company (EGC) and the most important of its thirty-seven licensees, the Union Carbide Company, operated. Two months later, moreover, in March 1895, Willson filed yet another acetylene patent, and on April 12 he and the Major signed an extensive series of indentures with officials of the EGC of New York. The new company's incorporators included Edward N. Dickerson, a patent attorney; Samuel Thorne, president of the Pennsylvania Coal Company; and George O. Knapp, chief operating officer of the People's Gas, Light and Coke Company of Chicago.[71]

These three indentures reveal Willson's skills as a negotiator and the extent to which the incorporators of the EGC intended it as a holding company. One indenture, signed by Willson and Morehead, "assigned to Electro Gas Company four (4) U.S. Patents and fourteen (14) U.S. Applications for Patent, all related to the manufacture and use of calcium carbide or acetylene." The other two indentures, both executed by the EGC, conveyed, respectively,

> to Thomas L. Willson a return license of some scope under part or all of the above-mentioned patent rights; and . . . jointly to Willson Laboratory Company [a company formed by Morehead and Willson to exploit the use of acetylene chemicals] and The Willson Aluminum Company a return license, exclusive but non-assignable, during the lives of such patents as might issue from [Willson's two recent patent applications] to make use and sell calcium carbide and related products and apparatus for generating and using acetylene for all purposes *other than* the generation of light, heat and power.[72]

The EGC got exactly what it wanted—"an exclusive license for the lives of the patents, issued and prospective, to make, use and sell calcium carbide and acetylene for light, heat and power"—and Willson and Morehead were equally pleased. Willson retained the right to license carbide companies outside the United States, while his and Morehead's new company, the Willson Laboratory Company, received the right to make and use carbide and acetylene for anything but the generation of light, heat, and power. Both men also received some EGC stock and immediately put it to good use.[73] Willson used his new-found prosperity to get married, cover his debts, and begin constructing a carbide plant near St. Catherine's, Ontario, while the Major used his gains to meet the demands of his North Carolina creditors and the carbide business. As his son, Mot, later recalled, the Major "received some stock in the Electro Gas Company for his interest. This he hypothecated, and when it got to any place where there was a sale for it he sold it all to apply on his debts."[74]

The Major also made some changes at Spray. He bought a new dynamo and electric arc furnace and hired a Dutch metallurgist, G. de Chalmot, to begin perfecting "the method of making high-content ferro-chromium, and ferro-silicon, and . . . to educate the steel business up to the use of these and other ferro-alloys." Indeed, when combined with the insights of Willson's earlier work on the bronze and aluminum cannon, de Chalmot's ferroalloy experiments soon prompted the Major to buy "water power on the James River from the State of Virginia," where he eventually constructed a plant to manufacture ferroalloys for "the makers of armor plate so that the projectile man couldn't shoot through it, . . . [and for] the projectile man so he could shoot through the armor plate."[75]

In the meantime Venable aggressively asserted his own claims to the acetylene discovery. In April 1895, at the same time that Willson and the Major signed their agreement in New York, the *Journal of the American Chemical Society* published "Some of the Properties of Calcium Carbide. By F. P. Venable and Thomas Clarke. Received February 7, 1895." The authors began their article by acknowledging the source of their research materials—"The calcium carbide used was prepared by the Willson Aluminum Company"—and then moved on to stress that the identification of acetylene predated recent publications on the topic. "Several authors have reported that the decomposition of this particular hydrocarbon caused the formation of acetylene. Experiments were carried out by us proving this fact, some time before there were any publications concerning it in the chemical journals, but we were not at liberty to publish anything concerning it at that time."[76]

Venable and Clarke ended their piece with a date, a description of their recent experiments at Chapel Hill, and a nod to Kenan. "In conclusion," they wrote, "we would give due credit to Mr. W. R. Kenan, who carefully verified some of the experiments here recorded. University of North Carolina, February 1893." This was roughly the date, of course, when Venable had provided the Willson Aluminum Company with his "full statement" of the properties of calcium carbide.

The publication of "Some of the Properties of Calcium Carbide" marked the beginning of a new chapter in the history of carbide, one characterized by competing patents, claims, personalities, and publications on the international level. In fact the early history of carbide is similar to other cases in which people working independently of one another invent or discover the same thing simultaneously.[77] In this instance, the experiments, inventions, and discoveries of the men in North Carolina overlapped to some extent with the work in Paris of two Frenchmen, Henri Moissan, and his assistant, Louis Michel Bullier.

According to Bullier's later testimony, he and Moissan produced "several kilogrammes" of calcium carbide in September 1893 as a result of experiments they had been conducting since May 1892 on the "various reactions obtainable by the use of the Moissan Electric Furnace." That was the same May, of course, that the Willson Aluminum Company first produced calcium carbide by using Willson's smelting process in the electric furnace at Spray. Only in February 1894, however, and only in France and Germany did Bullier first apply for carbide patents—long after Willson applied for (August 9, 1892) and received (February 21, 1893) U.S. patent no. 563,527 "for reducing calcium oxide and producing calcium carbide" through a process of electric reduction.[78]

The question of precedence did not arise until the end of February 1895, two weeks after Venable and Clarke submitted their article to the *Journal of the American Chemical Society*. On February 22 Bullier's Canadian lawyer submitted the Frenchman's patent applications for the production of calcium carbide ("Process & Manufacture of Earth-Metals & Extracts Therefrom") to the patent offices in Canada and the United States. The process described by Bullier was virtually identical to the one specified in the patents already awarded to Willson in the United States and in Canada. Thus began almost a decade of litigation in which, on more than one occasion, the article published by Venable and Clarke proved "crucial" to Willson's success.[79]

Kenan also helped defend Willson's patents in the late 1890s, but he appears to have been completely unaware of the interference question when he completed his teaching duties in the spring of 1895.[80] He was happy to be returning to North Carolina as a self-supporting member of the Kenan clan. He had earned "$1,200 for nine months work, in addition to all living expenses. I was so thoroughly occupied that I could not spend any money, so, at the end of the first year out of college, I had accumulated about $1,500."[81]

Thanks, moreover, to the University of North Carolina, which accepted him for graduate work in chemistry, Kenan continued to support himself after leaving Virginia. Not only did the university help him get a job with the General Electric Company, "installing a steam and electric plant for the University," but it also hired him as a physics and chemistry instructor for the 1895–96 academic year. He worked on the Chapel Hill plant throughout the summer and fall of 1895, putting up lights on campus streets "and standing on a stepladder and driving a screwdriver in the ceiling of the dormitories until my back was broken literally."[82]

He and Venable also decided that summer to sue Thomas "Carbide" Willson for breach of contract. Venable notified his father of their decision late in June, and the elder Venable, who was then in Ontario writing about his Civil War experiences as an aide-de-camp to General Robert E. Lee, was pleased with his son's decision. "I am very glad to learn from your letter that you propose to sue for your rights in the matter of the Gas Discovery. And I trust that you will consult Judge Manning in the different phases of the suit and by all means have written contracts with the lawyers whom you employ in the case. Where will the case be tried? I assume that your home is given to the Discovery."[83]

Will Kenan now became more attached than ever to Venable and the professor's family. A frequent visitor in their Chapel Hill home, his presence took on added meaning in August, when the professor left for Springfield, Massachusetts, to display and discuss some of the Willson Aluminum Company's products at a meeting of the American Chemical Society. Shortly after Venable left for the meeting, his wife, Sallie, wrote to assure him that "everything is going along very nicely, except if you wish to save Mr. Kenan from Laura's charms you had better hurry on & take possession of the Laboratory. She is decidedly bored now & wants to have some fun with him."[84]

Venable wanted Kenan around for more than his family's amusement, though. He was also worried about the safety of his copy of the 1893 carbide agreement, which was hidden in Sallie's clothes cabinet. "Do not forget to look after my little tin box in your wardrobe," he wrote to her at the end of August. "Its contents are very valuable to us. . . . I would feel much safer if you would have Mr. Kenan stay there until Isaac [Manning] can come over."[85]

THE WATERSHEDS OF 1895

It was off-campus, however, that some of the most important and enduring forces in the life of Will Kenan and his family now began to come together. Chief among these were the ideas and actions of Robert Worth Bingham and Henry Flagler.

Bingham and Mary Lily had been dating each other since the early 1890s, but their "affair," as she later described it, began to fade in the fall of 1894 after she visited Asheville, North Carolina, where he was teaching at his father's new school.[86] About that time Bingham met Eleanore Miller of Louisville, Kentucky. Four years younger than Mary Lily and an attractive woman in her own right, Miller arrived in Asheville with her family, including her ailing father, a wealthy capitalist, who was trying to recuperate from a recent nervous breakdown. She and Bingham soon became attracted to each other, and in February 1895 their budding romance got a boost from the comfortings that attended a tragedy: her father used a passing train to kill himself. Bingham did what he could to comfort the mourning Eleanore before she returned to Louisville with her family.[87]

Not long thereafter Bingham and Mary Lily ended their relationship, and he began pursuing Eleanore Miller. He wrote to her constantly from Asheville, where he continued to live and teach at his father's school. In the fall of 1895, at a time when he was asking permission to become engaged to Eleanore, Mary Lily enrolled in the School of Music at Peace College—the Raleigh school where she had befriended Bingham's sisters, Sadie and Mary. The school had recently hired an exciting new music teacher, Charles Gilmore Ward of Bethel, Vermont, and Mary Lily was eager to have him as her singing coach.[88]

It was also that fall that Henry Flagler began to have serious marital problems and to expand and consolidate the Florida empire that Mary Lily inherited and Will eventually ruled. Indeed, in September 1895, while the state of Florida was approving the incorporation of Flagler's Florida East Coast (FEC) Railway Company, the Kenan family first felt the impact of his activities there.

On September 19 the collector of customs for the port of Wilmington, Buck Kenan, wired the Treasury Department in Washington for instructions. Guns and ammunition, he believed, were being loaded onto the *Commodore*, a Colombia-bound North American steamer. Buck's telegram arrived in Washington at the same time that the State Department received one from Don Enrique Dupuy De Lôme, the Spanish minister to the United States. De Lôme, unaware of the *Commodore*'s arrival in Wilmington, reported that Cuban filibusters intended to use a vessel by that name to transport 20 boxes of guns and 450 boxes of ammunition from the North Carolina port to revolutionaries seeking to liberate Cuba from Spain.[89]

Federal officials descended on the *Commodore* and quickly confirmed the suspicions of Buck and De Lôme: the boxes contained guns, ammunition, and machetes. Buck was ordered to impound the vessel, which remained in Wilmington for the next five months, as the federal court tried and eventually acquitted its captain and crew of violating U.S. neutrality statutes. The *Commodore* immediately resumed the filibustering activities that made it one of the most notorious vessels involved in the Cuban revolution that preceded the Spanish-American War.

Expeditions like the *Commodore*'s continued to receive crucial logistical support from the southern railroads owned by Henry Flagler, Henry Walters, and Henry Plant. Support was forthcoming not, however, because the Henrys hoped to liberate the oppressed Cuban masses from Spanish control but because they hoped to expand and control further the transportation and tourist network they had been building between Florida, Cuba, and the Caribbean since the mid-1880s.[90]

The onset of the Cuban revolution coincided, in fact, with an expansion of Henry Flagler's activities in Florida. In the spring of 1895 he decided to extend his railroad from West Palm Beach to Miami and to build a hotel there called the Royal Palm—a decision that led to the creation of modern Miami. A few months later he started constructing the Palm Beach Inn at Palm Beach, where the year before his six-story Royal Poinciana Hotel had been completed. And in September, in preparation for building his railroad to Miami, Flagler had the state of Florida charter the company mentioned above, the FEC Railway Company. Put simply, although Will Kenan had yet to meet Henry Flagler, he would soon be following many of the tracks that the wealthy Florida developer was laying there. Indeed, Kenan's journey across those tracks would be two to three times longer than Flagler's.[91]

But the most far-reaching event of 1895, at least for the Kenan family as a whole, occurred in October of that year, when Flagler committed his second wife, Alice Shourds, to a mental institution in Pleasantville, New York. Alice, a former actress who supposedly served as a nurse for Flagler's first wife, had been acting very peculiarly toward her husband for more than a year. Her behavior became particularly bizarre in the spring of 1895 after Flagler's physician told her she was incapable of bearing children. Alice was devastated by the news. Not only had she hoped for her own heir to the Flagler fortune, but she also knew that her sixty-five-year-old husband wanted another child, especially since he and Harry Harkness Flagler, the only surviving child of his first marriage, had recently become estranged.

That the doctor's diagnosis weighed heavily on Alice is suggested by one of the more intriguing details he later offered as evidence of her insanity: her alleged fixation on three tiny pebbles. One of the pebbles had "cured many forms of paralysis," she claimed, while another could "produce pregnancy in a barren woman if she carries it with her for a month." Though Alice never revealed the purpose of the third pebble, she reportedly told the doctor, "I am going to send [it] to the Czar of Russia."[92]

Alice also upset her husband and friends by giving her manicurist a thousand-dollar check and spending hours with a Ouija board, from which she allegedly learned that the czar of Russia was in love with her and that she would marry him after Flagler's death. The disturbed woman also "carried on conversations with imaginary people, and laughed and joked with relatives who were nowhere near" and made harsh comments about the personal actions of Flagler and his friends. She often combined charges of his cruelty and unfaithfulness to her with excited discussions of William and Alva Vanderbilt's divorce case. Indeed, her "thoughts ran upon the general infidelity of men. Besides her husband, she accused many prominent New York people of all forms of immorality and crime."[93]

Two months after Alice was institutionalized, Will Kenan received a letter from the Carbide Manufacturing Company of Philadelphia. The letter was signed by the president of the company, Samuel Kent, and dated December 4, 1895.

> Dear Sir: We will have occasion about the 1st of January next to acquire the services of a man to do our Chemical and Clerical work and take charge of one shift of our plant for the manufacture of Calcium Carbide now being

installed at Niagara Falls. You have been recommended to us by Mr. J. M. Morehead and we write to ascertain if you are in a position to accept such a position as we have to offer to let you know what will be expected and to make you an offer of the situation.

In the event of your forming a connection with our Company you will have entire charge of the Laboratory and of the Office at all times.

We will expect you to work ten hours a day seven days a week. During six hours of this time you will have charge of the plant and of all the men at work at such time. During the rest of the ten hours we will expect you to make tests of the Carbide from each charge of the furnace and to make an occasional determination of the Lime in the furnace mixtures. There will also be submitted to you for analysis samples of lime and of coke. We will expect you also to keep the time of the other men, to make out the payrolls and to attend to the correspondence and the shipments of carbide and the receipts of lime and coke. The electrical apparatus will be delivered at Niagara Falls about the 26th of December. If you decide to accept the situation we will want you to report to work at Niagara Falls on Wednesday the 1st of January and assist in the erection and installation of the electrical equipment and of the wiring of the building for lights etc. under the supervision of the Engineer of the Company.

You probably will be associated with Mr. Jesse C. King, of North Carolina and Mr. Edgar F. Price, formerly of that state, now of Newark, N.J. who will have charge of the mechanical and electrical equipment respectively and of the other two watches. We will pay you twenty-five dollars per week.[94]

Will Kenan quit graduate school and moved to Niagara Falls.

The Columbus of Carbide

Will Kenan worked in the carbide industry during its most exciting early growth period, and it is telling that for him the economic uncertainties overwhelmed the excitement. He was constantly moved from place to place and from one set of corporate and personnel associations to another. He performed a variety of challenging tasks at carbide plants in the United States, Australia, and Germany and rode the rails between New York City, Philadelphia, and Chicago, investigating the patents and operations of electric arc furnaces. Only at the end of the century, with the formation of the great consolidator, Union Carbide, did the faces and places of his work become more consistent. But not for long.

Will Kenan arrived at Niagara Falls as both an outsider and an insider. Born, raised, and educated in the South, he spoke and acted differently than most western New Yorkers; yet he also shared a bond with the many bright and active college-educated scientists who also arrived there as outsiders. He considered himself a fellow migrant in "the Electro-Chemical development which brought to Niagara Falls bright and energetic young men from all over the country."[1]

Kenan was met at the train station by his friend and fellow Tar Heel John Motley Morehead, who immediately took him to the University Club at 315 Buffalo Avenue. The club was "an association of college graduates for the purpose of economical living," Kenan recalled—a purpose that suited him well. The members "rented a large house, had a housekeeper and full complement of servants and usually from twelve to fifteen men roomed and boarded at the Club. It was a delightful way to live and, of course, reduced the cost considerably. The qualifications to enter were, a graduate of some recognized college and pursuing an engineering or scientific vocation." Kenan moved into a room with Robert "Shorty" Goodman, an employee of the Niagara Railway, and on February 8, 1896, he became Member No. 13 of the University Club at Niagara Falls.[2]

Kenan was both captivated and intimidated by the Falls's "lively community of scientific and engineering professionals whose meetings, formal and informal, advanced both the theory and techniques of their common scientific discipline."[3] This was a world where knowledge and experience accounted for more than money, class, and family pedigree, and the confident, self-assured southerner became a shy, uncertain observer. "The first few months I lived at the Club I was amazed at the very full and deep discussions which took place. I simply sat and listened without saying a word."[4]

His demeanor was exactly the opposite of the older and more outspoken UNC graduate, Mot Morehead, who was one of the most popular figures at the Falls. Morehead had worked in the North since 1893; he had built carbide plants in England and Germany; and he was in charge of constructing the plant at Niagara Falls. Tall, confident, keen, and gregarious, he felt much more comfortable than Kenan in the social and intellectual atmosphere at the Falls. As an anonymous female poet noted in her description of the "fine" men at the University Club:

> Here's sweet young Haskins and Stoughton so cute,
> And the workers Will Dunlap and Kenan so mute.
> And funny man Givens and Tone isn't slow,
> And little Rob Goodman whom all of you know.
>
> Here's sweet cherub Wands and Storer so steady,
> And brilliant young Morehead, with wit ever ready.
> The men are all fine and the girls say 'tis clear,
> That Lincoln and Edmands are perfectly dear.[5]

By the time Kenan arrived at the Falls, the company he worked for had changed its name from the Carbide Manufacturing Company to Acetylene Light, Heat and Power Company (ALH&P). It also had hired the two "North Carolina Carbide Boys" who were not college graduates, Jesse King and Edgar Price. About a dozen men worked at the Niagara plant for the Philadelphia-based company, which was restricted to producing carbide for the city of Philadelphia and the parts of Pennsylvania covered by its licensing agreement.[6] Kenan, Morehead, Price, and King held four of the plant's seven supervisory positions, as chemical, construction, operating, and mechanical superintendents, respectively. The other workers included a foreman, a master mechanic, a power controller, four laborers, and a night watchman.[7]

The plant consisted of two adjoining structures. One building contained the equipment to crush, grind, screen, and mix raw materials (mainly lime and coke), and the other contained four pot-type Willson electric arc furnaces, an office, a laboratory, a transformer room, a control room, and a combined locker and motor room.[8] The plant was not a pleasant place to work. Conditions were dangerous, the pay was poor, and the hours were long. Kenan and

The "North Carolina Carbide Boys" at Niagara Falls. *Left to right:* Edgar F. Price, W. R. Kenan Jr., John Motley Morehead, Jesse C. King. (NgCHS)

the other superintendents worked about seventy hours a week at $20–25 per week, while the laborers received 15 cents per hour. According to one description of the plant,

> Operations were in the crude stage that marks most pioneer effort[s]. Moreover, they were conducted with the realization that hazardous conditions prevailed and in a dust-clouded, unhealthy atmosphere. Lime and coke, blended and reduced in a pebble-ball mixer, were introduced into the brick furnace's wrought iron crucible from overhead bins. After a run of about six hours, the crucible, mounted on wheels, was removed. In order to insure an almost continuous use of the power another crucible was immediately installed. By means of hand-operated crane and a three-ton chain hoist the 400-pound ingot, when cooled, was dumped on a platform provided to recover the reduced mixture. There was no equivalent for crushing or sizing the carbide.[9]

The plant baked its first carbide on April 27, 1896, three days before Kenan's twenty-fourth birthday. "It was a historic occasion. Calcium carbide was being manufactured commercially for the first time in America."[10] Kenan and the others quickly got a taste of what this meant. "The first introduction of personnel to carbide dust occurred on the day the plant was started," the power controller recalled. "There were four furnaces, built of brick, connected to a common flue. It contained baffles intended to settle the fine dust escaping the

The plant of the Acetylene Light, Heat and Power Company, Niagara Falls, 1896. (KC)

furnaces. The baffles killed the draft, and after operating for a few hours the furnaces were shut down and Mr. Morehead, putting on his overalls, entered the chamber, which was very hot, and sledged out the first baffle, followed in turn by other members of the organization, until the baffles were removed."[11]

Although no one was hurt sledging out the baffles, the first injury occurred shortly thereafter. On Memorial Day a furnace operator, "dopey" from a day of drinking and celebrating, fell asleep near the furnace at the end of the night shift. A "carbon holder slipped from the connecting bar and plunged into the crucible," one observer later recalled, "spraying the operator with hot mixture." The burns were "painful" but "not serious," and the injured operator returned to work after ten days of convalescence, during which he was paid "full time" by the company. "This practice was continued until long after the plant was on a full-time operating basis, but had to be discontinued because employees would stay away on account of the slightest injury."[12]

In addition to low wages, long hours, and hazardous working conditions, the carbide pioneers faced several other problems. One obstacle was a shortage of electrical power. Like the carbide industry, the electric power industry was still in its infancy. Although the power station at the Falls housed some of the largest and most advanced generating equipment in the world, it could not generate enough electricity for both the city of Buffalo and the rapidly expanding industrial complex at Niagara Falls, where the consumption of power soon exceeded that in Buffalo.[13] This created power shortages that initially restricted the ALH&P's operations "to a period between 6:00 P.M. and midnight, the working day being from 7:00 A.M. until noon and from 6:00 P.M. until midnight. During the morning the crucibles were emptied, returned to the furnaces and prepared for a new start. After 6:00 P.M. the furnaces were started and a run of about six hours made, after which the furnaces were shut down and allowed to stand until morning."[14] Not until June 1896 did the company get enough power to adopt "a 24-hour schedule, the employees working 12 hours a day, seven days a week." But even then the company failed to produce much carbide. "A good output for a horse power day in that early period was six pounds of carbide of a variable quality." The average daily production was even lower.[15]

The plant also suffered from the speculative mania that engulfed the carbide industry. Between 1895 and 1898, as investors eagerly responded to press reports of acetylene's potential as a source of municipal lighting, the EGC of New York sold regional distribution licenses to thirty-seven different carbide-acetylene companies in the United States, the last of which was the Union Carbide Company of Virginia. Some of the licensees were legitimate businesses; like the ALH&P, they intended to build plants and manufacture carbide. But others were stock-jobbing schemes, speculative ventures that led the *New York Sun* to warn its readers in 1896 to "Beware of Acetylene." At the height of the speculative boom, "between 20 and 30 million dollars worth of stock was in the process of being sold."[16]

Had acetylene lived up to the initial claims of its promoters, especially those of Thomas "Carbide" Willson, there would have been plenty of business for the ALH&P and the other original licensees. But it did not. Although acetylene could be used to enrich coal or water gas for city lighting and heating, it soon became obvious that acetylene could not compete with or replace them. Not only did most cities lack water power to generate electricity to manufacture carbide, but there was no way as yet either to produce acetylene on a large scale or to use it once it was produced. No safe and workable generators existed, and no burners or lamps could handle acetylene (until 1897). Despite Willson's patented "gas apparatus," widespread urban distribution of acetylene in pipes proved impracticable.[17]

All of these factors help explain why the ALH&P did not receive an order for its carbide until December 1896, some eight months after production began, and thus, also, the plant's poor performance. The company did not have the money to maintain its plant and pay its bills. When machinery broke down, as it often did, it remained unrepaired. On several occasions "the sheriff forced the company to close its doors and once, because of unpaid bills, the power company sawed off the lead-covered cables outside the plant."[18]

The plant's problems frustrated Kenan, but he used the time they provided to explore his surroundings and hone his skills as a chemist and engineer. The general manager of the Mathieson Alkali Works, Ben Thurston, asked Kenan "to organize their Chemical Laboratory and to purchase all the equipment and supplies for it. I had recently done the same thing for the Carbide Manufacturing Company." In April, moreover, he was sent to nearby Lockport, New York, "for the purpose of installing an electric furnace at the Cowles Aluminum Company, down on the creek in Lowertown."[19] The assignment inspired him to try his own hand at making aluminum and to get to know the women he met in Lockport. He and Shorty Goodman made "a high grade" aluminum in the carbide furnaces at Niagara Falls, but they quickly discovered "our process was much more costly than the Hall process then being used by the then called Pittsburgh Reduction Company . . . so nothing further was done."[20]

The handsome young southerner was more successful with the "crowd of young ladies who used to gather at the home of Marian Hall" in Lockport. Kenan told the women of "the nice crowd we had at the University Club at the Falls and the girls suggested that if I would bring over a crowd of men that they would give us a picnic. This was done, eight or nine came over on our bicycles and returned via train, the middle of May." Kenan clearly enjoyed the outing; it was spring, the end of his first winter in western New York, and the Niagara County countryside was much more appealing than the dusty, dangerous carbide plant. "The picnic was held during the afternoon at Hitchens Bridge, about a mile up the [Erie] Canal and we all had a grand time and every one rode out on their bicycle."[21]

Just as Kenan was beginning to enjoy himself, however, the EGC decided to send him on what became the most exciting journey of his young life. Kenan later described the company's decision as evidence of his successful work at Lockport and Niagara Falls. "I must have performed fairly well in connection with this difficult job because during the middle of June [1896] I was detailed to go to Australia for the purpose of developing and constructing a carbide plant."[22]

FRAGILE FRONTIERS

Australia had a great impact on Kenan. It made him see himself as more than a southerner. It convinced him he was an American scientist and businessman.

His chief business contact in Sydney was Samuel Hordern, president of the Australian Carbide Company. Hordern owned one of the largest department stores in Australia and was also interested in the state railroad system; thus, in addition to using acetylene to illuminate his department store, he may also have wanted to use it for lighting railroad cars. In any event, he was genuinely interested in developing a carbide business in Australia. As Kenan wrote to his roommate at Niagara Falls, Hordern planned to "erect one or two plants, if one locate it here [Sydney], costing about 25,000 pounds; if two, one here and one in Melbourne, costing about 17,000 pounds."[23]

With the exception of Hordern, however, Kenan spent most of his time with Americans and things American. He leased office space in "the handsomest building in the city," the ten-story Equitable Building, which, he proudly explained to his cousin, was an "American Building."[24] He also took pride in the Americanness of the new hotel in which he stayed. "I resided at the Australian Hotel, a modern American designed building of about 600 rooms, containing sufficient 'lifts' (elevators) and the first refrigerating plant installed on the continent of Australia. . . . It also had a typical American bar (called Pub) with a brass rail." It was "American in every way and . . . quite up to any of those in New York City."[25] What was more, the hotel was run by an American, Henry Edwin Moore, whose family became Kenan's closest companions. "The Moores had two young sons about 8 and 10 years old. They were fine boys and I was accustomed to play with them frequently. The greatest thrill they experienced was when I built them kites and we would fly them from the roof of the hotel."[26]

Kenan encountered the most convincing evidence of his Americanness outside the hotel. "The English money was quite confusing at first," he wrote his cousin, "but I readily 'got on' to it. Am however rather awkward with their manners and ways. They do everything in the most unheard-of way." The women, for example, "don't know how to dress—they wear elegant material + the brightest colors; and nearly every color of the rainbow all at once—the most peculiar combinations you ever saw."[27] Appearing equally peculiar to the aggressive young American was the combination of work habits and investment proclivities displayed by Australians. Rather than actively exploiting the tremendous potential of their country, the locals seemed content merely to enjoy its natural bounty. "I have seen a good bit of the country and it is wonderful, great resources," Kenan wrote to his roommate at Niagara Falls, "but the people are too slow to take advantage of them. They only work about four days a week, the rest being holidays." Kenan sounded much like a northern businessman, in fact, summarizing the land and people of his native South. "I can't say that I am very enthusiastic about this country. Everybody is so very slow and it is almost impossible to have anything done. I have worried myself out completely. Things have progressed exceedingly slow with us."[28]

The slow locals nevertheless imbued Kenan with a sense of power and prestige. "You just ought to see me here," he wrote to his cousin, "I swell around with the business men—all are trying to place an order with me, and anything I say goes. They don't know anything about our business and very little about Electricity. So you see I have full swing." But there was a touch of anxiety in Kenan's confidence. "I go up to my room some evenings and laugh to think that they take it so well. But you know this is the way of the world now—put on a bold face and know it all. I have been taken out driving quite a number of times and every one wants me to drink with them. The fact of the matter is that I feel a little out of place—'tho of course my opinion goes in every thing that we do here and they all know it."[29]

Kenan quickly learned, however, that the realities of the British imperial system made his power more perceived than real. "They manufacture absolutely nothing in these colonies so all equipment will have to be imported," he wrote his roommate at Niagara Falls. He could not import it directly from the United States, though; he had to get it through Englishmen and English companies that were unfamiliar to him. He "met opposition from every source" and was able to overcome it only "by degrees. From the present outlook," he wrote in December 1896, "it will be at least a year before I will be able to return to America."[30]

Kenan mentioned similar frustrations in a letter to his good friend Henry Walters, who tried to explain, in turn, the British mentality. "Englishmen are never anxious that other nationalities should succeed. . . . Their selfreliance is enormous and their desire to override all opposition is an inheritance of generations." Thus it was important for Kenan to "be infinitely more careful and deliberate in everything that you do than you would be if you were at home in America." Indeed, Walters warned, Kenan should be doubly cautious. "I think I once expressed to you that a friend of mine, who had watched the subject of acetylene gas, feared that its cost of production would be too great to make it of practical use, and upon this, of course, depends entirely its success. If you should find that my friend is correct the sooner you get out of any responsibility in the matter the better."[31]

Kenan had too much at stake, of course, to see anything but a bright future for the carbide industry and his own role in it, which was why the Australian project was so important to him. Everyone—from carbide's investors to his friends and family—was watching his performance. Several North Carolina newspapers carried stories on his trip to Australia, and these elicited praise and inquiries, in turn, from many old friends. "I was delighted to learn that my friends at Kenansville still took interest in me," Kenan responded to a letter from his cousin Owen, "and I trust that my method is agreeable to all." As for seeing his name in the Wilmington newspapers, "I haven't seen the clipping in the *Messenger* that you spoke of," Kenan noted, "but saw a small notice in the *Star*. I receive the *Star* about twenty papers at a time."[32]

Kenan showed much more interest in the news he received from his roommate at Niagara Falls. "I was delighted to hear of your doings and something about Niagara," he wrote to Goodman at Christmas. "I have met no one except those I come in contact with because of my business, so the evenings grow long and weary. I go to the theatre a good deal and have seen some very good plays but one does not enjoy pleasure of this kind unless you are accompanied by some one." Kenan longed to be back at the Falls. "I never will forget my time spent there in company with you. It has been the most pleasant part of my life and no one misse[s] you all as I do, over here. . . . Remember me to Miss Packard and Miss Drain and as well to all inquiring friends at the Falls."[33]

THE FOLKS BACK HOME

William also heard from his parents, it seems, but none of their letters has apparently survived. The news they sent him would not have been good. In addition to suffering a variety of physical ailments, Buck and Mollie confronted the pain of distressing family and political developments.[34]

In November 1896, in one of the heaviest turnouts in North Carolina's political history, Populists and Republicans staged a stunning "fusionist" victory in the state elections. Voters elected Wilmington attorney Daniel Russell as the state's first Republican governor since Reconstruction and sent seventy-two Republicans (eleven of them black), sixty-four Populists, and only thirty-three Democrats to the North Carolina general assembly. People like the Kenans were scared. "It was clear that the forces unleashed by fusion constituted a fundamental and severe threat to the traditional order."[35] The election of Republican president William McKinley also meant that Buck would lose his lucrative federal position as collector of customs for the port of Wilmington. Though his appointment lasted another year, he would undoubtedly be replaced by John Dancy, the black Republican who had preceded him as collector. There was also no doubt that Buck would have little to turn to to support his family thereafter. What the depression had not done to wreck his commission business, his inattention to it had.

The future also appeared dim for Will's oldest sisters, Jessie and Mary Lily, both of whom were living away from home. Jessie was in Macon, Georgia, with her husband, Clisby, and their one-year-old daughter, Louise, and she was very unhappy. Clisby frequently drank himself into a stupor for days at a time. Though he was never violent when he made himself "sick," he could not hold a job, and there was no guarantee that he would not become worse.[36] Mary Lily was not happy either. She was fast approaching her thirtieth birthday, and unlike her old flame Bob Bingham, who had recently gotten married, she had no immediate prospects of marriage. She was still living in Raleigh, still taking music lessons at Peace College, but seeing less and less of her closest friends, Henry Walters and the Pembroke Joneses, who now spent most of their time in New York.[37]

Mary Lily had also stopped traveling with Henry and Alice Flagler, whose future together appeared very uncertain. Henry felt happier than the Kenans, to be sure, with the way the 1896 elections turned out; his Republican friend from Ohio, William McKinley, had won the presidency. He was also pleased with his progress in Florida and the Caribbean. His FEC Railway reached Miami in April 1896, and his Royal Palm Hotel was completed there by Christmas. The FEC was also assisting the movement of filibusterers to Cuba, while Flagler himself was preparing to expand his empire into the British-controlled Bahamas. He planned "a one-half-million dollar hotel with a pier at Nassau, a one-quarter-million steamship service, and the improvement of the Royal Victoria Hotel, then owned by the British government."[38]

While Flagler was doing well on the Florida frontier, accommodating both Cuban revolutionaries and wealthy Americans alike, his life on the domestic front was clouded. His wife had been released from the institution at Pleasantville in June 1896, and he had tried to further her alleged improvement by having two of their favorite people, Eugene and Eliza Ashley of Lockport, New York, come and stay at his mansion on Long Island Sound. But shortly after the couple arrived, Alice secured a Ouija board and began referring again to her relationship with the Russian czar. In the fall of 1896 Flagler moved into a hotel room in New York City, leaving Alice alone with her doctors and the staff of the mansion at Mamaroneck.[39]

At this point Mary Lily reentered Henry Flagler's life. "During Alice's time of troubles," one Flagler biographer has written, "Mary Lily sang for him, and it was generally agreed among mutual friends that she was chiefly responsible for lifting him out of his heavy depression. Soon afterward, gossip spread that Flagler and Mary Lily were in love," and Alice was recommitted to the institution at Pleasantville, destined to be her home for the rest of her life. While Flagler began searching for a way to divorce his wife, "Eliza Ashley and Mary Lily spent the early months of 1897, the height of the Palm Beach season, at his Reef cottage on the Atlantic shore."[40]

Will Kenan was as unaware of these events, it seems, as he was of the simultaneous and equally far-reaching occurrences then shaping the future of the carbide industry in America. The situation he returned to would be even more turbulent and uncertain than the one he had left. During his absence the industry had entered a revolutionary new stage of its history, one created by the interpenetration of corporate, legal, and technological developments.

The men who created this revolution included George O. Knapp, William Smith Horry, and John Motley Morehead. Knapp was chief operating officer of the People's Gas, Light and Coke Company of Chicago and one of the original incorporators of the EGC of New York. He and his fellow investors were licensed by the EGC to distribute carbide in Chicago and Cooke County, Illinois, where they planned to use acetylene as a substitute for oil in the enrichment of water gas—the gas that People's and six other local companies piped into the businesses and homes of Chicago. In the summer of 1896, at the time Will Kenan left for Australia, Knapp incorporated the Lake Superior Carbide Company and initiated construction of its carbide plant at Sault Ste. Marie, Michigan, the "Soo."[41]

Knapp's chief engineer at the Soo was William Smith Horry, one of the most important figures in carbide's early corporate history and culture. In addition to being a skilled electrical engineer, Horry was a good businessman and an efficient manager. He not only built and equipped the power plant from which the Lake Superior Carbide Company received its electricity—a plant owned and operated by a paper mill on the Canadian side of the Soo—but he also strung two sets of electrical cables to the carbide plant on the American side of the Soo, some two miles away. Once he got the carbide plant up and running, moreover, Horry established an efficient system of production and record keeping and began experimenting with a rotary furnace—an invention that revolutionized the carbide industry.[42]

Horry got many of his ideas for the furnace from John Motley Morehead. The two men first discussed the project late in 1896, and in February 1897, after Morehead sent him a list of the patents held by the EGC, Horry sent Morehead an outline of the furnace and asked a favor. "Now that I have described this furnace I shall be obliged if you will criticize it severely & shall be pleased if you will come here & help me in developing it in the event of your liking the idea." There was just one problem: although both men worked for companies licensed by the EGC, no corporate connection existed between the Philadelphia-based ALH&P (which owned the Niagara plant where Morehead worked) and Knapp's Chicago-based Lake Superior Carbide Company (which employed Horry at the Soo plant in Michigan).[43]

Horry asked Knapp about Morehead before moving ahead. "Please indicate to me your position to Mr. Morehead, who says he will soon be here. Is he your employee? He is very good. I hope he will remain here some time especially attending to the new design of furnace which I think will be interesting work to him as well as to myself." Although Knapp demanded secrecy at the Soo, he also wanted Horry to work with Morehead. Morehead knew everything about Willson's electric arc furnace (the furnaces used in the carbide industry), and he also had seen the latest electric furnaces and smelting techniques in London, Paris, and Berlin. But these were the very attributes that worried Knapp. No one knew more about making carbide than Mot Morehead, and no one was in a better position than the UNC graduate to exploit Horry's furnace ideas.[44]

Horry wrote Knapp again after Morehead and several other men toured the Soo plant without Knapp's permission. "I am sorry about allowing Mr. Wood to see what we are doing here," he apologized. "I have taken steps to have no such error occur again and will show nothing to anybody without your order." Horry also had made "elaborate preparations against Mr. Morehead's visit, boarding up our self adjusting apparatus & we kept very quiet until we heard his story. I showed only the Dynamo to these men in Canada; then receiving no advice from you by wire in the morning, I showed them the furnaces &c They left at three o'clock & I got your telegram at 4:30."[45]

Mot Morehead liked the "self adjusting apparatus"—that is, Horry's model for a rotary furnace. He liked it so much in fact that he discussed his own ideas for a furnace with Horry and then gave him sketches of both it and a furnace made in Paris by a man named Piclel. Horry immediately wrote back to Morehead: "I very much like Piclel's arrangement in that it avoids all heating of the metal part. Yours too is very interesting in my opinion, but it does not occur to me at present how the wire can be carried out." Inspired by the sketch, Horry set about redesigning his rotary furnace and then paid to have a prototype made. "The crude idea for this was given to me by Mr. Morehead's illustration of Piclel's furnace [in] Paris France," he wrote to one associate. But the Frenchman's furnace, Horry stressed, "was not continuous and not rotary," thus differing from his own design.[46]

Horry now began referring to "our new furnace" in his correspondence with Morehead but used more discretion in his letters to Knapp, his boss in Chicago. "I send you herewith blue print of my new all iron furnace, it is being made by contract for 180^{00}$. It is continuous & if it succeeds in the way I expect it will revolutionise our system here. I am keeping it quiet & will patent it after trial. I promise you that it shall succeed & beat everything we have done yet in providing Carbide."[47] The test furnace worked beautifully, and at the end of March 1897 Horry prepared a four-page "specification & description" of it for patent purposes. The inventor spent a lot of time composing his description, for he believed that, with the crucial exception of its rotary or continuous operation, the new furnace was in many ways similar to the electric furnaces patented by others. As he wrote to his patent attorney, "The specification is of course incomplete but the blue print is not & I would like you to give especial care to the preparation of the document, as you know that the broad patents to which this is subject is in the hands of a strong corporation."[48]

The more Horry experimented with the furnace, the more he was convinced that it would quickly replace the old bricked-in, pot-type electric furnaces patented by Thomas Willson. Willson's furnace had one major problem: it could not make carbide continuously. It had to cool off before the carbide could be recovered and another seven-hour run started. It also required the work of several laborers simultaneously, an expense the struggling carbide producers could not afford.

Horry's rotary furnace worked on a completely different principle. It made carbide continuously, used electricity more efficiently, and could be operated by a single worker. It "looked like a steel water-wheel with its 'paddles' hidden by bolted steel plates. As this rotating, compartmentalized furnace was turned on its axis, batches of calcium carbide could be produced 24 hours a day, seven days a week." And one person did everything: "turning the furnace by hand, shoveling in the mixture, removing the outer plates after smelting had been completed, prying out the calcium carbide, breaking it up with a sledge hammer and axe, cleaning the product and packing it into drums."[49] As Horry

The first Horry electric rotary furnace, April 1897. (KC)

explained to Knapp in April 1897, "The new furnace will certainly produce a new article, all alike. I propose to call this 'New Process' carbide & it will command more money than 'Willson Process' carbide. We shall not produce any poor carbide when the 'New Process' is adopted. I feel very sure of it."[50]

Only one major obstacle remained: the patent office withheld Horry's application "in view of a probable interference, the other party to which has been given thirty days to prepare therefore." Specifically, there was little to distinguish Horry's rotary furnace from at least two others recently invented and little or no difference between its electrochemical processes and those employed by electric arc furnaces worldwide to make a variety of products, including the calcium carbide produced by the Willson and Moissan processes. Indeed, the "interference" litigation involving Willson and Moissan had become a major obstacle to the development and consolidation of the carbide industry in the United States.[51]

THE LONG VOYAGE HOME

Will Kenan completed his work in Australia sooner than anticipated. The Australian Carbide Company decided not to build a carbide plant in Melbourne, and once Kenan completed the plant at Sydney, his assignment down under was done. But as eager as he was to return to the United States, he also wanted to take the opportunity to see some more of the world. So he "booked passage to return via Borneo, Java, Sumatra, then China and Japan, sailing from Yokohoma [*sic*] to Vancouver."[52]

Three days before his departure, however, he "received a cablegram to proceed to London for instructions." After exchanging good-byes with Hordern and the Moore family, both of whom gave him generous farewell gifts, he was off on "the train to Melbourne and ship to Columbo. I remained a week on the Island of Ceylon, visiting Kandy and Kurunegala." From there he sailed through the Suez Canal to Brindisi, where he "took a train to Rome and Paris, enroute to London." Yet once he reached London he was immediately sent back to the continent, where he worked for "several months as Constructing and Consulting Engineer German Acetylene Company located south of Berlin, (Schoenberg)."[53]

The world traveler could hardly have been more disappointed with the situation he encountered upon his return to Niagara Falls in June 1897. Although his old plant was selling modest amounts of carbide, something it had not been doing when he left, the company that owned it, the ALH&P, was in default; Mot Morehead had moved to Chicago to become chief of research for the People's Gas company; and the workers who remained at the Falls were confused and uncertain about their future. Everyone had heard of Horry's new furnace and how it would doom the Willson furnaces at Niagara Falls. But they did not know when it would be ready and what changes it would bring.

Horry's first furnace was cast in August 1897, about the time that his Chicago boss, George O. Knapp, hired Kenan to investigate some of the legal and technical aspects of the patent question. Kenan spent hours on the train pursuing his assignment, commuting between New York, Chicago, Philadelphia, and the only three plants then producing carbide in North America: those at Niagara Falls, the Soo, and Appleton, Wisconsin. What he found was not encouraging. There was little to distinguish Horry's furnace from several others, and both it and the others employed almost exactly the same electric arc technology. What was more, the patent situation between the Willson Aluminum Company and the licensees of the EGC had become so crossed and intermingled that it was impossible to separate the two. The only advice Kenan could offer was to have Horry resubmit a revised and expanded description of the rotary furnace to the patent office.[54]

Horry sent his patent attorney a new "Description" of the rotary furnace in October 1897, along with an explanation of the "New Process" by which it made carbide. The attorney was not impressed. How, he responded, could Horry challenge the other furnaces? Easily, Horry answered; his was the only rotary furnace that met one of the most important criteria in pre-twentieth-century patent law: commercial success.[55]

Horry's furnace was a success, at least within the context of the struggling carbide industry. The Soo received a flood of carbide orders beginning in August 1897, just a few weeks before his first furnace was cast, and the orders continued to pour in throughout the fall. But why, one must ask, did the orders come when they did? What explains this sudden surge of demand for calcium carbide? Was it simply a ruse to have Horry's furnace meet the "commercial success" requirement of the patent laws? Or had a new commercial use for carbide and acetylene been discovered?

The demand was apparently greater than the deception. Although the Soo received most of its orders from either the EGC, the holding company that sold carbide licenses, or the Soo's competitor at Niagara Falls, the Philadelphia-based ALH&P, two inventions undoubtedly increased the demand for carbide. One was a safe and efficient acetylene burner, and the other was a maritime buoy lit by an acetylene flame—an invention made by Thomas "Carbide" Willson at his carbide plant on the Welland Canal near St. Catherines, Ontario. What was more, if the deluge of carbide orders reflected a deception, the perpetrators went to great lengths to carry it out. In August, Horry was transferred to the carbide plant in Appleton, Wisconsin, where he installed new electrical equipment and two of his first rotary furnaces.[56]

It is also clear, however, that the men backing Horry—Knapp and his wealthy associates in the People's Gas, Light and Coke Company of Chicago, C. K. G. Billings and Anthony N. Brady—viewed the rotary furnace as the key to controlling and dominating the carbide industry in the United States. Knapp believed that the invention would revolutionize the production and commercial potential of calcium carbide and that the company that owned the patent would dominate the industry. "I met Mr. Knapp in Chicago last week," Horry wrote to his patent attorney in November, "& he says that he wants a clean patent on the Rotary furnace even if he has to buy . . . claims to it. He wants it as a matter of policy, that others may not get hold of it & compete with him in Carbide making."[57]

Horry fully agreed with Knapp's assessment. Having just returned from Appleton to the plant at the Soo, where "we have suddenly been flooded with orders & are busy such as we never were before," he wanted the patent matter settled as soon as possible. "The Rotary Furnace is an improvement that it would pay any makers of Carbide to use even if they had to pay Royalties. . . . And it would never do to allow the Rotary Furnace to be used by competitors." There was also "another consideration" in favor of settling the competing patent claims. "The English company wants one of our Furnaces & I have by this mail a letter from Major [James Turner] Morehead who says that he will make some arrangements with Mr. Knapp to have some at his new plant in the South [at Holcomb Rock, Virginia]. So it is quite likely that with Royalties &c. we might find that the money paid . . . was paid wisely."[58]

Shortly thereafter Knapp and his associates decided to purchase all competing claims to the rotary furnace, all plants then producing carbide, and all rights, patents, and licensees of the EGC of New York. The carbide industry was about to join one of the largest business merger movements in American history.

Will Kenan spent the last few months of 1897 riding this emergent wave of corporate and technological change. "Well nothing surprises me these days," he wrote to his cousin Owen. "I had intended making another trip to New York but was rushed away from Niagara before I could complete the construction I was then on." Knapp had sent him to the Soo, "the most inaccessible place on the Continent," where he had remained for "ten days doing some construction work with Morehead on a Carbide Plant owned by the Chicago Gas Trust." From there he had been sent to Appleton to "take charge of this Plant. It has been poorly run and I am trying to straighten matters out. I am probably a fixture here for the Winter, but who knows what move I may make."[59]

Kenan hated the Wisconsin weather but remained optimistic if somewhat uncertain about his future. He had experienced "nothing but snow knee deep and zero weather" since leaving Niagara Falls. "You have to turn the thermometer upside down to keep from losing the mercury. You can even pick amperes off the electric wires—I am already sick and tired of it." Yet he still had hope. "I am now under the wing of the Chicago Gas—they just bought a Gas Company for $6,500,000.00 cash—it is a good crowd to be back of you—but I may make another change—have several matters in view. I am going to make some money or lose all I have."[60]

MONEY MATTERS

Because he was transferred from the Falls, Will Kenan missed what would have been his first meeting with Henry Flagler. In mid-November his sisters Mary

Lily and Sarah traveled with their maiden Aunt Annie to New York City, where Will was to have joined them to meet the wealthy oil magnate. Annie and her nieces had a grand time. They "dined at the Flaglers'" mansion on Fifth Avenue, "lunched at the [Pembroke] Jones's" mansion, and took "Five Ocl Tea with [the] Fleises." They also attended a horse show and "felt quite fine in one of the nicest Boxes & enjoyed the show immensely." Annie seemed pleased with Henry Flagler. "Mr. Flagler who seems a very kind old gentleman is going to Florida and we may go in his car from Washington home."[61]

Flagler had to stop in Washington to discuss several important matters with President McKinley and other officials. He wanted the federal government to help him pay for the deepening of Biscayne Bay at Miami and to support a bill in the Bahamian general assembly to subsidize his steamship service from Miami to Nassau. He also wanted McKinley to come to Palm Beach in February for an exclusive costume ball at the Royal Poinciana Hotel.[62]

When he arrived in St. Augustine in early December, Flagler asked Mary Lily, Sarah, and their parents to be his guests at the Ponce de Leon Hotel. Buck could not go down, however, probably because he had too much to do before turning over his duties as collector of customs to John Dancy. But the women went to St. Augustine, where Mary Lily sang in a special service at the Memorial Presbyterian Church, a magnificent building Flagler had built in memory of his deceased daughter, Jenny Louise. The Kenan women were back in Wilmington by Christmas, however, and attended the annual Christmas party at Pem and Sadie Jones's mansion on Wrightsville Sound.[63]

Flagler stayed in Florida for the holidays and then sailed to Nassau in January for a banquet celebrating approval of his new steamship service between Miami and the islands. Back in Florida in early February, he sent President McKinley a formal invitation to visit him. "My domain begins at Jacksonville," he wrote to the president on February 15. That same evening, the U.S. battleship *Maine* blew up in Havana harbor, killing 260 of the 354 marines and sailors on board.[64]

CONSOLIDATING THE CARBIDE INDUSTRY

Will Kenan was shivering at the Soo when the *Maine* blew up in sunny Havana harbor. Transferred from Wisconsin to the Lake Superior Carbide Company in January 1898, he was not happy about his return to Michigan. "This climate is too cold for me," he wrote his cousin, "3' of snow on a level and zero weather all the time—has been as low as −26° F. . . . I am not dead yet but I haven't long to live. . . . My blood is in bad condition or something. My skin itches and when I grow warm it feels as though pins were being stuck in me." He must not have been too sick, however, for he was "trying some of the Winter sports here and am now a fair skater, and don't think anything of snow-shoeing ten miles during an evening. It is great exercise." He even felt well enough to offer Owen a joke. "But say! Have you heard the story about the two eggs? Too bad—you know."[65]

The plant at the Soo was similar in size and industrial ambience to the one Kenan had worked in at Niagara Falls. It was unhealthy, dangerous, and burdened by power problems. Yet it also served Kenan and his fellow scientists well as a research laboratory. When he was not analyzing the plant's raw materials and the gas content of the carbide it produced, he was helping Horry and Mot Morehead experiment, with carbon pencils and carbon holders; with various methods of cleaning, scaling, and packing the carbide; and with a nine-foot version of Horry's original six-foot rotary furnace. Kenan also learned a great deal from Horry about managing a carbide plant efficiently. By instituting new bookkeeping procedures, cost analyses, daily production records, and standardized gas tests, Horry implemented, both on his own initiative and as a part of the consolidation of the carbide industry, an efficient, internal operating system.[66]

The chartering of the Union Carbide Company on March 30, 1898, marked the formal beginning of the consolidation process that Knapp, Billings, and Brady had been working on for the past several months. Five days later, on April 4, the new Virginia company purchased both the last license issued by the EGC of New York and the manufacturing licenses of the only three American companies (with the exception of the Willson Aluminum Company) that ever produced any carbide: the ALH&P, the Lake Superior Carbide Company, and Pettibone, Mulliken and Company (the owner of the carbide plant at Appleton). Only in 1903, however, in the aftermath of Willson's patent victories, would Union Carbide complete its monopoly of the American carbide industry by acquiring the assets of the EGC (which included Willson's American patents).[67]

While the creation of Union Carbide had little immediate impact on Kenan and his fellow workers, the confrontation between Spain and the United States did. It prompted Major J. T. Morehead to quit producing carbide in the Horry furnaces at his new plant in Holcomb Rock, Virginia.[68] "Just then the Spanish War came along and created a big demand for ferrochrome," the Major's son explained. "They specialized on ferrochrome, and sold it to the makers of armor plate so the projectile man couldn't shoot through it, then sold the same chrome to the projectile man so he could shoot through the armor plate. Some of the steel companies bought it for both purposes. He had one product used very largely at that time, which they called SAM alloy—Silica, Aluminum, Magnesia."[69]

Union Carbide eagerly filled the Major's carbide orders, and in the early summer of 1898 it sent Horry to reorganize and retool the old ALH&P plant at Niagara Falls. The plant now had a dependable supply of electricity, the one

The plant of the Union Carbide Company at Sault Ste. Marie, Michigan. Kenan learned to ice skate while managing the plant at the "Soo." (NgCHS)

thing the Soo plant lacked to make the rotary furnaces pay off, and the company planned to make the Falls facility the center of carbide production. Horry implemented the operating system he had organized at the Soo and replaced the old pot-type Willson furnaces at Niagara Falls. "It was decided to scrap all 24 and replace them with those of the rotary design. Three of the new furnaces, which were immediately installed, boosted production by 30 per cent." By September 1898 the Niagara plant was producing twelve to fourteen tons of carbide per day. "The product was finding a ready domestic outlet and a fair export business had sprung up."[70]

Things were not going as well back at the Soo, however, where Kenan had replaced Horry as manager. The power company was "always having trouble of some kind," he wrote to the home office, and this was creating all kinds of problems for the plant.[71] Poor carbide, decreased production, unfilled orders, and the expense of paying employees to wait for the electricity to be restored— the problems created by the power company's frequent and unexpected shutdowns—became regular topics of Kenan's correspondence with the Chicago office. But the men there simply ignored his reports or passed them on to Horry for comment. Horry was not kind to Kenan, for the latter blamed "all of this trouble" on the "poor design and poor construction" of the electrical equipment Horry ordered and installed in the generating plant on the Canadian side of the Soo.[72] The controversy came to a head in early September 1898, when Mot Morehead asked Kenan to respond to Horry's charge that the power plant had been in "good condition" when he left the Soo. "I can only say that this statement is an absolute falsehood," Kenan wrote Morehead, and in the four-page report that followed, he proved his point.[73]

Kenan continued to suffer "many setbacks and much ill-luck" at the Soo, including the news of the Wilmington race riot of November 1898.[74] Just how and when he learned of the deadly confrontation is not known, but he almost certainly read about it in the press before he got word of it from home. Although he eventually accepted what he heard about his father's role in the violence—that Buck helped quell the "riot of colored men" by directing the operations of a "riot gun on a wagon" and was "compelled to kill several persons"—the fact that Kenan remembered this happening when he was "a small boy" suggests that he was not entirely comfortable with the timing and memory of the event. The riot may even have been a source of embarrassment for him among the northern men with whom he worked.[75]

Conditions at the Soo got worse after Christmas. A fire destroyed the plant's grinding rooms, part of the roof, the cupola, two windows, and a bin containing ten tons of finely ground coke. The fire was "extinguished by our own men and the occurrence is not known around town," Kenan reported; but the water damage was severe. It "flooded everything on the 2nd and 3rd Floors and as far as I can judge 15 tons of mixture is damaged being soaking wet."[76] Yet Kenan remained hopeful. "I trust that our business this year will be such as to justify you in giving me a slight increase in salary," he wrote to Chicago on January 2.[77]

Kenan did not get his raise, however, and throughout the early months of 1899 the problems at his plant worsened. The power supply became even less dependable than before, and the damaged materials caused the furnaces to rotate "about ⅓ as fast as usual," precipitating a marked decline in both the quantity and quality of the carbide produced.[78] It was not easy to ship the carbide that was produced. The frozen lakes and canals forced Kenan to switch from waterborne traffic to railroads, which also proved susceptible to the harsh Michigan winter. A shipment of "30,000 lbs. did not go today for the reason that we have been unable to secure a car," Kenan reported in late January. "The railway is greatly troubled with so much snow and the handling of freight is delayed."[79]

More frustrating still for Kenan was the fact that the company continued to ignore his requests and complaints. He made regular reports to the Chicago office and wrote "in detail of my many troubles with suggestions as to how I expected to overcome them, but I got very few replies and no instructions."[80] His tiff with Horry was part of the problem; the latter was fast becoming a godlike figure within Union Carbide. The company also ignored Kenan because of the problems and plans it was confronting at Niagara Falls. The Horry furnaces were churning out ten to twelve tons of carbide a day at the Falls, but they were also creating a major environmental problem in the process. The black dust they spewed "began to settle about the neighborhood in increasing volume. Despite an elaborate system of collection installed in a separate dust house, it continued to present a source of extreme annoyance to residents of the area," who threatened to sue the company. The company thus decided to move the plant "to a less populated area. This was the reason for selecting a new factory location in Union (now 47th) Street." Also, the "site chosen had another advantage, excellent railroad connections." In late February 1899 Union Carbide broke ground for a huge new plant at Niagara Falls.[81]

It also began sending Kenan money at the Soo, but without any instructions or advice on how to use it. Indeed, only after a local resident threatened to sue Union Carbide for the black dust blowing from Kenan's plant did the company pay him any real attention.[82] It was hardly the kind of attention the frustrated manager expected. Not only was he ordered to shut down the plant, but he also received an unexpected visit from Knapp and several other Carbide officials, who thoroughly inspected everything. "Much to my surprise, Mr. Knapp called me into my office, where he was sitting at my desk, pulled out his personal checkbook, drew a check for $3,000.00 payable to me and handed it over, saying: 'We did not pay much attention to your operation here during the past year, but after inspecting the plant, I feel your salary should be supplemented by this amount.' "[83] Knapp then relieved Kenan of his duties and sent him to Niagara Falls as "Chemical Engineer, assisting in designing and constructing and operating 25,000 H.P. works of the Union Carbide Company."[84]

THE HAND OF HENRY FLAGLER

Knapp's generosity appears to have reflected more than his appreciation for Kenan's work. He probably also saw Kenan as a potential conduit to Henry Flagler's wealth. By the end of 1898, knowledge of the relationship between Flagler and Mary Lily had spread "to all the fashionable places in the country." Society writers were speculating on their future together, and in early 1899 Flagler made "his intentions known to Mary Lily while they were in Palm Beach. He wanted to marry her." He also gave her sister Jessie an expensive home in Macon, Georgia, and in March the sixty-nine-year-old oilman gave his thirty-two-year-old fiancée 1,000 shares of Standard Oil stock—a gift soon worth some $1 million.[85]

According to several recent writers the Kenan family pressured Flagler into taking these actions. As one favorite story goes, Mary Lily's grandmother was annoyed by the rumors and publicity surrounding the Flagler affair and demanded that something be done to end the speculation. Another tale has the Kenan family worried that Mary Lily might end up like her sister Jessie, whose husband, Clisby, "Kib," Wise, had allegedly abandoned her shortly after the birth of their daughter, Louise. In yet another story, moreover, Louise was not really the Wises' daughter but the illegitimate offspring of Mary Lily and Henry Flagler. Still another account has Will Kenan handling the stock transfers for Mary Lily; indeed, it speculates that he "may have prompted the transaction," for he "was a hard and effective businessman," and "Flagler, who had his own ruthless side, rather admired him for it."[86]

Like so much else recently written about the Kenans' relationship with Flagler and the Bingham family, these assertions are based on unfounded speculation. Will Kenan did not meet Henry Flagler until the summer of 1899. Both of his grandmothers had been dead for almost thirty years by then, and the publicity that allegedly annoyed one of them did not erupt until late that summer—long after Flagler had asked Mary Lily to marry him, after the Kenan family had stayed with him at his mansion on Long Island Sound, and after the New York Supreme Court had ruled on Alice Flagler's mental competency. Also, there is no evidence to suggest that Louise Wise was Mary Lily and Henry Flagler's child. Rather, the documentation that does exist—letters, interviews, and photographs—leaves little doubt that Jessie and Kib were indeed Louise's biological parents. While it is true that they did not have a happy marriage and that Kib abandoned Jessie and Louise, he did not leave them until the summer of 1901, two weeks before Mary Lily and Henry Flagler were married.[87]

As for Flagler caving in to pressure from Will Kenan and the Kenan family, this idea is both amusing and absurd. Henry Flagler was one of the most powerful men in America. He did only what he wanted to do. What, after all, could the Kenans threaten him with—a suit alleging adultery? This seems very unlikely; even if such charges were true, and there is no evidence that they were, the family, by making them public, would have unleashed publicity damaging to its own and Mary Lily's reputation. Certainly the Kenans worried about Flagler's relationship with Mary Lily, especially because of his marital status, but there was little they could do about it even if they had wanted to.

The evidence suggests another scenario: that Flagler and the Kenans shared a cordial, even warm relationship. The question of timing is important here, for it helps explain why Flagler made his gifts to Mary Lily when he did, some two and a half years before they were married. In addition to his marriage proposal and his feelings for Mary Lily, he had two things in mind when he gave her the Standard Oil stock: obtaining a divorce from his wife and the creation of Standard Oil of New Jersey. In April 1899 Flagler announced he was changing his residence from New York to Florida for business purposes. He wanted to be closer to his Florida enterprises, he told the press, and he also wanted to escape New York's excessive inheritance tax. What he did not say, however, was that he also hoped to obtain in Florida what he could not get in New York: a law that would allow insanity as grounds for a divorce. At the time Flagler announced his change of residence, his personal attorney, Eugene Ashley, was preparing a request to the New York Supreme Court to have Alice declared insane and incompetent.[88]

Flagler also timed his stock gift so that Mary Lily could benefit from both a dividend and the expected rise in its value. Flagler sent the stock transfer papers to her father, not to Will, and one month later, in April 1899, she received her first dividend check. This was the last dividend declared by the Standard Oil Interests, the twenty tightly held companies formed in 1892 in the wake of the dissolution of the Standard Oil Trust (the trust Flagler had devised in 1882). Indeed, at the time of Flagler's gift he and Standard Oil's other officers were reconstructing their corporate interests yet again. They were taking advantage of the new holding-company laws in New Jersey to consolidate their twenty companies into Standard Oil of New Jersey, a "holding company for their entire operation. Its capitalization was increased from $10 million to $110 million, and it held stock in forty-one other companies, which controlled yet other companies, which in turn controlled still other companies." By the time the consolidation was announced in June 1899, speculation in Standard Oil's securities had sent their value soaring.[89]

By then Flagler had invited many of the Kenans—including Will, his parents, his sisters, his cousin, Aunt Annie, and the Colonel and his wife—to come to stay with him at Lawn Beach, his mansion on Long Island Sound. "I am living in hopes each day to hear that the ladies of your family are coming to Mamaroneck at a very early day," he wrote to Colonel Thomas Kenan in early June. A few days later, in a letter to Buck Kenan, Flagler noted, "I am delighted with the prospect of having Jessie and Kib here next week. I hope he is better." It seems that Jessie's alcoholic husband was the only family member with whom Flagler showed any uneasiness, for Kib was often too "sick" to supervise renovations on the Macon mansion Flagler had given the Wises.[90]

Will Kenan arrived at Lawn Beach in early July, shortly after Eugene Ashley asked the New York Supreme Court to rule on Alice's mental status.[91] But he could not stay long; he had to get back to Niagara Falls, where Union Carbide was preparing to test the Horry furnaces at its new plant. Yet the two men did manage to initiate the relationship that defined much of their interaction over the next several years. They discussed technology. Specifically, they talked about the Kern Incandescent Gas Light Burner Flagler had ordered for his mansion. Although Kenan was unfamiliar with the burner, he did write Flagler about it after returning to the Falls, offering to test it for him. Flagler thanked Kenan for the "kind offer to make a test," but the burner had already been installed. Nevertheless, he promised, "If I succeed in getting in more of these lamps, will send you one."[92]

Neither Will nor his family was with Flagler in early August, however, when the New York Supreme Court declared Alice insane and appointed Eugene Ashley as committee of her property, and her doctor, Dr. Carlos MacDonald,

At Jackson's Sanatarium, Dansville, New York, 1899. *Left to right:* Buck and Mollie Kenan, Louise Wise, Jessie Kenan Wise, Annie Kenan, Will Kenan, Sarah Kenan, Mary Lily Kenan. (HMFM Archives)

as her guardian. The next day Flagler left with Ashley and Owen Kenan for a ten-day trip to Florida.[93]

THE DECISION OF A LIFETIME

Will spent some time with his family at Jackson's Sanatarium in Dansville, New York, while they waited for the publicity from Alice's case to die down. He went back to the Falls when they rejoined Flagler at Lawn Beach, however, only to be visited by them all again at the Falls, except for Buck and Aunt Annie, who returned to North Carolina. The girls wanted to see everything at the Falls, and Will showed it to them: the majestic mists, the men at the University

Club, and the new plant of the Union Carbide Company. But this did not take long, and the women quickly grew bored, especially Will's mother. As Flagler noted in a letter to Buck, Mollie "was very lonely at the Falls and wanted to get away, but did not want to go until the 1st prox. for fear William will be disappointed."[94]

William was already disappointed when his mother arrived. Although things had been bad for him at the Soo, he had nevertheless been in charge of the plant—something denied him at Niagara Falls. Union Carbide selected Edgar F. Price, one of the original employees at the Willson Aluminum Company in Spray, North Carolina, as the new plant's general manager.[95] Mollie must have told Flagler about her son's disappointment, for shortly after she returned to Lawn Beach, he began corresponding with Kenan about investing in a chemical company owned by a friend, thinking "maybe we could arrange a partnership for you in it, you putting in the capital (which I will furnish) if the prospect seems favorable."[96]

Kenan liked the idea, and Flagler immediately wrote his friend, Edward Taylor, to see if the latter felt "like taking a partner in your business who should put in all the capital necessary to put it on a firm strong basis." Flagler then offered a glowing description of Kenan. "My reason for asking this question is that I have in mind a young man of say 27 years, of excellent habits and character,—a son of a very dear friend. There is nothing I can say in his behalf that he does not deserve. During his college course, he was *first* in everything,— studies and games. During the past four years, he has been wholly absorbed in electricity."[97] Taylor agreed to take Kenan on as a partner. But Kenan, after visiting the company and inspecting its operations, decided that "the volume of business to be acquired could not be very extensive," and so he advised Flagler "not to invest in this enterprise."[98]

Kenan's bosses somehow got word that he was looking to make a large investment, and when he returned from inspecting the chemical company, they offered him the perfect place for his expenditure: Union Carbide. Kenan could not have been happier. Not only would such an investment ensure him a prominent position in Carbide's corporate hierarchy, but it would also earn him some money. The company had recently installed 120 of the efficient, money-saving rotary furnaces at the new Niagara Falls plant, and its financial prospects had never seemed brighter.[99]

Kenan took several weeks to make his decision, which turned out to be the most important of his life. He discussed the matter with Flagler, of course, but he also talked it over with Buck, who, after meeting with Flagler in New York City, toured the facility at Niagara Falls and met with Carbide's chief executive officer, George O. Knapp. Buck advised his son to make the investment and then returned to Wilmington.

But Henry Flagler wavered. One of his Standard Oil associates, William P.

Howe, had long been in "intimate contact with all the gas manufacturing companies in the United States" and knew a great deal about Union Carbide. He even "knew of the man in North Carolina who made the [carbide] discovery. I think he said his name was Morehouse," Flagler wrote to Kenan, "but perhaps I am mistaken." What bothered Flagler was the "doubt" Howe had expressed regarding the "future" of Union Carbide. Flagler had "no opinion" himself regarding the validity of Howe's pessimistic evaluation, but he did "have a suspicion that the men at the head of the Union Carbide Co. might more properly be classed as promoters than manufacturers. As to the wisdom of your buying some of the stock," he told Kenan, "I cannot form a satisfactory opinion. In all probability, the capital was largely watered when created. For all that it may be a good investment."[100]

Flagler talked with Howe immediately after writing this letter, however, and wrote Kenan again. Having found Howe "possessed of some considerable information, which he did not want to commit to paper," Flagler could only offer Kenan a warning. "I feel a hesitancy in doing so, but I am willing to say this to you,—I do not believe the parties at the head of the concern are men who would ever appreciate faithful service, such as yours, at its true worth. Mr. Knapp might, but I do not understand that he has any special influence aside from the manufacturing department."[101]

Early the next morning Buck wired Flagler that Knapp was on his way to see William at the Falls, and Flagler immediately wired William: "Do just as you think best in view of the letter I wrote you yesterday. In the event you decide to invest, I suggest you limit amount to twenty-five thousand dollars. There are other good things besides this." But Kenan could read between the lines—his financial backer was not enthusiastic about this investment.[102]

Kenan's decision not to buy the Carbide stock was clearly hard for him to make. In his letter informing Flagler of his choice, he included a copy of Francis Preston Venable's recent article in the *American Manufacturer*, "An Account of the First Production of Calcium Carbide and Acetylene in the United States." The article may have helped Flagler better understand Kenan's intimate association with the carbide industry, for it mentioned Kenan's name twice in conjunction with the seminal research. But Flagler had no regrets about the stock decision. He had since discussed Union Carbide with yet another friend who knew "the promoters of the enterprise thoroughly," and his friend had confirmed "the diagnosis given by Mr. Howe, and I am glad you have decided as you have. Although I do not come in contact with people much," he assured Kenan, "I shall keep an eye out for some opportunity for you to make an investment, coupled with a situation such as I feel you are able to fill. . . . I also return the article you sent me regarding the first production of Acetylene, which I have read with much interest."[103]

Kenan's decision drew a different reaction from his Carbide bosses, who quickly made it clear they were less than impressed. They not only curtailed his duties at the Niagara plant, but they also sent him out on the road. "During the Winter of 1900 I spent most of my time on the train between Chicago–Niagara Falls and New York City, making a round trip each week for the Union Carbide Company."[104]

NEW OPPORTUNITIES

Will Kenan reached the end of the line with Union Carbide in the spring of 1900. He resigned from the company rather than go to Vienna, Austria, to construct and operate a carbide plant for the German Acetylene Company. "This would have required at least a year," Kenan remembered, "so I declined it, because I was tired of living in a trunk and . . . I could not speak any foreign language." His break with the company was apparently amicable, however. When he told his boss he was leaving, Knapp replied, " 'Why not purchase Carbide stock and if you are unable to pay cash for the amount you wish to purchase I will be glad to endorse your note at our bank for any amount and carry it as long as necessary.' " Kenan refused Knapp's offer, but he did write an article on calcium carbide for the German Acetylene Company, "for which they paid me $500.00."[105]

Kenan's resignation had as much to do with the helping hand of Henry Flagler as it did with the way Union Carbide treated him. Flagler secured a position for the young scientist with the Traders Paper Company of Lockport, New York, a company recently reorganized and recapitalized by Eugene Ashley. Flagler, one of the company's major bondholders, also arranged for Kenan to buy some of the company's stock, and on June 1, 1900, William began working for Traders as assistant manager in charge of construction and operation.[106]

Kenan's move to Lockport also coincided with a number of changes and new opportunities for several of his friends and relatives. His cousin Owen got a job with one of Henry Flagler's physician friends in New York City, and Buck used a loan from Flagler to reorganize and become president of the Spiritine Chemical Company of Wilmington, North Carolina. This company, originally chartered in 1890 by the Kenans' next-door neighbor Ludwig Hansen, was closely intertwined with Hansen's Carolina Oil and Creosote Company—a firm created in the mid-1880s with the support of Flagler and Henry Walters. With the loan Flagler now provided, Buck and Hansen consolidated and reorganized both companies, and Buck purchased almost one-half of Spiritine's 200 shares.[107]

Kenan's move to Lockport also coincided with Francis Preston Venable's election as the new president of the University of North Carolina and the appointment of Charles Baskerville, Kenan's former roommate and fellow Gim Ghoul, as head of the university's chemistry department.[108] Also by then Baskerville was helping Louisville attorney Robert Worth Bingham investigate a gold mine in Asheboro, North Carolina. Indeed, the fact that Bingham subsequently purchased the gold mine and continued to work with Baskerville on other speculative ventures in North Carolina reflects his close association with the UNC professor as well as his growing prosperity and prominence in Louisville. In addition to profiting from his marriage to Eleanore Miller, Bingham had received his law degree from the University of Louisville in 1897, and in the fall of 1899 he and his new law partner, UNC alumnus and fellow Gim Ghoul Will Davies, started handling cases for the Louisville & Nashville Railroad.[109]

LOVELY LITTLE LOCKPORT

Will Kenan stayed in Lockport's Kenmore Hotel for several months before renting an apartment from the Traders' attorney, Eugene Ashley. Located on the corner of Genesee and Cottage Streets in a building Ashley had recently remodeled, the second-floor apartment gave Kenan a perfect view of the house next door, the home of his future wife, Alice Pomroy.[110]

Kenan found Lockport much as he had left it four years earlier: smaller than his native Wilmington and a very different kind of port city. Located twenty miles north of Buffalo in an area famous for its apple and peach orchards, Lockport was settled by Quakers in the early 1800s and was known as "Standing Up Hill" until a series of stone locks were constructed there as the final link in the Erie Canal (1817–25). The canal locks gave the village its name and reason for being, and during the four decades between its incorporation as a town (1829) and the chartering of the city of Lockport (1865), most of the population lived and worked on or near the canal.

Many of the more prosperous antebellum residents lived in stone houses adjacent to the canal, profiting as both merchants and mill owners. Their less affluent neighbors—mainly the poor Irish immigrants who built the canal, who worked on the locks, and who chose to remain at Lockport once construction was completed—lived in a shantytown of boardinghouses and small buildings near the locks, docks, and mills where they worked. Unlike Wilmington, moreover, Lockport had a thriving industrial base and very few African American residents. Although many blacks had passed through the village during the 1850s and 1860s, hiding in canalside houses as refugees, almost all had moved on to Canada and the West through the Underground Railroad.[111]

By the time Kenan made Lockport his home, the canal defined and divided the community. The area north of the canal and adjacent to both the lock corridors and Eighteen Mile Creek was known as "Lowertown," while the slopes of "Uppertown," the area where Kenan lived, rose above the canal south of the village. The upper and lower town designations also corresponded roughly with the class, ethnic, and political divisions of the community. Uppertown

Locks of the Erie Canal at Lockport, New York, ca. 1900. Uppertown is to the left of the canal; Lowertown, to the right. (NgCHS)

contained the splendid homes of the city's well-to-do Protestant, Anglo-Saxon natives, the bankers, mill owners, merchants, and real estate developers such as Republican activist Eugene Ashley. Lowertown was home to the Democratic masses, the mostly Catholic families of Irish, German, and Italian immigrants who served in a wage-earning capacity on the canal or at the locks, docks, and businesses that lined it and Eighteen Mile Creek.[112]

The canal and creek did more, however, than mark the social divisions that existed in Lockport. They formed the economic web that bound the community together. The canal provided direct employment for skilled and unskilled workers alike (temporary and uncertain though this often was); it also generated the water power that made the city's industrial base possible. From flour mills and iron foundries to textile plants, a canning factory, and Traders Paper Company—all depended on the power generated on the south side of the canal by the surplus descent of water to the locks.[113]

Kenan worked in Lowertown but lived and socialized in Uppertown with Henry Flagler's relatives. Flagler had lived near Lockport in the early 1840s, working as a teenager on one of the boats running out of Medina, a canal town twenty miles east of Lockport. His namesake uncle, Henry Flagler, had been a banker in Medina before moving to Lockport and opening a large dry goods store. Flagler's cousin Thomas Thorne Flagler had been one of the wealthiest and most prominent men in Niagara County. He had been president of Lockport's largest industrial enterprise (the Holly Manufacturing Company), president of the Niagara County National Bank, a Republican member of Congress, and a partner in Lockport's largest hardware store with his brother-in-law, Hopkins Chillingsworth Pomroy, the father of Alice Pomroy.[114]

Will first met Alice in the fall of 1900, shortly after becoming her next-door neighbor. But it was not across the hedgerow. They met, interestingly enough, at Henry Flagler's mansion in New York City. Alice had been traveling to Florida with Flagler and his niece Eliza Ashley since 1896, and like Ashley, who was receiving some $4,000 a year from the Standard Oil stock Flagler had given her, Alice was profiting from Flagler's gift of Federal Steel stock. For a while, at least, the already white-haired Alice had fancied more from Flagler than had Eliza and Eugene Ashley, who had comforted the wealthy oil magnate during his "considerable misfortune" with his institutionalized wife. According to one source, Alice Pomroy had competed with Mary Lily Kenan for Henry Flagler's hand.[115]

Will Kenan had neither the time nor the inclination for romance, though, when he first moved to Lockport. There was too much to do at Traders—"I had never seen a paper mill. It was all new to me." He was also playing the stock market with money and securities that Flagler had given him. "During the latter part of 1900 I thought I should like to do some trading in the stock market and with that in mind placed $20,000.00 and a goodly lot of Stock Exchange collateral with a broker in New York City. For a while I was very successful and since I was trading in one thousand shares at a time, my cash balance grew rapidly." So rapidly, in fact, that Kenan purchased a new Columbia Electric Stanhope automobile and built "a garage and charging station" for it at the Traders plant in Lowertown, "where I was able to get sufficient electric power."[116]

Simultaneously, Kenan proved his business and engineering skills to Flagler at the Breakers Hotel in Palm Beach. Originally known as the Palm Beach Inn, the hotel had been constructed in 1895 on the ocean side of Palm Beach—on the opposite side of the island, that is, from Flagler's Royal Poinciana Hotel and the luxurious marble mansion he was now constructing for Mary Lily. Flagler wanted to supply the Breakers with electricity, Kenan recalled, but could not decide whether "to build a new Power Plant at the Breakers or enlarge the capacity at the Poinciana and transmit electric power to the Breakers." Flagler had his own builders in Florida, but "no one to design the power plant, laundry, steam heating and refrigeration, and requested me to supply such a man. I knew of no one, and so informed him. At his suggestion I made a trip to Palm Beach, looked over the situation, and decided what could be done."[117]

Kenan suggested that Flagler install a separate power plant at the Breakers. "I made a detailed report including an estimate, and when I reached New York had it typed and presented to him." Flagler doubted the accuracy of the report, however, especially Kenan's construction estimates, which were far below what Flagler had paid for the power plant at his Colonial Hotel in Nassau. Ignore the Colonial, Kenan replied; the Breakers operated only three months a year and thus did not need the same kind of efficient and expensive machinery as the year-round Nassau hotel. The figures for the Breakers reflected the "simplest and the cheapest" machinery on the market. Flagler was still not convinced, however, and "so to prove my figures, I under took the job."[118]

To help him meet his obligations, Kenan hired twenty-two-year-old Schuyler Beattie as his private secretary. It was one of the best decisions he ever made. Beattie was a native of Lockport and an excellent stenographer. He knew everything about the village and its politics, and he had family connections among both the Irish in Lowertown and the gentry in Uppertown. "He knew everybody; everybody knew him," his daughter recalled. "He made it easy for Mr. Kenan. He kept things very, very smooth." And he did so for much of the next sixty-five years.[119]

Kenan immediately found Beattie "most generous in doing anything to assist me, coming to my apartment any time, day or night. We would sometimes work until midnight and he would be around the next morning at six o'clock." Beattie's assistance made it possible for Kenan to complete the drawings for the Breakers power plant, to contract for the plant's equipment, and to supervise its installation at Palm Beach, all at a cost "under my original figures." To be sure, Kenan had everything ready at the Breakers before the onset of the Palm Beach "season," and in early January he joined Flagler in Florida for an inspection of the new plant.[120]

Henry Flagler must have breathed a sigh of relief when he inspected the plant. Despite the fact that he was a no-nonsense businessman who suffered incompetence from no one, it would have been difficult for him to dismiss or embarrass the young engineer. But Kenan accomplished more than he had promised, and Flagler immediately displayed his pleasure and trust in him. He sent him to help inspect the water and power plants at hotels in Miami and Nassau and bestowed 500 shares of Traders stock on him—about half of the shares he owned in the company.[121]

Before Kenan returned to New York, Flagler also asked him to design and equip new water and power plants at several Flagler hotels and to serve as "a consultant in connection with the vapor heating, electric lighting, water and laundry" systems at Whitehall, the palatial residence at Palm Beach.[122] At the same time, Flagler also made it clear to his hotel builders that Kenan's advice would be accepted in all matters with which he was connected. Shortly after Kenan left him, for example, Flagler discovered that one of his builders had asked the engineer in charge of the Ormand Electric Plant to plan the new powerhouse for Flagler's Continental Hotel at Atlantic Beach. "This is all right," Flagler wrote to the builder, "but before it is adopted, I want it to be vised by Mr. Kenan, and if there are any differences of opinion, I want Mr. Kenan's views adopted. There are very few men of his age who have had as much experience and who are as competent as he. The successful working of the Breakers Plant proves this. We have got a plant in there with a greater measure of efficiency, and at least half of the cost of other plants of equal size."[123]

Kenan soon found it impossible, even with Schuyler Beattie's help, to keep up with his work for both the Traders Paper Company and Flagler. Beyond his normal managerial duties at Traders, where he worked six days a week from eight in the morning until six at night, Kenan now had to assist in the design and construction of several new mills for the company. "Therefore," Kenan recalled, "to accomplish my Florida work I got up each morning at 5 A.M. and retired at 12:30 each night." But even that was not enough, so in "order to fulfill my obligation to the Traders Paper Company I organized a small staff composed of one draftsman (and sometimes two) and one (frequently two) stenographers. I dug out enough work to keep this staff busy by working between 8 P.M. and 8 A.M."[124]

While Kenan struggled to get a few hours' sleep each night, Henry Flagler's lobbyists pressured the Florida legislature to make incurable insanity grounds for divorce in the state. Alice Flagler had been confined to the Pleasantville asylum for four years; the New York Supreme Court had ruled her insanity incurable; the court had appointed a guardian for her person and another for the fortune her husband had established for her; and Flagler himself was fast approaching the second anniversary of his status as a resident of Florida.

Most of these realities were embodied in the divorce law passed by the Florida legislature and signed into law on April 25, 1901. Many of the state's newspapers attacked the so-called Flagler Divorce Law and hinted that Flagler had bribed the legislature to get it passed. They were correct; recent estimates of his expenditures range from $50,000 to more than $100,000. The public outcry against the law increased in June, when Flagler filed for divorce in Miami, but dissipated in August after Eugene Ashley presented the circuit court with evidence bearing on Flagler's request. According to Ashley's financial statement, which was published in all of the Florida newspapers, Alice received an annual income of approximately $120,000 on the more than $2 million in cash and securities Flagler had given her. The court granted the divorce on August 13, 1901, after one day of hearings.[125]

Preparations for the wedding of Henry and Mary Lily were well under way by the time of the court's ruling. Dressmakers had been working on the bride's white chiffon gown for months, and workmen had been preparing Liberty

Hall, the old Kenan homeplace in Kenansville, North Carolina, for the wedding. Originally built with slave labor, Liberty Hall was now "completely refurbished from roof to cellar" with money made through Standard Oil, the world's mightiest industrial corporation. "Inside, rose Chinese silk wall paper covered dining and drawing room walls; rare Aubosson and Savoronne rugs were placed on the floors. Large vases of roses were set in corners. The only items left untouched by the workmen had been the family heirlooms gathered over the decades by the first Kenans who came to America in 1736."[126]

Henry Flagler arrived in Wilmington in his private railroad car shortly after noon on August 23, the day before the wedding. But there were no Kenans there to meet him. Mollie and Jessie had been in Kenansville for almost a week, and the rest of the family had headed there that morning on the ACL's northbound train. Only Mr. and Mrs. William Dick, who lived across the street from the Kenans, greeted their gray-haired visitor. Word soon spread that the wealthy oil magnate was in town, however, and by late afternoon Nun Street "was a jostling throng of the curious trying to get a glimpse of Henry at the supper table."[127]

Only a few curious onlookers were out at seven the next morning when Flagler, the Dicks, the Ashleys, and the other members of the small wedding party began the hour-long train ride to Duplin County. In addition to Flagler's private car, the locomotive pulled a baggage car containing members of the Hollowbush Orchestra and a beautiful carriage for the newlyweds to ride in. Henry Walters met the train at the Warsaw station, but the Pembroke Joneses were not in his private car with him. Sadie had spent the entire summer planning an elaborate dinner dance that she and Pem were giving at the Havemeyer villa in Newport, Rhode Island, and the invitations for the August 22 bash had already gone out by the time Flagler and Mary Lily set their wedding date. Sadie did send "a telegram and a substantial present to her closest friend, Miss Kenan," and Pem "also sent a telegram of congratulations as did several other cottagers" at Newport.[128]

Mary Lily was corseted and camouflaged when the coaches and carriages arrived at Liberty Hall, and she was not the stunning young bride she had dreamed of being. Her friends and family told her otherwise, but she knew the newspapers had come closer to the truth. She was thirty-four years old, and her hair was "streaked with gray. Although she cannot be termed graceful of figure," one paper reported, "she has an exceedingly pleasant face and her exquisitely gracious manners have won for her many friends and admirers throughout the country." Even more disappointing was the newspaper's prediction that she "will weigh approximately 125 pounds." Just when this would happen, though, the story did not say.[129]

While the stress of the situation had helped Mary Lily shed a few pounds, it had also drawn her nerves as tight as her corset strings. Her decision to marry

The Flaglers and their wedding guests at Liberty Hall. *Seated, left to right:* Molly Dick, Will Kenan, Louise Wise. *First row, standing, left to right:* Mollie Kenan, Jessie Kenan Wise, Mary Lily Flagler, Henry Flagler, unidentified woman. *Second row, standing, left to right:* Emily Kenan, Owen Hill Kenan, Sarah Kenan, Graham Kenan. Henry Walters stands directly behind Graham Kenan's left shoulder and directly in front of Buck Kenan. This is one of the few existing photographs of Walters. (HMFM Archives)

Henry Flagler had split Wilmington's First Presbyterian Church right down the middle. That was one reason why she chose Liberty Hall for the wedding and asked the church's former pastor, the Reverend Peyton Hoge, to return from his new church in Louisville, Kentucky, to perform the ceremony.[130] Thanks to Josephus Daniels, editor of the *Raleigh News and Observer*, the topic of divorce had been as hotly debated in North Carolina as in Florida. But unlike Florida, where the legislature liberalized the state's divorce laws as a result of Flagler's efforts, the North Carolina general assembly defeated similar legislation because of the antidivorce campaign waged by Daniels, who pontificated with his typical inerrant insight, "Every departure from the biblical rule is a step from sound morals and good public policy."[131]

The Kenans may well have found refreshment and relief from these tensions in the gifts that Flagler allegedly gave them at Liberty Hall. Thousands of shares of Standard Oil stock, Federal Steel securities, government bonds, and a check to Mary Lily for a million dollars were supposedly slipped under the proper plates by the black servants who prepared the wedding feast. If Will Kenan found anything under his plate, it was over and above what Flagler had already served up to him. "In commemoration of the happy event to take place one week from today," Flagler had written him on August 17, "I ask your acceptance of the 500 shares of Traders Paper Co. Stock (par value $50,000) which I enclose herewith as a mark of my esteem and sincere regard for you. No one but Mary Lily knows of this act and no one else will through me. With every wish for your success and happiness, I am Most cordially yours, H. M. Flagler."[132]

CHAPTER 6

For Better or Worse

Mr. Flagler's brother-in-law. That's what he heard himself called. Not William Rand Kenan Jr., scientist, engineer, and carbide discoverer. But Mr. Flagler's brother-in-law. Kenan never liked the description, but he did not hold it against Henry Flagler, at least not initially. He had so much work to do and so much money to make, and he knew all too well, even if others did not, that he was not just an empty barrel rolling on Mr. Flagler's wealth.

Between 1901 and 1905 Mr. Flagler kept Mr. Kenan very busy in Florida, where, as a construction engineer for the FEC Hotel Company, William first heard himself disparaged as Mr. Flagler's brother-in-law.[1] Yet Kenan worried less about the derogatory remarks of his fellow hotel workers than he did about how his family and friends perceived his relationship with Henry Flagler. He always let them know how hard he was working and how he was getting only a few hours of sleep a night. His father warned him to slow down. "I dislike to hear of your working 18 hours out of the 24 and, unless you quit it very soon," Buck wrote, "you will surely break down, for no one can abuse nature in that way without paying very dearly for it."[2] Frank Venable sent a more subtle warning just as Kenan was preparing to join his family for a winter vacation in Florida. The UNC president referred to the personal photograph Kenan had sent him: "I worry over it a little because I think I see some of those tired lines in the face that should be still fresh and young. I am glad to hear of your successes but fear you are working too hard. I trust you will rest some on your trip off. We shall certainly count on a visit from you."[3]

Kenan's Florida trip began an annual winter ritual that he and his family practiced for most of the rest of their lives. December meant St. Augustine and Christmas at the Ponce de Leon Hotel, while January meant Palm Beach and the luxury of Whitehall, the Flaglers' marble mansion. Will and his father never stayed as long as the rest of the family, however, especially the Flaglers, who usually remained at Whitehall until the end of the Palm Beach season in late March or early April.[4]

Whitehall, the Flagler mansion at Palm Beach, Florida. (Thomas S. Kenan III)

Will and his family enjoyed the comfortable lifestyle the Flagler wealth afforded, and they also appreciated the many jobs, loans, trips, and railroad passes Flagler secured for them and their closest friends. But there was one thing that Buck and William could not get from the wealthy oilman, and that was help playing the stock market. Flagler loaned them each $20,000 to invest in the market, but he refused to advise them where to invest it, because, he once told Buck, "I don't think there is a man in New York, who knows less of [stock] values outside of S[tandard] O[il] Trust, than I."[5] Buck and William placed most of their money with a New York stockbroker and, initially at least, Buck made most of their investment decisions. He bought common and preferred shares of both U.S. Steel and Southern Railway stock, and in early January 1902, apparently with the dividends from those purchases, he invested in two Wilmington firms: M. J. Corbett Company, a commission business, and the Electrical Supply and Construction Company.[6]

Buck and William received most of their investment advice from Flagler's financial manager, William Beardsley, and from their good friend Henry Walters. They could not have gotten better advice. Beardsley handled all of Flagler's stocks and bonds and was intimately familiar with the workings of Wall Street, while Walters was in a perfect position to help the Kenans speculate in railroad stocks. Not only was he on the verge of acquiring the Plant System's huge network of railroads in South Carolina, Georgia, Florida, and Alabama— a system that also included joint ventures with Henry Flagler in both the Florida Publishing Company and the Peninsular & Occidental (P&O) Steam-

The Kenans at Whitehall, 1902. *Left to right:* Sarah Kenan, Mollie Kenan, Will Kenan, Buck Kenan, Jessie Kenan Wise. (HMFM Archives)

ship Company—but he was also discussing with J. P. Morgan and Company a joint purchase by the ACL and Southern Railway companies of the Louisville & Nashville Railroad, which connected with the Plant System at Montgomery, Alabama.[7]

Buck may have been listening to Henry Walters in April 1902 when Beardsley obtained for him a six-month, 6 percent loan for $50,000 at the Metropolitan Trust Company of New York. Buck put up 328 shares of U.S. Steel preferred, 753 shares of U.S. Steel common, and 100 shares of soaring Southern Railway preferred as collateral for the loan, which he then used to buy more stocks, including 200 shares of increasingly valuable Louisville & Nashville common. When Beardsley renewed the loan for Buck at the end of October, the value of the securities in the Wilmington merchant's New York account approached $200,000, a figure that did not include the value of Buck's stocks in a number of North Carolina companies.[8]

By 1903 Will Kenan's father was no longer known as Buck. He was William Rand Kenan Sr., a UNC trustee, the white savior of the Wilmington race riot, and one the city's wealthiest and most prominent businessmen. Though far from the physically fit "muscular Christian" who had exercised with sit-ups and Indian clubs twice a day, Buck, at age fifty-seven, was in very good health. Only an occasional flare-up of rheumatism bothered him, and this he tried to ignore—an oversight, Henry Flagler joked, that Buck should not make. "You say your rheumatism is not very serious, and you think it will wear itself out in a few weeks. Be careful it doesn't wear you out."[9]

But it was not rheumatism that wore Buck out. It was amoebic dysentery. Struck by the disease in March 1903, he was rushed to Baltimore after appendicitis complicated his condition. Doctors at Johns Hopkins removed his appendix and "for a short time hope of his recovery was entertained, but that soon vanished and his friends and the family became resigned to the inevitable sad though it was." Buck died at 5 A.M. on April 14, 1903, surrounded by all of his immediate family except Mary Lily.[10] William wired the Flaglers and Henry Walters with the sad news and then telegraphed Beardsley to protect Buck's stock portfolio at J. H. Parker and Company. Other telegrams went out during the day to Wilmington, Raleigh, Kenansville, Atlanta, Louisville, and New York. Late that evening Will and his family left Baltimore for Wilmington, traveling with Buck's body on a special train provided by Walters.

Buck Kenan was buried on Thursday, April 16, an election day in Wilmington. The schools closed in his honor, the superior court gaveled a recess, and the Wilmington Light Infantry lowered its armory flag to half mast. A phalanx of infantrymen and Confederate veterans escorted Buck's casket to the First Presbyterian Church, where both the curious and the concerned packed the main auditorium and galleries for "one of the largest funerals in the history of the city." The eulogy, presented by the Reverend Peyton Hoge of Louisville, was "one of the prettiest ever delivered from a pulpit and greatly moved the large congregation."[11]

Buck was buried at Oakdale Cemetery amid musket fire and the lonely farewell of a bugler blowing taps. "It was a very sad blow to the family and to the community in which Mr. Kenan resided," Henry Flagler wrote. "I don't remember any case where such a genuine outburst of sympathy was expressed as by the citizens of Wilmington."[12]

NEW LIVING ARRANGEMENTS

Will Kenan did not take over as the man of the house. Henry Flagler did. The aging oilman now assumed an even greater role as protector and provider for the Kenan women. Less than a week after the funeral, he gave his mother-in-law 200 shares of Standard Oil stock and then had Beardsley sell all of Buck's

New York stocks, both to meet the loan at the Metropolitan Trust Company and to provide Mollie with some cash.

Flagler also began searching discreetly for some land on which to build Mollie and Sarah a new house in Wilmington. He soon abandoned the idea of building, however, and sought house-hunting help from Will Kenan's boyhood friend Thomas H. Wright. In his letters to Wright, who was a member of one of Wilmington's oldest families, Flagler continually stressed the need for strictest confidence. "I don't want my name ever to be known in connection with the purchase," he wrote to Wright. Not only would this make it easier "to induce [Mollie] to leave the home from which Mr. Kenan was buried," but it would also keep the cost of the new house down. "If anybody knew that I was thinking of purchasing," he explained to Wright, "the price would probably be double. I may say to you in confidence, that my only object in making the purchase is to make a present of the home to Mrs. Kenan."[13]

In late September 1903 Flagler purchased the Henry Latimer mansion on the corner of Third and Orange Streets "for a song,—$10,500," and asked Will Kenan to inspect it. "I want at my own expense to put the house in first class order," Flagler wrote, "[and] I am wondering whether you could not get away for a week or so and run down to Wilmington, take up the matter, see what is really necessary to be done and make contracts, leaving Tom Wright or someone else to see that the contracts are faithfully executed."[14]

Kenan had just returned to Lockport from Florida when the letter arrived. The Breakers Hotel had been destroyed by fire in June at a loss of $400,000 to Flagler, and Kenan, as the new consulting and construction engineer for the FEC Hotel Company, was pushing to have the hotel rebuilt in time for the Palm Beach season. Indeed, between rebuilding the Breakers and his own personal projects Kenan had not stopped working since his father's death. His life had become a blur of railway journeys, blueprints, business mergers, and stock dividends. He was caught in a confusing struggle between his own needs and those of the individuals and corporations with which he was connected.[15]

He was beginning to regret having accepted the job Flagler had obtained for him at the Traders Paper Company. His brother-in-law had obviously been wrong about the men behind Union Carbide. They were not speculators and promoters; they were legitimate businessmen, entrepreneurs who had created a monopoly in the carbide industry. They had started rebuilding Kenan's old carbide plant at the Soo, where a new hydroelectric plant, the Lake Superior Power Company, was also being constructed on the American side of the river. Also, Kenan had interrupted his busy assignment at the Breakers to travel to the Kanawha Valley in West Virginia, where, at the request of John Motley Morehead, he had analyzed the water power potential of a site on which Major James Turner Morehead soon built a new ferroalloy smelting plant—a plant that eventually became the nucleus of Union Carbide's ferroalloy business in "the Ruhr of the U.S. Chemical Industry."[16]

It now seemed to Kenan that the real speculators and promoters were his bosses at the Traders Paper Company, who were trying to monopolize the box and paperboard industry. Although he enjoyed the handsome dividends that attended their activities, their empire building robbed him of the individual recognition he desired. Like many businesses of the period, Traders was part of the great merger movement in American business. The $300,000 firm had been consolidated by its owners into a new creation, the United Box Board & Paper Company, which they then used in 1903 to create a $30 million holding company for an even larger consolidation, some sixty-eight heavy paper plants throughout the United States. Thus Kenan was much like Traders itself, an insignificant cog in a huge industrial corporation—something he would not have been at Union Carbide. Even if he now climbed to the top of United's Traders division, the merger diminished his chances of occupying a recognized position of status and power. As he later recalled, "I was not in sympathy with this move and so stated to my associates."[17]

Upset though he was with the changes, Kenan initially benefited from them in several ways. As a close associate of United's lawyer and leading consolidator, Eugene Ashley, and as a large stockholder in the Traders company himself, Kenan profited from the securities transactions that attended the merger. More important, he invested his profits in something completely unconnected with Henry Flagler: gas utilities. He used one of his first United dividends to help him buy the Saugerties Gas Light Company of Saugerties, New York, and to establish a business partnership with his former roommate at Niagara Falls, Shorty Goodman. "Together we joined forces and purchased Gas Plants at many places," Kenan remembered. "We modernized them, developed the business and sold them at a very handsome profit. . . . We concentrated our efforts on Gas Ranges, Gas Water Heaters and Internal Combustion Engines, which accounted for the very large increase in the sales of gas."[18]

Kenan also brought Goodman with him to inspect the Wilmington house that Flagler bought, and once this was done, the two gas men took the northbound ACL train to Wilson, North Carolina. The little town had not changed much in the thirty years since Kenan's uncle Colonel Thomas Kenan had been its mayor. But that was fine with Will and Shorty, at least for awhile, for they needed a small urban place to try to do what large syndicates of engineers and investors had done in almost every major city in the country: consolidate local gas and electric utilities.[19]

Kenan recruited several personal and family friends in Wilson to help him with this process, and by the time he and Goodman left North Carolina, they had worked out many of the preliminary details for the Wilson Lighting Company. They agreed to furnish 60 percent of the new firm's capital if their fellow local investors incorporated the utility, negotiated contracts with municipal officials, and sought other local investors for the $50,000 project. According to the company's prospectus, the "chief feature of the proposed development at this point is to be a gas plant for the purpose of making a low candle power light." At the same time, the organizers also proposed "to lease the municipal electric light plant on terms . . . that would eventually make this end of the business at least self-supporting" and "to investigate and develop, if practicable, a water power near Wilson, same to be used in operating the electric light plant."[20]

The Wilson Lighting Company was not the only North Carolina project Will Kenan hoped to develop. He also wanted to build a paper mill in Wilmington. He had been experimenting with "Short Leaf Pine, Long Leaf Pine or Hard Pine, in the manufacture of paper" and had shipped carloads of North Carolina pines to Lockport for his tests. "With these products I made Ground Wood, Sulphite Pulp and heavy papers." The experiments surprised Kenan as they appeared to contradict the prevailing wisdom in the paper industry that the high pitch content of southern pines precluded their use in such products. Kenan's experiments suggested otherwise. Southern pine worked as well as northern spruce. Indeed, he "shipped it out as Spruce product," and no one ever knew the difference. Thus the time seemed right to Kenan to build a paper mill in Wilmington. Not only was southern pine cheaper than northern spruce, but with the Wilson utility project and the repairs to the Latimer mansion to look after, he would clearly be spending more time in North Carolina.[21]

Kenan wrote Flagler about the paper mill during one of his inspection trips to the Latimer mansion in Wilmington. Having already interested several men in the project, he was wondering whether to accept their offer to provide raw materials rather than cash in return for stocks in the mill. Flagler said no, the stock proposal sounded like a bad idea. He also warned Will that if the prospects for the mill were as good as they seemed, then Kenan could expect competition. "Assuming that it won't be necessary to commit yourself on this point before we meet," he concluded, "I forbear further comment."[22] Flagler really hoped that Will would forget the mill and concentrate on the Flagler System in Florida. He wrote Kenan again the same day asking him to try to secure "confidential" information on the "question of building a steamship with Turbine propelling power, to run between Miami and Havana."[23]

Flagler then upped the ante to Will during the family's annual convocation in Florida. He announced Kenan's appointment as a director of both the FEC Hotel Company and the FEC Railway Company. Kenan thanked his brother-in-law and returned to Lockport. He had some tough decisions to make. He wanted to build the paper mill, but he needed Flagler's financial backing to do it. The mill would not only permit him to leave the Traders Paper Company, but it would also allow him to be the boss of his own business—a business based on his own research. What was more, he saw little meaningful work ahead for himself in Florida and the Caribbean. Flagler had no intention of building any more hotels; he was devoting his money and attention to his newest project, an "Overseas Railroad" to Key West. He had already hired several prominent engineers to realize this "Eighth Wonder of the World," so Kenan would only be needed in a supervisory role.

William was also concerned about his future with Alice Pomroy, to whom he had recently proposed marriage. Although he may have loved Alice and she may have loved him, their relationship was anything but spontaneous and passionate. They came together by arrangement, it seems, and not by mutual attraction. Alice was almost forty years old; Kenan, thirty-two. While she wanted to get married, he wanted to please their friends and families, especially Henry Flagler, who is said to have urged him to marry her. At the same time, William was also worried about Alice's financial relationship with Flagler. Although she had inherited land and stocks from her deceased parents, she derived much of her income from the stocks Flagler had given her. William could not replace him immediately in that respect, but the Wilmington paper mill was a good place to start. It was, after all, a Flagler-free and potentially profitable business—one he could call his own.

Kenan decided to resign from the United Box Board & Paper Company. In recalling his decision, he attributed it to the company's merger mania—to the fact that, as stated above, he "was not in sympathy with this move." He also recalled that he beat his bosses at their own game. After they placed United's new stock "on the New York Exchange, I sold my holdings and resigned,—this was in January of 1904, although I still held my position about four months longer at their request. It may be interesting to note that I was the only stockholder of the Traders Paper Company who got back their original investment." Indeed, the United Box Board & Paper Company soon failed.[24]

Kenan left his job at United just a few days before he married Alice Mary Pomroy. Alice was by all accounts a warm, beautiful, and full-figured woman. Her father, a hardware merchant, had spent almost half of his forty years in business with his wealthy Lockport brother-in-law, Thomas Thorne Flagler, Henry's cousin. Alice had attended the local public schools with her twin brother, Albert, and their older brother, Frederick, but unlike her brothers, she did not go on to college. She attended Mrs. Piatt's Girls Finishing School at Utica, New York, before returning to Lockport and becoming "active in community service and in the work of the Church. She taught a Sunday School class, and took her place with interest and loyalty in the Women's Missionary Society." Following her mother's death in 1895, she also had taken her place beside her friend, relative, and next-door neighbor, Eliza Ashley, as a regular traveling companion of Henry Flagler in Florida and the Caribbean.[25]

There are a number of rumors and stories about Will and Alice Kenan's relationship, most of which have been offered by people who disliked Kenan.

William and Alice Kenan at the time of their marriage, Lockport, New York, 1904.
(NgCHS)

According to one such source, Henry Flagler made it clear that Will Kenan should marry Alice Pomroy, while another suggested "that Kenan's move to Lockport and his choice of residence was a premeditated move and not the happy coincidence that he portrays in *Incidents by the Way*."[26] Another source recently recalled hearing stories as a child that Alice had "thought it would be nice to marry Mr. Flagler. Before Mary Lily did. Mary Lily thought it would not be nice, and she preferred to marry him herself. So they had a little word about that. . . . So Alice Kenan decided she would marry the next best, which was William. So she did. So that is Mrs. William Kenan."[27]

While these accounts are half-truths at best, there can be little doubt that Henry Flagler played an important role as matchmaker. William admitted as much in the first edition of his autobiography, in a passage designed primarily to reveal Flagler's opinion of him: "During the time I was courting my future wife, she was debating the fact that she was several years my senior. In speaking to Mr. Flagler about this, he replied: 'That young man was fifteen years old when he was born, so don't worry about that situation.' "[28]

Worried or not, Alice and William were married in Lockport on April 9, 1904, at her home on Genesee Street. A local newspaper described it as the "most notable wedding that has taken place in this city in some time." Henry and Mary Lily attended, as did Flagler's cousin and nephew, Horace and Thorne Flagler. Mollie, Sarah, Jessie, and Louise made the long trip north for the occasion, accompanied by the Colonel and Aunt Sallie and Will's cousin Owen. Following the ceremony some seventy-five guests enjoyed a "simple but handsome" reception where harpists from Buffalo provided the music. "The display of presents was one of the most magnificent ever seen in this city," the newspaper noted, "including a complete silver dinner and tea set, and many jeweled personal ornaments."[29]

Mr. and Mrs. William Rand Kenan Jr. spent six weeks on their honeymoon, riding the rails "to the West Coast, going via Denver & Rio Grande, stopping in Denver, Salt Lake City, San Francisco, Los Angeles, Pasadena, and returning the Southern route, through San Antonio and New Orleans." That is all that is known about their early relationship. Alice was undoubtedly the first woman Will was intimate with; he was probably her first sexual partner; and there were never any others for either of them, it seems. They moved into Alice's house after returning to Lockport and joined the Town and Country Club, and Will hired a chauffeur "to take Mrs. Kenan" around in their new Peerless touring car.[30]

NEW WORKING ARRANGEMENTS

Kenan was barely back from his honeymoon when he received a letter from Shorty Goodman. The Wilson Lighting Company had a problem: other utility investors had presented the city with a competing bid.

Although Kenan later claimed that the "deal fell through due to the survey disclosing an insufficient amount of water to produce the necessary power required," he and Goodman simply could not afford to counter the other offer. "Neither Mr. Goodman nor myself feel we are in a condition to handle this matter to our satisfaction just at this time," Kenan noted in a letter to a resident of Wilson. "We have taken hold of several properties which are panning out quite satisfactorily and until these are in a measure developed we do not feel inclined to go into anything unless the inducements are extraordinary." Put simply, their capital was tied up in the Saugerties gas company; in a gas plant in Bayonne, New Jersey; and in the Citizens Gas Company of Jacksonville, Florida, a utility that Flagler was helping them acquire.[31]

Shortly thereafter, Kenan received one of his first assignments as a director of the FEC Railway: "I was sent to Europe to investigate Automobile Railway Cars for use on branch lines." He and Flagler had been discussing the topic for almost two years, and they had become especially intrigued with a vehicle made by Ganz & Company of Hungary. The Ganz car generated its own electricity and thus required no wires, no poles, and no generating plant—just the kind of railway car, that is, that the FEC Railway needed for its branch lines on the Florida frontier.

Kenan took Alice with him to Europe, where they made lengthy stops in England, Scotland, France, Germany, Hungary, and Italy. Kenan eventually investigated the "Ganz Three-phase Traction Equipment on the Valtillina Railway, at Lake Coma, Italy. I purchased a Railway Autocar from Ganz & Company, Budapest, Hungary, for the Florida East Coast Railway. It had a Flash Steam Boiler with motors attached to the trucks. The cost of operation was very low. It was shipped to New Orleans and I went there to install the motive power and it was operated from New Orleans to St. Augustine by means of its own power. It was used in branch line service until it was worn out."[32]

Will and Alice got back from Europe in time to join the Flaglers at Whitehall for the Palm Beach season. It was a good news–bad news time for the occupants of the lavish, $3 million mansion. Jessie had decided to divorce Kib Wise for having "willfully and without just cause separated from and abandoned [her], and lived in adultery with a woman in Birmingham, Alabama."[33] What was more, Ida Tarbell's recently published exposé, *The History of Standard Oil*, was receiving national attention as "the most remarkable book of its kind ever written in this country," and the nation's newly elected president, Theodore Roosevelt, had recently launched a government investigation of Standard Oil and the oil industry.[34]

On the other hand, the Flaglers and Will Kenan had some happier news to share. Construction was about to begin on the Key West Extension, and Flagler, responding to the government's decision to build the Panama Canal, had added a codicil to his will that "not only allowed for the Key West Extension project after his death, but actively promoted it." At the same time, Kenan and Goodman assumed control of the Citizens Gas Company of Jacksonville, initiated an expansion program for it, and elected Will Kenan as a director of the company and chairman of the board.[35]

Mary Lily also told her family to mark their calendars for the dedication of a building she had financed in Wilmington: an armory in memory of Buck. The four-story, castlelike armory was also intended to serve as a home for the Boys' Brigade, a quasi-military organization for white boys between the ages of ten and seventeen. Buck "had been a sympathetic and wise counselor" for the brigade, which his best friend, Colonel Walker Taylor, had formed in 1896 as an extension of the efforts of local Presbyterians to provide "physical, mental, moral and religious training" to disadvantaged boys in the southern section of the city. The massive Norman structure was a fitting memorial to Buck. It was "complete in every detail, with large gymnasium, ample dressing-rooms and bathrooms, library and reception rooms, offices, large auditorium, dining-room, kitchen and pantry, bowling alleys, and rooms for guns and equipment."[36]

The new armory may also have prompted William to reconsider a Wilmington project he had recently discussed with Thomas H. Wright. Wright had "suggested that we join forces and build an apartment house. I was not interested and so he went it alone." But after Wright sent him the building plans (which were done by New York architect Robert Louis Shape, who also designed the New York Stock Exchange Building and the campus of New York College), Kenan not only wanted in on the deal, but he wanted to enlarge it, believing that "the whole thing was too small a scale." He "proposed that if [Wright] would let me get out some plans and supervise the construction, following it to completion, then he to take over from that point and I not to be called upon for any assistance, I would go along on a 50–50 basis." Wright accepted the proposal, and not long thereafter Kenan was elected president of the Carolina Apartment Company.[37]

Kenan's decision marked the first in a series of events that combined to alter many of his personal goals and relationships, especially those connected with Henry Flagler. In October 1905, while completing the power plant at the Breakers Hotel, he was instructed to lay down his tools and take the train to St. Augustine. Flagler was opening the Ponce de Leon Hotel for President Roosevelt, and he wanted Kenan to represent him.

Opening the Ponce out of season? Flagler had never done that for anyone but himself and his family, and he was now doing it for Roosevelt—for a man who appeared bent on destroying the company Flagler had helped create. The reason, Kenan assumed, was politics. The two men despised each other, but they also needed each other for a variety of reasons. Flagler, already feeling the heat from Roosevelt's attack on Standard Oil, could not afford to create additional problems for himself in Florida, where he had to work closely with the national government on the Key West Extension. And though he regarded Roosevelt's "stealing Panama . . . as the greatest piece of international burglary I have ever known," he was still "glad that [Roosevelt] did it." The canal would bring him one step closer to making southern Florida a gateway for trade and tourism between the United States, Latin America, and the Caribbean.[38]

Roosevelt cared little or nothing about Henry Flagler's Key West dreams, but he did have to reckon with the wealth and influence of Florida's most powerful man. Flagler not only controlled the most important newspaper in the state, the *Florida Times-Union* of Jacksonville, but also, as one of the South's leading Republican benefactors, Flagler shared Roosevelt's goal of strengthening the Republican party in the region. But that was the extent of their mutual interests. Whereas Roosevelt wanted to strengthen the party's black base in the region, Henry Flagler and his deceased friend, William McKinley, had written these black voters off. In October 1901, for example, Roosevelt invited Booker T. Washington to the White House to discuss southern political appointments. Their meeting "created a terrific furor in the white South, but it also advertised clearly that Roosevelt intended to allow the black constituency a new high level of consideration." More important, at least to Floridians and the residents of Jacksonville, Washington had been accompanied to the White House by Douglas J. Wetmore, one of Jacksonville's two black city councilmen.[39]

Roosevelt was not very friendly when Kenan greeted him at the Ponce de Leon Hotel in St. Augustine. He was uncomfortable staying under Flagler's roof, as it were, and things had not gone well for him in Jacksonville, the state's largest city and the center of Republican strength in Florida. The president had delivered a special speech, at Wetmore's request, to the city's "Colored People," the first such address on his tour of the South. Though well received by the city's black community, Roosevelt's decision did not sit well with the city's white establishment.[40]

The president's visit left William with his first real taste of the liabilities that attended his relationship with Henry Flagler. "Every possible thing was done for the comfort and pleasure of the President and he seemed to enjoy his stay," Kenan recalled, "but I am sure that he did not express his thanks to any one, either personally there, or to Mr. Flagler at a later date by letter." Kenan was upset and irritated when he returned to Palm Beach to complete the power plant at the Breakers, a job that ended his immediate engineering duties with the FEC Hotel Company.[41]

William now turned his attention to the paper mill and apartment projects in Wilmington, where he and Alice began making long visits with his family. They also stayed with the whole family at Liberty Hall in April 1906 while attending the funeral of William's maiden aunt, Annie Kenan, in Kenansville.

The visit brought back a flood of fond memories to William. He saw a host of cousins, friends, and old acquaintances and showed Alice the kitchen wall at Liberty Hall where he and his sisters had carved their initials. He also introduced her to Martha Cooper, who entered "the church with the family, dressed in deep mourning." The old black woman had been raised in the kitchen at Liberty Hall, where her mother, a slave, had cooked for Will's grandparents, and Martha herself had continued to cook for the Kenans and to live "in the yard" at Liberty Hall with her own children and grandchildren. One of her sons had cooked for Will's family in Wilmington, and two of her relatives now worked at the Flaglers' mansion in Palm Beach, one as a housekeeper and the other as the pedaling chauffeur of Henry Flagler's Afromobile.[42]

William now decided that he and Alice should move to Wilmington. He was no longer employed in Lockport, and the only thing keeping them there was Alice's attachment to the place. Indeed, they were already spending most of their time in the South, either in Florida or North Carolina, and he had spent thousands of dollars "making plans and drawing up specifications for a paper mill, employing George Freeman Rowe, of Lincoln, Maine, to do some of the drafting work and this labor alone on the drafting amounted to $2,112.50." In September 1906, moreover, Kenan paid $3,000 for "a site upon which to erect a mill at Wilmington, North Carolina, having connections with two railroads and also the Cape Fear River." He also "arranged to finance" $750,000 to construct the mill.[43]

Kenan never built his paper mill, however, which he eventually described as one of the potentially profitable "Opportunities in which 'I Missed the Boat.' " Exactly why the mill was never built is not clear. It may well have been, as he later recalled, that "I had too many irons in the fire already." But the deal apparently fell through because of the various legal and financial problems encountered by his major financial backer, Henry Flagler.

By the fall of 1906 the federal government was investigating rumors that the FEC Railway was illegally recruiting and retaining workers on Flagler's Key West Extension. In October a hurricane smashed into the Florida Keys, killing between 50 and 100 extension workers and destroying the company's buildings, equipment, and embankments at Long Key viaduct. One month later the Roosevelt administration filed an antitrust suit against Standard Oil, and in March 1907 a New York grand jury indicted three FEC employees and the railway's New York labor contractor on charges of violating an 1866 slave kidnapping law. Although Flagler had very deep pockets—deep enough to be financing the extension on his own—it was not the time to open them for an expensive paper mill using southern pines.[44]

William got the disappointing news shortly after he arrived at Whitehall for his winter visit with the Flaglers. He also received, either by chance or design, a letter from William E. Shaw, the president of the Western Block Company of

Lockport. The company's treasurer, Edward J. McGrath, wanted to retire, and Shaw suggested that Kenan buy McGrath's one-half interest in the block and tackle firm. Kenan knew almost nothing about Western Block; he had passed it for several years, "going to and from the Traders Paper Company, but had never been inside the plant." Yet the offer intrigued him, for he was eagerly looking for projects of his own. His paper mill plans were dead; he had no hotel projects in Florida; the Carolina Apartment building would soon be completed; and Goodman needed only occasional help with their gas plants. What was more, everything Kenan had heard about Western Block was positive, especially the rumor that it had recently paid out $12,000 in dividends.[45]

Kenan took the next train out of Palm Beach. "I at once returned to Lockport and inspected the plant. . . . I had on low shoes and no rubbers, there was so much snow that I got my shoes full walking around the grounds. I also inspected the books and then and there decided to purchase McGrath's stock for cash." Kenan began working for Western Block before the end of the Palm Beach season, and on April 6, 1907, he was elected treasurer and a director of the firm. He and Alice would not be moving to Wilmington.[46]

"Business was very active and everyone exceedingly busy" when the new treasurer plunged into his work at Western Block. According to Kenan, he and Shaw had a "private agreement": Shaw "was to handle the sales absolutely without any interference and I was to do the same with Finance, Purchases and Manufacturing." The two men worked with another man and two women in the front office, while twenty to thirty men worked in the factory itself, producing a variety of sheaves (grooved pulley wheels) and tackle blocks (sheave casings) for more than 200 businesses that used rope and wire pulley systems to move cargo, sails, and other materials.[47]

Kenan quickly found ways to improve the company's efficiency. "I saw the necessity of installing some labor-saving devices in the office and establishing a regular standard order system,—all of which was promptly done." Just as promptly, however, both he and the company suffered financial setbacks. Kenan's was mostly on paper. His stock portfolio had increased in value from $20,000 in 1900 "until it was approximately $130,000.00. This was the beginning of 1907. Then the panic of that year came and my profits were totally wiped out in a few months. Fortunately I had not taken anything out of this account so I ended up with about $300.00 profit for all my effort and trouble. Never again did I attempt to beat the stock market."[48]

Western Block was not so lucky. By the end of Kenan's first year with the company, it had "no business at all," and he came close to driving it completely under. He committed the company to enlarging its plant—the only decision, he recalled, over which he and Shaw ever "had any differences regarding [their] agreement. . . . I made some sketches of a building to fill in the vacant space along Market Street. I consulted Mr. Shaw and he approved, in a measure. I then made the plans and asked for bids on the steel." The bids were so low that Kenan decided "to complete the whole job, which was composed of five parts. We constructed each separately and had the steel distributed in the driveway and along the street between curb and sidewalk for nearly three years. We erected the steel and placed the concrete floors and roofs with our own employes,—only contracting for the brick work."[49]

THE SHADOWS LENGTHEN

Lockport's business community was now watching every move that Mr. Flagler's brother-in-law made. Kenan had originally moved there, after all, to work with Eugene Ashley, another Flagler man who had better connections, it seemed, than business sense. Ashley had married Flagler's Lockport niece and had handled Flagler's divorce. He had used Flagler money to invest in the Traders Paper Company, and he had recently led the Lockport firm into the United Box Board & Paper Company debacle—a financial nightmare that had wiped out the investments of many Lockportians not only in the Traders Paper Company but also in Ashley's huge Lockport real estate firm, the Holland Patent Realty Company. Was Western Block about to meet the same fate under Kenan? Was this southern parvenu overextending himself too?

Kenan says nothing in his autobiographies about the years between 1908 and Flagler's death in 1913. He moves from his first year at Western Block into a chapter recalling his activities as a trustee of the "H. M. Flagler Trust." This gap in Kenan's writing reflects the frustration and uneasiness he experienced during the last several years of Henry Flagler's life. The attacks on Standard Oil caused him considerable personal embarrassment, and the growth and expansion of Union Carbide made him particularly uncomfortable, for the company's success reinforced his misgivings about leaving the firm.

More to the point, if the treasurer of Western Block had stuck it out at Union Carbide, he would have been enjoying everything he now hoped for: personal wealth, work and recognition as a scientist, and the acknowledgment that he was more than Henry Flagler's brother-in-law. As Kenan recalled in his chapter titled "Opportunities in which 'I Missed the Boat,'" "I invested $50,000.00 in the Traders Paper Company which, had it been used to purchase Carbide stock, at the end of the first ten years, would have been worth $1,250,000.00." What Kenan failed to mention, of course, was that the man who bought and gave him this Traders stock, Henry Flagler, also persuaded him not to purchase Carbide stock.[50]

These were profitable years indeed for Union Carbide, which benefited greatly from the development of a safe and dependable acetylene generator. As homes and businesses bought the new apparatus, the "backwoods of America began to gleam with acetylene lamps, shiny contraptions, all knobs and valves throwing a fierce, white, immobile" light some twelve and a half times brighter than its nearest rival, coal gas. "Small towns began installing central-lighting generators, and at the peak in 1909 there were 235 U.S. towns glowing nightly with acetylene light." Acetylene likewise became an important source of lighting not only for railroad cars and automobiles but also for miners' lamps, providing a big advance in mine safety and lighting as well as a big advance in Carbide's profits. And on top of this, Carbide "took a hand in transplanting from France a new oxygen-acetylene technique for welding and cutting metals, a basic business that began to grow" and paved the way for revolutionary changes in the automobile industry.[51]

To help perfect this business Union Carbide purchased Niagara Research Laboratories and used it to turn the Niagara Falls carbide plant, now known as Electromet, into a research and development firm. One of Electromet's first major purchases, the Susquehanna Smelting Company of Lockport, led to business discussions between Kenan and Edgar F. Price, the North Carolina carbide boy whom Union Carbide had selected over Kenan in 1899 as the first manager of its new plant at Niagara Falls.

As part of the Lockport deal Price hired Susquehanna's Herbert Harrison as superintendent of the Electromet plant at Niagara Falls. But Harrison soon quit Electromet and returned to Lockport, where he started the Harrison Radiator Company. The radiator company "needed more capital," Kenan recalled, so Harrison "contacted Mr. Price, who came here and looked over the operation and stated he would furnish half of the necessary capital if I would furnish the other, about $200,000.00 total was necessary." Once again, though, Kenan missed the boat, just as he had with the Wilmington paper mill and the Carbide stock. He decided not to invest in the radiator company, and Harrison turned instead to W. W. Campbell, "a local attorney and friend of mine to organize a syndicate and raise the necessary capital. . . . The operation was most successful and after a few years they sold out to General Motors at a very handsome profit." Indeed, the radiator plant soon became, as it remains today, Lockport's major industry and largest employer.[52]

Kenan placed most of the blame for the radiator decision on what he perceived as Price's attitude toward him. "I was not looking for any investment and it looked to me that Edgar Price was planning to have me look after his investment as well as mine and he would not be required to give it any attention." In other words, Price seemed to be saying that he had more important things to do as vice-president of Union Carbide than Kenan did either as the treasurer of Western Block or as Mr. Flagler's "money-bags" brother-in-law. The slight, whether perceived or real, Kenan believed was confirmed by his own and Price's decision: "I did not invest and neither did he."[53]

Although Kenan gives the impression that he could have split the investment with Price if he had wanted to, the truth was otherwise. His major source of capital, Henry Flagler, had closed his pockets to everyone and everything except the Key West Extension, which was now putting "tremendous pressures" on his financial resources. Also, the delay caused by the government's peonage case against the FEC, a case dropped in 1908, had pushed the extension project beyond its targeted completion date. In January 1909 Flagler's chief engineer, Joseph C. Meredith, estimated that it would take at least $5 million and another year to reach Key West. What was more, Meredith died suddenly in April 1909, and in June, Flagler, who then owned all of the FEC's stocks and bonds, was forced to reorganize his railroad affairs and refinance the extension by offering a $10-million bond issue through J. P. Morgan and Company.[54]

October brought yet another hurricane to Florida and more damage to the extension. "It was most disastrous in its effects," Flagler wrote shortly thereafter, "costing more than a million of dollars to repair the damage[,] . . . but what is still more serious, was the lesson it taught: that we must abandon the character of the work we were doing, substituting more permanent work." According to Flagler's new engineer this new work would be very expensive. "His estimate of the cost of completing the work to Key West (including the loss by damage) is nine million dollars," Flagler continued, "and this does not include terminal expenses at Key West, which amount to upward of a million dollars."[55]

One month later the federal court in St. Louis ordered Standard Oil to dissolve itself. Although the company appealed the decision to the United States Supreme Court, Flagler believed the "Governmental raid upon the Standard Oil Co." would make it impossible for him to complete the Key West project "out of my income."[56] Yet the beleaguered builder tried to reassure his family that everything would be all right. "I hope you are not worrying over the St. Louis decision Saturday last," he wrote to William's wife at the end of November.[57]

Flagler was mad as hell, however, and decided to strike back by having his brother-in-law use the FEC Railway to challenge the new federal corporation tax. Although Kenan was a director of the FEC, only Flagler held stock in the company, and according to Julien T. Davies, whom Flagler asked about the matter, it was "very important" that a "bona fide stockholder" initiate a letter of complaint against the new tax. Thus, Flagler explained to Kenan, "I have had a certificate made out in your name for five shares. . . . When it reaches you, you may send me your check for $500., which I will keep in my possession and explain to you when you come South."[58]

Will sent the check shortly before he and Alice arrived in St. Augustine for Christmas. But within days of their arrival Flagler decided to drop the matter. As he explained to Davies, "Mrs. Flagler has so much fear that if I carry out the program you suggested regarding the Corporation Tax, that it will not only

Henry Flagler and Alice Pomroy Kenan at Daytona Beach, Florida, ca. 1910.
(HMFM Archives)

react upon me, but upon the Standard Oil Co., and she urges me not to do it; so suppose we let the matter hang up awhile?" Flagler also had been warned by former U.S. attorney general Wayne MacVeagh that the new Taft administration strongly supported the corporation tax. MacVeagh's "explanation was this," Flagler wrote to Standard Oil president John D. Archbold, "that the tax, being a scheme of the President's, he believed it would be upheld. He also stated most positively that he believed that the St. Louis decision would be supported by the Supreme Court."[59]

Will Kenan must have rejoiced at Flagler's decision not to challenge the corporation tax. Already embarrassed by the government's attacks on Standard Oil and the FEC Railway, the treasurer of the struggling Western Block Company hated the thought of having his name dragged into the federal courts in association with Flagler, whom John D. Rockefeller had described in testimony as the brains behind the Standard Oil Trust. Indeed, Kenan now began seeing Henry Flagler as little as politely possible, both in public and in private. He had to be prodded by Flagler "not [to] fail to be present" at the FEC's board meetings, and when he and Alice visited the Flaglers in Florida or New York, he left as soon as he could and returned to Lockport, citing his duties at Western Block.[60]

Kenan was not the only one responsible for this growing estrangement; Flagler contributed to it as well. He was concerned with little else but the Key West Extension, and he did not need Kenan for that. He already had gotten what he wanted from William: energy, enthusiasm, and technical expertise. What he now needed were doctors, lawyers, and engineers—men who could help him fulfill his Key West obsession. So intense was his desire to see the project through that his St. Augustine pastor believed Flagler might lose his will to live once the extension was completed. "I wanted him to see his undertaking completed," George Ward explained, "but I dreaded the withdrawal of this spur to living." Flagler wanted the extension to be a monument to himself and a reminder to his detractors, including John D. Rockefeller, that they had been wrong in regarding "my work in Florida . . . as a first-class 'folly.' "[61]

Flagler also began paying less attention to William than to William's cousins, especially Dr. Owen Kenan, who provided him with medical attention William could not give. Flagler was almost completely deaf and blind by the time of his eightieth birthday on January 2, 1910, and suffering from rheumatism and severe intestinal problems—maladies made less severe by Owen's ministrations.[62] Flagler also showed an unprecedented interest in the lives of Owen's brothers. Graham, a Wilmington lawyer, had started dating Will's sister Sarah and frequently joined her and the Flaglers in Florida. The Flaglers also invited Owen's Atlanta brother, Thomas Kenan, to visit them at Mamaroneck with his new bride, Annice Hawkins. And Flagler liked what he saw. "You will be glad to know that we were all very much pleased with Tom Kenan's wife," he wrote to a close friend, "—very much pleased; her father is President of a Bank in Atlanta. She is well educated, having studied two or three years in Paris, and is natural as clover."[63]

KEYS TO THE FUTURE

By the time the Supreme Court ordered the dissolution of Standard Oil in May 1911, the empire of the "Old House" was vast indeed.

> The company transported more than four-fifths of all oil produced in Pennsylvania, Ohio, and Indiana. It refined more than three-fourths of all United States crude oil; it owned more than half of all tank cars; it marketed more than four-fifths of all domestic kerosene and was responsible for more than four-fifths of all kerosene exported; it sold to the railroads more than nine-tenths of their lubricating oils. It also sold a vast array of by-products—including 300 million candles of seven hundred different types. It even deployed its own navy—seventy-eight steamers and nineteen sailing vessels.[64]

Two months later the company announced its plans to divide its holdings into several separate entities. The holding company, Standard Oil of New

Jersey (later Exxon), retained almost half of its former total net value and never lost its lead to the other new companies: the Standard Oil(s) of New York (Mobil), California (Chevron), and Ohio (Sohio, BP) as well as the Continental (Conoco) and Atlantic (ARCO, Sun) oil companies. "But if the dragon had been dismembered," one oil authority recently wrote, "its parts would soon be worth more than the whole. Within a year of the dissolution of Standard Oil, the value of the shares of the successor companies had mostly doubled; in the case of Indiana, they tripled."[65]

Henry Flagler had more than 2,500 men working on the Key West Extension when the Supreme Court ordered Standard Oil to dissolve itself. He also had exactly one year left in which to complete the railroad—a deadline set by the state and one that his engineers felt confident, in the absence of hurricanes (both natural and political), they could meet. They hoped in fact to have Flagler riding the rails into Key West by his birthday the following January.[66]

The Standard Oil decision coincided with a different sort of deadline for Will's seventy-three-year-old uncle, Colonel Thomas Kenan. In May 1911 the Colonel notified UNC president Francis Preston Venable that he was too ill to undertake his annual commencement duties as a university trustee and president of the Alumni Association. He had not been feeling well since his return from Richmond, Virginia, where he had helped select the contractors for the long-talked-of "Battle Abbey" Confederate Museum. The Colonel had secured a generous donation from Flagler for the museum, which was the largest of the many projects he had been promoting for the study and appreciation of North Carolina, southern, and Confederate history. In addition to being a founding member of the North Carolina Literary and Historical Society, the Colonel had promoted a Confederate memorial in Raleigh, and with the aid of Mary Lily, he had established the Kenan Fund at UNC for the acquisition of books and other printed materials related to the South, especially those that dealt with the Civil War and Reconstruction.[67]

Venable knew his old friend had not been feeling well, but he never anticipated that the Colonel would miss commencement. "I cannot tell you how much we will miss you," Venable wrote to the Colonel. "It is a real disappointment and sorrow to me that you cannot be present at this time but I know that it would be unwise for you to undergo the strain. I scarcely know how to get along without you, having been accustomed all during these years to rely so much upon your helpful presence."[68]

The Colonel died at his home in Raleigh on December 23, 1911, just as Will and his family arrived in St. Augustine for their annual Christmas celebration. Everyone but Flagler attended the funeral in North Carolina; having been assured by his engineers that the extension would be completed by the end of January, the excited builder wanted to inspect the line and be available for any last minute decisions.[69] Just how many Kenans came back to Florida for the extension festivities is not clear. Mary Lily did, of course; she and Henry left Palm Beach on January 21, 1912, and arrived in Key West, 250 miles away, at 10:43 the next morning as passengers on the first New York to Key West train. Flagler told the cheering crowd, "Now I can die happy. My dream is fulfilled."[70]

William was not in Key West for the celebration. He had been "visiting" in Kenansville in early January when his other uncle, Captain James Kenan, died in the overseers' cottage at Lockland plantation in southern Duplin County. The funeral was held on January 11, 1912, at Liberty Hall, where " 'Old Aunt Martha' . . . had charge of the 'big house' while absent members of the sorrowing family had gathered there for the last sad rites. Her presence and attentions gave a pathos to the funeral service of the last of those of the family with which she had grown up and to which she was markedly devoted."[71] Will might have gone to Key West had it not started to snow after the funeral. He and his family stayed at Liberty Hall "for several days, because of the severe cold." The old house was now a sad and lonely place of family relics and funeral gatherings; though Mary Lily owned it and was paying for its upkeep, it was no longer the warm, exciting Eden of Kenan's childhood.[72]

Fun and children were little more than hopes and memories for William. He still followed the fortunes of UNC's athletic teams and occasionally watched a baseball game in New York City, but he had not picked up a bat or a ball since leaving the South. Nor had he gone hunting or fishing. And children? He would soon be forty years old, and he and Alice, who was now forty-seven, still remained childless. Although they may have wanted it that way, it seems much more likely that the couple tried to have children but could not, either because Alice was too old or because William's carbide and paper mill work had made him sterile. Whatever the case, it was hard for him to hear the news his cousin Tom now shared with the mourners at Liberty Hall: he and Annice were expecting a second child.[73]

Kenan returned to Lockport after the funeral and purchased a house at 433 Locust Street. Located on a site known as "The Hill" in Uppertown, the historic mansion was surrounded by 6¾ acres of land and cost Kenan "$18,500.00." He took possession of it in April, shortly before his fortieth birthday, and immediately began renovations. "Did not have any architect or contractor," he recalled, "simply employing several carpenters, two plumbers and helpers and several painters." He had the men convert some things, rip out others, and help him install a "vapor heating system," "gas piping," "brass pipe for water with brass fittings," and "an Audiffren Refrigerating machine."[74]

The work was still going on in December when William and Alice attended the wedding of his sister Sarah and their cousin Graham Kenan. Sarah was now thirty-six years old, about the same age as Will and Mary Lily had been on their wedding days, and she was six years older than her cousin-husband—an age difference similar to that separating Alice and Will. The newlyweds moved in with Mollie at the mansion Flagler had purchased almost ten years earlier.[75]

The family's celebratory mood did not last long, however. On January 15, 1913, Henry Flagler fell at Whitehall and broke his hip. His secretary, Warren Smith, recalled that "Dr. Owen H. Kenan was on the spot, in charge of WHITEHALL. Fortunately guesting at the [nearby Royal Poinciana] Hotel, was a Dr. Newton Shaffer, orthopedic surgeon from New York, who was consulted. Mr. Flagler was ordered to bed, with sandbag reinforcement. He even tried to get out of this. As the weather grew hotter, and hotels closed, Mr. Flagler was transferred to a Company beach cottage."[76] His condition continued to deteriorate, however, and by April he was not sure where he was. "He has always dreaded going," his friend Andrew Anderson wrote, "but now he does not know it for his mind wanders. Most of the time he thinks he is in a railroad car."[77]

In early May, Mary Lily telegraphed her stepson in New York to come to Florida. It was not an easy thing for her to do. Harry Flagler had refused to see his father for almost twenty years. He had never met Mary Lily, and he had never visited Whitehall. Though he did both on his arrival, his father never recognized him. Flagler was heavily sedated and practically comatose by the time Harry arrived, and Owen and Mary Lily refused to allow them a deathbed reunion. Henry Flagler died on May 20, 1913, leaving Mary Lily an estate worth more than $100 million.

CHAPTER 7

Mary Lily and Her Families

Mary Lily was protecting her husband when she kept his son from him. Harry's sudden reappearance, she feared, would have been symbolically tantamount to administering unrequested last rites to Henry. Fearing, moreover, that Dr. Andrew Anderson might try to arrange a father-son reunion behind her back, Mary Lily attempted to prevent the physician from even entering Flagler's room. "She wouldn't let him in," Anderson's daughter recalled, "but he went in." And so did Harry, but not in time. As Harry later recalled in a statement meant to impugn the Kenan family's motives, his father "was kept constantly under drugs and was practically in a coma the three of four days after my arrival until his death."[1]

Dr. Anderson's daughter was away at boarding school when "Uncle" Flagler died, but she remembered much of what her father allegedly told her. "I told you that Mr. Flagler went to bed early . . . because he was tired and [Mary Lily] had to go too. He gradually got rid of her friends, and she didn't have much to do, no entertainment. She was not heavily endowed with brains, so that was not a relief to her. . . . Anyway, it was very tough for her, and I suppose she drank. She'd start, drink a little bit, a little bit more. I was by myself for a while, and it's very easy to do."[2]

Mary Lily appeared to be using more than alcohol at the time of Flagler's death—at least that is what Anderson assumed from an incident at the Palm Beach railroad depot. According to his daughter, Anderson was waiting with Mary Lily for Flagler's funeral train when suddenly, without warning, the grieving widow collapsed on him. The doctor was shocked and suspicious. "After she'd been most unpleasant and disagreeable to Daddy, . . . when the funeral train came up, there she was in [widow's] weeds and things, she fell on Daddy's neck, which was a surprise." It was neither the heat nor the sadness nor the exhaustion that wilted Mary Lily. It was "Dope!"[3]

The grieving widow had nothing more to do with Harry and Dr. Anderson once the black-draped funeral train reached St. Augustine. She took refuge with her family at the Ponce de Leon Hotel, and Harry and Anderson hurried off to the doctor's mansion. Things did not improve in the days that followed, especially for Harry. Although he knew his father would be buried in the Flagler mausoleum at the St. Augustine Memorial Presbyterian Church, he did not know what Anderson now told him: the dead patriarch had also arranged to have "buried in said Mausoleum the body of Mary Lily Flagler."[4] The atmosphere was icy in the crowded St. Augustine church—at least that's what Anderson told his daughter. Harry and the doctor sat "on one side, and the Kenans all sat on the other. Had nothing to do with each other at that time," she recalled. "They didn't like each other."[5]

To the extent that there was antipathy between the families, it was primarily of Harry Flagler's making. An elitist snob who considered the Kenans a taint on the Flagler name, he was also upset by the contents of his father's will. The will made it impossible for him to gain immediate access to his inheritance and thus to the funds he had been hoping to use for his pet project, the New York Philharmonic Orchestra. The elder Flagler had created a trust that named Joseph R. Parrott, William Beardsley, and William Rand Kenan Jr. as trustees. The trust, Flagler wrote in his will,

> shall continue for five years from the time of my death and if at the end of such five years the condition of the Florida East Coast Railway Company and the Florida East Coast Hotel Company (they being my Florida railroad and properties referred to) or either of them should be as to require financial aid from sources outside of themselves or itself, then I direct that such Trust shall continue so long as either or both of such last named companies shall require assistance but not longer, however, than a period of five years from the termination of the above mentioned or first period of five years.[6]

Once the trust was terminated, Mary Lily was to inherit the bulk of Henry Flagler's estate, Harry was to receive 5,000 shares of Standard Oil (of New Jersey) stock, and his three daughters were to divide equally another 8,000 shares.

More than this delay and relatively low inheritance disturbed Harry, however. He was already a wealthy man through his marriage to Annie Lamont, the heiress of financier Charles Lamont, and he held mounds of valuable stocks and bonds his father had given him—securities that yielded him, according to Flagler's will, "an average of $75,000 per annum in income." What bothered Harry was his father's explanation for the low inheritance: "My son has not shown for me the filial regard that would make me inclined to do more for him now than is done by this item of my will."[7]

Harry also resented the fact that his father appointed William Kenan as the family trustee of the estate. Harry could hardly have missed his father's message: Kenan had been more of a son to Henry Flagler. Where Harry had deserted his father and refused "to learn the hotel and the railroad business and gradually succeed him in the work," Kenan had embraced Henry Flagler and aided his plans in Florida. In fact, according to Flagler's first biographer, Sidney Walter Martin, who interviewed both Harry and William in the 1940s, Kenan "was the son that Harry Flagler wasn't. William R. Kenan was, in a way, the man that Flagler wanted Harry to be. And I believe, I honestly believe, that if Harry Flagler had gone to Florida and worked with his father, Kenan wouldn't have been in the picture quite as much as he was."[8]

NEW PICTURES

Neither William nor his family and friends fit the picture that several journalist-authors have recently painted of them. According to one writer, Mary Lily's "own family now deserted her, perhaps because they could not control the way she spent her money or persuade her to enrich them."[9] Another portrays her as "seemingly without friends and ignored by relatives. Shunned, as often happens with widows, rich and poor, for no reason other than she was *awkward*, difficult to place at a dinner table or a party, difficult to talk with."[10] Still others posit a cruel and uncaring relationship between the widowed matriarch and her family. "Flagler's death left Mary Lily wealthy beyond belief," they write.

> But it also left her in the hands of her domineering brother, Will. . . . All the same, she wished that he and the rest of the family would pay more attention to her. Overnight, she had gone from party frocks to widow's weeds, and instead of offering sympathy and companionship, Will and her happily married sisters, Sarah and Jessie, seemed to look upon her as the Kenans' cash cow. They issued stern warnings against remarriage, saying that any prospective mate was likely to be an opportunist hungry for her inheritance and, by implication, theirs.[11]

All of these accusations are patently absurd. Mary Lily was a "powerhouse" who refused to be dominated by anyone, including her family, who would never have presumed to issue her "stern" anythings.[12] She did make William one of her closest and most trusted advisers, but not the only one; as their niece Louise Wise later said, "My aunt draws careful, trusted, high-principled advisers about her and follows their advice—when she thinks it's good."[13] And while the shy, retiring Sarah may have been happily married, her sister Jessie, divorced for almost eight years, never was. Neither did the family see Mary Lily as a moneybag bovine to be milked at their demand. The dead, departed bull had provided them with most of what they needed, and she had given them much more—willingly, lovingly, and at her own devise.

In truth, Mary Lily's family and friends never deserted her, they never took her for granted, and they never had any trouble finding a place for her. Rather, they became closer to her than ever before.

Almost immediately after Flagler's death Mary Lily moved in with her oldest and dearest friends, Pem and Sadie Jones and Henry Walters, who invited her to stay with them at their New York City townhouse until she decided where she wanted to live. She apparently spent the first part of the summer of 1913 with her family near Asheville, North Carolina, and then moved to Newport, Rhode Island, to stay with Pem, Sadie, and Walters at the Joneses' enormous mansion, "Sherwood." While she may have felt sad and lonely at the exclusive resort, she did not get bored at Sherwood. According to one of her Newport friends the mansion was one of the resort's liveliest. "No one in Newport could produce mint juleps to equal those Mrs. Pembroke Jones dispensed every morning before luncheon to a select little coterie of the younger set at 'Sherwood.' . . . It was the most hospitable home in Newport; its owners were ideal hosts, they entertained on a splendid scale; their balls were famous."[14]

After returning from Newport, Mrs. Flagler and Mrs. Jones visited one of their favorite places, White Sulphur Springs, West Virginia. Both women had spent some of the happiest days of their lives at the "Old White," and they were eager to see the changes made by its new owner, the Chesapeake and Ohio Railroad (C&O), especially the resort's fabulous new hotel, the Greenbrier. Indeed, Sadie and Mary Lily were among the first to sign the Greenbrier's guest register on opening day, October 1, 1913, for they were there to help Frederick Sterry, the hotel's managing director, lure New York's most prominent families to the refurbished resort. Sadie, a well-established hostess among New York's elite "400," fit well into Sterry's campaign, as did his old friend Mary Lily, the "world's wealthiest widow." Sterry had been the first manager of Henry Flagler's Palm Beach Inn (the Breakers) and had managed it and the Royal Poinciana for Flagler. Flagler had left him $10,000 in his will, the same amount Mary Lily later left him.[15]

Sterry was also "noted for his role in opening the Plaza Hotel in New York City in 1907, which he continued to direct in conjunction with The Greenbrier. . . . In fact, in the years following The Greenbrier's 1913 opening, both The Plaza and The Greenbrier advertised their plush accommodations and facilities in a single brochure." Sterry soon completed a suite of rooms for Mary Lily at the Plaza Hotel, where her cousin Owen had lived almost since their friend Alfred Gwynn Vanderbilt had had the hotel built.[16]

Mary Lily also met several members of her family at the Greenbrier that autumn. Jessie was there with her eighteen-year-old daughter Louise, whom she brought "to meet eligible bachelors." Louise eventually married one of White Sulphur's most handsome and eligible bachelors, Lawrence Lewis, whose father, Thornton Lewis, a C&O official, was also president of the White Sulphur Springs Company and resided with his family at "The Meadows," a beautiful estate adjacent to the resort.[17]

The federal government also helped bring William and Mary Lily closer together that fall. Congress changed the federal corporation tax in October and also used the power of the recently ratified Sixteenth, or income tax, Amendment to pass a federal income tax measure. Both taxes affected and further confounded the intertwined fortunes of Mary Lily, her family, the Flagler System, and the Flagler Trust. Flagler had made Mary Lily very wealthy outside of the $100,000 a year she received from his trust, which he created primarily to support his Florida hotels and the FEC Railway—the total net profit of which, since 1892, was less than $10,000. In other words, Mary Lily owned but would not inherit the assets underlying the trust (and supporting the properties) until it was terminated, which might be ten years and many millions of dollars away.

More important, despite the fact that she controlled all of the stock of the Florida railroad, hotel, and land companies and thus had to pay taxes on them, she had nothing to say about their management and operation. Flagler had given that responsibility to his closest business associates, Joseph R. Parrott and William Beardsley, both of whom were also trustees with William of the Flagler Trust. Put simply, Parrott and Beardsley had the voting power to control the dispersal of trust funds to the Flagler properties they directed.[18]

The two trustees were not on the best of terms with William and Mary Lily. Parrott had been Flagler's Florida attorney since the early 1890s; he had been president of the FEC Railway since 1909; and at the time of Flagler's death Parrott was, Kenan recalled, "head of all our corporations as well as directing our Law Department." Unfortunately he and Kenan were also long-standing antagonists. Parrott had never been comfortable with the power of Mr. Flagler's brother-in-law. In 1903, in the wake of the fire that destroyed the Breakers Hotel, he had blamed Kenan for the water-pump problems that allegedly hampered the fire-fighting efforts—an accusation, Kenan recalled, that "provoked me considerably" and that he later proved to Parrott to be unfounded.[19]

Parrott created no real problems for William and Mary Lily, however, for he became ill shortly after Henry Flagler's death and returned to his home in Oxford, Maine. Beardsley thus had little choice but to cooperate with Mrs. Flagler and her brother, and this was not particularly difficult for him or them. His only transgression, it seems, had been to support a deathbed reconciliation between Henry and Harry Flagler—an understandable reaction given his long association with the Flagler family. Beardsley had been Henry Flagler's private secretary for almost thirty years. He had run Flagler's New York office for about that long, and for the past ten years he had handled the loans and securities Flagler had given Harry and the Kenans—a relationship that, for the Kenans at least, was both intimate and profitable.[20]

Parrott's death in October 1913 coincided with congressional approval of the federal income and corporation taxes and with Kenan's election as president and director of the Miami Electric Light & Power Company, the Miami Water Company, and the West Palm Beach Water Company—all of which he had worked on as an engineer. Kenan was also elected that fall as a director and a member of the executive committee of both the Record Company of St. Augustine (which owned the *St. Augustine Record*) and the P&O Steamship Company of Jacksonville (which ran cruise ships between Florida and the Caribbean). Although the utility companies became valuable properties, they were then little more than necessary appendages of the Flagler System. This was also true of the Record Company and of the P&O Steamship Company, which was jointly owned by the FEC Railway and the ACL and directed, for the most part, by Kenan's good friend Henry Walters.[21]

Kenan did not remain long on the periphery of power, however. In March 1914, while he and his family were wintering in St. Augustine, several top-level changes occurred within the Flagler System. Beardsley assumed Parrott's position as president of the FEC Railway, and Kenan was elected vice-president and director of all of the Flagler System's major properties: the FEC Railway, the FEC Hotel Company, the land companies, and the FEC Car Ferry Company (which carried freight and passenger railroad cars between Cuba and Florida). Kenan's next move, finding a replacement for Parrott as Flagler trustee and the system's general counsel, enabled him to exert some real authority over his dead brother-in-law's empire.[22]

In searching for a replacement, Kenan ignored Parrott's "two leading understudies," as "both of these men were very dictatorial and were difficult to get along with." He also ignored Beardsley's suggestion "that we should select a New York City lawyer of national reputation." Kenan "leaned to the most outstanding lawyer in the south and, preferably, a Floridian." (Which explains, perhaps, why he also ignored his cousin/brother-in-law, Graham Kenan, a young Wilmington lawyer.) William made "a survey" of the lawyers who fit his description and concluded that Judge William Alexander Blount of Pensacola, Florida, "was the man." Blount did not see it that way, however, and he turned Kenan down, stating that "he had a very fine practice, owned his home, and did not wish to move from Pensacola."[23]

Kenan may have sought out Blount on his own, but it seems much more likely that he heard about him from Henry Walters and that Walters also finally convinced Blount to take the job. Not only was Blount the Florida attorney for Walters's Louisville & Nashville Railroad, but Walters was Kenan's closest adviser after Henry Flagler's death. "Many things were in the development state," Kenan later recalled. "I was much concerned about our situation, especially in regard to our legal status. After much deliberation I decided to consult my good friend Mr. Henry Walters." And not long thereafter Blount, for whatever reasons and "after many interviews in Jacksonville," accepted Kenan's offer.[24]

Shortly after leaving Florida, William and Alice saw Mary Lily again, this

433 Locust Street, Lockport, New York, William and Alice's home on "The Hill" in Uppertown. (NgCHS)

time at their new home in Lockport. William undoubtedly gave his sister more information about 433 Locust Street than she wanted to know—its history, its cost, its ceiling measurements, the thickness of its walls, and the detailed minutiae of the renovations he made. He also took her out back to the old building he had converted into a barn for his milk cows. Though he knew nothing "whatever about a dairy cow," he had paid $100 to a local farmer for "Daisy," a grade Jersey cow, which the farmer considered "the best milker . . . [and] the best cow he possessed." Just in case "Daisy" went dry, moreover, Kenan had also purchased " 'Peg o' My Heart' 294352, an unbred heifer of St. Lambert breeding from the herd of H. M. Flagler, at St. Augustine, Florida, at a cost of $140."[25]

William probably also used the occasion to urge Mary Lily to make a large gift to the University of North Carolina. He had just made one himself while attending his twentieth reunion at Chapel Hill. He had donated his "Chemical Library consisting of more than 200 books. Also donated for the purchase of more books $8,981.16."[26] The atmosphere at the reunion had been gloomy and uncertain, however, as Francis Preston Venable had just resigned as the university's president. Venable had spent the past year in Europe trying to recover from a nervous breakdown, but the sabbatical had not been enough. "The nervous condition is easily brought on again and my medical adviser warns me against another breakdown," Venable wrote to the university's trustees from London. "I gave up my life work with much reluctance to undertake these less congenial duties. . . . I desire now to return to the work of my original choice."[27]

Mary Lily knew how much Venable meant to her brother and how impor-tant Chapel Hill and the university were to her family. She had earlier given $2,500 to the drive for $55,000 to the endowment of the Carnegie Library at UNC.[28] But she was now more interested in having William find her a new railroad car. She wanted to replace the masculine, memory-filled car that she and Henry Flagler had shared. William later recalled that "my sister (Mrs. Flagler) requested me to have constructed for her such a car as would be suitable for a lady's use." He conferred with the Pullman Company, and to-gether "we designed and they constructed an all steel car. . . . I enjoyed working out the many details and felt that we had produced a wonder job."[29]

Mary Lily was still using Flagler's private car when she left Lockport with William and Alice and joined the rest of the family in the mountains of western North Carolina. The Kenans had vacationed there since the 1880s, "either at Hendersonville, Asheville and later, Blowing Rock," and for the past six or seven years Mollie, Sarah, Jessie, and Louise had spent part of their summers either at Waynesville, Asheville, or Hot Springs, North Carolina. Yet more than tradition brought the family to the mountains during the summer of 1914. No one enjoyed the mountain climate more than their ailing mother, Mollie, who "got great enjoyment in driving about the country in a one-horse surrey with a coachman." The Kenans were also giving a special send-off that summer to Jessie's daughter, Louise Wise, who, thanks to her aunt Mary Lily's generosity, was preparing to leave for Miss Payen's fashionable school in Paris.[30]

The Kenans retained one of North Carolina's most prominent physicians, Dr. Samuel Westray Battle of Asheville, to monitor Mollie's health while she was away from Wilmington. Battle was the medical director of the Clarence Barker Memorial Hospital in nearby Biltmore and a close personal and profes-sional friend of the Kenans' private physician and neighbor in Wilmington, Dr. Edward Jenner Wood.[31] Dr. Battle's visits soon meant as much to Mary Lily as they did to her invalid mother, for the wealthy widow began taking long walks and buggy rides with Battle into the countryside. The Kenans would not have objected. Though not a wealthy man himself, Battle moved easily among the rich and powerful. He had been George and Edith Vanderbilt's physician at Biltmore since the late 1890s, and he had even delivered their daughter, Cor-nelia, at the magnificent Asheville estate. The sixty-one-year-old widower was also a handsome, humorous man whose "large and commanding presence, distinguished air and polished manner" was leavened by a winsome waxed moustache and a limp left wrist he had injured while serving as a navy physi-cian. All in all, he was a delightful, nonthreatening companion for Mary Lily and clearly not one of those fortune seekers that her family was allegedly so worried about.[32]

Exactly when Battle and Mary Lily began appearing together in public is not known. Perhaps it was that fall at White Sulphur Springs, or the following spring at Palm Beach when, as a guest at one of her own hotels, Mary Lily felt compelled to deny a report that she and Battle were engaged to be married. "If I were not still in deep mourning and not going around at all," she told the *New York Times*, "a statement like this perhaps wouldn't upset me so." She also said that "so long as she lived she would never thin[k] of selling or renting Whitehall, the Flagler Palm Beach estate, which several people have been reported to have made offers for." Her remarks did little to end the speculation regarding her romance with Battle, however, and rumors of their plans to be married continued to spread.[33]

BETWEEN BATTLES AND BINGHAMS

Though the United States did not declare war on Germany and its allies until the spring of 1917, from the opening of hostilities in August 1914 the events of World War I affected the lives of the Kenan family and their friends. One of the first to feel its impact was Mary Lily's nineteen-year-old niece, Louise Wise, who arrived in Paris just as the war broke out. By early September, as the Germans threatened to capture the French capital, she and her classmates at Miss Payen's school were busy making "things for the soldiers."[34]

Louise's situation worried Will's family, especially Jessie and Mary Lily, and in the spring of 1915, as Mary Lily contended with the rumors of her relationship with Battle, she and Jessie asked their cousin Owen to go to Paris and get Louise. Owen was the only unmarried adult male in the Kenan family, and he would soon complete his seasonal duties as house physician for the Palm Beach hotels. He was also as devoted to Mary Lily as she "was devoted to him. She spoiled him rotten," one family member recalled. "He had anything he wanted." He also had planned to return to Paris, it seems, to close up his house at 44 Rue de Bac, which "he had furnished with a beautiful collection of paintings and antiquities."[35]

Will and Mary Lily were already in New York with the rest of the family by the time Owen arrived at the Plaza Hotel. Their mother's heart condition had become critical in early April, and the family had taken her to New York to put "her under the care of a specialist." Though she was "improving very satisfactorily" by the end of April, the emergency interrupted William's efforts to sell his pulp mill property in Wilmington and forced him and his brother-in-law Graham Kenan to miss the inauguration of UNC's new president, Edward Kidder Graham. Both men had looked forward to attending the Chapel Hill ceremonies. The new president had been a freshman at the university during William's senior year, and the North Carolina legislature had just appointed Graham Kenan as a university trustee. "I want you to know that I was greatly disappointed because I was unable to be present for your inauguration," Graham Kenan wrote to Edward Graham. "I had kinder 'set my heart' on running up."[36]

Dr. Owen Hill Kenan. (HMFM Archives)

Most of the Kenans accompanied Owen to the docks in New York harbor early on the morning of May 1, 1915, for they were all familiar with the German embassy's repeated warnings to American tourists not to sail on enemy vessels. Indeed, on the very morning that Owen boarded the fastest and most luxurious British liner, the *Lusitania*, the *New York Tribune* published a notice from the German embassy warning Americans not to travel on British vessels. But if Owen saw the notice, he paid no attention to it, and neither, apparently, did his friend Alfred Gwynn Vanderbilt, who was sailing to England to check on his stable of prized thoroughbreds. Although news of the warning quickly spread through the 2,000 or so passengers and crewmen on the Cunard liner, it was soon forgotten in the days of uneventful cruising that followed. Uneventful, that is, until the afternoon of May 7, when the *Lusitania* was struck by torpedoes from a German U-boat and sank in less than twenty minutes.[37]

Owen Kenan spent his last few minutes on the sinking ship next to Alfred Vanderbilt and Vanderbilt's valet. The "valet put a life preserver over [Owen] and one over himself," Owen's great-nephew recalled. "Mr. Vanderbilt refused to put a life preserver on. He didn't think the ship was going to sink or something." Then, just as the *Lusitania* went down, Vanderbilt's servant "grabbed" Owen and together "they jumped overboard." The ship's whirlpool sucked them under and Owen "took one last breath knowing that that was the end. He breathed oxygen so he thought he had died and was in Heaven or someplace. But it was an enormous air bubble from one of the public rooms of the ship. It happened to have come up under him and buoyed him up. He had the life preserver on so he lost consciousness because of the force, but he landed with his head up. He came to a hospital. . . . [His] watch stopped at exactly 2:23 p.m. when he jumped overboard."[38] Vanderbilt was not as lucky as his servant and friend. He died along with 1,200 others in the deep waters off the coast of Ireland. Although Owen and Louise soon returned to the United States, the lucky doctor remained quite ill for several months with a severe case of tonsillitis.[39]

After dealing with the war, the worry, Dr. Battle, and her mother's bad heart, Mary Lily decided to prepare for the future. She brought most of her family to Asheville in mid-July and spent the next ten or twelve weeks with them at the Grove Park Inn, where she also began preparing her will.[40] The *Asheville Citizen* kept a constant watch on the "world's wealthiest widow," especially her appearances with Battle, which were reported in the newspaper's social column every few days between July 27 and August 17 (including their appearance together at his birthday party). Parties, teas, dinners, and dances indicated that the widow Flagler's black-clad days of public mourning were finally over.[41]

Mary Lily and her family also saw several members of the Bingham family that summer. The first to contact her were Major Robert Bingham, now called Colonel Bingham, and his daughters, Sadie Grinnan and Mary McKee, both of whom lived with their father and husbands at the Bingham Military Academy in Asheville. "She & my daughters were School mates at Peace College," the Colonel later explained, "& her foster-father, Col. Thos. S. Kenan & I were class mates at College & very close friends as long he lived. My daughters called & so did I, renewing the old friendship—& she spent a day here in the old, country way of 'spending the day' with friends. Her mother was not seeing visitors; but I begged to see her for old, Chapel Hill-time sake & we had a good, old time talk. My son & she [Mary Lily] had 'sweet hearted' a little years before, but had not met for 25 or 30 years."[42]

Only later that summer did Mary Lily receive a visit from her old beau Rob, as she called him, who was now Judge Robert Worth Bingham of Louisville. The Judge had lost his wife in a terrible car-train collision in April 1913, just a month before Henry Flagler died, and his three children, Robert, Henrietta, and Barry, had spent most of their holidays and summers in Asheville since that time. Indeed, Mary Lily probably saw the Judge's eldest son, the hell-raising, hard-drinking Robert, before she saw the Judge. Robert attended at least two parties in August where Louise Wise was also a guest, and he was also among the forty guests Louise invited to the party Mary Lily gave for her at the Grove Park Inn.[43]

The Judge arrived in Asheville in early September but left almost immediately for Virginia, where he enrolled his daughter as a first-year student at Stuart Hall and his son Robert as a freshman at the University of Virginia. Not until mid-September, it seems, after Mary Lily's family returned to Wilmington in her new "lady's car," did the Judge return to Asheville. He then paid a brief visit to Mary Lily and Louise at the Grove Park Inn—and only then, his father recalled, because "Mrs. Grinnan insisted on his going with us to call on her—& could hardly get him to go, lest he should be accused of fortune hunting."[44]

Indeed, if any of the Binghams showed an interest in the fortune Mary Lily was having written into her will, it was the Judge's father. "It has occurred to *me*," he wrote to UNC's president in early October, "(and it may have occurred to you & to others) that Mrs. Flagler, properly approached may be induced to do something for the University. She is the richest woman in the South. . . . Without saying a word to anybody but my son, I approached her on the subject & he rather opposed it on the ground that a rich woman is beset with beggars of all sorts and conditions, both of men & women." The Colonel claimed "absolutely no selfish motives" in approaching Mary Lily; he simply wanted her to do something for UNC. "Her attitude was favorable," he wrote. "She said she had been thinking of it. She did not favor a Flagler Foundation, but was not unfavorable to a Kenan Foundation."[45]

Of course Mary Lily was thinking of doing something for the university. Her ancestors had supported it since the late eighteenth century, and the list of Kenans among its recent students, trustees, and benefactors included herself, her brother, their father, their uncles, and most recently, their cousin/brother-in-law, Graham Kenan. And of course she "did not favor a Flagler Foundation." She not only wanted to honor the intertwined histories of her family and the university, but she also wanted to avoid the situation that had arisen a few years earlier when Flagler's old Standard Oil partner, John D. Rockefeller, withdrew his offer to contribute a new student union to UNC after hearing that several of the university's trustees, Josephus Daniels included, considered the Standard money "tainted."[46] The evidence suggests, in fact, that Mary Lily's will was already drafted by the time she saw the Binghams and that UNC was mentioned in it. What she had yet to do, however, was renew her romance with Rob Bingham. As his father wrote shortly after she and Louise left Asheville, "She is said to be about to marry Dr. Westr[a]y Battle."[47]

Mary Lily may have left Asheville with that intention, but she devoted the next several months to enhancing the marriage prospects of her twenty-one-year-old niece. Beginning in early October she and Louise spent several weeks at the Greenbrier Hotel in West Virginia and then returned to New York, where the rest of the family joined them for Louise's introduction to New York society. Mary Lily had willed most of her personal real estate to Louise, and she wanted her niece to meet some of the wealthiest and most eligible bachelors in the country. She also wanted to see Dr. Owen Kenan, who was returning to the war. The forty-two-year-old physician had taken a leave from his annual Palm Beach doctoring in order to join other men of social position in the American Ambulance Corps in France.[48]

William and his family broke with tradition that Christmas and gathered in Wilmington instead of St. Augustine. It was a season of mixed emotions for the family, especially Mary Lily. Her mother's declining health still worried her, as did Owen's planned departure for Europe, but the recent attentions of Battle, Bingham, and Louise helped lighten her spirits. She also enjoyed having her family around her. William and Alice were there, as was their Atlanta cousin, Thomas Kenan, who had his two young sons, James and Frank, with him. James later recalled that he and Frank regularly walked the "block or two" between their grandmother Annie's house and the house at 202 South Third Street "to see Mary Lily. And she was a very sweet person. At that time, it was the First World War, . . . and it was the national hymn of the French, very rousing, and when we would come in she'd always play that, and we'd rush all around the house. . . . The Marseillaise—quite really, it almost picks you up like Dixie! And she was nice to us; never got on us or anything. She was just a nice, lively person."[49]

Unfortunately, though, she also appears to have been battling a drinking problem. Although she was definitely an alcoholic at the time of her death, dating the onset of her dependency is difficult. Most recent authors have followed the line that she started drinking while waiting in the wings for Flagler's divorce; increased her intake during the final years of their marriage; drank more after his death, when her family and friends allegedly deserted her; and suffered full blown alcoholism by the time she married Bingham.

With the certain exception of the "family desertion" story, some of this scenario is undoubtedly true. Yet there is no way of knowing exactly when and why Mary Lily developed a dependency on alcohol. There is no indication, for example, of a genetic predisposition for alcoholism within the family, yet neither is there a history of abstinence. The Kenans had long made and drunk wine and whiskey at Liberty Hall, where Will, his sisters, and their cousins had all enjoyed siphoning off samples from the casks in the cellar. Buck and Mollie had never discouraged the consumption of alcohol at their Nun Street home, but they and everyone else in the family mourned the fact that Jessie married and divorced an alcoholic—a feeling that Mary Lily shared and could not forget. Indeed, the evidence suggests that when Mary Lily binged, she did so for only a day or two at the time and then tried to conceal her problem by hiding in her room.[50]

A series of sad events exacerbated whatever alcohol dependency Mary Lily had developed. The first occurred in early 1916, when her nearest and dearest relative, her Aunt Sallie Kenan, swallowed "a tiny piece of quail bone that lodged in the oceaphagus under her breastbone." Mary Lily "rushed to Raleigh," picked up her aunt, and took her to Johns Hopkins in Baltimore. She then went on to Palm Beach to reopen Whitehall after Sallie's condition appeared to improve. It was the first time she had opened the mansion since Henry Flagler's death.[51]

Mary Lily arrived at Palm Beach in her private railroad car with Henry's Lockport cousin Horace Flagler and with her close friend Janet Mitchell, the one person who had spent more time with the Flaglers at Whitehall than anyone else. The *Palm Beach Life* welcomed Mary Lily with open arms:

Although the past week's social calendar was replete with many notable events and hundreds of arrivals were chronicled at both hotels, quite the most important of the week's happenings was the opening of Whitehall and the arrival of Mrs. Henry M. Flagler.

The great sho[w] place of Palm Beach has been closed for nearly three years since the death of Mr. Flagler, and it is a genuine pleasure for her many friends to have Mrs. Flagler back in her accustomed place among them, not that it matters whether Mrs. Flagler be in her palatial mansion or in the most modest abode, for she is always the same and the many persons who are privileged to really know her well appreciate the sterling worth of this modest, unassuming little woman, so small of stature but so big of heart. However, it is a pleasure for everyone to see the big iron gates of Whitehall swung open once more, for we now feel that Mrs. Flagler is really here to stay.[52]

But she was not. Almost immediately after she arrived, Mary Lily got word that her aunt had died.[53]

If there was a point at which Mary Lily began bingeing on alcohol, it was within the context of Sallie's death and the flood of memories that attended the reopening of Whitehall and the closing of her aunt's house in Raleigh. Although Mollie was too weak to make the journey from Wilmington, where she remained at home with Sarah, Mary Lily was joined at the funeral by Will and Jessie, by their Kenan cousins, and by Dr. Samuel Westray Battle. She also sat next to "many of Mrs. Kenan's faithful servants [who] occupied seats near the casket."[54] It was a sad occasion for Mary Lily, and according to one family friend, she was "worn out" when she arrived at the Raleigh house Sallie had left to her. "She told the servants the day after the funeral, 'Don't let in a single person to see me today. I am going to sit by the fire all day in one of Aunt Sally's old wrappers, and I am not even going to wash my face.' "[55] Mary Lily never returned to Colonel Thomas and Aunt Sallie's house at Wilmington and Jones Streets, but she did take its most important occupant with her, their "kind, efficient and ever faithful" black servant, Mary Monk.[56]

Mary Lily got more bad news shortly after she returned to Whitehall. Her cousin Owen had been driving "on the crest of a hill" at Verdun when his ambulance took a direct hit from a German shell. "His automobile was struck and fell into a ditch, and Dr. Kenan himself lay for several hours with shells exploding all about him." Once again Owen was lucky; though the "dignified and fastidious" physician did not get a bath for three weeks, he did manage to escape serious injury. He also continued to transport and care for the wounded on the battlefield—a dangerous and uncertain pursuit that caused his family and Mary Lily endless worry.[57]

If these events were not enough to prompt Mary Lily to seek solace from a bottle, her mother's death on June 6 was. Mollie's funeral bore little resemblance to the spectacle that had attended Buck's death thirteen years earlier. There was no church funeral, no front-page headlines, no taps, no muskets, and no vast outpouring of sympathy from the local community. There was just a simple service at 202 South Third Street and a short notice tucked away on the inner pages of a local newspaper. "Mr. W. R. Kenan Jr., only son of the deceased, and family arrived yesterday morning from Lockport, New York."[58]

William says little in his autobiographies about his mother's death other than that "she lived to be 74 years old and died of a heart ailment which she suffered for several years." His only other reference to her death occurs within the context of his comments on his role in renovating the house that she and Sarah had received from Henry Flagler. "Her estate was left equally to her four children, but we all were of the opinion that Sarah should have the house and all contents, so this was done."[59]

William says even less about the momentous events that tied Mary Lily's fate with his own destiny and the Flagler fortune. He covers the entire period between 1913 and 1921 in a four-page chapter in the first edition of *Incidents* titled "H. M. Flagler Trust," almost half of which concerns his selection of

William A. Blount as legal counsel for the Flagler System. He says nothing about Mary Lily's marriage to Bingham and nothing about the scandal that surrounded her death. The chapter begins with Flagler's birth and death dates and ends with Kenan being treated for a "pain . . . just below my breast bone . . . as though a knife was struck in at that point and then twisted."[60]

By the time Mollie Kenan died, Mary Lily was experiencing chest pains of her own—physically, from a heart condition she may have inherited from her mother, and emotionally, from her renewed romance with Judge Bingham. Exactly when and where she and Bingham met is not clear. They may have met at the Plaza Hotel in New York City, but the press's constant scrutiny of Mary Lily makes this unlikely. More often than not, they probably rendezvoused at 5 East Sixty-first Street, where the Joneses and Henry Walters lived.[61] They definitely met in September 1916 at the Greenbrier Hotel, however, where Mary Lily suffered and recovered from an attack of myocarditis (a swelling of the heart muscle). They discussed their wedding plans with her family, and on September 23 Mary Lily signed her will.[62] She had been working on the document for at least a year, but the time had come to sign it. Her health was poor, she was planning to get married, and William was "much concerned" about the potential impact of the "Estate or Inheritance Tax," which Congress had revived two weeks earlier to prepare for war.[63]

Mary Lily named William and their sisters as her major beneficiaries, leaving them 40,250 shares of Standard Oil stock to "share and share alike"—stock that was then worth between $50 million and $60 million. She also earmarked $300,000 for her cousin Owen, $20,000 each for her cousins Emily and Tom, but nothing, directly, for her cousin/brother-in-law Graham. She made several smaller bequests of money and jewelry to family and friends and left the University of North Carolina $75,000 a year "for the purpose of paying the salaries of professors" and "in the interest of the youth of North Carolina, and also in memoriam of my father, Wm. R. Kenan, and my uncles, Thomas S. Kenan and James Graham Kenan, graduates of said University." She placed the rest of her estate in a twenty-one-year trust for the maintenance of the Flagler System's railroad and hotel properties and named her brother and William Blount as her trustees.[64]

The most frequently mentioned beneficiary was Mary Lily's "beloved niece," Louise Wise, who was to receive "all the real estate, wherever situated, which is now owned by me excluding from this devise any real estate the title to which is vested in the Trustees under the will of my late husband Henry M. Flagler." Louise was also to receive "Two Hundred Thousand ($200,000.00) Dollars annually" until she was forty years old, when she would then receive "the sum of Five Million ($5,000,000.00) Dollars."[65]

Louise got more good news that fall in the form of a marriage proposal from Lawrence Lewis, a handsome young man who shared her fondness for golfing and horseback riding. Lawrence was also the "black sheep" of his family and appeared to offer little more as a suitable mate than his good looks, saddle skills, and family pedigree.[66] Rather than attending college after his prep school days, Lawrence had returned to White Sulphur, where he was "riding in horse shows, going to social affairs . . . and had some sort of job either at the Hotel or with the C. & O."[67] He also had a wild streak that was not unlike the one that ran in Louise's alcoholic father. According to Louise and Lawrence's daughter, "Father was very full of himself. . . . Saturday night he would get roaring drunk and go down and shoot a goose, or one of the white swans [at the Greenbrier] and bring it back to his mother for Sunday lunch. And then his father would send him back to the coal mines for six weeks. He was just a hellion."[68]

LOVE AND HONOR

Most New York newspapers had a reporter on hand on November 5, 1916, when William Rand Kenan Jr. announced his sister's impending marriage to Judge Robert Worth Bingham. The stories they wrote mentioned Bingham's impressive credentials as a judge and as the Louisville mayor who "instituted a crusade against the saloons, took the Fire and Police Departments outside of politics and in general carried out reform work." But the stories focused on Mary Lily and her profession of love for Bingham.[69] "One of my friends said to me, 'Why, this is not a very brilliant match, is it?' 'Yes it is,' I replied to her. 'It is of the heart and what can be more brilliant than that?'" These matters of the heart, she explained, went back to the early 1890s. "You see, we had what you might call 'an affair' then, but our paths took us in opposite directions. In later years he married and three years ago Mrs. Bingham died. We met again when guests of a mutual friend at Asheville, North Carolina, about a year ago."[70]

If there is ample evidence of Mary Lily's affection for Bingham, almost nothing is known about how her family and friends viewed him at the time of the wedding. Certainly most of them hated him after her death, believing he had had something to do with it, and for the most part all who have recently written about these matters have had little good to say about him or the Kenans. They assume that the Judge sought out Mary Lily for her money, that he did so either on his own or in conjunction with the Louisville bankers to whom he allegedly owed huge sums of money, and that he was willing to do whatever it took, including murder, to get her money.[71]

As to what the Kenans and their kinfolk originally thought of Bingham, there is simply no evidence to support the claim that "despite their past family associations, the Kenans considered Bob, who had three children and considerable debt, an unsuitable mate, and they were not shy about showing it."[72] It is true that Bingham had three children, but to claim that this made him an unsuitable mate is to imply, once again, that Mary Lily's relatives were nothing but greedy will-watchers, people who hated the prospect of sharing their inheritance with Mary Lily's stepchildren.

There is not a shred of evidence that the Judge was being pursued by bankers to pay his debts. He was apparently doing quite well, in fact, as a member of one Louisville's best and most successful law firms.[73] As for the Kenans' alleged aggressiveness in voicing their displeasure with Bingham, this is simply not credible. Not only is there no evidence to support such a charge, but also, given the family personalities involved, it is hard to imagine these alleged money-hungry hopefuls, these relatives who had witnessed the public and private turmoil created by Mary Lily's relationship and marriage to Henry Flagler, challenging the presence of someone who obviously gave Mary Lily such pleasure. Surely there would have been no quicker way of losing the prospective inheritance that allegedly motivated their every movement.

Quite a different case can be made about the family's initial views of Judge Robert Worth Bingham. For one thing, he was a known quantity, a man who had old and very strong personal and family connections with the Kenans. More important, he was an old friend of William's. Indeed, it is impossible to understand the family's response to Bingham, both before and after Mary Lily's death, without taking this friendship into account. The two men had known each other since their prep school days; they had shared the same circle of friends, organizations, and athletic activities at UNC; and they had maintained these mutual friends and interests after leaving the school. Thus William not only trusted Bingham, but he was also happy to see his sister involved with someone who was giving her so much pleasure.[74]

Shortly before William announced his sister's wedding plans, Bingham requested a prenuptial agreement in which he renounced the half-interest in Mary Lily's estate to which he would be entitled under Kentucky law as her husband. He "insisted on a prenuptial contract to claim nothing from her estate if he should survive her," his father later noted, "& as she had no issue, under the law, he would have had some such a claim."[75] While no record survives of either the contract or the Kenans' feelings regarding it, Mary Lily reportedly said that "his act had been a very noble and voluntary act and she appreciated it."[76]

Mary Lily and the Judge were married at the Joneses' New York townhouse on Wednesday, November 15, 1916, a week before Thanksgiving. The event was neither lavish nor large; only fifteen or so family members and friends attended. Pem and Sadie and Henry Walters were there, as were William and Alice, Sarah and Graham, and Jessie and Louise, who served as Mary Lily's only bridesmaid. None of Bingham's children attended, however, and only Bingham's sister, Sadie Grinnan, and his best friend and best man, Dr. Hugh Young, represented the groom.[77]

From happiness to loneliness—this is the purported course of Mary Lily's life for the first two months after her marriage. Bingham's later detractors find little happiness in her life, choosing to speculate instead about the Judge's alleged lack of affection for Mary Lily and the supposed loneliness of her days in Louisville at the Seelbach Hotel. Poor Mary Lily; her "misery quickly became apparent," one recent observer notes. "She was a stranger in a new town, marooned in the small Seelbach suite, spending her days looking at suitable houses to rent. The Judge was away from Louisville for days at a time, seeking business with his newfound celebrity." Or, poor Mrs. Bingham: "The hotel was her daily prison, with her husband leaving in the morning and often not returning until late at night. Sometimes he would be gone for days." Or, poor Mary Lily Kenan Flagler Bingham: "Alone in a new city, with few intimates and her dreams of a warm family circle shattered, Mary Lily turned to her old friend—liquor."[78]

Almost all of these assertions are contradicted by the existing evidence, as are the claims that there "was no honeymoon" for the Binghams, that they "spent their honeymoon in the Flagler railroad car en route to Louisville that night," or that the Judge "doesn't even allow time for a honeymoon, leaving unaltered business appointments in Louisville, which a review of his correspondence shows could have been easily put off until December."[79] While reports of their honeymoon plans are admittedly confusing and inconclusive, the *New York Times* has the couple leaving for "their honeymoon in the South." The Wilmington, North Carolina, papers say the Binghams traveled to Canada and the Pacific coast, and the *Louisville Courier-Journal* says they planned to "spend [a] portion of their honeymoon here." But the first mention of the Binghams in Louisville does not occur until a week after their wedding, and there are no business appointments revealed in Bingham's correspondence.[80]

Whatever the Binghams did on their honeymoon, their return to Louisville was not attended by loneliness and boredom for Mary Lily. After spending her mornings house-hunting, she and the Judge kept busy during the afternoon and evening attending a series of well-publicized dinners, parties, and teas in their honor. Some were private, informal gatherings, such as the one given by Mary Lily's old friends from Wilmington, the Reverend and Mrs. Peyton Hoge; but most were lavish affairs thrown by Louisville's social elite: the Ballards (November 22 and 27), the Alexander Whittys (November 28), and the James Ross Todds (November 30).[81]

With the exception of the Hoges, however, Mary Lily was indeed "a stranger in a new town." This is a crucial and very important point, but not for the reason that Bingham's detractors make it: to impugn his character and to depict a lonely existence for Mary Lily. Put simply, Mary Lily remained a stranger in Louisville for the rest of her life. She had never visited the city, it seems, prior to November 1916 (in announcing her wedding plans, for example, the *Courier-Journal* noted, "Mrs. Flagler was Mary Kenan of Macon, Ga."), and she spent only a week or two in Louisville between the time of her marriage and her return from Louise's wedding in May 1917. As for her alleged unhappiness and loneliness in Louisville, that was not the impression she conveyed on November 28. She sent her family a telegram that day saying she was "the happiest woman in the world. I wouldn't trade places with any woman in the world."[82]

The Judge further reinforced her happiness on December 8, when he, his law partners, and their female stenographer met Mary Lily at the Seelbach Hotel to revalidate her will. Her signed statement was witnessed by the Judge's law partners and stenographer: "I, Mary Lily Bingham, wife of Robert W. Bingham of Louisville, Kentucky, being advised that my marriage to him may have revoked a last will and testament made by me on the 23rd day of September, A.D. 1916 do hereby republish, re-affirm and declare the aforesaid instrument as my present will and testament in like manner as if the said will and testament were now executed by me."[83] Bingham then honored whatever prenuptial agreement he had asked for. He signed the same paper and thereby gave "my assent to the re-publication, adoption and re-affirmation and re-declaration by my said wife of the said will." Thus in a single stroke Bingham, who was not mentioned in Mary Lily's will, gave up the half-interest in her estate to which he was then legally entitled.[84]

The happy couple then took the one o'clock train to New York City, where they stayed at the Plaza Hotel until a few days before Christmas. While their major purpose for returning to New York is not known, it was probably to attend a series of parties in their honor, to see yet another of Sarah Bernhardt's farewell stage appearances, and to give Mary Lily a chance to do her annual Christmas shopping in the city. For her long gift list now included the names of the Judge's three children: eighteen-year-old Robert, fourteen-year-old Henrietta, and ten-year-old Barry.[85]

The Judge's children arrived in Louisville the day after their father and stepmother returned to the Seelbach Hotel from New York. Mary Lily was excited when she invited them to her suite for what she hoped would be a happy surprise: stacks of beautiful, beribboned gifts. "To her shock, their reaction was sullen gloom—the children, resentful of their mother's replacement, set a tone of hostility which would last thereafter." Henrietta was allegedly so resentful of Mary Lily that the "moment she saw the presents, she threw them on the floor unopened and stalked out of the room."[86] Mary Lily was astounded. No one had ever treated her like this. But then again, she had never been in a situation like this. She had no children of her own, and suddenly she was forced to deal with three adolescent stepchildren who had lost their mother in a tragic accident and who found themselves in a situation in which their family relationships were being redefined and their profoundest emotions stirred.

Mary Lily was clearly angry and distraught when she and the Judge left Louisville separately in January 1917, he to take his children to school in Asheville and Virginia and she to take care of several matters in New York. "She railed against her stepchildren and said that they had been perfectly dreadful to her," Thomas S. Kenan III claims. "She said that she had never experienced such hate."[87] Unfortunately the experience also appears to have exacerbated her drinking and heart problems. As Bingham's former law partner W. W. Davies later explained, Mary Lily visited the Judge's longtime family physician, Dr. Michael Leo Ravitch, "before she went away from here to Palm Beach— along after Christmas. I think he attended her then because I remember she mentioned having been there when she had some sickness or indisposition of some sort."[88]

Why did she go to New York? Was she running from her problems? Seeking a place to drink in private? Possibly. She was undoubtedly exhausted from the social swirl of the past few months, and she had been rejected by her stepchildren at Christmas—her first Christmas without her mother and away from her own family. She was fast approaching her fiftieth birthday, she already had serious health problems, and if she had indeed appeared "young, radiant & full of life" at her wedding—a description provided by someone who was not there—it was impossible to ignore the fact that she had also outgrown the tender nickname "Pudgy" that Flagler had given her ten years earlier.[89]

Mary Lily did go to New York for business and personal reasons. For one thing, she was planning a surprise for the Judge; as W. W. Davies recalled, "She told me in the winter when she was here that she was setting aside property or securities for her husband Rob as she called him, that ought to give him an income of about $50,000.00 a year." At the same time, her cousin Owen had recently returned from France, where he had received the Croix de Guerre for his conduct at the front. The war-weary physician was in New York, but he would not be there for long, for he was preparing to resume his medical duties at the Flagler hotels in Palm Beach—a place that was also very much on Mary Lily's mind. She wanted to buy new clothes and accessories for her Florida debut as Mrs. Robert Worth Bingham.[90]

Mary Lily said nothing to the Judge about the securities she transferred to him in New York, some $696,000 in Standard Oil stocks, nor did she mention the gift when they returned to the city at the end of January, apparently for Louise's engagement announcement.[91] She waited until they arrived in Palm Beach, where they both received a warm welcome from the *Palm Beach Life*. "It was a joy to many friends of Mrs. Robert Worth Bingham, formerly Mrs. Henry M. Flagler, to see 'Whitehall' open once more and to know that Judge and Mrs. Bingham had arrived at Palm Beach for the season." While Louise would not be visiting them because of her wedding, the Binghams expected "Mr. and Mrs. Pembroke Jones, of New York, who will arrive in a day or two and who will be their guests at 'Whitehall' for several weeks. Though no plans have been laid for any large functions at 'Whitehall,' Judge and Mrs. Bingham will have a number of house guests from time to time and will entertain their large circle of friends informally."[92]

The Binghams spent a long and eventful season at Palm Beach—their first and last there. William and Alice came down from St. Augustine, as did Sarah and Graham Kenan, and in March Mary Lily added a codicil to her will providing $125,000 to the recently burned Flagler Hospital in St. Augustine—a codicil witnessed by her constant companion and physician, Dr. Owen Kenan. On Monday, April 2, moreover, President Woodrow Wilson summoned the Sixty-fifth Congress into special session and asked it to proclaim that a state of war existed between the United States and the Imperial German Government. Congress complied with the president's request, and on April 6 Wilson officially announced the entrance of the United States into the war.

The Judge was in Louisville when war was declared, securing temporary living quarters until repairs could be completed at "Lincliffe," the mansion he and Mary Lily had rented. As the *Louisville Courier-Journal* noted one week later, "Judge Robert W. Bingham and Mrs. Bingham, who have been spending the winter in the South, will return next week and will occupy 'Linden Hall' until they move to 'Lincliff[e],' their country home on the River road."[93] By then, however, the Judge had returned to Whitehall with his son Barry and his daughter, Henrietta; as the *Courier-Journal* had reported on April 7, upon his departure from Louisville, the Judge "left yesterday for Staunton, Va., where he will join his daughter, Miss Henrietta Bingham, and go to Asheville to meet his son, Barry Bingham, after which they will go to Palm Beach to join Mrs. Bingham for Easter."[94] Although Robert, the Judge's older son, may have wanted to join his family at Palm Beach, he appears not to have had any Easter holidays at the University of Virginia; and if Henrietta was unhappy with her stay at Whitehall, that was not the impression she gave to her classmates at Stuart Hall. The school's yearbook predicted that "Bing" would be "A Palm Beach Fan."[95]

By the time the Binghams returned to Louisville in late April, the town was alive with excitement, uncertainty, and talk of war. The wealthy couple had little time to talk and listen, however, and little time to relax. Not only did the Judge have to catch up on his legal work, but he was a candidate for county commissioner in the upcoming primaries. Mary Lily was equally busy settling into their temporary residence at Linden Hall, inspecting the final repairs at Lincliffe, selecting furniture and decorations to restore the huge mansion to its former splendor, and initiating the challenging task of organizing the move into their new home. There was also Louise's wedding to deal with. Mary Lily had to decide what to give her, what to wear, and what to do to help the family prepare for the occasion.

Given the circumstances in which she now found herself, it is not hard to imagine Mary Lily turning to liquor. She was still a stranger in a new town, her husband was preoccupied with his professional and political activities, and there was no love lost between her and her stepchildren. The war was also threatening again to disrupt her life and that of her loved ones. The Judge had been tentatively accepted into the Officers Reserve Corps, Owen had decided to volunteer for the nation's medical corps, and Lawrence, Louise's husband-to-be, was a prime candidate for the military.

The Binghams did not stay long in Louisville. They left again on April 28 to attend Louise's wedding in Wilmington. While Mary Lily undoubtedly wanted some time to visit with her family and help with the preparations, she and Bingham may also have wanted to be there in time to celebrate William's forty-fifth birthday on Monday, April 30.[96]

Lawrence and Louise were married on May 3 at her mother's new house "in the fashionable suburb of Carolina Heights," and with the exception of Dr. Owen Kenan, who sent a telegram apologizing for his absence, Mary Lily was once again in the company of her family and friends. The bride and groom received numerous telegrams and letters during the day (including one from Mary McKee, the Judge's sister in Asheville), and at five o'clock in the afternoon William performed the same function for Louise that he had performed for Mary Lily at her wedding the previous November: he "gave away" his niece. The ceremony was followed by "a reception held under a marquee on the lawn at the rear of the residence," and later "Mr. Lewis and his bride left on a private car without making their destination known."[97]

At this point, after returning to Louisville, the Judge became worried about Mary Lily's health. She was apparently not doing well when he left her during the third week of May 1917. Yet he was not gone for long, and he did not leave her alone. Her old friend from Wilmington, Hannah Bolles, arrived for a long visit, and Mrs. Peyton Hoge gave a luncheon in Mary Lily's honor during the last week of May. Mary Lily would not have objected to her husband's trip—at least not to the ostensible purpose for which he was making it: to say bon voyage to his best friend, Dr. Hugh Young, who was preparing to leave for the war. The two men had known each other since their college days at the University of Virginia, and Young had served as the Judge's best man the previous November, the last time he had seen Mary Lily.

Mary Lily did not know, though, that Bingham wanted to see Young for a more important reason, one that would not have made her happy. "Bob telegraphed me that he was in great trouble," Young later recalled, "and on his way to see me." The mysterious message came at an inconvenient time for Young, who was then only days from sailing to England with the commander in chief of the American Expeditionary Forces (AEF), General John J. Pershing. Not only was Young one of the most prominent surgeons on the staff of the Johns Hopkins Hospital in Baltimore, but he was also the world's leading expert in urology and a friend of President Woodrow Wilson's. His qualifications eventually earned him an appointment as head of the AEF's Division of Urology, a position that placed him in charge of devising a plan to control venereal disease among the AEF's troops in Europe.[98]

But Bob's "great trouble" was not venereal disease. "In May, 1917, Judge Robert Worth Bingham came to see me in great mental distress," Young later wrote, "because he said that he had discovered that his wife was intermittently a drunkard, who about once a month would become terribly inebriated for several days." Young listened closely to his friend's sad news. Was this the same Mary Lily he had seen in November?

> She was said to lock herself up and drink many bottles of gin until she was completely drunk, and remained in this condition for several days. As a result of this her health had rapidly declined, she was already in a very serious condition, and Judge Bingham implored me to see if medical aid could not be secured in curing her of this terrible habit.
>
> I accordingly made arrangements, which were to be carried out when and if she could be persuaded to come to Washington or Baltimore. In order that this might be consummated without suspicion, I personally arranged with Mr. Herbert Hoover, then Food Conservation Commissioner in Washington, to take Judge Bingham on his staff. The Judge was to move with his wife to Washington where it was hoped she could be persuaded to take a cure for her intermittent habit of drinking to inebriety.[99]

Bingham met briefly with Hoover before leaving Washington and then sent him a letter of application from Louisville.[100] But he soon left again to pick up his children from school and to attend a joint reunion of the Confederate and Federal Veterans in Washington, D.C.[101] Mary Lily and Hannah Bolles also appear to have left at the same time for a visit to New York, but all were back in Louisville on June 9, when the Binghams gave a lavish housewarming party at Lincliffe. There was dinner, dancing, card games, and a screening of perhaps the first film shown outdoors in Kentucky, a five-reel movie titled *Diplomacy*, which was shot, in part, in Palm Beach and around Whitehall.[102]

The party marked a turning point in Mary Lily's health and in the Judge's efforts to encourage her to seek treatment. Once again, it seems that a nasty confrontation between Mary Lily and her stepchildren set things off. While neither she nor they looked forward to spending the summer with one another, the Judge's children, especially Robert, looked forward to spending Mary Lily's money. They "were not so fond of her but wished to impose upon her in money matters," one observer later wrote. "She told Judge Bingham that she would not honor a sight draft of his grown son."[103]

More suggestive of the turmoil is the question put to W. W. Davies at the probate hearing for Mary Lily's will—a question that Davies never got to answer: "Mr. Davies, did you not know it to be a fact that what Mrs. Bingham termed the improper treatment of herself by Mr. Bingham's children and their lack of appreciation of what she had done for them had given her very great pain and the pain had gone to such an extent in the latter part of her life that she told Judge Bingham that his children could not come into her house?"[104] If she let them back into Lincliffe at all, it was not for long. Less than a week after the party, the Judge took his children to Asheville, where they remained until their stepmother's death.[105]

Mary Lily began seeing the Judge's longtime family physician, Dr. Michael Leo Ravitch, a Jewish dermatologist in Louisville. According to her cousin's grandson, Thomas S. Kenan III, she also began writing letters to her family in Wilmington. "They were remarkable because she was so sad and depressed," he is reported to have said in a recent interview. "Mary Lily used to write things like, 'I have been so very sad that Bob has said I should start going to a doctor. Now I go twice a week and he has been giving me a shot of something, a medication, and then I feel very good indeed until it wears off.'"[106] The medication she received was either morphine or its derivative, apomorphine, the most common form of treatment for alcoholics at the time. The drug worked as an emetic, causing nausea and vomiting in individuals who ingested alcohol while under the influence of the medication.[107]

Mary Lily turned fifty years old on June 14, and a day or two later, while the Judge was away in Asheville with his children, she asked his friend and former law partner W. W. Davies to draft a codicil to her will. Davies worked on several drafts of the codicil between June 15 and 19, and in addition to an initial conversation with her—"a very full one concerning the matter"—he held at least two more discussions with her while riding with her, her chauffeur, and her housekeeper "on the automobile drives which she would take very often in the middle of the day along about one or half past one or two o'clock."[108]

About noon or so on Tuesday, June 19, Mary Lily went to Dr. Ravitch's office with her chauffeur and housekeeper, and shortly after their arrival someone telephoned Davies to say that Mary Lily wanted to see him in Ravitch's office. No explanation was given, and Davies did not bring a draft of the codicil with him to the office. That is exactly why Mary Lily had summoned him, however; she wanted to sign the codicil. So he wrote it out on Ravitch's stationery from memory:

> I make this a codicil to my last will and it shall be a valid devise as such codicil and if at my death I have no will or have a will or wills made subsequently to this instrument it shall nevertheless be an independent devise to all times and under all circumstances of change, modification or revocation of my will or wills. I give and bequeath to my husband, R. W.

Bingham, five million ($5,000,000) Dollars to be absolutely his, and he shall have the option at my death of taking this from my estate in money or in such securities as he and the administering authorities of my estate may agree upon with respect to market values.[109]

Davies later testified that he did not know why Mary Lily was in Ravitch's office that day, that he did not know anything about the treatment she was receiving, and that "she had nothing in her manner" that day to indicate she had been treated with medication.[110] She simply signed the document, asked him and Ravitch to witness it, and then gave it to him. He then kept it for two or three days before "she asked me to return it to her that she might herself present it to Judge Bingham, and she did present it to him."

Less than a week later William Kenan arrived at Lincliffe for a visit. It was clearly not a social call, however, for if it had been, Alice would have been there too. Kenan was there, it seems, because the Judge had called him regarding Mary Lily's failing health. Yet William said nothing about her condition in a telegram he sent from Louisville to Louise on the latter's birthday, June 28: CONGRATULATIONS FROM THE BINGHAMS HANAH AND MYSELF.[111] Two weeks later, on July 12, Mary Lily "had a severe attack" of something, presumably connected with her cardiac problems, and according to one newspaper report, "Her brother, William R. Kenan, was summoned by Judge Bingham, and came. He conferred fully with Dr. Ravitch concerning Mrs. Bingham's condition, and approved everything that was being done."[112] On July 27, 1917, the day that Mary Lily died, the *Louisville Post* reported, "Mrs. Robert Worth Bingham is critically ill of heart trouble at her home, 'Lincliffe,' on the River Road. She has been a sufferer from myocarditis for some time, but has been confined to her bed only about two weeks. She became unconscious about 6:30 Thursday evening, and the physicians in attendance are fearful of the result. . . . The doctors say that her condition was improving, but regard her relapse Thursday as most serious."[113]

Mary Lily was not alone when the end came. Her sister Jessie had arrived two days earlier, and according to some accounts, William was back at her bedside when she died of what the death certificate described as edema of the brain. Bingham was also there, as were W. W. Davies, Hannah Bolles, several physicians and nurses, and a large staff of servants and maids. Jessie witnessed her sister's death certificate with Dr. Walter F. Boggess, one of the two physicians who had stayed with Mary Lily and treated her at Lincliffe.

The Reverend Peyton Hoge held a memorial service for Mary Lily the following day, but other than Jessie, it is not clear how many family members were there. Sarah and Graham were in Wilmington when Mary Lily died, Owen was in Pennsylvania, and Louise and Lawrence were in New York City. Most of the family was on the train with Bingham, however, when it left Louisville on Sunday night July 29. There was a general gathering of mourners the following day in Atlanta, where her cousin Tom and his family lived and where the funeral party grew to include a private railroad car of Flagler System officials. The train was on its way to Wilmington. Mary Lily was to be buried next to her parents in Oakdale Cemetery and not next to Flagler in St. Augustine.[114]

July 31 was one of the hottest days on record in Wilmington, with the temperature creeping past 100 degrees by the time the train arrived at 1 P.M. The funeral was held four hours later in Graham and Sarah's house at 202 South Third, where barely a year before, Mary Lily and her family had paid their last respects to Mollie. Henry Walters and the Pembroke Joneses were there, as were many other relatives and friends. While the active pallbearers were mostly officials of the Flagler companies in Florida, they also included W. W. Davies, who helped place Mary Lily's casket in the family plot at Oakdale Cemetery.[115]

DIGGING UP THE DIRT

Three days later Mary Lily's trustees, William Kenan and William Blount, walked into the county court at West Palm Beach, Florida, and filed her will along with the Flagler Hospital codicil and the revalidation statements that she and Bingham had signed. Although the Judge's codicil was not among the documents they filed, the evidence suggests that he showed it to the family immediately after the funeral.[116]

If the codicil surprised William and his family, they did not consider it suspicious until Graham Kenan received a letter and telephone calls from Rev. Peyton Hoge and Dr. R. Hayes Davis of Louisville. The accusations made by these two men, that Mary Lily had been mistreated by Ravitch, that she had been scaled off and possibly murdered at Lincliffe, naturally alarmed her cousin, who immediately contacted Lawrence and Louise in Louisville, where they had gone with Bingham to collect Mary Lily's jewelry and other effects. The newlyweds left on the next eastbound train without saying a word to Bingham.

Their sudden departure caught the Judge completely off guard. Not only was he unaware of the rumors Graham Kenan had received in Wilmington, but Bingham and Louise had also arranged for one of Louisville's most prominent attorneys, Judge Alexander Pope Humphrey, to represent them both at the probate hearings in Kentucky. As the *Louisville Courier-Journal* noted, "Judge Bingham left his home one morning to go to his office and when he returned in the evening he found that Mr. and Mrs. Lewis had slipped away from the house and out of the city, without saying good-bye or even mentioning their plans to depart."

Bingham knew exactly where to find Louise, however, and he immediately asked Judge Humphrey to contact her at the Greenbrier Hotel, where Lawrence's family was preparing for their annual horseshow. Rather than communicate directly with Louise, however, Humphrey telegraphed the president of the C&O, George W. Stevens, and on August 8 Stevens telegraphed Louise's father-in-law, Thornton Lewis, at the Greenbrier Hotel. "Judge Humphries [*sic*] wires that he represents Judge Bingham and expresses the opinion that there will be no conflict between representing him and also Mrs. Lewis, he desires conference with representative of Mrs. Lewis in order to explain Judge Bingham's attitude, Will you arrange."[117]

In the meantime Dr. Edward Jenner Wood slipped into and out of Louisville, where, at the request Graham Kenan, his friend and neighbor in Wilmington, he asked Hoge and Davis about their allegations. Though what happened next is not clear, Wood apparently went to Atlanta to share whatever they told him with Thomas Kenan, who then passed it on, it seems, to the family members who had gathered at White Sulphur Springs.[118] One newspaper reported that "several important family conferences were held at the Greenbrier Hotel and a contest of Judge Bingham's $5 million codicil was decided upon," but there was never any such challenge.[119] While many of the Kenans wanted to move, as one recent author claims they moved, "swift and hard, against Robert Bingham," William, the family patriarch, wanted no such thing. He had no intention of challenging his honorable friend and fellow Gim Ghoul on the basis of unsubstantiated rumors—rumors that originated, moreover, with men who, unlike himself and Bingham, had no idea what Mary Lily was being treated for or the treatment she had received.[120]

Challenging Bingham would also have created an ugly mess in the press, and William hated the thought of again seeing his family mentioned in connection with a scandal. There had been enough of that during the Flagler years. He much preferred the favorable publicity that was attending the news of Mary Lily's gift to UNC. On August 12, for example, the *New York Sun* noted, "Well may university lovers rejoice over the munificent benefaction, because it will definitely put Chapel Hill on a real university basis, swelling the State income to proportions that will make many things possible, and will doubtless break a broad way for future benefactions of great moment to the State and its venerable center of education."[121]

There were also practical reasons for avoiding a confrontation with Bingham, beyond William's sense of honor and responsibility. Even if the family found hard evidence that Mary Lily had been mistreated, which seemed very unlikely, they still had to face two complex and intertwined issues: Bingham's $5 million codicil and the "no squabble" clause in Mary Lily's will. The Kenans could only challenge the codicil after Bingham filed it *and* the will in Kentucky, where both he and Mary Lily were legal residents. Once he did that, however, the codicil was part of the will and thus subject to "Item Thirteenth" in the same, which made it very clear that if the will were challenged at any time and in any way by "any person named" or "interested" in it, that person would forfeit his or her interest therein.[122]

Bingham filed the will and codicil on August 28 in the Jefferson County court in Louisville, and on September 5 the probate hearing was held.[123] William and his cousin Graham were in the courtroom, but Bingham was not. He was in Virginia settling Robert and Henrietta into school. The only mention of a challenge to the codicil occurred when Bingham's lawyer, Judge Alexander Humphrey, objected to a question that Louise's lawyer, Helm Bruce, put to W. W. Davies regarding the rift between Mary Lily and the Judge's children.

Judge Humphrey: If the gentlemen [*sic*] wants to contest this codicil I demand that he shall say on whose part he is contesting it here.

Mr. Helm Bruce: I have a right to examine the witness.

Judge Humphrey: We have allowed very great latitude because we have absolutely nothing to conceal in the matter, but I am bound to object at this time when Mr. Bruce attempts to bring Judge Bingham's children in here.

The Court: I hardly think that is competent on this hearing. Let the objection be sustained to that question.[124]

William returned to Lockport immediately after the hearing, unaware, it seems, of what was about to happen. Private detectives, apparently hired by Graham Kenan, began investigating the rumors of Mary Lily's treatment. The aggressive hirelings did everything they could for their wealthy clients. They even manufactured evidence, when they could not find it, that might impugn Bingham, the treatment Mary Lily received, and the character of her caregivers. They pillaged Ravitch's office looking for narcotics records. They interviewed Mary Lily's nurses and offered them bribes. They apparently staged interviews with women who claimed to have been the Judge's mistresses. Although the Kenans have never made the detective's report public, it appears to have been a worthless jumble of hearsay and contrivance.[125]

The Kenans' world fell further apart in mid-September, when Graham and his brother Owen had Mary Lily's body exhumed. Graham made all the necessary arrangements in Wilmington, while Owen worked with Dr. John Marshall of the University of Pennsylvania to bring some of the country's leading pathologists to the North Carolina port.[126] The exhumation occurred about 3 A.M. on Tuesday morning, September 18, in the presence of Graham Kenan, the pathologists, a nurse, a stenographer, and, apparently, the Kenans' two closest physician-friends in Wilmington, Dr. Edward Jenner Wood and Dr. George Thomas. The pathologists removed vital organs from Mary Lily's body, returned her corpse to the grave, and then took the specimens to New York, Chicago, and Baltimore for examination.[127]

It took almost a week for the nation's newspapers to discover what had happened in Oakdale Cemetery, and when they did, they learned about it from Bingham's attorneys. On September 24, the day after Bingham's attorneys announced that the exhumation had taken place, an obviously embarrassed Graham Kenan told reporters in Wilmington, "The facts and circumstances relating to Mrs. Bingham's illness and death, as disclosed to members of her family, justified them in and made it their duty to consult leading physicians, who advised that an autopsy be performed. This has been done in the usual and regular way in the broad, open daylight by the best experts obtainable, but the results of their investigation have not yet been made known to the family."[128] That same day, moreover, the *Louisville Courier-Journal* noted that a person "vitally interested" in the case suggested "that among the Kenan heirs there is not the greatest of harmony, and the case may turn into a three or four-cornered legal battle, with certain relatives pitted against the others."[129]

This "vitally interested" person was the Judge's good friend from Atlanta, Shepard Bryan, who arrived in Wilmington on September 22 and broke the news of the exhumation to Bingham's attorneys in Louisville. There can be little doubt, moreover, as William Rand Kenan Jr. immediately made clear, that the rumors of family discord were true. On September 24, under the headline "William R. Kenan Denied that he Had Anything to Do With Action and Knew Nothing of It," the *New York Post* reported that "Mr. Kenan, when interviewed by the New York World on Saturday last [September 23], said that 'he had taken no action to exhume the body of Mrs. Bingham, and knew of no such action by other members of Mrs. Bingham's family.'"[130]

If William knew nothing about what his cousins had been doing, he immediately stepped in and took control of the investigation. He was clearly in command by September 27, when the *Louisville Courier-Journal* reported that the examination of Mary Lily's vital organs had been completed in New York and that "Dr. Norris is drafting his report. The findings of the expert will be communicated to William R. Kenan, Mrs. Bingham's brother. . . . The report may be made personally to Mr. Kenan at Wilmington."[131]

Despite predictions in the press that the report would soon be made public, the family has never released it. Their reluctance is easy to understand. As Bingham's friend Hugh Young later wrote of his interviews with the pathologists who examined Mary Lily's remains, "Two of the pathologists were my friends, and readily admitted that no evidence of poison had been found; that examination of the tissues showed she had died of alcoholism."[132]

CHAPTER 8

Between the Tracks

By the spring of 1918 Mary Lily's trustees, William Kenan and William Blount, were close to reaching a settlement with Judge Robert Worth Bingham. Short on cash but long on securities, the trustees wanted Bingham to take his $5 million in stock and take it quickly. "It is a matter of importance that the negotiation with him be concluded as soon as possible," Blount wrote in May 1918, "as under the proposition which we are now submitting all of these stocks to him, they are tied up until his decision is made, and not available to us for the purpose of raising money to meet the various taxes payable by the estate."[1]

The trustees had no settlement in sight, however, with the University of North Carolina, which badly needed its $75,000 annuity. The school had lost students and faculty alike to the war, and in expectation of funds from Mary Lily's estate, the university's trustees named five faculty members, including Dr. Francis Preston Venable, as the school's first Kenan professors and also promised higher salaries to them and other faculty members. Yet its requests for money had yielded nothing. As Blount explained to the university in early July 1918,

> I have received a letter from Mr. Wm. R. Kenan Jr., . . . and he suggests to me that I shall say to you that by reason of the necessity for payment of enormous inheritance taxes to the United States, to the State of Kentucky, and to various other States, corporations of which have issued stock held by this estate, it will be, he thinks, impracticable to settle up any of the legacies at the present time. Just as soon as these inheritance taxes are off of our hands, we will endeavor to give prompt attention to the annuity to the University of North Carolina and to others in like situation.[2]

Bingham received his legacy in cash and securities on July 27, 1918, exactly one year after Mary Lily's death, and one month later he paid $1 million for majority ownership of the *Louisville Courier-Journal* and the *Louisville Times*. UNC immediately responded with another request for its money, but once again it got only excuses and apologies. The estate faced inheritance and corporation taxes of "$14,000,000.00 or $15,000,000.00," Blount explained, "and in order to preserve the estate this must be paid before any payments can be made." The estate consisted largely of stocks, which "had to be worked off by slow degrees, and this accounts for the seemingly inexcusable delay in taking care of the legacies and annuities. I assure you," Blount concluded, "on behalf of Mr. Kenan and myself, that we will do the very best that is possible."[3]

The university wanted to hear from Kenan, however, and in mid-October Dr. Edward Kidder Graham called on him in New York City. It was their last meeting. Shortly after returning to Chapel Hill, the forty-two-year-old president died from pneumonia—another victim of the influenza epidemic then raging throughout the world. His death left it up to the university's business manager, Charles T. Woollen, to report on the meeting with Kenan, who appeared to Woollen to be doing everything possible to get the university its money. But the war was further confounding an already complicated problem. "Mr. Kenan said the trustees of the estate had been unable to raise enough money to pay the inheritance tax because of the fact that most of the estate consisted of railroad properties which were now in the hands of the United States Government, and could not be used as collateral."[4]

Furthermore, the university's annuity had to come from the stocks assigned to the twenty-one-year trust established under Mary Lily's will "for the maintenance and administration and development of the Florida East Coast Railway and the Florida East Coast Hotel properties . . . and the properties held by subsidiary Companies." Therein lay another problem: many of these stocks were not yet part of Mary Lily's trust. They were still in the H. M. Flagler Trust, which had just been extended for another five years by Henry Flagler's trustees (Kenan, Blount, and Beardsley).[5]

The pressure from UNC was nothing, however, compared with that confronting Kenan and Blount from other forces. Twenty states demanded some kind of taxes from Mary Lily's estate. The federal government wanted inheritance and corporation taxes, and the estate faced litigation in courts throughout the country. The pressure on Blount became so intense, in fact, that he had to seek medical treatment for stomach ulcers and abandoned his position as the Flagler System's general counsel.[6]

Kenan was headed in the same direction. In addition to the pressure of his trustee duties, he confronted a variety of demands related to the war and Mary Lily's death. Business was so good at Western Block that Kenan found it difficult to fill all of the private and government contracts generated by the war.[7] At the same time, the Flagler hotels overflowed with Americans who normally traveled to Europe. As a happy result, the FEC Railway generated enough revenue both to pay its operating expenses (for the first time in its history) and to meet the interest on its $37 million of bonds (a feat it would repeat for the next several years). Indeed, by 1918 the railroad, then in the hands of the federal government, had accumulated earnings of more than $3 million.[8]

William found no profit, however, in the pressure attending the "severe condemnation in Wilmington of the Kenan family's conduct" in exhuming Mary Lily's body. The city's mayor "publicly denounced" the county official who issued the exhumation permit, while the chastised official criticized Graham Kenan for failing "to advise him [as] to when the autopsy would be held, although Kenan had asked him to be present." The judge of the county court also demanded an investigation of the Kenans in order to determine "if an offense has been committed against the laws of the State by those who exhumed the body without the consent of Mr. Bingham or a court order."[9]

Worse still were the newspaper reports describing William and his family as criminals. "The heirs of the Flagler fortune continue the career of lawlessness by which that fortune and the power of the Standard Oil Trust was established." Mary Lily's trustees were lawbreakers: "The truth is that the unusual, if not the illegal, step of first filing the alleged will of a citizen of Jefferson County, Kentucky, in a Florida court clearly indicated a purpose to rob Kentucky of her inheritance dues, if courts could be misled by false issues raised, or clouds of witnesses mustered by the hired detectives, so often employed by the Standard Oil Trust." Indeed, the Kenans' hands had been soiled from the start. "Here on the stage is an unknown family in North Carolina dragged from obscurity to a kin[g]dom of unimagined power by a marriage which could be made legal only by packing, if not debauching, a Legislature of Florida, a province annexed to the Standard Oil domain by Henry Flagler."[10]

William's family dispersed in several directions after Mary Lily's death. Sarah moved with Graham from Wilmington to New York, "where his time and attention were required in dealing with matters of large moment." Dr. Owen Kenan left the country. Only a week or so after Mary Lily's exhumation, he embarked for Europe, where he joined the AEF's Medical Corps and the Relief Mission to Russia and Turkey.[11] Louise moved from one place to another. She went from Staten Island to Atlanta to be nearer her husband, Private Lawrence Lewis, who briefly commanded the army stables in Augusta, Georgia, before being transferred to Europe. Louise then moved in with her mother, Jessie, in Wilmington, where in July 1918 she gave birth to a son, Lawrence Lewis Jr.[12]

The joy that attended the end of the war also proved short lived for the Kenans. The family's old friend Pembroke Jones died two months after the armistice, at about the same time that William received a telephone call from Bingham's old friend Dr. Hugh Young demanding the release of Mary Lily's autopsy report. Young had interviewed the three pathologists who had examined her body, and he wanted William to permit these men "to make a statement to the effect that the findings were entirely negative, that no poison was present, or any evidence of foul play." But Kenan "absolutely refused" to release such a statement and ignored Young's (never fulfilled) threat to have Bingham publish one.[13]

The state of Kentucky also filed a pretrial brief against Mary Lily's trustees in early 1919, "alleging that Mrs. Bingham died seized and possessed of an estate of $99,584,866.44, all of which was subject to inheritance taxes, none of which had been paid." By the time the case came to trial, the money demanded by Kentucky included $4.5 million in inheritance taxes, an additional 10 percent in late fees, and $220,000 in taxes on her bequest to UNC.[14]

The intertwining of family and university affairs became even more pronounced when UNC appointed North Carolina attorney general Judge James Smith Manning to handle its legal affairs in Louisville.[15] Manning was the brother-in-law of Dr. Francis Preston Venable, he had been close friends with the Colonel and Mrs. Thomas Kenan, and he was on the university's board of trustees with Graham Kenan.[16] The Kenans also liked Manning's choice of legal counsel in Kentucky. He retained for UNC—at a "fee of 2½ percent and a further contingent fee of 5 percent if the University" won its case—the same Louisville law firm the family was using, Bruce & Bullitt.[17]

THE PERILS OF PROSPERITY

Mary Lily's gift helped transform UNC from a small teaching institution governed by personal and family relationships to a large, bureaucratic and research-oriented corporate enterprise. It was "the largest bequest ever made to this University," president Graham reported before he died, "and indeed one of the largest and one of the most wisely conceived ever made to any State institution in the Nation." Not only could the school double the "present strength" of its faculty with the gift, but it would "be so liberated from past restrictions that the youth of the State will have that quality of opportunity, judged by national standards, that equality of preparation and inspiration assures." The gift marked "a new era" in the university's development, Graham predicted, and he was right.[18]

It generated a debate about the use of the money and the future of the institution. Dormitories; a Kenan law school; an economic and sociology department; a department of public health; a school of art, architecture, and music; a department for training municipal officials; a coordinated college for women—the gift elicited endless suggestions from the university's alumni, faculty, and friends. The president heartily endorsed all of these proposals, expressing the hope that each would be realized at some point in the future (as most eventually were). But he decided on a pattern of expenditure in keeping with the stipulations in Mary Lily's will. The money was to be used to pay competitive salaries to the university's best professors.[19]

Graham Kenan, *far left*, with two unidentified friends, ca. 1918. (Thomas S. Kenan III)

The first Kenan professors were selected by an informal and personal procedure. Each faculty member submitted a secret ballot containing five names, the president of the university selected the finalists, and the school's trustees approved his list. The list included the only professor William Kenan wanted appointed, Dr. Francis Preston Venable, but it did not include Horace Williams, the man Graham Kenan considered the best teacher UNC had ever had. Yet Williams, a North Carolina native, had few friends on the Chapel Hill faculty. Most professors strongly disliked the philosophy teacher and considered him deficient in the "primary consideration" for selecting the first Kenan professors: "a widely recognized record of productive scholarship."[20]

Williams considered it "the worst blow" of his life not to have gotten one of the first Kenan appointments, and he shared his feelings with one of the university's youngest and most powerful trustees, Graham Kenan. Graham immediately demanded that Williams be appointed as a Kenan professor. "After all," he reportedly argued, "it was Kenan money, and to hundreds of University men Williams was 'the great teacher,' even if his colleagues might not think so."[21] Graham's demands raised two fundamental questions that still confront the university: institutional freedom and the value of research versus teaching.

Graham suggested the Williams appointment in a report to the new faculty chairman, Harry Woodburn Chase, who was one of three men recently nominated for the position of president of UNC. Chase, described by one journalist as "a damn-yankee, a genuine, blown-in-the-bottle Massachusetts blue-belly," had arrived in Chapel Hill in 1910 with no southern pedigree, no North Carolina connections, and no personal relationship with the Kenans. And he said no to Graham Kenan.[22] By intervening to make appointments, Chase explained, the trustees would usurp the power of university officials and create a precedent that would lead to confusion and reduced morale among the faculty. Chase got his way, at least temporarily. Graham Kenan withdrew his demand, and the trustees appointed Chase as the university's tenth president.[23]

The confrontation did not sit well with Cousin William. It not only placed additional strain on his relationship with the university, but it also involved Horace Williams, one of his least favorite people. He had never taken a class with Williams, and Williams strongly opposed Venable's promotion of science at UNC, having "gone out of his way to declare that science had swamped the University and to belittle his brother professors. Science he was constantly chiding depicting it as superficial. Its professors were particularists. . . . His associates were gatherers of unimportant facts and did not know what it was all about. In his own department he could see no good in any professor unless he was a Hegelian."[24]

Kenan did appreciate one result of the Williams incident, however, as did the university's trustees, faculty, and administrators. The confrontation led to the appointment of a joint faculty-trustee committee to recommend a general policy for the selection and payment of Kenan professors. The new policy must also have pleased Graham Kenan, for it made "teaching ability" a consideration for awarding future Kenan professorships.[25] Unfortunately, though, Graham never got the chance to see his former philosophy professor receive a Kenan appointment. On January 29, 1920, just two days after he and his fellow trustees approved the new Kenan professor guidelines, the thirty-six-year-old attorney signed his will in New York City. One week later he was dead, swept away by another flu epidemic. While his death shocked and saddened all of the family, Sarah, his cousin-wife, suffered the most. Like her long-divorced sister, Jessie, forty-four-year-old Sarah never remarried.

One month later William hired Henry Flagler's favorite architects, John Carrere and Thomas Hastings, to design and build a Kenan Memorial Fountain in Wilmington, North Carolina. But the monument was not in memory of his recently deceased brother-in-law, at least not directly. Kenan gave it to the city as a monument to his parents. Yet he clearly had more than filial piety in mind. In addition to serving as an apology for his family's recent scandals, the fountain embellished his local business interests. The huge, expensive monument was constructed at the intersection of Fifth and Market Streets—within the shadow of his Carolina Apartment building. It was still being designed when his alma mater provided a monument to Graham Kenan. In June 1920 UNC appointed three Kenan professors under the new guidelines, including Horace Williams for "outstanding merit as a teacher." The appointments brought to eleven the total number of Kenan professorships awarded but as yet unfunded.[26]

DUTIES AND DIVERSIONS

Will Kenan left the Flagler System's offices at 120 Broadway as soon as he got the news: C. I. Hood, the Sarsaparilla King, was having a sale the following day, June 3, at the Hood Farm in Lowell, Massachusetts. "I took the midnight express to Boston and motored out to Lowell, arriving there in the late morning."

He wanted "to talk with some individuals there to get a line on what I intended to do but, being late, this opportunity did not present itself." Fifteen hundred people were already jammed into the noisy tent by the time Kenan entered. He did not know anyone there, and though he had been studying the *Rural New Yorker* and *Country Gentleman*, he did not know how to interpret the pictures, pedigrees, and records printed in the Hood Farm catalog. Still, he was ready to bid, and he "sat down on the first row of seats just opposite the auctioneer."[27]

Kenan watched five or six sales before Sophie's Elberta brought him into the bidding. She was "a wonderful type animal with every indication of being a large producer," and William was determined to have her. He had recently lost Daisy and Peg o' My Heart to milk fever, and though he had replaced them with more expensive animals, he now wanted an exquisite specimen "to be used at my residence." But another bidder also wanted Sophie's Elberta, and by the time Kenan stopped dueling for her, his competitor had won with a bid of $6,300.

William was now into the spirit of the occasion, however, and began bidding on everything that came into the ring. Even on Sophie's Ethna, who was "bagged up so thoroughly that she laid down in the ring, and because of this, every other bidder dropped out and left me with this cow at a price of $2200. At the time, I did not know such a condition is liable to injure the cow." All he knew was that he was enjoying himself, and by the time the auctioneer gaveled for lunch, the Lockport millionaire had purchased Sophie's Ethna and four other Jerseys of Sophie's Tormentor breeding for $5,700. His aggressiveness did not go unnoticed. "During lunch time quite a number of people asked me where my herd was; if I had a farm and what I intended to do. I had to admit I had no plan, had no farm and only expected to purchase one family cow. The suggestion was made by quite a number that I should have a bull, and when the sale proceeded in the afternoon I did buy Sophie's 19th Son Eleventh 180565, at a price of $1600."[28]

Kenan shipped his Tormentors to Lockport by express rail and then herded them up the hill to Uppertown and the barns behind his house at 433 Locust Street. All of the animals survived the ordeal and "turned out to be splendid producers," particularly Sophie's Ethna, who despite her full-bag flop in the ring, proved to be "one of the best cows" Kenan ever owned. The only animals that suffered were two calves already living on the place. Bumped from their box stalls to make room for the new arrivals, the two young heifers died after chewing on a hastily built pen constructed from some wood "taken out of my house years prior, the same having been painted with white enamel." This incident, Kenan wrote, revealed "one of the very first things a beginner should learn; never use any paint composed of lead base around cattle and especially is this true regarding young calves."

Kenan's Uppertown residence now resembled an urban version of Liberty Hall, the North Carolina plantation where he had raised his first cows. Although there were no hogs or hog killings at 433 Locust Street, there were chickens, ducks, and turkeys; fresh milk, butter, and eggs; and vegetables, feed crops, and fruit trees on nine acres of "unimproved land to the rear and adjoining on Beattie Avenue." Like the black folks who once worked and lived at Liberty Hall, moreover, the white workers at Kenan's home were divided into household and outside staff. A cook, a butler, and several maids ran the house; a gardener tended the grounds and greenhouses; and a chauffeur and his assistant drove and mastered the mechanical needs of the new automobile William bought each year.

None of the servants welcomed more animals in the yard, however. Twice as many cows meant twice as much to do, Kenan recalled: "The men I had on my place were delegated to look after these animals and they were milked twice a day." What was more, the new Jerseys also required special attention: "The cows being on official test at Hood Farm, I concluded to continue this work, notifying Cornell and arranging the matter."

The Kenans' English gardener, Thomas Garrett, quit the Lockport plantation soon after the cows arrived, and William was especially "sorry to lose him." Garrett had saved and multiplied William's rarest and most prized plant, a hundred-year-old night-blooming cereus. He also had filled the greenhouse each fall with beautiful "mums, five or six feet tall, each with one flower and that would be practically the diameter of a human head." The chauffeur quit next, resigning in mid-December, just as William and Alice prepared to leave for St. Augustine. Fortunately, though, William did not have to abandon his beloved bovines to strangers. He hired one of his former chauffeurs, George Art, as the new gardener-milker, and another former chauffeur, Albert Chapman, as a part-time driver-milker.[29]

William and his family followed many of the old Flagler rituals during the winter of 1920–21, but they did not go to Palm Beach for the season. They remained in St. Augustine. The FEC's general offices were located just up the street from the Ponce de Leon Hotel, where William and Alice occupied a plush suite of rooms next to Jessie and Sarah's. Lawrence Lewis was also working at a "go-fer" job with the FEC in St. Augustine, where he and Louise lived with their son, Lawrence Jr., and their newborn daughter, Mary Lily, in "Kirkside," the old Flagler "cottage" adjacent to the Ponce.

William stayed particularly busy that winter. President-elect Warren G. Harding spent most of February at the Ponce de Leon Hotel, where amid "an endless chain of visitors and conferences, he settled down between sessions on the golf links to completing his Cabinet."[30] Also, for the first time in almost five years, the Flagler System (and not the United States Railroad Commission) controlled the FEC Railway, and there was plenty for Kenan and his lieutenants to do. Wartime steel shortages had forced the company to delay repairs to its tracks, which now needed to be inspected and scheduled for replacement. New freight cars also had to be ordered to replace those that had broken or deteriorated during the war. All of this had to be planned and paid for, moreover, within the postwar context of labor problems and economic recession. The FEC no longer needed the extra workers that war work and prolabor laws had forced it and most other railroads to hire, and it also wanted to reinstitute, as did most other railroads, prewar work rules and pay scales for its employees.

Kenan was working on these matters when the used Pullman he purchased arrived in Jacksonville. He immediately had the car prepared for the annual spring inspection of the Flagler System's properties. That night, however, while he and the FEC's president, William Beardsley, slept soundly on board, burglars managed to steal almost everything of value inside the car. Kenan awoke the luckiest of the two. Before retiring he had placed his "wallet and watch under my pillow and the only thing I lost was my sleeve buttons." Beardsley "lost everything of value," however, "his watch and chain, his wallet with considerable money in it. . . . He also lost his glasses." Kenan hired the "best detectives" he could find to investigate the incident; but the thieves left "no finger prints anywhere," and the case was never solved.[31]

Lawrence, Louise, and their son, Lawrence Lewis Jr., ca. 1919.
(Mary Lily Flagler Lewis)

When he returned to Lockport, moreover, Kenan discovered that his gardener and chauffeur were not very good milkmen. They had failed to pay "proper attention" to his cows, and so he "concluded the only thing to do was to get a capable and experienced man to take charge of the animals; and I immediately went East to places doing scientific feeding and testing, with the object in view of securing some one to look after my animals." The kind of herdsman Kenan wanted was hard to find. "I did not desire to get a manager or superintendent, but I wanted some one who was actually working in the barns and had technical and scientific knowledge of the work as well as ability to carry it out personally." Kenan offered the job to at least two men, but "neither one seemed inclined to accept, probably due to the uncertainty of a permanent position."[32]

Before Kenan could find a dairyman, however, Judge William Alexander Blount checked into the Johns Hopkins Hospital for an operation on his ulcerated stomach. The sixty-nine-year-old lawyer had been pushing himself too hard. In addition to handling the litigation connected with Mary Lily's estate, he had been devoting himself to his duties as president of the American Bar Association—the first Floridian to hold that office. Blount never made it to the operating room, however. He died of a heart attack on June 15, shortly before he was to undergo surgery.[33] The United States Supreme Court adjourned in his honor, while Kenan and Henry Walters, in Florida for the funeral, briefly halted their railroad operations in honor of the man who had served both them and their railroads so faithfully.[34]

Kenan went directly from Blount's funeral to the Hood Farm in Lowell, Massachusetts, where he succeeded in hiring the farm's "outside boss," Torrence E. Grow. As Grow's son later recalled, the agreement was convenient for both men. Hood Farm was cutting back on its operations, and Kenan and Grow "were in the right place at the right time. TE needed a job and WR needed a man."[35] Grow's performance at 433 Locust Street astounded Kenan: "The results were immediate. . . . Mr. Grow milked, fed, prepared the feed, bed and cleaned the stalls, in fact did all the work in connection with 11 cows, milking them three times a day, four, twelve and eight o'clock, from July 1st until the early part of March following, without missing a milking,—a record which to my mind is unsurpassed."[36]

Grow performed so well that Kenan "concluded he was too good a man not to have an opportunity and in the fall of 1921 I commenced to look around for a farm, the cause of which being due to Mr. Grow's work at my residence." Grow also helped Kenan find and purchase a farm that November. Located just beyond the interurban tracks on Chestnut Ridge Road, about three and a half miles east of Lockport, Kenan named the 350-acre farm "Randleigh"—a "constructed word," he noted, that Alice "composed of my middle name, 'Rand', and 'Leigh', a Scotch word meaning a pasture or meadow." While many of his friends considered the farm a folly, as "trouble for myself and nothing more," it made him happier and prouder than almost anything else in his life. It became crucial, in fact, to his quest for scientific recognition.[37]

Kenan initially used the farm, however, as a diversion, as an escape from the grueling affairs of his family and the Flagler System. Yet his hobby quickly contributed to the physical and psychological turmoil created by his other duties and responsibilities. "Shortly after Judge Blount died I had an attack of nervous indigestion," Kenan later wrote. "I had the pain for about nine months every hour I was awake and on some occasions it was so severe that I could scarcely stand up."[38]

His pain is easy to understand. Blount had been his shield and sword at the Flagler System, the Flagler Trust, and Mary Lily's estate, and though he now appointed Blount's assistant, Scott Loftin, as the system's legal counsel, he did not immediately fill Blount's trustee positions. Therefore he had no one to point to or turn to, as he had always had in Blount, when UNC asked for Mary Lily's money. In fact he had recently responded to one such request by writing "that I communicated with Mr. Blount, my co-Trustee, in connection with your suggestion. He has replied that it would be impossible for us to accede to either of the requests made by you. We regret this to be the condition of affairs but it will be necessary for us to await the action of the Tax Inheritance authorities, both Federal and the State of Kentucky."[39]

Kenan now had to face the pressure alone, and it was becoming more acute. On June 14, the day before Blount died, the university appointed two more Kenan professors, one of whom was Kenan's friend, history professor R. D. W. Connor. With thirteen Kenan professors now on its payroll, UNC was finding it increasingly difficult to pay their salaries. It got some of the money, ironically, from an emergency grant of $50,000 from the Rockefeller Foundation, but it also borrowed money from banks and dipped into its "Special Funds" account to meet the crisis. Worse still, the university was now having to pay for Mary Lily's gift: $4,000 a year for an appeal bond in connection with the state of Kentucky's efforts to assess the school for inheritance taxes.[40]

Kenan loved his alma mater and wanted it to get its money, but the Kentucky litigation also involved his personal reputation, family pride, and sense of honor. He and his family stood accused of continuing the "career of lawlessness" that allegedly built Standard Oil and the Flagler fortune, while he and Blount had been accused of acting maliciously and illegally by filing Mary Lily's will in Florida. Kenan wanted, in other words, to avoid any appearance of impropriety on his part or the university's.

Kenan was already feeling ill when he and Alice arrived at the Ponce de Leon Hotel in St. Augustine for Christmas. His sister Sarah then made things worse. She showed him a copy of her letter to professor Horace Williams. "I am enclosing a check for twenty-six thousand dollars—twenty-five thousand to be invested and the income used for establishing the Graham Kenan Fellowship in Philosophy, and one thousand dollars to meet the requirements for the coming year. I am sending it to you because I wish you as one of Graham's very dear friends to present it to the proper authorities of the University. You of course will award the fellowship annually."[41]

William doubtless wanted to scream. The gift could only complicate matters for him and the university. Rather than send the money directly to UNC, Sarah sent it to Horace Williams, the professor most disliked by his fellow faculty members, and she sent it in honor of her deceased husband, a man who had created a scandal on the professor's behalf. What was more, the gift reflected adversely on William himself. Recently he had only turned down the university's requests for Mary Lily's money, and though he had previously given gifts to his alma mater, these paled in comparison with those made by his sisters, neither of whom had attended the university.

Kenan's "nervous indigestion" now became so acute that he "consulted numerous doctors both in Lockport and at the Railroad Hospital at St. Augustine. Had my stomach pumped out many times, swallowed the thimble and on each occasion the digestive juices were analyzed and no one could find out the cause. I was beginning to think I had cancer."[42] He was having his juices analyzed in Lockport, in fact, in January 1922, when he received the strongest demand yet from UNC. Confident of victory in the Kentucky courts, the school's trustees had appointed a special committee, headed by Josephus Daniels, "to take up with the trustees of the Bingham estate the matter of the $75,000 annuity bequeathed to the University and demand payment of the same."[43]

This time Kenan sent his alma mater some money, but only part of what was owed and only after much explanation. The sticking point for him was still the Kentucky litigation. Although the university appeared "correct" in predicting victory in the courts, it was impossible, he wrote,

> to finally determine the question of taxes on this bequest to the University of North Carolina until the final decision by the higher court, which we estimate will be in the early summer. In view of this fact, we as individuals are not in a position to make payment at this time to the total amount of the bequest which has accrued up to this date [$225,000]. As you know, the total tax, if any, claimed by the State of Kentucky on this bequest is $194,639.45. They are also claiming interest at 6 percent from January 27, 1919 to date paid. With this fact in mind, we would be justified in making payment of $75,000., and are, therefore, enclosing herewith check for that amount.[44]

Kenan's pain did not let up, however. The Interstate Commerce Commission (ICC) was threatening to reduce freight and passenger rates, the railroads demanded wage reductions in return, and the railroad unions promised to strike if wages were reduced. Throughout the country, moreover, there was a general threat of labor unrest. Although President Harding had told the new head of the United Mine Workers, John L. Lewis, that the nation's miners had to accept wage reductions along with everyone else, Lewis promised to call a strike if the miners' wage levels did not remain the same after their contracts expired on March 31, 1922.[45]

Kenan's internal turmoil took a turn for the worse with the arrival in St. Augustine of President Harding and his entourage aboard the houseboat *Nahmeoka*. The president, bound "for a few mindless weeks of relaxation" at Palm Beach, decided to stop first for a couple of rounds of golf on the FEC's grass course in St. Augustine. He asked Kenan to be his partner for a match and Kenan accepted—with much trepidation. William wanted to do everything possible to advertise the Flagler System's golfing facilities in Florida, but he himself was no golfer. He had always been "too busy to play golf and never attempted it."[46]

Kenan played as well as Harding for most of the match, which the *St. Augustine Evening Record* called "the most interesting contest the President had while in the Ancient City." Thanks to three bisques granted by their opponents on the front nine, Kenan and Harding made the turn two points up. The lead changed several times on the back nine, however, until "one point down and the 18th hole to play, the President waded into the ball . . . and his first drive was at the edge of the bunker to the left. His second brassie was good and his third shot on the green. He sunk with two putts for a five . . . while Mr. Kenan took a seven and the President and Mr. Kenan lost the match by two points on the 18th green." Kenan hated losing at anything, especially sports, and his embarrassment at muffing the match for the president—and doing so in the glare of the public eye—made him promise himself he would learn the game as soon as he could.[47]

He had to get back to Lockport, however; it was time to transfer his cows to the farm. Grow had been preparing for the move since early March, working at the farm with Kenan's newest employee, Robert Howe, a professional herdsman from Connecticut. The two men "thoroughly cleaned out, fumigated and disinfected" the old barn and introduced a new set of feeds to the Jerseys. They replaced the old "commercial, ready-mixed ration" with a feed mixture used at Randleigh Farm for the next eight or nine years: "of ground oats, bran, gluten and corn meal with the proportion varied to meet the needs of the individual animal, but usually equal parts by weight."[48]

Kenan returned to Florida after the cows were moved and was elected executive vice-president of the FEC Railway Company, the FEC Hotel Company, and the FEC Car Ferry Company.[49] He then began his inspection tour down the coast. What he saw on his journey was better than what he heard: talk of a strike. More than a half-million U.S. and Canadian mine workers walked off their jobs on April 1, and the FEC's shop and maintenance workers threatened to join their counterparts throughout the nation in doing the same. The threat presented a particularly ominous problem for the FEC, as it depended directly on the activities of other railroads, especially those of Henry Walters's ACL, for freight and passenger service. Indeed, not only was the ACL one of the largest and most unionized railroads in the South; it had released thousands of workers from its bloated wartime payrolls, and its employees worked directly with the FEC's in Jacksonville.[50]

Kenan was badly in need of medical attention by the time he completed the Florida inspection and arrived in New York City for Henry Walters's wedding, but he tried his best to get into the spirit of the occasion. He loved his "second Father" and still looked to him, as one close associate noted, for advice and friendship: "Mr. Kenan continued to be guided by Mr. Walters, until his (Mr W's) death." Yet death now appeared closer to Kenan than to Walters. The seventy-three-year-old Walters was experiencing one of the happiest periods of his life. He was the wealthiest man in the South and enjoyed very good health. He still controlled the ACL's policies and practices but had turned its day-to-day operations over to his favorite nephew, Lyman Delano (who lived across the street from Kenan's sister Jessie in Wilmington). What is more, Walters now fulfilled his oldest and fondest dreams. On April 11, 1922, he married his longtime friend and lover, Mrs. Pembroke Jones.[51]

He also referred Kenan to a doctor. "In discussing my symptoms with Mr. Walters he suggested that I go to see Dr. Lodowick Kast of Madison Avenue, New York City," whom Walters "considered the most expert stomach specialist in the United States." Kenan took the suggestion and immediately went to see the Austrian physician, who started him on an extensive series of diagnostic tests. It was not the most pleasant way to spend one's fiftieth birthday, and the knife continued to twist in Kenan's gut. In May the ICC ordered the nation's railroads to reduce their freight and passenger rates by 10 percent, and the railroads responded by requesting the Railroad Labor Board to reduce the wages of shopmen by 12.5 percent—a request approved by the board over the objections of its labor members. The shop craft unions refused to accept the decision, however, and on July 1 over 400,000 railroad shopmen across the nation walked off their jobs.

The strike lasted several months and resulted in a great deal of violence and turmoil. Most of the problems stemmed from the desperate acts of the striking shopmen who saw their jobs taken by "scabs." Little is known about the actions and reactions of the FEC and its shopmen, except that someone, apparently a striking shopman, poured sand into the gas tank of Lawrence Lewis's automobile in St. Augustine. Yet it seems safe to assume that the company took many of the same actions as the ACL and experienced similar incidents. Over 90 percent of the ACL's shopmen joined the strike, and the company responded in turn by hiring more than 2,800 new workers. The ACL suffered cut air hoses on several locomotives and cars; its pump house at Lakeland, Florida, was dynamited; and an attempt was made in Tampa to blow up the dormitories of the railroad's shop employees.[52]

Kenan kept track of the situation from New York, where he continued to make periodic visits to the doctor's office on Madison Avenue. The Austrian specialist had no answers, however, and Kenan's pain continued to mount, aggravated by both the strike and a $33-million tax bill on Mary Lily's estate. And the bill did not include the levy in Kentucky, where the state demanded an amount based on the appraised value of her entire estate and not on its value after the payment of federal and state inheritance taxes. Thus, regardless of what the state of Kentucky was eventually paid, Mary Lily's trustees now owed almost one-third of the total value of her $99 million estate in taxes.[53]

Kenan turned to his farm in an effort to forget the pain. He helped Grow and Howe plan a "test barn," sink a six-inch well, and bury a storage tank and pipes to supply it with fresh spring water. He then spared no expense on the new barn, which was built of brick, hollow tile, and plaster and was attached "at right angles" to the old structure. He used "Insulite" to cover the "high ceilings" and hired "the Jamesway people of Elmira to install the ventilating system" and furnish "the stanchions, partitions, and gates. All of the box stalls as well as the stanchions had a concrete floor covered with cork brick. The barn was also equipped with individual drinking cups, steam heat and electric fans. . . . During this period two silos were constructed of glazed hollow tile ten feet and fourteen feet inside diameters, both forty-five feet high." Kenan also had two maternity stalls constructed in the old barn as well as a "rat-proof feed bin with a capacity of about two and a half carloads of grain."[54]

By early fall Kenan's doctor "had made every known test during ten visits and then reported that there was nothing organically wrong with me, it being a case of nerves, and I would have to cure myself." In explaining this diagnosis to Kenan, the Austrian doctor used a simile that his engineer-patient could appreciate. Kenan was like a " 'boiler operated beyond its capacity and neglected' " and he " 'would have to be scrapped' " if he did not give up his business for at least six months and " 'take it easy.' " But taking it easy was not Kenan's way. "I stated it would not be necessary to take a vacation if it were only nerves. I would stop being nervous by not worrying over anything. This I did."[55]

It took more than will power, of course, to stop Kenan's pain; it took changes in the environment provoking it. One such change occurred in mid-September, when the federation of shop craft unions acknowledged defeat and striking railroad workers accepted President Harding's "call" to return to work. On November 3, moreover, the court of appeals in Kentucky ruled that UNC did not have to pay inheritance taxes on Mary Lily's bequest and that all state and federal inheritance taxes paid by her trustees "were to be deducted from the total value of her estate to ascertain the amount upon which the state inheritance tax [in Kentucky] is to be computed."[56]

These decisions and the publicity given them in North Carolina made Kenan, his alma mater, and their attorneys all very happy. On November 5 Josephus Daniels announced UNC's victory in his newspaper, the *Raleigh News and Observer*, and shortly thereafter, at a meeting of the Executive Committee of the university's trustees, he "moved that $25,000 be set aside from the first moneys coming in from the Kenan legacy to cover services of Mr. Bruce and Judge Manning" as attorneys in the litigation. The motion was easily carried: "The sum of $25,000 had saved the University $240,000, a small price to pay, especially since it came out of the Kenan Fund anyway."[57]

Most of William's "nervous indigestion" was gone by the end of 1922. His test barn was completed in early December, and his cows were moved into their luxurious new, well-heated home just before he and Alice left Lockport for Florida on his railroad car, which he had recently named "Randleigh." It was also a warm, rewarding season for William in the Sunshine State. The strike was over, the hotels were full, and though the FEC railroad still needed extensive repairs to its tracks, roadbeds, and equipment, the company's freight and passenger business had more than recovered from the effects of the strike and the postwar recession.

Indeed, Kenan's return to Florida coincided with the onset of the Florida land boom. Beginning in 1923 and peaking in the summer and fall of 1925, millions of Americans flocked to Florida as tourists, homeseekers, and "get-rich-quick" land speculators. Lured by the extravagant publicity of real estate promoters and developers, they came by train, by car, and by bus. They bought land and left, or they bought land and stayed. They built on it or sold it, and then bought some more and quickly sold it to others who did the same. Their contagion also helped William add several new titles to his business pedigree. He was elected president and director of the St. Augustine Golf Development Company and of all of the Flagler System's busy land companies—the Model, Perrine, and Chuluota. To be sure, the boom could not have started at a better time for Kenan. The Flagler Trust expired in June, and Kenan transferred its assets to the twenty-one-year trust established under Mary Lily's will for the maintenance of the FEC Railway and hotel properties.

Kenan was as happy as he had been in many years when he and Alice returned to Lockport in early April, and the news he received upon his return made him even happier. Hood Farm was holding a dispersal sale on April 21— seventy of its prizewinning cattle would go to the highest bidder. Kenan immediately ordered "enough catalogues for all my boys at the farm,—every one being instructed to study its contents and list the animals which, in his judgement, we should purchase, the reasons, and at what price." Kenan then called everyone together for a meeting. "We digested the records of each animal thoroughly with the result that Mr. Grow and myself attended the sale with the object of securing ten animals . . . and we were successful in purchasing nine." Kenan paid $27,000 for the nine Sophie's Tormentors, including "the top price for a female at the sale and the highest price ever paid for an American-bred bull."[58]

CHAPTER 9

Up and Down the Line

William R. Kenan became a philanthropist and builder during the 1920s. He gave money to Lockport and to UNC, and he expanded the facilities of the Flagler System. But his renewed sense of hope and power soon succumbed to the doubt and uncertainty created by events beyond his control.

Kenan made one of his most fateful decisions in the early 1920s, when Henry Walters offered to buy the FEC Railway for the ACL. The offer must have appeared attractive to both men. Only the FEC stood between the ACL and the latter's control of freight and passenger traffic along the Atlantic Coast between Richmond and Miami. Though this had never been an issue for the two companies in the past—given Walters's close personal and business relationships with both Flagler and Kenan—the old Flagler road now struggled with the transportation demands attending the Florida land and building boom.[1]

The FEC could move people and goods in only one direction at a time on its single-track line, and even then it lacked the equipment to move them adequately. More to the point, the ACL was double-tracking its lines between Richmond and Jacksonville, and the FEC was disrupting its train schedules between Jacksonville and New York. During the first few months of 1924 alone, the FEC delivered the northbound "Florida Special" late to Jacksonville on 91 of its 108 runs from Miami.[2]

If a buyout appealed to Kenan, it also confronted him with some difficult decisions. He had a moral and legal responsibility, it seemed, to honor the major wish expressed by Flagler and Mary Lily in their wills: to maintain, administer, develop, and *keep together* the Flagler System's properties. Yet the time seemed right to cut a deal. He had just terminated the Flagler Trust, and with the brief exception of the years between 1915 and 1918, when the FEC's unprecedented earnings were "abnormal and due to war conditions," the road was never a moneymaker. The expanding Florida economy might make it one, but no one knew how long this peculiar frenzy would last. Indeed, the state's economic growth presented Kenan and the FEC with an ultimatum: either invest in an expensive expansion project or face direct competition from the ACL, which would be forced, in the face of the FEC's poor performance and in spite of Walters's friendship with Kenan, to build its own tracks into the FEC's sacred Flagler territory between Jacksonville and Miami.

Kenan decided to keep the FEC and to honor Flagler and Mary Lily's wishes by double-tracking the road between Jacksonville and Miami. Ironically, his decision coincided with the sale of the most visible symbol of Henry and Mary Lily's life together. On March 4, 1924, while vacationing in Havana, Louise Wise Lewis agreed to sell Whitehall to a group of New York businessmen. William apparently tried to control her negotiations. When the *New York Times* first announced the sale, it reported that Henry Bemis, the manager of the Flagler System's Royal Poinciana Hotel, had purchased Whitehall for a syndicate of investors who planned to use it "for a country club." Three days later, however, when the *Times* again reported on the transaction, there was nothing about turning Whitehall into a country club and no mention of Bemis.[3]

Rather, the newspaper noted that Douglas Gibbons and other New York businessmen had purchased the mansion to use "as an apartment and a centre for arts." Specifically, Gibbons said, they intended "to construct two new wings adjoining the present building, which will be converted into apartments."[4] What Gibbons did not mention, however, was that the new wings would be ten stories high and contain 300 hotel rooms. In other words, the Flagler System's Palm Beach hotels (the Royal Poinciana and the Breakers) would soon be competing with the Palm Beach Hotel and the new Whitehall Hotel.

The large, new hotel also promised more passengers for the FEC Railway—an important consideration to the company's officials. In March 1924, in anticipation of its double-tracking project, the FEC restructured its board of directors and elected new officers. Kenan replaced Beardsley as president of the FEC Railway, Hotel, and Car Ferry companies, while the aging, almost-blind Beardsley became chairman of the board of the Flagler System and gave up his inspection and supervisory duties in Florida to another newly elected FEC officer, Lawrence Haines, who had joined Kenan as a cotrustee of Mary Lily's trust.

Kenan spent much of the spring and summer of 1924 working on the FEC's expansion plans, and on July 1 he and the road's other officers signed an agreement with Bankers Trust Company of New York. The agreement involved the sale of $1.8 million in trust equipment certificates to fund the purchase of "20 mountain type locomotives, 5 switching engines, 3 steel passenger cars, 200 steel underframe box cars, 20 cabooses and 100 ballast cars." The FEC leased the new equipment from Bankers Trust, which quickly sold the equipment certificates to large institutional investors.[5]

Kenan and his advisers then made their most important and far-reaching agreement. They mortgaged all of the FEC's properties, rights, and franchises to Bankers Trust and Bethune W. Jones of New York as security for a $45 million issue of First and Refunding 5 Percent Mortgage Bonds (F&R 5s) to double-track the FEC. The ICC authorized the bond sale on September 23, and three days later the first group of F&R 5s was sold by J. P. Morgan and Company and two other prominent New York banks, First National Bank and the National City—all three of which also purchased substantial blocks of the bonds. Unfortunately for Kenan, these decisions put him even deeper into the shadow of Henry Flagler. By quadrupling the FEC's total bonded indebtedness, the F&R 5s set the stage for some of the longest and most grueling struggles of Kenan's life, struggles that emerged from the collapse of the Florida frenzy and the national depression that followed.[6]

In the meantime, however, the Flagler heirs entered a period of unprecedented prosperity, philanthropy, and building. Bolstered by a vigorous national economy, by the wild bulls on Wall Street, and for a time at least, by the widening gyre of speculation in Florida, William and "the girls" funded and contributed to a variety of public and private projects in New York, North Carolina, and Florida. They also spent money on themselves: William on his farm, his movie camera, his stock portfolio, and a new private railroad car, and his sisters and Alice on jewels, clothes, houses, securities, and vacations across Europe and North America.

William felt particularly proud of the large apartment he purchased at the Park Lane Hotel in New York City. He and Alice had "floated around the Grand Central Terminal" since the end of the war, staying, during their long and frequent visits to the city, "at the Biltmore, Commodore, and others, until we located at the Ritz-Carlton, remaining there nearly two years." After seeing the "grand results" achieved by the Park Lane's architect-designers, Schultze and Weaver, Kenan decided to buy an apartment there, and less than two weeks after signing the FEC's new mortgage, he and Alice moved into one of the hotel's grandest suites. Located on the top floor of the beautiful new building, the apartment contained four rooms, "two baths, a Kitchenette and entrance way on the top floor, at the rear of the building," and was also a "corner apartment having North, East and South exposures."[7]

They still called Lockport home, however, and began showing their community spirit there more than ever. They joined Frederick P. James in contributing to Alice's favorite local institution, the Lockport Memorial Hospital. Alice had been the only female on the hospital's governing board since 1920, when the city's Republican administration had appointed her to the position, and William had been providing the hospital with free milk and cream since that time. They now joined James, the president of the hospital board, in funding a new nurses' home adjacent to the hospital. James and Kenan each gave $25,000 to cover the cost of constructing the facility, and Alice donated $10,000 to equip it. When completed the following year, the Lockport Hospital Nurses Home "was one of the most completely equipped training schools for its size in New York State."[8]

William's hospital gift also coincided with his donations to the YMCA in Lockport. Like his father, who had been "much interested in the welfare of boys and . . . active in the work of the YMCA" in Wilmington,[9] William "was very fond of young people and doing for [them]," one female acquaintance recalled, "particularly for boys."[10] In addition to contributing $25,000 toward a new YMCA building in Lockport, William purchased seven acres of land for a YMCA camp on "the shore of Lake Ontario at Barker, N.Y. (which is about 18 miles northeast of Lockport) at a cost of $15,000."[11]

This became Camp Kenan and "a source of great satisfaction" to its benefactor. It allowed him to watch "these young fellows develop, not only physically, but in proper habits of life and conduct" and to shape the life and conduct of the camp itself. Kenan envisioned a place where "average working men could afford to send their children" and where the camp itself helped make this possible. "I stated very definitely that in my opinion there was no excuse for a camp that could not earn its operating expenses. Not to make money, but the rates charged should be sufficient to pay its way and build up a reasonable surplus for a rainy day." And Kenan got what he wanted; after operating at a loss for the first few years, the camp was able, Kenan noted, to build up a "nice surplus" while charging rates that were "much lower than any other camp of equal facility."[12]

This display of community interest in Lockport was unprecedented for Kenan, and for a variety of reasons it was all he ever showed. The place had more to do with the history of the Flagler family than with that of the Kenans. Only because Henry Flagler had gotten him a job at Traders Paper Company had William initially settled in Lockport, and he would have gladly returned to Wilmington if Henry had helped him with the paper mill project. What was more, William had spent much of his time since Flagler's death in New York City, working in the Flagler System's offices at 120 Broadway, and he and Alice left Lockport prior to some of the most important personal and community celebrations of the year, Christmas and New Year's. They did not return from Florida until April and soon left Lockport again to live in a hotel in New York City. Only in late July and August, in fact, did they spend much time at 433 Locust Street, and only then until the weather in western New York drove them back to their hotel in the city.

Kenan's local church and club connections did not fill him with any strong sense of community spirit either. Much of this was his own fault and fancy. He left the church-going to Alice and the golf-playing to others. Alice's family had been connected with the Presbyterian Society of the Village of Lockport since the mid-nineteenth century, and Alice, a Sunday School teacher, went to church every Sunday. But William rarely went; after getting back from New York City on Saturday nights, he spent his Sundays at Randleigh Farm, breaking only for lunch at the Town and Country Club, where unlike most of its male members, he never played golf. Although he soon started taking golf lessons, he did not join Alice's church until after her death in 1946.[13]

There was little community spirit for Kenan to catch in Lockport, anyway, and little sense of community among the residents themselves, at least not beyond their ethnic, religious, and neighborhood affiliations. "When I was a little girl," one former resident recalled, "people socialized pretty much within their church community. The Protestants were all very friendly. We did things sometimes together. We weren't ecumaniacs, but we sometimes got together, generally for political reasons and for general community. Protestants were pretty much on one side and the Roman Catholics on the other."[14] Increasing, too, were people on other sides of the community equation—the unknowns of the postwar influx of European immigrants. The Poles and Italians changed the sights and sounds of Lowertown, and the Ku Klux Klan appeared in the village. "The people who came in after World War I were mostly from southern Europe and spoke Italian. They were the green-grocers and they didn't fit. They were Roman Catholics too."[15]

Kenan fit into Lockport better than most of these newcomers, but he always occupied a class and category of his own. Born, raised, and educated in the South, he remained both an insider and an outsider. Most Lockportians knew him only by name, as the city's wealthiest resident, or by sight, as the man who walked back and forth between Uppertown and Lowertown. Although they occasionally saw him boarding or disembarking from his railroad car, being chauffeured in his Cadillac Victoria, or driving Alice to Olcutt Beach in a fringed surry drawn by two Morgan Walkers, few people knew anything more about him.

Not surprisingly, Kenan made few close friends in Lockport, not only because he was frequently away but because he was a hard man to get to know. Secrecy and formality had shaped his life since his college days and had become even more ingrained in his personality during the Flagler years and the Mary Lily fiasco. In truth, the only person he considered loyal to him in Lockport was Schuyler Beattie, his private local secretary, and he even kept his guard up with Beattie, who also acted as his purchasing agent at Western Block. "Mr. Kenan was always formal with my father," Beattie's daughter recalled. "I felt that Mr. Kenan basically relaxed with very few people. I always felt that he was very relaxed with Mrs. Kenan and with his sisters, to a degree that he wasn't even with my father, and even maybe a little bit with me."[16]

If there was anything about his secretary that made William uncomfortable, it was Beattie's social and political activities. Beattie was a leader of both the local Republican party and the local chapter of Freemasons, and though Kenan shared his secretary's party affiliation, he did not like politics and he did not like the Masons. This was never a problem for the two men, however, until 1925, when one of Beattie's fellow Masons, a Democrat, was elected mayor of Lockport and decided to make some changes in the Board of Managers at the city-run hospital.

LOSING TRACK

The FEC was double-tracking its line as quickly as possible during this period, but it could not keep pace with events in Florida. The state's population increased by an estimated 1.5 million in 1925 alone, and some of the most spectacular growth occurred in the old Flagler domain along the lower east coast. Between 1920 and 1925 Miami's population grew from 30,000 to 200,000, and in the wilderness to the north, about halfway between Miami and Palm Beach, the talented, gold-digging Mizener brothers began what they optimistically billed as the world's greatest resort: Boca Raton. Indeed, like many others, the Mizeners realized that automobiles and highways had erased the Flagler System's intertwined monopoly of transportation and tourist accommodations in the region.

The FEC's traffic volume increased by 70 percent between 1923 and 1925, mostly in the form of building materials, and the Flagler System's various land companies did an unprecedented amount of business. Everyone wanted to build "streets, houses and store buildings, along with elegant apartments and luxurious resort hotels. It seemed impossible to get enough, men, equipment, and materials to do it all soon enough, but the developers were trying. And then there were all the creature needs and wants of those hundreds of thousands of new people. The challenge proved too much for existing storage and transportation facilities."[17]

It certainly proved too much for the FEC's single-track line, which slowed the company's doubling-tracking project as well as construction projects all along the lower east coast. Yet the old Flagler road was not the only impediment. "There was not enough terminal and dock space to handle the shipments coming in by train and ships, partly because there were not enough auto trucks or horse-drawn drays to remove goods from loading docks or enough warehouses in the boom communities to receive the goods." And the boomers kept betting. Freight cars began piling up on the FEC's spurs, sidings, and yards in the spring of 1925, and it was not long before the "congestion backed up toward the northern part of the state as hundreds of additional freight cars jammed through the Florida gateways." The Flagler System had to do something to protect its road, and it had to do it quickly.[18]

It also had to do something at Palm Beach, where on March 18 the second

Breakers went up in smoke. Constructed in 1903 from tar-rich Dade County pine, the timbers of the famous hotel fueled the fire throughout the day and into the night. Some of the guests "flung furs and jewelry from the windows before they fled," but most watched the blaze from where they were when it erupted: on the beach and golf course. Luckily no one was injured, but the smoldering ruins "signaled the end of the era of wooden hotels in southeast Florida."[19]

William received the news with mixed emotions. On the one hand the building had been his most important monument in Florida. He had rebuilt its power plant in 1903 in the aftermath of the fire that destroyed the first Breakers, and he had also done its "steam, water, telephone, . . . Ice Plant and Laundry" systems. On the other hand, though, he now had a chance to further both his own personal goals and those of the Flagler System. By building a new Breakers on the site of the old ones and by making it a modern, luxurious facility, he would send a signal to the system's competitors and to others that he was committed both to tradition and innovation and that he was at least the equal of Henry Flagler as a builder. Kenan decided "we should rebuild with fireproof construction and attempt to make the Breakers the finest resort hotel in the World."[20]

The Flagler System badly needed to send such a signal. Most of its hotels had been built in the 1890s, and unlike their new concrete competitors, all but the St. Augustine hotels were built of wood. They were huge, Victorian structures, expensive to maintain and to operate, and as firetraps and outmoded relics of a bygone era, they were not as appealing as their "modern" competitors. And the FEC Hotel Company could not afford to lose out to its competitors in Palm Beach, for that was already happening to its hotels in St. Augustine. Both the Cordoba and the Alcazar were struggling to stay open, and for the first time in its history, the Ponce de Leon failed to earn its operating expenses.[21]

William had a different plan for resurrecting the fortunes of the Flagler System's St. Augustine hotels: golf. The game was all the rage among the wealthy and upper middle classes, and the Flagler System had a head start with it, especially in St. Augustine, where one of the state's few good, grass courses existed. Though neither he nor Alice nor Sarah cared for the game, Jessie and Louise loved to play, and so, too, in increasing numbers, did other women. "It was hoped to make St. Augustine the center for winter golf and several tournaments of national prominence were inaugurated," Kenan later wrote. "A women's tournament, the Florida East Coast Women's Championship for the Mrs. Wm. R. Kenan, Jr., Cup, was started in 1925." Two national men's tournaments were added later.[22]

By the time William returned from Florida to the Park Lane Hotel, the FEC's freight yards were completely filled with railroad cars, and its inability to clear them was causing endless delays for all of the railroads in Florida. Thus

Jessie Kenan Wise and her daughter, Louise Wise Lewis. (HMFM Archives)

the FEC "began refusing to accept cars destined for the Miami area from its connections at Jacksonville, which meant that the Southern and the ACL [railroads] had to stack cars on their sidings in Georgia and the Carolinas." This forced them in turn to place embargoes "on carload shipments bound for the busiest points in Florida. Since all traffic destined for points on the Florida

East Coast Railway and most freight for other parts of the state passed through Jacksonville, a serious bottleneck had developed there by late summer."[23]

In the meantime Kenan selected one of New York's most prominent hotel designers, Leonard Schultze, as the architect for the new Breakers. Schultze had designed the Park Lane Hotel and other buildings in the Grand Central Station area, including the station's terminal and the Biltmore, Commodore, Ambassador, and Waldorf-Astoria hotels. "I had never met the man," Kenan claimed, "so called him on the 'phone and asked him to call at my office, which he did." Kenan was impressed; already a fan of Schultze's hotel work, he liked the man he met. Schultze believed that "there should be uniformity in planning—Paris was his ideal."[24]

If William cared little about Schultze's Parisian ideal, he did share the architect's desire for uniformity in planning, and the two men quickly agreed on Italian architecture for the new hotel. They had little choice. Given both their penchant for uniformity and the prevailing architectural style in Palm Beach, they had to construct a building that would blend with yet stand out from the fashionable Palm Beach style: a "pseudo-Mediterranean village. The pastel stucco walls, variegated tile-roofs, lofty towers, and cast stone, wrought iron, and polychrome tile decorative details set amidst the lush semi-tropical landscapes."[25]

Italian architecture would also enable the Breakers to stand out from two of the most important new buildings on Palm Beach, the Everglades Club and Mar-a-Lago, the Hutton mansion. Soon to become the most fabulous private residence on Palm Beach, Mar-a-Lago's designs were described in May 1925 as "resembling a tiny Spanish village," a description not unlike that of the Everglades Club: "a little bit of Seville and the Alhambra, a dash of Madiera and Algiers." Outdoing the Everglades Club was particularly important to Kenan, for the exclusive club had eclipsed the Flagler tradition at Palm Beach. Financed by Paris Singer and designed by Addison Mizener, it had changed "forever the nature of Palm Beach as a winter resort."

> Until 1918 social life centered on the Flagler hotels and the Beach Club, Colonel Bradley's gambling casino. In the period after World War I, when growing wealth allowed America's middle class to plan winter vacations, society found its exclusiveness threatened. Almost anyone who could afford it could register at the Royal Poinciana, the Breakers or the Palm Beach Hotel. The Everglades Club, with its expensive restrictive membership, allowed for a new definition of society in the winter resort.[26]

Put bluntly, it gave Palm Beach society "a private club to escape the bourgeois guests at the hotels."[27]

Kenan did not give a damn about being part of Palm Beach society, and being thoroughly bourgeois himself, he did not resent the bourgeoisie paying to stay in his hotels. What he did resent, and what made the new Breakers so important to him, was the prospect of being perceived as anything less than Henry Flagler's equal. Mr. Flagler built the best and attracted the best. He had established the link between American society and his hotels, and that link had been broken on William's watch. That is why the new Breakers was so important to Kenan. He had a chance to reestablish that link with a new jewel in the Flagler System's crown. He sent Schultze to Italy to gather ideas.

Kenan may have been having chest pains again by the time Schultze left, for in August 1925 he did something totally out of character. He took a two-week vacation with several other men from Lockport. He went fishing for the first time since "I left the south to reside. . . . Five of my friends and myself went to Oak Orchard Lodge in the Kawatha Lake District, about 225 miles from Lockport." The trip made Kenan one of the boys again. "We took three motor cars loaded with our equipment, two men to each car; motored to Toronto and went northwest to Petersborough, Ontario, and back into the woods 16 miles. The nearest inhabitants was the Indian Village about five miles down Buckhorn Lake." The pace and pleasure also helped Kenan take his mind off his problems. "We fished each day from seven in the morning until six at night, taking about an hour and a half for lunch, which the guides always prepared."[28]

Kenan was back in New York City by mid-August, however, tackling the final details of the new Breakers. Schultze had returned from Italy with several design schemes for the hotel as well as sample furnishings for its public spaces, and Kenan now wanted him to do more. He asked him to pursue the uniformity of planning that characterized the Park Lane, to do the furnishings and equipment for the entire hotel, even the linens, china, and silverware. After some hesitation, Schultze agreed to accept the task, and his energy and efficiency amazed even Kenan, who considered him "the only architect I ever met that knew the value of a dollar."

> [Schultze] rented a loft in the city, built a typical bed room with bath and installed the windows, doors and all equipment including the hardware. He painted the trim, walls and ceilings many times to get the right combination, had several carpets woven and placed on the floor; about twelve different pairs of hangings for the windows; then put in the electric fixtures and made a completely equipped room. . . . He also prepared a book (which was called "the bible") which contained a description of each piece of furniture, sample of the upholstering and also samples of carpet and hanging in each public room and the location of each piece, as a record to be used for future information.[29]

While Schultze experimented, Kenan worked on the railroad mess in Florida. In late October he and the presidents of the state's other major railroads "agreed to impose a general embargo on carload shipments to all points in Florida. Exceptions were made for livestock, fertilizers, perishables, petroleum products, foodstuffs, and packaging materials for fruits and vegetables." Other exceptions could also be approved—an outlet that William badly needed to ensure the progress of the Breakers project. The railroads agreed to "issue permits for other traffic depending on their abilities to handle it and the willingness of cosignees to unload shipments immediately on arrival."[30] The freight cars continued to pile up, however, and there was a "lag of several more days when all the shipments initiated before the embargo gathered on Florida-bound lines. The situation peaked about mid-November, with south-bound movement of freight to Florida nearly paralyzed."[31]

Also in November, Louise Wise Lewis filed for a divorce from her husband, Lawrence. "I don't think there was any alcohol in that period," their daughter recently stated. "They were young. They were beautiful. They rode together—they were in horse shows together at the Greenbrier. Father had a black stallion and a black habit; and mother had a grey mare, and she wore a white linen side-saddle skirt . . . and her black hat with a veil. And they jumped tandem." But not at one gate. Lawrence "was too proud to cope with $66 million being thrown in his lap," his daughter exaggerated. "He just couldn't do it. . . . They were the most beautiful couple until she inherited $66 million, and that was the end of it. She just thought it was glorious and he couldn't handle it."[32]

The news in New York was not encouraging, either. Lockport's voters divorced themselves from five years of Republican control by electing Beattie's fellow Mason and political foe, Democrat Frank J. Moyer Jr., as mayor. And in New York City the FEC's chairman of the board, William Beardsley, lay dying in his home. Though he and Kenan had had their differences in the past, Beardsley knew the Flagler System from top to bottom; he was almost as important to Kenan and his family as Henry Walters. Not only was he the chief financial adviser for the system, for Louise Wise Lewis, and for Dr. Owen Kenan, but he also worked closely with Kenan and Walters on most postwar matters in Florida, from the strike, the boom, and the buyout offer to the double-tracking, Breakers, and embargo decisions. His death on Christmas Eve left a gap in the Flagler System that was never filled.[33]

In the meantime, moreover, the company hired to build the Breakers Hotel, the Turner Construction Company of New York, faced serious problems in Florida. It had assembled a team of supervisors and had procured permits for transporting materials to Palm Beach, but only a few carloads of the supplies arrived. As a result of the transportation bottleneck at Jacksonville, "construction conditions in Florida were at their worst. Everywhere large hotels and other projects were being rushed to completion to accommodate the winter influx of tourists for 1925–26."[34]

New tracks and a new hotel—the time seemed right for the FEC's president to have a new railroad car. He had not bought a cow for more than a year, and the Randleigh had been built, after all, for someone else. Kenan wanted to design his own car, one that reflected his wealth and position as well as the Flagler System's commitment to the finest accommodations.

Just as he and Schultze had done with the new Breakers, he "started from scratch" on plans for a new private railroad car. "I made many floor plans and some detail notes of what could be done and, during December, 1925, I sent the plans to the Pullman Company and ordered them to build a car for me. The agreement was on a cost plus basis, since I insisted that we use the best material and equipment obtainable, whether produced by the Pullman Company or other manufacturers." The only problem Kenan encountered involved the size of his new Pullman. He wanted a big, extra long one. "The car was 85'0" overall,—when built the longest car in existence. I had quite an argument with the builders because of the length."[35]

Otherwise, the Florida season went fairly well for William and Alice. Despite a lot of sadness and head-shaking over Lawrence, Louise, and their children, the divorce was quick and, apparently, without hostility. Louise got custody of Lawrence Jr. and Mary Lily for ten months a year, while their father reportedly "got $1,000,000 as a parting remembrance" from Louise.[36] At the same time, the completion of the FEC's double-tracking project facilitated work on the Breakers. "By the end of February the transportation situation cleared up rapidly and during March, for the first time, it was possible to make real progress on the work."[37]

William also received his new railroad car that spring. The thousand-ton Pullman cost him $92,000, and from its decor and air conditioning to its linens and china, this "longest car in existence" surpassed even William's desire for attention, luxury, and uniformity. "The car was an all steel car lined with American walnut waxed and had two large bed rooms with dressing rooms and toilet attached; two small bed rooms, with toilets; a large dining room, large observation room, butler's pantry and kitchen and crew quarters sufficient for three men. A bath room in the center of the car with regular porcelain tub and shower, also a shower and toilet for crew." The dining room was blue, the observation room was painted a sherry color, "Mrs. Kenan's room was apple green," and William's room was "tan." "All hangings, carpets, bed covers, etc., were in harmony with the separate colors of each room."[38]

Kenan stuck with the name "Randleigh" because it and his initials were monogrammed on all the equipment. "The car was air-conditioned throughout and was the best job I have seen. The control was so perfect that in any room you would not notice any circulation of air or draft." What you would notice were the car's exquisite furnishings. "The linen—both table and bed—

was all pure linen, made in Ireland. The blankets were all wool, first quality in color to match the rooms. The glass-ware was of special design and made in Czechoslovakia. The china was made in Bavaria. The carpets were of special design, made to match in color each room, by the Hartford Biglow Co."[39]

Kenan's new car arrived at the same time as a prospectus for a new stadium at Chapel Hill. The university's old stadium was adequate for baseball games and track meets, but its wooden stands could not accommodate the thousands of fans who showed up for football games and other outdoor pageants and programs "requiring large space combined with convenient seating arrangements."[40] William agreed to contribute to the stadium project on the same basis as the university's other alumni, but since he was already hoping, according to one source, to establish "some form of memorial to his father and mother" at UNC, the prospectus "suggested to him that the benefaction he contemplated might well take the form of a memorial stadium." William was also motivated by the intimate involvement of James and John Morehead in the project. James, a resident of Durham, was a member of the six-man alumni stadium committee, and he and his cousin John, William's old Union Carbide friend, had taken the lead in pledging donations for the proposed stadium. What is more, UNC had recently awarded John Motley Morehead an honorary doctor of laws degree.[41]

William handled the situation with strict formality and diplomacy, hoping thereby to avoid the turmoil created by his cousin Graham in the selection of the first Kenan professors. "With fine modesty and tact he indicated to the stadium committee the attraction the idea held for him. But at the same time he deferred to the whole body of alumni should they desire to erect the stadium according to the original plan. In case they should, he reiterated his desire to contribute on the same basis as the others." The stadium committee responded "immediately by unanimously approving the construction by him of a stadium of 24,000 capacity as a memorial to his father and mother."[42]

As the stadium went up, the Florida boom went bust. The "snarled railroad lines, overextended credit, the price cycle, buyer fears spawned by northern banker hostility to money fleeing their banks for dubious Florida real estate and, finally, rumors of intrusive action by the Internal Revenue Service" all contributed to the collapse, as did other, more sinister forces. The situation was similar, in fact, to the savings and loan scandals of the 1980s, in which the success of the system depended on fraud, greed, and continuous expansion.[43] Banks, brokers, and "binder boys" found it impossible to generate enough cash to keep their speculative schemes afloat, for people stopped buying and paying for land, the fuel that fired the development frenzy. "By the early weeks of 1926, there were already many worried people on the Gold Coast—people who held binders on lots for which they could not keep up the payments, people who were anxiously searching for suddenly scarce buyers."[44]

The situation also created serious financial problems for the banks in Georgia and Florida that fueled the boom and for their equally avaricious allies, the real estate developers. Without a continuous flow of new capital into the system, the developers could not repay the Florida banks that loaned them money for both their existing and planned projects. This meant, in turn, that the lending banks lacked the funds to keep the system churning. They had nothing to deposit, in short, in the Georgia banks from which they had been receiving high interest rates on deposits—rates and deposits that not only inflated the speculative bubble in Florida but also provided the Georgia money-center banks with capital to invest in risky projects of their own.[45]

The most ominous sign of the system's shakiness occurred in November 1925, when T. Coleman duPont resigned as chairman of the board of the Mizener Development Corporation (MDC), the largest and most unscrupulous development firm in Florida. The MDC was headed by Addison Mizener, Palm Beach's first "society architect," who succeeded in interesting duPont and duPont's friends, congressman George Graham and financier Jesse Livermore, in backing the MDC's development plans in Boca Raton and elsewhere. By the end of 1925, however, the MDC was so desperate for new business that it started offering newspaper coupons that prospective buyers could clip and use instead of money as a binder fee to buy land on promise of a later down payment. DuPont got out while the getting was good.

William allegedly learned of these and other developments from his cousin Tom's father-in-law, Frank Hawkins. A prominent Atlanta banker who also speculated in Florida land and hotel developments, Hawkins was apparently aware of the precarious position of the Atlanta-based W. D. Manley banking chain. The chain consisted of some 200 banks in Georgia and Florida, many of them directly linked to the speculative bubble in Florida. The Georgia banks acted as money-center banks for the chain's affiliated banks in Florida, including the four Palm Beach banks associated with the MDC, while Manley and his associates invested the deposits of the Florida banks in such speculative ventures as Morningside Heights in Atlanta.[46]

Kenan could do little, of course, to take advantage of these alleged warnings. He was not affiliated with the MDC or the Manly banking chain; the FEC already had been double-tracked and burdened with a huge new debt; and the FEC Hotel Company was now committed to the $6 million Breakers project. Indeed, William could only watch as the boom went bust. A banking panic began in Palm Beach in June 1926 with the failure of four local banks affiliated with Mizener and Manley. Mizener was immediately indicted for fraud, Manley was indicted in July, and within a ten-day period in July, 117 banks in Georgia and Florida also failed.

The panic coincided with the completion of the massive frame for the new Breakers Hotel. Constructed of reinforced concrete with a thousand tons of heavy structural steel, the building had been planned for "such sturdy construction that it would withstand without damage the violent storms that sometimes visit Florida between seasons." The planning now paid off, as natural disasters hastened the economic catastrophe. A huge storm hit Palm Beach in July, and two months later a hurricane smashed into the peninsula, causing widespread property damage along the lower east coast.[47] The storm ripped up portions of the Flagler System's Royal Palm Hotel in Miami and "deposited steam vessels on city streets, ruined hotels and apartment buildings and strewed mud and debris over many a handsome development community." The storms also delayed construction of the Breakers at Palm Beach, but "a most commendable spirit was maintained on the work and the whole-hearted co-operation of the various sub-contractors" made it possible not only for the builders to resume their work immediately but also to continue to hope that the hotel would be ready for the 1926–27 tourist season.[48]

William had the same hope when he left New York to inspect the Breakers in mid-November. The Flagler System badly needed the Breakers to open on time; having already lost one season of revenue from the famous hotel, it could not afford to lose another, especially since it now had to pay for the new structure. In Miami, moreover, the storm-damaged Royal Palm would not be reopened, while throughout Florida neither the system's officials nor anyone else knew how the banking panic and the storm might affect the tourist season. The Royal Poinciana probably would do well at Palm Beach, as would the Ormond Hotel at Ormond Beach and the system's relatively new hotel at Key West, the Casa Marina Hotel, which had become a popular stopover for wealthy travelers on their way to Havana, Cuba. But the prospects appeared bleak for the system's St. Augustine hotels. Even with the aid of the women's golf tournament, the Cordoba and the Alcazar barely covered their operating costs, and the Ponce recorded yet another unprofitable season.

William briefly visited the UNC campus before continuing to Palm Beach to inspect the Breakers. The trustees had selected a site for the stadium and a company to build it, and Kenan wanted to have a look at both. The proposed site lay in a "natural valley about two thousand feet from the center of the campus . . . just above the spot long known as The Meeting of the Waters." William approved both the site and the company and then formally announced his gift of $275,000 to carry out the project. Kenan Memorial Stadium would be built on a plot of land adjacent to the one his eighteenth-century ancestors had donated to the university.[49]

Already swelling with pride when he reached Palm Beach, the sight of the new nine-story Breakers heightened William's pleasure. Patterned after some of Italy's most famous Renaissance villas, especially the Villa Medici in Rome, the 500-room hotel was "nothing less than an Italian palace." It had twin belvedere towers and exquisite arches; elaborate stonework; ornamental iron balconies; sloping roofs of red, Old World tile; and a light-buff stucco finish—a beautiful exterior with no equal on the island. Its grand interiors were likewise unmatched. William marveled at the luxurious appointments as he wandered from room to room: beautiful painted ceilings, "15th century Flemish tapestries, frescoes, framed portraits, vaulted ceilings, the Great Stone Fireplace and a breathtaking Venetian chandelier of bronze." Hundreds of craftsmen were still at work, but the builders assured him that everything would be ready by the end of the year. His hotel would far surpass anything his brother-in-law had built.[50]

Almost everything seemed right in William's world as he boarded the Randleigh to return to Lockport. He had the world's longest railroad car, the world's finest resort hotel, Kenan Memorial Stadium, Camp Kenan, the Nurses Home and Randleigh Farm in Lockport, a beautiful fountain and apartment building in Wilmington, and the FEC's new double-track line in Florida. If the Flagler System faced problems and uncertainty in the crumbling Florida economy, William's own personal finances had never been better. He was enjoying the running of the bulls on Wall Street.

THE SEARCH FOR ORDER

Back in Lockport, however, William found Alice close to tears. The new mayor wanted her off the hospital board; she could either resign her position or be removed from it. William had a pretty good idea of the mayor's motivation, and he later revealed it to "Hank" the milkman, an employee at Randleigh Farm. "He said the mayor was all the time trying to get him to become a Mason, and Mr. Kenan would say, 'No, I don't want to be a Mason. . . . The Masonic Lodge wants to get all the wealthiest people and all the people in business to become Masons because then they could put pressure on these people for money and jobs. That's against my principles and I refused them.' . . . Anyway it broke her heart and Mr. Kenan was furious."[51]

Alice resigned from the hospital board in early December, and less than a week later William's lawyer allegedly presented the city of Lockport with a huge bill for the "free" milk and cream he had been giving the hospital. "And they shut down the city of Lockport period," the milkman claimed. "This lawyer had the papers from one of the state supreme courts. . . . It was a demand, and Lockport didn't have that much money in the treasury at that time. . . . The city had to scramble for a whole week before they could raise the money to pay the $36,000 that they owed."

Needless to say, the incident completely soured William's newfound community spirit. It "left a very bad taste in Mr. Kenan's mouth, and Mrs. Kenan, she was heartbroken," the milkman recalled. "She never got over that, being taken off the hospital board by a vindictive mayor. Mr. Kenan said from that day on he would do nothing to help the city of Lockport. . . . He told me, 'Young man, I will never do anything for the city of Lockport.' I just said, 'Mr. Kenan, the mayor was just one person.' He said, 'Yes, but he was a stinker. For that reason I never would give anything to the city of Lockport again.' "[52]

William also began developing a bitter estrangement from his divorced niece. Two days after Alice sent in her resignation, Louise's boyfriend, Hugh "Dick" Lewis, obtained a marriage license in New York City and reserved "the most luxurious suite" available on the Italian ocean liner *Duilio*. While William's sisters may have been aware of what was going on, especially Louise's mother, Jessie, neither William nor any members of Dick's family appear to have known that Dick and Louise were planning to get married.[53]

If Louise mentioned the subject at all to William and Alice, it was after they arrived in St. Augustine for Christmas. Although Louise liked Aunt Alice very much, Uncle William strongly irritated her. He tried to rule her life as he ruled the Flagler empire, and she resented it. He had opposed her divorce. He disliked her St. Augustine friends. He criticized her drinking and spending habits, and he thought she neglected her children. But she did not care what he thought. She did not even stay in Florida to celebrate the official opening of the new Breakers. She left St. Augustine in early January and traveled alone to New York City, where, on January 8, in her suite at the Hotel Vanderbilt, she and Dick Lewis were married by the Reverend Barton B. Bigler of St. Augustine. William did not give her away this time, however; no one did. In fact, no one from her immediate family attended the wedding. Her lone relative there was her cousin and childhood friend from Macon, Georgia, Iola Wise Stetson, who came with her husband, Eugene Stetson, a vice-president of the Guaranty Trust Company of New York.[54]

Most of what William and his family learned about the wedding came from the Florida papers that picked up the story from the Sunday *New York Times*. "FLAGLER HEIRESS IS WED SECRETLY," blared the front-page headlines in the *Times*, "BULK OF $70,000,000 ESTATE WAS LEFT TO HER—HE IS IN ICE BUSINESS." The most interesting part of the story concerned the alleged response of the Lewis family. "From friends of the bridegroom, who refused to give their names, it was learned that his family was opposed to the marriage and that his mother, Mrs. Albert Lewis, and his sister, Mrs. Charles M. Kliner, had arrived here several days before the time set for the wedding to make a final plea with him not to go through with the ceremony." The *Times* reporter tried to talk with the newlyweds after they boarded the *Duilio*, but "even on the steamer every precaution was taken to keep their marriage from becoming known. They locked themselves in their suite, where the door was guarded by a private detective, and refused to be interviewed."[55]

The Breakers Hotel at the time of its completion, 1927. (Thomas S. Kenan III)

If the christening of the Breakers was thus not as happy and fulfilling for William as it might have been, he did derive great pleasure from the public's response to the fabulous new hotel. "So anxious were many of the members of the Palm Beach winter colony here to partake in the opening of the New Breakers Hotel, that they arrived early in December and stayed at other hotels so that they could be at hand when the time came to move their things into The Breakers." Their time came on December 29, two weeks before the official opening of the hotel, when the management threw "open its beautiful new doors . . . [and] the Palm Beach official season opened." Everyone who saw the hotel considered it "the world's masterpiece," one source chirped, and destined to outdo its predecessors as "the center of all the activity of Palm Beach."[56]

Immediately after the opening festivities William rode the Randleigh back to St. Augustine, where he put into writing what he had expressed verbally to Henry C. Turner, the president of the Turner Construction Company. "In my opinion this is the best construction job I have ever seen, and your organization, in large part, is responsible for that result."[57] Yet Leonard Schultze was the man of the hour for Kenan. Schultze had done more than he promised and "still insisted that I could pay him anything," Kenan recalled. "After much discussion it was finally agreed that both of us would place an amount on a piece of paper and then expose it." Schultze's figures endeared him to Kenan, who was well aware of "the total cost of the work . . . and had some idea as to what would be fair and just. Strange as it may seem, when we exposed our figures they were both the same and every one was happy."[58]

But life was not rosy for long. Most of the guests who opened the new Breakers were winter colony regulars who "as usual spent the early season at The Breakers before moving over to the Royal Poinciana upon its opening" in mid-January. Other guests arrived to replace them, but the new hotel did not fill up. The banking panic had combined with the hurricane to diminish Florida's attraction for the rest of the country, and the pushing hordes of sunseekers and speculators had dwindled considerably. Rather than being impossible to obtain, reservations at the new Breakers were only "very difficult" to get. Finding a room was even easier in St. Augustine, where despite the third annual FEC Women's Golf Championship, the Flagler System's three hotels did not do well at all.[59]

Rather than give up his golf plans, however, Kenan expanded the system's investment in the game and tried to learn to play it himself. He had grass greens installed on the Royal Poinciana course in Palm Beach and added another tournament at St. Augustine, the men's National Championship of Golf Club Champions. He also "commenced taking lessons from Johnny Farrell, the Professional, in 1927 in St. Augustine. I played a number of times that winter season; purchased a leather bag with a complete set of clubs, balls, tees, etc."[60]

Unfortunately William's decision to take up golf had as much to do with his efforts to escape depressing family matters as it did with his desire to learn a game he hoped would improve his hotel business. The "girls" made depressing company that season; when they were not talking about Alice's forced resignation from the hospital board, they were wringing their hands about Louise and her children. Indeed, in mid-February they had to rush Lawrence Lewis Jr. to Johns Hopkins Hospital to be treated for some unspecified and short-lived illness. The *New York Times* tried to find out what was wrong, running the headline, "FLAGLER HEIR IN HOSPITAL," but his aunts "declined to discuss" his ailment. The newspaper could only report that he was being seen by a "noted" brain surgeon and that "the lad's mother, who is in Italy on her second honeymoon, has been summoned and the child's father, Lawrence Lewis of Richmond, Va., who was divorced from Mrs. Lewis two years ago, was reported on the way to Baltimore."[61]

The Kenans returned from Florida needing a vacation. William was still in good health at age fifty-five, but the physical and psychological burdens of the past year had eroded his seemingly endless supply of energy and enthusiasm. Alice, however, was not in good health. Several contemporary photographs

Kenan Memorial Stadium, ca. 1927. (NCC)

show the sixty-two-year-old woman supported by the steady arms and hands of William and others. Also, for the first time in several years, she, Jessie, and Sarah did not go to Europe. William took them on a long vacation in the Randleigh instead, to Yellowstone Park and the West Coast, along the "southern route." The only thing they had to do was get on board and enjoy the journey. William's secretaries made all the railroad connections and hotel reservations, while the Randleigh's three "excellent" black servants—a steward, a cook, and a porter—catered to the needs of the wealthy travelers. The trip, William noted, cost him "$4,263.00."[62]

Kenan continued to keep business at bay for the rest of the summer. He bought some cows, fished in the Canadian wilderness, purchased another "complete outfit" of golf equipment, and made his first appearance on the links in Lockport, playing "possibly a dozen times that summer."[63] Shortly after he returned from Canada, moreover, the University of North Carolina notified him that the stadium was finished and awaiting his inspection. On October 1, while on his way to Florida for the annual fall survey of the Flagler System, he "inspected the completed stadium, congratulated the builders on its beauty, and gave $28,000 for the construction of the field house."[64]

Kenan Memorial Stadium was dedicated on Thanksgiving Day, 1927, before the annual UNC-Virginia game. It was a wonderful day for William. He and Alice sat in the stands with the Venables and John and Genevieve Morehead, who had ridden down with them in the Randleigh.[65] The university band opened the ceremonies with a rousing rendition of "The Old North State," and John Sprunt Hill followed with the "Presentation of the Stadium on Behalf of the Donor." North Carolina governor Angus McLean spoke next, accepting the stadium on behalf of the state and the university. The ceremony ended with the band playing and 24,000 spectators singing "Hark the Sound of Tar Heel Voices."[66]

Then the game started. Carolina had lost twenty-one of the thirty-one previous contests and had not defeated Virginia since 1922. The "Program of Exercises" listed the final score of every game and included a photograph of the 1893 football team, showing Charlie Baskerville with his arm draped around his senior roommate, Will Kenan. William wished that Charlie could have been there with him and Dr. Venable that day. The recently deceased scientist would have relished UNC's stunning 14-13 upset win over Virginia.

After saying their good-byes to Venable and his wife, the Kenans and the Moreheads returned to Durham and boarded the waiting Randleigh for a trip to Spray, North Carolina, the birthplace of calcium carbide. Though Morehead was now a resident of Rye, New York, he had preserved his old family homestead and was in the habit, Kenan recalled, of returning there "each Fall for several days quail shooting. They had about a dozen hunting dogs and they fed the quail to keep them on the farm. Several New York City men joined us and they outfitted me completely, it was hunting under ideal conditions. I had not fired a gun in 32 years and of course was somewhat nervous as to the results. However, during two whole days my kill was just as good as those who had been hunting each year. To say that I enjoyed it is putting it mildly." Kenan never returned to Spray, however, and he never hunted again, "except to shoot a few starlings that attempted to roost in the trees at our home."[67]

Kenan did no more building, either. Instead he was forced to prevent the crumbling of what he had inherited and built. Not only were the Florida hotels continuing to lose money, but the FEC Railway was suffering a marked decline in revenues as a result of the slumping tourist trade and lower freight and passenger rates established by the ICC. At the same time motor trucks, which moved freight much more cheaply and efficiently than the railroads, began cutting into the FEC's freight business, while private autos and bus lines diminished its passenger business, especially on local routes. Americans now drove their "tin-lizzies" over newly constructed roads and highways to do business and pleasure in neighboring towns. By the time the Tamiami Trail opened in 1928, the FEC Railway was operating at a deficit.[68]

That did not stop the railroad's president from contemplating a proposal from two World War I aviators, Juan T. Trippe and John T. Hambleton, who had just launched America's first international air service: a mail route between Key West and Havana. "This operation was reasonably successful," Kenan wrote, but Trippe and Hambleton "concluded it would be better to operate from Miami and have operating connection with the railroads. Of course they needed additional capital and solicited help from the A.C.L. and the F.E.C. Ry."[69]

Kenan initially turned down Trippe and Hambleton. "When they discussed the matter with me, I felt that as a Trustee of an Estate it was too much of a gamble and declined their request." But he changed his mind after discussing the matter with Henry Walters. Walters advised Kenan that the ACL "would assist in the financing of the undertaking, but he felt that he would not only fail to receive any return on his investment but probably would not receive his investment back." Oddly enough, William then decided to make a personal investment in Pan American—for the good of the Flagler System. "When again approached on this matter I stated that our interest in Florida was such that we wished the undertaking to succeed and that I personally would subscribe just half of the amount that the A.C.L. took. I understood the Atlantic Coast Line would purchase 3,000 shares and I would personally purchase one-half or namely 1,500 shares."[70]

This was another example of the many ways in which Kenan and Walters cooperated for the mutual benefit of their intertwined business interests in Florida. The ACL exchanged all of its passenger and freight traffic bound for the east coast of Florida with the FEC, and the FEC depended mainly on the ACL for the same services at Jacksonville. Kenan also owned several thousand shares of ACL stock, while the Safe Deposit and Trust Company of Baltimore, the bank most closely identified with Walters and the ACL, held one of the largest blocks of the FEC's F&R 5s (double-tracking bonds). What is more, the FEC and the ACL each owned a one-half interest in the P&O Steamship Company, which ran several cruise ships between Miami, Tampa, Cuba, and the West Indies.

At the same time both the FEC and the ACL faced direct competition from the latter's old enemy, the Seaboard Railroad, which was about to break the FEC's monopoly along Florida's "Gold Coast." Not only was the Seaboard building into West Palm Beach from Sebring, Florida, but it received permission from the ICC to build a line paralleling the FEC's tracks from West Palm Beach to Miami and on to Homestead, Florida. Thus the ACL and the FEC, by investing in Pan Am and supporting the transfer of its airline terminal from Key West to Miami, hoped to secure favorable connecting schedules and passenger junkets with the fledgling airline. Pan Am's three or four planes could carry only eight to ten passengers at a time—all of whom, it was hoped, would arrive in Miami via the ACL and the FEC.

On August 9, 1928, as Pan Am began constructing its new airfield in Miami, Kenan paid $15,000 for 1,500 shares of the company's stock. The ACL, having decided to increase its holdings to 5,000 shares, paid $50,000 for its stock. The investment proved to be one of the best Kenan ever made. At the time of his death in 1965, he owned more than 77,000 shares of Pan Am stock, valued at more than $2 million.[71]

On the sixteenth of September,
In 1928,
God started ridin early;
He rode till very late.

He rode out on the ocean,
Chained the lightnin to his wheel;
Stepped on the land at West Palm Beach,
And the wicked hearts did yield.[72]

The 1928 hurricane hit Florida just a month before Pan Am's maiden flight from Miami. It slammed into Palm Beach with winds of up to 150 miles per hour and went on to be one of the deadliest storms in American history. Most of the destruction—2,000 people dead, another 2,000 injured, and $10 million in property damage—occurred in the agricultural settlements served by the FEC around Lake Okeechobee. "Three quarters of the victims were blacks, many from the Bahamas who had come as seasonal labor to work on the vegetable farms."[73]

The Breakers weathered the storm with only minor damage, but across the island the Royal Poinciana suffered heavy losses.[74] By destroying crops and croppers, moreover, the storm seriously diminished the freight revenues of the FEC. Agricultural shipments fell far below normal in November, the beginning of the harvest, and by the end of December the FEC had suffered a net loss of $1.7 million for the year. Shipments of agricultural products continued abnormally low throughout the winter, and in April 1929 things got worse. Fruit flies began ravaging Florida's citrus groves, attacking 70 percent of all trees. The infestation created a disaster for many citrus and vegetable growers and led to a further decline in freight revenues for the state's railroads. Florida was in an economic depression.[75]

Simultaneously, William and his family suffered the sad effects of a depressing personal storm: the divorce of Louise and Dick Lewis. Whatever attraction the couple had felt for each other was gone. "They drank a good deal," one close friend recalled. "I was staying with Whiffy Lewis, . . . Dick's sister in Bear Creek, Pennsylvania, and Louise came by from going to New York for a few days. She stopped where I was staying. And then she went home. And Dick tried to run her down . . . with a car. . . . She was on foot. So things were not very pleasant. I mean he was actively unpleasant."[76]

William's reaction to the divorce proved equally unpleasant. He tried to have a guardian appointed for Louise's children. This was the end of the line for Uncle William as far as Louise was concerned, and it also caused a breach between him and her children that never healed. "He didn't approve of her lifestyle, or anything about it," Louise's daughter recently explained, "and he

After Louise's second divorce. *Left to right:* Lawrence Lewis Jr., Mary Lily Flagler
Lewis, Louise Wise, Alice Kenan, Jessie Kenan Wise. (HMFM Archives)

wanted to have a guardian to take care of us, which just enraged my mother. . . .
He didn't think she was capable of taking care of us. Dreadful man—at least, we
thought he was."[77]

Once again William and the "girls" rode the rails west to try to escape from
it all. Early in the summer of 1929 they took a long trip in the Randleigh to the
Canadian Northwest. It was the most expensive ("$5,372.03") and memorable
vacation he ever took. It was memorable, in part, because of the breathtaking
beauty of Ranier and Glacier Parks, but mainly because he spent most of his

time shooting the scenery with his 16 mm Bell-Howell movie camera, "the best camera made at that time." Alice had given him the camera two years earlier, but "I was not interested in photography and for a time did not use it to any extent except occasionally taking some cattle pictures at the farm." His success on the trip changed his mind. "I took many pictures under all conditions and got remarkable results. These of course were only black and white pictures. From these results I got the bug."[78]

William was forced to shift his focus to North Carolina, however, after returning to Lockport. News arrived that his old friend Dr. Francis Venable was in poor health and that the North Carolina legislature had appropriated just one-half of UNC's budget request for the 1929–31 biennium.[79] William wanted to help Dr. Venable; but he wanted to do so through the university, and he did not want the professor to know about it. On October 24, 1929, just five days before the worst single day in stock market history, William sent UNC president Henry W. Chase a suggestion regarding Venable's "individual and special case." He asked Chase to "make an effort" to have Venable appointed "Emeritus Kenan Professor of Chemistry and continued at his same salary of $5,000.00; this to be paid from funds accruing from the Kenan Foundation which is supplying his present salary." Kenan clearly wanted the appointment made. "My personal interest and appreciation of Dr. Venable as a man and a Professor is beyond expression. The benefits accruing to me from my association with Dr. Venable during my college career were very great and I assure you that anything I could do which would make more comfortable the balance of his life would be cheerfully done."[80]

Kenan's request coincided with a plea from the university asking him and his family for their help in retaining history professor James G. de Roulhac Hamilton. Hamilton had been head of the university's history department since 1908; he had made it a leading center of graduate research in the South; and since 1920 he had been both a Kenan professor and director of the Southern Historical Collection, which he had created. Well respected for his research, teaching, and publishing record, which included one of the most important state studies of the aftermath of the Civil War and Reconstruction in North Carolina, Hamilton in the fall of 1929 was considering very attractive job offers from both the University of Virginia and "one of the larger universities in the country at a very much higher salary."[81]

Hamilton wanted to stay at UNC and complete his dream of establishing the Southern Historical Collection on a permanent basis, but given the university's recent budget cuts it now appeared very unlikely that the school would be able to help him do so. Enter the Kenans. Hamilton had taught at William's old prep school, the Horner Military Academy, and had served for several years as principal of Wilmington High School—the old Tileston School that William and his sisters had attended. After joining the faculty at UNC, moreover,

Hamilton was appointed to a committee charged with writing a history of the Order of the Gimghouls, and by 1929 the Kenan Collection of Civil War Materials, including the Kenan Confederate Pamphlet Collection, was a major part of the growing but not yet systematically developed Southern Historical Collection.[82]

William got what he wanted for Venable, and UNC held on to Hamilton and the collection with a gift from Sarah Kenan. At a meeting in January 1930 the trustees appointed Venable the first Kenan emeritus professor and allowed him "to retire in June, 1930, on his full salary of which $3800 came from the Kenan Professorships Fund." The trustees also accepted Sarah Kenan's $25,000 donation to establish a special fund to allow Hamilton to retain his Kenan professorship and devote himself full time to "my child," the Southern Historical Collection. "The thing is going well," he wrote of the collection in January 1930. "The promise of the future is very bright for it."[83]

William was at the Ponce de Leon Hotel when he received word of Venable's appointment, and he immediately wrote UNC's President Chase. "I am delighted at the satisfactory decision in regard to Dr. Venable for the reason that I think he fully deserves it and in this instance I do not believe it will create a precedent which, in years to come, might embarrass you or your successor." While William undoubtedly had his cousin's earlier run-in with Chase in mind, he was apparently referring to Chase's decision to resign from UNC to become president of the University of Illinois.[84]

NEW EXPERIMENTS

The 1930 commencement was the last for a while at which William felt comfortable. Indeed, it proved to be as much of a watershed in his relationship with UNC as it did in the history of the university itself. Former president Francis Preston Venable, retiring after fifty years of distinguished service to the school, received an honorary doctor of science degree, while the university also awarded an honorary doctor of laws degrees to its recently resigned president, Henry W. Chase. Finally Kenan got to meet the university's new president, Frank Porter Graham, whom the trustees had unexpectedly elected over the Kenan family's old friend R. D. W. Connor.[85]

William did not take an expensive trip on the world's longest railroad car that summer. He was too busy at Randleigh Farm. His chief herdsman for the past eight years, Robert Howe, resigned "because he obtained a better job and in accordance with our suggestions," and "we began to be worried about the physical condition of Dairylike Madcap." The cow had made

> two tremendous records before we purchased her and continued with this same production, making two records after she came here. This cow did not dry up and frequently she milked twenty pounds when she would calve

again. . . . During the summer she calved but seemed to lose flesh and shortly thereafter running around the paddock broke her hind leg. As she was a relatively old cow, all of the veterinarians I consulted suggested she be killed, but I was so impressed with the cow's records that I concluded to make every effort to save her and, with this in mind, telegraphed to Professor Oscar Erf, of Ohio State University, to come here and try to help us.[86]

Kenan's comments reflect his genuine concern for the injured animal but not what mattered most to him: "the performance of the herd" as a whole, its blood lines and milking records. These were his cows and his records, not Henry Flagler's. Unlike the family and the Flagler System he had inherited and over which, as events were now making clear, he had very limited control, almost everything at Randleigh Farm, from the choice of cows and the feed they received to the barns they inhabited and their breeding habits, was done under his expert direction. Randleigh Farm was William's laboratory, his place of control beyond the chaos.

By trying to keep Dairylike Madcap alive, moreover, Kenan wanted to vindicate himself and to demonstrate one of his major personal assumptions: any problem could be solved with the proper application of scientific principles. Unlike almost all of the cows he had purchased over the past several years, Dairylike Madcap was his personal choice. He had not consulted his superintendent, T. E. Grow, before buying her. He had bought her in June 1927 while Grow was buying cows in Oregon, and he had paid $5,700 for her—far and away the most expensive cow he had ever purchased. "She had made a very large record and was on test at the time I purchased her," Kenan wrote, "so we concluded to leave her at Meridale Farm until she finished before bringing her here." But something went wrong after Kenan got her. Although she did well after arriving at Randleigh Farm, she apparently "was unable to digest and assimilate or properly metabolize enough minerals to produce the large quantity of milk which she gave and, therefore, seemed to take it out of her own constitution."

That was the hypothesis, at least, of one of the nation's leading experts on animal nutrition, Professor Oscar Erf.[87] When Erf saw Dairylike Madcap, he did not offer Kenan much encouragement "on account of her age, being thirteen years, but was willing to make the effort," at Kenan's insistence, to save her. William spared no expense trying to rehabilitate the injured animal. "We placed a derrick in her stall and a sling around her body and raised her up and lowered her each day for approximately five months." They also fed her "scientifically germinated grains and minerals, including primarily calcium, phosphorus, iron and iodine," and exposed her "to the ultra-violet ray for about ten minutes twice each day by means of portable hand lamps of the carbon pencil type."[88]

William could not have been happier with the results. Dairylike Madcap's bone eventually "knitted, her physical condition was 100% and, while she limped, she was able to go around any place she desired to go." She also "produced two living calves fully developed after the above experience." Unfortunately for William, though, he could not control the chaos that increasingly reigned beyond his laboratory.

War on the Empire

William Rand Kenan experienced some of the worst years of his life during the 1930s. He watched his plans for outdoing Flagler in Florida destroyed, and he suffered repeated disappointments at the hands of his niece and his alma mater. The FEC Railway began the decade $2 million in the red, it lost $100,000 a month during the first two months of 1931, and in March it borrowed $2 million to pay the semiannual interest on its F&R 5 double-tracking bonds. It received a half-million-dollar loan from Mary Lily's trust and another $1.5-million loan from the Flagler System's most profitable subsidiary, the FEC Car Ferry Company.[1]

The Flagler System also razed the Royal Palm Hotel in Miami that spring, permanently closed the Royal Poinciana in Palm Beach, and shut down the Cordova and Alcazar hotels in St. Augustine, where the golf tournaments generated little, if any, extra business. William also quit the sport out of frustration. "I have a baseball swing and was much too fast for good results in golf, so I concluded that I could not play the game and gave it up." He began making the rounds with his camera instead, shooting a "very interesting record" of the women's golf tournaments.[2]

Kenan got his worst headache of the spring, however, on May 25, 1931, when Louise married her third husband, Freddie Francis, an ex-semipro baseball player giving golf and tennis lessons in his native St. Augustine.[3] Uncle William did not attend the wedding, nor did Aunt Alice or Aunt Sarah or Jessie, Louise's mother. They had already left St. Augustine for the season. But Louise made sure she had her children with her in the judge's chambers. According to the *New York Times*, only "Lawrence Lewis Jr. and Mary Lily Flagler Lewis, children of the bride, and Stanley Cole, a resident of [St. Augustine], were present" at the ceremony.[4] There were a lot of people at the sad party that followed, however, one of whom remembered that Louise "was very much upset at the large wedding reception, which I attended, was crying, became intoxicated and withdrew at the beginning of the party." Freddie had waited until they were married, it seems, to mention his homosexuality.[5]

One month later a fire destroyed most of the attic and second floor of Sarah Kenan's huge Wilmington mansion. No one was injured in the blaze, which firemen fought for several hours, but the mansion sustained between $25,000 and $35,000 worth of fire and water damage. William handled everything for Sarah. He dealt with the insurance companies, hired Leonard Schultze to help with the renovations, and made before and after movies of the house.[6]

Things did not get better until the fall when he started planning a dairy inn at Randleigh Farm. The purpose of the dairy "was to produce pure milk," he explained. "That is, not letting it come in contact with the human hand nor with the air." Kenan got the idea from Professor Oscar Erf, who "talked to me quite at length about his ideas in connection with a milking parlor, the idea being to take the cows out of the barns when milking." William was initially skeptical; his men kept the barns exceptionally clean, and there were electric insect screens to help control the flies. "At first I did not take much stock in it but eventually I seemed to see the light and during June, July and August of 1931 we experimented by constructing quite a number of wooden stalls carrying out the idea of Professor Erf. We developed these far enough so that we concluded to build a dairy inn and install the stalls."[7]

RUNNING ON EMPTY

Kenan also tried another, more portentous experiment that August in the Flagler System's offices at 120 Broadway in New York. "They called me into Mr. Kenan's room," George Cordwell recalled. "It was Mr. Kenan and Mr. Haines and this gentleman from Standard Oil of Kentucky. I took dictation."[8]

The secretary listened intently as he wrote. The FEC owed Standard $34,000 for fuel but was refusing to pay the bill. Yet there was no hostility in the room. The man from Standard Oil "was a very great friend of Mr. Kenan's," Cordwell explained, and had "visited us in St. Augustine several times." Indeed, it was agreed "that Standard Oil of Kentucky would bring a friendly suit against the railway for payment of indebtedness. . . . I remember this particularly because it happened just before lunch time," Cordwell noted, "and Mr. Haines told me, he said, 'Your notes,' he said, 'carry them with you wherever you go until you transcribe the notes. Then you destroy the notes and give me the typed statement or document.'"

Cordwell did as he was told, and on August 31 Standard made its move. It filed a bill of complaint in federal court in Jacksonville, Florida, "alleging the inability of the [FEC] Railway Company to pay its debts and the necessity for the appointment of receivers to conduct the future operations of the road." Federal Judge Louis Strum granted the request. He put all of the FEC's property under the court's protection and appointed the railroad's president, W. R. Kenan Jr., and its general counsel, Scott Loftin, as receivers for the road. The following day, September 1, the FEC failed to pay the semiannual interest on its $45 million of F&R 5s, causing the price of the bonds to fall to a new low of $13 on the hundred—well below the $95 to $98 that investors had originally paid.[9]

William issued a statement to the press before leaving for Florida, explaining that the FEC was not responsible for its predicament. The Florida land boom had forced the company to double-track its line, and the company had financed the expansion at a time when the "prospective demand for transportation facilities justified it and the earnings were ample to take care of not only existing fixed charges but also interest on the new financing." But from that point on, Kenan continued, the FEC was victimized by hurricanes and other forces beyond its control: the collapse of the Florida real estate boom, the fruit fly quarantine, the general business depression, competition from trucks and automobiles, and the "extension of the Seaboard Air Line to West Palm Beach and the paralleling of the East Coast road from that point to Homestead, under authority of the Interstate Commerce Commission." No one, Kenan stressed, could have predicted these developments at the time of the FEC's $45-million bond issue. "It may not be amiss to recall that in the years of 1923, 1924 and 1925 our net earnings, after paying fixed charges, were approximately two and one-half-times the fixed charges, whereas, due to the above reasons, during 1927, 1928, 1929 and 1930 the operation produced an actual deficit for each of those four years totalling for that period $6,720,000 approximately."[10]

The head of J. P. Morgan's bond department, Arthur M. Anderson, immediately organized a committee to represent the institutions (mainly New York banks and insurance companies) holding the largest blocks of F&R 5s (about 45 percent of the $45 million). He also called on the other bondholders to deposit their F&R 5s with the committee so that foreclosure proceedings could be initiated against the FEC.[11] This was exactly the response Kenan and his advisers had anticipated. By orchestrating a "friendly" maneuver with Standard Oil of Kentucky, one bondholder later explained, the "trustees of the Flagler estate were able to retain a certain control over the railroad and to forestall the appointment of receivers at the instance of unfriendly creditors and to obtain the appointment of receivers of their own choice." Indeed, William further reinforced his control over the FEC by obtaining a court "order granting such receivers power in their discretion and out of any funds coming into their hands, to pay the cost of maintaining the corporate existence of the Railway Company, including the salaries (to be fixed by the receivers) of necessary corporate officers, fees and other expenses."[12]

Kenan was also struggling to control the details of his new dairy inn. "We started construction in late October, 1931, and suffice it to say that when this was done we had no drawings whatsoever of a building and I simply stepped off the size we intended to have it and the building was designed as we went along with the construction." The improvisation gave Kenan complete command of the project, but it also gave him headaches: "We made many mistakes which not only increased the cost but delayed completion of the job."[13]

In the meantime Kenan became concerned with maintaining his family's status as UNC's leading benefactors. Mary Lily had put them in that position, and he and Sarah had helped keep them there with the Kenan Memorial Stadium, the Graham Kenan Fellowship in Philosophy, and the fund for the Southern Historical Collection. But their good friend, John Sprunt Hill, appeared to be closing in on them. He and his wife had contributed heavily to the university's new music hall, while Hill himself paid the entire cost of constructing the privately owned Carolina Inn on Cameron Avenue. Ironically, this new hotel replaced the old, recently demolished Chapel Hill landmark on Franklin Street, the University Inn, whose previous owners had included Kenan's parents.[14]

Still more disconcerting for Kenan was the dedication that fall of the Morehead-Patterson Bell Tower at UNC, a gift from John Motley Morehead and his cousin Rufus Lenoir Patterson. The twelve-bell, $100,000 tower was designed and constructed by the same firms that handled Kenan Memorial Stadium, and like the stadium it overlooks, the tower was built as a memorial. It was erected "to perpetuate the memory of those members of the Morehead and Patterson families who have from the foundation of this University been associated with its activities as trustees, teachers, or students."[15]

UNC dedicated the bell tower on Thanksgiving Day, 1931, at the UNC-Virginia football game—almost four years to the day after the Kenans and the Moreheads attended the dedication of Kenan Stadium. Frank Kenan, the youngest son of William's cousin Thomas Kenan, was then in his first semester at UNC, where his older brother, James, was beginning his junior year. "I just loved football," Frank recalled. "Weighed a hundred and forty pounds. . . . Played in the backfield."[16] But whether the Kenans watched with the Moreheads as the Tar Heels slipped past the Wahoos is not known. Neither is it clear that Morehead considered Kenan his competitor for the crown of UNC's preeminent benefactor. There is plenty of circumstantial evidence to suggest, however, that Kenan perceived Morehead as such a rival as early as 1931 and that by the late 1930s, when Kenan set out to refute Morehead's claim regarding the discovery of calcium carbide, his perceptions had become assumptions.

Morehead's accomplishments far surpassed those of William Rand Kenan Jr. Whereas Kenan inherited his wealth and reputation, Morehead earned his as a scientist, working and investing with Union Carbide. He was recognized nationally and internationally as both an author and an inventor in the chemical, gas, and acetylene industries. He had served on the General Staff of the United States Army during the war; worked closely with Bernard M. Baruch, chairman of the War Industries Board; and was chief of the Industrial Gases and Gas Products Division of the Council of National Defense. President of the

International Acetylene Association following the war, he served three consecutive terms as mayor of Rye, New York, in the 1920s. UNC awarded him an honorary doctor of laws degree in 1926, President Herbert Hoover appointed him U.S. minister to Sweden in 1930, and in 1931 the Royal Swedish Academy of Sciences awarded him its gold medal—an honor never before bestowed on a non-Swede.[17]

THE DEPTHS OF THE DEPRESSION

Less than a week after the bell tower game, Kenan lost his one true friend in life, Henry Walters, who died in New York City. His death could not have occurred at a worse time for Kenan, for now more than ever William desperately needed the advice, loyalty, and friendship of his "second Father."

In early February 1932 William and his sisters received an urgent appeal from the Emergency Student Loan Fund at UNC. The school had exhausted its regular loan fund, and it now confronted the unhappy prospect of "sending more than 500 students back to 'jobless' towns, and in many instances bankrupt homes."[18] The appeal did not surprise William and his sisters. The university always needed money, and the past two years had been particularly difficult for the school, especially for its new president, Frank Porter Graham. The state legislature ignored his appeals and slashed the university's appropriations while it simultaneously attempted to centralize and conserve the state's dwindling resources by creating the "Consolidated University," a system composed of UNC, North Carolina State College, and the Woman's College at Greensboro.[19]

Graham also faced a faculty crisis as a result of the financial difficulties. At least twenty of the school's professors received "offers from other institutions, sometimes at three times the salary they were making at Chapel Hill." Some of the professors decided to remain at UNC out of institutional loyalty and respect for president Graham, but many stayed because he created a pension fund from the Kenan Professorships Fund. "In this present financial crisis," one newspaper noted, "it is the testimony of President Graham that this money has helped the university to draw and hold on its faculty men of wide reputation for teaching and scholarship."[20]

Oddly enough, it was Jessie, William's older sister, who now made the largest Kenan contribution to UNC's Emergency Student Loan Fund. Completing her first year as a university trustee at the time, Jessie had never donated anything to the school and had made her only other recorded benefaction, the Kenan Memorial Chapel, Tower, and Spire at the First Presbyterian Church in Wilmington, in conjunction with William and Sarah. But she now gave $25,000 to the loan fund, while her sister Sarah contributed $1,000. Even more peculiar are the assertions made by the *Raleigh News & Observer* in April 1932 in a story on Jessie's donation to the fund. "She made the gift some time ago, Dr. Graham said, but preferred that no announcement be made. Later, however, 'she yielded to the realization of the value of such an announcement at this time might have on the further progress of the loan fund appeal and on university morale,' it was said."[21]

In truth, however, Jessie appears to have made her gift in anticipation of a lawsuit that threatened to cut off Mary Lily's bequest to UNC. In March 1932 the FEC again failed to pay its F&R 5 bondholders, and on May 12 the Bankers Trust Company and Bethune W. Jones, the trustees under the deed securing the $45-million bond issue, filed suit in federal court in Florida "for the foreclosure of said trust deed, alleging default in interest on September 1, 1931, and March 1, 1932, which suit was consolidated in this court with the original suit of Standard Oil Company."[22]

The threat to the university began four days later, on May 16, when the Florida court approved a petition from the FEC's attorney and coreceiver, Scott Loftin, to file suit in New York "against William R. Kenan, Jr., and Lawrence Haines, as trustees under the estate of Mary Lilly [sic] (Flagler) Bingham, and such other persons as might be necessary, for the purpose of obtaining a construction of item No. 9 of Mrs. Bingham's will." Specifically, Loftin was acting at the urging of the railroad's bondholders and creditors, whom he and Kenan legally represented as the FEC's receivers. The bondholders and creditors wanted the courts to determine whether item No. 9 of Mary Lily's will—the item establishing a twenty-one-year trust for the maintenance, development, and keeping together of Henry Flagler's railroad and hotel properties—required her trustees to contribute a substantial amount of money to the FEC, enough, that is, to pay the interest on the F&R 5s.[23]

The "other persons" Loftin could sue included the current and future beneficiaries of the trust: Louise Wise Francis, UNC, and William, Jessie, and Sarah. And sue them he did, in July 1932 in the supreme court of New York. Loftin claimed the FEC was in "imminent danger of destruction as a going concern by forced sale on foreclosure," and he asked for an immediate injunction "to prevent payments out of the [trust] fund except as ordered by the court."[24]

UNC thus started its new fiscal year not knowing when or if it might receive another $75,000 annuity. What it did receive was a court summons from New York, which prompted the university's business manager, Charles T. Woollen, to telegraph William in Lockport: THE UNIVERSITY HAS BEEN SERVED WITH SUMMONS IN RE SCOTT M. LOFTIN RECEIVER THE ANSWER RETURNABLE AUGUST FIRST WE DESIRE TO JOIN IN THE ANSWER AS YOU DEEM BEST THE NORTH CAROLINA ATTORNEY GENERAL AND A REPRESENTATIVE OF THE UNIVERSITY WILL BE GLAD TO COME FOR CONFERENCE IF YOU DESIRE ANY TIME AND PLACE.[25] There was no need for a conference, William wired back. He would simply have his attorney "draft a suggestion which you could use if you desire." But Kenan quickly changed his mind, finding "a number of points which ought to be discussed with you, particularly the necessity of your being represented by New York counsel, so that I now think it would be advisable to arrange a conference."[26]

The conference took place in New York City the following week, and after discussing the case, Kenan, Woollen, and North Carolina attorney general Dennis G. Brummitt decided that UNC should have a separate attorney, so that the school "would not be tied in with the more involved bequests." Woollen also used the occasion to raise the annuity question with Kenan. "I told Mr. Kenan we might find some slight difficulty in raising $75,000 for this year if the plaintiffs tied up the distribution of funds, as they could under their suit, and he made out this year's check and she is now on 4% deposit."[27]

Woollen then "went around to see Mr. Morehead and told him how much we would be able to do with $400,000 as a finishing sum for the Loan Funds. He left for Sweden next morning. Honestly, it wasn't because I tried to make a date with him for next day." Woollen had more luck with another North Carolina native and UNC graduate, George Gordon Battle, a prominent New York attorney whom he retained as the university's legal counsel. The arrangement was a strategic one. Battle was a cousin of Mary Lily's former beau, Dr. Samuel Westray Battle, and in the fall of 1917, at the time of Mary Lily's exhumation, his law firm had been serving as the New York counsel for Robert Worth Bingham. Woollen left New York feeling very much pleased with his work, believing that that suit would "doubtless be settled before another year rolls around." His prediction was off by about six years.[28]

OLD DEBTS AND NEW

In March 1933 the nation's new president, Franklin Delano Roosevelt, appointed two of the Kenan family's old antagonists to foreign posts. He made his old boss at the Navy Department, Josephus Daniels, ambassador to Mexico, and Judge Robert Worth Bingham became ambassador to Great Britain.

Daniels had never been on friendly terms with the Kenans, and he now made things worse for them. He led the trustee faction that treated William and his family as adversaries in the school's fight to retain and settle Mary Lily's bequest.[29] Bingham's appointment, however, caused the Kenans the most immediate concern. Not only did most of the family dislike the Judge, but his confirmation hearings also resurrected the sad matter of Mary Lily's death. Two of the Judge's old Kentucky adversaries, Abraham and Jacob Flexner, tried to scuttle his nomination by imparting the "murder" gossip to Bernard Baruch and Secretary of State Cordell Hull. At the same time Andrew Jackson May, a congressman from eastern Kentucky, delivered a speech on the House floor titled "From the Police Court to the Court of St. James's." He charged that

Mary Lily died from "mysterious and suspicious circumstances" and left her husband, "Robert Worthless Bingham," enough "filthy lucre" to purchase the *Louisville Courier-Journal* and to turn it into the "political harlot of the Republican Party" and the "Judas of the Democratic Party."[30]

Bingham survived the slanderous campaign against him, however, and in May 1933 he left the United States for London with his children and his third wife, Aleen Hilliard. While a few of Kenan's kinfolk undoubtedly relished the Judge's brief discomfiture and may even have contributed to the rumors against him, William himself did not. He already had enough problems and bad publicity to deal with concerning Mary Lily's legacies.[31]

In April 1933 Douglas Findlay, a citizen of Colorado and an FEC bondholder, filed suit in Jacksonville to prevent the New York courts from deciding the question Loftin wanted them to answer: whether item No. 9 of Mary Lily's will could be so construed as to make her trustees use the assets of her trust to keep the FEC from being destroyed as an ongoing concern. Findlay wanted the same question answered and answered in the same way, in the affirmative, but he wanted the Florida courts to make the ruling. He had not deposited his $75,000 F&R 5s with J. P. Morgan and Company; he was not a member of the "institutional" committee of bondholders that had; and he disagreed with the efforts of the committee to foreclose on the deed of trust securing the $45 million bond issue. He demanded instead that the Florida court "construe item No. 9 of Mrs. Bingham's will as creating an equitable asset of the railway company covered by the lien of the trust deed above mentioned; *that a separate receiver* be appointed in this cause to take into possession the rights of the railway company in and to the residuary trust fund, and to apply the proceeds of that fund in payment of the defaulted interest on plaintiff's [Findlay's] bonds and other bonds of said issue."[32]

Findlay lost his case, and William retained his position as coreceiver of the FEC. But the litigation helped delay the opening of Loftin's New York case until June 1934—a case that went on until January 1938, one month after Mary Lily's trust expired. The university got its first break in the case, however, on May 16, 1935, when New York Supreme Court Justice Aaron J. Levy appointed "a referee" to audit Mary Lily's trust "and to decide whether the Florida East Coast Railway . . . would be kept together by the payment of sums of bond interest or whether such payment would be merely a gift to the creditors of the railroad." On June 25, moreover, just three days before Louise Wise Francis's fortieth birthday—an event with strategic significance for UNC—the university's attorneys, Battle, Levy, Van Tine, and Fowler, asked Justice Levy for a separate decision on item No. 8 of Mary Lily's will, the item covering her legacy to the university.[33]

Justice Levy allowed Loftin to continue the item No. 9 suit against Mary Lily's trustees; but he exempted the university as a defendant in the case, and according to one UNC official, "the Kenan trustees aided the University in exempting its interests."[34] Levy concluded that the FEC had no basis in fact for claiming an interest in UNC's legacy, that the university was therefore entitled to a receive a legal judgment to that effect, and that a "separate and final" agreement be concluded between the university and the FEC's receivers. "Thus, by July 1, 1935," one observer later wrote, "the University had won its case, and the legacy was once more out of danger."[35]

What this meant, however, is not at all clear. The university did make some kind of agreement, but no record of it has been found. Apparently it combined a final settlement of UNC's bequest with the $5 million Louise was to receive on June 28, 1935, her fortieth birthday. As the university's New York attorneys noted on July 1, "the University is bound by the valuation placed upon the securities and consents to the payment of the legacy to Mrs. Francis. Valuation of the securities has been examined on behalf of Mrs. Francis and behalf of plaintiff [Loftin] and has been approved."[36] Yet UNC did not receive any securities from Mary Lily's trustees until the spring of 1940, and Louise may have been forced to wait for her $5 million. One newspaper later reported she received the money, but no other evidence has been found to suggest that she did.[37]

What is clear, though, is that the relationship between the Kenans and the university became strained, even antagonistic, and that once again William was only partially to blame. Most of this friction can be attributed to events beyond the control of both parties, and yet there was also a basic conflict between the assumptions and presumptions of both the benefactors and their beneficiaries regarding the use and abuse of wealth and power.

During the turning point in the New York trial, William's cousin Dr. Owen Hill Kenan received a fundraising appeal from the university's president, Frank Graham. UNC Press had reached the end of its "shoe string" budget, Graham wrote, and in order for it to continue to make its valuable contribution "to the productive scholarship and literary output of this University and the whole South," the press needed "a capital investment of fifty thousand dollars."[38] Owen did not even bother to respond to the letter, however, which arrived shortly after a similar missive from the director of the press. The physician was still irritated, it seems, with the university's response to his offer to have Randolph Churchill lecture at UNC. Although the university accepted Owen's offer, President Graham asked him to extend Churchill the invitation personally. To be sure, polite though it was, Graham's response was heavily qualified and not very enthusiastic, making it clear that Owen should arrange everything with his English friend on his own. For whatever reasons, Winston Churchill's son did not lecture at UNC.[39]

The university's president also asked Sarah Kenan to contribute to UNC Press, but she too, it seems, was in no mood to take out her checkbook. In early

July 1935 both she and her nephew James Kenan wrote Graham regarding a family friend, Lonnie London, who was about to graduate from UNC with his Ph.D. "At the risk of having you call me officious," James ventured, "I am writing to suggest that Lonnie be offered a place on the faculty of the Chapel Hill unit of the University. If there are no vacancies on the faculty at this time, I suppose it follows that he can't be offered a place, at this time."[40] Unfortunately, Graham responded, that was indeed the case; the university, he wrote to James and Sarah, could not find a place for Lonnie London.[41]

Prior to this exchange of letters, which took place in the week following the university's legal victory in New York, the relationship between the Kenans and Frank Graham appears to have been friendly, even warm. He frequently invited them to join him in the president's box for football games at Kenan Stadium, and after his marriage in 1932, his invitations included a pregame buffet at his official residence in Chapel Hill. William and his sisters occasionally accepted these invitations, but more often than not, either because of prior commitments or Alice's frequent illnesses, they had to send their regrets. Even more suggestive of the family's relationship with Frank Graham is the final paragraph of the letter to him from James Kenan regarding Lonnie London. "This Summer I'll be passing from time to time through Durham, where my brother Frank is now working, on my way to Wrightsville [Beach], and if you would like to take off there for a few days, we would of course be delighted to have you. Then the people of the Cape Fear country can see that you[r] bark is more radical than your bite." Graham did not go to Wrightsville Beach, however, and he and the Kenans apparently stopped exchanging social invitations after the fall of 1935.[42]

Several developments help explain the change. As James's comments suggest, Frank Graham's reputation as a liberal activist alarmed many North Carolinians and UNC supporters alike, one of whom was Sarah Kenan. According to one well-informed source, "On one occasion Sarah wrote to her brother concerning a Dr. . . . Graham. At the time he was coming into prominence from the University of N.C., by way of the 'educator' group who were gaining hold on the F. D. Roosevelt Regime—Sarah wrote that she consider[ed] Dr. Graham to be too 'radical' in his views, and she did not want any of her funds to be used by him."[43]

Indeed, by the fall of 1935 calls for Graham's resignation had reached a fever pitch. In addition to serving on various New Deal boards and councils, he defended the Chapel Hill speeches of controversial British philosopher Bertrand Russell and African American poet Langston Hughes. He also offered to make bond for former UNC student Alton Lawrence, secretary of the North Carolina Socialist party, who was arrested "for trespassing as part of a 'flying squadron' trying to close the Carolina Cotton and Woolen Mill of High Point."[44]

Of more immediate and personal concern to the Kenan family were Frank

Sarah Graham Kenan. (Thomas S. Kenan III)

Graham's response to the "Jewish quota" controversy and his plan for regulating intercollegiate sports. Graham, after discovering secret restrictions on the number of Jews accepted to UNC's medical school, ordered Dr. Isaac Hall Manning, the dean of the school, to end the policy immediately. But Manning resigned rather than comply.[45] The Kenans were not pleased. Not only was the doctor an old friend of William's, but he was also the brother-in-law of the ailing Dr. Francis Preston Venable, who moved to Richmond, Virginia, in the midst of the controversy and subsequently died there. Manning's resignation also created a tremendous uproar in Wilmington, where fourteen of the university's local medical school alumni, including the Kenans' good friend R. H. Bellamy, responded with a letter to Graham lamenting Manning's resignation and requesting "urgently and respectfully" that the doctor "be immediately made *Kenan Professor of Physiology*." Though there is no evidence that any of the Kenans intervened in the affair, Manning was immediately appointed Kenan professor and chairman of the Department of Physiology—the only Kenan appointment, it seems, left out of A. C. Howell's later work, *The Kenan Professorships.*[46]

Many of the Kenans also disliked Frank Graham's plan for reforming college athletics. Conceived in response to a Carnegie Foundation study recommending that college presidents take the lead in "rooting out" the evils of "recruiting and subsidizing of athletics" on college campuses, Graham's plan would have barred college athletes from receiving special financial aid. It also would have required athletes to file income statements, put athletics under faculty control, eliminated the payment of all noncollege funds to university staff, curtailed recruitment, provided for auditing and publishing of athletic accounts, and ended all postseason athletic contests.[47] William almost certainly supported the angry opposition of numerous individuals and organizations to the plan. He agreed on the need to eliminate the system's worst abuses, but he also makes it clear, in the autobiography he soon began, that both athletic activities and "book knowledge" proved equally important to his education at Chapel Hill. He considered it impossible, in fact, to have withstood "the physical grief of my career, were it not for the resistance built up by my years of athletics."[48]

Kenan also shared the genuine concern of many coaches, fans, and alumni that the Graham Plan would destroy intercollegiate athletic competition and thus, at UNC, the future use and significance of Kenan Memorial Stadium. As overblown and absurd as these concerns undoubtedly were, the Graham Plan came at a time when Tar Heel football was beginning to recover from an all-time low. Kenan was happy with the team's improvement, as was his newly graduated kinsman, Frank Kenan, who had played for some of the "sorriest" football teams Carolina had ever had.[49]

It was a natural disaster, however, that placed the greatest strain on the relationship between the Kenans and the university. On September 2, 1935, one of the most violent hurricanes in American history roared across the Florida Keys.[50] William immediately flew down to survey the damage. The "center of that storm was at Long Key," he later wrote, "at which point we lost the Fishing Camp, at a cost of approximately $300,000.00. The extent of the storm was approximately sixty miles wide. The second day after the storm I chartered a single motored cockpit plane and flew down the line about 1200 feet high and 1,000 feet to the west of the railroad track and took a motion picture showing the effects of the storm."[51]

The scene must have conjured up painful memories for Kenan. The damage was worse than that which Flagler had been forced to repair after the hurricanes of 1906 and 1909—the costly repairs, that is, that had forced William to abandon his dream of a paper mill at Wilmington, North Carolina. Indeed, the 1935 hurricane destroyed or damaged 40 of the 128 miles of FEC track between Homestead and Key West on the Key West Extension. The loss, in depression prices, was $2–3 million.[52]

THE TANGLED WEB OF FIRSTS AND 5S

By 1935 traffic on the Key West Extension was only 25 percent of what it had been during the line's best years, and the "Eighth Wonder of the World" was the FEC's "White Elephant." Yet in the aftermath of the hurricane the extension became the central focus in an epic struggle for control of the FEC Railway.

This struggle had its origins in Henry Flagler's decision to complete the extension by selling $12 million in bonds to the public rather than continuing to finance the project on his own. The bonds were sold in 1909 by J. P. Morgan and Company and two other New York banks, the First National and National City, the latter the principal banker of Standard Oil. These three banks, along with the two trust companies dominated by J. P. Morgan and Company—Guaranty Trust and Bankers Trust—had then constituted the so-called inner circle of the alleged "money trust" supposedly trying to concentrate "control of money and credit in the United States" prior to the world war. All of these financial institutions now wanted to control the fate of the FEC. Fortunately for Kenan, however, and for UNC, the 1909 bonds seriously complicated these efforts. Flagler had purchased $2 million for himself, and the banks had sold more than half the remaining $10 million to some of their biggest customers—the New York Life, Equitable, Prudential, and Mutual Life insurance companies—all of which were closely connected, in turn, through money and men, to the money trust banks.[53]

What made the 1909 bonds so important was the mortgage securing them: it appeared to be a first mortgage on all of the FEC's lines. The mortgage supposedly secured "in unequivocal terms, a first lien upon all the main line [of the FEC] . . . whether existing when the first mortgage was made in 1909 or whether later constructed." Put simply, this "after-acquired property clause" appeared to give the 1909 bondholders a first lien not just on the extension but on all of the FEC's lines, including the double-tracked main line financed with the F&R 5s in the mid-1920s.[54]

One has to assume that all of the major parties to the F&R 5 issue knew about the preeminence of both the 1909 first mortgage bonds and the after-acquired property clause underlying them. After all, the same money trust banks acted as underwriters and members of the selling syndicate for both bond issues. Yet in the flush times of the Florida boom, with the FEC's revenues rocketing to record levels, the thought of the old Flagler road defaulting on bond payments seemed remote. To be sure, the underwriting banks bought some $4 million of the F&R 5s for themselves. They also sold $2.3 million of the bonds to the Northwestern Mutual Life Insurance Company and another $1.5 million and $2.2 million, respectively, to two institutions that likewise held approximately $500,000 in 1909 bonds, the Metropolitan Life Insurance Company and the Safe Deposit and Trust Company of Baltimore (the chief financial backer of the ACL).[55]

Though it is unclear how many other F&R 5 purchasers knew about the preeminence of the 1909 first mortgage bonds, William and his fellow FEC officials definitely did. Never once in its twenty-five years of receivership and bankruptcy did the FEC fail to pay the interest on the 1909 first mortgage bonds, which explains, in turn, why the committee for the F&R 5 bondholders filed suit against the FEC in 1932 for foreclosure. The FEC defaulted on the 5s, not on the 1909 bonds. Indeed, the 1909 bondholders did not enter the fray until 1936, when the fate of the Key West Extension came into question.

This is not to say that the 1909 bondholders were not interested in the litigation against the FEC and Mary Lily's trustees. They definitely were. Not only were they closely tied, through personal, financial, and institutional affiliations, to the F&R 5 bondholders' committee, but also, if the FEC were forced into bankruptcy and compelled to reorganize, and/or if Mary Lily's will were so construed as to make her trustees pay the interest on the F&R 5s, the 1909 bondholders faced the prospect of the FEC defaulting on their bonds too. This close connection between the two bondholder groups led to one of the most significant developments in the case.

The F&R 5 committee halted its efforts to foreclose on and reorganize the FEC after being advised to do so by its attorney, former Democratic presidential candidate John W. Davis. As the committee's chairman, Arthur Anderson, later testified, "Early in the receivership the Committee was instrumental in having instituted the case of Loftin v. Kenan for construction of the will of Mary Lily Flagler Bingham. The committee was advised by its counsel [Davis] that it would prejudice the prosecution of this suit to attempt to present a plan of reorganization of the Railway Company pending final determination of the suit."[56] According to another summary of Davis's advice, however, one that better explains why Anderson's F&R 5 committee delayed foreclosure, Davis warned "very strongly against any action which would disturb the position of the [1909] first mortgage and might cause a foreclosure wiping out the stock" of the FEC. Revealingly, Davis was also the attorney for J. P. Morgan and Company, the attorney for Scott Loftin, and a director of at least one of the insurance companies that held FEC bonds.[57]

Deciding what to do about the hurricane-damaged Key West Extension seriously complicated matters for everyone concerned. Not only did it bring the 1909 bondholders into the negotiations, but also, by prolonging Loftin's suit for the construction of Mary Lily's will, it delayed the promised settlement between her trustees and UNC. The question involved appeared simple and clear: whether to abandon the Key West Extension entirely or repair the damaged section of its track, which amounted to almost one-third of the total mileage. But no one wanted to spend a large sum of money repairing a property that was already operating at a loss. Certainly the F&R 5 bondholders did not; they held no legal claim to the track and were receiving nothing from the FEC anyway. As for the 1909 bondholders, who did have a legal claim and were receiving FEC dividends, they saw no reason to burden themselves or the FEC with another debt that might endanger their interest payments. In fact, abandoning the road could only improve things for the 1909 bondholders, who claimed a first lien on all of the FEC's lines.

Therein lay the problem. Which group of bondholders owned a first lien on which FEC lines? The two groups discussed the problem but left it unresolved because of their close connections and the fact that resolving it might affect the course of Loftin's suit for a construction of Mary Lily's will. While there was no dispute regarding the rights of the 1909 bondholders to a first lien on both the Key West Extension and the main, double-tracked line between Jacksonville and Miami, both bondholder groups claimed a first lien on the Okeechobee Branch, the Bunnell Cutoff, and the Miami Belt Line.

The Okeechobee Branch accounted for about half of the FEC's revenues as a result of the huge fruit and vegetable shipments it carried from the farms around Lake Okeechobee. According to the 1909 bondholders the after-acquired clause of the mortgage underlying their bonds gave them a first lien on the Okeechobee Branch, while the F&R 5 bondholders based their first-lien claim "upon representations of the [FEC's] management in the letters signed by the President of the road [Kenan] (which letters were at the time approved by counsel for the Railway [Loftin]) that the 5% Bonds have a first lien on the entire Okeechobee Branch and upon the Bunnell Cut-off."[58] In other words, the F&R 5 bondholders believed that if anyone received bond payments based on the revenue of the Okeechobee Branch and the Bunnell Cutoff, they should, not the 1909 bondholders. Such a resolution seemed unlikely, of course, given the FEC's decision to continue to pay the interest on the 1909 bonds.

Negotiations on the fate of the Key West Extension began two weeks after the hurricane, when the FEC's receivers, Kenan and Loftin, turned the matter over to the courts. They promised to file a complete report on the hurricane damage with the U.S. district court in Jacksonville but lacked the authority, they claimed, as "mere agents" of that court, to decide the extension's future.[59] The first effort to influence the court's decision came in mid-November, but neither the FEC nor the bondholders initiated it. It originated with the Social and Economic Union of Cuba, whose president, José Manuel Casanova, sent cablegrams to President Roosevelt and his cabinet emphasizing the FEC's importance to both countries. "Components of Cuba's economic activity share the present misfortune of Key West as their own and respectfully entreat Your Excellency through your mediation to interpose your good offices toward the reestablishment at the earliest possible date of its railroad communication with the continent by the marvel of modern engineering which honors the United States and has been and still can be one of the greatest factors in friendly intercourse, cultural as well as commercial, between our two countries."[60]

But the road was not rebuilt. A week after Kenan and Loftin submitted their damage report to the court, the 1909 bondholders met to discuss the report and the future of the road. They met, interestingly enough, at the request of a new player in the game, the Guaranty Trust Company of New York, which had succeeded as trustee for the 1909 bonds another Morgan-dominated trust company, Bankers Trust, which still continued to serve, however, as trustee under the bond mortgage securing the F&R 5s. But by then, it seems, the decision on the extension had already been made. Shortly before Guaranty Trust called the 1909 bondholders together, the head of the F&R 5 committee "Arthur M. Anderson, partner in J. P. Morgan & Co., . . . announced that neither the bankers nor the Reconstruction Finance Corporation were interested in financing the repair of the line." And neither, the 1909 bondholders now announced, were they. The U.S. court at Jacksonville accepted the decision and ordered Kenan and Loftin to file an application of abandonment with the ICC.[61]

Things went from bad to worse for Kenan and the old Flagler road. In May 1936 the Federal Mediation Board held an election to determine which of two unions would represent the FEC's engineers in collective bargaining. The defeated union appealed the results to the U.S. district court in Jacksonville, which issued an injunction barring Kenan and Loftin from recognizing the winning union, which then successfully appealed the ruling to the Fifth Circuit Court of Appeals. By then, however, Bankers Trust had sold and bought at judicial auction all of the locomotives and all but three of the passenger cars securing the equipment trust certificates signed by the FEC in the mid-1920s.[62]

Simultaneously, moreover, the chairman of the F&R 5 committee, Arthur Anderson, announced that bondholders who wanted to withdraw their 5s from the committee could do so at that time, "because the deposit agreement provided that this step might be taken if no plan of reorganization [of the FEC] had been approved by the committee within five years after September 1, 1931."

Anderson suggested, however, that depositors keep their bonds where they were; the committee controlled almost $30 million, or 66 percent, of the total outstanding F&R 5s and thus was still the best vehicle for "continued united action" by the bondholders. As for when there would be any action, the committee considered " 'it wise to defer any recommendations as to a plan of reorganization until [the FEC's] earnings show improvement over a long period' and until litigation over the will of Mary Lily Flagler Bingham, widow of Henry M. Flagler, promoter of the Florida East Coast, is settled."[63]

On October 8, 1936, the FEC formally abandoned Henry Flagler's greatest monument, the Key West Extension, and two days later Louise Wise Francis filed for divorce from her third husband, Freddie Francis, accusing him of "extreme mental and physical cruelty."[64] If no one was shocked by the suit, it did come as a surprise to many. Despite Freddie's homosexuality, he and Louise appeared fairly happy as a couple, at least in public. They played golf and tennis together. She bought him the local baseball team, the St. Augustine Saints, and she flew him to the away games in her airplane. She also miscarried a set of twins Freddie had fathered.[65] In any event, shortly after she filed for divorce, Louise began seeing Phelps Dunham, a member of an old Chicago family, who limped because of a fused right knee. As one newspaper noted in late 1936, Louise's experience with men and money had been anything but a happy fairy tale: "So this Cinderella hasn't gotten any fun out of it yet, but it is said that she has rented a yacht and is going to make a fourth try at married happiness."[66]

William had enough problems of his own with men and money and could not worry about Louise, and the Flagler fortune was now more of a nightmare than a fairy tale for him too. It appeared very uncertain just how much would be left in Mary Lily's trust for him, his sisters, Louise, and UNC to inherit, for New York Supreme Court Justice Aaron J. Levy ruled against her trustees in Loftin's suit for a construction of item No. 9 of her will. The FEC, Levy decided, was entitled to a large sum of money from Mary Lily's trustees, and he "appointed a referee to determine the amount it should receive." Though Kenan and Haines appealed the decision, William was not optimistic about their chances for a reversal.[67]

The banks and bondholders applauded Levy's decision, but the University of North Carolina did not. Immediately prior to the ruling, the university's trustees rejected William's offer to settle Mary Lily's bequest by giving the school a group of marketable securities that could be sold for enough money to earn $75,000 a year on deposit at prevailing interest rates in North Carolina. Apparently, though, even if the university got full value for the securities Kenan offered, it could come "nowhere near" $75,000 a year at existing interest rates.[68]

Fortunately for all of Mary Lily's beneficiaries, however, Levy's decision was reversed on April 9, 1937, by the court of appeals. In explaining the ruling, Justice Alfred H. Townley cited the legal precedence of a similar case involving newspaper publisher Joseph Pulitzer's will and also the fact that the FEC's creditors were "strangers" to Mrs. Bingham. "Her intention in making the provisions which are found in the will were not charitable nor did she intend that her fortune should be consumed in contributions to these properties for sentimental reasons. Confirmation of this intention may be found in the nature of Mr. Flagler's transactions with these companies." Finally, Townley pointed out, "other beneficiaries and charities, including an annuity to the University of North Carolina, would be impaired if the decision were otherwise."[69]

William immediately sent UNC another settlement proposal. The time seemed right to him to put the matter to rest. The university's trustees met in June, Mary Lily's trust expired in September, and he planned to establish a voting trust to replace it.

LOOKING BACK

On May 2, 1937, two days after W. R. Kenan Jr.'s sixty-fifth birthday, the Electrochemical Society published "Early Days in the Carbide and Ferrochrome Industries," by August Eimer. Kenan knew about Eimer's long relationship with Thomas "Carbide" Willson, and he also knew that he disliked Eimer's article. Not only did he consider it "very deficient and incorrect regarding the early stages of this discovery," but it was the second time in the last several months that a writer had failed to do justice to the early days of the carbide industry.[70]

Only a few months earlier another journal, The Welding Engineer, had published an article by Ernest D. Findlay on the history of carbide and acetylene. Though Kenan was initially unaware of the piece, which was titled "History of the Oxy-Acetylene Industry in America," he later read a copy of it sent him by the journal's editor, F. L. Spangler, who knew that Kenan "had played a part in this history" and so had asked for "criticisms" of the article as well for "details of your early connections with the industry." The journal, Spangler explained, was planning a series of articles on the subject, and it wanted "to make these historical articles as complete as the space allotted will allow, and we hope you will be good enough to furnish us the details requested."[71]

Needless to say, Kenan obliged the editor with plenty of details. After offering his major criticism of the article, that "while it might apply accurately to oxy-acetylene, the early development of calcium carbide is entirely omitted," Kenan provided two, single-spaced pages of details—from the failed aluminum experiments at Spray to the tests that he and Venable had performed at Chapel Hill on the "waste product" obtained from these experiments. "Together we discovered that it was Calcium Carbide, determined it's [sic] formulae, and made known the fact that acetylene gas could be evolved from it. . . . I have considerable documentary evidence to substantiate the contents of this letter," Kenan assured the editor. He offered to send all of his documents to *The Welding Engineer* along with the article he had written in April 1900 for the German Acetylene Company, "with the distinct understanding that it will be returned to me."

The Welding Engineer never asked for the documents, but Spangler did write Kenan to explain why. The journal had scrapped the remaining carbide articles "because of some opposition to the series which we have met from one unexpected quarter." Though the journal had yet to make any "enemies," it had received complaints from "one or two powerful groups who do not want to offer their cooperation in the preparation of this series."[72] Spangler did not name names, and he did not have to. Kenan knew he was referring to Union Carbide.

Kenan's concern with these developments combined with several other events during 1937 to turn his attention to the past, or more precisely, to turn his thoughts to his own mortality and to his need to explain that he was more than Henry Flagler's brother-in-law. Indeed, in many respects 1937 rivaled 1917 as the most important year in Kenan's life. In addition to marking the end of the trust established by Mary Lily's will, it brought the deaths of three key characters in his life. It signaled a major shift, in short, in his temporal orientation. He became more concerned with the past than with the future.

This reorientation started, to some extent, in 1935 with the publication of his *History of Randleigh Farm* and was reinforced with the publication of the second edition in June 1937. But these were less an exercise in looking back than promotional tracts for the ongoing scientific investigations at the farm. It was the increasing public interest in the history of calcium carbide and acetylene that first prompted Kenan to concentrate on the past. Not only did the articles by Findlay and Eimer overlook Kenan's role in that history, but in 1937 the American Chemical Society awarded its Schoellkopf Medal to one of Union Carbide's chief executives, James G. Marshall, who had worked with Kenan at Niagara Falls at the turn of the century.[73]

In the midst of these developments, moreover, Kenan was forced to confront the realities of aging and the specter of death. In 1937 Alice's bachelor twin brother, seventy-two-year-old Albert Pomroy, moved out of Lockport's Tuscarora Club and into 433 Locust Street, where he subsequently died. The situation was undoubtedly difficult for both William and Alice. Not only was Alice growing increasingly senile, but her frequent illnesses also suggested that she too might soon share the fate of her fraternal twin.[74]

Next, in the middle of May 1937, only a month after Mary Lily's will case was settled, Henry Flagler's old Standard Oil partner, John D. Rockefeller Sr., died at his winter home in Ormond Beach, Florida. The FEC immediately arranged to transport his body back to New York. Long experienced in handling Rocke-feller's trips to Ormond Beach, the old Flagler road now provided tickets and guards for the funeral party traveling on the "Pioneer," Rockefeller's private car. Among the many thank-you letters later received by the FEC was one from John D. Rockefeller Jr. to "W. R. Kenan, Jr. and S. M. Loftin, Receivers The Florida East Coast Railway," expressing appreciation for what "you and your people did for us." Kenan replied, "We are all going to miss your father's trips to, and his neighborly spirit in Ormond and we hope that we shall find you and your family visitors to Florida in the future."[75]

Louise Wise Francis left St. Augustine about the same time as the train bearing Rockefeller's body. The train trip north was a happy one for Louise, however. Freddie Francis was out of her life, and perhaps in anticipation of the settlement of Mary Lily's trust, the forty-one-year-old heiress had recently established the Flagler Nursery School for Underprivileged Children at St. Augustine. Best of all, her children had met and liked the man she intended to marry, Phelps Dunham.[76]

Unfortunately, tragedy intervened. Just a day or two after arriving in Short Hills, New Jersey, for a visit with some friends, Louise got word that her fiancé had died in an automobile accident. "Stricken ill" by the sad news of Dunham's death, Louise was admitted to Overbrook Hospital, where on May 28, with her children and her mother at her bedside, she died "of an overdose of sedative taken through error, according to the official finding." In truth, however, Louise took her own life.[77] Her funeral was held in her mother's house at 1713 Market Street in Wilmington, and she was buried in the Kenan family plot at Oakdale Cemetery, next to Buck, Mollie, and Mary Lily. Hardly anyone was at the gravesite, however, which "was covered with a blanket of orchids and pink rosebuds."[78]

AMBASSADORS OF THE PAST

William and his family were still in mourning when the university buried his latest settlement proposal. He had offered the school a combination of cash and securities totaling $1.25 million—a package capable of producing $75,000 a year, he believed, through 6 percent dividends on the securities and 5 percent interest on the cash. A number of trustees and university officials wanted cash, however—enough, that is, to produce, when invested at 4 percent, $75,000 a year. These men included the university's president, Frank Porter Graham; the chairman of the trustees' finance committee, James A. Gray Jr; and the U.S. ambassador to Mexico, Josephus Daniels.[79]

Significant though these differences were, something else was clearly at work in the university's rejection of Kenan's proposals. In August 1937 the dean of UNC's law school, Maurice T. Van Hecke, discussed the rejections in a letter to North Carolina's attorney general. "The University trustees have not made their wishes sufficiently specific or clear," he wrote. "The Kenan trustees, on the other hand, have made two propositions since December and have persistently attempted a settlement. The tactics of the University trustees seem to be predicated upon the assumption that they are dealing at arm's length with adversaries. As a matter of fact, however, the Kenan trustees have displayed a wholly friendly interest in the development of the University." Van Hecke then listed many of the Kenan family's gifts to the university as well as the problems faced by the FEC and Mary Lily's trustees. He suggested that in order "to keep intact this demonstrated good will of the Kenan family," several of the school's representatives should "go to New York and deal directly in person with Mr. Kenan. . . . If Mr. Kenan is doing the best he can with the resources at his command the University ought to try to get the best possible compromise rather than risk jeopardizing the whole settlement by adopting an antagonistic attitude."[80]

Shortly after the trustees rejected Kenan's proposal, his principal adversary among them, Josephus Daniels, visited the U.S. ambassador to Great Britain, Robert Worth Bingham, in London. Though ostensibly a visit between old friends, Daniels was there to reassure Bingham that President Roosevelt did not intend to ask for the Judge's resignation. Bingham had recently created an international incident by making a speech in England, at Roosevelt's request, denouncing Adolf Hitler, and by the time Daniels arrived in London in August 1937, there were rumors that the president would ask Bingham to resign.[81]

Daniels immediately reassured Bingham that "Roosevelt had said to me 'Bob is doing a grand work in London and will stay there as long as he can be persuaded to do so.'" According to Daniels this "first hand appreciation gratified" Bingham and led to "many heart to heart talks" between the two men "about matters neither of us could unbosom ourselves to the world." Though there is no evidence that they discussed Mary Lily, the Kenans, or the settlement of her legacy to UNC, it is not implausible to assume that they did. It had been exactly twenty years since Bingham had filed his codicil to Mary Lily's will.[82]

The two newspaper owners never saw each other again. Bingham returned to the United States in early December 1937 and checked in to the Johns Hopkins Hospital in Baltimore, where he died of Hodgkin's disease on December 18, eight days after submitting his resignation to Roosevelt. Daniels, at his post in Mexico, immediately wrote a long letter to the Judge's youngest son, Barry. Full of praise for the Judge's "rich heritage of courage, good citizenship and distinguished public service," the letter also reveals why Daniels and the Judge were such close friends. "From their earliest recollections your father and my wife were chums and friends as well as cousins," Daniels wrote, and there were financial ties.

In the latter part of 1920, when I was closing my term as Secretary of the Navy, the News & Observer was in financial straits and borrowing money in Raleigh was impossible. I wrote your father stating my situation and asking the loan of ten thousand dollars. He did not wait to write but telegraphed "What I have is yours" and wrote me that aside from his love of my wife and his esteem for me he felt it a privilege to aid one who in the great war had been so dedicated to his country that he could not think of his own affairs. You may imagine what such friendship meant to us.[83]

Bingham had once shared family and financial ties with W. R. Kenan too, but it is doubtful that William felt as Daniels did about the deceased. The turmoil created by Mary Lily's death had been one of the saddest chapters in Kenan's life, and the publicity now surrounding the Judge's death brought back a flood of unpleasant memories. Yet the glowing reports of Bingham's career also helped stimulate Kenan to write about what he considered the most important event in his own career: the discovery and identification of calcium carbide.

Shared Knowledge and Self-Esteem

W. R. Kenan knew when he started writing his *Discovery and Identification of Calcium Carbide in the United States* that March 30, 1938, marked the fortieth anniversary of the Union Carbide Company. So did the men at Union Carbide. By the end of January they had compiled "Notes on Data of Pertinence to the Early History of Carbide," an annotated list of articles, speeches, notes, correspondence, and a book. All but two of the entries—the article from *The Welding Engineer* and Gilbert Pond's book, *Calcium Carbide and Acetylene*—were written, remembered, or delivered by men closely connected with that early history: August Eimer, John Motley Morehead, Joseph Scales, James G. Marshall, Francis Preston Venable, and William Rand Kenan Jr.[1]

The content of the documents listed in Carbide's "Notes" suggests why Kenan was so determined to tell his version of the story. Only Pond's book and Venable's 1898 article, "An Account of the First Production of Calcium Carbide and Acetylene in the United States," mention the roles played by the professor and his student. Also, Venable's article does not mention Major James Turner Morehead, who was the focus of John Motley Morehead's 1922 speech before the International Acetylene Association, "James Turner Morehead: Pioneer in American Industry." This selective and sentimental panegyric, which concentrates almost exclusively on the role played by the Major in the early stages of the carbide industry, was offered by his son on the occasion of the awarding of the association's "First Medal to Estate of James Turner Morehead—History of the Discoverer of Calcium Carbide."[2]

The Kenan documents Union Carbide then possessed are also revealing. In addition to copies of Kenan's correspondence with *The Welding Engineer*, there was a copy of the article he wrote for publication in Germany, "Calcium Carbide and the Process of Manufacture," and a copy of the 1895 letter offering him a position with the Carbide Manufacturing Company at Niagara Falls. While William may have sent all of these copies to Union Carbide himself, the evidence suggests that the company received them from Spangler, the editor of

The Welding Engineer, and that Union Carbide was the "powerful" group that Spangler mentioned as being opposed to the projected articles in the journal. In describing the first (and only) article in that series, "History of the Oxy-Acetylene Industry in America," one Carbide official wrote that the article "does not seem to give proper credit to the Union Carbide Company for its work in the field, and the series, of which it was a part, was discontinued after the appearance of the first article."[3]

By the time Kenan completed *Discovery* in the late fall of 1938, John Motley Morehead had served as the primary source for the two most important documents compiled by Union Carbide on its fortieth anniversary: "Early Workers in the Calcium Carbide Industry" and "Willson Aluminum Company in Relation to Electro Gas Company and Licensees." Many of Kenan's former co-workers are mentioned in the documents, and several, including John Motley Morehead, Jesse King, and William C. Horry, are given individual headings in "Early Workers." But Venable's name is missing from both documents, and Kenan is mentioned only in "Early Workers." Indeed, he is only referred to in connection with the 1895 letter offering him a job—a letter cited by the company not for Kenan's employment but for the light shed on the various names of Carbide's corporate predecessors.[4]

Kenan began searching for a publisher for *Discovery* as soon as the manuscript was completed. "I have recently written an article on the Discovery and Identification of Calcium Carbide," he wrote to the secretary of the Electrochemical Society on December 2. The society's only publication on the subject, Kenan noted, was Eimer's "very deficient and incorrect [article] regarding the early stages of this discovery. My article, I believe, would be of great interest to the members of the society and if you are in position to publish it I would be glad to submit it to you or the editor for consideration." Kenan then offered his credentials: "I have been a member of the Society ever since it's [*sic*] organization but am not now actively engaged in scientific work. An early reply will be appreciated."[5]

The society's secretary, Colin Frink, was "very pleased indeed to hear" from Kenan, and though Kenan failed to mention anything about the "length or other details" of the manuscript, Frink encouraged him to "send it on and we will have our Publication Committee pass on it." Kenan complied, and on December 10 Frink notified him that the article had been received and submitted to the society's Publication Committee.[6] Having heard nothing further by the middle of January, however, Kenan wrote back to ask about the delay. Frink's response surprised him. "We have received a report that the manuscript is being further considered but that there were a number of statements in your paper that did not seem to check with records of others acquainted with the early days of Carbide manufacture." Kenan was taken aback. "If you or your Publication Committee would give me some idea of just what your criticism refs to, I would make an effort to explain. I am sure that every word in that manuscript is the truth and I believe I can produce enough evidence to convince any one that such is the case."[7]

There can be little doubt that it was Union Carbide and John Motley Morehead who did not think that Kenan's story was accurate. Not only was the president of the Electrochemical Society, Robert L. Baldwin, an officer of the National Carbon Company, a subsidiary of Union Carbide, but Kenan's article contradicted almost everything Morehead had said about the early history of carbide. If Venable had not retrieved the "crystalline mass" from the "dump" in Spray, North Carolina, and if he and Kenan had not experimented with and identified it, Willson and the Moreheads would never have known the value of their "discarded" material. Yes, Kenan implied, both Moreheads had failed to recognize the value of the rubbish. "Mr. John Motley Morehead," Kenan wrote, "son of Major Morehead, was employed as consultant by his father, and has continued more or less in that capacity since."[8]

More offensive still to Major Morehead's son were the implications of Kenan's comments regarding the response of Willson and the Major to the discovery Venable and Kenan had made. "When our figures were checked and facts recorded," Kenan wrote, "Dr. Venable invited Mr. Morehead and Mr. Willson to Chapel Hill, where they witnessed the light and were informed of our discovery that acetylene was the gas evolved from the waste product of their furnace. At that time I presented Mr. Willson with my note book covering the work done. After a full discussion of the matter they were to apply for a patent, Dr. Venable was to receive a royalty and I was to have a job. But Willson applied for the patent in his own name and sold the rights covering different districts of the United States."[9]

In fact, every word in Kenan's manuscript was not the whole truth, and Morehead had reason to challenge at least one of the author's assertions. His father had not seen "the light" in Chapel Hill with Willson. It was the Major's brother-in-law, William R. Walker, who saw it, and Walker, acting as the Major's representative, signed the (never fulfilled) contract with Venable. Although Kenan later penciled in this correction on his manuscript, the damage was already done.[10]

The Electrochemical Society rejected his article without any additional explanation. "Because the original of your manuscript which you sent to us was badly soiled and somewhat damaged during transmittal to and from the Publication Committee, we have made a copy of it which were are enclosing herewith. Personally," Frink wrote, "I very much regret that we cannot publish your paper at this time." The society's secretary closed with a chirp of diplomacy, however: "We certainly hope to see you at the New York Meeting, September 11th has been officially set aside at the New York World's Fair as Electrochemical Society Day."[11]

William was more than angry. He wanted revenge. But he did not fire off a nasty letter. He did what he would do with all nine editions of the *History of Randleigh Farm* and with all five editions of his autobiography, *Incidents by the Way*. He had *Discovery* privately printed by the Record Company of St. Augustine, an old Flagler company. As soon as it came off the press in April, he informed the Electrochemical Society. He wrote to Frink: "Referring to the correspondence passing relative to article 'Discovery and Identification of Calcium Carbide' I have had this printed and enclose you a couple of copies thinking you might find them of interest." Frink did more than thank the author; he asked for additional copies. "If you have two or three more copies to spare I should like to keep these on reserve to supply inquiries about the early history of calcium carbide." Kenan was just as diplomatic. He immediately sent the society four more copies.[12]

FIRST THINGS FIRST

Two days later, Kenan was forced to shift his attention to the federal court in Jacksonville, Florida, where hearings began on plans to reorganize the FEC Railway. But the proceedings did not last long. The judge asked the chairman of the F&R 5 bondholders' committee, Arthur M. Anderson, whether "this committee would be willing to undertake the task of preparing a plan of reorganization. The Chairman agreed and the hearing was thereupon adjourned until October 20, 1939, for consideration of any plan of reorganization that the 5 per cent Committee might formulate and any different plan that any other party in interest might wish to present."[13]

William also found himself spending more time on matters at the Western Block Company in Lockport. The firm's longtime president, William Shaw, died just as the war in Europe began boosting the company's business, and in February 1939 Kenan was elected to replace him. Thus, when he was not riding the Randleigh back and forth to Florida, Kenan was busy commuting between New York City and Lockport. "During the summers prior to World War II, it was necessary for me to spend most of my time in New York City, going up to Lockport for the weekends only." He alternated his mode of travel each week, "going via plane one week and via train the next week. I would take the early morning plane from New York City to Buffalo on Saturday and return late Sunday afternoon. The following week I would take a night train via New York Central Railroad and return on Sunday night. I always used the American Air Lines and the New York Central Railroad."[14]

In between his Western Block and FEC duties, William also continued to negotiate with UNC and to promote his carbide pamphlet. Interestingly, "Dr. Frank" now proved helpful in both matters; after receiving a copy of the pamphlet and the 1895 letter offering Kenan a job at Niagara Falls, the university president wrote to thank Kenan for the documents and to suggest that additional copies be sent to the chemistry library at UNC.[15] More important, the two men finally worked out a settlement of Mary Lily's bequest to the university. In addition to $1.1 million in cash and securities from her trust, William and his sisters gave an additional $775,000 to the university. Yet the settlement prompted only a bland "Resolution of Thanks" from the university's trustees: "Governor Ehringhaus moved and Mr. Sutton seconded a resolution of thanks to Mr. Kenan, Mr. Haines, Mrs. Wise, Mrs. Graham Kenan, and the Finance Committee of the Board of Trustees severally and collectively, and to the Attorney General, expressing appreciation for the settlement and thanks for the manner in which the settlement was concluded."[16]

William was nevertheless in high spirits when he attended the Chapel Hill commencement that June. The ICC had delayed the FEC hearings again, the FEC had just paid the interest on its 1909 bonds, and Kenan was fresh from promoting his carbide article at the University Club's forty-fifth anniversary reunion at Niagara Falls. The club had become a local institution, a large organization of tuxedoed men who had done or were doing well at the Niagara Falls industrial complex—men, Kenan explained, who "made a great success financially as well as acquired outstanding position in the community in which they now reside." Some sixty-six of the club's eighty-four living members attended the reunion, including Kenan and John Motley Morehead, who sat at the banquet with only one member between them.[17]

One of the last things William did before leaving the Chapel Hill commencement was give a copy of his *Discovery* pamphlet to a local newspaper editor, and the editor did exactly as Kenan had hoped. "Louis Graves printed the story recently in *The Chapel Hill Weekly*," Frank Graham wrote to Kenan on July 1, "which has interested a good number [of] people." Graham was as pleasant and encouraging in his letter as he had been with Kenan at commencement. "When I mentioned the fact that you had written a pamphlet on this subject to Mrs. Sutton, who is Dr. Venable's daughter, she was very much interested in seeing a copy. She will be grateful to you if you will send her a copy if you have one available." Graham ended by urging Kenan to "please come to see us again. It is a joy to be with you, even for the few moments of time I had with you. Your coming meant much to us all."[18]

William was in the Canadian Rockies with Alice and his sisters when Graham's letter arrived, so Schuyler Beattie sent Venable's daughter the carbide article. It was William's first vacation with the "girls" since 1937, and he was on his way to making 1940 a year of spending liberally. In addition to the UNC settlement and the trip to the Rockies ("$4,218.25"), William took Alice and his sisters to Havana ("$485.75"). He gave $5,000 to UNC for stadium improvements, $5,000 to the Historical and Restoration Society of St. Augustine, and over $13,000 to the American Red Cross in Lockport.[19]

His most unusual donation, however, went to the cyclotron project at the University of California. He gave $2,500 to establish the William R. Kenan Jr. Fellowship in the radiation laboratory at Berkeley and promised another $2,500 for the fellowship in 1941. The gift was in large measure an extension of his carbide quest—of his growing need for scientific recognition—but not in the way one might imagine.

He apparently invested in the project as a favor to the Doctors Erf—Oscar, the father, a professor of animal research at Ohio State University, and Lowell, the son, a medical doctor and blood specialist. The elder Erf had been visiting Randleigh regularly since 1930, when Dairylike Madcap broke her leg. He had suggested the dairy inn at the farm and had organized the first scientific conference there in 1933 with two of his fellow professors at Ohio State, bacteriologist H. H. Weiser and biochemist J. F. Lyman. He also had organized the First Annual Scientific Conference at Randleigh Farm the following year, and at each conference since that time he and his son and Weiser and Lyman had presented research papers and planned Randleigh's annual experiments. By the late 1930s, in fact, Oscar and Lowell Erf were two of William's favorite people. Both displayed a genuine interest in his work at Randleigh Farm, and both got along well with him. Indeed, with the exception of William's Kenan kinfolk, Lowell Erf appears to be the only person to whom Kenan ever addressed a piece of correspondence using the recipient's first name.[20]

It was also Lowell Erf who prompted William's involvement with the cyclotron project at Berkeley. Clearly a rising star in blood research, Lowell had left the medical school at Ohio State University to accept a position as chief of hematology at the Rockefeller Medical Research Hospital in New York City. From there he had moved to Berkeley, to a temporary position in the radiation laboratory, where he worked closely with its director, Dr. Ernest Lawrence, and Lawrence's brother, Dr. John H. Lawrence. After learning that the Lawrences needed funds for the cyclotron project, Lowell arranged for John Lawrence to meet W. R. Kenan Jr. in New York.

Kenan listened to the plans for the cyclotron and came away from this "very interesting interview" impressed. "If there is anything I can do in connection with this matter I certainly want to help," he wrote to Erf in early January 1940. Needless to say Kenan quickly received letters from the Lawrence brothers. John included a copy of his article "Artificial Radiation," while Ernest described the cyclotron program and some of its funding problems. Kenan appreciated their research but readily admitted he had an imperfect understanding of the scope of the project. He found John's article "most illuminating and interesting but . . . far beyond my knowledge." To Ernest he wrote, "I am interested in your project. Think it one of the most remarkable developments ever brought to my attention. I cannot follow it very thoroughly but I can see wonderful possibilities to be obtained through a very large cyclotron."[21]

Kenan agreed to donate $5,000 to the project for the period 1940–41, and a week later, on March 2, 1940, a "tremendously pleased" Ernest Lawrence wrote back. He thanked Kenan for the gift and suggested that since the "project of the great cyclotron is at the present time under consideration by the Rockefeller Foundation," Kenan might consider allocating the money to the "groundwork" that needed to be done in the meantime—specifically, to "a fellowship stipend which would allow us to have an extra man on the laboratory staff, which would be a great help. Such a William R. Kenan, Jr. Fellowship here could be devoted to either medical or physical work or specifically to the design of the big cyclotron."[22]

William had no intention of funding groundwork for a potentially well-funded project, however, especially if it received Rockefeller money. He apparently conveyed his feelings in a letter to Lowell Erf, whose position in the radiation laboratory was about to expire. Erf showed the letter to the Lawrence brothers and made it perfectly clear to them, Ernest Lawrence wrote, "that, although he [Erf] had been offered an opportunity to return to the faculty of the medical school at Ohio State, he would welcome an opportunity to stay on here at least another year." Lawrence thus suggested that the $5,000 "be allocated as a Kenan Fellowship in our laboratory to be held by Dr. Erf."[23]

William sent his check for $2,500 on April 15, along with a letter noting the "suggestion relative to Dr. Erf. I think this would be a very happy solution of the situation and I will be very glad to cooperate with you in this connection." Thus, on July 1, 1940, Dr. Lowell Erf became the first (and last) recipient of the William R. Kenan Jr. Fellowship in the radiation laboratory at Berkeley, California.[24]

A CLEANER AND BETTER MILK FOR MANKIND

Keeping the Erfs happy was clearly as important to Kenan as the prestige of having his name associated with the Berkeley cyclotron project. Even more than Lowell, Oscar Erf had helped Kenan make Randleigh Farm one of the most important private centers of scientific dairy farming and research in the nation.

By the time Kenan published the third edition of his *History of Randleigh Farm* in June 1940, he had spent close to $150,000 stocking his herd. He had 200 head of prize Jersey cattle on the farm and another 80 calves, and between 75 and 100 of the cows were in milk, all of them reflecting Kenan's "idea of propagating the characteristics of size and high milk production of the Tormentor family with the refinement and high quality milk of the [Jersey] Island families."[25] Kenan kept most of the herd on Randleigh's 350 acres, but in 1939, "in connection with our experimental work on cow diseases," he purchased 122 acres for an "isolation" farm two miles east of Randleigh. "This arrangement

Randleigh Farm on the eve of World War II. (Francis B. Grow)

makes it possible for us to eliminate any animal at Randleigh Farm which tests only suspicious," Kenan wrote in the third edition, "and makes it possible to maintain a negative herd at this farm."[26]

One woman and more than twenty men worked on the farm at the beginning of World War II. The woman, a bookkeeper, worked in the dairy inn office with a man who made ice cream and served customers. And there were plenty of customers. Not only did Randleigh serve super-creamy ice cream, but visitors could sit and watch, through huge display windows, one of the cleanest and most advanced milking parlors in the world. Five cows got milked at a time, each in a separate display stall, at the rate of about fifty cows per hour, in an operation designed to produce "pure milk, that is, not letting it come in contact with the human hand nor with the air. This was accomplished by means of the DeLaval Magnetic Milker; to this was attached a specially designed set of vacuum receivers in which the milk was delivered, and out of which it was released into bottles or cans."[27]

Whatever mistakes William initially made in planning the dairy inn had long been rectified. Randleigh Farm was now an extremely efficient operation as both a factory in the field and a field laboratory. At the center of the parlor was the operator's room, a long, narrow chamber between the glassed-in ice-

The dairy inn at Randleigh Farm. (Kenan, *History*, 1)

cream observation room and the partition of windowed display stalls. From here the operator controlled the queued-up cows with compressed-air stall gates and cupped their teats to the milking machine "through a port-hole in the partition and these are the only openings in the partition, the rest of it being non-shatterable glass."

No milk was spilled to worry over. It passed from the cow to the magnetic milker to large Pyrex jars that had been manufactured by the Corning Glass Company "from designs and patterns made by us." Kenan described the process: "The milk is automatically weighed as it comes from the cow, each cow's milk being kept separate until weighed and sample is taken, when it passes through nickel bronze pipe or glass tubes to the storage glass jars at the end of the room, each with a capacity of 45 gallons. The milk is split into these two jars and is then sucked up into a center jar where it is mixed again. This operation is done for the purpose of getting a uniform milk and it is then bottled direct from the milking jar."[28]

The bottles arrived already washed at 250 degrees Fahrenheit in a "sterilizer, which has four compartments each sufficient to carry 400 bottles in cases, [and] was constructed under one end of the runway of reinforced concrete insulated with hair felt." Steam from the sterilizer also went "to heat the floor and gutters of the runway as also the stalls, provision being made so as to warm up the udder in cold weather, as we feel a little heat on the udder makes the cow let down the milk more freely."

Kenan took special pride in the "economical, efficient and satisfactory operation" of the inn's huge refrigerating plant. "The problem as presented was to cool the milk in bottles," Kenan explained, "it being bottled at the temperature it came from the cow." Kenan studied the problem himself before building the plant, and though he sent his report to "all refrigerating companies," none showed any interest "whatsoever in the problem." Indeed, it had taken Kenan, Erf, and Carroll Smith, a consulting engineer with the Flagler System, almost two weeks "to get any refrigerating company to even attempt to work out the problem. Eventually we got the York Manufacturing Company, of York, Pa., interested to such an extent that they agreed to furnish the air conditioners and compressors but without any guarantee whatever."

The resulting plant, Kenan wrote, was the first deep-freeze in existence and "beyond words."

> We have three boxes which operate for cooling milk, also one box containing a brine tank for bulk milk and ice making, with a capacity of 400 pounds per day. Also we have one large box for storage of dairy products which is controlled at about 38 degrees. We have a freezing room for the purpose of freezing fruits which we carry at between 10 and 12 degrees F. above zero. We have also an ice cream storage compartment that is carried at about the same temperature. Then we have a room with ammonia direct expansion aluminum plates as shelves and this is carried at about 20 degrees below zero. This is for hardening purposes and quick freezing.[29]

Most of the farm's employees worked outside the dairy inn on the farm itself, where they lived in buildings owned by Kenan. The complex contained "five dwelling houses and one boarding house for single men," Kenan noted. Two men also roomed "over the herdmen's office attached to the test barn and three men over the calf barn. The object of this is to have someone in both barns all the times." Kenan had only praise for his employees. "The question of help at the farm has never worried us in the slightest," he boasted. "As a matter fact, we have a greater number of applications than we are able to accommodate; therefore we believe we have the best boys and the best milkers available."[30]

While many of these men were simply glad to have a full-time job during the depression, they also enjoyed certain benefits from their employment at the farm. "We got free rent," the son of one recalled, "all the free milk we could drink and deep discounts (50% I think) on dairy products such as ice cream." Kenan also made sure "that the outside men, whose work was seasonal, were never laid off in the winter," which was "a plus in the 1930s when jobs (and free milk) were hard to get."[31]

Randleigh's superintendent, T. E. Grow, occupied the largest house on the farm. "We called it ours but of course it belonged to WRK," Grow's son explained. "Appropriately enough, it was called the Flagler house. About 1930, Norman Flagler went broke and TEG encouraged WRK to buy the place. We then moved in." Like other buildings on the farm, the Flagler house recycled materials from the Flagler System. "The house had two large living rooms at the front, both carpeted with red carpeting taken from one of the Florida East Coast hotels. Here the Randleigh Farm employees and spouses assembled for the annual showing of WRK's home movies. All home movies are boring but these were supremely so to me since the most of film was of Florida foliage and WRK and friends playing golf. I do, however, recall some spectacular aerial film of the results of the big hurricane of 193[5] showing the complete destruction of the Florida East Coast Railway from the mainland to Key West."[32]

By 1940 the economy was improving, and many of the farm's employees, especially the younger ones, started looking for better jobs. Their chores were no longer as simple as they once had been; the scientists and their experiments had changed all that. Strict records and regimens had to be maintained on everything, then changed again for new experiments: on individual cows and test groups, on the kinds and amount of feed they received, on the volume and quality of milk they produced, and on the length of their exposure to carbon lamps and radio music. According to one former employee, many of the workers—"the herdsmen and people like that"—believed Kenan thought more about science and the scientists than he did about the men who kept Randleigh running. These employees said of Kenan, "To prove a point, he spent quite a bit of money, but otherwise he was known to be tight."[33]

The rebellion of one field-worker, humorous though it was, presaged the general response of Kenan's employees to the extra work generated by the research at Randleigh. The occasion was the farm's first scientific conference. Grow "went around and told all the men to get the place looking as sharp as possible." In particular he spoke to Abe Willover (who had a rough exterior but a heart of gold) about the old truck that Abe used to haul manure from the manure pit to the fields. "This was a disreputable looking vehicle and Abe was instructed to clean it up. On the day of the conference the first order of business was to give the visiting dignitaries a tour of the farm. When the group got down by the manure pit, there was Abe's truck prominently displayed. Abe had cleaned it up as ordered but he added a touch of his own. On the side of the truck, in big white letters, was painted 'Abie's Shit Wagon.' "[34]

Nowhere is Randleigh's rise as a laboratory better reflected than in the first three editions of *History of Randleigh Farm*. The first edition, published in October 1935, contains 116 pages, three-quarters of which Kenan wrote himself. He describes his decision to start the farm; the date, number, and price of the animals purchased; the construction of the dairy inn; the medals of merit earned by his herd; and the experiments performed at Randleigh. The first experiments he describes were simple: analyzing the vitamin and mineral content of Randleigh's pasture grasses, inventing a bull exerciser, comparing the efficiency of electric fly screens, and measuring the impact on the nutritional value of milk of adding iodine to cow feed and exposing the cows to ultraviolet radiation. The second and third editions of the book are very different. Both approach 300 pages in length, and little of the writing is Kenan's. The contents are almost entirely the research papers originally presented by the scientists at Randleigh's annual conferences. Some of the pieces are original, some were previously published, but all deal with topics and test results from scientific experiments on cows and feed, mainly at Randleigh Farm. There are graphs, lists, tables, charts, and photographs of everything from cows and equipment to the tooth dentin of dead test rats.[35]

Kenan did not mind this change in his *History*, of course. He actively promoted and enjoyed it. He especially liked Erf's recruitment of Dr. Ondess L. Inman, a biologist at Antioch College in Yellow Springs, Ohio. As director of the Charles F. Kettering Foundation for the Study of Chlorophyll and Photosynthesis at Antioch College, Inman was a valuable source of prestige and information for Randleigh Farm. In addition to being a respected, well-funded scientist, he worked on cutting-edge research potentially useful to Kenan's goal of producing "A Cleaner and Better Milk for Mankind."[36]

Inman made his first visit to Lockport with Erf, Weiser, and Lyman in October 1936, on the occasion of the Third Annual Scientific Conference at Randleigh Farm. Like the previous one-day conferences, the third gathering was small; Erf and the professors did most of the talking while Kenan, Grow, and Inman listened. Inman finally spoke up at the end of the conference, during the planning session for Randleigh's research the following winter. He offered to test and evaluate the feed and milk associated with the farm's upcoming experiments with cod liver oil (vitamin D)—experiments originally suggested by E. R. Squibb & Sons, the makers of a vitamin supplement called Ultradol. Inman also suggested adding a vitamin A experiment involving alfalfa and carotene. The Kettering lab would test the feed and milk of the Randleigh cows fed with "ordinary hay plus cod liver oil with so many vitamin A units and with specially prepared alfalfa with large amounts of caretene [*sic*] in it."[37]

Kenan was so impressed with Inman's suggestions that he immediately wrote Squibb & Sons for information on the cod liver oil and other ingredients needed for the experiment. He also sent Inman a check for $300—money the professor then used to establish the Kenan Research Fund at Antioch College. Inman thanked the Jersey enthusiast for the money and "the opportunity to visit your dairy. I certainly learned much while there and I hope I may have the opportunity of visiting you again." Kenan sounded more professional than personal in his response. He sent Inman a copy of Squibb's suggestions along with a short note evaluating them. "It would appear to me that it is unnecessary for you to make a vitamin 'A' and 'D' test on this oil. However, I would like to have your opinion in this connection. It was a pleasure to have you here at the Farm and I hope that our experiments will prove of some benefit to humanity."[38] Kenan then sent an additional $200 for research, and Inman responded by offering to write an original article, "The Green Plant," for the second edition of Kenan's *History* (1937). Kenan published the article as the next-to-last chapter in the second edition; the final piece was "Blood, Life and the Progress of the Milk Industry," by Lowell Erf.[39]

From that point on, Inman worked closely with Kenan and Oscar Erf to expand the range and complexity of the scientific activities at Randleigh Farm. By 1940 the annual scientific conference lasted two days, and the number of participants had doubled. The farm had also added a "Nutritional Laboratory" containing an "Experimental Pasteurizer" and room enough for hundreds of white rats and a separate research herd, "in which all the cows are infected with mastitis," on the new isolation farm east of Randleigh. Kenan was also contributing between $500 and $1,000 a year to the Kenan Research Fund at Antioch College and probably twice that much to the Kenan Promotional and Investigational Fund at Ohio State University.[40]

Kenan clearly got as much out of this relationship as Erf and Inman. He liked both men personally, and his training as a chemist enabled him to understand their science and to shape and participate in the farm's experiments. He understood the purpose, procedure, and results of the work. He understood what Erf and Inman wanted to do there, and they knew that he understood. He made no admission of ignorance, for example, in responding to Inman's pamphlet on chlorophyll and photosynthesis. Rather, he displayed an understanding of both the subject and the author that proved prophetic. "This is one of the most interesting documents I have ever read and I can well appreciate why you are so enthusiastic about this work," he wrote to Inman. "Much has been discovered and yet it seems a long way to the end. I sincerely hope you will live long enough to obtain your objective."

In other words, Kenan was not a cash cow that Erf and Inman were milking. He was a scientist doing exactly what he wanted: work in which he found meaning. The research allowed him to demonstrate that his career as a scientist did not end with his resignation from Union Carbide. By the eve of World War II he could point to the farm, to its scientific conferences, and to the three editions of his *History of Randleigh Farm* as evidence of his continuing involvement in and publication of scientific research.

It was also clear by 1940 what Kenan meant by a cleaner and better milk for mankind and that his hopes of providing it were increasingly threatened by forces beyond his control. Kenan wanted to produce milk with the highest nutritional content possible and thus milk that had not been pasteurized. "The efforts of Randleigh Dairy Farm have been designated to improve the nutritional value of natural milk," one of Erf's assistants wrote in 1939, and the scientists working at the farm reinforced and redirected these efforts. "With the research staff employed by Randleigh Farm, the efforts have been intensified to the problem of development of foodstuffs for high record milk and butterfat production for several successive official test periods, as well as problems with reproduction, and improvement of nutrition of milk produced by these cows."[41] Randleigh's research reflected the basic principles enunciated in 1931 by Erf and another Ohio State professor, Dr. Ernest Scott, in the *Proceedings of the International Association of Dairy and Milk Inspectors*: "that milk is subjected to wide variation in its food value as affected by the type of food intake of the cow."[42]

While Kenan and Erf genuinely hoped to help mankind, they also wanted to prevent government-mandated pasteurization of milk. On one level these goals were consistent. Pasteurization kills bacteria, but it also destroys important nutrients in milk. Thus pasteurization should only be used, Erf wrote in the 1940 *History of Randleigh Farm*, where milk supplies were "unsafe." The factors that made them unsafe from the start, he continued, and thus in need of subsequent pasteurization, could initially be eliminated by frequently testing herds for infectious disease, by feeding them proper feeds, and by milking the cows "in a clean milking barn directly into the bottle with a good milking machine or the milk to be handled by men who have been tested and found free of (the) disease."

On another level, however, Erf's fight against government-mandated pasteurization suggests the extent to which a cleaner and better milk for mankind also meant a better deal for Kenan and his kind: owners of Jersey dairy herds. "A Board of Health cannot have as their ideal," Erf argued, "a milk supply that comes from miscellaneous sources where there are diseased cows and diseased people; to have a supply pasteurized might be considered a good makeshift for awhile but they should aim for a higher standard." That standard, he wrote, should be milk "delivered to the consumer in less than 48 hours and . . . kept below 40° during that time. It should be the standard for the Board of Health and all inspectors should aim to that point."[43]

Kenan and Erf had plenty of reasons, both past and pressing, to be contentious on the subject. Public officials pushing pasteurization came close to closing Randleigh's milking parlor before it opened. The parlor or "closed" system of milking was virtually unknown when the dairy inn was built, and the method proposed for cleaning the system was completely unique. "The idea of 'in-place-cleaning' was a new venture," professor Harry H. Weiser later recalled. "State and local Boards of Health were skeptical of such a fantastic plan. Fortunately, they were convinced that sanitary features could be maintained without disassembling the equipment"—fortunately, but not immediately. "After working with the Boards of Health and after 6 months of periodic checking, we agreed that good quality milk could be produced. Randleigh Farm Dairy was the first farm to operate under such a system."[44]

The parlor flap was also part of a wider, ongoing battle that included the impact of pasteurization on both the milk industry and Jersey cattle. State and local pasteurization laws forced thousands of small milk distributors out of business after World War I, and this led in turn to increasing control of milk distribution by a few giant companies. "Because the process involved a sizable capital investment in new equipment and returnable bottles, it drove out of business the small milk peddlers and storeowners whose overripe product and unhygienic cans and dippers had contributed to the problem [of unsafe milk]." The development of large-scale pasteurization after 1914 weakened the power and position of both the dairies themselves and the Jersey breed. Whereas dairies once controlled the industry—as producers and distributors—they now had to deal with the increasing power of a small number of very large distributors.[45]

As for those dairies with Jersey herds, pasteurization came as double blow. It placed the goals of safety and high production above that of nutrition—that is, above the quality that made Jersey milk so appealing, Jersey cattle the leading dairy breed in the nation, and Jersey milk the most expensive. In other words, pasteurization rendered Jersey milk just like other milk and thus less appealing, because of its higher price, to the giant holding companies such as National Dairy Products (Sealtest) and Borden's that, by the end of the 1920s, had gained control of milk distribution in most major cities.[46]

Jersey owners thus found themselves in an increasingly difficult position. "The giant milk distributors formed a national organization to inform the public of milk's nutritional value, inundating the schools with posters, pamphlets, and lesson outlines. Pictures of healthy children sipping their daily quart of milk (the recommended dose) smiled from the newspapers and magazines of the nation. In New York, Pennsylvania, and the midwestern states, powerful dairymen's leagues joined with milk distributors to encourage state departments of agriculture to study and propagate the good word about milk's healthful properties." While many Jersey dairymen supported these leagues, they did so halfheartedly, for the assumption shaping the government's "good word" for milk was that the milk supply would be pasteurized.[47]

Randleigh's place in these trends reflected a combination of Kenan's goals for the farm, his ownership of Jerseys, and the connections of the farm's research to the milk and dairy industry. Kenan's personal goals for Randleigh were clearly unique. He wanted to do science there, both to help humanity and to draw attention to himself and his career—to help him realize, as it were, his idea of himself. As such, he was indifferent to profit. "As a matter of fact, he wanted the farm to lose money," Schuyler Beattie's daughter recalled. "He wanted to see what would produce the best, and in my opinion, he did produce the best and showed it could be done, but he wasn't trying to make a profit."[48]

Beattie's daughter also remembered being so impressed with the research at Randleigh that it "had a lot to do later when I chose medicine as my career instead of something else." "I was interested from the very earliest in the work at Randleigh Farm. Of course my father was dealing with papers and the correspondence and a lot of scientific work that was being done there under Dr. Erf. Dr. Erf was at the house once in a while." And it was all very exciting. "It was a fascinating thing to be a part of all that. Mr. Kenan talked to me just as much as he would my father about things like that, and what they were doing and the nutritional benefits of feeding the cows properly. I remember he explained how important it was to keep the cows healthy, so that the milk was pure and people didn't get sick from it. They were some of the earliest people to use sulphur to control undulant fever in cattle."[49]

Randleigh's bookkeeper remembered another reason why Kenan did not want the farm to make a profit: taxes. "They always tried to prove to him that he got his living from Randleigh Farm," she explained, and he always tried to prove that he did not. "If he got an ice cream cone, he paid a nickel for it. Or a milk shake, he paid a dime for it. Always paid for his milk with ten cents or quarter or something like that. So they could not prove he got his living from Randleigh Farm. Otherwise, his taxes would be way up. . . . I remember they went to court out there from them."[50]

Regardless of Kenan's not-for-profit motivations, his farm operated within a web of corporate and personal relationships that made economic profit a high priority. He and his farm formed part of a larger nexus of manufacturers, drug companies, food processors, nutritional scientists, and Jersey cattle promoters. "The Milking Parlor idea or the closed system was promoted by De-Laval Separator Company," one Randleigh researcher recalled. "Such a system had been installed at The White Swan Farm [in Erie, Pennsylvania] with little success. However, Mr. Kenan, with the help of the manufacturers of milking machines, were convinced that such a system properly installed and efficiently operated would do a good job."[51]

There was always at least one representative, in fact, from some large corporate concern at Randleigh's annual scientific conferences. The farm used and tested products manufactured by the Veterinary Products Division of E. R. Squibb & Sons; it conducted experiments on Produlac, an antimastitis drug, for the National Distillers Products Corporation; and it worked with Nutritional Research Associates of Indiana, a manufacturer of carotene, in other experiments.[52]

Through Oscar Erf, moreover, Kenan and his farm also worked closely with America's leading animal nutritionists and some of the largest cattle and dairy organizations in the nation. Erf not only mobilized his professional colleagues to help at Randleigh Farm, but on the eve of World War II he also played a critical role in shaping the scientific and legal work associated with raising the standards of commercial dairy products. By 1940 his practical and scientific activities had earned him a "high standing among leaders in the dairy profession and industry."[53] Erf gave up his teaching duties, in fact, in the spring of 1940, at about the time that Kenan published the third edition of *History of Randleigh Farm*. The sixty-six-year-old professor began concentrating with Inman on "some chlorophyll problems under the Kenan Promotional and Investigational Fund. This pertained particularly to determining the chlorophyll and vitamin content of the feed that was fed various animals."[54]

Erf was now using Randleigh Farm and Kenan's money for more than shared knowledge and Kenan's self-esteem. He was wielding them as weapons in a fight by the nation's Jersey cattle interests—a fight that signaled the end of an era in Jersey history in the United States. For as long as anyone could remember, "milk had been judged primarily on its quantity of butterfat as manifested by a deep creamline seen through the glass bottle." And Jerseys, the queens of butterfat, "were in active demand because of their ability to produce a milk that was visibly more appealing as well as nutritionally superior." Yet all of this was changing as safety, not nutrition, became the chief criterion for judging milk and for the spread of pasteurization laws that Erf, Kenan, and other Jersey interests opposed.[55]

In responding to these challenges, Erf looked forward and backward. He confronted the pasteurization question with several assumptions about the future: that his and Inman's chlorophyll research would lead to a more nutritious milk supply, that pasteurization was here to stay, that more legislation was on the way, and that other changes on the industry's horizon, especially homogenization, pointed to the eventual dominance of a "fluid" milk supply. Erf thus decided to use the latest, most advanced scientific research to try to prevent pasteurization measures where possible and to shape such measures to the benefit of the Jersey interests where legislation appeared inevitable.[56]

Yet he pursued this strategy with the past in mind. He believed he could preserve the profit and reputation of the Jersey breed by implementing a "certification" system of milk inspection that was tried but abandoned by reformers at the turn of the century.[57] Put simply, where state and local governments could not be convinced to accept private policing of the milk supply, Erf advocated a system of public inspection that made room for a "certified" but unpasteurized milk.

Erf's strategy formed part of an aggressive campaign by the American Jersey Cattle Club (AJCC) to implement a private system of certification. The club had taken the first steps toward this goal in 1927 when it registered and copyrighted the "Jersey Creamline Products" trademark in order to issue "licenses to certain milk distributors to sell milk bearing this mark." Although the club's campaign languished in the economic turmoil of the depression, a new wave of state and local pasteurization initiatives had combined with slumping sales to prompt the formation of Jersey Creamline, Inc., on March 3, 1939. This new company immediately struck a deal with the AJCC "whereby it leased the Jersey Creamline Products trademark under terms mutually advantageous to both organizations." Apparently one of those terms was a marketing program that stressed both the nutritional superiority of Jersey milk and the safety of a privately regulated system of certification. That was the program, at least, which the AJCC's special Creamline Committee studied in December 1941 in order "to make any suggestions they thought would be helpful in improving this milk program thus bringing about more sales and a more successful Jersey milk promotion project."[58]

Both Kenan and Erf played important roles in the AJCC's activities. Kenan had joined the club in 1920, Randleigh was a licensee of Creamline Milk, and Kenan was elected vice-president of the club in 1943 at the same time that his friend and fellow UNC alumnus Junius G. Adams of Asheville was elected its president. Erf was a frequent contributor to the *Jersey Bulletin*, and much of what he published therein dealt with experiments at the most important private research facility involving Jerseys (and all breeds) in the nation, Randleigh Farm. Indeed, both men aggressively promoted the club's preference for a private system of milk certification.

The relationship between Kenan and Erf also shaped the geographical realignment of the club that began in the mid-1930s.[59] Although many factors account for this historical realignment—the most significant of which was the transfer in 1944 of the club's general offices from New York to Columbus, Ohio, the home of Ohio State University—certainly Oscar Erf and William Rand Kenan Jr. were critical. Not only did the two men serve as a bridge between the old Jersey interests in the East and the new Jersey interests in the Midwest and the South, but their work at Randleigh Farm served as both symbol and substance of the transition from dairy farming by gentleman-breeders to dairy farming by college-trained scientists. As the *Jersey Bulletin* noted in August 1944, two months after Kenan received an honorary doctor of laws degree from UNC, "The scientist, Dr. Erf, backed by the scientist, Dr. Kenan, proceeded to carry through regardless of expense, every experiment and every study that could be devised bearing upon the aim, to find out just what it is that makes the good cow give more milk of a better quality, live longer and bring forth a still better calf."[60]

Not surprisingly, Kenan received the greatest recognition for the work at Randleigh Farm. One writer, a former UNC classmate of Kenan's, wrote in the *Jersey Bulletin* that Kenan's honorary doctorate "was in recognition, not of his achievements in the field of chemistry, or as a construction engineer, or a business administrator, or by reason of his great philanthropies, but of his work with his Jersey cattle." Another contemporary writer noted that in the field of testing, Kenan's "Randleigh Farm herd is a giant. It has piled up big individual records in the American Jersey Cattle Club files and it dominates its state [New York]."

The honor Kenan prized most was the Master Breeder's Award, which he received from the AJCC in March 1945. "The justice of the award is above controversy," the *Jersey Bulletin* exclaimed, "for Mr. Kenan has achieved capably, magnificently for the Jersey in his wide range of activities and interest in the breed. He has built up one of the greatest breeding establishments in livestock history, and along with that he has contributed more to experiment in feeding and maintaining a healthy herd, and in the production of superior quality milk than any other private farm establishment of its kind." By working, moreover, with "men widely known and experienced in research," Kenan had compiled a catalog of research at Randleigh that "reads like the curriculum of a college of dairy science, and is 100 per cent Jersey."[61]

Kenan received more recognition than Erf partly because of Erf's withdrawal from scientific activity. The professor retired from Ohio State in 1945 at the age of seventy and returned to his birthplace in Monroeville, Ohio, where he died in the spring of 1947.

BETWEEN THE LINES

Erf's death came just two months after Alice Kenan's and only a few months after William Rand Kenan Jr. published the first edition of his autobiography, *Incidents by the Way*. Kenan wrote the first edition between 1940 and 1945 and then wrote four more editions, one every three years until 1958. When combined with the nine editions of his *History of Randleigh Farm* (the final edition appeared in 1959), Kenan's autobiographies represent his twenty-five-year struggle to escape the Flagler shadow by promoting his own achievements as a scientist and engineer.

He could not escape his brother-in-law's legacy, however. In late October 1940, after almost ten years of litigation, the federal court decided to submit the FEC's reorganization case to the ICC. Although the Jacksonville judge considered the Anderson plan both fair and equitable to the two largest groups of bondholders (Anderson's committee of F&R 5 bondholders and the institutional committee of 1909 first mortgage bondholders), he also agreed with the objections raised by an "independent" group of 1909 bondholders regarding the complex first lien question: "that he had no power in an equity proceeding to approve a plan of reorganization over the dissent of first mortgage bondholders. He, therefore, held that such a plan would have to be submitted to the Interstate Commerce Commission through Section 77 proceedings" of the federal Bankruptcy Act. Yet the ICC, citing the "public interest" as its chief concern, refused to consider the lien question and maintained that it would give top priority instead to putting the FEC under efficient, knowledgeable management. Its decision led to one of the longest railroad bankruptcy cases in American history.[62]

It also brought Ed Ball, a trustee of the Alfred I. duPont estate, to W. R. Kenan's doorstep. Ball was then fifty-two years old and in a position similar to what Kenan's had been twenty years earlier. He was at the height of his mental power; he controlled a $50-million estate left by his deceased brother-in-law, Alfred I. duPont; and he was a major force in the economic life of Florida. He was also president of both a Florida railroad company, the Appalachicola Northern Railroad, and a Florida land company, the St. Joseph Land & Development Company, and he owned hotels in Key West and elsewhere. But there the similarities ended.[63] Ball was a mean-spirited businessman who loved politics, despised Roosevelt, and hated the New Deal. He had already established a relationship with the FBI that would lead him to become friends with J. Edgar Hoover, to hire ex-FBI agents as corporate executives, and to become a contact for the FBI's special agent in charge in Florida.[64]

By 1940 Ball was also president of the St. Joe Paper Company in northwestern Florida and one of the most powerful men in the state. As he noted at the ICC-FEC hearing in 1941, the duPont estate controlled "six national and six state banks, referred to as the Florida National Group of Banks, having aggregate deposits at present, in excess of 100 million dollars, including the Florida National Bank of Jacksonville, Florida Bank & Trust Company at West Palm Beach, Florida Bank & Trust Company at Daytona Beach, and Florida National Bank and Trust Company at Miami."[65]

Ball asked Kenan to name a price for the FEC's stock, all but a few shares of which William owned and which he controlled for himself and his sisters through the voting trust he had created in 1938 after the expiration of Mary Lily's trust. The stock would give Ball a financial stake in the FEC and thus allow him to file a reorganization plan that would "cure the defects" which he believed "to inhere in the Five Percent Committee Plan." Although Ball considered Kenan's FEC stock to be worthless in monetary terms, both he and Kenan knew its strategic importance. Once Ball controlled it, he could appoint a new board of directors for the FEC and have them approve his plan for reorganizing the road, a plan that the ICC would then almost have to accept.

Kenan refused to put a price on the FEC's stock, however, for he wanted to continue to control the company as long as he could. As his FEC secretary George Cordwell explained, "When the railway went into bankruptcy, the stock was declared worthless but it continued to exist. Mr. Kenan maintained the corporate organization of the railway right through the receivership. As a matter of fact, I was one of the directors. There was a board of directors, and certain of us formed this board of directors. Met annually to preserve the corporate organization although they declared the stock had no value. We continued to publish every year an annual report on the railway." They also continued to pay the interest on the 1909 bonds. "There was a certain link between the corporate organization and bondholders," Cordwell noted, "they continued to pay the interest of the first issue."[66]

Undeterred by Kenan's response, Ball moved quickly to gain a financial interest in the road and thus the right to submit a reorganization plan to the ICC. The duPont estate acquired "the status of a creditor by purchase of the Railway Company's bonds," Ball explained a few months later. "The Estate directly acquired $10,000 principal amount of First Mortgage Bonds, and $100,000 principal amount of First and Refunding Bonds [the F&R 5s], and the Florida National Building Corporation, one of our subsidiaries, has acquired principal amount of $3,400,000 First and Refunding Bonds and $350,000 First Mortgage Bonds." Thus, by the early months of 1941 the duPont interests owned a small number of 1909 first mortgage bonds and more F&R 5s than any single bondholder.[67]

Ball's buying spree caught the eye of George Cordwell, who kept close track of the ownership certificates submitted by FEC bondholders. "My job was to go through these ownership certificates as they came in and watch to see if any organization was accumulating quantities of the bonds," Cordwell recalled. Which was exactly what Ball was doing—a move that Cordwell and others suggested Kenan duplicate. The F&R 5s were then "selling at 7 on 100, $7.00 for 100. Some of us in the New York office realized that this was ridiculous," Cordwell explained, "and we thought of buying some of these bonds. Finally, someone went to Mr. Kenan, and they said, 'Mr. Kenan, do you realize that you could gain possession of a sufficient number of these bonds to regain control?' "[68]

William was intrigued by the idea, but he worried about its legal and ethical implications. So he turned to his fellow FEC receiver, Scott Loftin, the FEC's attorney, for advice. According to Cordwell, "Mr. Loftin said, 'Mr. Kenan, you could do it but it would be very unethical, and you would be liable to be subject to very serious criticism.' Mr. Kenan went to some other legal body and asked them. They told him the same thing." William dropped the idea.[69]

In early 1941, moreover, in preparation for the ICC's preliminary bankruptcy hearings, Kenan ended his ten-year tenure as one of the FEC's coreceivers and selected as his replacement Edward W. Lane, president of the Atlantic National Bank of Jacksonville. The change further confounded the already complex and confusing FEC struggle, for unlike the receivership proceedings, which turned on the competing first-lien claims of the two closely linked groups of institutional bondholders, the ICC bankruptcy hearings involved an alliance of those two groups against the duPont estate and other groups of both F&R 5 and 1909 bondholders.

One of the first confrontations occurred over the question of whether the ICC should appoint Edward Lane as one of the railroad's trustees in bankruptcy. The federal court had nominated both Lane and Scott Loftin as bankruptcy trustees, but the independent committee of 1909 bondholders objected to Lane. Its reasons for doing so are very revealing, for in addition to shedding light on the alliances at work in the FEC's reorganization, they also demonstrate the extent to which Kenan's personal and business relationships shaped the railroad's long course through bankruptcy.[70]

Ball was naturally opposed to seeing Lane, the president of the duPont estate's largest banking competitor in Florida, appointed as trustee of the FEC. He and the independents also considered Lane, "by connection and interest, . . . not [to be] a disinterested person under the definition in Section 77 of the National Bankruptcy Act." They particularly objected to Lane's relationship with the other group of 1909 bondholders, the institutional group, which was led by the Guaranty Trust Company of New York. Not only was Lane's Jacksonville bank "the correspondent bank of the Guaranty Trust Company, trustee of the [FEC's] first mortgage issue," but Lane and his bank also used the same Jacksonville law firm as Guaranty Trust. What was more, Guaranty Trust was controlled by J. P. Morgan and Company, whose representative, Arthur M. Anderson, now presented the ICC with a reorganization plan that both major institutional groups of bondholders—the Anderson committee of F&R 5s and Guaranty's 1909 bondholders—had already agreed on. Indeed, in early March the independents rejected the Anderson plan and announced their support for an alternative plan submitted to the ICC by Ed Ball in the name of the duPont estate.[71]

Surely, too, both the independents and Ball objected to the close relationship that existed between Lane, the Kenans, and Guaranty Trust. The Kenans did most of their private banking with Guaranty, and Sarah Kenan had designated Lane's Atlantic National Bank as the successor trustee of her estate. In 1919, moreover, Lane's brother, Mills B. Lane of Savannah, Georgia, had merged his Citizens and Southern Bank with Frank Hawkins's Third National Bank of Atlanta. Hawkins, in addition to serving as a director and chairman of the board of the consolidated Citizens and Southern Bank, was the father-in-law of William's cousin, Thomas S. Kenan.[72]

The Kenans and all of these men also had close personal and business ties to Eugene Stetson, who in January 1941 was elected president of the Guaranty Trust Company. Stetson's climb to the top of the banking world was directly linked to the personal and financial power of these people, especially the Kenans. In 1916 Mills B. Lane's Citizens and Southern Bank had acquired the American National Bank of Macon, Georgia, a bank that Stetson's father had helped organize and for which Stetson himself had worked for several years. Between 1910 and 1916, moreover, the younger Stetson had been president of a small bank in Macon, Georgia, the Citizens National Bank, whose leading stockholder and director was Samuel Taylor Coleman II, the brother-in-law of both Stetson and Frank Hawkins.[73]

Stetson got his biggest break in the banking world on September 25, 1916, however, just two days after Mary Lily signed her will, when Charles H. Sabin, president of Guaranty Trust at the time, asked him to become a vice-president of the New York bank. While the offer partly reflected the Macon banker's abilities, Stetson's relationship with the Kenans was his best asset. He and Louise Wise's cousin and lifelong friend, Iola Wise, were married in 1915. They were invited to Louise's first wedding in 1917; they were her only guests at her second wedding in 1927; and they remained close to her until her death in 1937.[74] And if Stetson's relationships with the Lanes, the Kenans, and Guaranty Trust were not enough to disturb Ball and the independent bondholders, the banker's connections to the FEC were. Only a few months earlier, in the fall of 1940, Stetson, a director of the Illinois Central Railroad, had helped Kenan and Loftin convince that road to purchase a streamlined train for daily passenger service between Chicago and Miami via the FEC. The new service had started in December.[75]

The ICC rejected the objections to Lane's appointment, and both he and Loftin were serving as the FEC's bankruptcy trustees when the commission opened its formal hearings in Washington, D.C., in March 1941. The issue confronting the commission was whether to accept the Anderson committee's plan or the duPont estate's plan or to devise a reorganization plan of its own. It took the ICC more than a year to reach a decision.[76]

In the meantime the FEC's president continued to pursue his carbide quest. On April 21, 1941, while Ed Ball testified before the ICC in Washington, Mrs. Francis Preston Venable signed an affidavit for Kenan in Chapel Hill. It was not the one he originally asked her to sign, for that one had contained Kenan's error regarding Major Morehead. As she noted in a letter a few days later, "the affidavit I signed [was] not the one he sent me as his date & man Major Morehead was not correct."[77] Yet Kenan was just as pleased with the affidavit she did sign and send to him: "This is to certify that I was present and recall definitely when Mr. Walker, representing Major Morehead, and Mr. Willson came to Chapel Hill on March 27, 1893, to see the wonderful light produced there by Dr. Venable from calcium carbide. Further, it was agreed that Dr. Venable was to profit by this discovery, but the fact is and the result was he never received anything."[78]

Kenan immediately sent a letter to Colin Frink, the secretary of the Electrochemical Society, enclosing a copy of the affidavit and refreshing Frink's memory of the "manuscript relative to my experience with carbide." Kenan begged "to say, in view of the controversy arising I thought you would be interested in the photographic copy of an affidavit just received by me. I recently had an opportunity to see Mrs. Venable, wife of Dr. Francis P. Venable, and got her to give me this affidavit."[79] Kenan had indeed caused a controversy by publishing his *Discovery* pamphlet. Not only did it irritate the men at Union Carbide, but for some reason it also bothered the Venables' daughter, Cantey Sutton. As Mrs. Venable wrote to her son in April 1941, "I don't know who is bringing up this question to Mr. Kenan though I know there was some after Mr. Kenan's little book appeared last summer. Cantey was very indignant & wrote a letter to Mr. Kenan, fortunately she brought it over for me to read & I asked her not to send it, which she very reluctantly did not send him."[80]

Kenan's quest to be recognized for the carbide discovery took a turn for the worse on June 1, 1941, when *Fortune* magazine published the first in a series of extensive articles on Union Carbide: "A $365 million mystery corporation winding deep in the subterranean foundation of industry. It blows hot, blows cold, and profits haven't skipped a year in twenty-four." William, a subscriber to *Fortune* since its first issue, eagerly searched the article for references to himself and Venable. This was his best chance yet, maybe his best chance ever, to receive the widespread recognition he believed he deserved. Neither he nor Venable was mentioned in the article; only the work of Thomas Willson and Major James Turner Morehead was discussed.[81]

Kenan immediately wrote to the magazine's managing editor, Richard Wood. "In your June issue of Fortune there is a wonderful article on Union Carbide, the Corporation," Kenan began. "I have read this with a great deal of interest and I am surprised no credit is given Dr. F. P. Venable for discovering carbide in the United States." Kenan avoided mentioning his own role in the discovery, but he saw to it that the point was made. "In order that you may know the facts I am sending you, under separate cover, a little pamphlet written by me giving this situation." There were also other people, Kenan intimated, who would back up his story. "Mrs. F. P. Venable, the wife of the Doctor, is still alive and resides in Chapel Hill, North Carolina."[82]

Wood's response suggests that he was well aware of the controversy Kenan's pamphlet had already generated and that he probably also expected to hear from the disgruntled carbide researcher. The article clearly reflected hours and hours of interviews with Carbide officials—that is, with many of the men who knew about but refused to recognize Kenan's claims. Wood wrote to Kenan on June 9: "We knew of Dr. Venable's interest in carbide but from our research (and also the pamphlet which you very courteously sent to us) his part in the picture seemed to be in identifying the discovery which Mr. Willson had made—that the substance resulting from Willson's experiment in trying to make calcium out of lime and tar was calcium carbide and that the gas it gave off when sprinkled with water was acetylene."[83]

Wood then got to the heart of the matter, offering a summary that was closer to the truth than the Lockport millionaire was capable of admitting. "In other words Dr. Venable discovered that Mr. Willson had discovered carbide and it seems to me that your pamphlet claims no more for him. As a matter of fact, none of the encyclopedias which we checked makes any mention of Dr. Venable in connection with carbide nor does his biography in the Dictionary of American Biography." Kenan could hardly miss the implications of Wood's analysis: if the professor did not deserve recognition for the discovery, then certainly neither did his lab assistant.[84]

"I am not personally interested in this matter," Kenan responded disingenuously. "I only desire justice and I am amazed at the attitude you take." It was obvious, he argued, that Willson and Major Morehead "would have never known that the material thrown on the dump heap was carbide and that acetylene could be evolved from it if it had not been for the work Dr. Venable did. I do think Dr Venable ought to have credit for this discovery." Not surprisingly, Kenan also sent Wood a copy of the affidavit signed by Mrs. Venable and suggested that the editor keep it for "future reference."[85]

Wood responded politely to Kenan's letter in mid-July, two weeks after the magazine published its second article on Union Carbide. The new article also did not mention Kenan and Venable, and the editor did not back down. *Fortune* was "glad" to have Mrs. Venable's affidavit, he wrote to Kenan. "I was distressed, however, to know that you feel that FORTUNE has done Dr. Venable an injustice." Wood then gave what proved to be the magazine's final word on the matter, an assessment that officials at Union Carbide undoubtedly shared. "We have simply recorded the facts revealed by our research—namely, that Mr. Willson discovered a substance and that Dr. Venable identified it as calcium carbide thus putting him (Dr. Venable) more or less in the position of assayer. I am sorry indeed if this seems unfair."[86]

William did consider the analogy unfair, and he let Wood know it. "The trouble with the whole thing is you seem to have taken the wrong slant on this situation," Kenan complained. The proper slant, of course, was that he and Venable had analyzed something "thrown on the dump" by Willson and Major Morehead: a discarded and entirely accidental by-product of the failed aluminum experiments at Spray. In fact, Kenan wrote, "if it had not been for Dr. Venable's investigation, no one would have ever known about calcium carbide being made in this process." Venable "deserves the credit!" Kenan stressed, especially since the professor was robbed of financial recognition. "I might further say that there was some discussion of Dr. Venable applying for a patent but in view of his friendly relations with Major Morehead this was abandoned and I am certain that Dr. Venable never received a penny of compensation for this work."[87]

Fortune published the third and final article in its Union Carbide series in September 1941. The closing paragraphs predicted that the current war would treat the company even better than the First World War, when Union Carbide had become Union Carbide & Carbon Corporation by consolidating the National Carbon Company, the Linde Air Products Company, and the Prest-O-Lite Company. Indeed, with the addition of its profitable new subsidiary, the Carbide & Carbon Chemical Corporation, Union Carbide was prepared for unprecedented profits. "War booms chemicals as much as steel," *Fortune* cheered, "and Carbide's chemicals and plastics not only feed directly into such material as explosives, battleships and aircraft, but indirectly through all industry."[88]

The *Fortune* article ended with a paragraph that Kenan could have read both as a warning of the futility of his arguments and as a painful reminder of Ed Ball's efforts to acquire the FEC for the duPont estate. "Dupont, a brilliant developer of products, is usually given the palm for smart management in the chemical industry. Though Carbide's management is less well known, it may well be bracketed in that society. And with alloys and gases and carbon products still expanding, still pushing a frontier of new developments deep into the future, Carbide is today crowding duPont much more closely than anyone now thinks."[89]

Kenan appears not to have corresponded about the carbide matter again until August 1944, two months after UNC awarded him an honorary doctor of laws degree, when he felt he should have received a doctor of science degree instead. This lapse in his crusade had more to do, it seems, with the impact of World War II on his life than with any diminution in his quest for scientific recognition. As did most Americans, Kenan experienced profound changes as a result of the war. But unlike most Americans, he wrote an autobiography during the conflict and did so amid changes undermining his primary purpose for writing it: to promote his idea of himself as a natural-born scientist and much more than Henry Flagler's brother-in-law.

Incidents and the War

W. R. Kenan claimed he wrote his autobiography, *Incidents by the Way*, for a very specific reason. "Appreciation for my immediate family and for the younger generation of the Kenan family has induced me to record on the following pages recollections of my active life, which has been varied and to me most interesting."[1] Yet Kenan wanted to receive appreciation more than he wanted to show it. He wrote the first edition, as he did the four that followed, in response to events that threatened his perception of himself as a first-rate scientist and businessman, as a man who would have made a mark for himself even if he had not been the brother-in-law of Henry Morrison Flagler.

Kenan implied in *Incidents* what he argued explicitly before, during, and after World War II. In addition to promoting his version of the carbide matter, he made sustained efforts at the FEC's semiannual dinners to escape Henry Flagler's shadow. "I found out, at those dinners," one former FEC official recalled, "that Mr. Kenan was actually jealous of Mr. Flagler. One of the guests would invariably praise Mr. Flagler for his part in the development of the East Coast of Florida. Immediately Mr. Kenan would take charge of the conversation, repeating the same line, year after year." The line was about Flagler's plea for help in Florida: " 'William, I have got to have your help. These enterprises have grown too much for me. You have got to take charge.' " To this plea, Kenan said, he initially replied, " 'Mr. Flagler, I am much too busy. I have to manage my own block and tackle factory in Lockport, which is doing well. I am still engaged in an advisory capacity with the Union Carbide Company in Niagara Falls. I am in the process of redesigning and remodeling several paper mills.' " Eventually, though, Kenan helped Flagler out. " 'I agreed to redesign the engineering facilities of the Breakers and Royal Poinciana Hotels in Palm Beach, then finally to take over everything.' "[2]

Kenan's first autobiography also reflects the war's impact on his non-Flagler activities in Lockport. In the fall of 1941 union organizers succeeded in having the National Labor Relations Board grant the factory workers at Western Block

Picnic of Western Block "office fellows," Camp Kenan, Barker, New York, 1938. *Front row, left to right:* Burgess Lee, William Ferris, William Shaw, Reuben Olson, Schuyler Beattie, Fred Kinzly, Donald Smith. *Back row, left to right:* Willis Spinner, Wilbur LaFetra, Thomas Vogt, M. Clifford Oswald, William R. Kenan, Russel Van Norwick, Harry Whalen, J. C. Duncan. (Audrey Raff)

the right to vote on whether the Congress of Industrial Organizations (CIO) would represent them in collective bargaining. Conditions at the factory appeared to favor the union. The company had recently doubled the number of its office workers (from 12 to 25) and more than tripled the number of its shop employees (from 30 to 100) in an effort to satisfy the war's insatiable demand for its products.[3]

One former office worker, Audrey Raff, recalled, "Most of the men who worked in the factory looked at the end of the day like they had worked in the coal mines. . . . The wages at Western Block were very low, both in the factory and office." The work in both departments was also exhausting. "I think the most beautiful things I ever saw produced there were the tackle blocks made of lignum vitae. . . . That was a highly polished, very heavy wood. The blocks were enormous and had to be assembled on the flat-bed that took them to the shipyards during World War II. Everytime a government contract was filled I had a 13-page invoice with all the specs. And each net prices."[4]

William took a dim view of the union's organizing drive. Western Block was the most successful non-Flagler business he had ever directed. He was not Mr. Flagler's brother-in-law there; he was Mr. Kenan, the man in charge of the company's financing, purchasing, and manufacturing departments. More important, he was the company's president and largest stockholder, and until recently, at least, he knew most of his shop and office workers personally. He was irritated that the CIO appeared bent on destroying the mutual respect and loyalty that he believed the company and its employees shared.

To some extent Kenan's perceptions were accurate. The older employees of the firm, both in the office and in the shop, did feel a sense of loyalty to the company and its officials. Yet this had little to do with Kenan himself. It reflected the popularity of his private secretary, Schuyler Beattie, who also served as an officer and secretary of Western Block. As Raff, the former billing clerk, recalled, "Mr. Kenan did not take any ones personal problems to heart. Mr. Beattie was his man Friday and everyone loved him. Mr. Kenan was a very proud man and not too overly friendly." One can understand these sentiments, of course, at least as they pertain to Kenan. The Lockport millionaire had enough personal problems of his own to deal with. What was more, his attention to the Flagler System left him little time to spend at Western Block and made it necessary, in fact, for him to depend on Beattie to carry out his decisions at the factory.[5]

The factory workers defeated the CIO's bid to be their sole bargaining agent at Western Block, but the war helped to improve the union's chances. Not only did it make Western Block one of the largest, if not the largest, block and tackle company in the world, but it also forced the company to hire new workers to replace those who left for military service and other jobs. By 1945 the company was unionized and devoting virtually all of its output "to war work, the United States Navy and the Maritime Commission making immense demands upon its products. The United States Army and the armed forces in general," one contemporary source noted, "also demand block and tackle in their own campaigns all over the world, and depend upon the Western Block Company to supply its full quota."[6]

By the time Kenan completed the first edition of *Incidents*, the atmosphere at Western Block was dramatically different. Unrest had replaced loyalty as the defining feature of the company's management-employee relations, and Kenan was threatening to move the plant to the South. As Raff recalled, "They tried for years to get the union in Western Block and when they did, they were on strike whenever the contract came up for renewal. I worked every other week in 1946 because of a long strike."[7]

There were no strikes at Randleigh Farm during the early 1940s, but the war created labor problems for Kenan there too, "especially the years 1943, 1944 and 1945, [when] the labor conditions at the Farm were very severe and we were short in all departments, all of our employees being of draft age. Many volunteered and some were drafted." The labor shortage also "forced" Kenan and his men to search for as many "labor saving devices as possible, and as we were unable to purchase any equipment, decided to construct some at the Farm."[8]

They constructed it in a "very good shop . . . well equipped and heated, which included both an electric and an oxygen-acetylene welding outfit." One of their most unusual creations, a "Buck Rake," was made from "one of Mrs. Kenan's discarded Pierce Arrow motor cars." But they abandoned the peculiar vehicle after one season as "better progress could be made by baling the hay in the field." Yet they kept their homemade "manure loader." Constructed "on the steam shovel principle" and "attached to one of our tractors," the loader filled "a truck faster than four men when using forks. As loading manure is one of the most objectionable jobs on the farm," Kenan wrote, "everyone was enthusiastic about the operation of this device."[9]

Randleigh's labor and equipment problems also contributed to the most distressing wartime development Kenan faced at the farm: a curtailment of its scientific activities. The feed experiments were the first to go. In June 1941 in anticipation of expanding Dr. Ondess L. Inman's experiments on chlorophyll and carotene, Kenan purchased a 120-acre farm adjacent to Randleigh. Inman died in July 1942, however, just one month after Kenan published the fourth edition of the *History of Randleigh Farm*, and the "silage studies" on grass and alfalfa were abandoned. Inman's death was only part of the problem, however. "Of course, the barn work," Kenan explained, "such as milking, preparing the feed and cleaning the stalls and barns, had to be done and the farm work was neglected. This decreased our regular production of all kinds of feed, making it necessary to purchase more from other sources."[10]

World War II also marked a turning point in Jersey history and the nation's dairy industry. As did other promoters and licensees of Jersey Creamline Products, Randleigh Farm began to feel the impact of two fundamental changes: "(1) Widespread consumer acceptance of homogenized milk and (2) adoption of war time milk production subsidies which favored low test, higher production breeds." Despite an aggressive promotional campaign launched by Jersey Creamline, Inc., in January 1942, the number of active Creamline licensees never exceeded its 1941 peak of 434; instead, the number steadily declined. "Thus ended an important era in the history of Jerseys in the United States," the AJCC explained.[11]

Beyond the war's impact on his farm and factory, Kenan faced other developments that shaped the nature and purpose of his autobiography. The Flagler empire began unraveling, and he could not put it back together. In early April 1942, just a few weeks before Kenan's seventieth birthday, the Jacksonville federal court appointed former Florida governor John W. Martin to replace the recently deceased Edward W. Lane as coreceiver for the FEC. The ICC accepted Martin's appointment and offered a plan to reorganize the FEC that was a "compromise" between the Ball and Anderson plans. Unfortunately for Kenan the commission's plan declared the FEC's stock to be worthless and made no provision for him, the only stockholder that mattered, to participate in the reorganization.[12]

Ed Ball had no intention of accepting the ICC's plan, however, for it gave future financial control of the road to the F&R 5 bondholders and incorporated the Anderson committee's proposal for managing the road—a proposal that did not include a "manager" from the duPont estate. Thus the duPont trustee began buying all of the F&R 5s he could get, and he got a lot. George Cordwell remembered spotting Ball's bond activity. "It was found that a few organizations—and then all of a sudden they had sold their interest or their accumulation to the main one. The main one was the duPont interest in Jacksonville, a man by the name of Ed Ball. So Ed Ball, he became owner of quite an accumulation, so much so that he practically ran things."[13] Indeed, by the end of July 1942 Ball and his Miami ally, S. A. Lynch, jointly controlled a majority of the FEC's $45 million F&R 5s, a position that allowed them to challenge the ICC plan in district court, which they did.[14]

Of more immediate concern to Kenan and his family was the war's impact on the Flagler System's hotels and personnel. The federal government leased the Ponce de Leon Hotel as a training center for the United States Coast Guard and did not return it until the end of 1945, after which the hotel required extensive repairs and renovation. Though the lease provided the system with revenue, it also disrupted the lives of the Flagler heirs. Will and the "girls" had made the Ponce their winter home for almost forty years, and Jessie and Sarah had made it their legal residence since the early 1930s. For the rest of the war, however, they stayed in the Buckingham Hotel in St. Augustine.[15]

The government also enlisted the other Flagler hotels in the war effort. It paid $250,000 to use the Breakers as an army hospital between December 1942 and September 1943 and then paid to restore the luxury hotel in time for the 1943–44 social season.[16] It also used the Ormond Hotel near Daytona Beach and took over the Casa Marina Hotel in Key West, which it used to house naval officers and their families. But the Ormond and the Casa Marina were not returned in the best of shape, and shortly after the war the FEC Hotel Company sold them both. Also, from the end of 1942 until the end of 1945 Kenan was without the assistance of two of his three secretaries, Warren Smith and George Cordwell, both of whom joined the armed forces.[17]

The greatest spur to Kenan's autobiography during the war was the decline of his wife's health. By 1942 Alice Kenan had suffered several minor strokes and was showing signs of increasing senility. Moreover, according to Schuyler Beattie's daughter, who accompanied Alice to New York City in the fall of that year, "Mrs. Kenan, I think, was sort of lonesome." Not only was William spending little time at home in Lockport, but even when Alice and Beattie's daughter stayed with him at the Park Lane in New York City, they rarely saw him. "He had business, yes. He wasn't around."[18]

He was around more that winter, however, during their stay in Florida. One Lockport resident, Phyllis Van De Mark, who lived in St. Augustine during the war, remembered William and Alice visiting her and her family "every Sunday" during early 1943. "Mr. and Mrs. Kenan would walk out to our house which was, well, maybe two miles. Mrs. Kenan wasn't well at that time, and the doctor felt that it would be good for her to walk as much as possible. Of course, Mr. Kenan was a great walker. So Mrs. Kenan would get pretty tired at times but he always saw to it that she had her exercise. His quiet kindness always came through to me . . . although lots of people felt that he was austere and a little formidable."[19]

Alice had "a bad accident" after returning to New York, however. She fell "down the front hall stairs at our home in Lockport," William wrote. "She fractured her shoulder blade and struck her head and was knocked out completely. She was in the hospital several months and when she returned home she required the services of a trained nurse. During the Fall and Winter we had several and none of them was entirely satisfactory."[20]

Also that fall the Florida district court sided with Ball and rejected the ICC's compromise plan for reorganizing the FEC. The court declared the commission's plan "inequitable": first, because the cash accumulated by the FEC did not "afford due recognition to the rights of security holders" and, second, because the plan excluded the duPont estate from naming a reorganization manager. The case thus went back to the ICC, and Ball began acquiring more F&R 5s. But this time he used another duPont interest, the St. Joe Paper Company, which owned the Appalachicola and Northern Railroad Company in northwestern Florida, to acquire the bonds. By 1944 the duPont estate controlled almost $24 million F&R 5s, and the once-dominant Anderson committee held less than $1.5 million.[21]

William felt bemused and beleaguered by these developments. He had nursed the FEC through years of litigation and economic depression, and now, at a time of unprecedented prosperity for the road, he faced the prospect of losing it. The war dramatically altered the FEC's balance sheet. Gasoline rationing, submarine attacks, and the demand for oceangoing vessels combined to eliminate most of the railroad's freight-carrying competitors. In addition there was more of everything to carry, from service personnel and military equipment to civilian passengers forced to curtail their automobile travel because of gasoline rationing. Although no one knew what the future held, the FEC's revenues were soaring. By 1945 the railroad had a $20 million surplus.[22]

Much of William's world was falling apart, however. He found it particularly difficult to keep Alice comfortable. When they returned to St. Augustine at the end of 1943, "the nurse we brought with us was most unsatisfactory. We then obtained one in St. Augustine and took her to Lockport and although she remained until we returned to St. Augustine the following Winter, she was not a complete success." William and Alice also got a shock when they returned to Lockport in April 1944. Their cook and gardener were gone. William could not understand the married couple's behavior: "Although they had resided on the place, they left without saying 'good-bye,' nor telling anyone where they were going. I learned that they went direct to Pasadena, California."[23]

Kenan hired a new gardener and cook, but he had to leave Alice in the hands of an "unsatisfactory" nurse when he visited North Carolina in June 1944. That he had to leave her at all was very disappointing, for he was headed to Chapel Hill for his fiftieth class reunion and an honorary degree. Jessie and Sarah joined him for the occasion, however, and he enjoyed being inducted into UNC's Old Students' Club, which also elected him as its president. But what should have been the crowning moment of his visit, the commencement ceremony, did not turn out that way.

Everything seemed perfect at first. It was "a gorgeous night, full moon and very bright"; there were 2,500 spectators in Kenan Memorial Stadium; and Kenan himself was seated on a platform "in the middle of the field" with the three other "honorary degree men" and the commencement speakers. It took three hours to get around to the honorary degrees, however, and when they finally were handed out, someone else got the degree Kenan wanted and expected. "A citation was read by Dr. Graham, President of the University, as each individual stood up, the degrees being as followed: Doctor of Science, Doctor of Philosophy, Doctor of Medicine and I received a Doctor of Laws," Kenan recalled. "Being uninformed on such subjects I concluded that a mistake had been made in my case, as it should have been Doctor of Science."[24]

William did not mention the "mistake" to anyone until July, when he returned to North Carolina for a meeting of the AJCC at Biltmore, the Vanderbilt estate in Asheville. There he ran into Dr. Howard Odum, a fellow Jersey breeder who was also a distinguished Kenan professor and "one of the older professors" at UNC. When Kenan asked Odum about the degree, the professor explained with consummate tact "that Doctor of Laws was the highest degree that any university or college could bestow, as it not only required the marks necessary for other degrees, but must have rendered service to humanity, such as my work with Randleigh Farm and also my work with the Y.M.C.A., Camp Kenan."[25]

THE NORTH CAROLINA CONNECTION

When he returned to Lockport from the Biltmore meeting, Dr. Kenan sent UNC president Frank Graham a package of interesting materials. The aging alumnus was still not convinced, it seems, that he had gotten the appropriate honorary degree, for as Graham noted in his response to the package, the materials included "the pamphlet on the topic, 'Calcium Carbide,' and your correspondence thereon. With your permission," Graham wrote. "I am placing all of this in our Historical Collection."[26]

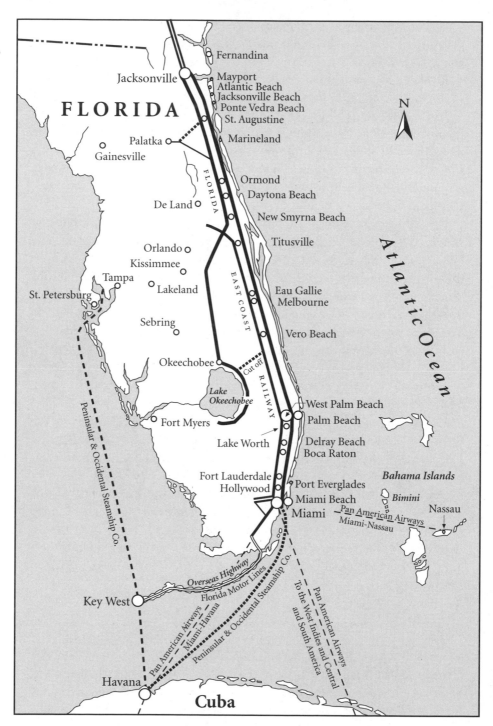

The Florida East Coast Railway, 1946. (Adapted from *The Story of a Pioneer: A Brief History of the Florida East Coast Railway* [N.p., 1946])

What was peculiar about Kenan's package was that he enclosed "a copy of the program with regard to the inter-American relations and the postwar world." While the nature of this program is not clear, the fact that Kenan sent it reflects his renewed hope of controlling and improving the Flagler System's fortunes. Henry Flagler had always wanted to profit from the exchange of freight and passenger traffic with Latin America, and though this trade never reached the heights he had hoped for, except in the case of Cuba, it was clear that World War II had ushered in a new and potentially profitable era of inter-American trade and diplomatic relations. More to the point, of all the major railroad companies in Florida, the FEC and the ACL were in the best position to reap the benefits.

Kenan had great expectations for both the FEC Car Ferry Company and the P&O Steamship Company. The ferries had been the Flagler System's biggest moneymaker prior to the war, and though they were then being used by the United States government, Kenan expected them to earn even greater profits once they resumed operations between Cuba and Florida. He was equally optimistic about the P&O Steamship Company, which was jointly owned by the FEC and the ACL. Although prowling German U-boats had temporarily ended the company's freight and passenger service between Miami and the Caribbean, this was no longer a problem, and the company fully expected its postwar receipts to swell as a result of pent-up tourist and consumer demand.[27]

Kenan had little more than these companies in mind when he thought about the future of inter-American relations. He and his sisters owned the FEC's one-half interest in the P&O Steamship Company; Kenan himself was vice-president and a director of the steamship company; and he was president of the FEC Car Ferry Company. Also, the FEC had always worked closely with the ACL, both before and since Henry Walters's death, to coordinate the activities of the steamships and railroad car ferries. As one intimate observer noted, William was particularly fond of his connection to the P&O: "After Mr. Walters' death, Mr. Kenan bought out to full control of P&O SS Lines. He must have liked shipping, for on one occasion he was given a Captain's hat, insignia, et al., and he showed great pleasure."[28]

Kenan's inter-American interests also reflected his negotiations with the ACL's new president, Champion McDowell Davis. Once again the ACL wanted to acquire the FEC, and once again Kenan wanted the company to have it—if he had to give it up. His family had been connected with the Coast Line since the 1830s, when his grandfather had used slaves to build the Wilmington and Weldon Railroad through Duplin County, North Carolina. His uncle Colonel Thomas Kenan had been an attorney for the Wilmington and Weldon when the Walters family acquired the road. Henry Walters and Henry Flagler had coordinated their railroad activities since the 1880s; Kenan and Walters had done the same thereafter; and so had Kenan and Walters's nephew, Lyman

Delano, who had lived in the Wilmington mansion now occupied by Sarah Kenan. What was more, the ACL's general offices had been located in Wilmington for almost fifty years.

Kenan had long been friends with Champ Davis. The two men had "formed a warm personal friendship early" in their lives, and this "continued uninterruptedly" until their deaths. Davis, who had often visited the Kenan home in the 1890s while serving as a messenger for the Wilmington and Weldon Railroad, recalled being one of the boys Buck Kenan "frequently entertained at his Nun street home during periods when Mrs. Kenan and the children were away at a resort. He would invite a group of hungry boys for sumptuous suppers, and after supper would talk with us and encourage character building, self-discipline, honesty of purpose, sincerity and other topics helpful to young men."[29]

Davis and the ACL became interested in acquiring the FEC after the district court sided with Ball and rejected the ICC's compromise plan for rescuing the FEC from bankruptcy. The ACL's controlling stockholder, the Safe Deposit and Trust Company of Baltimore, controlled a substantial number of the FEC's 1909 bonds and had held the largest single block of F&R 5s between the mid-1920s and 1942. Though the bank initially deposited its F&R 5s with the Anderson committee, it withdrew them in 1942 and refused to join the other former committee depositors in selling bonds to Ed Ball—even though the duPont trustee promised to make the ACL's chairman of the board, Lyman Delano, and the bank's president, G. C. Cutler, officials of the FEC once it emerged from bankruptcy. Both the ACL and the Baltimore bank wanted to shape the fate of the FEC, but they lacked the financial clout to intervene in the bankruptcy proceedings. Neither was among the FEC's many creditors, and the bank held only one-twentieth the number of F&R 5s controlled by Ball.[30]

According to Kenan, Ed Ball's erstwhile ally S. A. Lynch, a native of North Carolina, made it possible for the ACL to intervene in the FEC's bankruptcy hearings. In early August 1944, just a few days after the death of Lyman Delano, Lynch "approached" Champ Davis and the ACL's new chairman, Frederick B. Adams, "with a proposal whereby the Atlantic Coast Line would acquire majority ownership of the common stock of the new [FEC] company and would operate the property." Davis and Adams immediately took the proposal to Lockport, where on September 9, after a tour of Randleigh Farm, they reached an "understanding" with Kenan on the FEC's *existing* stock. According to Davis, "The understanding was that we [the ACL] would have an option on the stock, the common stock, all of the common stock of the Florida East Coast Railway and we would agree upon the price to be paid for the stock at the time we found it useful or needed it."[31]

There can be little doubt that the ACL would have struck a deal then and there if Kenan had agreed to put a price on the stock. But the FEC's president was reluctant to do so—not, it seems, because he harbored hopes of retaining control of the road, although that may have been possible, but instead because of the promises he had made and the ethical and legal implications of taking such an action. As he explained the "understanding" to Scott Loftin:

> We gave the matter due consideration and because of the neutral position with relation to the various creditors of the F.E.C. Ry. which we assumed you should preserve as Trustee of the property, we deemed it expedient not to inform you of the possible change in the ownership of the common stock of the F.E.C. Ry.
>
> However, because of recent developments, I now feel free to advise you that an option on the entire issue of the common stock has been given to the A.C.L.R.R., which option still remains in force.[32]

It was this evenhandedness, perhaps, that later prompted Davis to say, "In all the years I knew William Rand Kenan Jr., I think he was the most scrupulously honest man I've ever known. He never took advantage of anyone in any way and was extremely courteous to all."[33]

In November 1944 the ACL and the S. A. Lynch interests presented the ICC with a new reorganization plan that allowed the ACL to operate the FEC but permitted the bondholders to retain financial control of the road.[34] The ICC rejected the proposal as "impracticable," however, and offered instead a five-year "voting trust" to hold on deposit the new common stock of a reorganized FEC. The decision was a major victory for Ed Ball. The proposed trust would be managed by three trustees—one approved by the court and two appointed by Ball's St. Joe Paper Company.[35]

The decision depressed Kenan, who learned of it while working on his autobiography in St. Augustine. Yet it did not completely ruin his spring. In March the AJCC selected him to receive its highest honor, the Master Breeder Award, and shortly thereafter he persuaded Marion Godfrey, a longtime housekeeper at the Ponce de Leon Hotel, to return to Lockport to care for Alice. "The results were more than we could have hoped for," Kenan wrote. Godfrey "was most attentive and kind,—considerate to a degree and Alice was most happy all Summer."[36]

William was pleased also. Champ Davis refused to abandon the FEC to Ed Ball. Rather than accepting the trust proposed by the ICC, Davis offered to merge the FEC with the ACL and to exchange shares of Coast Line stock for the FEC's bonds. According to the ACL this new proposal marked a turning point in the case. Whereas the ICC had always concentrated on the "financial or security aspects" of the problem, the ACL was focusing on what should have been the ICC's primary concern all along: the "public interest." Indeed, the issue of public interest lay at the heart of the arguments offered in support of the ACL plan by Florida senator Claude Pepper, who in April and May 1945 called for the reopening of the FEC hearings "in consideration of the public interest." By accepting the duPont plan, Pepper claimed, the ICC "wholly renounced its function . . . to protect the public and promote the public welfare." The ICC announced it would reopen the FEC hearings later that year.[37]

Thus William's world showed some signs of improvement by the summer of 1945. He still had a hand in shaping the FEC's fate, and his powerful allies in the struggle held out hope of resolving the situation in a way that, given the alternatives, was the best he could hope for. Though Alice remained bedridden and almost completely senile, for the first time in almost two years she had a kind and caring attendant whose ministrations made her and her husband happy. What was more, the government had relinquished and renovated the Breakers; it was about to do the same for the Ponce de Leon; and William had two FEC employees, "Kenneth Calhoun Sr. and Alvin Grainger, the two negro men who were on my private railway car 'RANDLEIGH' for many years," serving "at my home in Lockport, as Chef and Butler." Plenty of problems remained, of course, such as those at Randleigh Farm and Western Block, but there were no strikes in progress and the winding down of the war promised changes in the labor situation at both places. Most uplifting of all, he was about to receive the AJCC's Master Breeder Award.[38]

The award represented the most significant recognition yet of Kenan's scientific efforts, and it was so important to him that he decided to forgo the annual meeting of the Old Students' Club at UNC, where he was expected to preside. In fact he probably shared the sentiments expressed at the awards ceremony by his fellow UNC alumnus Judge Junius G. Adams, president of the AJCC. In presenting Kenan the award, Adams said of him, "Among other of his outstanding accomplishments is that the University of North Carolina recognized him last year in bestowing a Doctors Degree on him. While I, like all the rest of us, would appreciate having an honorary degree from a University, I believe if I had my choice between the two—with all due respect to our old Alma Mater—I would choose this." Kenan accepted the honor graciously if somewhat disingenuously: "I never felt I had done very much. I was tremendously interested in what I was trying to accomplish. At the beginning it seemed I was all alone—everyone was opposed to my method of procedure. But I have stuck to it and I have had a wonderful time."[39]

AS THE WORLD TURNED

The aggressive actions of the ACL and Senator Claude Pepper signaled a new phase in the fight for control of the FEC, one that added deep-seated personal, political, and corporate animosities to the prevailing financial wrangling. The most decisive and far-reaching of these conflicts was the enmity between the Florida senator and Ed Ball.

The two men first squared off when Pepper spoke in behalf of President Roosevelt's veto of tax legislation that included clauses designed to benefit investors like Ball who had purchased bonds at depressed prices for speculative profits. Though the president's veto was overridden, Ball tried during the 1944 Democratic primaries to destroy the Florida senator "once and for all." He threw all his money and power behind J. Ollie Edmonds, Pepper's unsuccessful opponent in the primaries—a fact cited thereafter by the state's newspapers as the major source of friction driving the fight for the FEC. But this "was more of a symptom than a cause," one historian has written. "Pepper was diametrically opposed to all that Ball epitomized in the way of special interests, the arrogance of wealth and power, and 'monopoly.' "[40]

Throughout the summer and fall of 1945 Ball used every means at his disposal to mobilize Florida's east coast cities against the ACL proposal and to impugn Pepper's alleged motivations in supporting it. It was a shameful abuse of money and power; it was also very effective. By the time the ICC reopened its FEC hearings at West Palm Beach in November, almost every chamber of commerce and civic group in the cities touched by the FEC, and almost every FEC employee in the state, including all of the railroad brotherhoods, were denouncing both the ACL plan and the prolabor senator from Florida.[41]

One observer credited the opposition to Ball's publicity campaign. "It is my opinion that the duPont interests have done a very fine piece of advertising and salesmenship [sic] in selling their proposal to the public, principally in Jacksonville, Miami, St. Augustine and New Smyrna, but they have also done a good selling job in all the other East Coast towns. They have succeeded in getting public bodies like the Chamber of Commerce and the Luncheon Clubs to help them stir up the people in believing that ownership by their interests would be more advantageous to the state than ownership by the ACL would be."[42]

Fear and money, the writer suggested, explained Ball's success. "The Miami spot has been purchased by a promise from duPont that they will build a million dollar new depot in Miami. The New Smyrna sentiment is because they are afraid they will lose the shops and a large payroll." The sentiment in St. Augustine was "due to fear that the operating offices and the shops located between St. Augustine and Jacksonville will be abandoned and will cause an upset due to the loss of payroll and citizens. The Jacksonville sentiment is due to the influence of the Florida National Bank and they have been powerful enough to get the Chamber of Commerce and other civic organizations stirred up on it and I doubt if that could be reversed."[43]

Typical of the outcry from organized labor were the comments of FEC telegrapher B. C. Forte of New Smyrna, Florida. "The men are overwhelmingly against the ACL taking the FEC over," Forte wrote to Pepper, "and I believe a majority of the Officers feel likewise. Typical of the comment was, 'I thought

Senator Pepper was a friend of the Railroad men.' The reason for this feeling is that the Atlantic Coast Line is at heart strongly anti-union, and will slaughter the jobs of the men if they take over. They are noted thru-out the Southeast for their anti-union sentiments; in fact are the worst road in the Southeast in this respect." Forte fully expected the Coast Line to "abolish the freight agency in Jacksonville, as well as the Bowden Yards, also do away with the General Headquarters in St. Augustine and the Division offices in this city and then use the knife all along the line, throwing many men out of work."[44]

Pepper and the ACL did their best to counter such perceptions. The railroad promised not to cut jobs and shut down facilities, while the senator spent most of his time trying to dispel rumors that he was a lackey of the ACL and somehow stood to benefit from its proposal. He constantly reiterated his concern for the public interest and not the ACL, claiming that he supported the efforts of "any other competent rail carrier . . . to acquire or operate the Florida East Coast Railroad." But the St. Joe Paper Company, he argued, had no such credentials, and Ed Ball despised the working man. "If this road is put in the hands of the duPont interests," the embattled senator warned prophetically, "my friends among the workers will regret it to the end of their lives."[45]

Kenan wanted the ACL to prevail, but he hated the bad publicity generated by its merger proposal. For almost fifty years most of the residents of Florida's east coast had viewed the FEC as their economic lifeline and Henry Flagler as the region's creator and savior. While Kenan tried to reinforce and expand this tradition, his efforts had been undermined by events largely beyond his control. What was more, he believed that the FEC showed the same loyalty to its employees as Western Block did to its workers. Though never a friend of organized labor, neither he nor the FEC was its enemy. "Other than the usual confrontations between management and labor," the railroad's former chief surgeon recalled, "I never heard criticism from the rank and file employees."[46]

There was plenty of criticism, however, from both within the FEC and without, and most of it was directed at Kenan and his fellow FEC officials. As one journalist noted, the people of St. Augustine "know that the weakness in running that road for the past two decades has been at the top of the organization."[47] The most outspoken critic of the FEC's management was W. F. Howard, general chairman of the Brotherhood of Railway Clerks, who asked Pepper rhetorically, "Have you checked into the history of this carrier [FEC] to see how well they were succeeding before an unscrupulous management, in practically rebuilding the railroad during the so-called boom days, obligated the property unduly through waste of material and money and the awarding of contracts at unreasonable figures for the apparent sole purpose of obtaining personal graft."[48] Not only were Howard's charges ludicrous, but his motivations in offering them appear suspect at best. Although Howard's name appeared as author of two pro-duPont pamphlets condemning Pepper and the

ACL, the tracts actually were written by Ball's prominent St. Augustine ally Frank D. Upchurch.[49]

The criticism expressed by Upchurch and Howard represented more than their alliance with Ed Ball. It also reflected the genuine concerns of white- and blue-collar workers alike that a merger would lead to a loss of jobs, payrolls, and facilities—concerns that Ball exploited as much as possible. One ACL supporter noted that Samuel McDaniel, secretary-treasurer of the Flagler System's Model Land Company, "brought up the subject and made the same old arguments which the Ball-DuPont folks are putting out. Sam's attitude disclosed that what is left of the old Flagler interests are likely lined up with Ball. I think it means that all the Flagler interests including the Flagler hotels."[50] A more cynical local resident, Jim Caspar, reportedly "said that Ed Ball had everybody scared and panicky in St. Johns County, and nobody was opposing them [the duPont interests]. Jim said that the people of St. Augustine got the habit of kissing Flagler's so-and-so for so many years, and that they now seemed anxious to serve Ed Ball the same way."[51]

Kenan stood by the ACL, however. On October 18, 1945, three weeks before the ICC reopened the FEC hearings in West Palm Beach, he enhanced the ACL's position by making it one of the FEC's creditors. He "sold, assigned, transferred and set over [to the ACL] . . . any and all sums of money now due or to grow due upon the open account owing the Florida East Coast Car Ferry by the Florida East Coast Railway Company, . . . in the amount of One Million Five Hundred Thousand Dollars ($1,500,000.00)." He and Lawrence Haines also sold the ACL, "as Trustees under the Will of Mary Flagler Bingham, . . . all sums of money now due or to grow due upon the open account owing us as such Trustees by Florida East Coast Railway, . . . in the amount of Four Hundred Thousand Dollars ($400,000.00)." Thus in a matter of minutes the ACL, in exchange for "50% of whatever" it could collect on these debts (which had been on the books since 1930), became a creditor of the FEC to the tune of almost $2 million.[52]

The ACL presented 69 witnesses at the November hearings, and the duPont estate brought in 200, including Ed Ball, who testified that no "competent" FEC employee should worry "about his or her future" under the management of the St. Joe Paper Company. Ball failed to make a good impression on the commission, however, which later described him as a "hostile witness," who "while responsive in his answers to some of the questions . . . in answer to many other questions . . . was vague, indefinite, and adroit." His "unsatisfactory attitude" made it impossible for the commission to determine the "fitness" of the St. Joe Paper Company to control and manage a reorganized FEC.[53]

If Ball hurt his case by testifying, Pepper helped it by not being there. The Florida senator was in Europe, taking a trip he had planned since his father's death in July. The Coast Line's president, Champ Davis, cabled him that it would be "fatal" to miss the hearings, but Pepper ignored the warning and promised to file a written statement when he returned.[54] His decision hurt the ACL's case. As the Coast Line's attorney implied to Pepper's assistant, Ball had dug himself into a hole at the hearings, and the senator could have helped bury him: "I think we can also establish that as a witness Mr. Ball demonstrated that he is not the kind of a man who should be permitted to dominate a Class I railroad. . . . However, Mr. Ball's counsel established, and I have no doubt that Senator Pepper will find when he goes to Florida, that there is a strongly predominant sentiment on the east coast in Mr. Ball's favor at this time."[55]

There was a great deal of anger and uncertainty in St. Augustine when William and his family returned for the winter of 1946. Although they felt at home in their old suites at the Ponce de Leon Hotel, they received a cold reception outside the hotel. William especially felt the chill. He still walked back and forth to the FEC's offices twice a day, and he saw and was seen by hundreds of employees and residents alike. Pepper made things worse in February, when he finally filed his written statement with the ICC. According to one of the senator's correspondents, Pepper's "point that the railroad was not operated successfully by the Flagler estate, and therefore, would probably not be operated successfully by the trustees of the Dupont estate, is one which should be greatly appreciated by the residents of St. Augustine."[56]

In this context William completed *Incidents by the Way* and had it published in St. Augustine by the Record Company. The book contains 186 pages, almost half of which are full-page photographs. Much of it is a chronological narrative written by Kenan himself, but it also contains newspaper articles and other pieces written by other people. There is a long list of "Some Positions Held" by Kenan, of his "Automobiles" (with the annual expenses associated with operating each), and of the scientists who participated at Randleigh Farm's annual conferences. Yet only occasionally and briefly does the author mention the influence of others on his career, and he completely avoids the sad and most controversial incidents of his life. His only admission of failure or disappointment is in his chapter "Opportunities in which 'I Missed the Boat,'" in which he mentions the investments he wished he had made in Union Carbide, the paper mill in Wilmington, and the Harrison Radiator Company, Lockport's largest and most successful industry.

Incidents is a happy story that accurately reflects the hope, optimism, and enthusiasm of its author. If there is a hint of nostalgia in his childhood memories, it does not reflect his feelings of loss. It expresses his sense of indebtedness to the past, of the continuity of his experience as a person suited by temperament and training to the life of a scientist. Indeed, Kenan devotes one-half of his book to his work as a scientist and engineer at UNC, in the carbide industry, in Florida, and at Randleigh Farm.

Not surprisingly, there is nothing in *Incidents* about the FEC's post-Flagler history, which began a new chapter in October 1946 with the ICC bankruptcy hearings in Washington, D.C. The hearings proved the most rancorous yet: "The bitterness that had developed between Pepper and the duPont representatives was obvious." Pepper, who had filed a fifty-two-page brief with the ICC in August, continued to stress his role in the matter as one of upholding the public interest. He had "no connection with the Atlantic Coast Line," he asserted, which he fully expected to pay the " 'full, fair value of the property,' keep the Jacksonville gateway open to competitors, and deal fairly with the FEC employees."[57]

Pepper's reference to the Jacksonville gateway reveals the extent to which the matter had become further complicated and polarized by the entry of Florida's other major railroads into the dispute. As the ACL's Davis explained to Pepper's secretary, both the Seaboard and the Southern railroads, despite the Coast Line's promise "to keep open existing routes via Jacksonville," had aligned themselves with Ball. "I suspect, of course, that, just as Mr. Ball made a 'trade' with Southern Railway in case he acquires the FEC Railway, he has now made a somewhat similar trade with the Seaboard. Both of these railroads hope to benefit at expense of Coast Line should Mr. Ball be successful in acquiring the FEC."[58]

BY THE WAY

Alice Kenan died at the Ponce de Leon Hotel on February 12, 1947, two months before the ICC rendered its decision on the FEC. "She simply passed out gradually in her eighty-second year," Kenan wrote in the second edition of *Incidents.* "I shall miss her in every way, much more than I can ever express." Indeed, his description of her expresses little human emotion. "She was a splendid organizer, ran our house splendidly and did everything inside the house. . . . Alice was an expert shopper; she knew the value of most everything and especially was this true of silver, china, linens and laces. Her hobby was fans, and she had a splendid collection of more than one hundred and fifty."[59]

William was back in Lockport in April when the ICC announced its decision on the FEC, which completely reversed its 1945 order. In a 5-4 vote the commissioners approved the FEC's merger with the ACL, noting the "fairness of the Coast Line plan" to all concerned and the fact that the public interest would best be served by keeping the FEC an independent carrier. "It is clear from the evidence presented, that the St. Joe Paper Company would be in a position, if it controlled the reorganized debtor, to so control its operation as to further its own interests and the other interests of the duPont estate to the ultimate disadvantage not only of the State but to the detriment of the national transportation system as well."[60]

The struggle for the FEC was a long way from over, but the decision proved a bright spot for William in an otherwise gloomy and depressing spring. Oscar Erf died shortly after the ICC announced its report, and in Chapel Hill the university began planning John Motley Morehead's planetarium and art gallery. Although William was still in good physical health at age seventy-five, an incident that summer suggests he may have been losing some of his mental vigor, or else he was sending a very different message to his dead niece's children, Lawrence Jr. and Mary Lily, who came to Lockport with a plan for regaining control of the FEC. At one point during the discussion William leaned over to his great-niece and said, "By the way, who did you say you were?"[61]

A Place to Come To

William spent less and less time at 433 Locust Street after Alice's death. He stayed on the go, attending reunions, board meetings, cattle sales, and football games. He wintered longer in St. Augustine and extended his stays at the Park Lane, and when he was in Lockport, from June to September, he alternated between his Uppertown mansion and his large office at the farm, spending a week or so at a time in each place.

The 1947 commencement was not one of William's happiest. Each encounter brought expressions of sympathy for Alice's death, and well-meant as these undoubtedly were, they served to remind him of her recent demise. The aging alumnus also learned that the cornerstone of the new $2 million Morehead Planetarium would be laid in November. Worse still, at the Old Students' Club banquet he somehow ended up sitting next to Josephus Daniels—an arrangement that, to judge from a photograph of the reunion, neither he nor Daniels enjoyed.[1]

There were a few rewarding moments. "I talked with a young man who stated he had read my Graduation Thesis of 1894; that it was in the library." The wealthy alumnus also initiated what became a regular part of his commencement ritual thereafter. He visited Aunt Fanny McDade, a "small, slender, light-skinned woman" whose deceased husband, Bill, had been a janitor in South Building when Kenan resided there as a student. McDade had been born a slave on Kenan's grandmother's plantation, "the Hargrave place, where the Paul Greens live now," and he found her "very clever relating old times."[2]

William was barely back from commencement when the problems associated with the FEC Railway erupted again. In July 1947 Ed Ball challenged the legality of the ICC's April decision, and in October the commission again reopened the railroad's bankruptcy hearings. This time the arguments focused on the "constitutional question" of the ACL's plan to acquire and merge the FEC, and Ball had former Supreme Court justice James F. Byrnes in his corner. Byrnes had been a member of the Senate when Section 77 of the Bankruptcy

Act was amended, and he now argued that the ACL's plan amounted to an "involuntary merger" depriving the duPont trustees of their property without due process of law.[3]

William paid more attention to his cattle interests, however, than he did to the ICC hearings. In early October Randleigh Farm held its first scientific conference without Alice Kenan and Oscar Erf, and at the end of the month William journeyed alone to Columbus, Ohio, for a meeting of the AJCC's Research Committee. He also purchased several cows at the club's Sale of Stars, including Siegfield H. L. Popover 1454188 and her new calf.[4] Yet the farm was not the same without Erf and Alice. The professor had been one of Kenan's closest friends, and Alice had never wavered in her support for the farm. She had suggested its name, organized banquets for the visiting scientists, and helped William give tours of the dairy to schoolchildren.

In truth, Alice appeared to many observers to have been as much a mother as a wife and confidante to William. "I would say yes, in a way," Schuyler Beattie's daughter explained. "She'd never been a mother, and it's an aspect that maybe wouldn't occur to some people to think of but there were things about the way she related to other people, a kind of really seeing them and caring about them, that even though she was quite a formal lady, always a lady, it makes me think of more of a grandmother. . . . 'Would you like some more coffee? Would you like another cookie. Are you warm enough?' That kind of thing."[5] Indeed, William himself appears to have seen Alice in much the same way. As he wrote in the opening pages of the first edition of *Incidents*:

> Dedicated to my wife
> ALICE POMROY KENAN
> The Boy! What has the future in
> store for him?
> What will be his experience? And
> how will he handle it?

Incidents was William's answer, and he dedicated every edition of it to Alice.

Less than a month after the Columbus meeting, William again huddled around the family hearth at UNC, but not as the favorite son. Another alumnus, John Motley Morehead, also a recent widower, basked in the glow. The occasion was the laying of the cornerstone for the new Morehead Building and Planetarium. Morehead had been planning the facility since 1945, when he created the Morehead Foundation to build the planetarium and to establish a scholarship program to attract "to the University the most promising young people from across North Carolina and the nation."[6]

Morehead's gifts deepened William's concern with preserving his own and his family's reputation as the university's greatest benefactors. What concerned him most was the caption of a photograph taken at the cornerstone ceremonies for the Morehead Building and subsequently published in the university's *Alumni Review.*

Three of the University of North Carolina's greatest benefactors as they appeared at the cornerstone laying ceremonies of the two-million dollar Morehead Planetarium and Art Gallery at the University of North Carolina Saturday. Left to right, John Sprunt Hill, of Durham, donor of the Hill Hall, the Carolina Inn, and liberal contributor to the library and other university departments; John Motley Morehead, of New York, donor of the Morehead building and co-donor of the Morehead-Patterson bell tower, and William Rand Kenan, of New York, donor of the Kenan Stadium.[7]

That Kenan perceived this as a slight to the nature and extent of his own gifts to UNC is suggested by his subsequent benefactions and by the materials he included in the second edition of *Incidents* (1949). In 1940, at the time of his family's $1.875 million settlement with the university, the Lockport millionaire also gave $4,500 to help the school expand the stadium's end-zone and bleacher seating. He followed this with a $10,000 gift to the University Press in 1942 and an additional $5,000 for stadium improvements in 1946. But he now initiated a new phase of liberal contributions to his alma mater. In the three years that followed the Morehead cornerstone festivities, Kenan more than quadrupled the amount of his donations to the university over the preceding six years.

He began with gifts to expand the seating capacity of Kenan Memorial Stadium, which by 1946 could hold only 30,000 spectators. His new gifts made it possible for "the bleachers to be extended by the fifty-yard line and, at the same time, [to] raise the press and President's boxes so as to be over the above referred to bleachers. Also to have the structure three stories high, with the photographers on top, the radio men next, and the press under them, but all three floors being above the said bleachers."[8] Also, he wrote in the second edition of *Incidents*, "I have contributed during 1947–'48, $40,000.00 for this [stadium] work, and also $25,000.00 during 1949." He gave another $25,000 in 1950, "making my total contribution to the Stadium $443,139.75."[9]

The twenty-year-old stadium needed the extra seats to accommodate the huge postwar crowds that now flocked to Chapel Hill for football games. This was the era of Charlie "Choo-Choo" Justice, perhaps the greatest football player ever to don a Tar Heel uniform, and with the end of gas rationing and the return of peace, more people than ever wanted seats at Kenan Memorial Stadium. And Kenan loved making a place for them: "During the Fall of 1947 the smallest attendance was 36,000 and at two games there were 43,000 each. During 1948 at the Texas game we had 45,000."[10]

Kenan did not have to help with the expansion, of course. He and the university had shared the cost of earlier stadium additions, and given the facility's obvious moneymaking potential, the school would have paid for the expansion on its own. Yet the stadium was the most visible sign of Kenan's personal benefactions to the university, and he clearly wanted to keep it that way. He wanted to prevent it from being overshadowed by the gifts of others, especially those of John Motley Morehead.

To be sure, Kenan makes it clear in the second edition of *Incidents* that he perceived Morehead both as a personal rival and as a sibling vying for the attention and affections of their alma mater. Kenan published two, full-page photographs in his four-page chapter describing his gifts to Kenan Stadium. The first was taken in 1927, after the stadium dedication, and shows him and Alice standing next to Morehead's wife during their visit to the old Morehead homeplace in Spray, North Carolina. The second (the "benefactors" photograph described above) was taken at the dedication of the Morehead Building.[11] Kenan also noted in the second edition, perhaps in response to the benefactors caption, that "during June, 1948, I gave to the University of North Carolina (Chemical Library) 92 bound volumes of Electro Chemical Society and also contributed $500.00."[12]

Kenan wanted people to know that the stadium was not his only gift to the university—a point he had tried to make in the first edition of *Incidents*: "June 10, 1914, I gave to The University of North Carolina my Chemical Library consisting of more than 200 books. Also donated for the purchase of more books $8,981.16. Also have given each year since gift to the Library the Journals of the American Chemical Society."[13] In other words, he was just as interested as his sisters and Hill and Morehead in supporting the school's intellectual life. He never forgot the lesson he learned as a student at UNC: "Education should concern itself with the whole personality, not the brain alone."

The second edition of *Incidents* was the last in which Kenan overtly promoted his version of the carbide story. He devoted the next three editions to his own and the Flagler System's goals in Florida. He repeated his carbide contributions, of course, but he printed no old carbide documents and made none of the old carbide arguments. On the numerous occasions when the matter is mentioned, it is not in Kenan's own words; excerpts from newspaper articles summarize his brilliant career as a scientist, engineer, businessman, and philanthropist.[14]

The rivalry between Kenan and Morehead continued throughout the early 1950s, however, much to the delight of their alma mater. The Morehead Planetarium opened in 1949, and two years later the Morehead Foundation officially established the Morehead Scholarship Program at UNC: "the first nonathletic merit scholarship [awards] in the United States."[15] Morehead's scholarship program probably also prompted Kenan to start the William Rand Kenan, Jr., Scholarship Fund at UNC. Kenan continued to contribute to both athletic and intellectual pursuits at UNC. He donated between $250 and $500 a year to the school's Chemical Library, and in 1953 he donated $15,000 for "Television at U.N.C." Yet he changed the nature of his contributions thereafter because, he claimed, he was advised to do so. "It was suggested to me to let the Athletic Association pay for renewals and maintenance [at Kenan Stadium] and I give an endowment for scholarship."[16]

According to one "How I Spent My Money" list, Kenan gave $10,000 a year to this endowment between 1953 and 1956. In another list, he records a $15,000 gift to the "University of North Carolina Scholarship" in 1956, $68,000 in contributions to an "Endowment Fund" between 1953 and 1958, and $25,000 for the "Field House (Kenan Stadium)" in 1957. In any event, in 1954 Kenan gave $20,000 to establish the "William R. Kenan Scholarship Fund" for student athletes at UNC. Chancellor Robert B. House thanked him for establishing the fund. "We must maintain a fine, clean athletic program; we must get and encourage good boys who are athletes; and we must do this in a tough and highly competitive situation. Your action and generosity is a beginning of something which will get us on to a high level bye and bye and we are grateful for it."[17]

"Hank" the milkman offered a different reason why Kenan established the athletic scholarships: to help UNC compete with the Notre Dame football team. Though embellished in many respects, the milkman's story rings true, particularly with regard to the timing of Kenan's gift and his half-century love affair with Tar Heel football. "Hank" was a happy, gregarious Irish Catholic who always wore a Notre Dame cap while working at the farm, and he sat at a desk in front of Kenan's office. " 'Young man,' " Kenan said to him before the first UNC–Notre Dame game, " 'I see you're a Notre Dame fan. You wear that hat all the time. Would you like to make a gentleman's bet?' " Sure, the milkman said, certain of victory: "Ten dollars." " 'Oh . . . no,' " Kenan replied, " 'we've got to have a gentlemen's bet. . . . Fifty cents.' "[18]

UNC played its first game against Notre Dame at Yankee Stadium on November 12, 1949, almost fifty-six years to the day after Kenan and his teammates played Lehigh in New York in "the first game that a southern team ever played in the great metropolis."[19] The small former halfback must have recalled that historic game as he watched his Heels perform at Yankee Stadium. Even with the mighty Choo-Choo running, they quickly lost track to the Fighting Irish. The 42-6 defeat was no better than the 34-0 loss Kenan and his teammates had suffered in the university's football debut in the North.[20]

"Hank" found fifty cents on his desk when he finished his milk deliveries the following Monday morning, and he found the same amount after each UNC–Notre Dame game for the next several years. Then, one day "Mr. Kenan came and he said 'Young man, I want to show you something.' And he showed me a certified check from the Niagara County Bank for $150,000 made out to the University of North Carolina Athletic Department for football scholarships." The money did not work, at least not in Notre Dame's case. UNC did not defeat its powerful rival until the eleventh game in their series, in 1960.[21]

LIVING AND LIFE WRITING

Kenan published the second edition of *Incidents* in 1949, at the same time that the University of Georgia Press published *Florida's Flagler*, a biography of Henry Flagler by University of Georgia history professor Sidney Walter Martin. William was well aware of the coincidence and connections. Martin, a UNC Ph.D., had interviewed him in St. Augustine each winter since 1945, and they had been exchanging letters and information since that time. "He knew that I was a graduate of the University," Martin recalled, "and this may have had something to do with letting me talk to him. . . . I used to mention Kenan Stadium and things like that to him every once in a while. And he'd smile." Martin may also have mentioned that he had submitted the Flagler manuscript "to the University of North Carolina [Press] and they read it and kept it for some time, but then decided not to do it."[22]

Martin discerned in his dealings with Kenan what several other observers noticed about William's relationship with Henry Flagler. While Kenan displayed no "bitter feelings" toward his famous brother-in-law, Martin had "to admit, there wasn't a warmth between the two. I mean, he didn't speak in warm terms about Henry Flagler. . . . I don't think he held him in awe. . . . I don't believe he felt like a brother-in-law to him. I don't think there was any kinship feeling there, or feeling like 'You married my sister so you're special to me.' That wasn't there. It was strictly all business terms."[23]

Things had not been going well for William and the Flagler System when Martin interviewed him. Their first meeting took place in the winter of 1945–46, shortly before the publication of the first edition of *Incidents*, when much of St. Augustine and the Florida east coast was still in an uproar over the ICC hearings on the proposed ACL-FEC merger. The context of their next two interviews was much the same: Alice's demise and bitter ICC hearings.[24]

Florida's Flagler appeared at a time when the Flagler System was but a shadow of its former self. The system had terminated the operations of its greatest prewar moneymaker, the FEC Car Ferry Company, the company Kenan had hoped would profit from a new era in inter-American relations.[25] One observer blamed the change on William's decision not to challenge the operations of a competing ferry company. "When the Seatrain was opened out of St Louis [through New Orleans] paralleling the Car Ferry Boats, Mr Kenan was advised that he could make an appearance before the Maritime Board in Washington, as the opposition could hurt them. However he chose not to do so."[26] In truth, though, William's decision had more to do with trade-offs between the ACL and the FEC than with competition from Seatrain. Kenan not only sold the ACL the FEC's debts to the Car Ferry Company (in order to facilitate the Coast Line's intervention in the ICC hearings), but also, at some time before May 1948, when he became president of the P&O Steamship Company, Kenan apparently purchased the ACL's half-interest in that company.[27]

By the time *Florida's Flagler* was published, moreover, only the Breakers, the hotel that William had built, was showing a profit, and only one of the eight hotels originally built by Flagler in Florida, the Ponce de Leon Hotel in St. Augustine, had not been dismantled, closed, or sold.[28] The FEC Railway was showing more profit than it ever had in Flagler's day. William still controlled all but seven of the FEC's 375,000 shares of common stock, and he still controlled and managed the road almost as if it had never gone into receivership. But it was still in receivership, still under the protection of the district court, and still causing problems within both the system and the political and economic life of Florida.

The FEC struggle reached yet another turning point in early 1950, while Kenan and his sisters were at the Ponce de Leon Hotel. On January 17, 1950, as a result of appeals and counterappeals by Ball and the ACL, the Fifth Circuit Court of Appeals rejected the ACL's proposed merger with the FEC as a "forced merger . . . contrary to statute." The ACL immediately petitioned the United States Supreme Court for a writ of certiorari, but the court denied the writ in April 1950.[29]

The ACL's setback helped reinforce Ed Ball's vicious attacks on Senator Claude Pepper, who was again seeking the Democratic nomination for senator. Though William's feelings for the prolabor, "integrated liberal" are not known, the anti-Pepper appeals of men such as Frank Upchurch, chairman of the St. Augustine Chamber of Commerce, made Kenan uncomfortable. Upchurch wrote in a public letter to "friends" that Pepper supported the FEC's merger with the ACL to "rob St. Augustine of its principal payroll, one-third of its population, and reduce property values fifty-percent." Many FEC employees apparently agreed with Upchurch, as did many other residents of Florida's east coast, and with the help of both organized labor and the Dan Crisp advertising agency in Jacksonville, Pepper lost to Miami congressman George Smathers, who "fell into Ball's pot of senatorial campaign money and refused to struggle."[30]

Another southern liberal, one with closer ties to Kenan, was still running for senator when Kenan arrived for the Chapel Hill commencement in early June. Dr. Frank Porter Graham received more votes than either of his two Democratic opponents in North Carolina's May 27 primaries; but his total fell short of the majority needed for victory, and he found himself campaigning against Willis Smith in a runoff. Unfortunately the Smith campaign successfully portrayed Graham and the university as purveyors of dangerous, Communist-inspired racial and political ideas, and Smith, "assisted by U.S. Supreme Court decisions ordering racial desegregation and by his organization's distribution of defamatory racial leaflets and outright lies," narrowly defeated Graham in the runoff. "It was one of the meanest political campaigns in North Carolina history."[31]

Kenan got a taste of North Carolina politics himself when he returned to New York from Chapel Hill. The Kenan Memorial Fountain had become a political issue in Wilmington, with one newspaper calling on the city authorities "to buck up their courage and decide where the fountain may be relocated without constituting an accident hazard."[32] More to the point, Kenan found a letter awaiting him from Wilmington's city manager, J. R. Benson, who noted that the city council had "officially" considered moving the fountain from Fifth and Market Streets. There had been "numerous accidents there resulting in rather severe property damage and personal injuries and recently one fatality," Benson explained. "The fountain has been considerably damaged and its appearance greatly marred." The city had done everything it could, he continued, to try to prevent such accidents: "Traffic lights have been installed, stop signs erected, and no left turns allowed, but still the accidents continue. We have found it impractical to use the water to much advantage, as the spray is very objectionable to motorists and pedestrians."[33]

William was not pleased. The fountain stood at the center of his shrine to himself and his family. It not only memorialized his father and mother; it enhanced the most visible local monument to his engineering skills and civic pride, the Carolina Apartment building. Indeed, he and his apartment partner, Thomas Wright, had recently completed a massive renovation project on the 1906 building. Partly because the building needed it and partly, it seems, at the insistence of local building inspectors, the "entire plumbing was modernized, replacing all pipes with copper tubing and replacing all bath and toilet fixtures." Also, "we installed a complete sprinkler system. . . . The stairwell and the elevator shaft was reconstructed with fireproof material including all doors; also a steel spiral stairway was installed. All fire escapes were improved by 45 degree steel stairs, replacing the old ladders. A modern fire alarm system with auxiliary boxes on each floor was provided."[34]

Kenan responded politely to the city's request but made it clear he wanted the fountain to stay where it was. "My personal opinion is that the location of the fountain is a benefit from every point of view," he wrote to Benson. "I cannot help from feeling that its location has a retarding effect on automobile drivers speeding through the streets. I gave it to the city without any strings tied to it and I have no suggestion whatever to make in connection with relocating it."[35] Kenan sent a copy of his letter to the chairman of the New Hanover County Historical Commission, Louis T. Moore, who wondered, in a note to Benson, whether Kenan was not "deeply resentful of the continuing agitation relative to the fountain."[36]

The Carolina Apartment building and the Kenan Memorial Fountain, Wilmington, North Carolina. (*Incidents* 2)

Kenan was resentful, and he reacted much as he had when Alice was removed from the Lockport hospital board. "I washed my hands of the situation" in Wilmington.[37] The cleansing is clear in his autobiographies. He rarely mentions Wilmington after the first edition of *Incidents*, and when he does, it is not endearing. "For the Information of Some of My North Carolina Friends," he wrote in the third edition, "When Hugh McRae, of Wilmington, N.C., was operating the Tidewater Power Company 1904–05, formerly called Consolidated Gas & Light—and the street railways and was on the point of expanding considerably, he wrote me offering the job of General Manager. This I declined." In the fourth edition, which appeared in 1955, two years after the city removed a six-foot rim around the fountain, Kenan wrote, "The City of Wilmington finally got around to placing a bronze plaque on the Kenan Fountain at the corner of Market Street and Fifth Avenue. A matter of dispute for a number of years because it extended into the street on each side, the fountain was finally reduced in size and has now been lighted for the passerby."[38]

Kenan's break with Wilmington reflected his search for places where he and his philanthropy would be better appreciated. Although UNC was one such place, he faced competition there with other benefactors. He got more personal attention, at least for a time, in Kenansville, where in 1949 he gave $10,000 for the construction of Kenan Memorial Auditorium. There were no traffic lights in Kenansville and no apartment buildings, and only 674 people lived in the Duplin County seat when William and Sarah visited it in December 1950 to check on the auditorium.[39]

William enjoyed his visit. One reporter described him as "a young 'old' man," able to "carry on a conversation with the enthusiasm of a 16 year old boy. He and Mrs. Kenan reminisced over days gone by when they would play at the old Kenan home here and especially the big times they had at Christmas." They also expressed their pleasure "with the progress that has been made on the Kenan Memorial Auditorium. When it is finally completed Mr. Kenan said there will be nothing east of the Colliseum [sic] in Raleigh to compare with it. Mr. Kenan made an initial donation of $10,000 and Mrs. [Sarah] Kenan donated $5,000. The building is named for them and their families."[40]

William got just what he wanted from the locals. The *Duplin Times* described him as

one of the country's leading scientists, [with a] huge farm near Lockport, N.Y., on which he does extensive research in chemistry with cooperation from some of the nation's leading chemical and pharmaceutical houses. We could have sat and listened to him talk on for hours. Mrs. Graham Kenan was very charming and patiently quiet to let the men folks listen and interrogate Mr. Kenan. She, to me, as well as Mr. Kenan, represented the old time true Southern Aristocracy that we read about but seldom have the pleasure of knowing. They seem to take great pride in Kenansville and I think can truly be labled the patron saints of our home town.[41]

William's pride in Kenansville is evident in the first three editions of *Incidents*, which open with a chapter intertwining his family tree with the region. But the place and his forebears are rarely mentioned in the fourth and fifth editions, which are basically compilations of documents written by other people and previously published elsewhere. Also absent is any attempt at a chronological narrative; the only apparent organizing principle is a juxtaposition of pieces written about him and Henry Flagler. In truth, the third edition is the last in which Kenan's authorial voice is clear throughout, and to some extent that voice was already fading.

The last editions of *Incidents* reflect Kenan's obsession with his reputation and events in Florida. The fourth opens with four photographs taken at St. Augustine between 1905 and 1954, all suggesting the importance of the Ponce and the Kenans to St. Augustine's social life. The text begins with articles from New York newspapers extolling the soundness of the Ponce's coquina structure in late 1954, and these are followed by reprints of pieces from various sources regarding the Flagler Memorial Presbyterian Church in St. Augustine—"Our Church's Story" and "A Beautiful Memorial," the latter a summary of the gifts from William and his family to the church.

A long review of *Florida's Flagler*, reprinted from a Palm Beach newspaper, comes next, and this is followed by "Flagler's Greatest Dream," a short article by George Cordwell. Flagler is also the subject of the next piece, "Building out to Sea: The Key West Extension of the Florida East Coast Railway," a twenty-page speech originally delivered by former extension employee Carlton J. Corliss to the Mississippi Valley Historical Association. The speech summarizes Flagler's "courageous" fight to overcome the problems associated with the building of the Key West Extension, and it ends with the receivership of the FEC and the replacement of the hurricane-damaged extension by the Overseas Highway. "If Flagler's aim was to create homes and employment opportunities for the people, then his efforts were immensely successful. The Overseas Highway as well as the Florida East Coast Railway, stand as monuments to his memory, as symbols of his courage and faith in the future of this good land." Most of the remaining 80 or so pages of the 128-page book are dedicated to articles about William Rand Kenan Jr.

As much of this suggests, the fourth edition represented more than Kenan's ongoing efforts to escape the shadow of his famous brother-in-law. It also reflected a peculiar blend of his declining mental powers and the Flagler System's response to events in the FEC's bankruptcy case. William was not only beginning to conflate his own carbide experience with that of Francis Preston Venable; he was also remembering as his own many of Henry Flagler's activities in Florida. As his great-nephew Lawrence Lewis Jr. recalled, "I think he told the stories so many times that it just became a fact in his mind that he did a lot of the things that Mr. Flagler actually did."[42]

There is more method than misremembering in William's fourth edition, however—be it his own or someone else's method. Put simply, the fourth edition formed part of the system's publicity campaign to promote the ACL-FEC merger and to make peace with the people and places that might be affected by the alliance. This helps explain the photographs that open the book: Mary Lily with fifty guests at the Ponce in 1905, William and Alice with twenty guests on the hotel patio in 1910, William and Alice with another couple at a St. Augustine costume party, and William and his sisters with several Flagler System officials and their wives beside the "Ponce de Leon Swimming Pool, Sunday, February 28, 1954."

This last photograph was taken less than two months before the United States Supreme Court rendered one of the most important legal decisions in the FEC's epic bankruptcy case. On April 5, 1954, just a month before the historic *Brown v. Board of Education* desegregation decision, the Court overturned the ICC's 1951 approval of yet another ACL merger plan, which Kenan had approved but Ed Ball had appealed all the way to the high court. The court ruled that the ICC could not order an involuntary, or "forced," merger of the FEC and the ACL.[43]

Within days of the decision ACL president Champ Davis visited W. R. Kenan Jr. at the Ponce de Leon Hotel—not, however, to buy his old friend's FEC stock, but instead to get William's written approval of the 1951 reorganization plan. By doing so, one lawyer argued, the ACL might take advantage of

Justice Felix Frankfurter's footnoted opinion that there was "no reason why, just because it was in the Bankruptcy Court, a carrier should not be in a position to merge with another carrier, if the two carriers wanted to." In other words, Kenan's explicit support for the 1951 plan would demonstrate that the merger of the two railroads was not involuntary and thus that the ACL had a reason to return to the courts and the ICC.[44]

William signed Davis's document consenting "to the execution by the Florida East Coast Railway Company of an adoption of such a plan," and the lawyers returned to the courts. But William's word did little good. The Supreme Court denied the ACL a rehearing, and the district court then approved Ed Ball's request to abandon the reorganization proceedings under the Bankruptcy Act, whereupon the ACL petitioned the circuit court in New Orleans to reverse the district court's decision.[45]

FLORIDA'S KENAN

William had the fourth edition of *Incidents* ready for publication on April 30, 1955, his eighty-third birthday, when he was interviewed in the FEC's St. Augustine offices by a reporter from the *St. Augustine Record*, a former Flagler company. On May 1 and again on June 1 the *Record* published the reporter's story on the "incredible" achievements of this "inventor, discoverer, business man, engineer, scientist, dairy farmer, and cattle breeder." Then in August, in connection with his dedication of Florida Power & Light's huge new generating station at Cutler, Florida, Kenan was the subject of stories in the *Florida Times-Union* (a paper owned by the ACL, the FEC, and the Seaboard Railroads), the *Miami Daily News*, and the *Miami Herald* (also a former Flagler paper). The stories recognized Kenan's achievements as a Florida Power & Light director and "Utility Pioneer" in Florida, and as an "83-year-old veteran of the era of empire builders, who built the first 200 kilowatt plant in Miami in 1904" and who now turned on the company's giant new "140,000 kilowatt electric power generator—largest ever installed in the state."[46]

The publicity was good for Kenan and the Flagler System. He was not described as Henry Flagler's brother-in-law; he was "a long-time associate of the late Henry M. Flagler" and an "engineering consultant and top advisor to the late Henry M. Flagler." About this time, moreover, the Flagler System began receiving praise for the sale of its West Palm Beach Water Company and a 17,000-acre "watershed" to the city of West Palm Beach. The money was not bad either: the system received a total of $8.5 million for the land and the utility.[47]

While some of this publicity reflected the Flagler System's efforts to improve its image, most of it was intended to help Kenan and the ACL improve theirs. Indeed, Kenan was now the single most important actor in the struggle for control of the FEC. As such he was facing intense public criticism from the attorneys representing the duPont interests, one of whom went so far as to accuse him of "acting as the catspaw of Atlantic Coast" and engaging in a conspiracy with Davis to conceal "unlawful transactions."[48]

Kenan cooperated with Davis and the ACL, but there was nothing fraudulent or conspiratorial about his transactions—all were a matter of public record. Kenan's attorney argued that these allegations were made "because Mr. Kenan has been given a standing by the Supreme Court's opinion to act on a merger and because his views as to a desirable merger, a desirable reorganization, coincided with those of the Interstate Commerce Commission, which found that it would be against the public interest for the St. Joe Paper Company to acquire control of the debtor railroad by an internal reorganization, and that it would be in the public interest for the Atlantic Coast Line to acquire the Florida East Coast by merger."[49]

One of the best descriptions of Kenan's role in the case came from another antimerger attorney, Robert McCracken, who offered his opinion during hearings in the circuit court in New Orleans in December 1955. "Mr. Kenan is in a dual position," McCracken argued. "He is a trustee, sole trustee, for the Bingham Estate and the sole stockholder of the railroad, and president of the railroad—really a quadruple situation—and he is—by virtue of that doctrine of law he acts as a fiduciary for these creditors [the bondholders]." It was clear to McCracken what Kenan should do. "Now there is just one thing I submit for Mr. Kenan, who is, I understand, a highly honorable gentleman. I have just one thing for Mr. Kenan to do, and that is withdraw his activity and permit the others who have an interest in this property to work out a plan."[50]

William was in too deep to withdraw even if he wanted to. In late 1955 the New Orleans circuit court confirmed its order to reopen the FEC's reorganization proceedings, and in early January, while Kenan was in St. Augustine, the FEC's vice-president, A. R. MacMannis, met with the ACL's attorneys in New York and worked out a merger plan that the railroads presented jointly to the ICC. The ACL played its Kenan card, hoping to exploit the principle Justice Frankfurter had noted. It was also hoping, despite previous rulings, that since the FEC was "returning higher revenues almost every year and meeting all of its current fixed charges," the ICC and the courts might "now acknowledge that some ownership rights still resided with the sole stockholder of the old company"—William Rand Kenan Jr.[51]

Both the FEC and the ACL also hoped that the Florida Railroad and Public Utilities Commission had been listening to the favorable publicity given Kenan and the Flagler System with regard to the Miami and West Palm Beach utilities. The commission's opinion would weigh heavily in the ICC's consideration of the new merger proposal, and competition for the agency's approval was keen. The ACL offered to build a new $1.5-million railroad terminal in Miami on the site of the old facility, while Ed Ball offered $4 million to construct a new passenger station at a new location.[52]

Neither the new merger plan nor the decision to reopen the ICC hearings met with a warm reception in Florida. "We can't get excited about the latest plan to end a quarter-century of litigation for control of the Florida East Coast Railway," the *Miami Herald* sighed in February 1956. "All that's new about this plan, apparently, is that it has the formal endorsement of William R. Kenan, Jr., president and sole stockholder of the bankrupt FEC company. His support of the ACL's bid has been a matter of court record for some time."[53] The Florida Railroad and Public Utilities Commission did not think much of the new merger plan either. On May 7, 1956, one month before the ICC hearings opened in Washington, D.C., the state agency filed a statement with the ICC supporting the St. Joe–Ed Ball–duPont plan. Not only was the latter's terminal offer superior to the ACL's, but also, the agency argued, a merger would significantly reduce the number of railroad workers in the state.[54]

William attended the UNC commencement only days before the ICC hearings opened in Washington, D.C. Slow of foot and uncertain of his memory, the eighty-four-year-old alumnus was undoubtedly uneasy with the changes occurring in his native region and university. The furor on race was rising, fueled by the *Brown* decision and demands from the North for change. In December Rosa Parks had refused to give up her seat on a Montgomery bus, and by the spring of 1956 a black boycott of the city's transit system was being led by the Reverend Martin Luther King. What was more, UNC's president, Gordon Gray, had resigned his position to return to government service in Washington, and in March 1956 the university's board of trustees appointed thirty-five-year-old William C. Friday as the school's acting president. Friday, a graduate of both North Carolina State and the Law School at Chapel Hill, became president of UNC that October and served in that position until his retirement in 1986, when he became executive director of the William Rand Kenan, Jr. Charitable Trust at Chapel Hill.

Kenan was not in Washington when the ICC opened its hearings. Champ Davis was there, however, and so were Ed Ball and his sister Jessie Ball duPont, who, at age seventy-two, looked "stylish in a navy and white suit and matching hat."[55] The first witness, Davis's senior assistant at the ACL, George Cain, spent two hours testifying about their discussions with Kenan on the new merger plan. But the high point of the morning occurred when Robert K. Frey, vice-president of the ACL's largest stockholder, the Safe Deposit and Trust Company of Baltimore, presented the commission with a list of the ACL's thirty largest stockholders. Kenan's name was last on the list.

When Frey was asked about this Kenan connection, however, he could not help the St. Joe–Ed Ball–duPont attorney. He did not know Kenan, he did not know when Kenan had bought the ACL stock, and he did not know if the FEC's

Kenan was the same Kenan listed as the owner of 6,300 shares of ACL. Another antimerger attorney asked for the same information a few minutes later, but all Frey could do was offer to try to get the information during the lunch recess. "Some listeners looked wise," the *Miami Herald* noted, "thinking the date might have something to do with Kenan's 12-year support of the ACL."[56] But Frey testified after lunch that the FEC's president had acquired all of his ACL shares prior to 1948. "Our records show that between the dates of February 8, 1917 and April 9, 1932, 2,000 shares of Atlantic Coast Line stock went to his [Kenan's] name. An additional hundred shares went to his name on June 4, 1948, making 2100 shares. On February 11, 1955, there was issued to him an additional 4,200 shares, in connection with the three-for-one split [the previous year], thus making his holdings 6,300 shares, as shown in Exhibit 498."[57]

Although William was absent from the hearings again the following day, he was scheduled to appear as a witness on June 27. The date was set by his attorney, Joseph Schreiber, of Dewey, Ballantine, Bushby, Palmer and Wood of New York, and by the man who subpoenaed Kenan in the first place, I. R. Turney, the St. Joe–Ed Ball–duPont attorney. Turney, apparently hoping to use William's fading memory against him, noted cynically to the ICC examiner, "Mr. Kenan is a year or two older than I am, and we felt that we aged people should not be imposed upon, so we agreed that, subject to your approval . . . Mr. Kenan will be here on Wednesday of next week, and will testify on that day." Kenan's attorney quickly qualified the arrangement, however. "May I add, Mr. Examiner, that we have just discussed the definitive date this morning and I have not yet had a chance to talk to Mr. Kenan. He is 84 years of age, and I will produce him if he is available to appear at that time. If there is any difficulty about it, I will notify the Hearing Examiner."[58]

This exchange occurred after several hours of testimony by A. R. Mac-Mannis, who spent most of the morning being grilled by Turney and the other antimerger attorneys regarding the special meetings at which the FEC's directors and stockholders approved the ACL plan. More to the point, Turney tried to paint MacMannis as Kenan's dupe, as nothing more than a rubber stamp for some nefarious but unmentioned conspiracy hatched and carried out by Kenan and Davis. "Is it true, then," Turney asked MacMannis, "that so far as any participation in this plan by you, . . . you were merely acting under the complete order, direction and domination of Mr. Kenan?"[59]

The *Miami Herald* was excited. "FEC Called Slave of 'Master' Kenan," it blared, and in another story, "Brother-Sister Teams to Star at FEC Hearing," the paper noted that William and his sister Jessie would join Ed Ball and his sister Jessie as witnesses in front of "two dozen lawyers" and "nearly 100 persons . . . in the high-ceilinged, wood paneled room." But the courtroom drama was pretty much over; neither William nor any of the other members of the brother-sister teams ever testified. The ICC hearings were transferred to

West Palm Beach in September and ended there in November—fifteen years and 20,000 pages of transcripts later.[60]

The drama now shifted to the boardrooms of the ACL, where many of the company's stockholders and officials had grown as tired, impatient, and disgruntled as the people of Florida with the epic railroad struggle. The railroad had spent millions of dollars in the fight but had nothing as yet to show for it. The finger of blame was pointed at Kenan's old friend, Champ Davis, the seventy-seven-year-old president of the ACL, and it should have been. The FEC struggle was more than a business deal for Davis; it was a matter of personal integrity and personal loyalty. Beyond his friendship with Kenan, Davis had grown to despise Ball, who constantly referred to him in private and in public as "Chump" Davis.

Davis resigned as the ACL's president in May 1957, a year before the ICC rendered its decision. The "more influential members" of the ACL's board had decided to end his "relentless pursuit of the FEC struggle." Though they asked him to continue as one of the company's directors, Davis refused, probably to avoid being associated with the changes they urged him to make. Shortly after his resignation, the company's board of directors approved a plan to transfer the ACL's general offices from Wilmington, North Carolina, to Jacksonville, Florida, and by the end of 1957 the bulldozers were clearing and filling in the new building site in Jacksonville. Ironically, it was not the FEC's workers who now had to worry about relocating; it was 1,000 ACL families in Wilmington who had to move.[61]

Kenan was undoubtedly upset with these events, and the ICC's decision made things worse. On April 18, 1958 the commission rejected the ACL-FEC merger plan and recommended the adoption, with certain modifications, of the reorganization plan proposed by the St. Joe–Ed Ball–duPont interests. The courts agreed with the commission's decision, and the ACL withdrew from the field. As the company's new president, W. Thomas Rice, explained to Mrs. Jessie Ball duPont, "Continued litigation . . . was certainly not in the interests of either the people living on the east coast of Florida or the railroads involved."[62]

William published the fifth and final edition of his autobiography shortly before the ICC handed down its final decision in the FEC case. The book opens with the "Hotel Ponce de Leon," an article written in the late nineteenth century by the hotel's architects, Thomas Hastings and John Carrere, describing the "Great Architectural Achievement Envisioned and Built By Henry M. Flagler in St. Augustine, Florida." The article is accompanied by a photograph of William and his two sisters, "pictured recently at the Hotel Ponce de Leon, their winter home." Although William may have selected the materials for his 132-page book, he appears to have written only two paragraphs in it. Both appear early and consecutively and concern his relationship with Henry Walters and Henry Flagler.

Most of the reprinted articles in the fifth edition repeat the old stories of Kenan's association with UNC, Randleigh Farm, Camp Kenan, Union Carbide, and Florida. But there are two stories on a new topic. In March 1958, just a month before he lost the FEC Railway, the Florida State Chamber of Commerce announced it would name an eight-acre tract surrounding its new state headquarters in Jacksonville as the William R. Kenan Jr. Floral Gardens. The chamber wanted to honor Kenan's "labor in the upbuilding of Florida, through his association with the late Henry M. Flagler, who developed the Florida East Coast Railway and other Flagler System properties."[63]

By the time the chamber dedicated the Kenan Floral Gardens in February 1959, the steel skeleton of the ACL's Jacksonville headquarters was three stories high. Construction was completed in July 1960, and in August of that year 950 Coast Line families were transported across the 500 miles of track from Wilmington. "I've often been told since that was the best thing that ever happened to our town," Wilmington native David Brinkley later recalled, "that it woke Wilmington up from a long afternoon nap. A very long nap—about 100 years." Unfortunately, W. R. Kenan did not live long enough to share that perspective.[64]

CHAPTER 14

Disembarking

The minister always found William sitting at the window, kicking gently at the worn-out carpet. "I'd call on him in his home, I guess, about once a month through the years," Dr. James Westhafer recalled. "And he sat there in his living room. . . . That was his regular place, his chair by the window. There he'd watch the high school kids coming down the street from high school." The visits always ended with a prayer and a query from Kenan, who thought like an engineer until the end. "And almost every time I saw him, I think, after the prayer, he would say, 'Did you construct that yourself?' "[1]

William spent a lot of time at that window during the last five or six years of his life, especially after he lost his driver's license and his chauffeur died. "He didn't pay any attention when he went out the driveway whether anybody was coming," a neighbor recalled. "He reached that point in his life, you see. He wasn't looking. And you would hear brakes screech." His accelerator jammed and the public be damned, William drove like he owned the road, ignoring stop signs and pedestrians alike. Roaring up the road to Camp Kenan or rumbling out to Randleigh Farm, he eventually messed up. He injured a boy or bruised a girl or the sheriff just got tired of giving out warnings and tickets—no one who knew William remembers exactly why he lost his license.[2]

No one remembers because no one but the preacher visited him. "I would talk to some of his old friends and encourage them to go to see him," Westhafer explained. "I think when he became a little bit senile, a lot of people assumed, you know, it was no use to go and unfortunately kind of dropped him. He was very lonely, I think." Indeed, he rarely saw any of his family. Jessie and Sarah spent most of their time in North Carolina, which was once again their legal residence. In 1962 the courts declared Sarah mentally incompetent and a charge of her nephew, Frank H. Kenan, of Durham, North Carolina, who became her trustee and legal guardian. Though Jessie remained much more active than either William or Sarah, she concentrated on her grandchildren, Lawrence Jr. and Mary Lily, who now had children of their own and who

W. R. Kenan Jr. in the late 1950s. (*Incidents* 5)

wanted, for various reasons, to have as little to do with "Uncle" William as possible.[3]

William also gradually lost or got rid of most of his servants and maids. As for the house, "he didn't keep it up, and things really did go to pieces." Part of the servant problem was the expanding economy; with business good it was difficult to find dedicated domestics. But Kenan also grew "more and more penurious" in his eighties, and after Miss Godfrey quit, he "had trouble keeping housekeepers because he tried to pay them so low. . . . He brought in part-time maids. All they did was clean and change the linen and dust and do the whole house." William appeared to be "very stingy with his help, extremely stingy. He even counted the soap they used." He was especially stingy, it seems, with his black servant and cook—not because they were black but because they worked for the FEC and had to be paid union wages. "To off-set this expense he charged them for their living quarters and meals. When his bill for electricity was increased, he took away their electric heater and it can get very cold in the early A.M. in upstate New York."[4]

The biggest changes occurred in 1961, after the FEC passed into the hands of St. Joe–Ed Ball–duPont. The black servants did not return to Locust Street—much to their delight—and Schuyler Beattie hired a full-time, live-in cook-housekeeper for William. "She had a little apartment off the kitchen," "Hank" the milkman recalled, "three bed-room apartment. She had a television set in there. . . . She wasn't as old as Mr. Kenan but she was close to it. . . . She watched the television set . . . and she always left the door open because she knew Mr. Kenan would come in, and he did. He used to come in and watch television with her for hours and hours." But he never bought a television himself. "He stuck to his radio."

Kenan preferred his old appliances, too. "Mr. Kenan had a 1920 wood and coal and natural gas stove, and that's what they cooked on. He also had a 1927 Frigidaire. He had two of them, two 1927 model Frigidaires in his kitchen, and when he died he still had those '27 Frigidaires."[5] To be sure, the only indication that this was the home of an "Electric Power Pioneer," of the man who had "blueprinted and built Miami's first major electric plant," were two six-slice toasters. Otherwise, there was just "one light in the kitchen from a wire with a double socket in it to which the maid attached the iron."[6]

William tried to make sure, however, that the house's exterior continued to look good, for that had been his job while Alice was alive. She had "handled everything inside the house," and "I employed the gardener's force and chauffeur and attended to everything on the property, except the operation of the inside of the house."[7] One neighbor recalled William being "right there" to see that all of the outside work got done, and that even in his old age he tried to keep on top of things. "You know, he would even get up and clean the eaves out. They had a terrible time with him because they knew he shouldn't get on those ladders. He wanted to know it was done."[8]

By the late 1950s William's outside workforce consisted of only one man, George Rossman, who lived alone above the old cow barn behind the big house. William got along well with Rossman, who had been his gardener since 1944. "He is a remarkable individual," Kenan wrote of Rossman in 1949, "very active, efficient, and can do anything; always in good humor; understands poultry of all kinds, and has been an excellent gardener."[9] Rossman did a little bit of everything on the twenty-five-acre Locust Street plantation. He "took care of the chickens and fed them and cleaned them and gathered the eggs." He also tended the fruit trees in the orchard behind the house and "took care of the lawn and all the ground work, all the trimming and the feeding the grass and cutting the grass and trimming and all the bush work."[10]

Rossman devoted most of his attention to Kenan's large garden and green-house. The short, tobacco-chewing gardener raised a variety of crops in the fields adjacent to the house, including some six-foot pea plants allegedly descended from the original pod found in the tomb of King Tutankhamen in the early 1920s. Like the eggs he collected and the chickens he killed, Rossman's vegetables were served in the big house, and the surplus was distributed by Kenan to his Uppertown neighbors and the men in the office at Western Block. More than one neighbor remembered William's peculiar blend of generosity and thriftiness with the garden's abundance. After delivering a large, eight quart basket of vegetables, the Lockport millionaire would invariably tell the recipient, "I'll wait for the basket."[11]

Both William and his gardener took special pride in the greenhouse, where they raised and experimented with flowers and vegetables. The facility accounted for the largest item in William's household budget and it was "beauti-ful. In the summer, it would be a lovely experience," one neighbor recalled. Kenan's most cherished plant was a cactus, the night-blooming cereus, which blooms with white, fragrant, lilylike flowers. The "rare old" plant had been growing in the "poorly located" original greenhouse, and William had had it transplanted to the new greenhouse, where one of his previous gardeners had successfully propagated a number of the plants in tubs and boxes.[12]

William became obsessed with the cereus after Alice's death, keeping strict records of the dates and times when the blooms appeared as well as the total number of flowers produced between June and September. But this involved more than his normal penchant for record keeping and scientific analysis. He used the flowers to show his love, to reach out to the people Alice had touched for them both. At first he wanted a sign that his love was appreciated: "I now have a lot of fun each season surprising my friends between 9 and 10 o'clock at night when I deliver them, as they are always startled and thrilled by these beautiful flowers which when fully open are extremely fragrant."[13]

Eventually, though, William became a silent messenger. "Every once in a while in the summer," a friend recalled, "I'd go to the front door and here would be two or three night-blooming cereus hanging on the front door. They'd collapse when it's daytime, but the fragrance was just wonderful." Kenan took the same shadowy approach to some friends up the street. "Every year when the plant was in bloom," their son explained, "my father and mother would get a bloom, and every year it was invariably we'd be out for the evening and come home and my mother would say, 'Oh, Mr. Kenan has been here.'"[14]

Almost all of Kenan's cereus friends were people he knew from the First Presbyterian Church of Lockport. The church was the oldest institution and one of the only ones to which he developed a strong attachment in Lockport. Yet it was only strong after Alice's death. Whether from disinterest, disbelief, or the antebellum divisions that continued to separate Presbyterians, "he did not join the church until after Alice died. As a tribute to her," the church's former minister explained, "he suddenly became an active member." Another church member remembered that William "wasn't interested at all" in the church prior to Alice's death. "I don't think he ever discouraged her in any way, and he'd go along with many of her gifts, but . . . all at once after she was gone, he appeared in church and came very regularly when he was in the city." Indeed, shortly after Alice died, William gave the church a stained glass window in her memory—something she had done in memory of her parents.[15]

By 1960 William depended almost entirely on his Lockport secretary, Schuyler Beattie, a Methodist, to get him to church and everywhere else around town. Although William walked to church and to Western Block during most of the 1950s, the hills between the canal and Uppertown eventually proved too much of a strain. "He was not as alert as, of course, he had been earlier in his life," Rev. Westhafer noted. "He required a good bit of supervision. Mr. Beattie went over every Sunday morning to pick him up to take him to church. Mr. Kenan's question always was, 'Have you got the dollar?' Every Sunday he put a dollar bill in the offering plate. Of course, Mr. Beattie saw to it that we had a sizable check each June."[16]

Beattie became more than his employer's principal link to the local community. He became the most important person in W. R. Kenan's life. He drove him down to Western Block in the morning, out to Randleigh Farm in the afternoons, and then back to Locust Street for supper. He also made sure that William made it to board meetings of the Marine Midland Bank. Organized in 1856 and known for most of its history as the Niagara County National Bank, the bank was one of Lockport's oldest and most important financial institutions. Alice Kenan and Henry Flagler's kinsman, T. Thorne Flagler, had been among its first elected officers, as had George W. Rogers, whose house formed the foundation of William's—its walls now a part of 433 Locust Street. Since 1949, however, the chairman of the board of this local institution had been a native-born southerner, William Rand Kenan Jr., who "used the bank board meeting as an opportunity to catch a few Z's. He would drop off to sleep as soon as he called the meeting to order. When the meeting was over Douglas Patterson, a bank director who always sat on WRK's right, would say in a loud voice, 'Very good meeting, Mr. Kenan.' Those words served to arouse WRK from his slumber."[17]

The only woman Kenan was seen with after Alice's death was her old friend Pauline Zwicker, a widow who occasionally had more than Sunday dinner with

Schuyler Beattie and his cat, Chan, in the 1950s. Beattie served as Kenan's private secretary in Lockport for almost sixty-five years. (Guila B. Janssen)

him at the Lockport Town and Country Club. According to one observer, William decided on one such occasion, his birthday, to break a long-standing personal practice. He "always limited himself to one bourbon before dinner but at the birthday dinner he decided to have second one even though Pauline strongly advised him against it. He took a couple of sips of bourbon #2 and started to go to sleep, picking up the tablecloth and starting to use it as a blanket. Pauline's quick reaction saved the china and silverware from going all over the country club floor."[18]

If William took in little of what went on at the club and the bank board meetings, he was almost certainly aware, if only fleetingly, of the most exciting development at Western Block in years. In March 1961 the company announced that the "world's first nuclear powered aircraft carrier, the U.S.S. Enterprise, will be equipped with 113 different types of tackle blocks supplied by the Western Block Co."[19] The contract marked a watershed of sorts in the history of the company. Western Block was once again benefiting from war—hot and cold alike—but its long relationship with increased profits and government contracts steadily declined thereafter. Although the factory operated for almost twenty years after the death of its president and major stockholder, W. R. Kenan Jr., and for almost eight years after the death of its secretary, Beattie, the "effects of an industrial recession" forced the company to close its doors in March 1985, "resulting in the loss of 72 jobs."[20]

Beattie made his greatest contribution to Kenan at Randleigh Farm, where the watershed years came much sooner than at Western Block. The changes began in 1953 when the farm's manager-superintendent, T. E. Grow, decided to retire. According to Grow's son, Kenan was "extremely upset" when the elder Grow announced "he was going to retire and move to Florida. . . . Never having retired himself, he [Kenan] just couldn't see why anybody else would want to retire, particularly at the youthful age of 65." Kenan tried to change Grow's mind, but "TEG was naturally stubborn and refused. Thus a long, productive and friendly relationship ended in bitterness on both sides."[21]

Grow's departure forced Beattie to do more at the farm. He not only assumed the superintendent's correspondence, but he also began supervising the farm's record keeping, a duty previously performed by the herdsman, Frank Stedman, who now became Grow's replacement. At the same time Beattie also began dealing with William's pasteurization problems and helping A. R. Mac-Mannis with Kenan's fight against the Internal Revenue Service. The IRS still wanted to prove that William made his living from Randleigh Farm, but he still paid for his ice cream cones and dairy products. He also ignored a new state law requiring the pasteurization of all raw milk. "It really crushed him when they had to pasteurize milk," one employee recalled. "In fact, he didn't, you know, for quite awhile. He would just let it slide—that he didn't know anything about it." In truth, William left it up to Beattie and Stedman to see that the farm complied with the law.[22]

Beattie also assumed Grow's responsibilities for organizing Randleigh's annual scientific conferences. Kenan still enjoyed the meetings, and he still contributed $1–2 thousand a year to Ohio State University; but that was about all he did. He could no longer assist in the research himself, and he could no longer grasp the significance of most of the experiments he funded—such as "Cis-Trans Isomerism and Photoisomerization of Some Carotenoids" and "A Study by Electrophoresis and Microbiological Tryptophan Assay on Biochemical Changes in Induced Casein from Skim Milk Inoculated with Certain Lacto-bacteriaceae."[23] Though Beattie knew even less than Kenan about the meaning and significance of this research, he had been working with the scientists and their publications for quite some time. As he did with every edition of *Incidents*, Beattie helped Kenan organize and compile every edition of the *History of Randleigh Farm.*[24]

By 1958 Kenan may not have been tired of his books and conferences, but Beattie, then eighty, almost certainly was. In September 1958, shortly after the fifth and final edition of *Incidents* appeared, Randleigh Farm hosted its twenty-fifth and, apparently, final science conference. The guests included representatives from the University of Rochester; Cornell University; Inorganic Bioelements, Inc., of Cleveland, Ohio; and North Carolina State College in Raleigh. Most of the guests came from Ohio State University, however, which honored Kenan with a plaque "In recognition of 25 years of loyal support through gifts to The Ohio State University Development Fund which has permitted a continuous research program to be conducted at The Ohio State University in Bacteriology and Biochemistry." Not long after the conference, the ninth and final edition of the *History of Randleigh Farm* was published by the Record Company of St. Augustine.[25]

If Beattie welcomed an end to the books and conferences, he also wanted to see Kenan honored by the city and people of Lockport. Florida had recognized Kenan's contributions, UNC had given him its highest honor, and so had the AJCC. Wilmington had placed a plaque on his fountain, the University of Buffalo had presented him with a citation for distinguished public service, and now Ohio State University had recognized his contributions to its research programs. But the city and the people of Lockport had done nothing to recognize Kenan. Beattie's daughter recalled her father's disappointment. "I know my father felt that Lockport did not appreciate what Mr. Kenan wanted to do for them, because he always wanted to see some response. He wanted to see that they appreciated what he was doing, and frankly, I think he misjudged the community. Lockport wasn't that kind of a community, to appreciate what he was able and willing to do. So I think my father appreciated that aspect of Mr. Kenan and understood maybe that Lockport would not appreciate it much."[26]

Both Beattie and Kenan felt particularly offended, it seems, by the city's response to an extremely generous offer from William. According to one source, Kenan made the offer in the early 1950s, when the site for a new senior high school was being hotly debated. The most popular site, at least to the wealthy, Republican Protestants of Uppertown, was just up the street from William's house, on the corner of Locust Street and Lincoln Avenue. But this was not the first choice of the working-class Democrats who lived in the ethnic enclaves of Lowertown, and the city's voters defeated several referenda on the matter. Then William allegedly offered the city "the money for that school if they had named it the William Rand Kenan Jr. High School. And they turned him down."[27] They did build the Lockport Senior High school on Lincoln Avenue, however, and its students were the ones Kenan watched from his window.

That the city rejected Kenan's offer is not surprising. He was part of the old and very divisive social and geographical realities of Lockport. "The Erie Barge Canal—I've always called it the Berlin Wall," one resident recently complained.[28] The canal created and symbolized the mental and physical realities dividing the people in Uppertown and Lowertown, and Kenan was no exception. He lived on the highest hill in Uppertown, and he was Lockport's wealthiest citizen. Though Kenan was largely apolitical by experience and choice, many of his friends, especially Beattie, had always been dedicated, active Republicans. In truth, Beattie's long and intimate association with the party helps account for the divided city's failure to honor Kenan—a fact that undoubtedly helps explain Beattie's own disappointment. Indeed, in 1955, the year Lockport Senior High School opened on Lincoln Street, Beattie's old Democratic and Masonic nemesis, Frank J. Moyer Jr., again became mayor of the city—some thirty years after he had removed Alice Kenan from the hospital board.

Yet Kenan himself failed to win the affection and appreciation of the local population. Though he had worked and lived in the city since 1900, he had never been *of* Lockport, and to a large extent his Locust Street property set him apart from everyone else in the city. It had more in common with Liberty Hall than with the urban realities that surrounded it. And there can be little doubt that Kenan wanted it that way, that he tried to re-create in Lockport his idealized memories of Liberty Hall.

Kenan devoted most of his twenty-five urban acres to one aspect of the old plantation's goal of self-sufficiency: foodstuffs. He provided dairy products to the lone servant who lived "in the yard," tended crops in the fields, raised and roasted turkeys and chickens, collected eggs, and harvested the fruit from the orchard out back—a setup that Kenan often recalled from Liberty Hall. "And of course, this was a farm," one neighbor stressed. "This they used as a farm. I can remember hearing the chickens crowing." Also, another friend recalled, Kenan "would not buy any meat that was not produced on the farm and all of these [house] employees tired of eating turkey. The housekeeper bought lamb chops, at her own expense."[29]

Kenan made his last and most obvious effort to re-create Liberty Hall at Locust Street in 1963. He offered to build his church a new structure, Kenan Memorial Church, on the Bishop property "north and adjacent to my place." His grandfather had done something similar in 1856 by donating land adjacent to Liberty Hall for the site of the new Grove Presbyterian Church in Kenansville. Apparently William also wanted a church on his property. Dr. James Westhafer had just arrived as the church's senior minister, the old church needed work inside and out, and, Westhafer noted, the site offered by Kenan "would be in some sense a better location in terms of the affluent personnel of the community." Yet the minister "discouraged" accepting the offer "because that would be a poor stewardship. . . . It would have evoked a great deal of criticism and disturbance," especially over the question of "the old church that had a lot of history, built in 1858."[30]

By the early 1960s much of Kenan's urban plantation resembled the grounds and boarded-up big house at Liberty Hall. Though 433 still looked good on the outside, the old Bishop house, next door, did not. Kenan had done nothing with it since buying it in 1939; "vandalized" and "very much deteriorated," it was "quite a hazard." George Rossman had also become too fat and blind by then to do much as William's gardener and caretaker. "There were a few duck barns but it wasn't being farmed or gardened. The orchard had degenerated." Worst of all, there were no more cereus blooms for Kenan to deliver. "One winter the heat went off and froze the things in the greenhouse, and he never replaced them."[31]

ONE OF AMERICA'S WEALTHIEST FAMILIES

On June 23, 1965, just a month before W. R. Kenan died in his sleep at Locust Street, the *Lockport Union-Sun & Journal* ran a long story, "The Fabulous Fortune of the Kenan Family." The piece covered most of page twenty-one in the newspaper as well as half of page thirty-six, the last page of that day's edition. It included photographs of Dr. William R. Kenan Jr. and Dr. Kenan's Locust Street home, of Mary Lily Flagler, of Jessie and Sarah, of the Flagler wedding party on the porch at Liberty Hall, of Whitehall at Palm Beach, and of Kenan Stadium. Appropriately, the story did not originate with the local press; it consisted mainly of quotes and paraphrases from "a copyrighted story in the Miami Herald, written by Nixon Smiley and released to the Union-Sun and Journal for reprint."

The Lockport paper began its story quoting the prefatory note to the *Miami Herald*'s piece: "Many people have believed that Henry M. Flagler dissipated the fortune he made as John D. Rockefeller's partner in the Standard Oil Co., on the Florida East Coast Railway and other Florida ventures. This is not true, and in the following articles, Nixon Smiley tells how Flagler's heirs have pyramided their inheritance in excess of $300 million." The Lockport story then mentioned Smiley's comments about the modest living of the wealthy Kenans and the fact that Sarah's incompetency had led to the revelation that she was worth between $90 million and $120 million. "Mr. Smiley noted that 'presumably, her brother and sister hold a similar portfolio of investments.' "[32]

The local story went beyond the *Miami Herald*'s, however, in giving a detailed summary of the career of William Rand Kenan Jr.—based, of course, on the Lockport reporter's reading of *Incidents*. Also woven into the local story was an explanation of the Kenan family's connection with Henry Flagler and Flagler's connection with Lockport—that he "was well-known by numerous Lockport area residents" and that he had "two nieces who lived in Lockport, the late Mrs. Eugene Ashley and her sister, the late Mrs. John Arnold." A "few" Lockport residents had even visited the Flaglers at Whitehall, the newspaper noted, and many more had toured the building since its conversion to the Henry Morrison Flagler Museum in 1959 by Mrs. Roger Mook, one of the oilman's three granddaughters, who "set up a non-profit corporation to operate the museum, then paid for having the incongruous 10-story tower behind the mansion dismantled."

Though generally favorable toward Kenan and his family, the local story contained several interesting statements that perhaps reveal something about Lockport's view of him. One comment refers to his financial status at the time he became associated with Western Block: "It is generally known that Dr. Kenan was worth $1 by the time he reached 36 years of age." Whether this was a misprint or a mischievous omission is hard to say, and it is equally unclear just what the newspaper meant in the editor's note that opens the piece: "A story of Dr. Kenan's wealth comes as no surprise to the people of Lockport, however, because they are surrounded by his many philanthropies, all bearing his name." Yet the first "of Dr. Kenan's philanthropies" mentioned by the paper is Randleigh Farm, which "costs him more than $50,000 a year to maintain. For each quart of milk delivered at a customer's home (there is always a waiting list), he has a cost of about $2 for its production."

Only at the end of the story did the newspaper mention Kenan's other local philanthropies. He had made two in the 1920s—Camp Kenan at Barker, New York, and the Kenan-James nursing building at the Lockport Memorial Hospital—and two more since 1963. "His latest Lockport contributions are toward the Kenan Recreation Center to be built by First Presbyterian Church and the Kenan Wing under construction at the Lockport Town and Country Club." In other words, Kenan gave nothing to the city of Lockport itself after the 1920s.

The church's recreation and community centers have come closest to serving the people of Lockport, and Kenan was probably unaware that he had given them. He died before either was realized. In the summer of 1963, shortly after William returned from his last winter in St. Augustine, Schuyler Beattie asked Dr. James Westhafer "if the church would have any use for Mr. Kenan's house. . . . So we said we certainly would be interested. We had a committee, and we proposed to Mr. Kenan the development of the Kenan Community Center, and he seemed favorably disposed. Of course, this decision was not made by him so much as by Mr. MacMannis in New York and Mr. Gray, his advisers." Although several church members considered the proposal too expensive and "spoke against it," the congregation voted to accept both the house and the idea of the center. One can only hope that William knew what was going on when Westhafer asked him to stand in church one Sunday morning and the "congregation gave him an ovation and applause for what he was offering to do."[33]

The church made it clear from the start that it would own the center but that a community board would operate and control the facility. The church's first plan was to build a community center along the lines of the "lighted schoolhouses" established by the Mott Foundation in Flint, Michigan, where there were "more students in the schoolhouses . . . after four o'clock than before four o'clock, with activities for all ages, adult education, recreation." Unfortunately the church "got a cold shoulder from the board of education who are very cost conscious and very conservative."

The church then decided to build a facility the community did not already have: a skating rink that "would cost about $600,000. So we were told by Mr. Kenan that he would, if the church would raise $100,000, he would give the balance, which was $474,000." Kenan's advisers had the cost sharing "figured down to the dollar, very precisely," Westhafer recalled. "Apparently this was his plan of operation with his philanthropies. There had to be some show of interest by the recipients, some responsibility. . . . So the church people with some struggle raised the one hundred thousand dollars."[34]

William died and was buried in Lockport before the Kenan Arena was constructed at the back of his property on Beattie Avenue. The arena served for a time as the church hoped it would, as "a real community center and very active place." But insurance costs eventually made it too expensive to operate, and the skating rink was closed. The church has had more success with William's house at 433 Locust Street, which is known as the Kenan Center. The center is always among the principal points of interest mentioned in Lockport tourist brochures: "The Kenan Center, with its 25-acre campus and gardens, is the heart of Lockport's cultural activities. It includes an elegant 1853 mansion that hosts art exhibits and classes in arts, crafts and literature; a separate sports and recreational arena; an excellent nursery school; an education building; and the Taylor Theatre where the prize-winning Four Seasons Players perform outstanding productions periodically."[35]

Kenan's cows and farm met a different fate. They did not become, as he had always hoped, his greatest legacy to Lockport. In late 1964 he signed a codicil to his will that left them to the University of North Carolina at Chapel Hill with the option of relocating them near North Carolina State University in Raleigh. Plans to sell the farm began almost immediately after Kenan's death in July 1965, and in early 1966 UNC sold Randleigh Farm for $300,000 to Dr. Ralph M. Lewis, a veterinarian who also chaired the Kenan Center Building Committee of Lockport's First Presbyterian Church. Shortly thereafter, with the temperature dipping down around zero, thirty-seven cows and forty-one heifers began their own trip across fortune's tracks, traveling by train to their new home at North Carolina State University. In 1971, with funds from the sale of the farm and a grant from the $2 million Randleigh Foundation created by Kenan's will, the 420-acre William R. Kenan Jr.–Randleigh Farm was dedicated in south-eastern Wake County. Thus the college whose creation had caused so much concern for William's family and friends in the 1880s now benefited from his largess.[36]

William outlived UNC's other major benefactors, John Sprunt Hill and John Motley Morehead, but died several years before his two sisters. Jessie passed away at her home in Wilmington in January 1968 at age ninety-seven, and two months later Sarah, bedridden and under the care of nurses since 1962, died at home at age ninety-two. By then their old winter home, the Ponce de Leon Hotel, had been closed and sold for use as a private college. Known today as Flagler College, its chief benefactors have been Jessie's grandchildren, the late Lawrence Lewis Jr. and his sister, Mary Lily Wiley. By 1968, moreover, the remaining Flagler System properties had been reorganized by Lawrence Lewis Jr. and Frank and James G. Kenan into the Flagler System, Inc., which still owns and controls the only surviving Flagler System property, the Breakers Hotel.

About $95 million of W. R. Kenan's $161 million estate went into the William R. Kenan, Jr. Charitable Trust, which is now housed in the Kenan Center on the UNC campus in Chapel Hill. Evolving over time in both its mission and its methods, the trust began by establishing William R. Kenan Jr. professorships at well-known institutions of higher education. By 1991 it had endowed ninety-two chairs at fifty-six universities and colleges. Yet UNC and its Kenan-Flagler School of Business will continue to be the major beneficiaries of the trust's primary focus on contributing to education in the United States.[37]

The trust has also supported a variety of other projects and funds over the years, from restoring Liberty Hall to funding family literacy centers and making challenge grants to secondary schools. Since 1966 it has distributed grants exceeding $219 million from the annual incomes produced by its assets, which in 1991 totaled approximately $250 million. With recent grant commitments of $20 million to each of two new independent funds in North Carolina—the William R. Kenan, Jr. Fund for the Arts and the William R. Kenan, Jr. Fund for Engineering, Technology and Science—the William R. Kenan, Jr. Charitable Trust will continue to reinforce the strength of North Carolina's modern power triangle of government, business, and universities.

Kenan would approve of this record, one assumes, and of the trust that bears his name. Yet he would also disagree with much that appears in this trust-funded story of his life, particularly the suspicion that there would be no Kenan trust and no Kenan biography without the Flagler fortune. His protests would not be difficult to accept. Even if he had never met Henry Flagler, William Rand Kenan Jr. would almost certainly have made a noteworthy journey on his own.

NOTES

BHNC   Ashe, Samuel A., series ed. *Biographical History of North Carolina: From Colonial Times to the Present.* 8 vols. Greensboro, N.C.: Van Noppen, 1905–17.

CR   Chancellor's Records, University Archives, University of North Carolina, Chapel Hill

DAB   Malone, Dumas, ed. *Dictionary of American Biography.* 10 vols. New York: Charles Scribner's Sons, 1936.

DB   Deed Book

DNCB   Powell, William S., ed. *Dictionary of North Carolina Biography.* 5 vols. Chapel Hill: University of North Carolina Press, 1979–92.

DUMD   Duke University Manuscript Department, Durham, N.C.

FLb   Henry Morrison Flagler Letterbook. This abbreviation is followed, where possible, by the number of the letterbook being cited. A few of the letterbooks are unnumbered.

HMFM   Henry Morrison Flagler Museum, Palm Beach, Fla.

Incidents   Kenan, William Rand, Jr. *Incidents by the Way.* Privately printed. St. Augustine, Fla.: Record Co. Kenan wrote, compiled, and published five different editions of this, his autobiography. The *Incidents* abbreviation is followed by the number of the edition being referred to.

KC   Klotzbach Collection, Lewiston, N.Y. This private collection of documents, letterbooks, pamphlets, and photographs related to the history of Union Carbide is in the possession of Robert J. Klotzbach of Lewiston, N.Y. According to Klotzbach, a former Carbide employee who has long been interested in the company's history, he asked for and was given these documents shortly before they were to be destroyed as part of the general weeding-out process that attended the transfer of records from the company's local office.

Kenan, History	Kenan, William Rand, Jr., *History of Randleigh Farm.* Privately printed. St. Augustine, Fla.: Record Co. Kenan published nine different editions of his *History.* The abbreviation is followed by the number of the edition.
KLb	Kenan Letterbook, Klotzbach Collection, Lewiston, N.Y.
KLF-OKL	Kettering Laboratory Files, Olive Kettering Library, Antioch College, Yellow Springs, Ohio
LBL	Lawrence Berkeley Laboratory, University of California, Berkeley
LbLSCC	Letterbook of the Lake Superior Carbide Company, Klotzbach Collection, Lewiston, N.Y.
LWL Scrapbook	Louise Wise Louis Scrapbook, Richmond, Va. This scrapbook is in the private collection of the Lewis family in Richmond, Va.It consists mainly of invitations, telegrams, and newspaper and magazine clippings.
M&BBF	Mary and Barry Bingham Fund, Louisville, Ky.
M&CPP	Mildred and Claude Pepper Papers, Florida State University, Tallahassee
MC-ECU	Manuscript Collection, East Carolina University, Greenville, N.C.
MD-FC	Manuscript Department, Filson Club, Louisville, Ky.
MLKFB Will	Mary Lily Kenan Flagler Bingham Will, Duplin County Courthouse, Kenansville, N.C. Copies of Mary Lily's 1916 will can be found in many different places, including the Kenan Family Papers in the Southern Historical Collection and the University Archives, both at the University of North Carolina, Chapel Hill. This abbreviation, however, refers to a document filed in the Duplin County Courthouse in May 1920. This thirty-two-page document is dated March 14, 1918, and is titled "Certified Copy of Last Will and Testament With Codicils There To of Mary Lily (Flagler) Bingham Deceased and Probate Proceedings Thereon in the Jefferson County Court of Kentucky." As the title suggests, this document includes copies of other documents presented for probate in Louisville, Ky., in September 1917.
NCAB	*National Cyclopedia of American Biography.* 64 vols. New York: White, 1891–1984.
NCC	North Carolina Collection, University of North Carolina, Chapel Hill
NCDAH	North Carolina Division of Archives and History, Raleigh, N.C.
NCHR	*North Carolina Historical Review*

NgCHS   Niagara County Historical Society, Lockport, N.Y.
OCR   Orange County Records, Orange County Courthouse,
                Hillsborough, N.C.
POR   President's Office Records, University Archives, University of
                North Carolina, Chapel Hill
SHC   Southern Historical Collection, University of North Carolina,
                Chapel Hill
SM, ICC-FEC Stenographer's Minutes, Interstate Commerce Commission–
   Hearings   Florida East Coast Railway Hearings. The ICC began
                bankruptcy hearings on the FEC in March 1941. Some thirty
                boxes of stenographer's minutes of these and related hearings,
                as well as other published and unpublished documents
                regarding the case (which went on until the late 1950s), are in
                the author's possession. They are part of the huge Atlantic
                Coast Line Railroad Collection donated by the CSX
                Corporation to the Southern Historical Collection in 1991.
StAHS   St. Augustine Historical Society, St. Augustine, Fla.
Transcript   Transcript of Record, Court of Appeals of Kentucky, Louisville
   of Record   Trust Company, etc., Appellant, *versus* Robert W. Bingham
                and William R. Kenan and William A. Blount, Trustees,
                Appellees, November 1917.
TWP-NAC   Thomas Willson Papers, National Archives of Canada, Ottawa,
                Ontario, Canada
UA   University Archives, University of North Carolina, Chapel Hill

CHAPTER ONE

1. *Incidents* 1:19.

2. Outlaw, *Official Directory*, 4–15; McGowen and McGowen, *Flashes*, 180–83; De Van Massey, "British Expedition," 403. The best source of Kenan family genealogy is Register, *Kenan Family*. Except where otherwise noted, the following discussion is based on the sources mentioned in this note.

3. In addition to the sources mentioned in the previous note, see correspondence in the Kenan Family Papers, SHC.

4. Powell, *Four Centuries*, 286–87. For information on Sarah Graham and the Graham family, see Kenan Family Papers, SHC, and Sadler, "Dr. Stephen Graham's Narration," 359–67. Documents in the Kenan Family Papers suggest that Owen acted as legal guardian for Sarah and for one, if not both, of her brothers. The Wilmington and Weldon was chartered (as the Wilmington and Raleigh Railroad) during Owen's tenure in the state legislature and was built through Duplin in the late 1830s.

5. For a list of the slaves who worked on Lockland and the Graham plantations, see Kenan Family Papers, SHC.

6. *BHNC*, 3:253–57.

7. Ibid.; Orange County Estates, "Hargrave Estate, 1866–1869," NCDAH; *Smaw's Wilmington Directory*, 103. According to one source, William H. McCrary, who died in 1882, "was very successful in his business undertakings and during the years of his active business life amassed a large fortune by his prudence, energy and foresight." See McCrady and Ashe, *Cyclopedia of Eminent and Representative Men*, 2:519–20.

8. North Carolina, New Hanover County, 18:108, in R. G. Dun & Co. Collection, Harvard University.

9. North Carolina, Duplin County, 8:414 c/6, in ibid.

10. Unidentified, undated newspaper clipping, Thomas S. Kenan Scrapbook, NCC (quotation); *BHNC*, 3:247–52.

11. Register, *Kenan Family*, 21, 30–35.

12. Quoted in McGowen and McGowen, *Flashes*, 258.

13. Except where otherwise noted, all quotations are from *Incidents* 1.

14. Quoted in *Incidents* 3:80.

15. *Incidents* 1:18.

16. Green, *Fit for America*, 183.

17. *Wilmington Star*, April 23, 26, May 1, 1872.

18. Ibid., July 28, 1872.

19. Evans, *Ballots and Fence Rails*, 166–67.

20. John Lyon Holmes to S. A. Ashe, April 26, 1872, Samuel A. Ashe Papers, NCDAH.

21. A. M. Waddell to S. A. Ashe, March 13, 1872, in ibid.

22. Evans, *Ballots and Fence Rails*, 188–92; John Lyon Holmes to S. A. Ashe, April 26, 1872, Ashe Papers, NCDAH (quotation). Holmes was Buck Kenan's third cousin. See Register, *Kenan Family*, 130.

23. *Wilmington Star*, October 15, 1872.

24. Adelaide Savage Meares Notebook, 37, Meares Papers, DUMD; Evans, *Ballots and Fence Rails*, 188–92.

25. Watson, *Wilmington*, 106.

26. Wilmington's third railroad company was the Wilmington, Charlotte and Rutherford.

27. Prince, *Atlantic Coast Line*, 105. Except where otherwise noted, the following discussion is based on chaps. 1, 2, and 3 of Hoffman, "History of the ACL."

28. Dozier, *History of the Atlantic Coast Line*, 122–25; *Incidents* 2:14; "Special Edition" of the Wallace *Enterprise*, n.d. [ca. September 1968], in the Katie Murray Papers, Special Collections Department, Wake Forest University, Winston-Salem, N.C.

29. W. T. Hildrup to Owen Rand Kenan, July 26, 1872, Kenan Family Papers, SHC; *NCAB*, 27:216.

30. *DAB*, 19:399–401; Kernan, "William and Henry Walters," 102–12.

31. *Incidents* 1:41–42.

32. Akin, *Flagler*, 42.

33. *Wilmington Star*, May 11, 1872; Foster, *Ghosts of the Confederacy*, 36–62; Cashman, *Cape Fear Adventure*, 75.

34. *Wilmington Star*, May 8, 1872.

35. Ibid.

36. C. S. Wooten, "Col. Thos. S. Kenan—A Sketch," *Charlotte Observer*, June 11, 1905.

37. Eric Anderson, *Race and Politics*, 10; Evans, *Ballots and Fence Rails*, 102.

38. North Carolina Officers' Committee to Vance, March 30, 1864, Thomas S. Kenan Papers, NCDAH; *DNCB*, 2:361–62.

39. T. J. Bostic to Frank Hall, July 11, 1881, Hall Family Papers, DUMD; *DNCB*, 2:362; *BHNC*, 3:249–52, 4:477–94; *Confederate Veteran*, May 1898, 229; June 1898, 246; April 1902, 153–54; March 1911, 106; Yancey, "Soul Train," 21.

40. Daniels, *Tar Heel Editor*, 175–76.

41. Ibid., 168–69 (quotation); Eric Anderson, *Race and Politics*, 36–38; C. S. Wooten, "Col. Thos. S. Kenan—A Sketch," *Charlotte Observer*, June 11, 1905; *DNCB*, 2:362.

42. *Wilmington Star*, July 28, 31, November 2, 1872.

43. Eric Anderson, *Race and Politics*, 38–39.

44. *Wilmington Star*, October 2, 1872; Evans, *Ballots and Fence Rails*, 114–16.

45. For the best description of Bradley and the Tileston School, see Cashman, "Yankee Transplant." Except where otherwise noted, the quotes and summary that follow are from this source. Account books documenting the cost and tenure of the Kenan children at Tileston can be found in the Amy Morris Bradley Papers, DUMD.

46. Miss Emily M. Coe, quoted in the *Tileston Recorder*, January 1884, Bradley Papers, DUMD.

47. *The* [Tileston] *Lighthouse*, October 1882, Bradley Papers, DUMD.

48. Ibid. The "poor" and "paid" designations appear in the Tileston account books in the Bradley Papers, DUMD.

49. Cashman, "Yankee Transplant," 12–13.

50. Escott, *Many Excellent People*, 164–65.

51. *Wilmington Star*, November 10, 1872. Byrne acted as an agent for both the New York Life Insurance Company and the Imperial Fire Insurance Company of London.

52. The formation of Wooten Richardson & Company is mentioned in ibid., December 22, 1872, and Buck's affiliation with the company is noted in his obituary in ibid., April 15, 1903. For the Hargrave real estate transactions, see DB 41:360, 537–38, DB 44:229, 321, 335–36, 344, DB 46:194–96, OCR. Mollie's brothers sold separately as individuals the specific landholdings they had inherited from their father, mother, and uncle. But they almost certainly maintained the practice they had followed since the 1850s of sharing the proceeds from the sale of these lands (and other inherited assets) with one another and with Mollie. See Orange County Estates, "Challenge to Hargrave Estate, 1856–1857" and "Hargrave Estate, 1866–1869," NCDAH. For the attempts to resuscitate the university between 1872 and

1873, see Battle, *History of UNC,* 2:43–50, and Brabham, "Defining the American University," 427–55.

53. Evans, *Ballots and Fence Rails,* 191–92; Watson, *Wilmington,* 116.

54. Hoffman, "History of the ACL," chap. 2, p. 7.

55. Gaston, *New South Creed,* 17–32.

56. *Wilson Institute Quarterly,* July 8, 1873.

57. Brabham, "Defining the American University," 448–49; *BHNC,* 6:84.

58. Brabham, "Defining the American University," 449–50.

59. Vickers, *Chapel Hill,* 18, 22–23, 34 (quotations), 35. According to Vickers, the 221-acre "Old Chapel Tract" donated by Christopher Barbee "now includes Polk Place, much of McCorkle Place, the area north to Cobb Terrace, and land west along Cameron Avenue."

60. Ibid.

61. North Carolina, Orange County, 19:225, in R. G. Dun & Co. Collection, Harvard University; Jesse Hargrave Will, June 2, 1854, OCR.

62. Robert Bingham to Edward Kidder Graham, October 6, 1915, and Bingham to Graham, n.d. [1917] (quotation), both in CR, House Series.

63. Vickers, *Chapel Hill,* 65.

64. Brabham, "Defining the American University," 429.

65. Vickers, *Chapel Hill,* 65; Orange County Estates, "Hargrave Estate, 1866–1869," NCDAH.

66. David and Mary McCauley to William R. Kenan, December 1, 1875 [recognizing 1871 transaction], DB 44:229; William R. Kenan to David and Mary McCauley, January 24, 1876, DB 44:321; David McCauley and Mary McCauley to William R. and Mary Hargrave Kenan, January 26, 1876, DB 44:335, all in OCR; Orange County Estates, "Challenge to Hargrave Estate, 1856–1857" and "Hargrave Estate, 1866–1869," NCDAH; Willis Barbee Will, May 13, 1869, OCR; Vickers, *Chapel Hill,* 61, 78–83, 109–10; Shields et al., *Study of the Barbee Families,* 54; Long, *Son of Carolina,* 1–15. The hotel took its name from its owner, Hugh Guthrie, one of Chapel Hill's most despised Republican officials and the husband of Jane Cave, Mollie Kenan's cousin. Guthrie purchased the hotel in 1853 from Nancy Segur Hilliard, the town's most beloved innkeeper, who called it the "Eagle Hotel."

67. Carosso, *The Morgans,* 180–81.

68. Hoffman, "History of the ACL," chap. 2, pp. 18–20, and chap. 3, p. 1; W. T. Hildrup to O. R. Kenan, June 6, 1873; J. W. Ellis to Messrs. W. S. & D. J. Devane, August 22, 1874; W. S. & D. J. Devane to O. R. Kenan, October 22, 1874; and E. K. Hines to O. R. Kenan, May 12, 1877, all in Kenan Family Papers, SHC.

69. *Incidents* 1:12.

70. Ibid., 25.

71. Ibid.

72. W. R. Kenan to David McCauley, January 24, 1876, DB 44:321, OCR.

73. Robert W. and Mollie Hargrave to Mollie Kenan, February 12, 1876, DB 44:344–45, OCR.

74. *Wilmington Star*, August 11, 1876 (emphasis in original). For Buck's bad-check case, see *Bank of New Hanover v. Kenan*, in *North Carolina Reports*, 340–46.

75. *BHNC*, 3:249–52.

76. Thomas S. Kenan to Gov. Vance, November 8, 1876, in McKinney and McMurry, *Papers of Zebulon Vance*, reel 1.

77. Powell, *Four Centuries*, 404–5.

CHAPTER TWO

1. North Carolina, New Hanover County, 18:241, in R. G. Dun & Co. Collection, Harvard University (quotation); Sheriff, *Sheriff's Wilmington*, 66, 78, 96; Reilly, *Past, Present, and Future*, 109.

2. *Incidents* 1:12.

3. *Laws and Resolutions of the State of North Carolina*, 230–37. The board consisted of five men, one from each ward in the city, appointed by the governor to two-year terms.

4. The 1884 mortgage is mentioned in National Bank of Wilmington to W. R. Kenan, April 3, 1886, DB 49:116, OCR.

5. Reilly, *Past, Present, and Future*, 109.

6. See Chapter 1, above, for a discussion of Buck and Mollie's tenure as owners of the Chapel Hill boardinghouse. Robinson to Kenan, September 9, 1892, DB 51:301, OCR, does not mention the boardinghouse; it records Mollie's repayment of the mortgage on the Chapel Hill town lots. But this indenture coincided with the sale of the boardinghouse and almost certainly reflects Mollie's use of a portion of the proceeds from that sale to pay off the mortgage on the lots.

7. "Account Book, Wilmington Mission & Tileston Normal School, 1866–1895," 122–26; "Record Book & Scrap Book: Tileston Normal School, 1882–1891," 14; and *Tileston Recorder*, January 1884 (quotation), all in Bradley Papers, DUMD.

8. For more than a century, Masonry had been as important as both the Presbyterian church and military matters in defining the social identity of the Kenan men. Buck's great-grandfather General James Kenan was a founder and ruling elder of the Presbyterian church in Duplin County and the founder and first master of St. John's Masonic Lodge No. 13 in Duplin. Buck's grandfather, father, and brothers all followed this tradition, as did Buck himself. See McGowen and McGowen, *Flashes*, 169–70. Buck and several other Masons eventually demitted from the old Wilmington Lodge and formed a new one. See *Orient Lodge No. 395, AF&AM*, pamphlet, Lower Cape Fear Historical Society, Wilmington, N.C.

9. *BHNC*, 3:251–57; *Orient Lodge No. 395*.

10. "Hank" the milkman recollections; Westhafer interview.

11. *Incidents* 1:27.

12. Ibid.

13. For reports of the murder, see *Wilmington Star*, December 18–25, 1886, January 14, 15, 16, 21, and February 12, 1887. Bingham's support for the college is

noted in Lockmiller, "The Establishment," 284, and mentioned in Yancey, "Spare the Rod," 24.

14. Lockmiller, "The Establishment"; John H. Cooper, *Walter Hines Page*, 66–81.

15. Eric Anderson, *Race and Politics*, 96. In August 1881 North Carolina voters overwhelmingly defeated a popular referendum on a law that, in addition to prohibiting the manufacture of all liquors except wine and hard cider, would also have prevented the sale of intoxicating beverages except by druggists or physicians licensed to sell the same. The defeat of the referendum reinvigorated the temperance forces, which in 1882 and again in 1884 put forward candidates for state office who favored Prohibition. See Lefler and Newsome, *North Carolina*, 544–45.

16. "Notes from Mr. Guion's Address," n.d., Kenan Family Papers, SHC; *Incidents* 1:22, 2:14.

17. *Fifth Annual Catalogue of Wilson College*, 5–6; Daniels, *Tar Heel Editor*, 191–92 (quotation). The author would like to thank Virginia Pou Doughton for the reference to the Wilson College catalog.

18. Daniels, *Tar Heel Editor*, 192.

19. BHNC, 2:120–25; DNCB, 2:362; *Raleigh Observer*, November 27, 1884.

20. *Raleigh Observer*, November 27, 1884 (quotation), December 13, 1955; NCAB, 32:178; DNCB, 2:65–66, 3:324–25; Reilly, *Past, Present, and Future*, 81; "Comments of Mrs. Fussell of Landfall"; New Hanover County, Wills and Estate Records, Platt K. Dickinson and Ann H. Dickinson, NCDAH; Wharton Jackson Green to Lucy Polk, December 12, 1881, and Green to Polk, February 19, 1882, Lucy Williams Polk Papers, NCDAH; Conte, *History of the Greenbrier*. Jones was president of Carolina Rice Mills, Wilmington's largest rice-milling company, which also had offices in New Orleans. He was related to the Kenans through his aunt and female guardian, Anne Dickinson, whose sister, Sally, was the wife of Buck's Wilmington cousin, John Lyon Holmes.

21. *Raleigh Observer*, November 27, 1884.

22. James Sprunt to H. Walters, February 18, 1895, Sprunt Papers, DUMD; Tony P. Wrenn, *Architectural and Historical Portrait*, 53–55.

23. Hoffman, "History of the ACL," chap. 5; Sister Bridget Marie Englemeyer, letter to William Johnston, February 4, 1990, Walters Art Gallery, Baltimore, Md.

24. Hoffman, "History of the ACL," chaps. 4 and 5; Akin, *Flagler*, 8–10, 113–18.

25. Lynette B. Wrenn, "Cottonseed Price-Fixing," 411–37; BHNC, 1:167–70; Hoffman, "History of the ACL," chaps. 3–6; *Wilmington Star*, December 22, 1887, January 6, 1888; W. H. Beardsley to E. E. Eagan (Asheville Ice & Coal Co., Asheville, N.C.), July 8, 1890; H. M. Flagler to Norwood Giles (Carolina Rice Milling Co., Wilmington, N.C.), September 17, 1890; Flagler to Judge A. C. Haskell (Loan & Exchange Bank, Columbia, S.C.), October 1, 1890, FLb 53; Flagler to Mess. Hallgarten & Co. (New York), October 6, 1890, FLb 56; Flagler to Pem Jones, November 26, 1890, FLb 58, HMFM.

26. Henry Flagler later made it possible for Buck Kenan to join Hansen in forming the Spiritine Chemical Company, the creosoting company's corporate

successor. See *Carolina Oil and Creosote Company;* Evans, *Ballots and Fence Rails,* 201–3; Tony P. Wrenn, *Architectural and Historical Portrait,* 258–62; *Wilmington Review,* June 6, 1887; Reilly, *Past, Present, and Future,* 112; *Facts about the Spiritine Chemical Company; Wilmington Messenger,* September 5, 1894; W. R. Kenan Sr. to J. R. Parrott, May 17, 18, 1900, Florida East Coast Railway Collection, StAHS; *Wilmington Dispatch,* May 16, June 20, 1900; *Wilmington Star,* May 26, 1900; *Wilmington, the Metropolis,* 60. Walters also backed the formation of the Wilmington Savings and Trust Company, whose directors included Pem Jones, several local Democrats, and George French Jr., a member of one of Wilmington's leading Republican families.

27. Akin, *Flagler,* 91–128.

28. Ibid.

29. The author would like to thank Dr. Robert Fales of Wilmington, N.C., for this information, which is based on traditional oral accounts of the Jones-Kenan relationship and which Fales repeated in a conversation with the author at the New Hanover County Library, Wilmington, N.C., on August 16, 1989. While the only hostesses Fales mentioned by name were Mary Lily and Jessie Kenan, the names of Sadie's other young hostesses appear in one or more sources referring specifically to the Joneses between 1884 and 1892. See *Raleigh Observer,* November 27, 1884; McKoy, *Early Years of the Cape Fear River,* 255–56; Henry M. Flagler to Pem [Jones], July 14, 1890, FLb 53, HMFM; *Wilmington Messenger,* August 17, 1892.

30. *Wilmington Star,* January 4, 1888.

31. That Flagler was in the audience for one of Mary Lily's two performances is suggested by Edward A. Oldham in his newspaper column, "North Carolina in New York," *Winston-Salem Sentinel,* 1937.

32. *Wilmington Star,* December 24, 29, 31, 1887.

33. Ibid., January 10, 1888.

34. Evans, *Ballots and Fence Rails,* 201–3; H. M. Flagler to William Kennish (Kenan?), October 3, 1890, FLb 56, HMFM. See Hugh MacRae Papers, DUMD, for correspondence related to the MacRae's landholdings in Florida and Fernandina. Donald MacRae was vice-president of the Navassa Guano Company, an important local stockholder of the Wilmington and Weldon Railroad, and close friends with the Walters family. See, for example, Donald MacRae to Donald MacRae Jr., November 10, 1881, MacRae Papers, DUMD.

35. For the origins of this controversy, see L. L. Polk to Gov. Z. B. Vance, April 18, 1877; Vance to Thomas S. Kenan, April 19, 1877; Vance to Col. John Ott, August 23, 1877; Vance to Barbee & Latta, January 24, 1878, reel 14; Barbee & Latta to Vance, January 24, 1878; Polk to Vance, March 8, 1878; K. P. Battle to Vance, February 8, 1878; Polk to Vance, March 27, 1878; Vance to Thomas S. Kenan, March 28, 1878, reel 28, all in McKinney and McMurry, *Papers of Zebulon Vance.* See also Battle, *History of UNC,* 2:121–23, 136–39, for the connection between the reopening of UNC, use of the Land Grant Fund, the Agricultural Experimental Station at UNC, and the controversy with Polk and others concerning the station and fertilizer taxes. For Polk's resignation as commissioner of agriculture, see Daniels, *Tar Heel Editor,* 296.

36. Lefler and Newsome, *North Carolina*, 542.

37. Several alliance agents arrived in North Carolina from Texas in 1887, and in the fall of that year a state farmers' alliance was formed and quickly absorbed Polk's organization. Known commonly as the Southern Alliance, this secret, non-political organization had originated in Texas in the 1870s with the goal of ending rural depression. See Bromberg, " 'Worst Muddle,' " 20.

38. Hoffman, "History of the ACL," chaps. 4–6; Hunt, "Making of a Southern Populist," part 1, p. 75 n.

39. Hoffman, "History of the ACL," chap. 6, p. 7. For Thomas Kenan's earlier ruling, see "Amendment to Railroad Charter—Effect of—Opinion of Attorney General," document 31, *North Carolina Executive and Legislative Documents.*

40. Lefler and Newsome, *North Carolina*, 544–46; Hunt, "Making of a Southern Populist," part 1, p. 72; Bromberg, " 'Worst Muddle,' " 20; Escott, *Many Excellent People*, 244; Powell, *Four Centuries*, 424.

41. Bromberg, " 'Worst Muddle,' " 20–21.

42. Quoted in ibid., 28.

43. Thomas S. Kenan to Sen. Z. B. Vance, July 9, 1890, in McKinney and McMurry, *Papers of Zebulon Vance*, reel 34.

44. *Branson's Alphabetical Directory of Raleigh*, 169; *Laws and Resolutions of the State of North Carolina*, 683–84.

45. Battle, *History of UNC*, 2:788.

46. Ibid., 459; William H. S. Burgwyn to W. J. Peele, January 9, 1890, and "University of North Carolina, Chapel Hill, July 25, 1890," both in William L. Saunders Papers, DUMD.

47. W. R. Kenan Sr. to Sen. Z. B. Vance, February 1, 1890, in McKinney and McMurry, *Papers of Zebulon Vance*, reel 10.

48. Hoffman, "History of the ACL," chaps. 6 and 7; H. M. Flagler to Henry Walters, December 1, 1890, FLb 58, HMFM.

49. *Incidents* 1:41–42; Daisy Cronly to Mary [?], April 19, 1889, Cronly Family Papers, DUMD; H. M. Flagler to Pem Jones, July 7, 14, 1890, and Flagler to Henry Walters, July 19, 1890 (quotation), FLb 53, HMFM.

CHAPTER THREE

1. Horowitz, *Campus Life*, 5; Battle, *History of UNC*, 2:464, 488, 501.

2. Quoted in Warren Smith Reminiscences, Warren Smith Collection, HMFM. According to Kenan, however, Flagler said that he, Kenan, was eighteen years old when he was born. See *Incidents* 1:66, and Chapter 6 at n. 28, below.

3. *Incidents* 1:27.

4. William Frederick Harding Memoir, MC-ECU, 13.

5. Ibid.

6. *Incidents* 1:28. Room prices are for 1891 as listed in Faculty Journal, August 19, 1891, 244, UA. The $10 rent for rooms in New East is based on the statement that

"students occupying rooms alone in other Building[s] than the South shall pay an additional fee of $5.00 per *term.*" Prices for rooms in South Building are listed on the same page.

7. Harding Memoir, MC-ECU, 13.

8. Ibid., 13–14; *Incidents* 1:29–31.

9. Harding Memoir, MC-ECU, 13.

10. *Incidents* 1:31; Student Records and Faculty Reports, 5 (1882–97): 146, UA.

11. J. L. Gilmer to Pat [Patterson], September 21, 1890, Patterson Family Papers, NCDAH (emphasis in original).

12. Ibid.

13. Harding Memoir, MC-ECU, 13–14.

14. Ibid., 14.

15. Gilmer to Patterson, September 21, 1890, Patterson Family Papers, NCDAH.

16. Escott, *Many Excellent People*, 245.

17. Harding Memoir, MC-ECU, 15.

18. Ibid.

19. Ibid.

20. *Incidents* 1:31.

21. Battle, *History of UNC*, 2:465.

22. Sumner, "North Carolina Inter-Collegiate Foot-Ball Association," 283.

23. Memorandum, "Raleigh, North Carolina, January 3, 1891," William L. Saunders Papers, DUMD.

24. *Incidents* 1:29–32.

25. Ibid., 12–13.

26. *BHNC*, 3:252.

27. *Incidents* 1:34.

28. Conte, *History of the Greenbrier*, 84.

29. Quoted in ibid.

30. *Incidents* 1:25; Blanche Williamson to Owen Hill Kenan, August 3, 1894, and Annie Kenan to Owen Hill Kenan, October 1, 1894, Kenan Family Papers, SHC; Edmunds, *Blandwood*, 36.

31. Sam Patterson to Mama, February 2, 1890, Patterson Family Papers, NCDAH.

32. Thomas S. Kenan III interviews; *Macon City Directory*, 418; *DNCB*, 3:150.

33. *Wilmington Messenger*, June 16, 1892.

34. Comments on and the specifics of Kenan's performance as a baseball player can be found in spring issues of the weekly student newspaper, the *Tar Heel*, in 1893 and 1894. See ibid., May 11, 1894, for his statistics as a senior.

35. *Incidents* 2:60.

36. *Tar Heel*, April 13, 1894.

37. Ibid.

38. Ibid., March 16, 1893.

39. Ibid., March 23, 1893.

40. Ibid., February 16, 1894.

41. Ibid., February 23, 1894.

42. Ibid., May 4, 1894.

43. Ibid., May 11, 1894.

44. Ibid., December 7, 1893.

45. Harding Memoir, MC-ECU; Tifft and Jones, *The Patriarch*, 30.

46. Harding Memoir, MC-ECU, 16.

47. Battle, *History of UNC*, 2:470. See also Harding Memoir, MC-ECU, 16.

48. Andrew Patterson to Mother, May 25, 1890, Patterson Family Papers, NCDAH.

49. Bursey, *Carolina Chemists*, 76–79; *Wilmington Star*, February 5, 1902; Hugh L. Miller to Robert Worth Bingham, January 26, March 25, 1901, and Purden Smith to Bingham, February 21, 1901, Robert Worth Bingham Papers, MD-FC.

50. Gaston, *New South Creed*, 172–73.

51. Janssen interview, September 21, 1990. Dr. Janssen's father, Schuyler Beattie, was William Rand Kenan Jr.'s private secretary from about 1900 until Kenan's death in 1965.

52. For one explanation of the club's origins, see Cherry, "Gimghouls' Castle," 64–65. The origin of the name is usually attributed to the legend of the alleged seventeenth-century ghostly city of Gimghoul.

53. *Incidents* 1:32.

54. Ibid., 31.

55. See Venable, "The Educational Value of College Athletics," Venable Papers, SHC.

56. *Tar Heel*, February 23, 1893.

57. Ibid., March 30, 1893.

58. Sumner, "North Carolina Inter-Collegiate Foot-Ball Association," 283.

59. *Tar Heel*, May 18, 1893.

60. Ibid., September 25, 1893.

61. W. R. Kenan Jr. to Owen Kenan, March 20, 1894, Kenan Family Papers, SHC.

62. Schlereth, *Victorian America*, 172.

63. Thomas P. Hughes, *Networks of Power*, 122–39.

64. W. R. Kenan Jr. to Owen Kenan, August 24, 1893, Kenan Family Papers, SHC.

65. For a description of the victory celebration, see John Patterson to Mamma, December 1, 1892, Patterson Family Papers, NCDAH.

66. *Tar Heel*, October 12, 1893.

67. *Incidents* 1:31.

68. *Tar Heel*, September 25, 1893.

69. Ibid., October 6, 1893 (first quotation), and November 2, 1893 (second and third quotations).

70. *Incidents* 2:60.

71. *Tar Heel*, November 23, 1893.

72. Ibid. (first and second quotations), and ibid., December 7, 1893 (third quotation).

73. Venable and Clarke, "Some of the Properties of Calcium Carbide," 307. Venable was born in Virginia in 1856. His father, Charles Scott Venable, was an aide-de-camp to General Robert E. Lee during the Civil War, a professor of mathematics at the University of Virginia, and chairman of the faculty there. See Bursey, *Francis Preston Venable*, 1–18.

74. Bursey, *Francis Preston Venable*.

75. Quoted in Midgette, *To Foster the Spirit*, 25.

76. Bursey, *Francis Preston Venable*, 36.

77. Midgette, *To Foster the Spirit*, 30.

78. Bursey, *Francis Preston Venable*, 38; Bursey, *Carolina Chemists*, 76; DNCB, 1:111; *Wilmington Star*, February 5, 1902.

79. Venable to Wife, August 21, 1890, Venable Papers, SHC.

80. *Incidents* 1:138.

81. Venable, "An Account," 875.

82. Ibid.

83. *Incidents* 1:139–40.

84. Quoted in Bursey, *Francis Preston Venable*, 61–62.

85. Evidence of these developments can be found in almost every issue of the *Tar Heel* published in the spring of 1894. See also Powell, *First State University*, 125.

86. *Tar Heel*, April 13, 1894.

87. *Incidents* 2:16–25.

88. *Tar Heel*, May 4, 1894.

89. W. R. Kenan Jr. to Owen Kenan, March 20, 1894, Kenan Family Papers, SHC.

90. T. L. Willson to James T. Morehead, June 4, July 12, 1894, TWP-NAC. See S. Walter Martin, *Florida's Flagler*, 171, for Alice Flagler's mental breakdown.

CHAPTER FOUR

1. Kenan's account can be found in one form or another in each of the five different editions of *Incidents*. His most complete account of the story, however, is in W. R. Kenan Jr. to F. L. Spangler, December 5, 1936, KC. Morehead deals with the early carbide story in his "James Turner Morehead," KC. The chief sources of the Canadian version of the carbide story are Carter, " 'Carbide' Willson," 12–14, and *Thomas "Carbide" Willson*, KC, a pamphlet apparently published by the National Archives of Canada.

2. Robert Cluett to H. G. MacNeill, September 7, 1988, Morehead Foundation, Chapel Hill, N.C.; Cluett interview. Cluett is a descendant of the Morehead family.

3. Except where otherwise noted, information on the Major's activities is taken from "James Turner Morehead," KC.

4. For information on Ledoux, see Battle, *History of UNC*, 2:137, and *NCAB*, 12:449–50. See *NCAB*, 14:193–94, for information on Eimer.

5. *NCAB*, 7:91–92; *DAB*, 9:471.

6. *Thomas "Carbide" Willson*, 3–5, KC; Thomas Willson to Mr. Walker, April 3,

1890, TWP-NAC. Willson's earlier troubles with patent lawyers and creditors can be found in his correspondence between 1888 and 1890 in TWP-NAC.

7. Battle, *History of UNC*, 2:463–64; "James Turner Morehead," 2–3, KC.

8. Battle, *History of UNC*, 1:814; W. R. Kenan Jr. to F. L. Spangler, December 5, 1936, KC (quotation); Edmunds, *Blandwood*, esp. 36.

9. F. P. Venable to Wife, October 23, 1890, Venable Papers, SHC.

10. Thomas Willson to Messrs. Seward and Morehead, November 17, 1890, and Willson to My dear Botsworth, December 7, 1890, TWP-NAC.

11. Thomas Willson to My dear Botsworth, December 7, 1890, TWP-NAC.

12. John Motley Morehead to Andrew Patterson, June 12, 1891, Patterson Family Papers, NCDAH.

13. "James Turner Morehead," 2–3, KC.

14. Thomas Willson to Carpenter Steel Co., June 13, 1893, TWP-NAC; *DAB*, 9:471. Willson purchased four tons of copper for the Willson Aluminum Company in February 1891 while he was still in New York. He used most of it, it seems, in his experiments to find an alloy to make artillery guns both more elastic and stronger than existing iron and steel armaments. See Willson to J. T. Morehead, February 14, 1891, TWP-NAC.

15. *Thomas "Carbide" Willson*, 7, KC.

16. "James Turner Morehead," 3, KC.

17. Carter, " 'Carbide' Willson," 13.

18. "James Turner Morehead," 3, KC.

19. Ibid., 3–4.

20. Ibid., 4.

21. W. R. Kenan Jr. to F. L. Spangler, December 5, 1936, KC.

22. F. P. Venable to Wife [Sallie Venable], June 8, 1892, Venable Papers, SHC.

23. Ibid.

24. F. P. Venable to Wife, June [20?], 1892, Venable Papers, SHC.

25. F. P. Venable to [?], November 12, 1904, in ibid.

26. W. R. Kenan Jr. to F. L. Spangler, December 5, 1936, KC.

27. Lord Kelvin to Thomas Willson, October 3, 1892, TWP-NAC.

28. Venable, "An Account," 875.

29. Ibid. (quotation). Venable did not receive an immediate answer to his letter of February 6, 1893, so he wrote another a week later, which also received no immediate reply. Although neither letter has survived, their content is summarized in J. Turner Morehead to F. P. Venable, February 28, 1893, Venable Papers, SHC.

30. J. Turner Morehead to F. P. Venable, February 28, 1893, Venable Papers, SHC.

31. Thomas Willson to A. N. Fraser & Co., March 14, 1893, TWP-NAC. A copy of the March 16, 1893, patent can be found in the TWP-NAC, along with correspondence describing its importance in establishing claims of precedence in the carbide and acetylene discoveries.

32. Charles Venable to Mother [Mrs. F. P. Venable], August 18, 1937, Venable Papers, SHC.

33. *Incidents* 1:139–40. That the agreement preceded the demonstration is mentioned in Thomas Willson to F. P. Venable, January 13, 1895, Venable Papers, SHC.

34. A handwritten copy of the contract is in the Venable Papers, SHC.

35. "James Turner Morehead," 4, KC.

36. *Tar Heel*, May 11, 1893.

37. Thomas Willson to J. Turner Morehead, April 15, 1893, TWP-NAC.

38. Ibid. (question mark in original). Venable apparently made this statement in a letter addressed to Major Morehead and dated April 14, 1893. See Willson to Venable, April 17, 1893, Venable Papers, SHC.

39. Thomas Willson to J. Turner Morehead, May 4, 1893, TWP-NAC.

40. Ibid.

41. Thomas Willson to Edward N. Dickerson, June 21, 1893, TWP-NAC.

42. Thomas Willson to A. C. Fraser & Co., June 13, 1893, TWP-NAC.

43. Thomas Willson to Adam McCalister, January 14, April 2, 1893; Willson to Edward N. Dickerson, June 13, 21, 1893; Willson to Carpenter Steel Co., June 13, 1893 (quoting Ingersoll's letter of June 4, 1893); R. R. Ingersoll to Willson, November 3, 1893 (second quotation); Willson to Robert M. Thompson, November 8, 1893, all in TWP-NAC.

44. Thomas Willson to A. C. Fraser & Co., May 8, 1893, TWP-NAC.

45. Thomas Willson to A. C. Fraser & Co., June 13, 1893, TWP-NAC.

46. Thomas Willson to F. P. Venable, April 17, June 20, 1893, Venable Papers, SHC.

47. *DAB* 9:471–72.

48. "James Turner Morehead," 4–5, KC. The timing, sequence, and explanation of events presented in this, Mot Morehead's account of his father's activities between 1893 and 1895, is confusing and contradictory. The narrative presented here is based on a combination of this account, Willson's correspondence, and other primary and secondary sources.

49. *NCAB*, 14:193–94, 43:426–27.

50. Thomas Willson to J. Turner Morehead, January 30, 1894, TWP-NAC.

51. "James Turner Morehead," 5, NAC. The Pintsch Company provided gas lighting for railroad cars. See Albro Martin, *Railroads Triumphant*, 89.

52. Thomas Willson to J. Turner Morehead, January 30, 1894, TWP-NAC.

53. Thomas Willson to J. Turner Morehead, February 15, 1894, TWP-NAC.

54. Thomas Willson to J. Turner Morehead, February 23, 1894, TWP-NAC.

55. Thomas Willson to J. Turner Morehead, n.d., TWP-NAC.

56. Thomas Willson to J. Turner Morehead, March 7, 1894 (first quotation), and Willson to Morehead, March 31, 1894 (second quotation), TWP-NAC.

57. For Willson's description of these experiments, see his correspondence between February and June 1894 in TWP-NAC. For the research on water gas and coal gas, see "James Turner Morehead," 5, KC.

58. Thomas Willson to J. Turner Morehead, March 20 [23?] 1894, and Willson to Morehead, May 9, 1894, TWP-NAC.

59. Thomas Willson to J. Turner Morehead, July 12, 1894, TWP-NAC; W. R. Kenan Jr. to Pat Patterson, July 9, 1894, Patterson Family Papers, NCDAH.

60. Thomas Willson to E. N. Dickerson, June 20, 1894, TWP-NAC. For laboratory conditions at UNC, see Bursey, *Carolina Chemists*, 55. The question of burners and acetylene-air mixtures is briefly discussed in Charles Venable to Mother (Mrs. F. P. Venable), August 18, 1937, Venable Papers, SHC.

61. Thomas Willson to J. Turner Morehead, June 20, 1894, TWP-NAC.

62. Ibid.

63. Ibid.

64. Thomas Willson to J. Turner Morehead, July 17, 1894, TWP-NAC.

65. "Willson Aluminum Company," 1–2, KC.

66. Thomas Willson to J. Turner Morehead, September 19, 1894, TWP-NAC.

67. *Incidents* 1:34–35.

68. Annie Kenan to Owen Kenan, October 1, 1894, and W. R. Kenan Jr. to Owen Kenan, December 14, 1894, Kenan Family Papers, SHC.

69. J. Turner Morehead to F. P. Venable, January 23, 1895, Venable Papers, SHC.

70. Ibid.

71. "Early Workers," 4, and "Story of Union Carbide Metals," 3, both in KC. See also *NCAB*, 25:274.

72. "Early Workers," 4 (emphasis in original), KC.

73. Ibid.

74. "James Turner Morehead," 6, KC.

75. Ibid.

76. Venable and Clarke, "Some of the Properties of Calcium Carbide," 306–10.

77. Smith, *From Monopoly to Competition*, 8–9.

78. The details of all of these developments are covered in the voluminous legal materials in TWP-NAC. Bullier applied for the French patent on February 9, 1894, and received it on April 30, 1894; he applied for the German patent on February 19, 1894, and received it on May 21, 1894. Although Bullier applied for and received these and other patents, he was acting on behalf of Moissan, who, as a member of the French Academie des Sciences, was prohibited from patenting or engaging in any commercial venture. According to Willson, Moissan announced his own discovery of calcium carbide to the French Academy on December 12, 1892. See Thomas Willson to Hon. Sydney Fisher, December 18, 1897, TWP-NAC.

79. Bursey, *Francis Preston Venable*, 50. Willson applied for his Canadian patents in August 1894. See legal correspondence in TWP-NAC.

80. Not until August 1895 did the Canadian patent office notify Bullier that his patent applications were in "interference" with those submitted a year earlier by Willson. See R. Pope to L. M. Bullier per O. N. Evans, August 13, 1895, TWP-NAC.

81. *Incidents* 1:36.

82. Ibid., 37; Faculty Minutes, University of North Carolina, 338, UA.

83. Charles S. Venable to Frank [F. P. Venable], July 24, 1895, Venable Papers, SHC.

84. Sallie Manning Venable to F. P. Venable, August 3, 1895, in ibid.

85. F. P. Venable to Sallie, August 21, 1895, in ibid. Isaac Manning was Sallie's brother.

86. Annie Kenan to Owen Kenan, October 1, 1894, Kenan Family Papers, SHC.

87. Chandler and Chandler, *Binghams of Louisville*, 43–47; Brenner, *House of Dreams*, 81–89; Tifft and Jones, *The Patriarch*, 30–34; Louise Wise Lewis's notes on undated, unidentified newspaper clipping, "Mrs. Flagler's Life Long Vain Quest for Happiness," LWL Scrapbook.

88. Robert Worth Bingham to Henrietta Miller, undated [August 1895], Robert Worth Bingham Papers, MD-FC; Battle, *History of UNC*, 2:524; *Annual Catalogue of Peace Institute, 1895–'96*, 43; Jean Bradley Anderson, *Durham County*, 203–4. There is a great deal of disagreement among the secondary sources mentioned in the preceding note regarding the timing of the Millers' arrival in Asheville and the exact date of Bingham's undated "proposal" letter. The late summer or early fall of 1895, however, seems the most logical time. See Thomas, "Let the Documents Speak," 313–14.

89. Halkiotis, "Guns for *Cuba Libre*," 60–75.

90. Proctor, "Filibustering," 84–88; Rickenbach, "Filibustering," 231–53; Schellings, "Florida and the Cuban Revolution," 175–86, and "Advent of the Spanish American War in Florida," 311–29. For the activities of the three Henrys in Florida, see Hoffman, "History of the ACL"; Coleman and Gurr, *Georgia Biography* 2:800–801; Chandler, *Henry Flagler*, 126–27; William T. Walters to Donald MacRae, June 30, 1887, Hugh MacRae Papers, DUMD.

91. Akin, *Flagler*, 134–73; Chandler, *Henry Flagler*, 173–74.

92. Shelton Testimony, Flagler Divorce Proceedings, August 12, 1901, Seventh Judicial Circuit, Miami, Fla., quoted in S. Walter Martin, *Florida's Flagler*, 172.

93. S. Walter Martin, *Florida's Flagler*, 173.

94. Samuel Kent to W. R. Kenan Jr., December 4, 1895, quoted in *Incidents* 1:38–40.

CHAPTER FIVE

1. *Incidents* 1:49.

2. Ibid.

3. Smith, *From Monopoly to Competition*, 81.

4. *Incidents* 1:49.

5. Ibid., 2:33.

6. "Willson Aluminum Company," KC.

7. "Niagara Makes Carbide," 7, KC.

8. Ibid., 9.

9. Ibid., 8–9.

10. Ibid., 7.

11. Marshall, "Reminiscences of the Carbide Industry," 158–59.

12. Ibid., 159.

13. Thomas P. Hughes, *Networks of Power*, 139.

14. Marshall, "Reminiscences of the Carbide Industry," 159; "Niagara Makes Carbide," 10, KC.

15. "Niagara Makes Carbide," 10, KC.

16. Ibid., 7; "Story of Union Carbide Metals," KC.

17. Scales, "Union Carbide Company," 89–90; "Union Carbide I," 123.

18. "Niagara Makes Carbide," 9, KC.

19. *Incidents* 2:26–27.

20. Ibid., 1:43. Kenan says this happened in early 1897, but this appears to be a mistake. He wrote to Goodman from Australia in December 1896, and his account (in ibid.) of his return trip from there as well as his letter to his cousin Owen, May 26, 1897, Kenan Family Papers, SHC, suggests that he did not get back to Niagara Falls until late May or June 1897.

21. *Incidents* 2:27.

22. Ibid., 1:40.

23. Ibid., 3:37; W. R. Kenan Jr. to Robert B. Goodman, December 9, 1896, quoted in ibid., 2:28. For information on Hordern, see Nairn et al., *Australian Dictionary of Biography*, 4:423.

24. W. R. Kenan Jr. to Owen Kenan, October 14, 1896, Kenan Family Papers, SHC.

25. *Incidents* 1:40–41.

26. Ibid., 41.

27. W. R. Kenan Jr. to Owen Kenan, October 15, 1896, Kenan Family Papers, SHC.

28. W. R. Kenan Jr. to Robert B. Goodman, December 9, 1896, quoted in *Incidents* 2:28.

29. W. R. Kenan Jr. to Owen Kenan, October 15, 1896, Kenan Family Papers, SHC.

30. W. R. Kenan Jr. to Robert B. Goodman, December 9, 1896, quoted in *Incidents* 2:28.

31. Walters to W. R. Kenan Jr., January 14, 1897, quoted in ibid., 4:123.

32. W. R. Kenan Jr. to Owen Kenan, October 15, 1896, Kenan Family Papers, SHC.

33. W. R. Kenan Jr. to Robert B. Goodman, December 9, 1896, quoted in *Incidents* 2:28.

34. That Kenan corresponded with his parents is suggested in Henry Walters to W. R. Kenan [Jr.], January 14, 1897, quoted in ibid., 4:123. This letter also mentions Buck and Mollie's complaints about their health. Buck suffered from rheumatism, and Mollie had a heart ailment.

35. Escott, *Many Excellent People*, 252 (quotation); Crow and Durden, *Maverick Republican*, 73.

36. O'Neal interview, May 14, 1989. Clisby Wise was Mrs. Margaret Wise O'Neal's uncle.

37. Hoffman, "History of the ACL," chap. 5, p. 28; *Annual Catalogue of Peace*

Institute, 1896–'97, 53; James Sprunt to Henry Walters, February 18, 1895, Private Letterpress Book, 1893–1900, Sprunt Papers, DUMD.

38. Akin, *Flagler,* 162–69; Rickenbach, "Filibustering," 231–41.

39. S. Walter Martin, *Florida's Flagler,* 178–79.

40. Chandler, *Henry Flagler,* 117. According to S. Walter Martin, *Florida's Flagler,* 183, Flagler went to and returned from Florida during November 1896. But other evidence suggests that the Florida developer spent the first months of 1897 vacationing at his Palm Beach cottage and supervising the opening festivities of his new Royal Palm Hotel in Miami. The man who handled Flagler's real estate activities in Miami, for example, James Ingraham, referred to Flagler's presence in Florida during the first months of 1897 in a 1920 address to the Miami Women's Club. His references are quoted in Chandler, *Henry Flagler,* 180–81.

41. Robert J. Klotzbach to F. A. Smith, June 15, 1979, KC.

42. "Early Workers," 3, KC.

43. W. S. Horry to J. M. Morehead, February 3, 1897, LbLSCC.

44. W. S. Horry to George O. Knapp, February 3, 1897, LbLSCC.

45. W. S. Horry to George O. Knapp, February 18, 1897, LbLSCC.

46. W. S. Horry to J. M. Morehead, August 15, 1897 (first quotation), and Horry to F. H. Clerque, March 1, 1897 (second quotation), both in LbLSCC.

47. W. S. Horry to George O. Knapp, March 7, 1897, LbLSCC.

48. W. S. Horry to Augustus Stoughton, March 26, 1897, LbLSCC. Horry's four-page brief immediately precedes this letter.

49. *Thomas "Carbide" Willson,* 10, KC.

50. W. S. Horry to George O. Knapp, April 9, 1897, LbLSCC.

51. Ibid.

52. *Incidents* 1:41.

53. Ibid.

54. Ibid., 43; "James Turner Morehead," 7, KC.

55. W. S. Horry to A. B. Stoughton, October 19, 1897, LbLSCC.

56. See LbLSCC.

57. W. S. Horry to E. N. Dickerson, November 6, 1897, LbLSCC. Dickerson had handled the legal transactions between Willson, Morehead, and the EGC and was also an officer of the EGC.

58. W. S. Horry to E. N. Dickerson, November 6, 1897, LbLSCC.

59. W. R. Kenan Jr. to Owen Kenan, December 7, 1897, Kenan Family Papers, SHC.

60. Ibid.

61. Annie Dickson Kenan to Owen Kenan, November 20, 1897, Kenan Family Papers, SHC.

62. Akin, *Flagler,* 166–70.

63. *Wilmington Star,* December 17, 21, 24, 1897.

64. Akin, *Flagler,* 168, 190.

65. W. R. Kenan Jr. to Owen Kenan, February 26, 1898, Kenan Family Papers, SHC.

66. Edward Thompson to R. G. Marshall, May 28, 1924, KC. For Horry's system-building, see LbLSCC.

67. "Willson Aluminum Company," and "Early Workers," both in KC. The Lake Superior Carbide Company was licensed to sell carbide in Cook County, Illinois, including the city of Chicago, while Pettibone, Mulliken and Company held a license to Wisconsin and Illinois outside Cook County. For the involvement of Knapp, Billings, and Brady, see "Union Carbide I," 124.

68. The Major had been making carbide "night and day" at his plant in Spray, N.C., and was continuing to do so at Holcomb Rock, Va., where he had been forced to move after the sale of the cotton mill adjacent to the Willson Aluminum Company at Spray. See "James Turner Morehead," 6, KC, and Morehead and de Chalmot, "Manufacture of Calcium Carbide," 311.

69. "James Turner Morehead," 6, KC.

70. "Niagara Makes Carbide," 11, KC.

71. W. R. Kenan Jr. to W. P. Martin, August 8, 1898, KLb.

72. See KLb for Kenan's problems at the Soo. The quote is from W. R. Kenan to W. P. Martin, August 15, 1898, KLb.

73. W. R. Kenan Jr. to J. M. Morehead, September 5, 1898, KLb. This letter quotes Horry's letter.

74. *Incidents* 1:46.

75. See ibid., 15, for Kenan's memory of the Wilmington race riot. One of the best accounts of the riot is Edmonds, *The Negro and Fusion Politics in North Carolina*. Less reliable but more detailed is Prather, *We Have Taken a City*. For a psychosexual interpretation of the riot, see Williamson, *Crucible of Race*, 195–201. See Cronly Family Papers and Clawson, "The Wilmington Race Riot of 1898," Clawson Papers, both in DUMD, for comments of Wilmingtonians who witnessed the riot.

76. W. R. Kenan Jr. to George O. Knapp, December 27, 28, 1898, KLb.

77. W. R. Kenan Jr. to George O. Knapp, January 2, 1899, KLb.

78. W. R. Kenan Jr. to W. P. Martin, February 19, 1899, KLb.

79. W. R. Kenan Jr. to W. P. Martin, January 28, 1899, KLb.

80. *Incidents* 1:46.

81. "Niagara Makes Carbide," 12, KC.

82. W. R. Kenan Jr. to W. P. Martin, February 11, March 25, April 5, May 10, 23, 1899, KLb.

83. *Incidents* 1:46–47.

84. Ibid., 43.

85. S. Walter Martin, *Florida's Flagler*, 193 (first quotation); Chandler, *Henry Flagler*, 189 (second quotation). The timing of Flagler's gift to Jessie Kenan Wise is suggested by the correspondence in FLb 99A, HMFM, and information in McKay et al., *Guide*, 30–31.

86. Chandler, *Henry Flagler*, 190. Bingham, *Passion and Prejudice*, 144–45, contains the most direct and complete statement of the "pressure" and paternity arguments. Tifft and Jones, *The Patriarch*, 59, repeats the pressure scenario implied

in Chandler's *Henry Flagler*, 189–90, and in Chandler and Chandler, *Binghams of Louisville*, 85–87, both of which also offer the annoyed "grandmother" hypothesis. For the Kenan family's alleged worries about the parallel between Mary Lily's situation and that of her sister Jessie, see Akin, *Flagler*, 149.

87. *Jessie K. Wise v. J. C. Wise*, New Hanover County, Divorces, Jessie Kenan Wise, NCDAH; O'Neal interviews (Mrs. O'Neal was Louise Wise's cousin and her childhood playmate in Macon, Ga.); Gibbs interview (Mrs. Gibbs was the daughter of Henry Flagler's best friend, Dr. Andrew Anderson); *Twelfth Census*, 1900, Bibb County (Macon), Ga., Washington, D.C., microfilm copy. Photographs of Louise Wise as a child and as an adult show a striking resemblance to both her father and uncle; see photograph of Basil and Clisby Wise and photographs of Louise Wise and her cousin Margaret as children in Nancy Briska Anderson, *Macon*, 101. When asked about Louise's parentage, Mrs. O'Neal noted in her March 7, 1989, telephone interview with the author that she had never heard of the Flagler–Mary Lily rumor and doubted "that it was true because there was such a strong resemblance between Louise Wise and her Grandmother Clisby."

88. See the letters from Flagler to Ashley in FLb 99B, HMFM, and S. Walter Martin, *Florida's Flagler*, 186.

89. Yergin, *The Prize*, 98. For Flagler's stock transfers to Mary Lily, see W. H. Beardsley to H. M. Flagler, March 21, April 1, 15, 1899, and Beardsley to W. R. Kenan [Sr.], April 3, 1899, FLb 99A, HMFM.

90. H. M. Flagler to Col. Thomas S. Kenan, June 3, 1899, and Flagler to W. R. Kenan Sr., June 9, 1899, FLb 99B, HMFM. For Flagler's concern with the mansion renovations and Kib's drinking, see Flagler to P. E. Dennis, June 16, 1899, FLb 99B, HMFM.

91. S. Walter Martin, *Florida's Flagler*, 184–85; H. M. Flagler to Dr. [Andrew] Anderson, June 29, 1899, FLb 99B, HMFM.

92. H. M. Flagler to W. R. Kenan Jr., July 28, 1899, FLb 99B, HMFM.

93. H. M. Flagler to Eugene Ashley, July 31, 1899, in ibid.; S. Walter Martin, *Florida's Flagler*, 184–85; Louise Wise Lewis Photo Album, Richmond, Va.

94. H. M. Flagler to W. R. Kenan Sr., August 28, 1899, FLb 99C, HMFM.

95. "Niagara Makes Carbide," 13, KC.

96. H. M. Flagler to W. R. Kenan Jr., September 5, 1899, FLb 99C, HMFM.

97. H. M. Flagler to Edward R. Taylor, September 9, 1899, in ibid. (handwritten underlining of typewritten original).

98. *Incidents* 2:49–50.

99. "Niagara Makes Carbide," 13, KC; H. M. Flagler to W. R. Kenan Jr., September 20, 1899, FLb 99C, HMFM.

100. H. M. Flagler to W. R. Kenan, Jr., October 18, 1899, FLb 99C, HMFM.

101. Ibid.

102. H. M. Flagler to W. R. Kenan Sr. and W. R. Kenan Jr. (telegrams), October 19, 1899, and Flagler to W. R. Kenan Jr. October 19, 1899, FLb 99C, HMFM.

103. H. M. Flagler to W. R. Kenan Jr., October 23, 1899, in ibid.; Venable, "An Account," 875.

104. *Incidents* 1:47.

105. Ibid., 47, 60.

106. Ibid., 51; Pioneer Association, *Souvenir History*, 176; H. M. Flagler to Eugene Ashley, July 5, 1899, FLb 99B, HMFM.

107. *Wilmington Dispatch*, May 16, 1900; *Wilmington, the Metropolis*, 60; Spiritine Chemical Company, *Facts*, NCC; W. R. Kenan Sr. to J. R. Parrott, May 12, 1900, Florida East Coast Railway Collection, StAHS; Tony P. Wrenn, *Architectural and Historical Portrait*, 261; New Hanover County, Wills and Estates, William Rand Kenan Sr., May 1903, NCDAH. Although there is no documentation for the source of Buck's capital—the Flagler letterbooks are missing for this period—it is safe to assume, given Buck's financial status, that the money came from Flagler.

108. Bursey, *Francis Preston Venable*, 67.

109. Robert Worth Bingham to Joseph Holmes, April 21, 24, 1900; Charles Baskerville to Bingham, August 7, October 3, 10, 12, 22, 26, 1900; Bingham to Baskerville, October 22, 1900, all in Robert Worth Bingham Papers, MD-FC; Chandler and Chandler, *Binghams of Louisville*, 54–60.

110. *Incidents* 1:84, 2:40, 48–49.

111. Colbey interview; Way, "Evil Humors and Ardent Spirits," 1426–27. According to Pioneer Association, *Souvenir History*, 178, citing the census of 1900, the population of Lockport was 16,581 in 1900. This was down from the estimated population of 19,570 in 1891.

112. Pioneer Association, *Souvenir History*; Janssen interviews.

113. Pioneer Association, *Souvenir History*, 172–78; *Lockport, N.Y.: Electrical and Industrial.*

114. S. Walter Martin, *Florida's Flagler*, 6–7; New York, Niagara County, 463:80, 104, and 465:442, 525, in R. G. Dun & Co. Collection, Harvard University; Ashley, Adriance, Flagler, and Pomroy Family files in the Niagara County Historian's Office and in the Genealogical Library, Niagara County Historical Museum, both in Lockport, N.Y.

115. *Incidents* 2:40; H. M. Flagler to George W. Wilson, May 26, 1899; Flagler to W. Murray, May 26, 1899; Flagler to J. M. McDonald, July 28, 1899, FLb 99B; Flagler to Alice M. Pomroy, January 11, 1901, FLb 127, HMFM; Ashley file, Niagara County Historian's Office, Lockport, N.Y.; Gibbs interview.

116. *Incidents* 1:61 (second quotation), 2:75 (third quotation), and 4:58 (first quotation).

117. Ibid., 1:53.

118. Ibid., 51–53.

119. Janssen interviews. At the time Kenan hired him, Beattie was commuting between Lockport and Buffalo, where he worked as the private secretary for Warren Bissell, Grover Cleveland's former law partner.

120. *Incidents* 1:53 (second quotation) and 2:38 (first quotation).

121. H. M. Flagler to C. H. Bradley, January 18; Flagler to W. H. Beardsley, January 20, 1901, FLb 127, HMFM.

122. *Incidents* 1:1–55.

123. H. M. Flagler to J. A. McGuire, January 30, 1901, FLb 127, HMFM.

124. *Incidents* 1:57 (first quotation) and 4:58 (second quotation).

125. S. Walter Martin, *Florida's Flagler*, 186–90. The Florida divorce law required four years of incurable insanity, recognition of the condition by a competent court, financial support from the husband (in the case of his wife's incompetency), and at least a year's residence in the state.

126. McGowen and McGowen, *Flashes*, 186–89.

127. *Wilmington Star*, August 24, 25, 1901; Smith and Smith, "Mary Lily Kenan," 12, private collection, Chapel Hill, N.C. (quotation).

128. *New York Times*, August 23, 1901; *Wilmington Star*, August 25, 1901 (quotation).

129. Unidentified, undated newspaper clipping in the Kenan Family file at the Lower Cape Fear Historical Society, Wilmington, N.C.

130. That Mary Lily's marriage caused a division within the church was made known to the author by one of the older members of the church during the author's presentation "The Kenans of Wilmington" to a meeting of the Lower Cape Fear Historical Society at Wilmington's First Presbyterian Church in October 1989. The church member heard the Mary Lily story from his parents, who were also members of the church.

131. Daniels, *Editor in Politics*, 383–84.

132. H. M. Flagler to W. R. Kenan Jr., August 17, 1901, quoted in *Incidents* 4:122. (The Flagler letterbooks for this period have not survived.)

CHAPTER SIX

1. *Incidents* 2:35. Except where otherwise noted, the narrative that follows is based on the correspondence of Henry M. Flagler and his secretaries in the Flagler Letterbooks, 1901–1905, HMFM.

2. W. R. Kenan Sr. to W. R. Kenan Jr., November 14, 1901, quoted in *Incidents* 4:58.

3. F. P. Venable to W. R. Kenan Jr., November 18, 1901, quoted in ibid., 59.

4. *Incidents* 1:92.

5. H. M. Flagler to W. R. Kenan [Sr.], June 9, 1899, FLb 99B, HMFM.

6. *Wilmington Dispatch*, January 9, 1902; *Wilmington Star*, January 30, 31, 1902.

7. Hoffman, "History of the ACL," chaps. 8 and 9.

8. This figure is based on the securities pledged as collateral for the Metropolitan loan as well as on those in Buck's account with J. H. Parker and Company. See W. H. Beardsley to H. M. Flagler, April 20, 1903, FLb 138A, HMFM. For a listing of Buck's stockholdings in Wilmington companies, see New Hanover County, Wills and Estates, William Rand Kenan Sr., May 1903, NCDAH.

9. H. M. Flagler to W. R. Kenan Sr., February 13, 1901, FLb 127, HMFM.

10. *Wilmington Star*, April 15, 1903. The *Star*'s account says nothing about Buck's appendicitis, only that he had undergone "an operation for a complication of

stomach troubles." *Incidents* 1:12 identifies Buck's stomach troubles as amoebic dysentery, while a coded telegram from W. H. Beardsley to H. M. Flagler, April 20, 1903, FLb 138A, HMFM, mentions appendicitis.

11. *Wilmington Star*, April 17, 1903. Buck had been a member of School Committee No. 2 in Wilmington.

12. Ibid.; H. M. Flagler to Dr. G. G. Shelton, May 18, 1903, FLb 138A, HMFM.

13. H. M. Flagler to Thomas Wright, September 27 (second quotation), September 28 (third quotation), and September 30, 1903 (first quotation), FLb 142, HMFM. For information on Wright, see Block, *Wrights of Wilmington*, 109–16.

14. H. M. Flagler to W. R. Kenan Jr., October 5, 1903, FLb 142, HMFM.

15. *Incidents* 1:51, 59.

16. "Carbide & Carbon Chemicals," 63 (quotation); Scales, "Union Carbide Company," 91; "Early Workers," KC; H. M. Flagler to W. R. Kenan Jr. (c/o J. A. McDonald), telegram, September 8, 1903, FLb 141, HMFM.

17. *Incidents* 1:57; Pioneer Association, *Souvenir History*, 176.

18. *Incidents* 1:63; H. M. Flagler to W. R. Kenan Jr., November 19, 1902, FLb [unnumbered, September 24–December 16, 1902], HMFM.

19. The correspondence related to the Wilson Electric Company is located in the W. R. Kenan Jr. Papers, NgCHS.

20. "Wilson Lighting Company . . . Prospectus," September 26, 1903, in ibid. George D. Green and George Whitfield Connor were Kenan's most important contacts. Green was the owner of Wilson's largest hardware store and a close friend of Colonel Thomas Kenan, and Connor was an attorney who had attended UNC with Will Kenan. Connor's father, Henry Groves Connor, was Wilson's most prominent jurist and Democratic politician and a close associate of Colonel Thomas Kenan.

21. *Incidents* 1:60–61.

22. H. M. Flagler to W. R. Kenan Jr., October 16, 1903, FLb 142, HMFM.

23. Ibid.

24. *Incidents* 1:57–58; Lamoreaux, *Great Merger Movement*, 88–89.

25. *Incidents* 3:74 (quotation); Pomroy family file, Niagara County Historian's Office, Lockport, N.Y.

26. R. J. Klotzbach to Dr. B. T. Britten, May 8, 1980, KC.

27. Gibbs interview.

28. *Incidents* 1:66.

29. *Lockport Journal*, April 9, 1904.

30. *Incidents* 3:84–85.

31. Ibid., 1:64, 2:86; W. R. Kenan Jr. to W. L. Cantwell, June 9, 1904, Kenan Papers, NgCHS.

32. *Incidents* 1:64–65.

33. New Hanover County, Divorces, Jesse Kenan Wise, NCDAH.

34. Quoted in Yergin, *The Prize*, 105.

35. Akin, *Flagler*, 213.

36. Sprunt, *Chronicles of the Cape Fear River*, 588–91 (quotations); *Wilmington, the Metropolis*, 68–69.

37. *Incidents* 1:1–69.

38. H. M. Flagler to George Wilson, November 23, 1903, FLb 142, HMFM.

39. Williamson, *Crucible of Race*, 350.

40. *Florida Times-Union*, October 16, 18, 1905; Meier and Rudwick, "Negro Boycotts," 525–33.

41. *Incidents* 2:35–36.

42. Laura Moore Gavin to Mrs. Robert Love Kenan, September 21, 1941, Kenan Family Papers, SHC.

43. *Incidents* 1:60; *Wilmington Dispatch*, September 10, 1906.

44. Yergin, *The Prize*, 108; Akin, *Flagler*, 214; *Incidents* 4:41.

45. *Incidents* 1:70–72.

46. Ibid.

47. See untitled, undated manuscript on the Western Block Company in the Local History Collection of the Lockport City Library, Lockport, N.Y.

48. *Incidents* 1:61–62.

49. Ibid., 70–71.

50. Ibid., 60.

51. "Carbide & Carbon Chemicals," 124.

52. *Incidents* 1:60–61.

53. Ibid., 61; Price letter to author. Kenan and Price appear to have had an otherwise long and cordial relationship, which probably accounts for the naming of Price's grandson, John Kenan Price.

54. Akin, *Flagler*, 199. Flagler's decision to finance the extension through a bond issue can be followed in the Flagler letterbooks for 1909, HMFM.

55. H. M. Flagler to John M. Carrere, January 4, 1910, FLb, HMFM.

56. Ibid.

57. H. M. Flagler to Alice Kenan, November 22, 1909, FLb, HMFM.

58. H. M. Flagler to W. R. Kenan Jr., December 4, 1909, in ibid.

59. H. M. Flagler to Julien T. Davies, December 7, 1909 (first quotation), and Flagler to J. D. Archbold, December 15, 1909 (second quotation), in ibid.

60. H. M. Flagler to Dr. Peyton Hoge, January 4, 1909; Flagler to Sister Julia, January 7, 1909; Flagler to W. R. Kenan Jr., June 8, 1909; Flagler to Mrs. W. R. Kenan, July 8, 1909, FLb 169, in ibid.

61. H. M. Flagler to George W. Perkins, April 17, 1909, FLb 172, in ibid. (second quotation); first quotation quoted in Akin, *Flagler*, 226.

62. H. M. Flagler to Owen Kenan, January 12, 1909, FLb 169; J. C. Salter to Wm. S. Kenney, May 14, 1909, and Salter to Dr. Andrew Anderson, April 29, 1909, FLb 172; Flagler to James Parrott, July 30, 1909, FLb 174; Flagler to Dr. George Ward, August 19, 1910, and Flagler to Butler Ames, September 16, 1910, FLb, HMFM.

63. H. M. Flagler to Janet Mitchell, August 10, 1909, FLb, in ibid.

64. Yergin, *The Prize*, 110.

65. Ibid., 112–13.

66. Akin, *Flagler*, 221–23.

67. W. H. Beardsley to H. M. Flagler, February 24, 1899, FLb 99A, HMFM; Rush, *Library Resources*, 31, 194; Louis R. Wilson, *University of North Carolina*, 476–77; *Confederate Veteran*, May 1898, 229; April 1902, 153–54; and March 1911, 106; Brown, "State Literary and Historical Association," 157. The Colonel was on the Executive Committee of the Confederate Memorial Association for many years.

68. F. P. Venable to Col. Thos. S. Kenan, May 15, 1911, Thomas S. Kenan Papers, DUMD.

69. *Raleigh Times*, December 23, 1911.

70. Chandler, *Henry Flagler*, 257.

71. *Wilmington Star*, January 12, 1912. James's death at Lockland is discussed in Laura Moore Gavin to Mrs. James Love Kenan, September 21, 1941, Kenan Family Papers, SHC.

72. Laura Moore Gavin to Mrs. James Love Kenan, September 21, 1941, Kenan Family Papers, SHC.

73. See author's interviews with Frank Hawkins Kenan, Phyllis Van De Mark, Lawrence Lewis Jr., Francis M. Delahunt, and Dr. Guila B. Janssen.

74. *Incidents* 1:84–87.

75. Ibid., 64; Register, *Kenan Family*, 55.

76. Warren Smith Collection, HMFM.

77. Dr. Andrew Anderson to Clarissa [Anderson], April 10, 1913, Anderson Papers, StAHS.

CHAPTER SEVEN

1. Gibbs interview; Harry Flagler's margin note in S. Walter Martin, *Florida's Flagler* (quotation), copy in HMFM.

2. Gibbs interview.

3. Ibid.

4. Trust Agreement, May 29, 1911, Presbyterian Church Records, Memorial Presbyterian Church, StAHS; Graham, *The Awakening*, 217. Flagler was buried next to his daughter Jennie (Harry's sister) and Jennie's infant daughter. He had built the church in their memory.

5. Gibbs interview.

6. Quoted in *Incidents* 1:73.

7. Quoted in Akin, *Flagler*, 227.

8. S. Walter Martin, *Florida's Flagler*, 126 (first quotation); Martin interview (second quotation).

9. Bingham, *Passion and Prejudice*, 152.

10. Chandler and Chandler, *Binghams of Louisville*, 100.

11. Tifft and Jones, *The Patriarch*, 60–61.

12. Thomas S. Kenan III, quoted in Chandler and Chandler, *Binghams of Louisville*, 104.

13. Unidentified, undated newspaper clipping in LWL Scrapbook.

14. Lehr, *"King Lehr,"* 157 (quotation). It was probably in Newport, moreover, that Mary Lily met Lewis Cass Ledyard, the New York attorney to whom Henry Walters referred William R. Kenan for specific legal advice regarding the Flagler Trust and Florida properties. See Amory, *Last Resorts*, 245–46, and *Incidents* 1:77. Mary Lily's presence in Asheville in 1913 is suggested by George T. Winston to Edward Kidder Graham, August 22, 1916 [1917], CR, House Series. Her presence in Newport that summer is suggested in Chandler and Chandler, *Binghams of Louisville*, 100.

15. For Flagler's legacy to Sterry, see Akin, *Flagler*, 227. For Mary Lily's legacy to Sterry, see MLKFB Will.

16. Conte, *History of the Greenbrier*, 108; Akin, *Flagler*, 147, 227; MLKFB Will; H. M. Flagler to Owen Kenan, October 3, 1911, FLb, HMFM; Patterson, *Vanderbilts*, 242. Owen Kenan's connection to Alfred Gwynn Vanderbilt is discussed further below.

17. Mary Lily Flagler Lewis interview (quotation), and Lawrence Lewis Jr. interview, September 24, 1991.

18. *Incidents* 1:73–75; Akin, *Flagler*, 232–33.

19. *Incidents* 1:103, 2:35; Akin, *Flagler*, 208.

20. Gibbs interview; Akin, *Flagler*, 107.

21. *Incidents* 1:73–74; Akin, *Flagler*, 171–72.

22. *Incidents* 1:73–75.

23. Ibid.

24. Ibid.; Muir, "William Alexander Blount," 458–76.

25. Kenan, *History*, 2:15–16.

26. *Incidents* 1:119.

27. Quoted in Bursey, *Frances Preston Venable*, 89–90. Venable had suffered a nervous breakdown the previous year, in the aftermath of a fatal hazing accident to UNC student Isaac William Rand, and he had taken a leave of absence to travel in Europe with his family.

28. According to George T. Winston, "The summer after Mr. Flagler died Mrs. F[lagler] spent in Asheville and was near my home. In an interview one day she consulted me about managing her large estate; and this gave me an opportunity to advise a large bequest to the University in memory of her father & uncles." See Winston to President Graham, August 22, 1916 [1917], CR, House Series. Mary Lily probably did see Winston in the summer of 1913, but she would not have asked him to manage her estate. Parrott, Beardsley, and her brother were doing that. Also peculiar is the fact that Winston dated his letter August 22, 1916, when he actually wrote it in August 1917, one month after Mary Lily's death, at the same time that Colonel Bingham was also writing UNC's president to take credit for having originally inspired Mary Lily to make a gift to the university. See Col. Robert Bingham to Dr. Graham, n.d. [August–September 1917], in ibid.

29. *Incidents* 1:103.

30. Ibid., 25 (first quotation) and 12–13 (second quotation); H. M. Flagler to W. R. Kenan Jr., July 30, 1909, FLb 174, and Flagler to Janet Mitchell, September 5, 1911, FLb, HMFM. For Louise's schooling prior to going to Paris, see Flagler to Sarah Kenan, September 10, 1909, FLb, HMFM.

31. The family's presence in the mountains during the summer of 1914 is suggested by a variety of sources, including those cited in the previous note. The Kenans were creatures of habit and tended to do the same thing at the same time, year after year. Moreover, according to Kenan (*Incidents* 1:12) his mother died on June 6, 1916, at the age of seventy-four, from "a heart ailment which she suffered for several years." That she was an invalid by the summer of 1915 is stated in Col. Robert Bingham to Dr. [Edward Kidder] Graham, n.d. [1917], CR, House Series. Like Wood, his father, Thomas Fanning Wood, and the Kenans' other Wilmington physician, Dr. George Thomas, Battle served on the North Carolina Board of Health for many years. See *Incidents* 1:25; *DNCB*, 1:117; and George M. Cooper, "The Woods."

32. The author would like to thank Kathleen Baldwin of Biltmore House for providing information regarding Battle's relationship with the Vanderbilt family. See *DNCB*, 1:117, for a biographical sketch of Battle, and 1:109–19 and 2:7, for his family connections. Battle also appears to have been the source for "Dr. Montague," a character in the fictionalized account of Mary Lily's life written by Metta Folger Townsend, *On Golden Hinges*. Battle was also friends with both the new trustee of the H. M. Flagler Trust, William A. Blount, whom he had known since his days as a navy surgeon in Pensacola, Fla., and with Colonel Robert Bingham and Bingham's daughters, Sadie Grinnan and Mary McKee, all of whom lived at the Bingham School in Asheville. The doctor's first wife, moreover, Alice Maude Belknap, who died in Asheville in 1899, was a distant relative of the prominent Belknap family of Louisville, Ky. Indeed, it seems quite likely that Mary Lily and Battle discussed the Binghams, the Belknaps, and the Vanderbilts during the summer of 1914. George Vanderbilt died in March after an emergency appendectomy; Judge Robert Worth Bingham had lost his wife in April of the previous year; and William B. Belknap, one of the judge's political protégés in Louisville, had recently died there at his mansion, "Lincliffe." Mary Lily and the judge would rent the empty Lincliffe mansion in January 1917, and she would die there the following July.

33. *New York Times*, March 20, 1915; Col. Robert Bingham to E. K. Graham, October 6, 1915, CR, House Series.

34. "Was It a Lucky Day for Judge Bingham when Mary Lily Flagler Jilted Him?," unidentified, undated magazine article [ca. November 1917], in LWL Scrapbook.

35. *Raleigh News & Observer*, May 8, 1915; Thomas S. Kenan III interview, September 15, 1987.

36. Graham Kenan to Edward Kidder Graham, April 29, 1915, UNC Papers, UA.

37. Simpson, *The Lusitania*, 112–15, 162–64; Bailey and Ryan, *Lusitania Disaster*, 89–91, 170–93.

38. Thomas S. Kenan III interview, September 15, 1987.

39. Laura Moore Gavin to Mrs. Robert Love Kenan, September 21, 1941, Kenan Family Papers, SHC.

40. That Mary Lily drafted her will during the summer of 1915 is suggested by Louise Wise's margin notes on an undated and unidentified article in LWL Scrapbook. The article is titled "Mrs. Flagler's Life Long Vain Quest for Happiness," and part of it notes that "Judge Bingham himself suggested that the bulk of her [Mary Lily's] great wealth, its burdens and obligations, should be bequeathed to her much beloved niece, Louise Wise. Which was done within a month of the aunt's nuptials [November 1916]." Louise underlined this last sentence and wrote, "Done a year before."

41. *Asheville Citizen*, July 8, 18, 24, August 8, 13, 19, 20, 21, 25, September 10, October 2, 1915. Although the newspaper continued to make almost daily references to Mary Lily until she left in early October, the only subsequent mention of Battle came on September 10, when the newspaper noted that he had returned to Asheville from visiting a sick friend in Tennessee.

42. Col. Robert Bingham to Dr. [Edward Kidder] Graham, n.d. [August–September 1917], CR, House Series.

43. Eleanore Bingham died from injuries sustained when an interurban trolley struck the automobile in which she and her family were riding. See Thomas, "Let the Documents Speak," 323–24.

44. *Asheville Citizen*, August 15, 1915; *University of Virginia Catalogue, 1915–1916*. The University of Virginia gave entrance examinations between September 13 and 18, and lectures began on September 20. See *University of Virginia Record, 1915–1916*.

45. Col. Robert Bingham to Dr. [Edward Kidder] Graham, October 6, 1915, CR, House Series.

46. Louis R. Wilson, *University of North Carolina*, 248–49.

47. Col. Robert Bingham to Dr. [Edward Kidder] Graham, October 6, 1915, CR, House Series. See n. 40, above, for the timing of Mary Lily's decision to draft her will.

48. LWL Scrapbook; Seymour, *History of the American Field Service in France*, 437, 481.

49. James Graham Kenan interview.

50. Her drinking habits are discussed further below.

51. Laura Moore Gavin to Mrs. Robert Love Kenan, September 21, 1941, Kenan Family Papers, SHC.

52. *Palm Beach Life*, February 15, 1916.

53. *Raleigh News & Observer*, February 16, 1916.

54. Ibid.

55. Laura Moore Gavin to Mrs. Robert Love Kenan, September 21, 1941, Kenan Family Papers, SHC.

56. Wake County, N.C., Wills, Sallie Dortch Kenan, NCDAH.

57. For Owen's ambulance accident, see the undated newspaper clipping from the "American Notes" section of the *New York Herald* in LWL Scrapbook (first

quotation). Owen's fastidiousness is mentioned in Laura Moore Gavin to Mrs. Robert Love Kenan, September 21, 1941, Kenan Family Papers, SHC (second quotation).

58. *Wilmington Star*, June 8, 1916.

59. *Incidents* 1:64.

60. Ibid., 77–79.

61. Brenner, *House of Dreams*, 102–3; Chandler and Chandler, *Binghams of Louisville*, 105; Tifft and Jones, *The Patriarch*, 61. Bingham and his good friend Shepard Bryan were both related to Pem Jones, and the latter's townhouse would be the site of the Judge and Mary Lily's wedding.

62. *Asheville Citizen*, July, 1917; Tifft and Jones, *The Patriarch*, 62. Mary Lily's heart problems may account for the fact that one of the three men who witnessed her will, Dr. S. B. Capito, was the resort's chief physician. The other two witnesses were Owen J. MacLaughlin, the Greenbrier's chief room clerk, and Howard Slocum, the hotel's resident manager. Robert Conte, telephone interview, August 12, 1993.

63. *New York Times*, September 8, 1916; *Incidents* 1:73.

64. The most numerous and valuable of the oil stocks Mary Lily designated for her siblings were 16,000 shares of Standard Oil of New Jersey and 12,000 shares of Standard Oil of New York. See MLKFB Will.

65. Ibid.

66. Mary Lily Flagler Lewis interview. Lawrence's mother, Elizabeth Harrison Lewis, was a great-granddaughter of President William Henry Harrison and a niece of former Union general and Republican president Benjamin Harrison. His father, Thornton Lewis, was a native of Ohio who worked with the C&O in Cincinnati before moving to West Virginia as president of the railroad's White Sulphur Springs Company.

67. Lawrence Lewis Jr. interview, September 24, 1991.

68. Mary Lily Flagler Lewis interview.

69. *New York Times*, November 4, 1916. Rumors of their engagement began in the New York press on the day before William announced the wedding plans.

70. *New York Herald*, November 6, 1916.

71. Chandler and Chandler, *Binghams of Louisville*, 103; Brenner, *House of Dreams*, 117; Bingham, *Passion and Prejudice*, 143; LWL Scrapbook.

72. Tifft and Jones, *The Patriarch*, 62.

73. Thomas, "Let the Documents Speak," 324; Bingham, *Passion and Prejudice*, 135; "Errors and Misstatements in *Passion and Prejudice*," M&BBF.

74. See Chapter 3, p. 22, and Chapter 5, pp. 129–30, above.

75. Col. Robert Bingham to E. K. Graham, August 1917, CR, House Series.

76. Transcript of Record, 77–78.

77. *New York Times*, November 16, 1916.

78. Brenner, *House of Dreams*, 107 (first quotation); Chandler and Chandler, *Binghams of Louisville*, 114 (second quotation); Tifft and Jones, *The Patriarch*, 63 (third quotation).

79. Tifft and Jones, *The Patriarch*, 63 (first quotation); Brenner, *House of Dreams*, 105 (second quotation); Chandler and Chandler, *Binghams of Louisville*, 112 (third quotation).

80. *New York Times*, November 16, 1916; *Wilmington Star*, November 16, 1916; *Louisville Courier-Journal*, November 16, 23, 1916; Robert Worth Bingham Papers, MD-FC.

81. *Louisville Courier-Journal*, November 22, 1916; Thomas, "Let the Documents Speak," 326.

82. This telegram (Mary Lily Bingham to Graham Kenan, November 28, 1916), is quoted in the private detective's report prepared for the Kenans in September 1917. Because the report cannot be quoted directly, however, the author has relied on the reported paraphrasing of the telegram provided by Thomas S. Kenan III, who appears to have offered a slightly different version of it to each author who interviewed and quoted him on the topic. Chandler and Chandler, *Binghams of Louisville*, 105, offers one version of Kenan's description of the telegram but clearly uses that description, incorrectly, to describe Mary Lily's feelings for Bingham while they were allegedly courting in New York—almost a year before the telegram was actually written. See Brenner, *House of Dreams*, 102, and Tifft and Jones, *The Patriarch*, 63, for examples of the quotations attributed to Kenan.

83. MLKFB Will.

84. Ibid.

85. Transcript of Record, 86; *New York Times*, November 16, December 9, 10, 1917.

86. Chandler and Chandler, *Binghams of Louisville*, 115 (first quotation); Tifft and Jones, *The Patriarch*, 64 (second quotation). Chandler offers no source for this information, but it almost certainly came from his August 1984 interview with Thomas S. Kenan III, whose November 19, 1986, interview with Tifft and Jones is cited by them, 525 n., for Henrietta's response.

87. Quoted in Brenner, *House of Dreams*, 108.

88. Transcript of Record, 78–80.

89. Ethel Thacker to Robert Worth Bingham, August 5, 1917, Bingham Papers, MD-FC.

90. Quotation from the "American Notes" section of an undated copy of the European edition of the *New York Herald* in LWL Scrapbook; Seymour, *History of the American Field Service in France*, 437, 481; *New York Times*, July 13, 1963; Owen Hill Kenan, Veterans C-File, Veterans Administration, Winston-Salem, N.C., Regional Office. Mary Lily also arranged during her trip to New York to sell her million-dollar lot on Fifth Avenue to the Pembroke Joneses' architect son-in-law, John Russell Pope. See Robert Worth Bingham to J. R. Pope, January 25, 1917, box 1, folder 22, Bingham Papers, MD-FC.

91. "Errors and Misstatements in *Passion and Prejudice*," M&BBF.

92. *Palm Beach Life*, February 20, 1917.

93. *Louisville Courier-Journal*, April 13, 1917.

94. Ibid., April 7, 1917.

95. Ibid.; *Inlook*; *Stuart Hall Catalogue*; *University of Virginia Catalogue, 1916–1917*; *University of Virginia Record, 1916–1917*; Pardee interview.

96. *Louisville Courier-Journal*, April 29, 1917.

97. *Wilmington Star*, May 4, 1917. According to the *Star*—which was still unaware of, or covering up, Jessie's divorce—the wedding occurred "at the residence of the bride's parents, Mr. and Mrs. J. K. Wise." Although the *Star* does not mention the presence of Lawrence's family at the wedding, a report in the *Louisville Courier-Journal*, April 27, 1917, noted that the "entire" Lewis family would attend the wedding.

98. Hugh H. Young, Memorandum, February 14, 1940, M&BBF; Brandt, *No Magic Bullett*, 99, 102–4. Young's memorandum is one of two he prepared on the subject. He prepared the first in 1933. See n. 99, below.

99. Statement of Hugh Young, March 13, 1933, Alan Mason Chesney Medical Archives, Baltimore, Md. See also Thomas, "Let the Documents Speak," 335.

100. Robert Worth Bingham to Herbert Hoover, May 28, 1917, M&BBF.

101. Bingham mentions his plans to attend the reunion in Robert Worth Bingham to E. K. Graham, February 11, 1917, box 31, UNC Papers, UA.

102. *Louisville Courier-Journal*, June 10, 1917.

103. Laura Moore Gavin to Mrs. Robert Love Kenan, September 21, 1941, Kenan Family Papers, SHC.

104. Transcript of Record, 81.

105. Ibid., 76, 85; Bingham, *Passion and Prejudice*, 163.

106. Quoted in Brenner, *House of Dreams*, 111. Brenner interviewed Kenan in the late 1980s. Whatever letters Mary Lily wrote have never been made public. That she wrote them at all is very strange indeed. Only one or two fragments of letters she wrote are known to have survived. These are in HMFM.

107. See Bowman and Jellinek, "Alcohol Addiction and Its Treatment," 149–50, for the use of morphine and apomorphine in treating alcoholism at the turn of the century. Apomorphine was also used as part of the most famous treatment for alcoholism at the time: the Keeley "cure." See Keeley, *Non-heredity of Inebriety*. The use of morphine is also mentioned in the summary of the 1917 detective's report prepared for Thomas S. Kenan III. Hypodermic injections are mentioned in Transcript of Record, 80 and 85. For other arguments regarding the nature of Mary Lily's illness and the treatment she received, see Tifft and Jones, *The Patriarch*, 66–70, and Chandler and Chandler, *Binghams of Louisville*, 200–210.

108. Mary Lily was also accompanied by her housekeeper, Ida Remley, on at least one of these automobile drives, and Remley went to Ravitch's office with her on the day Mary Lily signed the codicil. Remley had started working for Henry Flagler in 1890. See Chandler and Chandler, *Binghams of Louisville*, 83.

109. MLKFB Will.

110. Transcript of Record, 73, 80.

111. LWL Scrapbook.

112. Undated and unidentified newspaper clipping, in ibid. A similar report appears in the *Louisville Courier-Journal*, September 24, 1917.

113. *Louisville Post,* July 27, 1917.

114. *Wilmington Star,* July 31, August 1, 1917; *New York Times,* September 24, 1917; Thomas, "Let the Documents Speak," 337–41. Chandler and Chandler, *Binghams of Louisville,* 130, and Tifft and Jones, *The Patriarch,* 70, say that William was with Mary Lily when she died, but they do not cite any source for this assertion.

115. *Wilmington Star,* July 31, August 1, 1917.

116. Laura Moore Gavin to Mrs. Robert Love Kenan, September 21, 1941, Kenan Family Papers, SHC; MLKFB Will.

117. LWL Scrapbook.

118. Summary of detective's report. This document summarizes the report compiled for Graham Kenan by the private detectives he hired in the fall of 1917. The summary was prepared in the early 1990s by friends of the Kenan family and was made available to the author on the condition that it not be quoted and its authors not be contacted.

119. *Louisville Evening Post,* August 27, 1917.

120. Ibid.; Brenner, *House of Dreams,* 117 (quotation); LWL Scrapbook.

121. Quoted in Howell, *Kenan Professorships,* 17. The gift was first reported in the *Asheville Times,* August 11, 1917, after a resident of Palm Beach passed the newspaper a copy of Mary Lily's will. The Asheville paper was one of the few North Carolina papers to get the story correct. Most misunderstood the nature of Mary Lily's bequest to the university, reporting incorrectly that it provided only a one-time gift of $75,000.

122. MLKFB Will. According to the Court of Appeals of Kentucky, Mary Lily "died a resident of Jefferson county [Kentucky]." See *Louisville Trust Co. et al. v. Bingham et al.,* 199 *Southwestern Reporter* 59.

123. Transcript of Record, November 14, 1917.

124. Ibid., 80–81.

125. To the extent that the summary of the detective's report accurately reflects the actual report itself, the latter was a compilation of anti-Semitic innuendo, political backbiting, and wartime anxieties over Prohibition and woman suffrage. See *Louisville Courier-Journal,* September 22 and 23, 1917, for the break-in at Ravitch's office and the nurses' interviews.

126. Summary of detective's report; *NCAB,* 18:146–47, 32:499; *Who's Who in America* (1916–17), 9:1581; "Errors and Misstatements in *Passion and Prejudice,*" M&BBF. The pathologists included Dr. Ludvig Hektoen of the University of Chicago; Dr. William George MacCallum, the chief pathologist at Johns Hopkins; and Dr. Charles Norris, director of laboratories at Bellvue and Allied Hospitals and, after 1918, chief medical examiner of New York City.

127. Memo of Hugh Young, quoted in Thomas, "Let the Documents Speak," 347–51.

128. *New York Times,* September 24, 25 (quotation), 1917.

129. *Louisville Courier-Journal,* September 24, 1917.

130. *New York Post,* September 24, 1917.

131. *Louisville Courier-Journal,* September 27, 1917.

132. Unwitnessed affidavit-statement of Hugh H. Young, February 14, 1940, M&BBF.

CHAPTER EIGHT

1. William A. Blount to Helm Bruce, May 23, 1918, M&BBF.

2. William A. Blount to R. D. W. Connor, July 1, 1918, quoted in Howell, *Kenan Professorships,* 44.

3. William A. Blount to R. D. W. Connor, September 16, 1918, quoted in ibid., 45.

4. Howell, *Kenan Professorships,* 46.

5. MLKFB Will; *Incidents* 1:73.

6. Muir, "William Alexander Blount," 473–74. Blount's assistant, Scott Loftin, assumed the position of general counsel for the Flagler System. See *NCAB,* 46:500–501, for a biographical sketch of Loftin.

7. "Western Block Company History," undated, unpublished manuscript in Local History Collection, Lockport Public Library, Lockport, N.Y.

8. 196 *Kentucky Reports* 342–43.

9. *Louisville Courier-Journal,* September 25, 1917 (first, second, and third quotations); *New York Times,* September 25, 1917 (fourth quotation).

10. *Louisville Evening Post,* September 26, 1917.

11. "Memorial Sketch of Graham Kenan," in Andrews, *Proceedings,* 118–19. It is not clear what these "matters of large moment" were, but they were probably connected in some way with the Flagler properties in Florida and the legal work surrounding the settlement of Mary Lily's estate. Howell, *Kenan Professorships,* 9.

12. Owen Kenan to Lawrence Lewis [Sr.], September 17, 1917, telegram, and unidentified, undated newspaper clippings in LWL Scrapbook; Lawrence Lewis Jr. interview, September 24, 1991.

13. Thomas, "Let the Documents Speak," 349.

14. 220 *Southwestern Reporter* 728 (quotation); Howell, *Kenan Professorships,* 49.

15. Howell, *Kenan Professorships,* 49.

16. *DNCB,* 4:212–15; *Raleigh News & Observer,* February 16, 1916. Manning was one of the pallbearers at Mrs. Thomas S. Kenan's funeral. See *Raleigh News & Observer,* February 16, 1916.

17. Howell, *Kenan Professorships,* 49–52.

18. Ibid., 40–42.

19. Ibid., 32.

20. Ibid., 40, 56 (quotation), 60, 177–82.

21. See ibid., 54.

22. Quoted in Snider, *Light on the Hill,* 169. See Howell, *Kenan Professorships,* 54–55, and Louis R. Wilson, *University of North Carolina,* 505–6, for information on the Williams matter.

23. Louis R. Wilson, *University of North Carolina,* 505–6.

24. Winston, *Horace Williams*, 195–204.

25. Howell, *Kenan Professorships*, 55.

26. Ibid., 57–58.

27. Kenan, *History*, 1:13. Except where otherwise noted, the following narrative is based on this source.

28. Ibid., 14.

29. *Incidents* 2:50, 3:27–28, 83–84.

30. Russell, *President Harding*, 432.

31. *Incidents* 2:70–71.

32. Kenan, *History*, 2:19.

33. Muir, "William Alexander Blount," 475.

34. Ibid.

35. Grow letter to author, December 29, 1990.

36. Kenan, *History*, 2:19.

37. Ibid.

38. *Incidents* 1:78–79.

39. Quoted in Howell, *Kenan Professorships*, 50.

40. Ibid., 50, 58–59, 115–21. Connor was a former principal of the old Tileston School that William and his sisters had attended in Wilmington.

41. Ibid., 60. Howell cites the date of Sarah Kenan's gift, incorrectly, as December 1920. It was December 1921. See Louis R. Wilson, *University of North Carolina*, 460.

42. *Incidents* 1:79.

43. Quoted in Howell, *Kenan Professorships*, 51. Daniels had just received a loan for his newspaper, the *Raleigh News & Observer*, from Judge Robert Worth Bingham. See Chapter 10 at n. 83, below.

44. Quoted in Howell, *Kenan Professorships*, 51.

45. Russell, *President Harding*, 536–37; Hoffman, "History of the ACL," chap. 12.

46. *Incidents* 2:63.

47. *St. Augustine Evening Record*, March 11, 1922, quoted in *Incidents* 3:51–54.

48. Kenan, *History*, 1:38.

49. *Incidents* 1:95.

50. Hoffman, "History of the ACL," chap. 12.

51. Warren Smith Reminiscences, Warren Smith Collection, HMFM; *NCAB*, 37:288–89; Broadfoot, "Kenan House," 1–2.

52. Hoffman, "History of the ACL," chap. 12, pp. 1–8. The incident involving Lawrence Lewis's car was recalled by his son. See Lawrence Lewis Jr. interview, September 24, 1991.

53. 220 *Southwestern Reporter* 728; Howell, *Kenan Professorships*, 50; Thomas, "Let the Documents Speak," 338–39; "Errors and Misstatements in *Passion and Prejudice*," M&BBF.

54. Kenan, *History*, 1:18.

55. *Incidents* 1:79.

56. 196 *Kentucky Reports* 319.

57. Howell, *Kenan Professorships*, 52–53. Kentucky received approximately $3.3 million in inheritance taxes from Mary Lily's trustees, a figure based on the $67 million remaining in her estate after payment of federal and other state inheritance taxes. See Thomas, "Let the Documents Speak," 338–39, and "Errors and Misstatements in *Passion and Prejudice*," M&BBF.

58. Kenan, *History*, 1:23.

CHAPTER NINE

1. Thomas S. Kenan III interview, February 24, 1992.

2. Hoffman, "History of the ACL," chap. 12, p. 32.

3. *New York Times*, March 5, 1924.

4. Ibid., March 8, 1924.

5. Ibid., August 25, 1934. Prior to the agreement the company owned approximately 150 engines, 1,500 freight cars, and 150 passenger cars.

6. The bonds were sold in 1924, 1925, and 1926. See ibid., September 2, 1931.

7. *Incidents* 1:101.

8. Lockport Memorial Hospital Guild, *Lockport Memorial Hospital*, 7.

9. *NCAB*, 43:210.

10. Van De Mark interview.

11. *Incidents* 1:113.

12. Ibid., 112.

13. Strauss, *Our First One Hundred and Fifty Years*, 68–69; Janssen interview, September 21, 1990.

14. Janssen interview, September 20, 1990.

15. See ibid. for quotation. For the Klan's activities in Lockport, see Delahunt interview.

16. Janssen interview, September 21, 1990.

17. Hoffman, "History of the ACL," chap. 12, p. 34.

18. Ibid., p. 35.

19. Hass, "View of Times Past," 16–21.

20. *Incidents* 1:59, 81.

21. Kaylene Hughes, "Flagler Was the Founder," 25.

22. *Incidents* 2:63–64. The National Championship of Golf Club Champions began in 1928, and the National Amateur-Professional Best-Ball Match Play Championship started in 1935.

23. Hoffman, "History of the ACL," chap. 12, pp. 35–36.

24. *Incidents* 1:81–82 (first quotation); *New York Times*, August 26, 1951 (second quotation).

25. Curl, "Joseph Urban's Palm Beach Architecture," 436–37.

26. Ibid.

27. Melusky, "Palm Beach," 18.

28. *Incidents* 1:90.

29. Ibid., 82.

30. Hoffman, "History of the ACL," chap. 12, p. 36.

31. Ibid.

32. Mary Lily Flagler Lewis interview.

33. See Warren Smith Collection, HMFM.

34. Hosmer, "How the New Breakers Was Built," 27. See also R. C. Wilson, "New Breakers Hotel."

35. *Incidents* 1:103.

36. Newspaper clipping, *American Weekly*, 1936, in Florida East Coast Railway Collection, StAHS.

37. R. C. Wilson, "New Breakers Hotel," 10.

38. *Incidents* 1:103.

39. Ibid., 104.

40. *Kenan Memorial Stadium.*

41. Ibid. The author would like to thank Megan Mazzocchi of the Morehead Foundation for providing information on Morehead's honorary degree.

42. *Kenan Memorial Stadium.*

43. Bush, "Sun-Bound Highways," 110.

44. Hoffman, "History of the ACL," chap. 12, p. 43.

45. Except where otherwise noted, the details of the 1926 Florida banking failure are based on the author's telephone interviews with Raymond Vickers, June 18 and 19, 1991. Vickers, a former assistant comptroller of Florida, was one of the first, if not the first, researcher to gain access to the records of private banks that failed. He used this information for his 1991 dissertation at Florida State University, "Prelude to Panic: The Florida Banking Crisis of 1926."

46. Frank Hawkins Kenan interview, September 3, 1987, and various interviews with Thomas S. Kenan III.

47. R. C. Wilson, "New Breakers Hotel," 10.

48. Hoffman, "History of the ACL," chap. 12, p. 46 (first quotation); R. C. Wilson, "New Breakers Hotel," 10 (second quotation).

49. *Kenan Memorial Stadium*; Powell, *First State University*, 372.

50. Kaylene Hughes, "Flagler Was the Founder," 23.

51. "Hank" the milkman recollections. Hank says this incident took place sometime in the 1930s, but it appears to have occurred in late 1926 and early 1927. See *Proceedings of the City Council of Lockport: 1927*, "Minutes No. 2," 1, for a reprint of Alice's letter of resignation.

52. "Hank" the milkman recollections.

53. *New York Times*, January 9, 1927.

54. Ibid.

55. Ibid.

56. *Palm Beach Life*, January 18, 1927.

57. W. R. Kenan Jr. to Henry C. Turner, January 17, 1927, reprinted in R. C. Wilson, "New Breakers Hotel," 14.

58. *Incidents* 1:83.

59. *Palm Beach Life*, January 18, 1927.

60. *Incidents* 2:63.

61. *New York Times*, February 20, 1927.

62. *Incidents* 1:104.

63. Kenan, *History*, 1:25–26.

64. *Kenan Memorial Stadium.*

65. *Incidents* 1:89.

66. *Kenan Memorial Stadium.*

67. *Incidents* 1:89.

68. Bush, "Sun-Bound Highways," 113; Hoffman, "History of the ACL," chap. 12, pp. 45–55; *New York Times*, September 2, 1931.

69. *Incidents* 2:96. Hambleton was the son-in-law of the ACL's president, George Elliott.

70. Ibid.

71. Ibid.; Niagara County Records, William Rand Kenan Jr., Estate Tax Return, 1965, Rider to Schedule B, Niagara County Court House, Lockport, N.Y.

72. "The 1928, or West Palm Beach, Storm," folksong quoted in Kennedy, *Palmetto Country*, 39.

73. Winsberg, *Florida Weather*, 125.

74. The FEC Hotel Company used one wing of the Poinciana for several years as a nursery to supply flowers and plants to the rest of the Flagler hotels. Dismantling of the hotel began in 1934. See Cordwell interview.

75. U.S. Treasury Department, "Florida East Coast Railway Company Reorganization Proceedings," 129; Colburn and Scher, *Florida's Gubernatorial Politics*, 190.

76. Gibbs interview.

77. Ibid.

78. *Incidents* 1:97.

79. Louis R. Wilson, *University of North Carolina*, 335–57.

80. W. R. Kenan Jr. to H. W. Chase, October 24, 1929, quoted in Howell, *Kenan Professorships*, 62–63.

81. Howell, *Kenan Professorships*, 147; J. G. Hamilton to James Southall Wilson, January 4, 1930, J. G. Hamilton Papers, SHC.

82. Howell, *Kenan Professorships*, 245–47; folder 199, Robert Worth Bingham Papers, MD-FC; Rush, *Library Resources*, 31, 194; *Raleigh News & Observer*, January 8, 1939.

83. Howell, *Kenan Professorships*, 63 (first quotation); J. G. Hamilton to James Southall Wilson, January 4, 1930, Hamilton Papers, SHC (second quotation).

84. W. R. Kenan Jr. to H. W. Chase, January 25, 1930, CR, House Series.

85. Louis R. Wilson, *University of North Carolina*, 597; Snider, *Light on the Hill*, 207–8.

86. Kenan, *History*, 1:36.

87. *Ohio State University Bulletin.* After graduating from Ohio State University in 1899, Erf received his Ph.D. in science at the Vonn Behring Physiological Institute in Germany and returned to Ohio State University, where, between 1907

and his death in 1947, he taught and conducted research in the College of Agriculture. See Biographical Files, University Archives, Ohio State University, Columbus, Ohio. The author would like to thank Miss Bertha L. Inhat, archives assistant for manuscripts in the University Archives at OSU, for sending him this information. Erf's other qualifications and accomplishments are discussed further in the chapters that follow.

88. Kenan, *History*, 1:37.

CHAPTER TEN

1. *New York Times*, July 16, 1932; U.S. Treasury Department, "Florida East Coast Railway Company Reorganization Proceedings," 129.

2. *Incidents* 2:63–64.

3. See author's interviews with Gibbs, Lawrence Lewis Jr., and Mary Lily Flagler Lewis. See also Lockwood letter to author, October 18, 1991, for information on Freddie Francis.

4. *New York Times*, March 26, 1931.

5. The source of this quote wishes to remain anonymous.

6. *Incidents* 1:91–92. Additional details of this exciting event can be found in Broadfoot, "Kenan House," 3.

7. Kenan, *History*, 1:44.

8. Cordwell interview. Cordwell became Kenan's private secretary in New York and St. Augustine in January 1927.

9. U.S. Treasury Department, "Florida East Coast Railway Company Reorganization Proceedings," 128–29. See *New York Times*, September 2, 1931, for bond prices.

10. *New York Times*, September 2, 1931.

11. Ibid., September 8, 1931; U.S. Treasury Department, "Florida East Coast Railway Company Reorganization Proceedings," 134.

12. U.S. Treasury Department, "Florida East Coast Railway Company Reorganization Proceedings," 132.

13. Kenan, *History*, 1:44.

14. Louis R. Wilson, *University of North Carolina*, 391–405.

15. Ibid., 399.

16. Frank Hawkins Kenan interview, September 3, 1987.

17. "John M. Morehead Honored," *Carbidea*, May 1929, p. 6; John Motley Morehead Foundation, "Annual Report," 6; Scales, "Union Carbide Growth," 109. The author would like to thank Megan Mazzocchi of the Morehead Foundation for information on Morehead's awards.

18. *Raleigh News & Observer*, April 14, 1932.

19. Snider, *Light on the Hill*, 202–16.

20. Ibid., 209 (first quotation); *Raleigh News & Observer*, April 14, 1932 (second

quotation). For Graham's creative use of the money from the Kenan professorships to help retain faculty, see Howell, *Kenan Professorships*, 64–65.

21. *Raleigh News & Observer*, April 14, 1932; Cromartie, *Pointing the Way*, 17. Destroyed by fire at the end of 1925, the church was rebuilt in 1928. Though neither William nor his sisters appear to have then been members of the church, they each gave approximately $17,000 to construct the chapel, tower, and spire as a memorial to their mother and father. See *Incidents* 1:119.

22. See *Findlay v. Florida East Coast Ry. Co.*, 3 Federal Supplement 393, 397.

23. Ibid.

24. *New York Times*, July 16, 1932.

25. Quoted in Charles T. Woollen to Dennis G. Brummitt, July 21, 1932, CR, House Series. Woollen sent the telegram in Dr. Frank Porter Graham's name because Graham got married that same day and left on a month-long honeymoon in Canada.

26. Ibid. (first quotation); W. R. Kenan Jr. to Frank P. Graham, July 21, 1932, CR, House Series (second quotation).

27. Charles T. Woollen to Frank P. Graham, [1932], Frank Porter Graham Files, POR.

28. Ibid. For information on Battle, see *NCAB*, C:195–96, and *DNCB*, 1:109–18. The *New York Evening Journal*, September 27, 1917, mentions Battle's law firm as the New York counsel for Bingham.

29. Tifft and Jones, *The Patriarch*, 124; Maurice T. Van Hecke to A. F. Seawell, August 18, 1937, Graham Files, POR.

30. *Congressional Record*, March 15, 1933, 491–94; Morgan, *FDR*, 393; Thomas, "Let the Documents Speak," 350–51.

31. If any of the Kenans aided the campaign against Bingham, it was William's cousin, Dr. Owen Kenan. Though there is no documentary evidence of Owen's complicity in the 1933 move against the Judge, he knew the Flexner brothers well and appears to have dealt with Jacob Flexner in 1917 when the latter floated rumors regarding "foul play" in Mary Lily's death. In 1937, moreover, Owen's good friend Randolph Churchill, the son of Winston Churchill, would use the columns of an English newspaper to resurrect the foul-play rumors against the U.S. ambassador to Great Britain, Robert Worth Bingham. See Robert Worth Bingham to Lord Beaverbrook, November 1, 1937, and Beaverbrook to Bingham, November 1, 1937, in M&BBP.

32. *Findlay v. Florida East Coast Ry. Co.*, 3 Federal Supplement 393, 397 (emphasis added).

33. Howell, *Kenan Professorships*, 68.

34. Maurice T. Van Hecke to A. F. Seawell, August 18, 1937, Graham Files, POR.

35. Howell, *Kenan Professorships*, 68.

36. Ibid. What makes this passage so peculiar is that item No. 8 of Mary Lily's will says nothing about securities; it mentions only cash. Her trustees had the right, if they deemed "it compatible with the interests of my estate and the purpose of the trust hereby created," to pay to the university, "at any time prior to the

expiration of the trust, . . . such sum in cash at the rate of interest then current in North Carolina [as] will produce an annual income of seventy-five thousand ($75,000.00) Dollars, the amount of such sum to be determined by my said Trustees." See MLKFB Will.

37. "Excerpts from the minutes of the full Board of Trustees covering its regular meeting on June 7, 1940: '4. Settlement of Kenan Trust Fund,'" CR, House Series; Howell, *Kenan Professorships*, 68–73; *Raleigh News & Observer*, June 1, 1937.

38. F. P. Graham to Owen Hill Kenan, May 30, 1935, Frank Porter Graham Papers, SHC.

39. F. P. Graham to Owen Kenan, February 19, 1931, Graham Papers, SHC. The letter from W. T. Couch, director of UNC Press, to Owen Kenan is mentioned by Graham.

40. James Kenan to F. P. Graham, July 8, 1935, and Sarah Kenan to F. P. Graham, July 11, 1935, Graham Papers, SHC.

41. F. P. Graham to James Kenan, July 11, 1935, and Graham to Sarah Kenan, July 17, 1935, both in ibid.

42. James Kenan to F. P. Graham, July 8, 1935, in ibid.

43. Warren Smith Collection, HMFM.

44. Snider, *Light on the Hill*, 202–22.

45. Halperin, "Frank Porter Graham," 385–410.

46. Ibid., 403; Howell, *Kenan Professorships*; Bursey, *Francis Preston Venable*, 108. Manning was also appointed Kenan professor emeritus upon his retirement in 1939. See *NCDB*, 4:212.

47. Snider, *Light on the Hill*, 220. Though the details of his plan were not released until January 1936, Graham first mentioned his general ideas to UNC's Board of Trustees in November 1934.

48. *Incidents* 1:31–32.

49. Frank Hawkins Kenan interview, September 3, 1987.

50. Winsberg, *Florida Weather*, 119.

51. *Incidents* 2:68.

52. *New York Times*, February 27, 1936.

53. Carosso, *The Morgans*, 606, 628.

54. Testimony of Alfred E. Myers, vice-president and treasurer of the New York Life Insurance Company, SM, ICC-FEC Hearings, March 17, 1941, 129–34.

55. Testimony of Arthur M. Anderson, vice-president of J. P. Morgan and Co. Incorporated, SM, ICC-FEC Hearings, March 17, 1941, 91–92.

56. Ibid., 94–95.

57. Question of Edgar G. Crossman, in ibid., 278–79.

58. Exhibit 35, March 18, 1941, in ibid., 481.

59. *New York Times*, September 16, 1935.

60. Quoted in ibid., November 17, 1935.

61. Ibid., February 20, 21 (quotation), 27, 1936.

62. Ibid., September 26, 1936, January 21, 1937. Bankers Trust paid $328,000 for the equipment and announced that the equipment might be resold for as much as $500,000.

63. Ibid., September 24, 1936.

64. Ibid., October 22, 1936.

65. Lawrence Lewis Jr. interview, September 24, 1991, and Mary Lily Flagler Lewis interview.

66. Lawrence Lewis Jr. interview, September 24, 1991, and Mary Lily Flagler Lewis interview; *American Weekly*, 1936, clipping in StAHS (quotation).

67. *New York Times*, April 10, 1937.

68. Maurice T. Van Hecke to A. F. Seawell, August 18, 1937, Graham Files, POR.

69. Quoted in *New York Times*, April 10, 1937.

70. The date of Eimer's article is mentioned in W. R. Kenan Jr. to Dr. Colin Frink, December 2, 1938, Kenan Family Papers, SHC. Another source, "Notes on Data of Pertinence to the Early History of Carbide," KC, notes the publication date of Eimer's article as 1927. A search of the periodical literature for the period turned up no mention of Eimer's article. See *NCAB*, 14:193–94, for a biographical sketch of Eimer, and Chapter 4, above, for his earlier involvement with Willson and the Willson Aluminum Company.

71. F. L. Spangler to W. R. Kenan Jr., November 13, 1936, KC.

72. F. L. Spangler to W. R. Kenan Jr., December 23, 1936, KC.

73. See "Notes on Data of Pertinence to the Early History of Carbide," KC.

74. Janssen interview, September 21, 1990; Mary Lily Flagler Lewis interview; biographical files, Niagara County Historian's Office, Lockport, N.Y.

75. Robert D. Gumbel to J. D. Rahner, June 9, 1937; John D. Rockefeller Jr. to W. R. Kenan Jr. and Scott Loftin, August 9, 1937 (first quotation); and W. R. Kenan Jr. to John D. Rockefeller Jr., August 16, 1937 (second quotation), Rockefeller Archive Center, North Tarrytown, N.Y.

76. *Raleigh News & Observer*, June 1, 1937; Lawrence Lewis Jr. interview, September 24, 1991.

77. *Raleigh News & Observer*, June 1, 1937; Mary Lily Flagler Lewis interview.

78. Laura Moore Gavin to Mrs. Robert Love Kenan, September 21, 1941, Kenan Family Papers, SHC.

79. Howell, *Kenan Professorships*, 70–71.

80. Maurice T. Van Hecke to A. F. Seawell, August 18, 1937, Graham Files, POR.

81. Chandler and Chandler, *Binghams of Louisville*, 197. For Daniels's visit with Bingham in London, see Josephus Daniels to Barry Bingham Sr., December 19, 1937, M&BBP.

82. Josephus Daniels to Barry Bingham Sr., December 19, 1937, M&BBP.

83. Ibid.

CHAPTER ELEVEN

1. "Notes on Data of Pertinence to the Early History of Carbide," KC.

2. See ibid. and "James Turner Morehead," KC.

3. "Notes on Data of Pertinence to the Early History of Carbide," KC.

4. See "Willson Aluminum Company" and "Early Workers," both in KC.

5. W. R. Kenan Jr. to Colin Frink, December 2, 1938, Kenan Family Papers, SHC.

6. Colin Frink to W. R. Kenan Jr., December 5, 1938, in ibid.

7. W. R. Kenan Jr. to Colin Frink, January 17, 1939; Frink to Kenan, January 25, 1939 (first quotation); Kenan to Frink, January 27, 1939 (second quotation), all in ibid.

8. Kenan, *Discovery*, December 2, 1938, copy in ibid.

9. Ibid.

10. Ibid.

11. Colin Frink to W. R. Kenan Jr., February 28, 1939, Kenan Family Papers, SHC.

12. W. R. Kenan Jr. to Colin Frink, April 6, 1939 (first quotation); Frink to Kenan, April 10, 1939 (second quotation); Kenan to Frink, April 12, 1939, all in ibid.

13. Anderson testimony, SM, ICC-FEC Hearings, March 17, 1941, 95.

14. *Incidents* 2:68.

15. W. R. Kenan Jr. to F. P. Graham, April 7, 1939, and Graham to Kenan, May 1, 1939, Frank Porter Graham Papers, SHC; Howell, *Kenan Professorships*, 70–71.

16. Howell, *Kenan Professorships*, 70–72. According to the minutes of the June 7, 1940, meeting of the UNC trustees, the university received "the following marketable securities and cash:"

6,000 shares American Power & Light Company $6 Preferred Stock
4,000 shares Standard Oil of California Stock
14,000 shares Socony-Cacuum Oil Company, Inc., Stock
7,000 shares National Fuel Gas Company Stock
$600,000 principal amount American Power & Light Company 6% Debenture
    Bonds due 2016
$560,000 in cash.

The American Power & Light stocks and bonds were among the AP&L securities in Mary Lily's trust that Kenan received from the utility holding company in exchange for the Flagler System's water and electric companies in Miami. See *Incidents* 3:43–44 and "Settlement of Kenan Trust Fund," Excerpts from Trustees' Meeting, June 7, 1940, CR, House Series.

17. *Incidents* 1:49–50; Anderson testimony, SM, ICC-FEC Hearings, March 17, 1941, 98–100.

18. F. P. Graham to W. R. Kenan Jr., July 1, 1940, Graham Papers, SHC.

19. *Incidents* 1:119.

20. W. R. Kenan Jr. to "My dear Lowell" [Lowell Erf], January 3, 1940, Ernest O. Lawrence Records, LBL. The author would like to thank Lori Hefner of the Archives and Record Office at Berkeley for photocopying the Kenan correspondence in the Lawrence Records.

21. W. R. Kenan Jr. to John Lawrence, January 22, 1940 (first quotation), and Kenan to Ernest O. Lawrence, February, 22, 1940 (second quotation), Lawrence Records, LBL.

22. Ernest Lawrence to W. R. Kenan Jr., March 2, 1940, in ibid.

23. Ernest Lawrence to W. R. Kenan Jr., April 4, 1940, in ibid.

24. W. R. Kenan Jr. to Ernest Lawrence, April 15, 1940, in ibid.

25. Oscar Erf, "Minerals and the Development of the Sophie Tormentors," in Kenan, *History*, 2:171.

26. Kenan, *History*, 3:235. See ibid., 2, and 2:3, for figures on herd size and cost.

27. Ibid., 2:50.

28. Ibid., 55.

29. Ibid., 58–59.

30. Ibid., 156.

31. Grow letter to author, December 29, 1990 (second quotation), and February 6, 1991 (first quotation).

32. Ibid., December 29, 1990.

33. Groff interview.

34. Grow letter to author, December 29, 1990.

35. Both the cows and their feed were exposed to ultraviolet lights made by the National Carbon Company's Solarium Lamps. See the first three editions of Kenan's *History*.

36. Information on Inman comes from photocopies of newspaper clippings, letters, and pamphlets in both the Antiochiana Collection and the KLF-OKL. See, for example, "Professor at Antioch Says Cows Need Vitamins, Too," *Dayton Daily News*, January 19, 1937; "Finding out Why Grass Is Green," *Cleveland Plain Dealer*, May 14, 1939; Inman, *Kettering Foundation*; and Oscar Erf to A. D. Henderson, July 31, 1942, Antioch College Letters, Antioch College, Yellow Springs, Ohio.

37. O. L. Inman to W. R. Kenan Jr., October 28, 1936, and Inman to D. G. Perkins, November 2, 1936 (quotation), KLF-OKL.

38. W. R. Kenan Jr. to O. L. Inman, November 3, 1936, KLF-OKL.

39. Kenan, *History*, 2:285–97.

40. See Kenan Correspondence in KLF-OKL.

41. Hildreth, "Experiments in Nutritional Value of Milk," in Kenan, *History*, 3:214.

42. Ibid.

43. O. Erf, "Pasteurization," in Kenan, *History*, 3:254.

44. H. H. Weiser, speech at Randleigh Farm, September 1958, in ibid., 9:xiv.

45. Levenstein, *Revolution*, 134.

46. Ibid., 41, 154.

47. Ibid.

48. Janssen interview, September 20, 1990.

49. Ibid.

50. Groff interview.

51. Weiser, speech at Randleigh, September 1958, in Kenan, *History*, 9:xiv.

52. See the second and third editions of Kenan, *History*, and Kenan Correspondence, KLF-OKL, for these developments.

53. "Oscar Erf," biographical file, Ohio State University News Bureau, Ohio State University Archives, Columbus, Ohio.

54. Ibid.; Oscar Erf to A. D. Henderson, July 31, 1942, Antioch College Letters, Antioch College, Yellow Springs, Ohio; Crews, *American Jersey Cattle Club*, 6–79.

55. Crews, *American Jersey Cattle Club*, 79.

56. "Oscar Erf," biographical file, Ohio State University Archives.

57. Levenstein, *Revolution*, 130.

58. Crews, *American Jersey Cattle Club*, 77–78.

59. See Crews, *American Jersey Cattle Club*, for the club's geographical realignment.

60. *Jersey Bulletin*, August 1944, reprinted in *Incidents* 1:127.

61. *Jersey Bulletin*, March 1945, reprinted in ibid., 129.

62. *New York Times*, February 22, 1941 (quotation); SM, ICC-FEC Hearings, March 17, 1941, 99–100; Stoesen, "Road from Receivership," 136.

63. For information on Ball's background, see Griffith, *Ed Ball*; Mason and Harrison, *Confusion to the Enemy*; and Wall, *Alfred I. du Pont*.

64. Ball's relationship with the FBI is covered, with several strategic deletions, in Ed Ball File, Federal Bureau of Investigation, Washington, D.C. Copy obtained through the Freedom of Information Act; copy in possession of author.

65. Ed Ball Testimony, SM, ICC-FEC Hearings, April 21, 1941, 662.

66. Cordwell interview.

67. Ball Testimony, SM, ICC-FEC Hearings, April 21, 1941, 666–67.

68. Cordwell interview.

69. Ibid.

70. *New York Times*, February 22, 1941.

71. Ibid.

72. "Last Will and Testament of Sarah Graham Kenan, Dated March 20, 1951," copy in William T. Joyner Papers, SHC; Walter G. Cooper, *Official History of Fulton County*, 616–23.

73. For information on Stetson, see Bond, *Eugene W. Stetson*. On the Coleman-Stetson-Hawkins connection, see Young et al., *History of Macon, Georgia*, 633, and Coleman Family Reference Files, Genealogical & Historical Room, Washington Memorial Library, Macon, Ga.

74. Bond, *Eugene W. Stetson*, 59; Iola and Eugene Stetson to Louise Wise, May 3, 1917, LWL Scrapbook; *New York Times*, January 9, 1927; Nancy Briska Anderson, *Macon*, 101. Iola Wise's uncle, Joseph Clisby Wise, was Louise's father.

75. Bond, *Eugene W. Stetson*, 134; Scott Loftin Testimony, SM, ICC-FEC Hearings, March 18, 1941, 227.

76. The Anderson and duPont plans are covered in detail in the testimony presented at the ICC-FEC hearings. The basics of the two plans are presented in *New York Times*, March 9, 18, 27, 1941. The best summary of the plans and of the subject is Stoesen, "Road from Receivership."

77. Mrs. F. P. Venable to Charles S. Venable, April 24, 1941, Venable Papers, SHC.

78. Reprinted in *Incidents* 2:99.

79. W. R. Kenan Jr. to Colin Frink, May 3, 1941, Kenan Family Papers, SHC.

80. Mrs. F. P. Venable to Charles S. Venable, April 24, 1941, Venable Papers, SHC.

81. "Union Carbide I."

82. W. R. Kenan Jr. to Richard Wood, June 5, 1941, Kenan Family Papers, SHC.

83. Richard Wood to W. R. Kenan Jr., June 9, 1941, in ibid.

84. Ibid.

85. W. R. Kenan Jr. to Richard Wood, July 1, 1941, Kenan Family Papers, SHC.

86. Richard Wood to W. R. Kenan Jr., July 18, 1941, in ibid.

87. W. R. Kenan Jr. to Richard Wood, July 23, 1941, in ibid.

88. "Carbide & Carbon Chemicals," 154.

89. Ibid.

CHAPTER TWELVE

1. *Incidents* 1:6.

2. Lockwood letter to author, September 15, 1991. Lockwood was the FEC Railway's chief surgeon in Florida between 1930 and 1960.

3. "50 Years—1941," *Lockport Union-Sun & Journal*, September 9, 1991.

4. Raff letter to author, March 11, 1991.

5. Ibid.

6. *History of Northwestern New York*, 3:314.

7. "50 Years—1941," *Lockport Union-Sun & Journal*, September 9, 1991; Raff letter to author, March 11, 1991 (quotation).

8. Kenan, *History*, 5:1.

9. Ibid., 1–3.

10. Ibid. For Kenan's purchase of the Wendt Farm in 1941, see ibid., 4:1. Letters concerning the first silage studies in 1939–40 can be found in Kenan Correspondence, KLF-OKL. Inman's death is mentioned in Oscar Erf to A. D. Henderson, July 31, 1942, Antioch College Letters, Antioch College, Yellow Springs, Ohio.

11. Crews, *American Jersey Cattle Club*, 78.

12. *New York Times*, April 12, 14, 1942.

13. Cordwell interview.

14. *New York Times*, July 31, 1942. Lynch's role in the FEC's reorganization is very interesting if not exactly clear. He was apparently a native of North Carolina and an acquaintance of Kenan's good friend from Wilmington, N.C., Champion McDowell Davis, who became president of the ACL in 1942. Lynch owned $5 million F&R 5s, which he initially deposited with the Anderson committee. Though not particularly comfortable with the committee's reorganization plan, he opposed Ball's efforts to present a competing scheme to the ICC in Washington, D.C., in the spring of 1941. What made him withdraw his bonds from the committee in 1942, however, and form an alliance with Ball is not clear. But, as mentioned further below, he broke with the duPont trustee in 1944, when the ACL made a bid for the FEC—a bid supported by W. R. Kenan Jr. For a summary of Lynch's bond pur-

chases, see his testimony in SM, ICC-FEC Hearings, March 19, 1941, 526–34; for his opposition to Ball's plan, see his cross-examination of Ball, April 21, 1941, 698–718; for his alliance with Ball, see *New York Times*, July 31, 1942; and for his relationship with ACL president Champ Davis, see photocopy of an undated newspaper article from the *Orlando Sentinel* in box 39, folder 2, series 201, M&CPP. There are also papers pertaining to Lynch and the FEC in the Special Collections Department of Baker Library, Harvard University; see "FEC Railway Reorganization."

15. Kaylene Hughes, "Flagler Was the Founder," 25; *Incidents* 1:92. Jessie and Sarah transferred their legal residence from North Carolina to Florida in order to escape North Carolina's income and inheritance taxes. Florida had neither an income tax nor an inheritance tax. In the 1950s, however, both women again became legal residents of North Carolina.

16. Kaylene Hughes, "Flagler Was the Founder," 25; "Annual Report—Ream General Hospital, 1943," Unit Annual Reports, World War II Administrative Records, 319.1, RG 112, National Archives, Washington, D.C.

17. Kaylene Hughes, "Flagler Was the Founder," 25; *Incidents* 2:20–25.

18. Janssen interview, September 21, 1990.

19. Van De Mark interview.

20. *Incidents* 2:65.

21. "Deposition of Mr. Ed Ball," SM, ICC-FEC Hearings, Jacksonville District Court, November 9, 1948.

22. Hoffman, "History of the ACL," chap. 14; Stoesen, "Road from Receivership," 135. The war's impact on the FEC is discussed in almost every ICC hearing from 1941 on.

23. *Incidents* 3:28.

24. Ibid., 1:111 (quotation), 2:93.

25. Ibid., 1:111.

26. F. P. Graham to W. R. Kenan Jr., August 16, 1944, Kenan Family Papers, SHC.

27. Prince, *Atlantic Coast Line*, 57.

28. Warren Smith Collection, HMFM (quotation); *Incidents* 1:96; Prince, *Atlantic Coast Line*, 57.

29. "Kenan Gives $350,000 to Davis Nursing Home," undated [ca. 1965] unidentified [Wilmington] newspaper clipping in the Lower Cape Fear Historical Society, Wilmington, N.C.

30. Cutler testimony, SM, ICC-FEC Hearings, Washington, D.C., May 3, 1944, 1166–74; "Deposition of Mr. Ed Ball," SM, ICC-FEC Hearings, Jacksonville District Court, November 9, 1948, 202–3; Hoffman, "History of the ACL," chap. 14, p. 20.

31. W. R. Kenan Jr. to Scott Loftin, November 3, 1944 (first quotation), and Davis testimony (second quotation), both in Transcript of Proceedings, June 21, 1954, United States District Court, Southern District of Florida, Jacksonville Division, 41–55.

32. W. R. Kenan Jr. to Scott Loftin, November 3, 1944, in ibid., 54.

33. "Kenan Gives $350,000," unidentified, undated newspaper clipping in the Lower Cape Fear Historical Society, Wilmington, N.C.

34. Stoesen, "Road from Receivership," 137.

35. Ibid., 137–38.

36. *Incidents* 3:65.

37. Stoesen, "Road from Receivership," 139–40.

38. *Incidents* 3:67.

39. Ibid., 1:135.

40. Stoesen, "Road from Receivership," 139.

41. Ibid. For information on the nature and extent of Ball's activities, see series 201, boxes 38–45, M&CPP.

42. Moorman M. Parrish to W. R. Fokes [Pepper's secretary], December 20, 1945, series 201, box 39, folder 5, M&CPP.

43. Ibid.

44. B. C. Forte to Claude Pepper, May 30, 1945, series 201, box 39, folder 4A, M&CPP.

45. Quoted in Stoesen, "Road from Receivership," 141.

46. Lockwood letters to author. According Lockwood, the FEC always worked closely with the railroad brotherhoods in the area of medical care, showing a strong interest in helping the railroad's "employees to obtain hospital and medical benefits at very reasonable rates. These benefits were begun in Mr. Flagler's time and were carried on during Mr. Kenan's tenure as president of the railway."

47. J. A. Cawthon to Claude Pepper, February, 24, 1946, series 201, box 40, folder 4, M&CPP.

48. W. F. Howard to Claude Pepper, September 1, 1946, in ibid.

49. Stoesen, "Road from Receivership," 140–41.

50. "Interview with 'Samuel C. McDaniel (St. Johns),'" n.a., n.d., series 201, box 41, folder 1, M&CPP.

51. "Interview with 'Jim Caspar (St. Johns),'" in ibid.

52. Transcript of Proceedings, June 21, 1954, United States District Court, Southern District of Florida, Jacksonville Division, 56–63.

53. "ACL Witnesses . . . Dupont Witnesses," series 201, box 38, folder 4, M&CPP. The remarks by Ball and the ICC are quoted in Stoesen, "Road from Receivership," 142.

54. Stoesen, "Road from Receivership," 141–42; Champ Davis to Claude Pepper, July 10, 1945, and Pepper to John L. Rogers, July 26, 1945, series 201, box 39, folder 4A, M&CPP.

55. Edward W. Bourne to James C. Clements, December 8, 1945, series 201, box 40, folder 2, M&CPP.

56. J. A. Cawthon to Claude Pepper, February 24, 1946, series 201, box 40, folder 4, M&CPP; Stoesen, "Road from Receivership," 144.

57. Stoesen, "Road from Receivership," 144.

58. Champ Davis to W. R. Fokes, September 27, 1946, series 201, box 41, folder 1, M&CPP.

59. *Incidents* 2:40–41.

60. Quoted in Stoesen, "Road from Receivership," 146.

61. Mary Lily Flagler Lewis interview.

CHAPTER THIRTEEN

1. *Incidents* 2:58.

2. Ibid., 3:77–79.

3. Stoesen, "Road from Receivership," 148.

4. *Incidents* 2:87.

5. Janssen interview, September 21, 1990.

6. Morehead Foundation, "Annual Report," 6 (quotation); *Incidents* 2:95.

7. *Incidents* 2:56.

8. Ibid., 55.

9. Ibid. (first quotation) and 3:35 (second quotation).

10. Ibid., 2:55.

11. Ibid., 54–57.

12. Ibid., 88.

13. Ibid., 1:119.

14. See the third, fourth, and fifth editions of *Incidents*.

15. Morehead Foundation, "Annual Report 1989," 6. According to this report, Richard Moll, *The Public Ivys* (1985), makes the claim that the Morehead Awards were the "first" such scholarships.

16. *Incidents* 4:89.

17. Robert B. House to W. R. Kenan Jr., June 23, 1954, CR, House Series. For the scholarship fund, see Trust Agreement, November 27, 1954, in ibid. According to this agreement, the income from the fund was to be "used first for the purpose of awarding scholarships and grants in aid to deserving students who have demonstrated proficiency in one or more athletic programs at the University and have been awarded Numerals or Monograms or the equivalent recognition for athletic achievement." Any surplus income could be used for the upkeep of the facilities and surrounding grounds of Kenan Stadium, and if for any reason the fund could be used in the future for athletic scholarships and the stadium, the income it generated could be "used for scholarships and grants in aid to worthy students."

18. "Hank" the milkman recollections.

19. See Chapter 3 at n. 72, above.

20. *UNC Football Media Guide, 1993*.

21. "Hank" the milkman recollections; *UNC Football Media Guide, 1993*. It was also in 1960 that NASA astronauts first came to Morehead Planetarium to study celestial navigation. In 1975, when the astronauts ceased using the planetarium, UNC lost the last game it played against Notre Dame, leaving the Tar Heels with a miserable 1 and 15 record in the series. The two teams did not play in 1957, and after 1960 they met at irregular intervals: 1962, 1965, 1966, 1971, and 1975.

22. Martin interview.

23. Ibid.

24. Stoesen, "Road from Receivership," 145–48.

25. *Miami Herald*, April 18, 1965.

26. Warren Smith Collection, HMFM.

27. Ibid.; *Incidents* 2:62; Prince, *Atlantic Coast Line*, 57–59.

28. See Kaylene Hughes, "Flagler Was the Founder," for the fates of the Flagler hotels. The Casa Marina in Key West was planned before Flagler's death in 1913. Construction began in 1918 but was interrupted by the First World War and other difficulties, and the hotel was not completed until 1921.

29. Stoesen, "Road from Receivership," 148–49.

30. Ibid., 150–52.

31. Snider, *Light on the Hill*, 236.

32. See "Another Fountain Accident," unidentified newspaper clipping, 1950, Louis T. Moore Collection, New Hanover County Public Library, Wilmington, N.C.

33. J. R. Benson to W. R. Kenan Jr., June 13, 1950, in ibid.

34. *Incidents* 2:43.

35. W. R. Kenan Jr. to J. R. Benson, June 21, 1950, Moore Collection, New Hanover County Public Library, Wilmington, N.C.

36. Louis T. Moore to W. R. Kenan Jr., July 1, 1950, in ibid.

37. W. R. Kenan Jr. to Louis T. Moore, September 21, 1951, in ibid.

38. *Incidents* 3:42 (first quotation) and 4:79 (second quotation).

39. O. P. Johnson, F. W. McGowan, and V. H. Reynolds, "Sketch on Duplin County," manuscript, n.d., Dorothy Whitener Library, Kenansville, N.C.; *Incidents* 2:89.

40. *Duplin Times*, December 29, 1950, reprinted in *Incidents* 3:80–82.

41. Ibid.

42. Lawrence Lewis Jr. interview, September 24, 1991.

43. On October 25, 1951, in a decision that effectively reversed the district court's 1949 "forced merger" ruling, the ICC approved yet another reorganization plan under which the assets of the FEC would be vested in the ACL. But this plan was also rejected by the district court, which likewise dismissed the ICC proceedings too, only to have its ruling reversed by the court of appeals, which reinstated the plan. Ed Ball and the duPont trustees then filed a petition for certiorari with the U.S. Supreme Court, and the justices agreed to hear the case. Stoesen, "Road from Receivership," 148–53; Hoffman, "History of the ACL," chap. 15, pp. 27–29.

44. Arguments of Robert T. McCracken, SM, ICC-FEC Hearings, United States Court of Appeals for the Fifth Circuit, New Orleans, La., December 6, 1955, 4–5.

45. Stoesen, "Road from Receivership," 148–53; Hoffman, "History of the ACL," chap, 15, p. 28.

46. *Miami Herald*, August 16, 1955; *Miami Daily News*, August 16, 1955; *Florida Times-Union*, August 16, 1955. The *Buffalo News* and the *Lockport Union-Sun* also ran stories on August 16, 1955, regarding Kenan's role in dedicating Florida Power

& Light's new power station at Cutler and his long association as both an electrical engineer and director of the power company and its predecessor, the Miami Electric Light & Power Company. All of these newspaper stories, including those from the *Record*, are reprinted in *Incidents* 5:61–65, 126.

47. *Miami Herald*, April 18, 1965.

48. Arguments of Edwin W. Cooney, SM, ICC-FEC Hearings, Transcript of Proceedings, United States District Court, Southern District of Florida, Jacksonville Division, April 27, 1955, 86.

49. Arguments of Joseph Schreiber, SM, ICC-FEC Hearings, United States Court of Appeals for the Fifth Circuit, New Orleans, La., December 6, 1955, 67.

50. Arguments of Robert McCracken, in ibid., December 6, 1955, 27.

51. Hoffman, "History of the ACL," chap. 15, p. 28.

52. Ibid., p. 29.

53. Ibid.

54. Ibid.

55. *Miami Herald*, June 21, 1956.

56. Ibid.

57. Robert K. Frey testimony, SM, ICC-FEC Hearing, Washington, D.C., June 19, 1956, 7568–79.

58. Schreiber response, in ibid., June 20, 1956, 7692.

59. A. R. MacMannis testimony, in ibid., 7687.

60. *Miami Herald*, June 20, 21, 1956.

61. Hoffman, "History of the ACL," chap. 16, p. 18.

62. Quoted in Hewlett, *Jessie Ball duPont*, 243.

63. Quoted in *Incidents* 5:124, from a reprint of a story in the *St. Augustine Record*, March 23, 1958.

64. Quoted in Junior League of Wilmington, *Old Wilmington Guidebook*, 6.

CHAPTER FOURTEEN

1. Westhafer interview.

2. Henrietta Lewis interview.

3. Thomas S. Kenan III, *Sarah Graham Kenan Foundation*, 8–12; Lawrence Lewis Jr. interviews; Mary Lily Flagler Lewis interview.

4. Henrietta Lewis interview (first and fourth quotations); "Hank" the milkman recollections (third quotation); Lockwood letter to author, September 15, 1991 (second and fifth quotations).

5. "Hank" the milkman recollections.

6. Westhafer interview.

7. *Incidents* 2:40–41.

8. Henrietta Lewis interview.

9. *Incidents* 2:28.

10. "Hank" the milkman recollections.

11. Storrs interview. See Lewis L. Fawcett to W. R. Kenan Jr., Spring 1951, in *Incidents* 3:31–32, for the history of the King Tut peas.

12. *Incidents* 2:50.

13. Ibid.

14. Henrietta Lewis interview (first quotation); Storrs interview (second quotation).

15. Westhafer interview; Henrietta Lewis interview.

16. Westhafer interview.

17. Grow letter to author, December 29, 1990. Grow was a trust officer at Marine Midland. Kenan mentions his own appointment as chairman of the "advisory" board of "Marine Trust Company of Western New York" in *Incidents* 3:42. The Flagler-Rogers connection to Marine Midland's corporate predecessor, the Niagara County National Bank, is noted in *Lockport Union-Sun & Journal*, August 4, 1965. For information on Rogers and others connected with the house at 433 Locust Street, see I. Richard Reed to Roger G. Reed, October 4, 1982, Kenan File, Niagara County Historian's Office, Lockport, N.Y.

18. Grow letter to author, December 29, 1990.

19. *Lockport Union-Sun & Journal*, March 24, 1961.

20. Ibid., May 31, 1985.

21. Grow letter to author, December 29, 1990.

22. Groff interview.

23. See Kenan, *History*, 7:1 and 9:192.

24. Janssen interview, September 21, 1990.

25. See a facsimile of the plaque in Kenan, *History*, 9:x.

26. Janssen interview, September 21, 1990.

27. Storrs interview.

28. Ibid.

29. Henrietta Lewis interview (first quotation); Lockwood letter to author, September 15, 1991 (second quotation).

30. Westhafer interview; Strauss, *Our First One Hundred and Fifty Years*, 54–55.

31. Westhafer interview (first quotation); Henrietta Lewis interview (second quotation). The descriptions of the Bishop house are taken from both of these interviews. See *Incidents* 2:51 for Kenan's acquisition of the Bishop property. On Rossman's condition, see "Hank" the milkman recollections.

32. *Lockport Union-Sun & Journal*, June 23, 1965. Smiley's story appeared in the *Miami Herald* on April 18, 1965. The Lockport paper actually misquotes the *Herald*'s opening note, which said the Flagler's heirs "have pyramided their inheritance into hundreds of millions of dollars."

33. Westhafer interview.

34. Ibid.

35. Lockport Tourism Committee and Lockport Common Council, *Welcome to Lockport*, brochure.

36. "Last Will and Testament of William R. Kenan, Jr.," Niagara County Court-house, Lockport, N.Y., 4–8; *Raleigh News & Observer*, October 2, 1965; *Buffalo Evening News*, February 27(?), 1966; *Greensboro Daily News*, May 17, 1971 (quotation); Department of Agricultural Communications, North Carolina State University, *Ten Years of Research at Randleigh Farm*, 2; Westhafer interview.

37. William R. Kenan, Jr. Charitable Trust, *First Twenty-Five Years.*

BIBLIOGRAPHY

INTERVIEWS AND RECOLLECTIONS

Cluett, Robert. Interview by author. Chapel Hill, N.C., April 26, 1990.

Colbey, Howard J., Jr. Interview by author. Lockport, N.Y., May 17, 1991.

Cordwell, George. Interview by author. Chapel Hill, N.C., September 25, 1987.

Delahunt, Francis M. Interview by author. Lockport, N.Y., May 16, 1991.

Gibbs, Clarissa Anderson. Interview by author. St. Augustine, Fla., May 27, 1989.

Groff, Delia. Interview by author. Lockport, N.Y., April 28, 1988.

"Hank" the milkman. Taped recollections regarding William Rand Kenan Jr. Lockport, N.Y., February 1991.

Hardiman, Charles V. V. Taped recollections regarding William Rand Kenan Jr. Delray Beach, Fla., January 1991.

Janssen, Guila B. Interviews by author. Portland, Ore., September 20, 21, 1990.

Kenan, Frank Hawkins. Interviews by author. Chapel Hill, N.C., September 3, 1987, and June 26, 1991.

Kenan, James Graham. Interview by author. Atlanta, Ga., June 10, 1991.

Kenan, Thomas Stephen, III. Interviews by author. Chapel Hill, N.C., September 15, 1987, and February 24, 1992.

Lewis, Henrietta. Interview by author. Lockport, N.Y., April 27, 1988.

Lewis, Lawrence, Jr. Interviews by author. Richmond, Va., May 10, 1988, and September 24, 1991.

Lewis, Mary Lily Flagler (Mrs. James L. Wiley). Interview by author. Middleburg, Va., September 24, 1991.

Martin, S. Walter. Interview by author. Valdosta, Ga., February 3, 1990.

O'Neal, Margaret Wise. Interview by author. Chapel Hill, N.C., May 14, 1989.

——. Telephone interview by author. Macon, Ga., March 7, 1989.

Pardee, Jeanne. Telephone interview by author. Charlottesville, Va., August 17, 1993.

Raff, Audrey, and Helen Griffin. Interview by author. Lockport, N.Y., May 16, 1991.

Storrs, William. Interview by author. Lockport, N.Y., May 16, 1991.
Van De Mark, Phyllis. Interview by author. Lockport, N.Y., April 28, 1988.
Vickers, Raymond. Telephone interviews by author. Tallahassee, Fla., June 18, 19, 1991.
Westhafer, James. Interview by author. Lockport, N.Y., April 27, 1988.

LETTERS TO AUTHOR

Grow, Francis B. From Jamestown, N.Y., December 29, 1990, and February 6, 1991.
Lockwood, Vernon A. From St. Augustine, Fla., September 15 and October 18, 1991.
Price, James Kenan. From Lewiston, N.Y., August 7, 1989.
Raff, Audrey. From Lockport, N.Y., October 17, 1990, and March 11, 1991.

MANUSCRIPTS

Baltimore, Maryland
  Alan Mason Chesney Medical Archives, Johns Hopkins Medical Institutions
  Walters Art Gallery
    Letters, interviews, and other materials compiled by Bill Johnston for
      biography of William and Henry Walters
    "Comments of Mrs. Fussell of Landfall." N.d. [ca. 1985]
Berkeley, California
  Archives and Record Office, University of California
    Lawrence Berkeley Laboratory, Ernest O. Lawrence Records
Cambridge, Massachusetts
  Special Collections Department, Baker Library, Harvard University
    R. G. Dun & Company Collection, Credit Ledgers
Chapel Hill, North Carolina
  Morehead Foundation
    Correspondence files
  North Carolina Collection, University of North Carolina
    Thomas S. Kenan scrapbook
  Private Collection, Thomas S. Kenan III
    Smith, Ralph Kenan, and Nancy King Smith. "Mary Lily Kenan." January 18,
      1989. Unpublished manuscript.
    Summary (1991) of Detective's Report (1917)
  Southern Historical Collection, University of North Carolina
    Frank Porter Graham Papers
    J. G. Hamilton Papers

William T. Joyner Papers
Kenan Family Papers
Francis Preston Venable Papers
University Archives, University of North Carolina
Chancellor's records
Faculty minutes
President's Office records
Student records and faculty reports
Columbus, Ohio
University Archives, Ohio State University
Ohio State University News Bureau
Biographical file
Durham, North Carolina
Manuscript Department, Perkins Library, Duke University
Amy Morris Bradley Papers
Clawson Papers
Cronly Family Papers
Hall Family Papers
Hugh MacRae Papers
William L. Saunders Papers
Adelaide Savage Meares Papers
Sprunt Papers
Greenville, North Carolina
Manuscript Collection, East Carolina University
Elias Carr Papers
William Frederick Harding Memoir
Hillsborough, North Carolina
Orange County Courthouse
Orange County deeds
Orange County wills
Kenansville, North Carolina
Duplin County Courthouse
Duplin County wills
Liberty Hall
Lewiston, New York
Private Collection, Robert J. Klotzbach
"James Turner Morehead: Pioneer in American Industry, An Address
   delivered by the Honorable John Motley Morehead before the
   International Acetylene Association, Chicago, Illinois, October 27, 1922."
"Notes on Data of Pertinence to the Early History of Carbide, Memo,
   February 2, 1938."
"Early Workers in the Calcium Carbide Industry. September 15, 1938."
"Willson Aluminum Company in Relation to Electro Gas Company and
   Licensees: Information Given Verbally Today by Mr. John M. Morehead,

Modified, Amplified and Checked from Various Sources, Including Many Documents. September 14, 1938."

"Niagara Makes Carbide and Ferro-Alloys: A History of the Niagara Works of the Metallurgical Company." N.d. [ca. 1943].

"The Story of Union Carbide Metals." N.d. [ca. 1950].

"Niagara Makes Carbide and Ferro-Alloys: A History of the Niagara Works of the Metallurgical Company." N.d. [ca. 1941].

Thomas "Carbide" Willson. N.p, n.d.

Letterbook of the Lake Superior Carbide Company. November 23, 1896– January 14, 1898.

William Rand Kenan Jr. Letterbook at the Lake Superior Carbide Company. July 30, 1898–September 1, 1899.

Lockport, New York
  Lockport Public Library
    Local History Collection
  Niagara County Courthouse
    Wills and estates
  Niagara County Historical Museum
    William Rand Kenan Jr. Papers
    Genealogical Library
  Niagara County Historian's Office
    Individual and family files

Louisville, Kentucky
  Manuscript Department, Filson Club
    Robert Worth Bingham Papers
  Private Archives, Mary and Barry Bingham Fund
    Letters
    "Errors and Misstatements in *Passion and Prejudice*"

Macon, Georgia
  Genealogical & Historical Room, Washington Memorial Library
    Reference files

North Tarrytown, New York
  Rockefeller Archive Center
    Correspondence with FEC Railway, 1937

Ottawa, Ontario, Canada
  National Archives of Canada
    Thomas Willson Papers

Palm Beach, Florida
  Breakers Hotel
  Henry Morrison Flagler Museum
    Henry Morrison Flagler Papers
    Henry Morrison Flagler Letterbooks
    Warren Smith Collection

Raleigh, North Carolina
    North Carolina Division of Archives and History
        Samuel A. Ashe Papers
        Davidson Collection
        Thomas S. Kenan Papers
        New Hanover County, wills and estate records
        New Hanover County, divorces
        Orange County, estate records
        Patterson Family Papers
        Lucy Williams Polk Papers
        Wake County, wills and estate records
    Library of Peace College, Peace College
        Records of the Peace Institute
Richmond, Virginia
    Private Collection, Lawrence Lewis Jr.
        Louise Wise Lewis Scrapbook
        Louise Wise Lewis Photo Album
St. Augustine, Florida
    St. Augustine Historical Society
        Anderson Papers
        Florida East Coast Railway Collection
        Memorial Presbyterian Church Records
Tallahassee, Florida
    Pepper Library, Florida State University
        Mildred and Claude Pepper Papers
Wilmington, North Carolina
    Lower Cape Fear Historical Society
        Individual and family files
    North Carolina Room, New Hanover County Public Library
        Louis T. Moore Collection
Winston-Salem, North Carolina
    Special Collections Department, Wake Forest University
        Katie Murray Papers
Yellow Springs, Ohio
    Olive Kettering Library, Antioch College
        Antiochiana Collection
        Kettering Laboratory files

NEWSPAPERS

Florida
    Florida Times-Union (Jacksonville)
    Miami Herald
    Palm Beach Life

St. Augustine Evening Record
St. Augustine Record
Kentucky
Louisville Courier-Journal
Louisville Evening Post
Louisville Herald
New York
Buffalo Evening News
Lockport Union-Sun & Journal
New York Evening Journal
New York Herald
New York Post
New York Times
North Carolina
Asheville Citizen
Charlotte Observer
Duplin Times
Greensboro Daily News
Lighthouse (Wilmington)
Raleigh Daily News
Raleigh Daily Times
Raleigh Observer
Raleigh News & Observer
Tar Heel (UNC, Chapel Hill)
Tileston Recorder (Wilmington)
Wallace Enterprise
Wilmington Dispatch
Wilmington Messenger
Wilmington Review
Wilmington Star
Virginia
Richmond Times

CATALOGS, DIRECTORIES, REPORTS,
AND GOVERNMENT PUBLICATIONS

Annual Catalogue of Peace Institute . . . For the Academic Year 1895–'96. Raleigh: E.
    M. Uzzell, 1896.
Annual Catalogue of Peace Institute . . . For the Academic Year 1896–'97. Raleigh: E.
    M. Uzzell, 1897.
Branson's Alphabetical Directory of Raleigh. Raleigh: Branson, 1891.
Carolina Oil and Creosote Company. Washington, D.C.: N.p., n.d.

Department of Agricultural Communications, North Carolina State University. *Ten Years of Research at Randleigh Farm.* Raleigh: North Carolina State University, 1981.

Facts about the Spiritine Chemical Company. N.p., n.d.

Fifth Annual Catalogue of Wilson College. Wilson, N.C.: Office of the Wilson Advance, 1876.

Inlook. Yearbook. Stuart Hall. Staunton, Va., 1917.

William R. Kenan, Jr. Charitable Trust, *The First Twenty-Five Years.* N.p., 1991.

Kenan Memorial Stadium. N.p., n.d. [ca. 1927].

Laws and Resolutions of the State of North Carolina . . . 1876–1877. Raleigh: News Publishing Co., 1877.

Lockport, N.Y.: Electrical and Industrial. N.p., n.d.

Macon City Directory, 1890–1891. Macon, Ga.: N.p., 1891.

John Motley Morehead Foundation. "The John Motley Morehead Foundation, Annual Report, 1989." Chapel Hill, 1989.

North Carolina Executive and Legislative Documents, Session 1881. Raleigh: News & Observer, 1881.

North Carolina Reports. Raleigh: Raleigh News, 1877.

Ohio State University Bulletin. May 5, 1947.

Smaw's Wilmington Directory. Wilmington, N.C.: Smaw, 1867.

Stuart Hall Catalogue, 1916–1917. Staunton, Va., 1916.

University of North Carolina Alumni Report. Summer 1992.

University of Virginia Catalogue, 1915–1916. Charlottesville, Va., 1915.

University of Virginia Catalogue, 1916–1917. Charlottesville, Va., 1916.

University of Virginia Record, 1915–1916. Charlottesville, Va., 1916.

University of Virginia Record, 1916–1917. Charlottesville, Va., 1917.

U.S. Treasury Department. "Florida East Coast Railway Company Reorganization Proceedings." Vol. 2, "Receivership Record." Document 109.

BOOKS

Akin, Edward N. *Flagler: Rockefeller Partner and Florida Baron.* Kent, Ohio: Kent State University Press, 1988.

Amory, Cleveland. *The Last Resorts.* New York: Harper and Brothers, 1948.

Anderson, Eric. *Race and Politics in North Carolina, 1872–1901: The Black Second.* Baton Rouge: Louisiana State University Press, 1981.

Anderson, Jean Bradley. *Durham County: A History of Durham County, North Carolina.* Durham: Duke University Press, 1990.

Anderson, Nancy Briska. *Macon: A Pictorial History.* Virginia Beach: Donnin, 1987.

Andrews, A. B., ed. *Proceedings of the Twenty-Second Annual Session of the North Carolina Bar Association.* Raleigh: N.p., 1921.

Ashe, Samuel A., series ed. *Biographical History of North Carolina: From Colonial Times to the Present.* 8 vols. Greensboro, N.C.: Van Noppen, 1905–17.

Bailey, Thomas A., and Paul B. Ryan. *The Lusitania Disaster: An Episode in Modern Warfare and Diplomacy.* New York: Free Press, 1975.

Battle, Kemp Plummer. *History of the University of North Carolina.* 2 vols. Raleigh: Edwards and Broughton, 1907, 1912. Reprint, Spartanburg, S.C.: Reprint Co., 1974.

Bingham, Sallie. *Passion and Prejudice.* New York: Knopf, 1989.

Blakey, Arich Fredric. *The Florida Phosphate Industry.* Cambridge: Harvard University Press, 1973.

Block, Susan. *The Wrights of Wilmington.* Wilmington, N.C.: Wilmington Printing Co., 1992.

Bond, Adrienne Moore. *Eugene W. Stetson.* Macon, Ga.: Mercer University Press, 1983.

Brandt, Alan. *No Magic Bullett: A Social History of Venereal Disease in the United States since 1880.* New York: Oxford University Press, 1985. Paperback, expanded ed., 1987.

Brenner, Marie. *House of Dreams: The Bingham Family of Louisville.* New York: Random House, 1988.

Brooks, Aubrey Lee, and Hugh Talmage Lefler, eds. *The Papers of Walter Clark.* Vol. 1. Chapel Hill: University of North Carolina Press, 1948.

Bursey, Maurice. *Carolina Chemists: Sketches from Chapel Hill.* Chapel Hill: University of North Carolina, Chemistry Department, 1982.

——. *Francis Preston Venable.* Chapel Hill: Chapel Hill Historical Society, 1989.

Carosso, Vincent P. *The Morgans: Private International Bankers, 1854–1913.* Cambridge: Harvard University Press, 1987.

Cashman, Diane Cobb. *Cape Fear Adventure: An Illustrated History of Wilmington.* Woodland Hills, Calif.: Windsor, 1982.

Chandler, David Leon. *Henry Flagler: The Astonishing Life and Times of the Visionary Robber Baron Who Founded Florida.* New York: Macmillan, 1986.

Chandler, David Leon, and Mary V. Chandler. *The Binghams of Louisville.* New York: Crown, 1987.

Colburn, David R., and Richard K. Scher. *Florida's Gubernatorial Politics in the Twentieth Century.* Tallahassee: University Presses of Florida, 1980.

Coleman, Kenneth, and Charles Stephen Gurr, eds. *Dictionary of Georgia Biography.* Athens: University of Georgia Press, 1983.

Conte, Robert S. *The History of the Greenbrier: America's Resort.* Charleston, W.Va.: Pictorial Histories Pub. Co., 1989.

Cooper, John H., Jr. *Walter Hines Page.* Chapel Hill: University of North Carolina Press, 1977.

Cooper, Walter G. *Official History of Fulton County.* Atlanta: Brown, 1934. Reprint, Spartanburg, S.C.: Reprint Co., 1978.

Crews, Guy M., ed., *The American Jersey Cattle Club: 100 Years.* Greenfield: Greenfield Printing and Publishing, 1968.

Cromartie, Susan Taylor. *Pointing the Way: A History of the First Presbyterian Church Building, Wilmington, North Carolina, 1928–1978*. Wilmington, N.C.: Session's Committee on Commitment, 1978.

Crow, Jeffrey J., and Robert F. Durden, *Maverick Republican in the Old North State: A Political Biography of Daniel L. Russell*. Baton Rouge: Louisiana State University Press, 1977.

Crowell, John Franklin. *Personal Recollections of Trinity College, North Carolina, 1887–1894*. Durham: Duke University Press, 1939.

Daniels, Josephus. *Editor in Politics*. Chapel Hill: University of North Carolina Press, 1941.

——. *Tar Heel Editor*. Chapel Hill: University of North Carolina Press, 1939. ·

Doyle, Don. *New Men, New Cities, New South*. Chapel Hill: University of North Carolina Press, 1990.

Dozier, Howard Douglas. *A History of the Atlantic Coast Line Railroad*. Boston: Houghton Mifflin, 1920.

Durden, Robert. *The Dukes of Durham, 1865–1929*. Durham: Duke University Press, 1987.

Edmonds, Helen G. *The Negro and Fusion Politics in North Carolina, 1894–1901*. Chapel Hill: University of North Carolina Press, 1951.

Edmunds, Mary Lewis Rucker. *Governor Morehead's Blandwood*. Greensboro, N.C.: Greensboro Printing Co., 1976.

Escott, Paul D. *Many Excellent People: Power and Privilege in North Carolina, 1850–1900*. Chapel Hill: University of North Carolina Press, 1985.

Evans, W. McKee. *Ballots and Fence Rails: Reconstruction on the Lower Cape Fear*. Chapel Hill: University of North Carolina Press, 1966. Paperback ed., New York: Norton, 1974.

Foster, Gaines M. *Ghosts of the Confederacy*. New York: Oxford University Press, 1987.

Gaston, Paul. *The New South Creed: A Study in Southern Mythmaking*. Baton Rouge: Louisiana State University Press, 1970.

George, Paul S., ed. *A Guide to the History of Florida*. New York: Greenwood, 1989.

Graham, Thomas. *The Awakening of St. Augustine: The Anderson Family and the Oldest City, 1821–1924*. St. Augustine, Fla.: St. Augustine Historical Society, 1978.

Green, Harvey. *Fit for America: Health, Fitness, Sport, and American Society*. New York: Pantheon, 1986. Paperback ed., Baltimore: Johns Hopkins University Press: 1988.

Griffith, Leon Odell. *Ed Ball: Confusion to the Enemy*. Tampa, Fla.: Trend House, 1975.

Hewlett, Richard Green. *Jessie Ball duPont*. Gainesville: University Press of Florida, 1992.

History of Northwestern New York. Vol. 3, *Personal and Family History*. New York: Lewis Historical Pub. Co., 1947.

Horowitz, Helen Lefkowitz. *Campus Life.* New York: Knopf, 1987.

Howell, A. C. *The Kenan Professorships.* Chapel Hill: University of North Carolina Press, 1956.

Hughes, Thomas P. *Networks of Power: Electrification in Western Society, 1880–1930.* Baltimore: Johns Hopkins University Press, 1983.

Inman, Ondess L. *The C. F. Kettering Foundation for the Study of Chlorophyll and Photosynthesis.* N.p., 1937.

Junior League of Wilmington. *Old Wilmington Guidebook.* Wilmington, N.C.: Junior League of Wilmington, 1978.

Keeley, L. *The Non-heredity of Inebriety.* Chicago: Griggs, 1896.

Kenan, Thomas S., III. *Sarah Graham Kenan Foundation: A History.* Privately printed, 1984.

Kenan, William Rand, Jr. *History of Randleigh Farm.* Privately printed. St. Augustine, Fla.: Record Co., 1st ed., 1935; 2d ed., 1937; 3d ed., 1940; 4th ed., 1942; 5th ed., 1947; 6th ed., 1950; 7th ed., 1953; 8th ed., 1956; 9th ed., 1959.

——. *Incidents by the Way.* Privately printed. St. Augustine, Fla.: Record Co., 1st ed., 1946; 2d ed., 1949; 3d ed., 1952; 4th ed., 1955; 5th ed., 1958.

Kennedy, Stetson. *Palmetto Country.* Tallahassee: Florida A & M University Press, 1942. Reprint, 1989.

Lamoreaux, Naomi. *The Great Merger Movement in American Business, 1895–1904.* Cambridge: Cambridge University Press, 1985.

Lefler, Hugh Talmage, and Albert Ray Newsome. *North Carolina: The History of a Southern State.* 3d ed. Chapel Hill: University of North Carolina Press, 1973.

Lehr, Elizabeth Drexel. *"King Lehr" and the Gilded Age.* Philadelphia: Lippincott, 1935.

Levenstein, Harvey. *Revolution at the Table.* New York: Oxford University Press, 1988.

Lockport Memorial Hospital Guild. *Lockport Memorial Hospital, 1903–1983.* Lockport: Lockport Memorial Hospital Guild, 1983.

Long, Augustus White. *Son of Carolina.* Durham: Duke University Press, 1939.

McCrady, Edwards, and Samuel A. Ashe. *Cyclopedia of Eminent and Representative Men of the Carolinas of the Nineteenth Century.* Vol. 2. Madison, Wis.: Brant & Fuller, 1892.

McGowen, Faison Wells, and Pearl Canady McGowen, eds. *Flashes of Duplin's History and Government.* Kenansville, N.C.: N.p., 1971.

McKay, John J., Jr., Nelle Edwards Smith, and Spencer B. King Jr., eds. *A Guide to Macon's Architectural and Historical Heritage.* Macon, Ga.: Middle Georgia Historical Society, 1972.

McKinney, Gordon B., and Richard M. McMurry, eds. *The Papers of Zebulon Vance.* Frederick, Md.: University Publications of America, 1987 (microfilm edition).

McKoy, William Berry. *Early Years of the Cape Fear River.* Wilmington, N.C.: N.p., n.d.

Martin, Albro. *Railroads Triumphant: The Growth, Rejection, and Rebirth of a Vital American Force.* New York: Oxford University Press, 1992.

Martin, S. Walter. *Florida's Flagler.* Athens: University of Georgia Press, 1949. Reprint, 1977.

Mason, Raymond K., and Virginia Harrison. *Confusion to the Enemy: A Biography of Ed Ball.* New York: Dodd, Mead, 1976.

Members of Pennsylvania Sigma Phi, comps. *History and Catalogue of the Sigma Alpha Epsilon Fraternity.* Harrisburg, Pa.: Meyers Printing House, 1893.

Midgette, Nancy Smith. *To Foster the Spirit of Professionalism: Southern Scientists and State Academies of Science.* Tuscaloosa: University of Alabama Press, 1991.

Morgan, Ted. *FDR: A Biography.* New York: Simon & Schuster, 1985.

Nairn, Bede, Geoffrey Serle, and Russel Ward, section eds. *Australian Dictionary of Biography.* Vol. 4. Melbourne: Melbourne University Press, 1972.

Outlaw, A. T., comp. *Official Directory of Duplin County, North Carolina, 1749–1935.* Kenansville, N.C.: N.p., 1935.

Patterson, Jerry D. *The Vanderbilts.* New York: Abrams, 1989.

Peace College. *The Inauguration of Garrett Briggs as Eighth President of Peace College.* Raleigh: N.p., 1989.

Pioneer Association of Niagara County. *Souvenir History of Niagara County New York.* Lockport, N.Y.: N.p., 1902.

Powell, William S., ed. *Dictionary of North Carolina Biography.* 5 vols. Chapel Hill: University of North Carolina Press, 1979–92.

———. *The First State University: A Pictorial History of the University of North Carolina.* 3d ed. Chapel Hill: University of North Carolina Press, 1992.

———. *North Carolina through Four Centuries.* Chapel Hill: University of North Carolina Press, 1989.

Prather, H. Leon, Sr. *We Have Taken a City: Wilmington Racial Massacre and Coup of 1898.* Cranbury, N.J.: Associated University Presses, 1984.

Prince, Richard E. *Atlantic Coast Line Railroad: Steam Locomotives, Ships, and History.* Green River, Wyo.: Richard E. Prince, 1966.

Register, Alvaretta Kenan. *The Kenan Family.* Statesboro, Ga.: Kenan Print Shop, 1967.

Reilly, J. S. *Wilmington: Past, Present, and Future.* Wilmington, N.C.: N.p., 1884.

Rush, Charles E., ed. *Library Resources of the University of North Carolina.* Chapel Hill: University of North Carolina Press, 1945.

Russell, Francis. *President Harding: His Life and Times, 1865–1923.* London: Eyre and Spottiswoode, 1969.

Schlereth, Thomas J. *Victorian America.* New York: HarperCollins, 1991.

Seymour, James W. D., ed. *History of the American Field Service in France: "Friends of France," 1914–1917.* New York: Houghton Mifflin, 1920.

Sheriff, Benjamin R. *Sheriff's Wilmington, N.C. Directory and General Advertiser for 1877–78.* Wilmington: N.p., 1877.

Shields, Ruth Herndon, Belle Lewler West, and Kathryn Crossley Stone. *A Study of the Barbee Families of Chatham, Orange, and Wake Counties in North Carolina.* Boulder, Colo.: Privately printed, 1971.

Simpson, Colin. *The Lusitania.* Boston: Little, Brown, 1972.

Sklar, Martin J. *The Corporate Reconstruction of American Capitalism, 1890–1916.* New York: Cambridge University Press, 1988.

Smith, George David. *From Monopoly to Competition: The Transformations of Alcoa, 1888–1986.* New York: Cambridge University Press, 1988.

Snider, William. *Light on the Hill.* Chapel Hill: University of North Carolina Press, 1992.

Spiritine Chemical Company. *Facts about the Spiritine Chemical Company.* Wilmington, N.C.: N.p., n.d. [ca. 1923].

Sprunt, James. *Chronicles of the Cape Fear River, 1660–1916.* 2d ed. Raleigh: Edwards & Broughton, 1916.

Strauss, Gertrude. *Our First One Hundred and Fifty Years, 1823–1973.* Lockport, N.Y.: First Presbyterian Church of Lockport, New York, 1973.

Tifft, Susan, and Alex Jones. *The Patriarch.* New York: Summit, 1991.

Townsend, Metta Folger. *On Golden Hinges.* New York: Broadway, 1917.

Vickers, James. *Chapel Hill: An Illustrated History.* Chapel Hill: Barclay, 1985.

Wall, Joseph Frazier. *Alfred I. du Pont.* New York: Oxford University Press, 1990.

Watson, Alan D. *Wilmington: Port of North Carolina.* Columbia: University of South Carolina Press, 1992.

Wilmington, the Metropolis and Port of North Carolina. N.p., n.d. [ca. 1912].

Williamson, Joel. *The Crucible of Race: Black-White Relations in the American South since Emancipation.* New York: Oxford University Press, 1984.

Wilson, Leonard, ed. *Johnson's Series: Makers of America.* Vol. 3. Washington, D.C.: B. F. Johnson, 1917.

Wilson, Louis R. *The University of North Carolina, 1900–1930.* Chapel Hill: University of North Carolina Press, 1957.

Winsberg, Morton D. *Florida Weather.* Orlando: University of Central Florida Press, 1990.

Winston, R. W. *Horace Williams, Gadfly of Chapel Hill.* Chapel Hill: University of North Carolina Press, 1942.

Woodman, Harold D. *King Cotton and His Retainers.* Lexington: University of Kentucky Press, 1968. Reprint, Columbia: University of South Carolina Press, 1990.

Wrenn, Tony P. *Wilmington, North Carolina: An Architectural and Historical Portrait.* Charlottesville: University Press of Virginia, 1985.

Yergin, Daniel. *The Prize.* New York: Simon & Schuster, 1991.

Young, Ida, Julius Gholson, and Clara Nell Hargrove. *History of Macon, Georgia.* Macon, Ga.: Macon Woman's Club, 1950.

ARTICLES AND MISCELLANEOUS PAPERS

Altman, Burt. " 'In the Public Interest?' Ed Ball and the FEC Railway War." *Florida Historical Quarterly* 44 (July 1985): 32–47.

Bowman, Karl M., and E. Morton Jellinek. "Alcohol Addiction and Its
  Treatment." *Quarterly Journal of Studies on Alcohol* 2 (June 1941): 98–176.
Brabham, Robin. "Defining the American University: The University of North
  Carolina, 1865–1875." *North Carolina Historical Review* 57 (October 1980): 427–
  55.
Broadfoot, Mary Bason. "Kenan House." *Lower Cape Fear Historical Society, Inc.,
  Bulletin* 15 (January 1972): 1–4.
Bromberg, Alan B. " 'The Worst Muddle Ever Seen in N.C. Politics': The Farmers'
  Alliance, the Subtreasury, and Zeb Vance." *North Carolina Historical Review* 56
  (January 1979): 19–40.
Brown, William Burlie. "The State Literary and Historical Association: 1900–
  1950." *North Carolina Historical Review* 27 (April 1951): 156–97.
Bush, Gregory W. "Sun-Bound Highways: The Growth of Florida as an
  Independent State, 1917–1940," in *A Guide to the History of Florida*, edited by
  Paul S. George, pp. 107–16. New York: Greenwood, 1989.
"Carbide & Carbon Chemicals." *Fortune*, September 1941, pp. 57–67, 154.
Carter, Margaret. "Thomas Leopold 'Carbide' Willson." *Stelco Today*, August
  1988, pp. 12–14.
Cashman, Diane Cobb. "A Yankee Transplant in Southern Soil: Amy Morris
  Bradley—The Wilmington Years, 1866–1904." *Lower Cape Fear Historical
  Journal* 31 (June 1989): 1–22.
Cherry, T. Kevin B. "The Gimghouls' Castle." *Carolina Alumni Review*, Spring
  1993, pp. 64–65.
Cooper, George M. "The Woods—Father and Son." *Southern Medicine and
  Surgery* 90 (December 1928): 787–94.
Curl, Donald. "Joseph Urban's Palm Beach Architecture." *Florida Historical
  Quarterly* 71 (April 1993): 436–57.
De Van Massey, Gregory. "The British Expedition to Wilmington, January–
  November, 1781." *North Carolina Historical Review* 66 (October 1989): 387–411.
Dorsey, John. "Mount Vernon Place." *Baltimore Sun Magazine*, June 14, 1970, pp.
  19–20.
Halkiotis, Stephen H. "Guns for *Cuba Libre*: An 1895 Filibustering Expedition
  from Wilmington, North Carolina." *North Carolina Historical Review* 55
  (January 1978): 60–75.
Halperin, Edward C. "Frank Porter Graham, Isaac Hall Manning, and the Jewish
  Quota at the University of North Carolina Medical School." *North Carolina
  Historical Review* 67 (October 1990): 385–410.
Hass, Renita. "A View of Times Past." *Traditions*, 1990, pp. 16–21.
Hoffman. Glenn J. "History of the Atlantic Coast Line Railroad." Unpublished
  manuscript in the Legal Department of the CSX corporation, Jacksonville, Fla.
Hosmer, L. S. "How the New Breakers Was Built." *Turner Constructor* 4 (February
  1927): 26–30.
Hughes, Kaylene. "Flagler Was the Founder of Tourism on Florida's Eastern
  Coastline." *Florida Hotel & Motel Journal*, June 1986, pp. 12–26.

Hunt, James L. "The Making of a Populist: Marion Butler, 1863–1895." *North Carolina Historical Review* 62 (January 1985): 53–77; (April 1985): 179–202; (July 1985): 317–43.

Johnson, Frontis W. "The North Carolina Historical Commission, 1903–1978." In *Public History in North Carolina, 1903–1978*, edited by Jeffrey Crow, pp. 1–15. Raleigh: North Carolina Department of Cultural Resources, Division of Archives and History, 1979.

Kernan, Michael. "William and Henry Walters." *Smithsonian* 20 (August 1989): 102–12.

Lockmiller, David Alexander. "The Establishment of the North Carolina College of Agriculture and Mechanic Arts." *North Carolina Historical Review* 16 (July 1939): 273–95.

Marshall, J. G. "Reminiscences of the Carbide Industry in Niagara Falls." *Tapping Pot*, May 10, 1921, pp. 158–59.

Meier, August, and Elliott Rudwick. "Negro Boycotts of Segregated Streetcars in Florida, 1901–1905." *South Atlantic Quarterly* 69:525–33.

Melusky, Robert. "Palm Beach: The First Hundred Years." *Traditions*, 1987, pp. 15–23.

Morehead, J. T., and G. de Chalmot. "The Manufacture of Calcium Carbide." *Journal of the American Chemical Society* 18 (April 1896): 311–31.

Muir, Thomas, Jr. "William Alexander Blount: Defender of the Old South and Advocate of a New South." *Florida Historical Quarterly* 67 (April 1989): 458–76.

Proctor, Samuel. "Filibustering aboard the *Three Friends*." *Mid-America* 37 (1956): 84–100.

Rickenbach, Richard V. "Filibustering with the *Dauntless*." *Florida Historical Quarterly* 28 (April 1950): 231–53.

Sadler, Lynn Veach. "Dr. Stephen Graham's Narration of the 'Duplin Insurrection': Additional Evidence of the Impact of the Nat Turner Rebellion." *American Studies* 12 (1978): 359–67.

Scales, Joseph. "Union Carbide Company: 'The Mother of Us All.'" *Carbidea*, June 1926, pp. 88–92.

———. "Union Carbide Growth Creates Subsidiaries." *Carbidea*, July 1926, pp. 108–12.

Schellings, William J. "The Advent of the Spanish American War in Florida, 1898." *Florida Historical Quarterly* 39 (April 1961): 311–29.

———. "Florida and the Cuban Revolution, 1895–1898." *Florida Historical Quarterly* 39 (October 1960): 175–86.

Stoesen, Alexander R. "Road from Receivership: Claude Pepper, the Dupont Trust, and the Florida East Coast Railway." *Florida Historical Quarterly* 42 (October 1973): 132–56.

Sumner, Jim L. "The North Carolina Inter-Collegiate Foot-Ball Association: The Beginnings of College Football in North Carolina." *North Carolina Historical Review* 65 (July 1988): 263–86.

Taylor, Rosser H. "Fertilizers and Farming in the Southeast, 1840–1950." *North Carolina Historical Review* 30 (July 1953): 305–28; (October 1953): 483–523.

Thomas, Samuel W. "Let the Documents Speak: An Analysis of David Leon Chandler's Assessment of Robert Worth Bingham." *Filson Club History Quarterly* 63 (July 1989): 307–61.

"Union Carbide I: The Corporation." *Fortune*, June 1941, pp. 61–68, 123–24, 126, 128, 130, 133–34.

"Union Carbide II: Alloys, Gases, and Carbon." *Fortune*, July 1941, pp. 49–56, 92, 94, 96, 98, 100–101.

Venable, Francis Preston. "An Account of the First Production of Calcium Carbide and Acetylene in the United States." *American Manufacturer*, December 16, 1898, p. 875.

Venable, F. P., and Thomas Clarke. "Some of the Properties of Calcium Carbide." *Journal of the American Chemical Society* 17 (April 1895): 307–10.

Way, Peter. "Evil Humors and Ardent Spirits: The Rough Culture of Canal Construction Laborers." *Journal of American History* 79 (March 1993): 1397–428.

Wilson, R. C. "The New Breakers Hotel, Palm Beach, Florida." *Turner Constructor* 4 (February 1927): 4–25.

Wrenn, Lynette B. "Cottonseed Price-Fixing in Eastern North Carolina, 1903–1907." *North Carolina Historical Review* 67 (October 1990): 411–37.

Yancey, Noel. "Soul Train." [Raleigh, N.C.] *Spectator*, July 19, 1990, p. 21.

——. "Spare the Rod and Spoil the Child." [Raleigh, N.C.] *Spectator*, June 29, 1989, p. 24.

INDEX

Acetylene gas: Venable and Kenan in discovery of, 71, 75, 82, 84, 85, 86, 93, 97, 261; Willson and discovery of, 75, 93, 282; lighting applications of, 85, 92, 93, 108, 117, 153–54; Willson's attempts to commercialize, 87–88, 92, 93, 94, 107; Willson's patents on production of, 89, 96, 261

Acetylene Light, Heat and Power Company (ALH&P), 113, 116, 117; Niagara Falls plant, 104–5, 120–21; calcium carbide production, 105–7, 121

Adams, Frederick B., 294

Adams, Junius G., 276, 296

Alexander, Sydenham B., 45

Aluminum production, 70, 77, 83, 108

Amend, Otto Paul, 90, 92

American Association for the Advancement of Science, 70

American Chemical Society, 255

American Jersey Cattle Club (AJCC), 275–76, 288, 304; Master Breeder's Award to Kenan, 277, 295, 296, 327

American Manufacturer, 128

Anderson, Andrew, 160, 161–62

Anderson, Arthur M., 239, 250, 252–53, 262, 277, 280

Andrews, Alexander, 50

Andrews, William, 50

Antioch College, Kenan Research Fund, 270, 271

Archbold, John D., 156

Arnold, Mrs. John, 330

Art, George, 199

"Artificial Production of Petroleum" (Kenan), 72

Ashley, Eliza, 112, 132, 145, 330

Ashley, Eugene, 112, 124–25, 129, 130–31, 134, 143, 153

Asheville Citizen, 171

Asheville Times, 365 (n. 121)

Atlantic Coast Line (ACL) Railroad Company: Walters's operation of, 20, 41–42, 43, 44, 45, 48, 293; "Florida Special" train, 44; agrarian movement and, 45, 46, 48; cooperation with FEC, 205, 230, 293; labor strike of 1922, 205–6; attempts to acquire FEC, 209, 293–96, 297–300, 301, 303–4, 308–9, 313–14, 315–18; competition with FEC, 209–10; investment in Pan American, 229–30; Davis's operation of, 293, 318; Kenan's investment in, 316–17; move from Wilmington to Jacksonville, 318, 319

Australian Carbide Company, 116

Baldwin, Robert L., 261

Ball, Ed: control of duPont estate, 278; attempts to acquire FEC, 278, 295, 301; investments in FEC, 279, 289, 290, 294; reorganization plan for FEC, 280, 315–16, 318; hostility toward Pepper, 296–97, 309; opposition to ACL-FEC merger plans, 297, 298–99, 303, 313, 314, 382 (n. 43); and ICC hearings on

FEC reorganization, 299, 300, 303, 317; hostility toward Davis, 318
Bankers Trust Company of New York, 210, 242, 249, 252
Barbee, Christopher ("Old Kit"), 27
Barbee, William, 27
Baruch, Bernard M., 240, 243
Baskerville, Charles, 229; as UNC student, 64, 65, 66, 67; friendship with Kenan, 62, 63; as UNC professor, 129–30
Battle, George Gordon, 243
Battle, Herbert Bemerton, 69–70
Battle, Kemp P., 53, 54, 61
Battle, Samuel Westray, 243, 360 (n. 32); relationship with Mary Lily Kenan, 168–69, 171
Beardsley, William: and Kenan family investments, 139, 140, 141–42; as trustee of Flagler estate, 162, 165; as FEC officer, 166, 199, 210, 219; death of, 219
Beattie, Schuyler, 263; as Kenan's private secretary, 133, 213, 322, 324, 330, 354 (n. 119); in Republican party, 213–14, 328; as Western Block officer, 287; and Randleigh Farm, 326–27
Belknap, Alice Maude, 360 (n. 32)
Belknap, William B., 360 (n. 32)
Bellamy, R. H., 248
Bemis, Henry, 210
Benson, J. R., 310
Bigler, Rev. Barton B., 225
Billings, C. K. G., 117, 120
Bingham, Barry, 172, 180
Bingham, Eleanore Miller, 99–100, 130, 361 (n. 43)
Bingham, Henrietta, 172, 180, 182
Bingham, Mary Lily Kenan. See Kenan, Mary Lily
Bingham, Robert (father of RWB), 26, 27, 29, 38, 171–72
Bingham, Robert (son of RWB), 172, 180, 184
Bingham, Robert Worth, 129–30; as UNC student, 60, 62; relationship with Mary Lily Kenan, 62, 99, 172, 173;

176; marriage to Mary Lily, 62, 177–79, 180; friendship with Will Kenan, 62, 178; marriage to Eleanore Miller, 99–100, 111, 130; children of, 172, 180–81, 182, 184–85; Mary Lily's will and, 176, 178, 180, 181, 185–86, 188, 189, 191; and Mary Lily's illness and death, 183–84, 186, 187–88, 243–44, 372 (n. 31); as ambassador to Britain, 243, 244, 257; marriage to Aleen Hilliard, 244; death of, 257, 258; friendship with Josephus Daniels, 257–58
Bingham, Walter, 38
Blount, William Alexander, 166, 175–76, 187, 191, 192, 201, 202
Boca Raton, Fla., 214
Boggess, Walter F., 186
Bolles, Hannah, 183, 184, 186
Bradley, Amy Morris, 23–24, 36
Brady, Anthony N., 117, 120
Breakers Hotel (Palm Beach, Fla.), 132–33, 227, 309, 332; burned in fires, 142, 165, 214–15; reconstruction in 1925–27, 215, 218, 219, 220, 222–24; during World War II, 289, 296
Bridgers, Robert, 19
Brinkley, David, 319
Bruce, Helm, 189, 207
Brummitt, Dennis G., 243
Bryan, Shepard, 62, 190
Buffalo, N.Y., 106
Bullier, Louis Michel, 97–98, 348 (nn. 78, 80)
Byrne, J. A., 24
Byrnes, James F., 303–4

Cain, George, 316
Calcium carbide: Venable and Kenan in discovery of, 69, 71, 75, 82–84, 85, 97–98, 254–55, 281, 282–83; derivation of acetylene from, 71, 82, 86, 254–55; Mot Morehead on discovery of, 75, 80, 81–82, 259, 260, 261; Willson and discovery of, 75, 81, 83–86, 261, 282–83; Major Morehead and discovery of, 75, 83, 85, 88, 89, 90–91, 259, 261, 282, 283; Willson's patents on production of,

85, 94, 98; commercial production of, 86, 94, 96, 105–6, 114–15, 117, 121
"Calcium Carbide and the Process of Manufacture" (Kenan), 259
Calhoun, Kenneth, Sr., 296
Cameron, J. Donald, 19
Campbell, W. W., 154
Camp Kenan (Barker, N.Y.), 212, 330
Cape Fear and Yadkin Valley Railroad, 76–77
Capito, S. B., 362 (n. 62)
Carbide Manufacturing Company, 65, 101–2, 104. See also Acetylene Light, Heat and Power Company
Carnegie Foundation, 248
Carolina Apartment building (Wilmington, N.C.), 149, 310
Carolina Central Railway Company, 25
Carolina Oil and Creosote Company, 43, 44, 129
Carolina Rice Mills, 340 (n. 20)
Carpenter Steel Company, 88
Carrere, John, 197, 318
Casa Marina Hotel (Key West, Fla.), 289
Casanova, José Manuel, 252
Caspar, Jim, 299
Cataract Construction Company, 65
Cave, Jane, 338 (n. 66)
Chadbourn, W. H., Jr., 23–24
Chalmot, G. de, 97
Chapel Hill, N.C., 25, 26, 27
Chapel Hill Weekly, 263
Chapman, Albert, 199
Chase, Harry Woodburn, 196, 233, 234
Chesapeake and Ohio (C&O) Railroad, 164
Chicago World's Columbian Exposition (1893), 65
Churchill, Randolph, 245, 372 (n. 31)
Citizens Gas Company of Jacksonville, 149
Clarke, Thomas, 95, 97, 98
Cole, Stanley, 237
Coleman, Samuel Taylor, II, 281
Congress of Industrial Organizations (CIO), 285–86, 287
Connor, George Whitfield, 356 (n. 20)

Connor, R. D. W., 202, 234
Cooper, Martha, 8, 9, 151
Cordwell, George, 238, 278–79, 289, 312
Corliss, Carlton J., 312–13
Corning Glass Company, 267
Cotillion Club (Wilmington, N.C.), 43
Cowles Aluminum Company, 108
Cuba, 100, 112, 252, 293
Cutler, G. C., 294

Dancy, John, 111, 119
Daniels, Josephus, 22, 39–40, 303; as newspaper editor, 46, 136, 207; and Mary Lily's bequest to UNC, 173, 203, 207, 243, 256; as ambassador to Mexico, 243, 257; friendship with Robert Worth Bingham, 257–58
Davies, Julien T., 155
Davies, William W., Jr., 62, 130, 181, 185–86, 187, 189
Davis, Champion McDowell, 378–79 (n. 14); attempts to acquire FEC, 293, 294, 295, 300, 301, 313–14, 315, 316, 318; friendship with Kenan, 294, 318; on Kenan's honesty, 295
Davis, John W., 250–51
Davis, R. Hayes, 187
Delano, Lyman, 205, 293–94
DeLaval Separator Company, 274
De Lôme, Enrique Dupuy, 100
Dick, William, 135
Dickerson, Edward N., 96
Discovery and Identification of Calcium Carbide in the United States (Kenan), 259, 262, 263, 282
Dortch, Sallie. See Kenan, Sallie Dortch
Douglass, Frederick, 22
Drewey, T. J., 38
Dunham, Phelps, 253, 256
Duplin Rifles, 6
Duplin Times, 312
DuPont, Alfred I., estate, 278, 279, 284, 290, 299, 301, 304, 315
DuPont, Jessie Ball, 316, 317
DuPont, T. Coleman, 222

E. R. Squibb & Sons, 270, 274

Edmonds, J. Ollie, 297

Eimer, August, 77, 79, 90–91, 92, 259; "Early Days in the Carbide and Ferrochrome Industries," 254, 255, 260

Electrochemical Society, 254, 260, 261

Electro Gas Company of New York (EGC), 95, 108; calcium carbide and acetylene patents, 94, 96; licenses for carbide manufacturing, 96, 107, 112, 117, 120

Electromet carbide plant (Niagara Falls, N.Y.), 154

Elisha Mitchell Scientific Society, 69, 72

Empie, Theodore, 10

Erf, Lowell, 264, 265, 271

Erf, Oscar: work at Randleigh Farm, 235, 238, 264, 265, 270, 271, 274–75, 276; as Ohio State professor, 235, 264, 370–71 (n. 87); friendship with Kenan, 264, 304; and pasteurization laws, 272, 275; death of, 277, 302, 304

Erie Canal, 130, 328

Everglades Club (Palm Beach, Fla.), 217

Farmers' alliances, 44–45, 46, 342 (n. 37)

Farrell, Johnny, 227

FEC Railway. *See* Florida East Coast Railway Company

Federal Bureau of Investigation (FBI), 278

Ferroalloy production, 97, 120, 142

Findlay, Douglas, 244

Findlay, Ernest D., 254, 255

First National Bank of New York, 249

Flagler, Alice Shourds, 101, 111, 112, 124–26, 134

Flagler, Harry Harkness, 101, 160, 161–63

Flagler, Henry, 131–32

Flagler, Henry Morrison, 210, 319, 351 (n. 40); operation of Standard Oil, 20, 125; partnership with Rockefeller, 20, 156, 329; relationship with Mary Lily Kenan, 21, 112, 123–24; and Buck Kenan's finances, 36, 129, 139, 141–42, 340–41 (n. 26), 354 (n. 107); collaboration with Walters, 41–42, 43, 293; construction of hotels in Florida, 43, 44, 100, 111–12, 132–34, 142; Florida railroad investments, 48, 111–12; appreciation of Will Kenan's abilities, 49, 127, 133, 162–63; and wife Alice's illness, 74, 101, 112, 124–26, 134; influence on Kenan, 99, 332; interests in Cuba, 100, 112, 293; incorporation of FEC, 100–101; estrangement from son Harry, 101, 160, 161–63; and McKinley presidency, 111, 119, 150; gift of stocks to Mary Lily, 123, 124, 125; change of residence to Florida, 124–25; and Kenan's investments, 127–28, 129, 139, 144, 151, 153; promotion of Kenan's career, 129, 132–34, 138, 142, 144, 285; connections in Lockport, 131–32, 330; and Kenan's marriage to Alice Pomroy, 132, 145, 147; gifts of stock to Kenan, 133, 137; divorce of wife Alice, 134; and Florida divorce law, 134, 136; marriage to Mary Lily, 134–37; Kenan's resentment of, 138, 218, 255, 285, 308, 313; purchase of house for Mollie and Sarah Kenan, 142; construction of Key West Extension, 145, 148–50, 151, 154–55, 157, 158–59, 249, 312–13; relations with Theodore Roosevelt, 149–50; and federal corporation tax, 155–56; friendship with Kenan family, 157; death of, 160, 161–62, 163; Mary Lily's inheritance from, 160, 162, 165; trust created by, 162, 165, 209; role in development of Florida, 285, 298; Martin biography of, 308

Flagler, Horace, 174

Flagler, Jenny Louise, 119

Flagler, Mary Lily Kenan. *See* Kenan, Mary Lily

Flagler, Norman, 269

Flagler, Thomas Thorne, 132, 145, 324

Flagler College, 332

Flagler Nursery School for Underprivileged Children (St. Augustine, Fla.), 256

Flagler System, 166, 308, 314, 332; Mary Lily's will and, 176, 209; and FEC bankruptcy, 199, 313; Kenan elected president of, 207; Flagler's will and, 209; hotels of, 210, 215, 237, 289; highway construction and, 214; World War II and, 289

Flagler Trust. *See* H. M. Flagler Trust

Flexner, Abraham, 243

Flexner, Jacob, 243, 372 (n. 31)

Florida: Flagler Divorce Law, 134, 136, 355 (n. 125); land boom of 1923–25, 207, 209–10, 221–22, 227, 239; population growth, 214; railroad congestion in, 214, 218–19; hurricane of 1928, 231; hurricane of 1935, 248–49; Railroad and Public Utilities Commission, 315, 316

Florida East Coast (FEC) Car Ferry Company, 166, 237, 293, 308–9

Florida East Coast (FEC) Hotel Company, 138, 142, 162, 166, 192, 215, 289

Florida East Coast (FEC) Railway Company: incorporation of, 100–101; construction to Miami, 111–12; purchase of railway cars, 148; federal peonage case against, 151, 155; construction of Key West Extension, 151, 155, 249; and federal corporation tax, 155; Flagler Trust and, 162, 165, 192; Kenan elected vice-president of, 166; Mary Lily's will and, 192, 242, 244, 250, 251, 253–54; profitability of, 192–93, 290, 309; federal government control of, 193, 199; World War I and, 199; labor strike of 1922, 204–5, 207; cooperation with ACL, 205, 230, 293; ACL's attempts to acquire, 209, 293–96, 297–300, 301, 303–4, 308–9, 313–14, 315–18; Florida land boom and, 209–10, 214, 215–17, 239, 250; Kenan elected president of, 210; construction of double-track lines, 210, 214, 220, 239; mortgage bond sales of 1924, 210–11, 237, 250; investment in Pan American, 229, 230; declining revenues and losses, 229, 231, 237; hurricane damage to, 231, 251–52, 269; default on bond interest payments, 238–39, 242, 250; Kenan and bankruptcy proceedings, 239,

278–79, 290, 294–95, 299, 308–9, 314–15; Loftin foreclosure suit and, 242, 244–45, 251; bond sales of 1909, 249–50; interest payments on 1909 bonds, 250, 251, 263, 279; Okeechobee Branch, 251; Anderson reorganization plan, 252–53, 262, 277, 280; abandonment of Key West Extension, 253; and Rockefeller funeral, 255–56; ICC bankruptcy hearings on, 277–78, 279–80, 281, 295–96, 297, 299–300, 301–2, 303–4, 316–18; Ball's efforts to acquire, 278, 295, 301; Ball's investments in, 279, 289, 290, 294; ICC reorganization plans for, 288–89, 290, 294, 295, 313, 315, 382 (n. 43); World War II and, 290, 293; Supreme Court and bankruptcy case, 309, 313–14, 315; St. Joe–Ball–duPont acquisition of, 318, 322; employee benefits, 380 (n. 46). *See also* Key West Extension

Florida National Group of Banks, 278

Florida Power & Light Company, 314

Florida Times-Union, 150, 314

Forshee, J. M., 34, 35

Forte, B. C., 297

Fortune, 282, 283–84

Francis, Freddie, 237, 253, 256

Frankfurter, Felix, 313–14, 315

French, George Zadoc, 22

Frey, Robert K., 316–17

Friday, William C., 316

Frink, Colin, 260, 261, 262, 281

Ganz & Company, 148

Garrett, Thomas, 198–99

General Electric Company, 98

German Acetylene Company, 129

Gibbons, Douglas, 210

Gilmer, John Lash, 51

Gim Ghouls, Order of the, 60–63, 64, 344 (n. 52)

Godfrey, Marion, 295

Goodman, Robert B. ("Shorty"), 103, 108, 110, 143, 147–48, 149

Gore, Joshua, 54

Graham, Edward Kidder, 169, 192, 194

Graham, Frank Porter: as UNC president, 234, 241, 246–47, 248; and Kenan family donations to UNC, 241, 242, 245–46, 256; relations with Kenan family, 246, 262–63; award of Kenan's honorary doctorate, 291; senatorial election campaign, 309–10

Graham, George, 64, 222

Graham, Sarah Rebecca. *See* Kenan, Sarah Rebecca Graham

Graham, Stephen, 5

Grainger, Alvin, 296

Grant, Ulysses S., 22, 24

Graves, Louis, 263

Gray, Gordon, 316

Gray, James A., Jr., 256

Greeley, Horace, 22

Green, George D., 356 (n. 20)

Green, Sadie. *See* Jones, Sadie Green

Green, Wharton Jackson, 21, 40

Greenbrier Hotel (White Sulphur Springs, W.Va.), 164

Grinnan, Sadie, 171, 172

Grow, Torrence E.: work at Randleigh Farm, 201, 204, 206, 208, 235, 269; retirement of, 326

Guaranty Trust Company of New York, 249, 252, 280

Guthrie, Hugh, 338 (n. 66)

H. M. Flagler Trust, 162, 165, 192, 207, 209

Haines, Lawrence, 210, 238, 299

Hambleton, John T., 229–30

Hamilton, James G. de Roulhac, 233–34

Hansen, Ludwig, 43, 129, 340–41 (n. 26)

Harding, Warren G., 199, 204, 206

Harding, William Frederick, 50–52, 53–54

Hargrave, Jesse (grandfather of WRK), 27

Hargrave, Margaret Barbee (grandmother of WRK), 27

Hargrave, Mollie. *See* Kenan, Mary Hargrave

Hargrave, Robert W. (uncle of WRK), 25, 31

Hargrave, William F. ("Freddie") (uncle of WRK) , 25, 34–35

Harrisburg Car Factory, 19, 30

Harrison, Herbert, 154

Harrison Radiator Company, 154

Hartford Biglow Company, 221

Hastings, Thomas, 197, 318

Hawes, Archie, 24

Hawkins, Annice. *See* Kenan, Annice Hawkins

Hawkins, Frank, 222, 280

Hayes, Rutherford B., 32

Hemenway, Mary Tileston, 24

Henry Morrison Flagler Museum, 330

Hill, Annie. *See* Kenan, Annie Hill

Hill, John Sprunt, 228, 240, 305, 332

Hilliard, Aleen, 244

Hilliard, Nancy Segur, 338 (n. 66)

History of Randleigh Farm (Kenan), 255, 262, 265, 269–70, 271, 272, 277, 327

Hoge, Mrs. Peyton, 179, 183

Hoge, Rev. Peyton H., 56, 136, 141, 179, 186, 187

Holden, William Woods, 17

Holland Patent Realty Company, 153

Holmes, John Lyon, 17, 18

Hood, C. I., 197

Hood Farm (Lowell, Mass.), 197, 201, 207

Hoover, Herbert C., 184, 241

Hordern, Samuel, 108

Horner, Jerome, 38

Horner's Military Academy, 36, 38

Horry, William Smith, 112–13, 120–22, 260; rotary furnace invention, 113–18, 120, 121, 122–23

House, Robert B., 307

Howard, W. F., 298–99

Howe, Robert, 204, 206, 234

Howe, William P., 127–28

Howell, A. C.: *The Kenan Professorships*, 248

Hughes, Langston, 246

Hull, Cordell, 243

Humphrey, Alexander Pope, 187–88, 189

Incidents by the Way (Kenan), 16, 262, 300, 308, 314, 318–19, 329–30; on

Kenan's parents, 13, 175; on Alice Pomroy Kenan, 147, 301, 304; and Kenan's relations with Flagler, 175–76, 277, 285, 301, 312–13; on Kenan's gifts to UNC, 305, 306; on discovery of calcium carbide, 306; on Wilmington, 311
Ingersoll, Royal Rodney, 77, 89, 90; *The Elasticity of Guns*, 80
Ingraham, James, 351 (n. 40)
Inman, Ondess L., 270–71, 275, 288
Internal Revenue Service, 326
International Acetylene Association, 259
Interstate Commerce Commission (ICC), 239, 263; and railroad rate reductions, 203, 205, 229; and FEC bond sales, 211; FEC bankruptcy hearings, 277–78, 279–80, 281, 295–96, 297, 299 300, 301–2, 303–4, 316–18, FEC reorganization plans, 288–89, 290, 294, 295, 313, 315, 382 (n. 43)

J. P. Morgan and Company, 249, 280
James, Frederick P., 211–12
Jersey Bulletin, 276, 277
Jersey Creamline, Inc., 276, 288
Jones, Bethune W., 211, 242
Jones, Pembroke, 43, 135, 164, 187, 340 (n. 20); marriage to Sadie Green, 40, 41; death of, 193
Jones, Sadie Green, 40–41, 43, 135, 164, 205
Journal of the American Chemical Society, 97, 98
Justice, Charlie ("Choo-Choo"), 305, 307

Kast, Lodowick, 205
Kelvin, William Thomson, Baron, 84–85, 91
Kenan, Alice Mary Pomroy (wife of WRK), 130, 156, 159, 233, 295, 313; gift of stock from Flagler, 132, 145; marriage to Kenan, 145–47; and Randleigh Farm, 201, 304; involvement with Lockport Hospital, 211–12, 224–25; membership in Lockport Presbyterian Church, 212–13, 324; in poor health, 227–28, 255, 289–90, 291, 296; death of,

301, 303, 324; Kenan on, 301, 304; and house in Lockport, 322
Kenan, Annice Hawkins, 157, 159
Kenan, Annie (aunt of WRK), 5, 8, 95, 118–19, 150–51
Kenan, Annie Hill (aunt of WRK), 7, 8
Kenan, Daniel, 5
Kenan, Emily (cousin of WRK), 8
Kenan, Frank H. (second cousin of WRK), 173, 240, 248, 320, 332
Kenan, Graham (cousin of WRK), 8, 157, 166; marriage to cousin Sarah Kenan, 159; as UNC trustee, 169, 196; and Mary Lily's death, 187, 188, 189, 190, 193, 365 (n. 118); death of, 196–97
Kenan, James (great-great- grandfather of WRK), 5, 339 (n. 8)
Kenan, James (uncle of WRK), 5, 6, 7, 8, 19, 32, 159
Kenan, James G. (second cousin of WRK), 173, 240, 245–46, 332
Kenan, Jessie (sister of WRK; later Jessie Kenan Wise), 8, 43, 135, 291, 317; birth of, 7; unhappy marriage of, 39, 111, 123–24, 163, 174; marriage to Clisby Wise, 56; residences of, 123, 289, 379 (n. 15); and daughter Louise, 124, 164, 169; divorce from Wise, 148; and Mary Lily's death, 186; enjoyment of golf, 215; donations to UNC, 241–42; grandchildren of, 320–21; death of, 332
Kenan, Mary Hargrave ("Mollie") (mother of WRK), 23, 127, 135, 168, 174; marriage to Buck Kenan, 6; children of, 6, 8, 21; Kenan's memories of, 12, 13; background, 27–29; properties in Chapel Hill, 29, 31, 35–36; death of, 175, 360 (n. 31)
Kenan, Mary Lily (sister of WRK; later Mary Lily Kenan Flagler Bingham), 8, 118–19, 159, 313, 359 (n. 28); birth of, 6; childhood and adolescence, 12, 44, 55–56; Henry Walters and, 20, 41; relationship with Henry Flagler, 21, 112, 123–24; alcoholism of, 39, 173–75, 184, 190; friendship with Pembroke and Sadie Jones, 43, 48, 55, 164; relation-

ship with Robert Worth Bingham, 62, 99, 172, 173, 176; marriage to Flagler, 74, 134–37, 147; friendliness with Morehead family, 79; musical studies, 100, 111; Flagler's gift of stocks to, 123, 124, 125; financing of Wilmington armory, 149; donations to UNC, 158, 168, 172–73, 176, 188, 194, 240, 365 (n. 121), 372–73 (n. 36), 375 (n. 16); and Flagler's death, 160, 161–62, 163–64; inheritance from Flagler, 160, 162, 165; visits brother in Lockport, 166–67; relationship with Dr. Battle, 168–69, 171; will and codicil to, 171, 176, 180, 182, 185–86, 187, 188–89, 361 (n. 40); friendship with Bingham family, 171–72; and mother's death, 175; affection for niece Louise Wise, 176, 182–83, 361 (n. 40); and operation of Flagler System, 176, 209, 210; heart condition, 176, 362 (n. 62); marriage to Bingham, 177–79, 180; married life in Louisville, 179–80; stepchildren's dislike of, 180–81, 184–85; death of, 186–87, 243–44, 258; exhumation and autopsy, 189–90, 193–94; UNC's struggle for bequest of, 191–92, 202, 203, 206–7, 242–43, 244–45, 253, 254, 256–57, 263; taxes on estate of, 192, 194, 206–7, 368 (n. 57); FEC and trust of, 237, 242, 244, 250, 251, 253–54

Kenan, Owen (grandfather of WRK), 5, 8, 19, 30

Kenan, Owen Hill (cousin of WRK), 8, 164; as UNC student, 50, 51; medical studies, 56–57; as physician for Flagler, 129, 157, 160, 169, 181; and cousin Mary Lily, 169, 182; voyage on *Lusitania*, 170–71; in World War I, 173, 175, 181, 183, 193; and Mary Lily's death, 189, 372 (n. 31); and UNC fundraising, 245; friendship with Randolph Churchill, 245, 372 (n. 31)

Kenan, Sallie Dortch (aunt of WRK), 7, 174–75

Kenan, Sarah Graham (sister of WRK), 8, 118–19, 157, 280, 291; marriage to cousin Graham Kenan, 159, 163; inheritance of mother's house, 175; and Mary Lily's death, 193; and Graham Kenan's death, 197; donations to UNC, 202–3, 234, 240, 241, 245–46; fire at house of, 238; sued by Loftin, 242; residences of, 289, 379 (n. 15); contribution to Kenan Auditorium, 311–12; declared legally incompetent, 320, 329; wealth of, 329; death of, 332

Kenan, Sarah Rebecca Graham (grandmother of WRK), 5, 7

Kenan, Thomas (cousin of WRK), 8, 157, 159, 173, 186–87, 188

Kenan, Thomas (great-grandfather of WRK), 5

Kenan, Thomas S. (uncle of WRK): birth of, 5; law practice, 6, 7, 293; in Civil War, 6, 21; in state legislature, 7; as mayor of Wilson, 17, 21, 22, 25; promotion of education, 25–26; friendship with Robert Bingham, 26, 171; as state attorney general, 32–33, 35; and temperance movement, 39–40; agrarian movement's hostility toward, 45, 46, 47; as UNC trustee, 47, 49–50, 54, 70, 158; death of, 158

Kenan, Thomas S., III (third cousin of WRK), 181, 185, 363 (n. 82)

Kenan, William Rand ("Buck") (father of WRK), 127, 128, 138, 174, 294; birth of, 5; in Civil War, 6; marriage to Mollie Hargrave, 6; children of, 6, 7, 8, 21, 22; career in business, 6, 13, 24–25, 29, 30, 32, 34–35; involvement in politics, 7, 15, 17, 21, 30, 48; house in Wilmington, 10; influence on son Will, 13, 20, 36; Kenan's memories of, 13–16; in militia companies, 16, 36; in Wilmington race riot, 16, 122; Chapel Hill real estate investments, 27, 29, 31, 35–36; membership in Wilmington Presbyterian Church, 30, 36; on Wilmington Board of Audit and Finance, 35; as Wilmington collector of customs, 36, 100, 111, 119; Flagler and finances of, 36, 129, 139, 141–42, 340–41 (n. 26), 354

(n. 107); in Wilmington social set, 43; and agrarian movement, 46, 47, 48; stock market investments, 139, 140; illness and death of, 141, 355–56 (n. 10); Wilmington armory memorial, 149

Kenan & Forshee, 35

Kenan Foundation, 233

Kenan Memorial Auditorium (Kenansville, N.C.), 311–12

Kenan Memorial Fountain (Wilmington, N.C.), 197, 310–11

Kenan Memorial Stadium (Chapel Hill, N.C.), 221, 223, 228–29; expansion of, 305–6, 307

Kenan Recreation Center (Lockport, N.Y.), 330

Kenansville, N.C., 5, 311–12

Kenansville Grove Presbyterian Church, 328

Kenan Trust. See William R. Kenan, Jr. Charitable Trust

Kent, Samuel, 101–2

Kentucky: and Mary Lily Bingham estate taxes, 194, 206–7, 368 (n. 57)

Kern Incandescent Gas Light Burner, 125

Key West Extension: construction of, 148–50, 151, 154–55, 157, 158, 249, 313; opening of, 158–59; hurricane damage to, 251–52; FEC's abandonment of, 253

King, Jesse C., 80, 87, 102, 104, 105, 260

Kinnear, Annie, 8

Kliner, Mrs. Charles M., 225

Knapp, George O., 96, 112, 120, 123, 129; and Horry rotary furnace, 113, 116, 117–18

Ku Klux Klan, 16, 52, 213

Lake Superior Carbide Company, 112, 120, 352 (n. 67); Sault Ste. Marie carbide plant ("the Soo"), 112–13, 118, 120, 121–22, 142

Lake Superior Power Company, 142

Lamont, Annie, 162

Lamont, Charles, 162

Lane, Edward W., 279, 280, 281, 288

Lane, Mills B., 280

Latimer, Henry, 142

Lawrence, Alton, 246

Lawrence, Ernest, 264, 265

Lawrence, John H., 264

Ledoux, Albert R., 77, 87, 88, 89

Ledyard, Lewis Cass, 359 (n. 14)

Levy, Aaron J., 244–45, 253–54

Lewis, Mrs. Albert, 225

Lewis, Elizabeth Harrison, 362 (n. 66)

Lewis, Hugh ("Dick"), 225, 231

Lewis, John L., 204

Lewis, Lawrence: marriage to Louise Wise, 164, 176–77, 183; and Mary Lily's death, 187; in World War I, 193; employed by FEC, 199, 205; divorce from Louise, 219, 220, 227

Lewis, Lawrence, Jr., 199, 220, 227, 237; birth of, 193; Kenan and, 302, 313, 320–21; and Flagler College, 332

Lewis, Louise Wise. See Wise, Louise

Lewis, Mary Lily Flagler (later Mary Lily Wiley), 199, 220, 237, 302, 320–21, 332

Lewis, Ralph M., 331

Lewis, Thornton, 164, 188, 362 (n. 66)

Lewis, Whiffy, 231

Liberty Hall (Kenansville, N.C.), 3, 5, 8, 9, 134–35, 332

Lincliffe mansion (Louisville, Ky.), 182

Linde Air Products Company, 283–84

Lippert (chemist), 77, 79

Livermore, Jesse, 222

Lockport, N.Y., 130–31, 354 (n. 111); Kenan's house in, 166–67; Kenan's relations with, 212, 213, 224–25, 327–28, 330

Lockport First Presbyterian Church, 324, 328–29, 330–31

Lockport Hospital Nurses Home, 211–12, 330

Lockport Town and Country Club, 330

Lockport Union-Sun & Journal, 329–30

Loftin, Scott M.: appointed Flagler System legal counsel, 202; and FEC bankruptcy, 238, 279, 280, 281, 295; and Mary Lily's estate, 242, 244, 251, 253

London, Lonnie, 245–46

Louisville Courier-Journal, 179–80, 182,

187, 190; Bingham's purchase of, 191, 244

Louisville Post, 186

Louisville Times, 191

Lusitania, 170–71

Lyman, J. F., 264

Lynch, S. A., 289, 294, 295, 378–79 (n. 14)

McCauley, David, 29, 31

McCracken, Robert, 315

McCrary, William H., 336 (n. 7)

McDade, Bill, 303

McDade, Fanny, 303

McDaniel, Samuel, 299

MacDonald, Carlos, 125–26

McGrath, Edward J., 152

McKee, Mary, 171, 183

McKinley, William, 111, 119, 150

MacLaughlin, Owen J., 362 (n. 62)

McLean, Angus, 228

MacMannis, A. R., 315, 317, 326, 330

MacRae, Donald, 341 (n. 34)

McRae, Hugh, 311

McRary, William H., 6

MacVeagh, Wayne, 156

Mallet, John, 69

Manning, Isaac Hall, 247–48

Manning, James Smith, 194

Mar-a-Lago mansion (Palm Beach, Fla.), 217

Marine Midland Bank, 324

Marshall, James G., 255, 259

Marshall, John, 189

Martin, John W., 288

Martin, Sidney Walter, 163; *Florida's Flagler*, 308, 309, 312

Masons, 339 (n. 8); Kenan's dislike of, 36, 214, 224

Mathieson Alkali Works, 107–8

May, Andrew Jackson, 243–44

Meredith, Joseph C., 155

Metropolitan Life Insurance Company, 250

Miami, Fla., 100, 214

Miami Daily News, 314

Miami Electric Light & Power Company, 165–66

Miami Herald, 314, 316, 317, 329

Miami Water Company, 165–66

Miller, Eleanore. *See* Bingham, Eleanore Miller

Miller, Hugh, 62, 70, 79

Mitchell, Janet, 174

Mizener, Addison, 217, 222

Mizener Development Corporation, 222

Moissan, Henri, 97–98, 116, 348 (n. 78)

Monk, Mary, 175

Mook, Mrs. Roger, 330

Moore, Henry Edwin, 109

Moore, Louis T., 310

Morehead, Genevieve, 228

Morehead, James, 221

Morehead, James Turner ("the Major"): friendship with Kenan family, 70, 79; and discovery of calcium carbide, 75, 83, 85, 88, 89, 90–91, 259, 261, 282, 283; background, 76–79; operation of Willson Aluminum, 79, 80, 83, 87–88, 92; financial troubles, 87, 88, 90; licenses for carbide and acetylene production, 94, 95–97; production of ferroalloys, 97, 120, 142; and Horry rotary furnace, 118

Morehead, John (Major's brother), 76, 77

Morehead, John Motley ("Mot"), 97, 121–22, 142, 332; on discovery of calcium carbide, 75, 80, 81–82, 259, 260, 261; as UNC student, 77–78, 79; work for Willson Aluminum, 78–79, 80, 87; friendship with Kenan, 79; work in carbide industry, 94, 102, 104, 106, 112, 113; in University Club of Niagara Falls, 103, 104, 263; and invention of Horry rotary furnace, 113–14; work for People's Gas of Chicago, 116; and Kenan Stadium construction, 221, 228; donations to UNC, 221, 240, 302, 304–5, 306; awarded honorary doctorate, 221, 241; hunting trip with Kenan, 229; Kenan's rivalry with, 240, 304, 306; success in industry and politics, 240–41

Morehead Foundation, 306

Morehead-Patterson Bell Tower (Chapel Hill, N.C.), 240
Morehead Planetarium (Chapel Hill, N.C.), 303, 304–5, 306, 381 (n. 21)
Morgan, J. P., 65
Mott Foundation, 331
Moyer, Frank J., Jr., 219, 328

National Bankruptcy Act, 280, 303–4, 314
National Carbon Company, 283–84
National City Bank of New York, 249
National Dairy Products, 273
National Farmers' Alliance, 46, 48
National Labor Relations Board, 285–86
Niagara County National Bank, 324
Niagara Falls, N.Y.: ALH&P carbide plant, 104–5, 120–21; industrial complex, 106; Union Carbide plant, 123, 127, 154
Niagara Research Laboratories, 154
New York Post, 190
New York Stock Exchange, 29
New York Sun, 107, 188
New York Times, 179, 210, 225, 227, 237
New York Tribune, 170–71
North Carolina: secession of, 6; elections of 1872, 17–18; elections of 1876, 32; A&M college controversy, 38–39, 45, 47–48, 53; agrarian movement in, 44–45, 46, 53; elections of 1896, 111; elections of 1950, 309–10; temperance movement in, 340 (n. 15)
North Carolina Farmers' Alliance, 47
North Carolina Farmers' Association, 45
North Carolina Literary and Historical Society, 158
North Carolina State College/University, 241, 331–32
Northwestern Mutual Life Insurance Company, 250

Odum, Howard, 291
Ohio State University, 326, 327; Kenan Promotional and Investigational Fund, 271
Ormond Hotel (Daytona Beach, Fla.), 289

Palm Beach, Fla., 217, 222
Palm Beach Inn, 100, 132
Palm Beach Life, 174, 181
Panama Canal, 148, 150
Pan American Airways, 230
Park Lane Hotel (New York, N.Y.), 211
Parks, Mary, 77
Parrott, Joseph R., 162, 165, 166
Patterson, Douglas, 324
Patterson, Rufus, 240
Patterson, Sam, 56
Peninsular & Occidental (P&O) Steamship Company, 166, 230, 293, 309
Pennsylvania Railroad Company, 19, 30
People's Gas, Light and Coke Company, 112, 117
Pepper, Claude, 295–300, 301, 309
Pettibone, Mulliken and Company, 120, 352 (n. 67)
Phillips, William B., 69
Pintsch Company, 91
Pittsburgh Reduction Company, 108
Plant, Henry, 100
Plaza Hotel (New York, N.Y.), 164
Polk, James K., 50
Polk, Leonidas Lafayette, 45, 46, 47
Pomroy, Albert, 145, 255
Pomroy, Alice. *See* Kenan, Alice Mary Pomroy
Pomroy, Frederick, 145
Pomroy, Hopkins Chillingsworth, 132
Ponce de Leon Hotel (St. Augustine, Fla.), 44, 289, 309, 312, 332
Pond, Gilbert: *Calcium Carbide and Acetylene*, 259
Prest-O-Lite Company, 283–84
Price, Edgar F., 80, 87, 102, 104, 127, 154
Proceedings of the International Association of Dairy and Milk Inspectors, 272
Proceedings of the Naval Institute, 89
Progressive Farmer, 47
Prohibition movement, 39, 340 (n. 15)
Pullman Company, 168, 220

Raff, Audrey, 286, 287
Railroad Labor Board, 205
Raleigh News and Observer, 207, 241

Rand, Isaac William, 359 (n. 27)
Randleigh Farm (Lockport, N.Y.):
    Kenan's purchase of, 201–2; and
    Kenan's scientific aspirations, 202, 235,
    271; dairy research experiments, 204,
    234–36, 238, 265–75, 277, 288; Kenan's
    expenditures on, 235, 265, 269, 273–74,
    326, 330; Kenan's history of, 255, 262,
    265, 269–70, 271, 272, 277, 327; annual
    scientific conferences, 264, 269, 270,
    271, 274, 304, 326–27; Jersey cattle rais-
    ing, 265, 273, 275, 276–77; labor short-
    ages at, 287–88; bequeathed to UNC,
    331–32
Randleigh Foundation, 332
Randleigh railroad car, 207, 220–21
Ravitch, Michael Leo, 181, 185, 186, 187,
    189
Record Company of St. Augustine, 166,
    262, 300, 327
Richmond Times, 48
Rice, W. Thomas, 318
Rockefeller, John D., Sr., 20, 156, 157,
    172–73, 255–56, 329
Rockefeller, John D., Jr., 256
Rockefeller Foundation, 202, 265
Rogers, George W., 324
Roosevelt, Franklin D., 243, 257, 297
Roosevelt, Theodore, 148, 149–50
Rossman, George, 322–23, 329
Rowe, George Freeman, 151
Royal Palm Hotel (Miami, Fla.), 100,
    111–12, 223, 237
Royal Poinciana Hotel (Palm Beach,
    Fla.), 100, 237, 370 (n. 74)
Russell, Bertrand, 246
Russell, Daniel, 111

Sabin, Charles H., 281
Safe Deposit and Trust Company of
    Baltimore, 230, 250, 294
St. Albans School (Radford, Va.), 94–95
St. Augustine, Fla., 215
St. Augustine Evening Record, 204
St. Augustine Golf and Development
    Company, 207
St. Augustine Record, 166, 314

St. Joe Paper Company, 290, 295, 298,
    299, 301, 315
Saugerties Gas Light Company, 143
Sault Ste. Marie, Mich., carbide plant
    ("the Soo"), 112–13, 118, 120, 121–22,
    142
Saunders, William L., 52
Scales, Joseph, 259
Schreiber, Joseph, 317
Schultze, Leonard, 217, 218, 226–27, 238
Scott, Ernest, 272
Seaboard Railroad, 230, 301
Sewanee Times, 72
Seward, George Frederick, 77, 79, 88
Shaffer, Newton, 160
Shape, Robert Louis, 149
Shaw, William E., 151–52, 262
Sherwood mansion (Newport, R.I.), 164
Singer, Paris, 217
Slocum, Howard, 362 (n. 62)
Smathers, George, 309
Smiley, Nixon, 329
Smith, Andrew, 43
Smith, Carroll, 268
Smith, Warren, 160, 289
Smith, Willis, 309–10
Southern Railroad, 301
Southern Railway Project, 18
Spangler, F. L., 254, 255, 259–60
Spanish-American War, 120
Spiritine Chemical Company, 129, 340–
    41 (n. 26)
Springfield Gas Machine Company, 91
Standard Oil Company, 20, 125; and
    acetylene gas lighting, 92, 93; Roo-
    sevelt's antitrust investigation of, 148,
    149–50, 151, 153; dissolution of, 155,
    156, 157–58; and FEC, 238, 239
Stedman, Frank, 326
Sterry, Frederick, 164
Stetson, Eugene, 225, 280–81
Stetson, Iola Wise, 225, 281
Stevens, George W., 188
Strum, Louis, 238
Susquehanna Smelting Company, 154
Sutton, Cantey, 263, 282

Tarbell, Ida M.: *The History of Standard Oil*, 148
Tar Heel, 57, 58, 59, 60, 64, 65, 67, 72
Taylor, Edward, 127
Taylor, Walker, 149
Thomas, George, 189
Thorne, Samuel, 96
Thurston, Ben, 107–8
Townley, Alfred H., 254
Traders Paper Company, 129, 134, 137, 142, 143, 153
Trippe, Juan T., 229–30
Turlington, Lizzie, 38
Turner, Henry C., 226
Turner Construction Company, 219
Turney, J. R., 317

Union Carbide & Carbon Corporation, 283–84
Union Carbide Company: license for carbide and acetylene production, 96, 107, 120, 153–54; carbide industry monopoly, 120, 142; Niagara Falls carbide plant, 123, 127, 154; Kenan and investment in, 127–29, 142, 153; and historical accounts of calcium carbide discovery, 255, 259–60, 261; *Fortune* articles on, 282–84
United Box Board & Paper Company, 143, 145, 153
United States Coast Guard, 289
United States Supreme Court, 201; and Standard Oil dissolution, 155, 157, 158; and corporation tax, 156; and FEC bankruptcy, 309, 313–14, 315; and racial desegregation, 309–10
University Club (Niagara Falls, N.Y.), 103, 104, 263
University of Buffalo, 327
University of California, 264–65
University of Georgia Press, 308
University of North Carolina, 25, 26–27; establishment of A&M college and, 27, 38–39, 47–48, 53; Kenan as student at, 48, 49–51, 53, 54, 56, 57, 71, 72; blacking ritual, 51–53; football team, 54, 64, 65–67, 229, 248, 305, 307–8; baseball

team, 57–60; Gim Ghouls society, 60–63, 64; enrollment, 64–65; Kenan's graduation from, 72; Kenan's graduate studies in chemistry, 74, 98; Kenan Fund, 158; Mary Lily Kenan's donations to, 158, 168, 172–73, 176, 188, 194, 240, 365 (n. 121), 372–73 (n. 36), 375 (n. 16); Kenan's book donations to, 167, 306; Carnegie Library, 168; in fights over Mary Lily's estate, 191–92, 202, 203, 206–7, 242–43, 244–45, 253, 254, 256–57, 263; Mary Lily Kenan professorships, 194–96, 197, 202; Sarah Kenan's donations to, 202–3, 234, 240, 241; construction of Kenan Memorial Stadium, 221, 223, 228–29; John Motley Morehead's donations to, 221, 240, 302, 304–5, 306; Southern Historical Collection, 233–34; John Sprunt Hill's donations to, 240, 305; financial difficulties at, 241; Kenan Professorships Fund pensions, 241; Jessie Kenan's donations to, 241–42; Jewish quota dispute, 246–48; athletics reform controversy, 248; Kenan awarded honorary doctorate by, 276–77, 284, 291, 327; expansion of Kenan Stadium, 305–6, 307; William Rand Kenan, Jr., Scholarship Fund, 306–8, 381 (n. 17); Kenan's bequest of Randleigh Farm to, 331; Kenan-Flagler School of Business, 332
University of North Carolina Press, 245, 305, 308
Upchurch, Frank D., 298–99, 309

Vance, Zebulon Baird, 21, 32, 45, 46–47
Van De Mark, Phyllis, 289–90
Vanderbilt, Alfred Gwynn, 164, 171
Vanderbilt, Cornelia, 168
Vanderbilt, Edith, 168
Vanderbilt, George, 168, 360 (n. 32)
Van Hecke, Maurice T., 256–57
Venable, Charles Scott, 98–99, 345 (n. 73)
Venable, Francis Preston, 313, 359 (n. 27); Kenan as research assistant to, 49, 69, 70–71, 84; belief in value of athletics,

54, 63–64; doctoral students of, 62, 69–70; Kenan's friendship with, 67–69, 99, 138; promotion of science at UNC, 69, 70, 196; calcium carbide experiments, 70–71, 83–84, 97, 281, 282–83; acetylene experiments, 71, 82, 85–86, 92, 93; zirconium experiments, 72; role in discovery of carbide and acetylene, 75, 82, 83–84, 85, 93, 97, 259, 260, 261, 282–83; Mot Morehead's studies with, 78; agreement with Willson Aluminum Company, 86–87, 88, 89–90, 95, 99; "Some of the Properties of Calcium Carbide," 97, 98; lawsuit against Willson, 98–99; "An Account of the First Production of Calcium Carbide and Acetylene in the United States," 128, 259; as president of UNC, 129, 158, 167; appointment to Kenan professorship, 191, 195; appointment as emeritus professor, 233, 234; death of, 247–48

Venable, Sallie, 99, 281–82, 283

Waddell, Alfred Moore, 17–18
Walker, William R., 85–86, 261, 281
Walters, Henry, 19, 53, 135, 166, 187, 201, 340–41 (n. 26); influence on Kenan, 10, 20, 41, 110; operation of ACL Railroad, 20, 41–42, 43, 44, 45, 48, 293; friendship with Pembroke and Sadie Jones, 40, 41, 164; and Cuban revolution, 100; and Kenan family finances, 139–40; marriage to Sadie Jones, 205; and FEC bankruptcy, 209, 230; death of, 241
Walters, Jennie, 19
Walters, William T., 19
Ward, Charles Gilmore, 100
Ward, George, 157
Washington, Booker T., 150
Weiser, Harry H., 264, 272–73
Welding Engineer, 254, 255, 259–60
Western Block Company, 151–53, 192, 262, 285–87, 326
Westhafer, James, 320, 324, 328–29, 330–31

West Palm Beach Water Company, 165–66, 314
Wetmore, Douglas J., 150
White and Blue, 72
Whitehall (Palm Beach, Fla.), 138, 174, 181, 210, 330
White Sulphur Springs, W.Va., 164
Whitney, William C., 89
Wiley, Mary Lily. *See* Lewis, Mary Lily Flagler
William R. Kenan, Jr. Charitable Trust, 332
William R. Kenan, Jr. Floral Gardens (Jacksonville, Fla.), 319
William R. Kenan, Jr. Fund for the Arts, 332
William R. Kenan, Jr. Fund for Engineering, Technology and Science, 332
Williams, Horace, 54, 195–96, 197, 202
Willover, Abe, 269
Willson, Thomas Leopold ("Carbide"), 74; in discovery of calcium carbide, 75, 81, 83–86, 261, 282–83; attempts to produce aluminum, 77, 80, 83; experiments with cannons, 77, 80, 88–89, 90, 346 (n. 14); incorporation of Willson Aluminum, 79; electric arc furnace invention, 113, 114; and Venable's role in calcium carbide discovery, 83–84, 86, 88, 89–90, 93, 282–83; patents for calcium carbide and acetylene production, 84, 85, 89, 94, 96, 98, 261; partnership with Major Morehead, 87–88, 91, 94, 96; attempts to commercialize carbide and acetylene, 87–94, 107, 116, 117; partnership with Eimer, 90–92, 254; sale of licenses for carbide production, 96
Willson Aluminum Company: and Venable's calcium carbide experiments, 69, 70, 83–84; attempts to produce aluminum, 70, 80, 83; production of calcium carbide, 75, 80–81, 97, 98; incorporation of, 79; agreement with Venable, 86–87, 95; attempts to commercialize calcium carbide, 87, 88, 91,

92; contract with Electro Gas Company, 95, 96, 117
Willson Laboratory Company, 96
Wilmington, N.C., 319; race riot of 1898, 16, 122; elections of 1872, 17, 20; economy of, 18; Confederate Memorial, 20–21; public education in, 23; Board of Audit and Finance, 35; Kenan Memorial Fountain, 197, 310–11
Wilmington and Weldon Railroad, 18–19, 41, 45
Wilmington, Charlotte and Rutherford Railroad Company, 25
Wilmington, Columbia & Augusta (WC&A) Railroad, 18–19, 25, 30
Wilmington First Presbyterian Church, 136, 241, 372 (n. 21)
Wilmington Savings and Trust Company, 340–41 (n. 26)
Wilmington Star, 22, 32, 44, 364 (n. 97)
Wilson, Henry Lane, 22, 24
Wilson, Rev. Joseph R., 30
Wilson, Woodrow, 182, 184
Wilson Lighting Company, 143–44, 147–48
Winston, George T., 53, 54, 359 (n. 28)
Wise, Iola, 225, 281
Wise, Jessie Kenan. *See* Kenan, Jessie
Wise, Joseph Clisby ("Kib"), 56, 111, 123–24, 125, 148
Wise, Louise, 172, 227, 281; childhood, 111, 123–24, 353 (n. 87); on Mary Lily

Kenan, 163; marriage to Lawrence Lewis, 164, 176–77, 182–83; at school in Paris, 168, 169; inheritance from Mary Lily, 173, 176, 219, 242, 245, 361 (n. 40); and Mary Lily's death, 187–88; children of, 193, 199, 220; sale of Whitehall, 210; enjoyment of golf, 215; divorce from Lawrence Lewis, 219, 220, 227; marriage to Dick Lewis, 225; dislike of Kenan, 225, 231–32; divorce from Dick Lewis, 231; marriage to Freddie Francis, 237; divorce from Francis, 253; engagement to Phelps Dunham, 256; death of, 256
Woman's College of the University of North Carolina, 241
Wood, Edward Jenner, 168, 188, 189
Wood, Richard, 282–83
Woollen, Charles T., 192, 242, 243
Wooten Richardson & Company, 24–25, 29, 31, 32
World War I, 169, 182
World War II, 288; and Union Carbide, 283–84; and Western Block, 286, 287; and Flagler hotels, 289; and FEC, 290, 293
Wright, Thomas H., 142, 149, 310

York Manufacturing Company, 268
Young, Hugh H., 178, 183–84, 190, 193–94

Zwicker, Pauline, 324–25